MERGERS,
RESTRUCTURING, AND
CORPORATE CONTROL

MERGERS,
RESTRUCTURING, AND
CORPORATE CONTROL

J. Fred Weston

Anderson Graduate School of Management
University of California, Los Angeles

Kwang S. Chung

College of Business Administration
Chung-Ang University, Seoul

Susan E. Hoag

Anderson Graduate School of Management
University of California, Los Angeles

PRENTICE HALL, Englewood Cliffs, NJ 07632

Library of Congress Cataloging-in-Publication Data

Weston, J. Fred (John Fred)
    Mergers, restructuring, and corporate control / J. Fred Weston,
  Kwang S. Chung, Susan E. Hoag.
        p.   cm.
    Includes bibliographical references.
    ISBN 0-13-577172-2 :
    1. Consolidation and merger of corporations--United States-
  -Finance. 2. Consolidation and merger of corporations--United
  States--Management.   I. Chung, Kwang S.,   II. Hoag,
  Susan. III. Title.
  HG4028.M4W47 1990
  338.8'3'0973--dc20   89-49014
                                                                CIP

Editorial/production supervision and interior design: **Maureen Wilson**
Cover design: **Ben Santora**
Manufacturing buyer: **Mary Ann Gloriande**

 © 1990 by Prentice-Hall, Inc.
A Division of Simon & Schuster
Englewood Cliffs, New Jersey 07632

Printed in the United States of America
10 9 8 7 6 5 4 3 2 1

ISBN 0-13-577172-2

Prentice-Hall International (UK) Limited, *London*
Prentice-Hall of Australia Pty. Limited, *Sydney*
Prentice-Hall Canada Inc., *Toronto*
Prentice-Hall Hispanoamericana, S.A., *Mexico*
Prentice-Hall of India Private Limited, *New Delhi*
Prentice-Hall of Japan, Inc., *Tokyo*
Simon & Schuster Asia Pte. Ltd., *Singapore*
Editora Prentice-Hall do Brasil, Ltda., *Rio de Janeiro*

Overview

Contents

Chapter 4
Merger Types and Characteristics   82

PART V   DEAL STRUCTURING

PART VI   RESTRUCTURING

Chapter 14
Joint Ventures   330

Chapter 15
ESOPs AND MLPs   360

Chapter 20
Takeover Defenses   481

Preface

Dramatic events in mergers, takeovers, restructuring, and corporate control fill the newspaper headlines almost daily. Mergers, takeovers, restructuring, and corporate control issues have become central public and corporate policy issues. To some, M&As, restructuring, and corporate control activities represent a new industrial force that will lead the United States and other economies that practice these arts to new heights of creativity and productivity. To others, these same activities are regarded as a blight on our economy—a symptom of the larger malaise of greed and gambling that is rotting the core of American society. Regardless of which view is held, M&As, restructuring, and corporate control represent a major force in the modern financial and economic environment. This is an area with potential for both good and harm.

The RJR Nabisco leveraged buy-out at $25 billion in 1988 was the blockbuster takeover for the wave of merger and acquisition (M&A) activity that began in 1980. Other large transactions in recent years were the purchases by Chevron of Gulf Oil for $13.3 billion, by Philip Morris of Kraft for $12.6 billion, by Texaco of Getty Oil for $10.1 billion, by General Electric of RCA at $6.1 billion, by Eastman Kodak of Sterling Drug for $5.1 billion, by General Motors of Hughes Aircraft for $5.0 billion. Buy-outs and takeovers have been the U.S. form of restructuring just as *perestroika* has been for the USSR. Is the U.S. form of restructuring good for business? For the economy? For investors? For consumers? For workers? This book seeks to provide increased understanding related to these questions.

M&A activity has stimulated a veritable deluge of published material in the last decade. Compact summaries of these materials or synthesis articles cannot cover the material adequately. This book seeks to provide a more complete treatment of the leading topics related to mergers, takeovers, restructuring, and corporate control. In the future, shifts in the levels of these activities may occur with fluctuations in the economy and with changing regulatory environments. However, takeovers, restructuring, and leveraged buy-outs will continue to be major forces in the economy. Additionally, to analyze takeovers and restructuring, some key topics such as valuation, cost of capital, and strategic financial planning—essential to the subject of financial economics—are involved. So important analytical concepts must be mastered.

We have no ax to grind in this book. We see some positive benefits from increased emphasis on financial strategy and restructuring. Undoubtedly, there have been excesses as typically occur in waves in speculative markets. We have to separate the good from the bad. We come not to praise, criticize, or condemn, but to increase understanding. Our central aim is to provide a conceptual framework that will help the reader put into perspective and to increase his or her understanding of events that are headlined almost daily in the financial and general press.

The main audience we have in mind is the academic user. Increasingly, M&A courses deal with all or part of the subject matter of this book. For that reason, we have included end-of-chapter questions to stimulate discussion and to focus the key subject matter. But we have also kept in mind two other audiences—the businessperson and the general public, including legislators and other policy makers. We have tried to keep the level of treatment accessible by avoiding excessive jargon. We have tried to develop the technical materials from the ground level up so that both the academic reader and the general reader will be able to master the material and, we hope, experience intellectual growth in the process.

What we think will be of value to academics for future use and for business-people is the ability to answer natural and practical questions that arise. For the bidding firm, how much will my early investment in the target increase in value if I use cash versus stock as a method of payment? For the target, what is a reasonable premium for me to expect from a bidder? How much will my firm increase in value if I engage in a sell-off or divestiture? What will be the effect on a firm's share price on average if it engages in stock repurchase? What will be the impact of my firm's share price if it makes a stock or debt issue? What will the share price effect be if a proxy contest is started? What will be the effect of paying greenmail? What value changes take place with going private, particularly through a leveraged buy-out? If my firm establishes two classes of stock, which one will have the greater value—the one that pays more income or the one that has more voting power?

There is a rich body of empirical material that can provide a basis for answering such questions. This book attempts to bring that empirical material together in a systematic way. At the same time it tries to lay bare the theory or principles and the logical analysis which give meaning to the empirical findings. These and related materials will provide the general reader with a basis for understanding and judgment about the continued flow of proposals to alter public policy toward M&As and corporate restructuring that are introduced into every session of Congress.

We are grateful to the following people for their helpful comments: Nickolaos Travlos, Boston College; Michael J. Sullivan, Florida State University; Kenneth W. Wiles, University of Texas at Austin; George J. Papaioannou, Hofstra University; Douglas V. Austin, University of Toledo; Maclyn L. Clouse, University of Denver; Matthew Spiegel and Michael Salinger, Columbia University; Nikhil P. Varaiya, Southern Methodist University; Robert F. Bruner, University of Virginia; and Ralph A. Walkling, Ohio State University.

Our appreciation also to the many scholars whose writings have enriched the literature on M&As and corporate control. They are listed in the Author Index, and those with multiple citations deserve our special gratitude. We were also helped by our colleagues at UCLA whose writings and discussions have stimulated our thinking: Armen Alchian, Bhagwan Chowdhry, David Hirshleifer, Narasimhan Jegadeesh, Ivan P-L. Png, Richard Roll, and Sheridan Titman.

Dan Asquith prepared the Subject Index and he with Tim Opler were valuable advisors on many substantive matters. Marilyn McElroy helped on so many aspects of the development of the book that she was virtually a co-author. We appreciate the complete cooperation of the people at Prentice Hall, particularly Scott Barr, Editor–Finance, and his associates, Teresa Fernandez, Leah Neel, and Maureen Wilson.

This subject matter area is so dynamic and the flows of articles and other materials are so voluminous that there will be need for future updating. Our hope is that our initial efforts will justify further developments and improvements in subsequent editions. We invite reactions, comments, and suggestions from our readers.

J. FRED WESTON
KWANG S. CHUNG
SUSAN E. HOAG

Anderson Graduate School of Management
UCLA
Los Angeles, CA   90024-1481
(213) 825-2200

MERGERS, RESTRUCTURING, AND CORPORATE CONTROL

CHAPTER 1

Overview

INTRODUCTION

Takeovers and related activities in the 1980s are much broader in scope and raise more fundamental issues than previous merger movements. The daily newspapers are filled with case studies of mergers and acquisitions (M&As), tender offers (both friendly and hostile), spin-offs and divestitures, corporate restructuring, changes in ownership structures, and struggles for corporate control. Dramatic insider trading charges have been raised. In recent years, leverage ratios for some companies have increased and newer forms of financing have proliferated, including an increase in the use of bonds with ratings below the first four grades (below Baa3 by Moody's or BBB− by Standard and Poor's, referred to as "junk bonds"). Thus, the traditional subject matter of M&As has been expanded to include takeovers and related issues of corporate restructuring, corporate control, and changes in the ownership structure of firms. For brevity, we refer to these and related activities as M&As.

Mergers and industrial restructuring (M&As) have raised important issues both for business decisions and for public policy formulation. No firm is regarded safe from a takeover possibility. On the more positive side, M&As may be critical to the healthy expansion of business firms as they evolve through successive stages of growth and development. Both internal and external growth may be complementary in the long-range evolution of firms. Successful entry into

1

new product markets and into new geographical markets by a firm may require M&As at some stage in the firm's development. Successful competition in international markets may depend on capabilities obtained in a timely and efficient fashion through M&As. Some have argued that mergers increase value and efficiency and move resources to their highest and best uses, thereby increasing shareholder value (Jensen, 1984).

Others are skeptical. They argue that companies acquired are already efficient and that their subsequent performance after acquisition is not improved (Magenheim and Mueller, 1988; Ravenscraft and Scherer, 1988). Others aver that the gains to shareholders merely represent a redistribution away from labor and other stakeholders (Shleifer and Summers, 1988). Another view is that the M&A activity represents the machinations of speculators who reflect the frenzy of a "Casino Society." This speculative activity is said to increase debt unduly and to erode equity resulting in an economy highly vulnerable to economic instability (Rohatyn, 1986).

Even individual businesspersons have expressed skepticism of the power of mergers (Buffett, 1981). Warren Buffett (1981, pp. 4–5) observed:

> Many managements apparently were overexposed in impressionable childhood years to the story in which the imprisoned handsome prince is released from a toad's body by a kiss from a beautiful princess. Consequently, they are certain their managerial kiss will do wonders for the profitability of Company T(arget) . . . investors can always buy toads at the going price for toads. If investors instead bankroll princesses who wish to pay double for the right to kiss the toad, those kisses had better pack some real dynamite. We've observed many kisses but very few miracles. Nevertheless, many managerial princesses remain serenely confident about the future potency of their kisses—even after their corporate backyards are knee-deep in unresponsive toads . . .
>
> We have tried occasionally to buy toads at bargain prices with results that have been chronicled in past reports. Clearly our kisses fell flat. We have done well with a couple of princes—but they were princes when purchased. At least our kisses didn't turn them into toads. And, finally, we have occasionally been quite successful in purchasing fractional interests in easily-identifiable princes at toad-like prices.

In this volume, we seek to sort out these opposing views. A major task of the present book is to present a general hypothesis to explain the merger phenomenon. In order to provide factual content to the hypothesis, we critically examine the vast literature of empirical evidence and present new data on the firm, industry, and macroeconomic levels.

The theoretical interest is directed to three questions. First, it is concerned with motivation behind M&As. A related question is why firms choose M&As rather than internal growth. Second, the theory should be able to predict the types of firms engaging in M&As, that is, which firms are likely to be acquiring, which acquired, which divesting, and so on. Third, the theory should have implications on aggregate merger activity. Why do we see more mergers in some periods than in others?

Given a theory to explain various aspects of merger activity, it should be possible to offer guidelines for such practical matters as M&A planning by firms and valuation of combining firms. Further, the theory and empirical evidence have implications for social and economic policies towards mergers. Thus, another purpose of the present work is to provide a framework to evaluate alternative business and social policies involving M&As.

FORMS OF CORPORATE RESTRUCTURING

Business firms engage in a broad range of activities including expanding, shrinking, and otherwise restructuring asset and ownership structures. To provide an overview of these many kinds of practices, they are summarized in Table 1.1. The grouping is somewhat arbitrary but indicates the direction of the emphasis in these various practices. Each type of activity will be briefly explained.

Expansion

Under expansion, we have listed mergers, tender offers, and joint ventures. Mergers are like a marriage in the romantic tradition. Usually there is a period of courtship leading to the joining of two or more separate entities into one, after which the parties hope to live happily ever after.

TABLE 1.1
Forms of Restructuring Business Firms

I. *Expansion*
   Mergers and Acquisitions
   Tender Offers
   Joint Ventures

II. *Sell-offs*
   Spin-offs
      Split-offs
      Split-ups
   Divestitures
      Equity Carve-outs

III. *Corporate Control*
   Premium Buy-backs
   Standstill Agreements
   Antitakeover Amendments
   Proxy Contests

IV. *Changes in Ownership Structure*
   Exchange Offers
   Share Repurchases
   Going Private
   Leveraged Buy-outs

to the outside offer and the restructuring may make the target less attractive to the bidder.

Joint ventures involve the intersection of only a small fraction of the activities of the companies involved and usually for a limited duration of ten to fifteen years or less. They may represent a separate entity in which each of the parties makes cash and other forms of investments.

Sell-Offs

The literature describes several kinds of sell-offs. The two major types are spin-offs and divestitures. A spin-off creates a separate new legal entity; its shares are distributed on a pro rata basis to existing shareholders of the parent company. Thus, existing stockholders have the same proportion of ownership in the new entity as in the original firm. There is, however, a separation of control, and eventually the new entity as a separate decision-making unit may develop policies and strategies different from those of the original parent. Note that no cash is received by the original parent. In a sense, a spin-off represents a form of a dividend to existing shareholders. A variation of a spin-off is the split-off, in which a portion of existing shareholders receives stock in a subsidiary in exchange for parent company stock. Still a different variation of the spin-off is a split-up, in which the entire firm is broken up in a series of spin-offs, so that the parent no longer exists and only the new offspring survive.

In contrast to the class of spin-offs in which only shares are transferred or exchanged is another group of transactions in which cash comes into the firm—divestitures. Basically, a divestiture involves the sale of a portion of the firm to an outside third party. Cash or equivalent consideration is received by the divesting firm. Typically, the buyer is an existing firm, so that no new legal entity results. It simply represents a form of expansion on the part of the buying firm.

A variation on divestiture is the equity carve-out. An equity carve-out involves the sale of a portion of the firm via an equity offering to outsiders. In other words, new shares of equity are sold to outsiders which give them ownership of a portion of the previously existing firm. A new legal entity is created. The equity holders in the new entity need not be the same as the equity holders in the original seller. A new control group is immediately created.

The distinctions between these various forms of spin-offs are somewhat arbitrary, and some writers view them all as simply various forms of stock dividends, except for transactions that involve the sale of shares to parties other than existing shareholders.

Corporate Control

The third grouping of activities in Table 1.1 we have referred to as "corporate control." Premium buy-backs represent the repurchase of a substantial stockholder's ownership interest at a premium above the market price (called greenmail). Often in connection with such buy-backs, a standstill agreement is written. This represents a voluntary contract in which the stockholder who is bought out agrees not to make further attempts to take over the company in the future. When a standstill agreement is made without a buy-back, the substantial stockholder simply agrees not to increase his or her ownership which presumably would put him or her in an effective control position.

Antitakeover amendments are changes in the corporate bylaws to make an acquisition of the company more difficult or more expensive. These include (1) supermajority voting provisions requiring a high percentage (for example, 80 percent) of stockholders to approve a merger, (2) staggered terms for directors which can delay change of control for a number of years, and (3) golden parachutes which award large termination payments to existing management if control of the firm is changed and management is terminated.

In a proxy contest, an outside group seeks to obtain representation on the firm's board of directors. The outsiders are referred to as "dissidents" or "insurgents" who seek to reduce the control position of the "incumbents" or existing board of directors. Since the management of a firm often has effective control of the board of directors, proxy contests are usually regarded as directed against the existing management.

Changes in Ownership Structure

Changes in ownership structure represent the fourth group of restructuring activities listed in Table 1.1. One form is through exchange offers, which may be the exchange of debt or preferred stock for common stock, or conversely, of common stock for the more senior claims. Exchanging debt for common stock increases leverage; exchanging common stock for debt decreases leverage.

A second form is share repurchase, which simply means that the corporation buys back some fraction of its outstanding shares of common stock. Tender offers may be made for share repurchase. The percentage of shares purchased may be small or substantial. If the latter, the effect may be to change the control structure in the firm. For example, it has been said that the substantial share repurchase activity by Teledyne, Inc. has increased the effective control position of H. E. Singleton, the chairman and chief executive officer of the company. The company purchased shares from other shareholders, but Mr. Singleton did not reduce his already substantial holdings. The fixed holdings of Mr. Singleton thereby became a larger percentage of the new reduced company total.

In a going-private transaction, the entire equity interest in a previously public corporation is purchased by a small group of investors. The firm is no longer subject to the regulations of the Securities and Exchange Commission, whose purpose is to protect public investors. Going-private transactions typically include members of the incumbent management group who obtain a substantial proportion of the equity ownership of the newly private company. When the transaction is initiated by the incumbent management, it is referred to as a management buy-out (MBO). Usually, a small group of outside investors provides funds and, typically, secures representation on the private company's board of directors. These outside investors also arrange other financing from third-party investors. When financing from third parties involves substantial borrowing by the private company, such transactions are referred to as leveraged buy-outs (LBOs).

Issues Raised by Restructuring

Clearly, many forms of business and financial activities are covered by Table 1.1. These activities have stirred much controversy. Are they good or bad for the economic health of the nation? Do they divert the energies of managers from bona fide economic activity to financial manipulation? Do they use up financial resources which otherwise would be employed in "real" investment activities? Why has such heightened merger activity been a phenomenon of the last 20 years? In short, we need a theory or theories to explain the restructuring of corporate America. The materials we present throughout the book seek to shed light on these basic questions. In the effort to accomplish this, we begin by reviewing the major merger movements that have taken place in the United States since the 1890s.

EARLY MERGER MOVEMENTS

Several major merger movements have occurred in the United States (Golbe and White, 1988), and each was more or less dominated by a particular type of merger. All of the merger movements occurred when the economy experienced sustained high rates of growth and coincided with particular developments in business environments. According to the general hypothesis developed in the following chapters, this is not a mere coincidence. In our hypothesis, mergers represent resource allocation and reallocation processes in the economy, with firms responding to new investment and profit opportunities arising out of changes in economic conditions and technological innovations impacting industries. Mergers rather than internal growth may sometimes expedite the adjustment process and in some cases be more efficient in terms of resource utilization.

One reason why merger activity is concentrated in periods of high business activity may be that firms are not motivated to make large investment outlays when business prospects are not favorable. Only when future benefits accruing to a business endeavor exceed its costs is the action warranted. When such favorable business prospects are joined with changes in competitive conditions directly motivating a new business strategy, M&A activities will be stimulated.

The 1895–1904 Merger Movement

The combination movement at the turn of the century consisted mainly of horizontal mergers, which resulted in high concentration in many industries, including heavy manufacturing industries. The period was one of rapid economic

TABLE 1.5
Merger Activity: The Grimm Series

YEAR	(1) TOTAL DOLLAR VALUE PAID[a] ($ BILLION)	(2) TOTAL[b]	(3) NUMBER OF TRANSACTIONS VALUED AT $100 MILLION OR MORE	(4) NUMBER OF TRANSACTIONS VALUED AT $1,000 MILLION OR MORE	(5) GNP DEFLATOR (1982=100)	(6) 1982 CONSTANT-DOLLAR CONSIDERATION
1968	43.6	4,462	46	—	37.7	115.6
1969	23.7	6,107	24	—	39.8	59.5
1970	16.4	5,152	10	1	42.0	39.0
1971	12.6	4,608	7	—	44.4	28.4
1972	16.7	4,801	15	—	46.5	35.9
1973	16.7	4,040	28	—	49.5	33.7
1974	12.4	2,861	15	—	54.0	23.0
1975	11.8	2,297	14	1	59.3	19.9
1976	20.0	2,276	39	1	63.1	31.7
1977	21.9	2,224	41	—	67.3	32.5
1978	34.2	2,106	80	1	72.2	47.4
1979	43.5	2,128	83	3	78.6	55.3
1980	44.3	1,889	94	4	85.7	51.7
1981	82.6	2,395	113	12	94.0	87.9
1982	53.8	2,346	116	6	100.0	53.8
1983	73.1	2,533	138	11	103.9	70.4
1984	122.2	2,543	200	18	107.7	113.5
1985	179.6	3,001	270	36	110.9	161.9
1986	173.1	3,336	346	27	113.9	152.0
1987	163.7	2,032	301	36	117.7	139.1
1988	246.9	2,258	369	45	121.3	203.5

[a]Based on the number of transactions which disclosed a purchase price.

[b]Total: Net merger-acquisition announcements. The W. T. Grimm & Co. Research Department records publicly announced formal transfers of ownership of at least 10 percent of a company's assets or equity where the purchase price is at least $500,000, and where one of the parties is a U.S. company. These actions are recorded as they are announced, not as they are completed. Cancelled transactions are deducted from total announcements in the period in which the cancellation occurred, resulting in net merger-acquisition announcements for that period.

SOURCE: Columns (1–4): W. T. Grimm & Co. *Mergerstat Review*, Chicago, IL; column (5): *Economic Report of the President* (Table B-3) January 1989, *Economic Indicators*, U.S. Government Printing Office, August 1989, p. 2; column (6): column (1) divided by column (5).

course, include all of the large transactions. Column (2) shows that the net number of merger-acquisition announcements in 1985 was only about half the level of 1969. However, because the number of transactions valued at $100 million or more or $1 billion or more was much larger in later years, column (6) shows that the constant dollar consideration involved in mergers was higher in 1985 than in 1968 or 1969, the previous high years. In fact, it was not until 1984 that the constant dollar consideration in mergers approximated the level that had been reached in 1968. However, during 1985 the constant dollar consideration in mergers-acquisitions was 40 percent higher than the level of 1968.

Another measure of the economic magnitude of the M&A activity in recent

TABLE 1.6
M&As in Relation to Size of the Economy

YEAR	(1) DOLLAR AMOUNT OF M&As ($ BILLION)	(2) GNP IN CURRENT DOLLARS ($ BILLION)	(3) M&As AS % OF GNP
1968	43.6	892.7	4.9
1969	23.7	963.9	2.5
1970	16.4	1,015.5	1.6
1971	12.6	1,102.7	1.1
1972	16.7	1,212.8	1.4
1973	16.7	1,359.3	1.2
1974	12.4	1,472.8	0.8
1975	11.8	1,598.4	0.7
1976	20.0	1,782.8	1.1
1977	21.9	1,990.5	1.1
1978	34.2	2,249.7	1.5
1979	43.5	2,508.2	1.7
1980	44.3	2,732.0	1.6
1981	82.6	3,052.6	2.7
1982	53.8	3,166.0	1.7
1983	73.1	3,405.7	2.1
1984	122.2	3,772.2	3.2
1985	179.6	4,014.9	4.5
1986	173.1	4,240.3	4.1
1987	163.7	4,526.7	3.6
1988	246.9	4,880.6	5.1

SOURCES: Column (1): W. T. Grimm & Co.; *Mergerstat Review,* Chicago, IL; column (2): *Economic Report of the President* (Table B-1) January 1989; *Economic Indicators,* U.S. Government Printing Office, August 1989, p.1.

years is to express M&A activity in relation to the economy as a whole. This is done in Table 1.6 in which the dollar amount of M&A activity is expressed as a percent of gross national product (GNP) for the years 1968–1988. By this measure, M&A activity, despite the large size of major mergers in 1984–1986, did not match the earlier peak of 1968 until 1988. Some would argue that this evidence shows that recent M&A activity has not been excessive, but rather has produced restructuring that has contributed to the economic vigor of the 1980s.

Other evidence has also been cited to argue that in a broader economic perspective, the M&A activity of recent years merely parallels the growth of the economy. Such a measure is provided in Table 1.7 which presents the total assets of all corporations as the reference metric. Only in the years 1968, 1984, 1985, and 1988 did M&A activity exceed 1 percent of the total assets of all corporations.

But since M&A activity often involves equity values alone, the relevant base might also be total equities. In Table 1.8 this comparison is made. In 1981, for the first time M&As exceeded 5 percent of all equities. But a decline took place in 1982 and 1983, before rising to the historical high of 6.9 percent in 1988. Both M&A data and total equity values have been pushed upward by the bull

TABLE 1.7
M&As in Relation to the Corporate Universe

YEAR	(1) TOTAL ASSETS ALL CORPORATIONS ($ BILLION)	(2) M&As TOTAL DOLLAR VALUE PAID ($ BILLION)	(3) M&As AS % OF TA
1967	2,476		
1968	2,712	43.6	1.76
1969	2,910	23.7	0.81
1970	3,127	16.4	0.52
1971	3,455	12.6	0.36
1972	3,880	16.7	0.43
1973	4,333	16.7	0.39
1974	4,826	12.4	0.26
1975	5,292	11.8	0.22
1978	7,542	34.2	0.45
1979	8,624	43.5	0.50
1980	9,789	44.3	0.45
1981	10,927	82.6	0.76
1982	11,639	53.8	0.46
1983	12,572	73.1	0.58
1984	13,807	122.2	0.89
1985	15,147	179.6	1.19
1986	16,640	173.1	1.04
1987	17,792	163.7	0.92
1988	19,504	246.9	1.27

SOURCE: Column (1): Federal Reserve Statistical Release C.9, *Balance Sheets for the U.S. Economy, 1947–87*. Data for Nonfarm Noncorporate plus all Corporate, pp. 16–30. Washington, DC: Board of Governors of the Federal Reserve System.

market in equities that began in the late summer of 1982 and appeared to end on October 19, 1987. Also, M&A activity has the effect of shrinking the denominator in this ratio. It has been estimated by Salomon Bros. and financial research organizations that during the years 1984–1986, the total amount of equity values that have disappeared as a consequence of M&A activity has totaled $110 billion per year.

Table 1.9 shows that M&A activity over the years has been highly correlated with plant and equipment expenditures. For most of the years shown in Table 1.9, M&A activity has averaged about 20 percent of total plant and equipment expenditures. But in the earlier peak year 1968 and in 1985, 1986, and 1988 the M&A activity has risen to over 45 percent of plant and equipment expenditures. Some view the data as showing that M&As substitute for "real" economic investments. Others argue that while numerous factors influence M&As, the level of investment activity is a strong causal factor. They suggest that similar kinds of economic forces influence both forms of investment activity and that a similar economic rationale for both is operating.

TABLE 1.8
M&As in Relation to the Market Value of All Equities

YEAR	(1) TOTAL MARKET VALUE OF ALL EQUITIES ($ BILLION)	(2) M&As AS % OF ALL EQUITIES
1967	868.2	2.1
1968	1,032.6	4.2
1969	913.9	2.6
1970	906.2	1.8
1971	1,059.2	1.2
1972	1,197.1	1.4
1973	948.1	1.8
1974	676.9	1.8
1975	892.5	1.3
1976	1,052.0	1.9
1977	991.3	2.2
1978	1,034.2	3.3
1979	1,229.0	3.5
1980	1,636.0	2.7
1981	1,565.0	5.3
1982	1,798.0	3.0
1983	2,134.0	3.4
1984	2,158.0	5.7
1985	2,824.0	6.4
1986	3,361.0	5.2
1987	3,358.0	4.9
1988	3,600.9	6.9

SOURCE: Column (1): Board of Governors of the Federal Reserve System, *Flow of Funds Accounts: Financial Assets and Liabilities,* various years.

Mergers and acquisitions since 1976 have been concentrated in such service industries as commercial and investment banking, finance, insurance, wholesale, retail, broadcasting and health care, and in the natural resources area. The increase in mergers involving firms in service industries reflects the increasing importance of these industries in the U.S. economy. In particular, the financial service industry which represented over 15 percent of all mergers since 1976 has been undergoing restructuring caused by deregulation of the industry. The restructuring involved both consolidations within the industry, especially in the banking sector following the arrival of interstate banking, and production-extension, market-extension, and pure conglomerate acquisitions. It has been the consensus among bank merger participants that it will take significant size to compete effectively once interstate banking is completely allowed. Greater size would enable the banking organizations to capitalize on economies of scale in data processing, back-office operations, trust management, and in lending and financing. On the other hand, major industrial companies with

TABLE 1.9
M&As in Relation to Plant and Equipment Expenditures

YEAR	(1) DOLLAR AMOUNT OF M&As ($ BILLION)	(2) PLANT & EQUIPMENT EXPENDITURE ($ BILLION)	(3) M&As AS % OF P&E
1967	18.0	83.7	21.5
1968	43.6	88.8	48.4
1969	23.7	98.6	24.1
1970	16.4	102.1	16.1
1971	12.6	104.4	12.1
1972	16.7	116.8	14.3
1973	16.7	136.8	12.2
1974	12.5	149.2	8.4
1975	11.8	147.1	8.0
1976	20.0	164.6	12.2
1977	21.9	190.4	11.5
1978	34.2	221.1	15.5
1979	43.5	279.7	15.6
1980	44.3	282.8	15.7
1981	82.6	315.2	26.2
1982	53.8	310.6	17.3
1983	73.1	304.8	24.0
1984	122.2	354.4	34.5
1985	179.6	387.1	46.4
1986	173.1	379.5	45.5
1987	163.7	388.6	42.1
1988	246.9	429.7	57.5

SOURCES: Column (1): W. T. Grimm & Co.; *Mergerstat Review,* Chicago, IL; column (2): *Economic Report of the President* (Table B-51) January 1987 and *Economic Indicators,* U.S. Government Printing Office, August 1989, p. 10.

mature or declining product markets and in search of investment opportunities entered this field through acquisitions of nonbanking, financial service companies. Product department-store concepts have been pursued by Merrill Lynch, American Express, and others.

Changes in regulatory conditions have helped increase merger activity in broadcasting and health services industries. Acquisitions in broadcasting increased sharply in 1984 due to a less restrictive Federal Communications Commission rule governing the ownership of television and radio stations. Due to revised Medicare/Medicaid guidelines and private efforts to control medical costs, hospital occupancy rates declined. In response, hospital management companies have taken such short-term measures as cutbacks in staffing, supplies and purchases of equipment and the long-term strategy of acquiring businesses in growing alternative-care fields such as home health services, nursing homes, urgent-care centers, and rehabilitation and psychiatric hospitals.

Both wholesalers and retailers have been merging to improve operational

efficiency. Customer and supplier pressure on distributors to become more sophisticated in their operations such as automation, more service, and larger
inventories has led them to merge with larger firms for professional management and financial assistance. Retail companies have faced limits in their internal growth through new construction of major shopping malls and opted for
growth through acquisition.

Acquisition activity in the natural resources area significantly increased
since the increases in the prices of energy and minerals. Oil, gas, and mining
properties represented more than 20 percent of dollar value paid in all transactions during the ten-year period since 1975. Large oil companies were engaged
in vertical integration by acquiring additional oil reserves and also acquired other
natural resources. The forces that have driven the oil industry toward vertical
and horizontal consolidation are the earlier perception that the oil industry's
domestic resource base is declining and the more recent need to improve operating efficiencies.

Another characteristic of the current wave of merger activity is that divestitures became a substantial portion of acquisition activity. Table 1.10 shows that
divestitures accelerated following the conglomerate merger movement of the late
1960s. Divestitures also increased following the 1981–1982 recession. Throughout
the 1980s, they have represented over 35 percent of all mergers and acquisition
transactions.

Many factors influence divestitures (Chapter 9 treats this subject more
fully). In some cases acquired firms were comprised of segments that were
sought by the bidder and other segments that were intended to be sold for lack
of fit or to help pay for the parts retained. Divestitures were sometimes businesses having little relationship to the core activities of the company or having

TABLE 1.10

Divestitures, 1966–1986

YEAR	NUMBER	PERCENT OF ALL TRANSACTIONS	YEAR	NUMBER	PERCENT OF ALL TRANSACTIONS
1966	264	11	1977	1,002	45
1967	328	11	1978	820	39
1968	557	12	1979	752	35
1969	801	13	1980	666	35
1970	1,401	27	1981	830	35
1971	1,920	42	1982	875	37
1972	1,770	37	1983	932	37
1973	1,557	39	1984	900	36
1974	1,331	47	1985	1,237	41
1975	1,236	54	1986	1,259	38
1976	1,204	53	1987	807	40
			1988	894	40

Source: W. T. Grimm & Co., *Mergerstat Review,* 1988, Chicago, IL, p. 75.

management and financial needs that were out of proportion with their performance. Some companies instituted divestiture programs that were as active as their acquisition programs. These companies have shifted operations to serve markets with promising investment opportunities or redeployed assets to support core businesses.

EFFECTS ON CONCENTRATION

Impact on Macroconcentration

The high rate of divestitures is one of the reasons why merger activity in recent years has not greatly affected aggregate concentration in the economy. The share of assets of the largest 200 U.S. corporations to the assets of all nonfinancial corporations was about 38 percent in 1970. Their share declined to 36 percent by 1980 and to 34 percent by 1984 (Golbe and White, 1988, p. 277). These data give a view that is biased upward in that the largest 200 firms in the numerator are the ones that rank highest in each year of measurement—the individual firms in the list change. If the same 200 group of firms is followed over a period such as 1970 to 1984, their share of assets or sales of all nonfinancial corporations would decline more substantially. The significance of the changing composition of the largest 200 firms from an economic point of view is that it reflects the vigor of competitive forces in the economy. Over time, some firms rise in relative size while others decline, depending on their relative success in the marketplace.

International competition also needs to be taken into account. If aggregate concentration were measured in global terms, the share of the top 200 would be smaller. These data have not been compiled because of the difficulty of obtaining data for the denominator on a world basis.

Impact on Microconcentration

Concentration measures have also been calculated for individual industries. These are called measures of microconcentration. Historically, the most widely used measure has been the share of the four largest firms of industry sales, assets, employment or the value added in manufacturing, with the last receiving most emphasis. When the four-firm concentration ratio exceeds 40 percent, one view holds that competition in the industry may be diminished to some degree. But this view has also been disputed both on theoretical and empirical grounds. The degree of concentration varies widely among individual industries. When measured by value added, the weighted average level of concentration in individual industries has stayed relatively constant at about 40 percent over the years during the decades of the 1960s and 1970s (Scherer, 1980). Since no measure is available for the 1980s, the impact of the merger and takeover activity of the most recent years is not yet known.

However, the published microconcentration measures are based on U.S. domestic data, without taking international factors into account. This impact can be conveyed by measures of concentration for individual markets. In an earlier study, for example, we found that the share of the largest four U.S. firms in steel production in the United States was 52 percent. The share of the largest four steel companies (two were non-U.S.) of world steel production for the same year was 14 percent (Weston, 1982). More generally, we found that 75 manufacturing industries could be identified as having international markets. The four-firm concentration ratio (the sales or value added of the largest four firms to the industry total) for these 75 industries averaged 50 percent, somewhat higher than the 40 percent average concentration ratio for all manufacturing industries (about 450 in total). However, when adjustments are made for the international nature of the 75 markets, the average four-firm concentration ratio for these industries declines from 50 percent to 25 percent (Weston 1982).

SUMMARY

In this chapter we describe how merger activity has broadened into a much wider range of corporate restructuring and control issues. In addition to mergers and acquisitions in the traditional sense, we have seen an increased use of tender offers and joint ventures. Also in recent years divestitures have been involved in as much as 40 percent of merger activity. Other changes in ownership structure have taken place. Exchange offers and share repurchases have altered the ownership shares in firms. The greater use of leverage and increased use of lower-rated bonds have taken place. We have also seen public corporations of even relatively large size move back into private ownership. Often these represent management buy-outs and they are typically highly leveraged and referred to as leveraged buy-outs (LBOs).

Corporate control issues have come to the fore. Managements have sought to prevent takeovers by a number of methods. One is to repurchase shares held by major owners through premium buy-backs. Antitakeover amendments and golden parachutes have been used in the attempt to discourage takeovers. Increasingly state laws have been changed to make it difficult for takeovers to be accomplished.

To put these developments in perspective, we have traced the major merger movements since the turn of the century. All of the merger movements coincided with sustained growth of the economy and with significant changes in business environments. The horizontal merger movement in the 1890s was associated with the completion of national transportation systems making the United States the first broad common market. Mergers in the 1920s were represented by both forward and backward vertical integration. They appeared to represent responses to radio, which made national advertising feasible, and to the automobile, which facilitated national distribution systems. The conglomerate merger movement of the 1960s appeared to reflect changes in management technology that had developed in the 1950s. These were associated with improved methods of financial planning and control, long-range planning, and the emergence of the methodology of strategic analysis.

The recent trends in mergers and divestitures have represented activities of much broader scope than those of the previous merger movements. Some have ascribed the increase of mergers in recent years to changes in antitrust policy by the federal government. However, the changes in policy took place in 1980. Yet after increased merger activity in 1981, merger activity sharply declined during the 1982 economic downturn. The economic recovery that began in late 1982 has continued into 1989 and has been accompanied by a high level of merger and LBO activity. Thus an argument can be made that the merger movement of the 1980s, like previous merger movements, represents a response to fundamental characteristics of the economic environment.

One of the tasks of the chapters to follow is to evaluate whether or not the M&A activity of recent years makes sense for business firms and is good or bad for the economy and society. Many dimensions of corporate mergers, restructuring, and control are covered. We begin by seeking to understand mergers, restructuring, and corporate control in the context of the fundamental nature of business firms. Therefore, the following chapter treats the theory of the firm. It discusses why firms exist and the functions they perform in the effort to understand better the new dimensions of corporate activity that have been observed in recent years.

QUESTIONS

1. What are the major forms of M&A activity encountered in the 1980s?
2. What were the major merger movements prior to the 1980s in the United States, and what were the major factors involved in each?
3. What were the major factors explaining the increased merger activity of the 1980s?
4. What is the relationship between plant and equipment expenditures (investment) and merger activity?
5. Does merger activity differ from real investment in that the funds involved are no longer available for real investment?
6. What is the magnitude of divestiture activity in relation to merger activity?
7. Do you have any judgment of the effects of M&A activity in recent years on trends in aggregate concentration?

REFERENCES

BUFFETT, WARREN E., Berkshire Hathaway Inc., *1981 Annual Report*, pp. 4–5.

BUTTERS, J. K., JOHN LINTNER, and W. L. CARY, *Effects of Taxation on Corporate Mergers*, Cambridge, MA: Harvard University Press, 1951.

DEWING, ARTHUR STONE, *The Financial Policy of Corporations*, Vol. 2, New York: The Ronald Press Company, 1953.

GOLBE, DEVRA L., and LAWRENCE J. WHITE, "A Time-Series Analysis of Mergers and Acquisitions in the U.S. Economy," Chapter 9 in Alan J. Auerbach, ed., *Corporate Takeovers: Causes and Consequences*, Chicago: The University of Chicago Press, 1988, pp. 265–309.

JENSEN, MICHAEL C., "Takeovers: Folklore and Science," *Harvard Business Review*, 62, November–December 1984, pp. 109–120.

LIVERMORE, SHAW, "The Success of Industrial Mergers," *Quarterly Journal of Economics*, November 1935, pp. 68–96.

LYNCH, HARRY H., *Financial Performance of Conglomerates*, Boston: Division of Research, Graduate School of Business Administration, Harvard University, 1971.

MAGENHEIM, ELLEN B., and DENNIS C. MUELLER, "Are Acquiring-Firm Shareholders Better Off after an Acquisition?" Chapter 11 in John C. Coffee, Jr., Louis Lowenstein, and Susan Rose-Ackerman, eds., *Knights, Raiders, and Targets*, New York: Oxford University Press, 1988, pp. 171–193.

MARKHAM, JESSE W., "Survey of Evidence and Findings on Mergers," *Business Concentration and Price Policy*, National Bureau of Economic Research, Princeton, NJ: Princeton University Press, 1955.

MOODY, JOHN, *The Truth About the Trusts*, New York: Moody Publishing Company, 1904.

RAVENSCRAFT, DAVID J., and F. M. SCHERER, "Mergers and Managerial Performance," Chapter 12 in John C. Coffee, Jr., Louis Lowenstein, and Susan Rose-Ackerman, eds., *Knights, Raiders, and Targets*, New York: Oxford University Press, 1988, pp. 194–210.

ROHATYN, FELIX G., "Needed: Restraints on the Takeover Mania," *Challenge*, 29, May–June 1986, p. 30.

SALTER, MALCOLM S., and WOLF A. WEINHOLD, "Diversification via Acquisition: Creating Value," *Harvard Business Review*, 56, July–August 1978, pp. 166–178.

———, *Diversification Through Acquisition*, New York: The Free Press, 1979.

———, "Merger Trends and Prospects for the 1980s," U.S. Department of Commerce, Harvard University, December 1980.

SCHERER, F. M., *Industrial Market Structure and Economic Performance*, Chicago: Rand McNally College Publishing Company, 1980.

SHLEIFER, ANDREI, and LAWRENCE H. SUMMERS, "Breach of Trust in Hostile Takeovers," Chapter 2 in Alan J. Auerbach, ed., *Corporate Takeovers: Causes and Consequences*, Chicago: The University of Chicago Press, 1988.

STIGLER, GEORGE J., "Monopoly and Oligopoly by Merger," *American Economic Review*, May 1950, pp. 68–96.

———, "The Division of Labor is Limited by the Extent of the Market," *Journal of Political Economy*, June 1951, pp. 185–193.

STOCKING, G. W., "Commentary on Markham, 'Survey of Guidance and Findings on Mergers,' " in *Business Concentration and Price Policy*, Princeton, NJ: Princeton University Press, 1955, pp. 191–211.

W. T. GRIMM, *Mergerstat Review, 1987*, and previous years.

WESTON, J. FRED, "Domestic Concentration and International Markets," Chapter 7 in

J. Fred Weston and Michael E. Granfield, eds., *Corporate Enterprise in a New Environment*, New York: KCG Productions, Inc., 1982, pp. 173–188.

———, "Will the Restructuring Movement Continue?" ms., 1988.

———, and SURENDA K. MANSINGHKA, "Tests of the Efficiency Performance of Conglomerate Firms," *The Journal of Finance*, 26, September 1971, pp. 919–936.

CHAPTER **2**

Theory of the Firm
and Corporate Activity

We observe that firms engage in joint ventures, enter into other types of complex contracts, buy other firms, divest segments, and restructure in many different ways. Why do firms engage in such diverse activities? Why don't they just produce products and keep life simple? Even relatively pure production activities involve the structure of authority within the firm and organization control.

This chapter seeks to develop a foundation for understanding the many topics covered in the remaining chapters of this book. To understand the many aspects of mergers and acquisitions, corporate restructuring, and the diverse issues of corporate control, we need an understanding of why firms come into being and why they engage in the wide range of observed activities. In short, we need a theory of the firm. We try to summarize the vast literature on this subject in a form that helps explain the many diverse activities of firms described in subsequent chapters.

Among the important questions we analyze are the following:

1 Rationale for the firm—why does it come into being?
2 Firm versus market—why do some transactions take place within the firm while others make use of the market?
3 The corporation—why is the corporate form of business organization dominant in terms of the volume of business transacted?
4 Separation of ownership and control—is this an advantage or disadvantage?
5 Organization structures—who has authority in the firm and how is it exercised?
6 Organization learning—how is it achieved and why is it worth preserving?

7 Organization reputation—of what value is this to a firm?

8 Organization spirit—how is it achieved, and how does it increase efficiency?

9 Multiple stakeholders—in what sense do consumers, suppliers, workers, creditors, and the government have an investment in the long-run performance of private business firms?

These basic issues are involved in the major topics of this book. Some of the key subjects to be treated involve the following:

1 Internal versus external investments—when should a firm build capacity from within or acquire it by taking over another firm?

2 Acquisitions and divestitures—what role should they perform in the long-run development of a firm?

3 Takeovers—should the purpose be to improve operations or to engage in a "bust up" in which the parts are sold?

4 Executive compensation—how is this related to performance and the takeover market?

5 Dual stock—is it justified for certain shareholders to have superior voting rights?

6 Golden parachutes—is there any justification for giving executives special payoffs if a firm is taken over?

7 Management buy-outs—why do some managements take their firms private while others go public?

8 Poison pills—should shareholder approval be required for the enactment of provisions that seek to prevent the firm from being taken over?

These are the kinds of issues that are encountered. In order to have a basis for analyzing and evaluating matters of this kind, a theory of the firm is required.

Therefore, this chapter reviews, interprets, and synthesizes the diverse theories on the nature of the firm, its organizational and related problems, and the internal and market mechanisms to control these problems. More importantly, the implications and relevance of each theory on major corporate activities are analyzed.

The classical theory of perfect competition was concerned mainly with the price system but had little to say about the internal organization of firms. Authority or commands that we now understand to characterize the firm played no role in coordinating the allocation of resources. Organization and management to control owners of factor inputs which seek their own interests found no place in the theory.

These limitations of the theory were the natural consequences of the fundamental assumption of the theory that information is freely available. Perfect competition theory was a useful framework for explaining how a price system makes possible a decentralized organization of production and distribution (Demsetz, 1987).

The development of the theory of the firm since the seminal study by Coase (1937), however, has been rich in concepts and multifaceted. An overview of the literature on the theory of the firm is encompassed by the following outline:

   I. Rationale for the existence of the firm
    A. Transaction cost efficiency
    B. Production cost efficiency
    C. Firm as nexus of contracts
   II. Organization forms
    A. Vertical structure
    B. Horizontal structure
   III. Organization behavior
    A. Shirking
    B. Agency problems
    C. Contractual performance
    D. Investment behavior
    E. Capital structure decisions

The materials fall into three broad areas: (1) rationale for the existence of the firm, (2) organization forms, and (3) organization behavior. The rationale for existence treats transaction cost efficiency and later developments which encompass production costs to take all costs into account. It also discusses the institutional approach that the essence of the firm is the nexus of contracts among input owners restraining their behavior. Organization forms seek to explain vertical structures although one view is that the existence of the firm itself represents a vertical structure in some sense. Horizontal structure encompasses new developments such as the M-form structure, conglomerates, and multinationals. The third area deals with organization behavior. Here the firm is increasingly viewed as a nexus of contracts. New issues emerge dealing with problems such as shirking, agency considerations, contractual performance, investment behavior, and capital structure decisions.

    Using the framework as outlined, we develop the central themes in the development of the theory of the firm.

RATIONALE FOR THE EXISTENCE
OF THE FIRM

Based on considerations of transaction cost and production cost, a number of themes have developed, including those related to the contractual aspects of the firm. These are outlined in Table 2.1.

Transaction Cost Efficiency

The first approach to the theory of the firm hypothesizes that the costs involved in market transacting lead to organizational innovations (that is, firms) to reduce those costs. A transaction represents the transfer of a good or service across a technologically separable interface (Williamson, 1971, 1973). The transaction may be smooth, or the parties to the transaction may disagree on the quality of

TABLE 2.1
Rationale for the Existence of the Firm

SUBJECT	CONTRIBUTOR	CENTRAL THEMES	ACTIVITIES EXPLAINED
Transaction cost efficiency	Coase (1937)	Market transactions versus transactions within the firm	Formation of firms; investments
	Williamson (1971, 1975)	Bounded rationality; opportunism and small-numbers bargaining	Internalization of transactions; vertical integration; hierarchical decomposition of organizational structure
Production cost efficiency	Alchian and Demsetz (1972)	Team production	Horizontal integration; investments
	Prescott and Visscher (1980); Rosen (1972); Rubin (1973)	Organization capital; firm expansion	Growth of firms; mergers; joint ventures; financial reorganization to avoid bankruptcy and preserve organization capital; diversification
Firm as nexus of contracts	Williamson (1985); Alchian and Woodward (1987, 1988)	Holdup and specificity; moral hazard and plasticity	Determination of ownership structure and organization forms; joint ventures; capital structure decisions; management defenses and buyouts

the good or service and haggle over the terms of exchange. Obviously a smooth transfer is preferred; this could be achieved by an organizational arrangement between the transactors to provide for each other's needs. However, the costs of coordinating or managing transactions within the organization (that is, the firm) may offset the benefits of a smooth transaction. It will be efficient to substitute firms for markets only if the costs of transacting across markets become larger than the costs of managing the firm. The proposition of Coase is that a firm will substitute market transactions as long as management costs are less than transaction costs.

BOUNDED RATIONALITY AND OPPORTUNISM   Under market circumstances where competitive supply conditions are not satisfied, transactional friction can arise and may be avoided by complex contingent claims contracts. These contracts would envisage all of the changes that might take place in the future and take all possible contingencies into account. However, Williamson (1971, 1975) argues that a set of environmental factors together with a related set of human factors cause such contracts to be costly to write, execute, and enforce. He attempts to identify these sources of friction which ultimately lead transactions to be executed within a firm rather than across a market.

The environmental factors contributing to market failure, as identified by Williamson, are uncertainty and exchange relations between a small number of bargainers. These factors, when joined with such human factors as *bounded rationality* and *opportunism*, impede market transactions, as explained in the following paragraphs.

BOUNDED RATIONALITY AND UNCERTAINTY/COMPLEXITY   Bounded rationality refers to the limited capacity of the human mind for processing information and formulating and solving complex problems of the real world. Bounded rationality can take either computational or language forms. Bounded rationality resulting from language limitations refers to the inability of transactors to communicate successfully about the nature of the transaction through the use of words or symbols that are contractually meaningful.

The pairing of computational capacity and language limitations with uncertainty makes a complete contingent claims contract infeasible or very costly to write. Incomplete contracting exposes the contracting parties to risk of opportunistic behavior. Internal organization provides an efficient review and monitoring process that would be required to determine contractual performance, and serves to curb such opportunism, thereby relaxing the need for complete contracts. Also, the hierarchical structure of the firm facilitates the specialization of decision making and economizes on communication expense through idiosyncratic coding economies, through specialization of information collection and dissemination, and by promoting convergence of expectations. Convergent expectations serve to attenuate uncertainties that are generated when interdependent parties make independent decisions with respect to changing market circumstances.

OPPORTUNISM AND SMALL NUMBERS   Opportunism involves self-interest seeking with guile and includes shirking, cheating, and other suboptimal behavior. It can involve data distortion or the making of self-disbelieved promises.

In the absence of the small-numbers condition, opportunistic inclinations do not imply that markets are flawed. Rivalry among large numbers of bidders will render opportunistic inclinations ineffectual. However, when opportunism is joined with a small-numbers condition, the transactional dilemma arises where each party seeks terms most favorable to it through opportunistic representations and haggling. To avoid the bargaining costs and indirect costs of the process, the parties can be joined. The hierarchical structure of the firm permits incentive and control techniques to bear in a selective manner, thereby serving to curb opportunism. Further hierarchy permits small-numbers bargaining problems to be resolved by fiat.

The problem arising from opportunism and small-numbers bargaining is clearly illustrated by Klein, Crawford, and Alchian (1978) for the case of specialized assets. Their proposition is that the greater the degree of asset specificity, the more likely that transactions will be carried out more efficiently within organizations.

In general, an asset's productivity increases with its specialization to other inputs used in the production process. However, specialization also increases the risk of loss to the owner of the complementary asset if the other inputs are withdrawn. The owners of the other inputs ("unique" inputs) have the owner of the specialized complementary asset ("dependent" or "reliant" input) over a barrel. By threatening to remove the unique inputs, their owners can expropriate or "hold up" the owner of the dependent asset by taking a larger share of the return from the process. The expropriable amount is a part of the quasi-rent value of the specialized asset. A quasi-rent is the excess above the return necessary to maintain its current service flow. A quasi-rent represents a recovery of sunk costs when profits are not included in its measurement. The quasi-rent value is the present value of a stream of quasi-rents and equals the excess of its value in current use over its salvage value. The potentially expropriable specialized portion of the quasi-rent of a dependent asset is called the composite quasi-rent and equals its return in current use minus its prospective return in the second highest-valued use. In the absence of recourse, the owner of the dependent input has little choice but to allow expropriation up to the composite quasi-rent. There can also be reciprocal complementarity in which each input's value is dependent on the participation and behavior of the other. In this case, all the owners have incentive to engage in expropriative rent seeking.

Input owners thus have incentives to make preinvestment arrangements to discourage rent seeking and promote confidence in joint use of assets. They will choose the organizational form which minimizes transaction costs. The greater the transaction costs relative to the value of the output unique to the joint use of the resources, the more critical the search for an economizing form, particularly in competitive industries where cost economies are essential to firm survival. Long-term explicit contracts are one solution to the problem. Another is common ownership of the complementary assets which leads to joint ventures, or vertical or horizontal integration.

Contractual arrangements may be explicitly stated, legally enforceable contracts, or implicit guarantees enforced by withdrawal of future business if rent-seeking behavior occurs. However, a flexible contract may inadequately deter rent seeking, while a comprehensive contract will be costly both to write and to enforce. These costs may outweigh the benefits of the reduced expectations of rent seeking. Even if contracts are able to enumerate all contingencies and are legally binding, enforcement might require litigation and delay. The threat alone of litigation might cause large costs to the owner of an input with large expropriable quasi-rent, and to avoid these costs he or she might endure expropriation by the owners of other inputs. The use of arm's-length contracts is more likely where expropriable quasi-rent is smaller.

Common ownership of complementary assets is more appropriate where expropriable quasi-rent is larger. If the owner of asset 1 invests in asset 2 (which is dependent on asset 1), he or she has less incentive to behave opportunistically, that is, to later require the owner of asset 2 to pay more for the continued use of asset 1.

Production Cost Efficiency

Whether individuals produce independently and transact across markets or co-operate through a multiperson firm depends on the extent of scale economies to management and production as well as transaction costs. Even if transaction costs were zero and management costs were positive, it might be in the interest of a firm (possibly a one-person firm) to expand and produce its own inputs inhouse.

TEAM PRODUCTON   Alchian and Demsetz (1972) argue that team production is the distinguishing characteristic of the firm, along with the existence of a centralized agent in the contractual arrangements of all inputs. Team production results in greater output than the sum of the output produced by the team members working independently; that is, there is a synergistic effect. The team continues in existence only if the team output is sufficiently greater than the sum of output under independent production to justify the costs of organizing and monitoring team members.

The increased output of team production comes about as a result of the team and cannot be unambiguously attributed to any individual team member. This gives each team member a greater incentive to shirk than under independent production. The costs of shirking by a team member would be shared by all the team members and the chances of detection would be less. Market competition among potential team members could be a mitigating force; for example, an outside input owner might promise greater inputs or demand fewer rewards than current, shirking team members in order to secure a place on the team, but once on the team, his or her incentive to shirk is no less than any other team member's. Alchian and Demsetz argue that the firm provides the policing mechanism devised to detect shirking when team production is present. Monitoring is unlikely to eliminate shirking altogether. In fact, firms will monitor only to the extent that the marginal benefits of detection activity (reduced shirking) are equal to the marginal costs of detection activity. Various types of monitoring activities and programs to reduce the incentive to shirk result in varying types of ownership structures under alternative conditons.

According to Alchian and Demsetz, two simultaneous conditions lead to the formation of the classical free-enterprise capitalist firm:

1 The possibility of increased productivity through team production (in which the detection of shirking is costly).
2 The ability to economically estimate marginal input productivity by observing and specifying behavior.

Thus, the classical firm is characterized by team production and the existence of a specialized monitor common to the contracts of all joint inputs. The nexus of contracts assigns him or her a bundle of rights. Thus, input owners agree to be monitored to increase productivity which is in the interest of all. The specialist monitor has disciplinary power to revise all input contracts independently, and for compensation is given residual claimant status. This owner-monitor reserves the right to sell those rights.

ORGANIZATION CAPITAL   The efficiency and survival of firms may also relate to their informational advantages. Any entrepreneur could assemble a collection of previously independent inputs to achieve a certain end. However, an employer with a team already in place might achieve superior results, not because of any innate superiority of inputs, but because of superior knowledge about the relative productive performance and interaction of inputs within the team.

This theme of Alchian and Demsetz is expanded by Prescott and Visscher (1980). They identify three types of information which are collectively named as organization capital: (1) information used in assigning employees to tasks that they can best fulfill, (2) information used in matching employees for formation of teams, and (3) information that each employee acquires on other employees and on the organization itself. Productivity is enhanced with accumulation of organization capital within the firm.

Because of the presence of these informational assets specialized to the firm, employees cannot costlessly leave the firm. They are bonded to the firm, which signifies the existence of an implicit long-term contract between the firm and its employees. This in turn motivates both the firm and employees to make firm-specific investments in information, skills, choice of residential location, and so on.

The Firm as a Nexus of Contracts

A later development in the theory of the firm focuses more directly on the institutional aspect of the firm and views the essence of the firm as a nexus of long-term contracts restraining the behavior of transactors (Jensen and Meckling, 1976; Williamson, 1985; and Alchian and Woodward, 1987, 1988, hereafter A/W). In this view, which follows the tradition of the transaction cost efficiency approach, the essence of the firm does not lie in teamwork but in the nexus of contracts, even though it is recognized that teamwork always involves contractual restraints (A/W, 1987). The reason is that the form of organization—franchises, mutuals, partnerships, joint ventures, and so on—is determined by a nexus of contracts governing the special relations among people and physical assets which constitute the team. A/W argue that it is of little value to try to set the boundary of the firm and to define the firm as any particular form; what is more relevant is to examine each organizational form of group activity to understand the reasons for and consequences of different organizational forms found in social clubs, sporting groups, or production of goods and services for sale. Thus, a more useful concept than the firm is a *coalition*, which is a set of resource owners bound by contractual relations. As we shall see, the "nexus of contracts" view of the firm emerges as a generalization encompassing the various theories explaining different aspects of organizational behavior.

Williamson and A/W suggest teamwork always creates dependencies calling for contractual restraints. Initially, various input owners organize a team to benefit from the continuous use of costly, long-lived information (mutual knowledge) specialized to the activity of the team. The presence of teamwork is an indication of the costliness and durability of the information. The team has to solve two problems in addition to organizing the team: monitoring team resources to assure the delivery of promised productivity and controlling the potential for team members to renege on the original agreement for the sharing of income. Different levels of monitoring costs and vulnerability to opportunistic behavior lead to different ways of stabilizing the teamwork. A/W distinguish two kinds of opportunism, holdup and moral hazard, to more carefully identify the factors shaping contractual restraints.

HOLDUP AND DEPENDENCE (SPECIFICITY)   Whenever a resource is dependent on (specialized to) the rest of the team, there is the temptation for some contractors to hold up the dependent resource to expropriate its quasi-rent. Each resource in the team is likely to have made team-specific investments and thus be dependent on the other resources within the team and vulnerable to expropriation by holdup. Further, inside a firm, value is created by the teamwork (by organization capital). Therefore, the firm must solve the problem of how to apportion the value created to each input owner. To minimize the costs involved in the apportioning process, appropriate contractual terms are sought.

MORAL HAZARD AND PLASTICITY   Moral hazard arises when one party (a principal or input owner) relies on the behavior of another (an agent or input owner) and information about that behavior is costly. In this situation the first party can bias his or her actions more toward self-interest. Within the context of the firm, moral hazard will arise in employee/employer relations, debtor/creditor relations, and in the general problem of how owners and nonowners manage assets. Shirking by employees, increasing the riskiness of the assets by the debtor (the firm) and managing nonowned assets without adequate care are examples of morally hazardous behavior. A/W call resources or investments "plastic" when a wide range of discretionary decisions can be employed by the user. When plasticity is combined with high monitoring costs, moral hazard problems are likely to develop.

In A/W's view, moral hazard due to plasticity and monitoring costs and holdup due to team-specific investments and information of input owners are the two key problems giving rise to a set of contractual relations called the firm.

OWNERSHIP INTEGRATION   Common ownership of dependent resources provides protection from holdup. Further, moral hazard problems in the case of plastic assets are also solved by ownership integration since residual claimants are the owners. However, ownership integration can have its own problems if the ownership is shared by many people as in corporations. Problems also arise if the firm-specific resources are not all owned in common, for example, if some stockholders own firm-specific resources not shared in common by all other shareholders or if some nonstockholders such as employees own firm-specific resources (skills, information, and so on).

Shareholders may disagree about the best course of action, but this difficulty can be mitigated by making shares transferable. Limited liability lowers the transaction costs associated with transferable shares, since shareholders under limited liability need not investigate the wealth of each shareholder.

Diffuse ownership puts the shareholders, the primary owners of team-specific resources, at the risk of opportunistic exploitation. Thus, the board of directors as agents of team-specific resource owners becomes a means of safeguarding their investments. Still delegation requires monitoring and this is provided by certain shareholders who control large blocks of shares. These large shareholders suffer the cost of a less well-diversified portfolio and, therefore, must be compensated by the "outside" shareholders. This compensation can take the form of higher salaries for owner-managers and profits from insider trading (Demsetz and Lehn, 1985). In the theory of Williamson and A/W, firms with higher costs in monitoring their activities will be organized with substantial owners as managers. On the other hand, when they remain outside the firm, they can profit from engaging in frequent takeover activity although they may not be able to obtain proportionately greater shares of the profit than smaller shareholders (Shleifer and Vishny, 1986).

INCOMPLETE OWNERSHIP INTEGRATION   Owners of general (independent, nonfirm-specific) resources value the right of control less highly than owners of heavily dependent resources. This is because the value of general resources is not (or less) affected by the actions of the team. Competition among the resource owners will result in contracts in which firm-specific resource owners opt for the right to control by placing higher value on it and owners of more general resources choose prespecified rewards. Thus, the general resource owners become "employees" who sell their services to the owners of the firm-dependent resources.

In many cases, employees make highly firm-specific investments and have accumulated rights for future benefits. Then they will seek representation on the board of directors or other means of enforcing their contractual arrangements. In general, any resource whose value has become firm specific will seek some form of control. Labor unions collectively protect employees' firm-dependent values by restraining employers from expropriating firm-specific rewards. However, organized labor or labor representation on the board may have the reverse risk of employees expropriating employers' quasi-rents, especially in heavy manufacturing where large quasi-rents arise due to significant sunk costs (Ippolito, 1985). Firms safeguard against this risk not only by being committed to large interest and debt repayments through increased financial leverage, but also by underfunding pension plans.

In some firms, labor is more dependent on the firm than capital. Consequently, labor becomes the owner of these firms as in law and accounting firms where the manager-director-owners form well-matched teams and thus become strongly interdependent. This consideration suggests the notion that capital is the boss and hires labor is misleading.

In many firms, managers may make and accumulate personal, firm-specific investments over time. This will lead the managers to seek protection of their firm-specific investments, for instance, by owning more shares or through such defensive devices as golden parachutes (A/W, 1988, p. 71). Management buyouts may also be explained by such desires of managers.

Dependence can also develop outside the directly cooperating members of a team. Customers of a firm's product who depend on the firm's continued activity for service and supply of parts are owners of firm-specific resources. This dependence, when it becomes dominant, may lead to organization of the firm as a mutual (often in banks, insurance companies, country clubs, and so on) in which customers own the firm. Two firms such as a subcontractor and a prime contractor that are mutually dependent will create a coalition with contractual relationship. Their resources may be owned separately but specialized to each other. In this case, each would want representation or influence on the other's board, but the conflict of interests may increase divisiveness and the cost of making decisions.

When the ownership of all interdependent resources is not integrated, protection from opportunism is provided by credible commitments. For instance, stock options given to executives are such a commitment for reward to their personal, firm-specific investments. Joint ventures that can avoid expropriation by sharing common ownership are also a form of credible commitments. When both parties are reliant on an end product whose provision is subject to significant economies of scale, common ownership of the venture will prevent the holdup problem. Also, when two interreliant resources are owned separately, a joint venture by their owners will avoid expropriation of the composite quasi-rents.

ORGANIZATIONAL FORMS

Writings on the theory of the firm have resulted in a rich literature which seeks to explain important developments in the organization structures of business firms. Key contributions are outlined in Table 2.2 as an overview for the following discussion.

Vertical Structure

The emerging theory of the firm also provides increased insights over developments both in vertical relationships within the firm as well as in the development of parallel horizontal structures. A number of historical developments in the

TABLE 2.2
Organizational Forms

SUBJECT	CONTRIBUTORS	CENTRAL THEME	ACTIVITIES EXPLAINED
Vertical structure	Williamson (1971, 1975)	Haggling; adaptive, sequential decision making; moral hazard; information impactedness; convergence of expectations	Vertical integration
	Klein, Crawford, and Alchian (1978)	Specialized assets; appropriable quasi-rents	Contracts; vertical integration; joint ventures
Horizontal structure	Williamson (1975, 1985); Ouchi (1984)	M-form structure; conglomerate organization; internal capital markets; multinationals	Product-extension mergers; conglomerate mergers; foreign direct investments

economy provided the rationales for both forward and backward integration. For forward integration, an important emphasis was to control distribution quality. This was to avoid product adulteration at lower levels in the chain of distribution.

To illustrate, suppose that a manufacturer has developed a product that is of higher quality than competitors' but requires more servicing during and after the distribution process. The manufacturer may develop a reputation for this product so that it commands a price premium. The manufacturer sells its product to various distributors. A distributor may take shortcuts in the required servicing to lower costs, which cause the product to be less useful. If the distributor can still sell the product at the same price as other distributors who provide adequate service, the distributor's personal wealth will be increased at the expense of the manufacturer's reputation and other distributors who do not take the cost-cutting, quality-reducing shortcuts. The existence of this type of externality or "free riding" leads to common ownership of manufacturing and distribution channels within the same firm, that is, forward integration.

An additional rationale for forward integration was provided by the development of national communication networks by radio and television. It resulted in economies of mass advertising, preselling products, and obtaining the benefits of national markets. There was also increased recognition that the sales organization itself could be an important tool for market research.

Forward integration also increased the ability of firms to provide back-up service on big-ticket items. This would be true on a range of products from computers through other household items such as refrigerators and heating and cooking units.

An important incentive for backward integration was to control component quality. In addition, important forms of organization learning take place from the design and manufacture of key components and parts of the firm's product. Backward integration also facilitates the balance and use of specialized manufacturing facilities. The notable example here is the integration advantages in the exploration and production of oil combined with the refining operations.

Williamson (1971, 1975) provides a comprehensive account of affirmative rationales for internal organization and the reasons for market failures which involve transaction costs that can be attenuated by substituting internal organization for market exchange. Briefly, the affirmative rationales fall into three categories: incentive, control, and inherent structural advantages. Interests tend to be harmonized within an organization and free of opportunistic misrepresentations for fear of alienation. The firm can utilize a wider variety of control, reward, and penalty instruments than the market and has low-cost access to requisite data to perform more precise self-performance evaluations than can a buyer. The firm may also realize economies of information exchange through common training and experience, through repeated interpersonal interactions, and through the possible development of a compact code.

Williamson (1971) lists five sources of reductions in transaction costs. First, bargaining costs involved in bilateral monopoly or oligopoly situations can be avoided through vertical integration. Second, for products that are technically complex or that require periodic redesign or volume changes, contracts are likely to involve ambiguities that can be resolved only by haggling. Integration harmonizes interests, reconciles differences, often by fiat, and permits efficient (adaptive, sequential) decision making. Third, where strategic misrepresentation risks are large due to uncertainty, internalization reduces the incentives to exploit uncertainty opportunistically, allows superior access to the relevant data, reduces the moral hazard problem of contracting, and can selectively utilize the control machinery. Fourth, integration improves information processing through observational economies, convergence of expectations, and dissipation of "information impactedness" conditions. Fifth, integration facilitates institutional adaptations to circumvent regulations, avoid taxes, and so on. Internalization of productive activity also makes possible a specialization of risk-bearing function when members of a population have different degrees of risk aversion.

As noted earlier, Klein, Crawford, and Alchian consider the potential appropriation problem when an asset is specialized to other inputs. They examine a wide range of contractual forms of avoiding the problem. It is observed that long-term contracts may take two basic forms. One is an explicitly stated contractual guarantee legally enforced by an outside institution. Alternatively, there may be an implicit contractual guarantee enforced by the market mechanism of withdrawing future business if opportunistic behavior occurs. The defect of explicit long-term contracts are the costs of specifying possible contingencies and the costs of detecting violations and enforcing the contract in the courts. The smaller the appropriable specialized portion of quasi-rent, the more likely the transactors will rely on a contractual relationship. However, their central proposition is that if an asset has a substantial portion of quasi-rent which is strongly dependent on another asset, both assets tend to be owned by one party.

Horizontal Structure

The development of widespread railroad networks in the nineteenth century was an important event for organization theory. Asset specificity militated for common ownership of independently owned end-to-end rail systems; however, common ownership alone did not assure smooth operations with minimal transaction costs. In response, the railroads developed the first decentralized *line-and-staff* organizations and created formal administrative structures manned by full-time salaried managers. The system exemplified hierarchical decomposition of internal organization and enabled railroads to function more efficiently by separating support activities from operations.

The twentieth century saw the development of the *multidivisional corporation* (M-form organization), first in Du Pont and General Motors. Williamson (1975) explains this phenomenon with the transaction cost approach. Growing firms using a unitary (U-form) structure began to experience communications overload (bounded rationality) and the problem of functional areas within the firm pursuing subgoals (opportunism). Integration of firms as safeguard against opportunism arising from specialized resources can use the M-form to avoid these problems of U-form organization. The multidivisional form is a refinement of the hierarchical decomposition beyond basic line and staff. M-form organizations can achieve greater efficiency by using profit centers to reduce the need for information flows across divisions and to guide the allocation of resources to their highest-valued uses and by greater capability in strategic planning, monitoring, and control.

From the viewpoint of production cost efficiency, the multidivisional organization structure developed primarily to obtain the benefits of large fixed investments in general office expertise which could be utilized over a number of individual decentralized operations. The advantage of the decentralized operations was to place decision making on specific management functional activities closer to the level of activities. Thus, in General Motors, the prototype of the M-form of organization (Williamson, 1975; Ouchi, 1984), the general office and staff functions included research, economics, financial planning and control, and legal functions. But manufacturing and marketing were in decentralized, semi-autonomous divisions whose activities were specialized to some degree and oriented for close interaction with production and marketing requirements. Some activities, such as design and market research, required interaction between the corporate level and the divisions.

The multidivisional form was developed in General Motors at a period when the largest proportion (by dollar volume) of its output was automotive products segmented by groups of product characteristics. But General Motors also subsequently added activities related generally to transportation, such as buses, locomotives, and tractors; there were also household appliances and a range of high-technology activities in connection with government defense contracts.

Subsequently, in other firms, the multidivisional form involved more diversified activities. To be successful in more diversified activities, it appears desirable that some relatedness exist on some dimension of the activities, for example, research, production, or marketing. The fundamental requirement is that the activity as a part of the M-form organization should benefit from scale economies or learning advantages that the unit would not possess standing alone or as part of another organization. As Williamson stated (1975, p. 137): "The resulting structure displays both rationality and synergy; the whole is greater (more effective, more efficient) than the sum of the parts."

The M-form was carried to its most developed form in the conglomerate corporation. By definition, the conglomerate corporation carried on activities or produced products that were unrelated. Diversification reduces the variance or risk of an activity by combining activities, among which there is less than perfect correlation. If activities were perfectly related, then there is no diversification benefit from combining them. The conglomerate firm was said to combine unrelated activities, and even zero correlation yields benefits of diversification. The highest benefits of diversification come when the activities have perfect negative correlation.

However, portfolio diversification was not an adequate explanation for the proliferation of conglomerates. In the conglomerates that exemplified the best performance there appeared to be important elements of carry-over of capabilities to different business activities, at least at the generic managerial level. In companies like ITT in the days of Harold Geneen, the carry-over was in the effectiveness of financial planning and control. In Litton Industries, its early success resulted from the carry-over of technological capabilities and a general systems approach to many business lines.

Thus, in conglomerate firms, there was usually a carry-over of at least generic managerial capabilities. In addition, some of the internal transactions advantages argued by Williamson for vertical integration also were applicable to the conglomerate firm. The advantages included the benefits stemming from the internal learning process, the ability to shift resources more promptly and the internal feedback system. These allowed the conglomerate firm to function as an efficient internal capital market by curtailing capital allocations to some activities and redirecting them to more promising activities. In addition, the central office of a conglomerate served as a sort of agent for the shareholders in monitoring the operations of constituent parts, with the informational advantage of an internal versus external monitor.

Multinational firms extend M-form organization to direct foreign investment, and the rise of multinationals appears to be directly related to the prevalence of the M-form structure. They are particularly important in high research and development (R&D) industries where technology transfer is critical in extending operations. Recurring complex contracting to achieve international goals is superseded by the multinational firm to economize on contracting costs.

The holding company (H-form) is similar to the M-form organization in that it has profit centers and one central headquarters. But the control from the top officer is limited to decisions on the relative amounts of dividends and reinvestment from each profit center's income. Williamson (1985) suggests that when the common use and interdependence of physical and informational resources are limited, the organization will employ the H-form rather than M-form.

ORGANIZATION BEHAVIOR

The foundations for introducing behavioral aspects of the theory of the firm were set out by Cyert and March in their pathbreaking, *A Behavioral Theory of the Firm* (1963). Among others, the book analyzes the implications of individual self-interest in the functioning of the firm viewed not simply as a mathematical equation representing a production function, but as an organization of people. This framework stimulated consideration of behavioral aspects of the firm as reflected in the topics outlined in Table 2.3. This led to a substantial literature which is summarized in the materials of this section.

Monitoring and Ownership Structure

Alchian and Demsetz's focus on monitoring leads them to analyze the qualities of various types of organizations which lend themselves to successful performance monitoring under various circumstances.

Profit sharing is a method to reduce the incentive to shirk by encouraging self-monitoring. However, in larger organizations, profit sharing does little to reduce the incentive to shirk, since detection of shirking is as difficult as in alternative organizational structures, and the shirker bears only a fraction of the costs of his or her action.

On the other hand, consider professional or artistic organizations, regardless of size. It is exceptionally difficult to evaluate productivity by observing behavior in these types of endeavors. Mozart composed symphonies with relative ease, while poor Salieri slaved away doggedly; the observer of behavior might be led to conclude, therefore, that Salieri's productivity was superior. A brilliant lawyer might see to the heart of a problem in an instant, while another might require hours of painstaking analysis. Thus, the self-monitoring of profit-sharing organizations (such as partnerships) is likely to be most effective in relatively small and/or artistic or professional firms.

The corporation is the dominant organizational form in our economy. It enables more economical accumulation of capital by allowing many risk-averse investors to contribute a small amount each for a fractional ownership share with limited liability. The greater part of monitoring activity is carried out by management to which shareholders delegate decision-making authority for more effective control. Management, in turn, is monitored by both internal competition (from other managers within the firm) and external competition (the overall market for managerial labor and the market for corporate takeovers).

TABLE 2.3

Overview of Organizational Behavior

SUBJECT	CONTRIBUTORS	CENTRAL THEME	ACTIVITIES EXPLAINED
Shirking behavior	Alchian and Demsetz (1972)	Monitoring; residual claimants	Choice of ownership structure; profit sharing
Agency problems	Jensen and Meckling (1976)	Agency costs	Ownership restructuring; optimal capital structure
	Fama and Jensen (1983, 1983a)	Separation of decision management and decision control	Decision-making process; boards of directors; take-over contests
	Manne (1965)	Market for corporate control	Mergers; share repurchases
	Fama (1980)	Managerial labor market	Managerial wage contracts
	Shleifer and Vishny (1986)	Role of large shareholders	Tender offers
Contractual performance	Klein and Leffler (1981)	Reputation (brand-name capital)	Nonsalvageable investments; brand-name capital
	Cornell and Shapiro (1987)	Implicit claims and multiple stakeholders; organization capital	Signaling by financial policy; diversification
Investment behavior	Fama and Jensen (1985)	Organization forms and investment decision rules;	Choice of organization forms
	Jensen and Meckling (1976); Myers (1977)	Financial distress and investment behavior; risk shifting	Underinvestment of levered firms and by managers
Capital structure decisions	Jensen and Meckling (1976); Titman (1984); Fama (1985); Chung and Smith (1987); Cornell and Shapiro (1987); Alchian and Woodward (1987), Ippolito (1985), Jensen (1986)	Agency costs; intangible assets and signaling; contract costs; plasticity of assets and investment; expropriation by labor and management	Cross-sectional variation in capital structure; optimal capital structures

The monitoring of management by shareholders is enhanced by the unrestricted saleability of stock and by proxy machinery. Shareholders dissatisfied with management performance can bail out by selling their shares if they find they are unable to control management; presumably those who retain an ownership interest in the firm are those who are either satisfied with management performance or do not feel powerless to make a change. Alternatively, share votes can and do frequently congeal into voting blocs to effect decisive changes; this results in a phenomenon akin to the classical firm in which the monitoring power is concentrated in those who hold claim to the residual cash flows.

Alchian and Demsetz also address the issue of team spirit and loyalty which can enhance the common interest in nonshirking and improve the success of self-monitoring even in larger organizations.

Control of Agency Problems

Agency problems arise because of a divergence in interest between the agent and the principal. In the context of the theory of the firm, the relevant agency relationships are those between (1) owners and managers, (2) equity holders and debt holders, and (3) the firm and noninvestor stakeholders such as employees, suppliers and customers. Agency problems would not exist if contracts between principals and agents could be costlessly written and enforced. In general, an agency relationship gives rise to (1) costs of contracting, (2) costs of monitoring and controlling the agent's behavior, (3) costs of bonding to ensure that agents will make optimal decisions or principals will be compensated for the consequences of suboptimal decisions, and (4) the residual (welfare) losses that arise due to imperfect control of the agent's behavior despite contracting and enforcing activities.

At the most basic level, agency costs arise whenever the management of a firm is not the sole owner. Variations range from the entrepreneur who has had to sell external equity to raise funds for investment, but who retains substantial ownership and control, to the case where managers (without ownership shares) are simply hired hands to whom equity owners have delegated authority for more effective control. As in the case of team production, less than 100 percent ownership by management increases the incentive for management to shirk since the costs of shirking are not fully borne by the shirker. Shirking by management can take a number of forms, perhaps most notably the excessive consumption of perks, which may increase a manager's personal utility, but do little to enhance the value of the firm. Shirking can also take the form of working less vigorously to seek out positive net present value investment opportunities.

The significance of the conflict between ownership and control, principal and agent, is a matter of debate. Jensen and Meckling (1976) suggest that the problem is mitigated somewhat by the fact that burden of agency costs is borne entirely by the owner/manager. This is because outside investors will reduce the price they will pay for an ownership interest by their estimate of value loss caused by the increased incentive to shirk involved in a reduced ownership interest for the owner/manager. However, while the decline in total firm value may be borne entirely by the owner/manager, his or her total welfare loss is not so great due to the ability to consume nonpecuniary benefits (perks). Thus, the problem is mitigated, but certainly not eliminated.

SEPARATION OF OWNERSHIP AND CONTROL   Despite potential agency problems, many organizations are characterized by separation of ownership and control, where decision agents do not bear the major wealth impact of their decisions. This separation of risk-bearing and decision functions is found in open corporations, large professional partnerships, financial mutuals, and non-profit organizations.

The common stock of open corporations provides *unrestricted* residual claims in the sense that these claims are freely alienable, they have unlimited time horizon, and the shareholder is not required to hold any other role. Barring agency problems, unrestricted residual claims would be superior for all organizations. Fama and Jensen (1983, 1983a) hypothesize that organizations in which ownership and control are separated survive because they have found an effective means of dealing with resulting agency problems. They argue that agency problems are controlled by separating decision management and decision control in complex organizations.

It is generally recognized that the decision process involves at least the following elements:

1 *Initiation* of proposals for resource allocation and structuring contracts.
2 *Selection* among alternative decision choices.
3 *Implementation* of ratified decisions.
4 *Monitoring*—measurement of the performance of decision agents.
5 *Incentive* and *reward* system.

Fama and Jensen formalize into a predictive model the separation of the decision process. They hypothesize that the separation of residual risk bearing from decision management leads to the separation of decision control (selection, monitoring, and reward systems) from decision management (initiation and implementation). Their view is that the separation is efficient in complex organizations. Because the knowledge needed for decisions is diffused among many agents, decision management is delegated to agents who possess the relevant information—the hired professional managers in the firm. Decision control is placed in residual claimants. The advantages to having residual claims in widely diffused ownership are twofold. First, the large risk of uncertain net cash flows is shared by many. Second, this enables corporate enterprise to raise substantial funds for buying assets and for bonding payments to creditors.

The common features of decision control systems involve (1) a decision hierarchy, (2) a mutual monitoring system among employees and managers, and (3) top-level decision control which usually resides in the board of directors. The ultimate source of internal control is the expert board of directors. Some argue that the inside, or management, board members are more influential than outsiders (who are often nominated by the insiders). One view is that the insiders thereby control the outside board members. An alternative view is that the insiders have better knowledge of the complementary skills required and select outside board members to round out the breadth of capabilities required for effective control of the firm. Since the outside members are often decision agents of other organizations, the value of their human capital is at stake, which prevents them from simply acquiescing to pressures from inside management.

Fama and Jensen observe that open corporations are characterized by almost complete separation of decision management and residual risk bearing. This specialization enhances adaptability to environmental changes. They point to a number of mechanisms which exist to control agency problems that may arise. Two of these mechanisms are external. One is the stock market by which prices signal a wide perception of the effectiveness of internal decisions. The other external mechanism is the takeover market by which outsiders can oust incumbent managers by direct appeals to residual claimants.

THE MARKET FOR CORPORATE CONTROL   Control of the agency problem through the market mechanism has been the subject of a vast number of studies. Manne (1965) argues in his seminal paper that the alleged separation of ownership and control is considerably weakened by the existence of the market for corporate control. This market conveys to small shareholders both power and protection commensurate with their interest in corporate affairs.

The market for corporate control requires and presumes a high positive correlation between corporate managerial efficiency and stock price. The stock price of a poorly managed company declines relative to its industry or the market as a whole. A lower stock price facilitates takeover by giving the prospect of a large capital gain to those who believe that they can manage the company more efficiently. Thus, the takeover market provides some assurance of competitive efficiency among corporate managers and thereby affords strong protection to small, noncontrolling shareholders.

Shleifer and Vishny (1986) suggest a mechanism for active monitoring and takeover involvement by "outsiders." In a diffusely-held corporation, any one of the small shareholders does not have the incentive to monitor the management. However, the presence of a large minority shareholder provides a solution to this free-rider problem. In their model, large shareholders could initiate a takeover and gain, after the costs of the takeover, from the increase in the share price resulting from the changes in corporate policy brought about by the takeover. Or, third-party takeovers will be facilitated by the presence of large shareholders who are willing to split their large gains on their own shares with the bidder. Shleifer and Vishny provide empirical evidence that large shareholdings are prevalent among the largest corporations in the United States.

Fama (1980), on the other hand, places great faith in the disciplinary force of the managerial labor market. While equity holders are traditionally thought to perform the function of risk bearing in an organization, their risk as to the success or failure of a particular firm is far less than that of firm managers as long as capital markets efficiently price all securities and enable their sales at low transaction costs. Managers, however, are likely to have a good deal of their personal wealth, in the form of their human capital, at stake. Future rental rates for their human capital in the managerial labor market are dependent on the success or failure of their firm. As long as managerial compensation is adjusted regularly (and noise deviations in the measurement of performance are not excessive), over a manager's career, compensation will fully reflect his or her performance to result in what Fama refers to as full ex post settling up, and the incentive to shirk will be virtually eliminated. Whether or not actual managerial compensation in practice results in full ex post settling up is an empirical issue not addressed by Fama.

Implicit Contractual Performance and Reputation

The preceding considerations of the behavioral aspect of the firm focus on the ownership structure for efficient monitoring of resource owners and the separation of ownership and control in diffusely-held corporations. The questions considered are mainly related to the internal organization of the firm.

Klein and Leffler (1981) extend the theory of the firm by explicitly considering the implicit contractual relationship between the firm and its customers—the external market. They are concerned with the mechanism which ensures that a firm, in supplying a particular product, delivers the quality expected by customers. The question addressed is important under the real-world situation of informational asymmetry between the firm and its customers. It is a well-known proposition that if information about product quality cannot be acquired prior to purchase, only the lowest-quality product (that is, the "lemons") will be supplied. Klein and Leffler suggest that in such cases a firm may signal its commitment to a higher level of quality by provision of a "bond" in the form of nonsalvageable investment (investment in assets with no salvage value). The bond functions as a quality guarantee if the cost to the firm of lowering quality, the loss of the bond, exceeds the immediate gain from cheating, that is, lowering quality below the expected level.

The nature of the nonsalvageable investment is such that the firm expects to earn a normal return on the investment through repeat business with its customers provided it does not depreciate product quality, but less than a normal return otherwise. Customers perceive evidence of nonsalvageable investment as an implicit guarantee of product quality, and are willing to pay for it with a price premium sufficient to yield a normal return on the investment. The existence of expenditures on nonsalvageable assets may thus be regarded as giving rise to firm reputation or "brand-name capital." Nonsalvageable investments may take many forms. They will typically include advertising that does not provide specific information on a product or price, nonmarketable information resulting from research and development, and firm-specific aspects of fixed-asset investments or organzational development.

Thus, in the framework of Klein and Leffler, the firm is composed not only of tangible assets but also of intangible assets, including reputation. Liquidation of a firm necessarily involves the loss of its brand-name capital and reorganization under financial distress reflects this consideration. Further, mergers and acquisitions should be distinguished from new investments in physical assets as the former involve acquisition of intangible assets. In fact, some mergers and acquisitions appear to be motivated by the need to acquire established reputation in addition to the organization capital discussed earlier.

MULTIPLE STAKEHOLDERS AND IMPLICIT CLAIMS   While Klein and Leffler (1981) focus on the relationship between the firm and its customers, it must be recognized that all input factors—labor, suppliers, customers, and other societal groups—are impacted by the activities of purposive organizations and thereby become stakeholders. The production function of the firm therefore necessarily becomes multivectored in the sense of having to take into account the goals and preferences of alternative stakeholders. In recent years, this broader viewpoint of residual claimants has been well documented. For example, when labor unions are asked to accept wage reductions either in negotiations or as a consequence of formal bankruptcy or reorganization filings, they are typically compensated by a grant of a portion of the common stock of the firm; this formalizes labor's position as a residual claimant. The position of consumers is adjusted in a number of ways. Major lawsuits against business firms such as Johns Manville and A. H. Robins dramatize the ability of consumers to assert their stakeholder position in formal terms.

Cornell and Shapiro (1987) analyze the dependence of corporate policy on the existence of noninvestor stakeholders. They recognize that firms issue both explicit contractual claims, such as wage contracts and product warranties, and implicit claims, such as the tacit promise of continuing service and delivery of expected quality to customers and job security to employees. Implicit claims are embedded in every business transaction of the firm and cannot be unbundled from the goods and services the firm buys and sells. Explicit claims are essentially risk free as long as bankruptcy probability is low. However, firms can default on implicit claims without being in financial distress.

Cornell and Shapiro define organizational capital (OC) as the current market value of all future implicit claims the firm expects to sell, and organizational liabilities (OL) as the expected costs of honoring both current and future implicit claims. (Note that this definition of OC is different from the use of the term by Prescott and Visscher and in most of this text.) In this context, the firm creates value by selling implicit claims at an average price that exceeds (the present value of) the average cost of honoring them.

The price of implicit claims and thus the value of OC depends on stakeholder perceptions of the firm's ability and willingness to honor claims. If the total risk of the firm rises, stakeholders will recognize that the probability of default on their implicit claims is higher. Misinformation on the part of stakeholders will be a serious problem since implicit claims are embedded in every transaction and the firm cannot wait for current information to be dispersed. Expected opportunism on the part of the firm can also reduce the price of the implicit claims, which will lead the firm to find ways to certify itself.

These considerations result in important predictions about firm behavior. To reduce the total risk (rather than simply the systematic or market risk) of its residual cash flows, the firm will keep its debt/equity ratio lower, the greater the fraction of its total value attributable to OC. Also, diversification at the firm level becomes predictable behavior. Firms with high levels of OC will be reluctant to invest in unproven products. Rather, these firms will want to merge with smaller firms with innovative products which are established enough not to put the acquirers' OC at risk. Since OC is not separable from operation of the firm, high-OC firms will expand (worldwide) by direct investment rather than licensing, for example. For high-OC firms contemplating product line extension, there is a tradeoff between exploitation of OC and the risk of contamination. The contamination effect arises because failure to honor implicit claims in one product line affects stakeholder beliefs about the firm's ability or resolve to honor claims in other lines. In order to mitigate contamination, the firm could maintain financial slack to be able to drop a failed product without financial distress. The firm could also adopt a conglomerate structure, although this may require the firm to bear the cost of developing a separate reputation for each product line. Firms with high levels of OC will have above-average liquid assets and excess lines of credit to signal stakeholders that the firm has resources to cope with competitive threats without having to default on implicit claims. Further, the higher the OC, the more careful the firm will be to set dividends at a maintainable level, since dividend cuts are likely to have larger negative impact than dividend increases have positive impact.

Investment Behavior

Organizations can be distinguished by the characteristics of their residual claims on net cash flows. Different restrictions on residual claims lead to different investment behavior.

ORGANIZATION FORMS AND INVESTMENT DECISIONS   Fama and Jensen (1985) analyze the relationship between characteristics of residual claims and investment behavior.

The common stocks of large corporations are the least restricted residual claims in the sense that residual claims:

1 have property rights in net cash flows for an indefinite horizon;
2 are separable in that stockholders are not required to hold any other role in the organization; and
3 are alienable without restriction.

Large corporations whose residual claims are characterized by these properties are called *open corporations* by Fama and Jensen. They also define *closed corporations* as those that are generally smaller and have residual claims that are largely restricted to decision agents.

The unrestricted nature of the common stocks of open corporations fosters the development of an efficient capital market. When the common stocks are traded without transaction costs in a perfectly competitive capital market and their prices correctly reflect available information, a corporation's stockholders all agree that all decisions of the corporation should be evaluated according to the *market value rule*. That is, decisions should be judged only by their contribution to the current market value of residual claims of the stockholders. This is because, under the given conditions, the consumption streams that a stockholder can realize in future periods are constrained only by current wealth. When the optimal consumption stream of an investor is different from the payoff stream implied by the value-maximizing investment decisions of an open corporation, the stockholder can use the capital market to exchange residual claims in the corporation for other claims with the same market value but with a different payoff stream.

Market value reflects agency costs. Therefore, an important investment choice of open corporations is control of the decision process. Market value maximization requires extending decision control mechanisms to the point where the value of improved decisions of agents equals the cost of improved control.

Residual claims of closed corporations, proprietorships, and partnerships are generally restricted to decision agents (that is, management). This restriction avoids costs of controlling agency problems between decision agents and residual claimants of these organizations. However, there are costs in the form of inefficiency in residual risk bearing and underinvestment (deviation from the market value rule). The limited personal wealth of these firms causes them to invest less in capital projects than open corporations. Moreover, the residual claimants of these firms forego optimal portfolio diversification so that only an appropriately small number of agents have rights for both decision making and residual claims. Since diversification is limited, the implicit price of risk (or discount rate) applied by the residual claimants in evaluating projects tends to exceed the market price of risk (or discount rate) used by open corporations. This causes closed corporations, proprietorships, and partnerships to invest less in risky projects. Further, the restricted alienability of residual claims generates uncertainty about a residual claimant's ability to capture the full value of *future* claims when he or she leaves the firm. This uncertainty causes these firms to choose lower levels of investment in long-term capital projects than open corporations. Closed corporations, proprietorships, and partnerships survive in the face of these inefficiencies because they avoid agency costs incurred by open corporations.

AGENCY RELATIONSHIPS AND INVESTMENT BEHAVIOR   When firms are financed by debt as well as equity, their investment behavior will be different relative to the case of no financial leverage.

STOCKHOLDERS VERSUS BONDHOLDERS. Myers (1977) shows that there are situations where the residual claimants of a levered firm refuse to contribute equity capital to undertake projects with positive net present values. This occurs because any increase in firm value is shared by stockholders and bondholders. Therefore, it may not be in the interest of stockholders to contribute new capital even if a project has positive net present value.

Theoretically, all firms with outstanding debt will be affected by this problem, but the problem becomes more serious when firms are under financial distress. When the default risk is higher, bondholders will gain more from new investments that increase firm value.

The current market value of a levered firm reflects the possibility of skipping profitable investment opportunities in the future. Thus, Myers argues that firms with more growth opportunities will tend to use less debt. Nevertheless, as long as firms use debt, their investments are likely to be smaller because of the particular agency problem between bondholders and equity holders.

We also see in the following discussion of capital structure that a levered firm has the incentive to increase its level of risk by choosing a project with higher risk even when another project with the same net present value but with lower risk is available. This would imply that the firm may undertake risky projects even with zero or negative net present value.

OWNERS VERSUS MANAGERS. It has been argued in the literature that the agency relationship between managers and shareholders may result in underinvestment. Jensen and Smith (1985) discuss three sources of this agency problem. First, as Jensen and Meckling argue, new investments usually require additional efforts on the part of managers. But, in the absence of appropriate incentives, managers may be reluctant to put in additional efforts. Second, managers have investments in the firm in the form of specialized human capital and thus tend to dislike risky investment projects which would increase the total risk of the firm. Third, managers may forego investments in long-term capital and research and development projects if there is informational asymmetry between the stock market and the management, and thus the stock price does not fully reflect the true value of the project, or if managers are compensated based on short-term accounting performance results rather than on the market value of the firm.

Most of these problems may be mitigated by the threat of takeover or ex post settling up of managerial compensation in the market or by the institution of an incentive compensation program to avoid shirking and pursuit of self-interest by managers. However, these market forces or internal control devices may be too costly and imperfect to completely resolve the agency problem of underinvestment.

ASSET STRUCTURE AND INVESTMENT BEHAVIOR   The preceding discussions on reputation and implicit claims have implications for investment behavior of firms. A firm whose asset structure involves a large amount of such intangibles will want to reduce its total risk rather than simply systematic or market risk. Therefore, these firms will tend to invest less in risky capital projects than others whose assets mainly consist of physical investments.

Financial Decisions

The theory of the firm also has implications for corporate financial policy, particularly on capital structure and dividend decisions. The literature on agency costs (Jensen and Meckling, 1976) suggests that there will be an optimal capital structure for a firm which minimizes its total agency costs. There is a tradeoff between the agency costs of using outside debt and those of using external equity. Alchian and Woodward (1987, 1988) argue that the moral hazard cost of debt will be larger for more plastic assets and thus the debt/equity ratio will be low for firms with more plastic assets. A recent development in the theory of capital structure focuses on the effect of a firm's intangible assets (reputation, the value of implicit claims to be sold, and so on) on corporate capital structure decisions (Chung and Smith, 1987, Cornell and Shapiro, 1987, Titman, 1984). There are also "enlist the bondholders" theories based on the monitoring expertise of financial specialists (debt holders). Their expert monitoring helps reduce the contract cost between the firm and its suppliers (Fama, 1985) and also the efforts of equity holders to monitor managers. The "commit the quasi-rents" view is that committing quasi-rent income to interest and debt payment avoids expropriation by labor (Ippolito, 1985) and by management (Jensen, 1986). With regard to dividend policy, both agency and information-signaling effects may perform roles. Easterbrook (1984) suggests that dividends may provide a low-cost method of monitoring managers and may be useful in adjusting the levels of risk that may be selected by managers and by different classes of investors. These materials will be developed more fully in Chapter 5.

EXTENSIONS AND CONCLUSIONS

Organization Learning, Organization Capital, Brand-name Capital, and Economic Rents

Organization learning is defined in the literature as the improvement in skills and abilities through learning within the firm. This can have at least two dimensions. One is the increased efficiency of individual workers with experience; this would be represented by products that have long volume runs. This is referred to as moving down the learning curve with the experience of the individual workers and worker groups. The second aspect is team effects. As members of an organization work together over a period of time, the Williamson principles can take effect, as discussed earlier. Inside the organization, information flows more efficiently and transactions costs are reduced.

Organization learning has been distinguished from the concept of organization capital, which has been defined as firm-specific informational assets. Among individual managers and workers, a part of learning experience could be firm-specific informational assets. In addition, there would also be team effects arising from specialized information, which can be carried over to either other firms in the same industries or across industries only if the team is transferred as a whole.

In reality, organization learning and organization capital exist in combinations and may not be separable. When organization learning and organization capital reside in generic managerial capabilities such as research, and planning and control, they would appear to be transferable across firms and across industries. But both organization learning and organization capital could also be industry specific. In this case, they are more likely to be other than generic managerial capabilities. When organization learning and organization capital reside in non-managerial human capital, they are more likely to be firm-specific.

A related concept has been the view of the firm as a set of contractual relationships. The firm is viewed as a set of interrelated contracts among the factor input suppliers and the purchasers of final outputs. Many different stakeholders have long-term interests in the firm. When a firm has achieved organization learning and developed organization capital, it has valuable assets.

These assets together with brand-name capital give rise to an ability of the firm to sell either or both explicit and implicit claims to stakeholders on favorable terms, thereby earning quasi-rents. These intangible assets make input owners interdependent and call for long-term contracts among residual claimants and other stakeholders, which will permit one or more groups of stakeholders to earn economic rents. This recognizes that economic rents accrue not only to residual claimants in the traditional sense. All stakeholders who enter into implicit or explicit contracts which constitute the firm may have the ability to extract quasi-rents. To illustrate, prior to the 1970s, when American mass-production industries were low-cost producers and sold in the large U.S. market free from external competition, rents were earned by the more efficient firms in the industry. Some argue that these rents were received not only by the stockholders, but by labor and consumers as well. Labor had become effectively organized through the industrial labor movement of the mid-1930s. With industrywide unions, strong union leadership (sometimes with government support) exerted market power for its members. In addition, the price trend performances of these industries were superior, with price increases lower than general price indexes. (Presumably, the low price increases partly reflected organization learning and accumulation of organization capital.) Thus, labor and consumers shared the economic rents (quasi-rents). With unequal cost conditions among the firms in these industries, shareholders of low-cost firms earned positive economic rents, while shareholders of high-cost firms earned negative economic rents.

Investment, M&As, and Restructuring

Finally, we bring together some of the propositions previously developed to provide some perspective on the role of mergers, acquisitions, and corporate restructuring. These are all forms of investment activity. Investment opportunities may be defined as the ability to earn rent from a firm's organization capital and brand-name capital by placing resources in projects with positive net present value. Investment opportunities can take at least three forms. Internal investments are the continuation or expansion of existing projects or the addition of new projects internally. Investment activity can also be external in the form of horizontal, vertical, product-extension, and geographic market-extension mergers or conglomerate merger activity. Restructuring refers to liquidating projects in some areas and redirecting assets to other existing or new areas. The concept of restructuring has also been applied to changing the ownership structures or financing patterns in firms. Of course, different sets of the major themes developed for the nature of the firm should be able to explain different restructuring activities.

Expanding existing product-market activities would appear to involve the least risk in that the firm is moving into areas in which it has had previous experience. But sales-to-capacity relations and profitability prospects may be relatively unfavorable in a firm's traditional product-market areas. Some of the most attractive prospects may appear to be in new areas, whether entered internally or by external transactions. Totally new business areas may appear more attractive because they represent important innovations or because the new area is not adequately understood by the firm. Launching into new product-market areas internally may be less efficient because the firm lacks critical capabilities in the new area, or because other firms with good track records and high capabilities have already made investments which will come to fruition earlier.

On the other hand, the disadvantage of external diversification is that the firm may not adequately understand the new area. In addition, external diversification by merger or tender offer means competing as a bidder in an efficient capital market with a high degree of perfect competition. Thus, unless an acquiring firm is able to transfer some capability to an external diversification activity, it can only hope to be a bidder among equals and such projects will, at best, be zero net present value projects. If the company has organization learning, organization capital, or brand-name capital to transfer, then there may be real synergy, which increases the probability that the project will have a positive net present value.

Looking Ahead

We did not explicitly resolve the many issues posed at the beginning of this chapter. The issues were set forth to provide a motivation for the relatively abstract materials on the nature of the firm summarized in the chapter. The framework provided by this chapter is applied in analyzing and evaluating many important topics that are covered in the following chapters.

QUESTIONS

1. What are transactions costs?
2. How are the following related to transaction cost efficiency: bounded rationality; opportunism; and specialized assets?

3. Explain the concepts of the unitary versus M-forms of business organizations.

4. What are the problems in the use of long-term contracts?

5. How do firms help solve the problems of bounded rationality and opportunism?

6. What are agency problems and how do they arise? What mechanisms can be used to mitigate agency problems?

7. Define and distinguish between decision management and decision control according to Fama and Jensen.

8. What are the advantages and disadvantages of the separation of ownership and control in the modern corporation?

9. Distinguish between organization capital and brand-name capital.

10. What are implicit claims and what role do they perform?

REFERENCES

ALCHIAN, ARMEN, and HAROLD DEMSETZ, "Production, Information Costs and Economic Organization," *American Economic Review,* December 1972, pp. 777–795.

ALCHIAN, ARMEN, and S. WOODWARD, "Reflections on the Theory of the Firm," *Journal of Institutional and Theoretical Economics,* March 1987, pp. 110–136.

———, "The Firm is Dead; Long Live the Firm: A Review of Oliver E. Williamson's *The Economic Institutions of Capitalism,*" *Journal of Economic Literature,* March 1988, pp. 65–79.

CHUNG, K. S., and R. L. SMITH, "Product Quality, Nonsalvageable Capital Investment, and the Cost of Financial Leverage," in T. E. Copeland, ed. *Modern Finance and Industrial Economics,* New York: Basil Blackwell, 1987, pp. 146–167.

COASE, R. H., "The Nature of the Firm," *Economica,* November 1937, pp. 386–405.

CORNELL, BRADFORD, and ALAN SHAPIRO, "Corporate Stakeholders and Corporate Finance," *Financial Management,* Spring 1987, pp. 5–14.

CYERT, RICHARD M., and JAMES G. MARCH, *A Behavioral Theory of the Firm,* Englewood Cliffs, NJ: Prentice-Hall, Inc., 1963.

DEMSETZ, H., "The Theory of the Firm Revisited," ms., 1987.

———, and K. LEHN, "The Structure of Corporate Ownership: Causes and Consequences," *Journal of Political Economy,* 1985, pp. 1155–1177.

EASTERBROOK, FRANK H., "Two Agency-Cost Explanations of Dividends," *American Economic Review,* September 1984, pp. 650–659.

FAMA, EUGENE, "Agency Problems and the Theory of the Firm," *Journal of Political Economy,* 1980, pp. 288–307.

———, "Contract Costs and Financing Decisions," working paper, University of Chicago, 1985.

———, and MICHAEL C. JENSEN, "Separation of Ownership and Control," *Journal of Law and Economics,* 1983, pp. 301–325.

———, "Agency Problems and Residual Claims," *Journal of Law and Economics,* 1983a, pp. 327–349.

————, "Organizational Form and Investment Decisions," *Journal of Financial Economics*, 1985, pp. 101–119.

IPPOLITO, R. A., "The Labor Contract and True Economic Pension Liabilities," *American Economic Review*, December 1985, pp. 1031–1043.

JENSEN, M. C., "Agency Costs of Free Cash Flow, Corporate Finance, and Takeovers," *American Economic Review*, Papers and Proceedings, 76, May 1986, pp. 323–329.

————, and WILLIAM H. MECKLING, "Theory of the Firm: Managerial Behavior, Agency Costs and Ownership Structure," *Journal of Financial Economics*, October 1976, pp. 305–360.

JENSEN, MICHAEL C., and CLIFFORD W. SMITH, "Stockholder, Merger, and Creditor Interests: Applications of Agency Theory," *Recent Advances in Corporate Finance*, E. I. Altman and M. G. Subrahmanyam, eds., Homewood, IL: R. D. Irwin, 1985, pp. 93–131.

KLEIN, BENJAMIN, and K. B. LEFFLER, "The Role of Market Forces in Assuring Contractual Performance," *Journal of Political Economy*, August 1981, pp. 615–641.

KLEIN, BENJAMIN, R. G. CRAWFORD, and A. ALCHIAN, "Vertical Integration, Appropriable Rents, and the Competitive Contract Process," *Journal of Law and Economics*, 1978, pp. 297–326.

MANNE, H. G., "Mergers and the Market for Corporate Control," *Journal of Political Economy*, 1965, pp. 110–120.

MYERS, S. C., "Determinants of Corporate Borrowing," *Journal of Financial Economics*, November 1977, pp. 147–176.

OUCHI, WILLIAM G., *The M-Form Society*, Menlo Park, CA: Addison-Wesley Publishing Company, 1984.

PRESCOTT, E., and M. VISSCHER, "Organization Capital," *Journal of Political Economy*, June 1980, pp. 446–461.

ROSEN, S., "Learning by Experience as Joint Production," *Quarterly Journal of Economics*, August 1972, pp. 366–382.

RUBIN, P., "The Expansion of Firms," *Journal of Political Economy*, July/August 1973, pp. 936–949.

SHLEIFER, A., and R. W. VISHNY, "Large Shareholders and Corporate Control," *Journal of Political Economy*, 94, 1986, pp. 461–488.

TITMAN, S., "The Effect of Capital Structure on a Firm's Liquidation Decision," *Journal of Financial Economics*, March 1984, pp. 137–152.

WILLIAMSON, OLIVER E., "The Vertical Integration of Production: Market Failure Considerations," *American Economic Review*, May 1971, pp. 112–123.

————, "Markets and Hierarchies: Some Elementary Considerations," *American Economic Review*, May 1973, pp. 316–325.

————, *Markets and Hierarchies: Analysis and Antitrust Implications*, New York: The Free Press, 1975.

————, *The Economic Institutions of Capitalism*, New York: The Free Press, 1985.

CHAPTER **3**

Strategy, Diversification,
and Mergers

M&A activity should take place within the framework of long-range planning by business firms. Therefore, it is useful to present a review of the planning process and the role of diversification and mergers in strategic planning.

STRATEGY

Many different theories and approaches to strategy formulation and implementation are presented in the literature. Some writers distinguish between strategy as a concept and strategy as a process. Others emphasize that strategy is a way of thinking. However defined, strategy is concerned with the most important decisions made in an enterprise. The central thrust of these decisions is the future of the organization. While the horizon is the long view, strategy to be implemented properly must also take account of mid-term and short-run decisions and actions.

Strategy is formulated in many different ways. The strategic planning process can be performed on the basis of a set of formal procedures and/or informally in the minds of managers. Strategy is not static. Individual strategies, plans, policies, or procedures are utilized, but they are not the whole story. Strategic planning is behavior and a way of thinking, requiring diverse inputs from all segments of the organization. Everyone must be involved in the strategic planning processes.

Ultimate Responsibility

Since strategic planning is concerned with the future of the organization, it follows that ultimate responsibility resides in the top executive (group). While many others perform important roles and have responsibilities for strategic planning processes, the chief executive (group) must take ultimate responsiblity for its success or failure. The chief executive officer (CEO or group) is responsible for the strategic planning process for the firm as a whole; the top manager of a division must be responsible for strategic planning for that division and for conforming it to the strategic planning for the organization as a whole.

Basic Steps in Strategic Planning

While different approaches to strategic planning may be found, they include the steps set forth in Table 3.1.

Table 3.1 indicates the critical activities involved in strategic planning processes. These procedures are described at length in the vast literature on strategy. Whether these represent formal or informal procedures, they are elements to be covered. In each of the strategic planning activities, both staff and line personnel have important responsibilities in the strategic decision-making processes.

DIVERSITY IN STRATEGIC PLANNING PROCESSES

Some general elements required for all strategic planning activity have been identified. In other aspects of strategic planning wide diversity is encountered. These involve a number of different activities and aspects involved in strategic planning.

Monitoring Environments

A key to all approaches to strategic planning is continuous monitoring of the external environments. The environments should encompass both domestic and international dimensions and include analysis of economic, technological, political, social, and legal factors. Different organizations will give different emphasis and weight to each of the categories.

Stakeholders

The strategic planning processes must take into account the diverse stakeholders of organizations. These are the individuals and groups which have an interest in the organization and its actions. They include: customers, stockholders, credi-

TABLE 3.1
Essential Elements in Strategic Planning Processes

1 Assessment of changes in the environments.
2 Evaluation of company capabilities and limitations.
3 Assessment of expectations of stakeholders.
4 Analysis of company, competitors, industry, domestic economy, and international economies.
5 Formulation of the missions, goals, and policies for the master strategy.
6 Development of sensitivity to critical external environmental changes.
7 Formulation of internal organization performance measurements.
8 Formulation of long-range strategy programs.
9 Formulation of mid-range programs and short-run plans.
10 Organization, funding, and other methods to implement all of the preceding elements.
11 Information flow and feedback system for continued repetition of preceding and for adjustments and changes at each stage.
12 Review and evaluation of preceding processes.

tors, employees, governments, communities, media, political groups, educational institutions, financial community, and international entities.

Writers disagree on the appropriateness of the stake of each of the groups listed. One view is that the firm need only maximize profit or shareholder stock values to maximize the long-run interests of every group. Another is that by balancing properly the interests of major stakeholders, the long-range interests of all will be maximized.

Organization Cultures

How the organization carries out the strategic thinking and planning processes will also vary with its cultures. Illustrative organization cultures are:

1 Strong top leadership versus team approach.
2 Management by formal paperwork versus management by wandering around.
3 Individual decision versus group consensus decisions.
4 Rapid evaluation based on performance versus long-term relationship based on loyalty.
5 Rapid feedback for change versus formal bureaucratic rules and procedures.
6 Narrow career paths versus movement through many areas.
7 Risk taking encouraged versus "one mistake and you're out."
8 Big-stakes (bet-your-company) decisions versus low-risk activities.
9 Narrow responsibility assignments versus "everyone in this company is a salesman (or cost controller, or product quality improver, and so on)."
10 Learn from the customer versus "we know what is best for the customer."

Some of the preceding examples may appear to be caricatures, but they are encountered in practice. In addition, they convey the wide variations in corporate cultures and how the strategic thinking and planning processes may be affected.

Alternative Strategy Methodologies

We draw a distinction between different strategy methodologies and different analytical frameworks employed in developing strategy. First, some alternative approaches to methodologies used in strategy formulation are considered in Table 3.2.

The first twelve in the list will be described somewhat more fully. The remainder are well known or self-explanatory and do not appear to require elaboration.

WOTS UP ANALYSIS   Identifying strengths and weaknesses and opportunities and threats would appear to be easily accomplished. However, much subjectivity is involved. Different managers may have different judgments. While opportunities may exist, the differences in cost may require a careful balancing of considerations. On balance this approach may provide a useful starting point for

TABLE 3.2
Alternative Strategy Methodologies

1 SWOT or WOTS UP—inventory and analysis of organizational strengths, weaknesses, environmental opportunities, and threats.
2 Gap Analysis—assessment of goals versus forecasts or projections.
3 Top-Down and/or Bottom-Up—company forecasts versus aggregation of segments.
4 Computer Models—opportunity for detail and complexity.
5 Competitive Analysis—assess customers, suppliers, new entrants, products and product substitutability.
6 Synergy—look for complementarities.
7 Logical Incrementalism—well-supported moves from current bases.
8 Muddling Through—incremental changes selected from a small number of policy alternatives.
9 Comparative Histories—learn from the experiences of others.
10 Delphi Technique—iterated opinion reactions.
11 Discussion Group Technique—stimulating ideas by unstructured discussions aimed at consensus decisions.
12 Adaptive processes—periodic reassessment of environmental opportunities and organization capability adjustments required.
13 Environmental Scanning—continuous analysis of all relevant environments.
14 Intuition—insights of brilliant managers.
15 Entrepreneurship—creative leadership.
16 Discontinuities—crafting strategy from recognition of trend shifts.
17 Brainstorming—free-form repeated exchange of ideas.
18 Game Theory—logical assessments of competitor actions and reactions.
19 Game Playing—assign roles and simulate alternative scenarios.

developing a strategic planning process and to stimulate strategic thinking in an organization.

GAP ANALYSIS   In the assessment of goals versus forecasts or projections, goals may be first formulated. These may be expressed in quantitative terms, such as sales of $2 billion by 19XX or net income of $100 million by 19XX or a return on shareholder equity of 15 percent. But a reasonable assessment of the future based on the firm's existing capabilities may indicate that these goals cannot be achieved by the target dates. The divergence may stimulate an assessment of whether the goals should be revised or how the organization could augment its capabilities in order to close the gap between goals and projections.

TOP-DOWN VERSUS BOTTOM-UP FORECASTS   In the history of strategic planning, a variety of approaches can be observed. In some companies overall projections are made with an assignment of requirements for individual segments so that the overall company results could be achieved. At the other extreme, the projections of individual segments could be added up with the result representing the outlook for the company as a whole. Good practice avoids both extremes.

There is evidence that successful companies begin with planning premises formulated at the overall corporate level. These planning premises begin with the outlook for the economy and the industry, translated into what appears plausible for the particular firm. The planning premises are supplied to the individual segments who use them as a basis for their own individual forecasts. The individual segment forecasts are aggregated to provide an outlook for the company as a whole. Meetings and discussions between the corporate level and the individual segments take place. A communication process is developed and iterations of meetings continue until a consensus is reached. The desired goal is a company plan that is understood and reasonable from the standpoint of the various segments and results in an overall company outlook that is satisfactory from the standpoint of top management.

COMPUTER MODELS   Computer models provide the opportunity for considerable detail and complexity. However, the models must reflect a theory or logic to guide their content. Otherwise, there is a great risk that the methodology will be overwhelmed by the resulting complexity.

COMPETITIVE ANALYSIS   A number of approaches to competitive analysis may be found (see, for example, Porter, 1979). Our approach is conveyed by Figure 3.1. Basically, what is conveyed is that a firm's competitive position is determined by important factors involved in demand conditions and in supply conditions. On the demand side, what is critical is the degree of feasible product substitutability. On the supply side, the nature and structure of costs are critical. Of particular importance is the ability to switch among suppliers of inputs. This may be critically affected by switching costs—the costs involved in shifting from one supplier to another. Supply competition from other firms including potentials for capacity expansion are also major influences on the competitive position of the firm.

FIGURE 3.1   Competitive Analysis

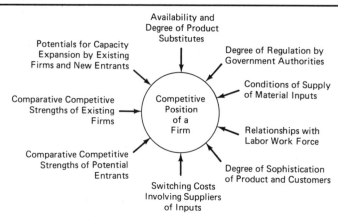

SYNERGY   Synergy represents the two plus two equals five effect. The concept of synergy was highly regarded at an earlier period, but then subsequently
came into disrepute. What is critical is how the extra gains are to be achieved.
One example of synergy is found in the history of the pharmaceutical industry
when after World War II the major firms shifted from producing bulk chemicals
for others to process to an emphasis on basic research and packaging products
that were ready for final sale. A sales organization was also required. After a
number of years, synergistic mergers took place involving companies strong in
research or marketing with companies that had complementary strengths and
weaknesses. Synergy can be a valid concept if it has a basis in reality.

LOGICAL INCREMENTALISM   After extensive field interviews, Quinn
(1977, 1980) concluded that major changes in strategy are carried out most effectively when the changes involved are relatively small or on an incremental basis.
In addition, he emphasized that a number of steps are required to involve the
organization as broadly as possible. The process he emphasized also involved
the exercise of effective leadership qualities.

MUDDLING THROUGH   This represents another form of the incremental
approach. Lindblom (1959, 1965) called the approach "muddling through." He
also used the term "disjointed incrementalism" to describe the process. The basic
idea is that instead of attempting an evaluation of a wide range of alternatives,
decision makers focus only on those policy alternatives that differ incrementally
from existing policies. An iterative process is then employed to formulate and
implement decisions.

COMPARATIVE HISTORIES   This methodology is widely used by many
firms in monitoring the behavior of their rivals. It was used in a fundamental
research mode by Chandler (1962) in an analysis of the interrelationships among
the economic environments of firms, their strategies, and their organization

structures. Chandler compared the history of organizational changes among 50 large companies during a century beginning with the period after the Civil War in the United States. From his studies he developed theories about the relationship between a firm's strategy and its organization structure at various stages of development. Individual firms continuously monitor the policies, actions, and reactions of rivals.

DELPHI TECHNIQUE   A questionnaire developed to obtain information on problems or issues is distributed by mail to informed individuals. The responses are summarized into a feedback report and returned with a second questionnaire designed to probe more deeply into the ideas generated by the first questionnaire. Several iterations can be performed.

DISCUSSION GROUP TECHNIQUE   The group leader begins with a statement of the problem. An unstructured group discussion ensues for the purpose of generating ideas. Information and judgments are generated. The goal is to reach a consensus decision or to make a decision based on a majority voting procedure.

ADAPTIVE PROCESSES   In some sense all approaches to strategy employ adaptive processes. The approach was first formalized by Ansoff (1965). The nature of the problem is structured on a tentative basis. Analysis is facilitated by

TABLE 3.3
Alternative Analytical Frameworks

1 Product Life Cycles—introduction, growth, maturity, decline stages with changing opportunities and threats.
2 Learning Curve—costs decline with cumulative volume experience resulting in first mover competitive advantages.
3 Competitive Analysis—industry structure, rivals' reactions, supplier and customer relations, product positioning.
4 Cost Leadership—low-cost advantages.
5 Product Differentiation—develop product configurations that achieve customer preference.
6 Value Chain Analysis—controlled cost outlays to add product characteristics valued by customers.
7 Niche Opportunities—specialize to needs or interests of customer groups.
8 Product Breadth—carry-over of organizational capabilities.
9 Correlations with Profitability—statistical studies of factors associated with high profitability measures.
10 Market Share—high market share associated with competitive superiority.
11 Product Quality—Customer allegiance and price differentials for higher quality.
12 Technological Leadership—keep at frontiers of knowledge.
13 Relatedness Matrix—unfamiliar markets and products involve greatest risk.
14 Focus Matrix—narrow versus broad product families.
15 Growth/Share Matrix—aim for high market share in high growth markets.
16 Attractiveness Matrix—aim to be strong in attractive industries.
17 Global Matrix—aim for competitive strength in attractive countries.

a series of checklists or analysis of matrix relationships. Successive iterations take place until a basis for formulating policies and reaching decisions is achieved. The method emphasizes developing a strong information feedback system to achieve flexibility in organization capability adjustments to its environmental changes.

The remainder of the approaches in Table 3.2 do not require further elaboration. The list conveys the profusion of methodologies encountered in strategic planning. The particular approaches to strategy adopted by individual firms and consultants involves selection from alternative strategy methodologies as listed in Table 3.2 combined with different groups of alternative analytical frameworks of the kind discussed next.

Alternative Analytical Frameworks

Many different alternative analytical frameworks are employed in the formulation of strategy. Their nature is indicated by the list in Table 3.3.

Many of the items in Table 3.3 are self-explanatory. Others are described in the references provided. We should like to comment on the wide use of matrix patterns of strengths and weaknesses or alternative approaches to markets.

A simple approach is the product-market matrix shown in Figure 3.2. It is based on the relatedness concept that is widely used in formulating strategy. The thrust of Figure 3.2 is that in developing new product markets the lowest risk is to stay "close to home." The highest risk is to venture forth into unrelated products and unrelated markets. This analysis clearly depends on how risk is defined. It may be very risky to stay where you are if, for example, the prospects for growth of existing products and markets are unfavorable and the industry has excess capacity.

Figure 3.3 portrays one formulation of a competitive-position matrix. It suggests a choice of emphasis between product differentiation versus cost leader-

FIGURE 3.2   Product-Market Matrix

Product / Market	Present	Related	Unrelated
Present	Low Risk		High Risk
Related			
Unrelated	High Risk		Highest Risk

FIGURE 3.3   Competitive-Position Matrix

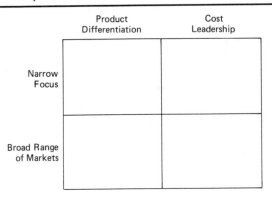

ship. In addition, the focus may be on a narrow market segment or niche or product representation to provide presence in a broad range of markets.

The matrix shown in Figure 3.4, the growth-share matrix, has been associated particularly with the Boston Consulting Group. Products for which the firm has a high market share in an industry with favorable growth rates are potential "stars" with high profitability. As an industry matures, its growth slows so that if a firm continues to have high market share, the attractive profits are available for investment in markets with more favorable growth rates so the products become "cash cows." Products and markets with low growth where the firm has a small market share are "dogs" and the firm should discontinue such products, according to the simple product portfolio approach.

A variant of the growth-share matrix is the strength-market attractiveness matrix shown in Figure 3.5. The greatest opportunities for investment and

FIGURE 3.4   Growth-Share Matrix

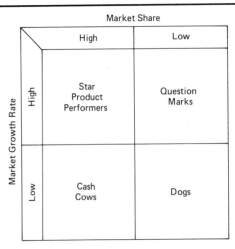

FIGURE 3.5 Strength-Market Attractiveness Matrix

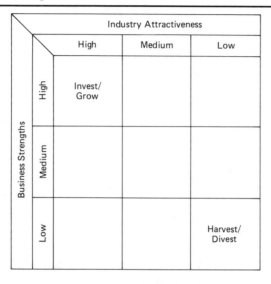

growth are where the outlook for an industry is attractive and the firm has high capabilities for performance in that industry. Where the industry outlook is unfavorable and the firm has weakness in such markets, the firm should divest or close down such businesses.

Figure 3.6 moves the analysis to an international basis. In the international setting the most attractive countries in terms of growth or political stability in which the firm has competitive strengths offer the most favorable growth opportunities. The opposite, of course, occurs in countries of low attractiveness where the firm's competitive strengths are low.

FIGURE 3.6 Competitive Strengths

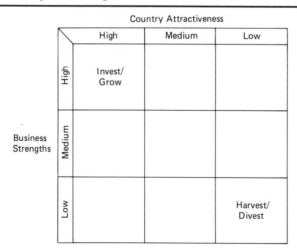

In our view the preceding examples of the matrix approach to strategy represent in spirit the checklist approach to formulating alternatives. They are useful devices for suggesting factors to take into account in formulating strategies.

The different analytical frameworks set forth in Table 3.3 are not mutually exclusive. In strategic planning a wide range of analytical approaches may usefully be employed. Their use is facilitated by a checklist and adaptive approach to strategic planning. Practicing consultants as well as individual firms have employed a combination of methodologies and analytic approaches with considerable success. Three approaches which combine different methodologies and alternative analytic approaches are described next.

APPROACHES TO FORMULATING STRATEGY

Many different schools of thought in the strategy field can be observed. Each represents some combination of the methodologies and/or analytical frameworks in the preceding lists. Three approaches are discussed more fully to illustrate how alternative methodologies and analytical frameworks are used in practice. They are: (1) the Boston Consulting Group, (2) the Porter approach, and (3) adaptive processes.

The Boston Consulting Group

The Boston Consulting Group (BCG) historically emphasized three concepts: the experience curve, the product life cycle, and portfolio balance (Boston Consulting Group, 1985; Henderson, 1984).

The experience curve represents a volume-cost relationship. It is argued that as the cumulative historical volume of output increases, unit costs will fall at a geometric rate. This is said to result from specialization, standardization, learning, and scale effects. The firm with the largest cumulative output will have lower costs, suggesting a strategy of early entry and price policies to develop volume.

The product life cycle holds that every product or line of business proceeds through four phases: development, growth, maturity, and decline. During the first two stages, sales growth is rapid and entry is easy. As individual firms gain experience and as growth slows in the last two stages, entry becomes difficult because of the cost advantages of incumbents. In the decline phase of the product line (as other product substitutes emerge) sales and prices decline; firms which have not achieved a favorable position on the experience curve become unprofitable and either merge or exit from the industry.

Related to the product life cycle is the concept of portfolio balance. In the early stages of the product life cycle, rapid growth may require substantial investments. Such business segments are likely to require more investment funds than are generated by current profitability levels. As the requirements for growth diminish, profits may generate more funds than required for current investment requirements. Portfolio balance seeks to combine attractive investment segments (stars) with cash-generating segments (cash cows), eliminating segments with unattractive prospects (dogs). Overall, total corporate cash inflows will roughly balance total corporate investments.

While the volume-cost relationships implied by the experience curve have been documented for some industries, particularly commodity-type products, their general applicability has not been substantiated. Microeconomics would suggest that the emphasis on cost advantage neglects opportunities provided by product quality, variety, and innovation. The emphasis on growth and/or portfolio balance may be inconsistent with maximization of shareholder value. The practical application of the BCG strategy to develop a dominant market share in an emerging industry may be difficult to implement; if many firms try to do the same thing their efforts may become self-cancelling. Some argue also that substantial aspects of experience are a part of knowledge that rapidly diffuses across firms and industries (Thomas, 1986).

The Porter Approach

Michael Porter has elaborated his views in a number of writings (Porter, 1980, 1985, 1987). His approach can be summarized into three parts: (1) select an attractive industry, (2) develop competitive advantage through cost leadership and product differentiation, and (3) develop attractive value chains.

Porter (1987, p. 46) defines an attractive industry or strategic group as one in which

> entry barriers are high, suppliers and buyers have only modest bargaining power, substitute products or services are few, and the rivalry among competitors is stable. An unattractive industry like steel will have structural flaws, including a plethora of substitute materials, powerful and price-sensitive buyers, and excessive rivalry caused by high fixed costs and a large group of competitors, many of whom are state supported.

The difficulty of generalizing about industries is demonstrated by Porter's example. During the past decade minimills have flourished and by 1988 some major steel firms had returned to profitability. In addition, there appears to be an inconsistency in that high fixed costs are considered to be an entry barrier in Porter's theory.

Second, Porter formulates a matrix for developing generic strategies. Competitive advantage may be based on cost leadership or on product differentiation. Cost advantage is achieved by consideration of a wide range of checklist factors including BCG's learning curve theory. The focus of cost advantage or of product differentiation can be on narrow market segments, or niches (for autos, the luxury car market—Cadillac, Continental, BMW, Mercedes, and so on) or broader market groups (compact and standard cars) or across the board (GM).

Porter's third key concept is "the value chain." A matrix relates the support activities of infrastructure, human resource management, technology development, and procurement to the primary activities of inbound logistics, operations, outbound logistics, marketing-sales, and service. The aim is to minimize outlays in adding characteristics valued by customers.

Porter's prescriptions can be interpreted as finding an industry or industry sector in which a small number of firms can "cooperate" (collude) behind high entry barriers. While many insights are found in the related checklists developed, the basic philosophic orientation is flawed. It is similar in spirit to the structural theory of industrial organization economics which evidence in recent years has controverted (Weston, 1978, 1982, and references cited). If barriers to entry are high, the costs of entry or acquisition will permit only a normal rate of return. Moreover, the dimensions of products and prices are so numerous and subject to such rapid change that collusive efforts could not achieve sustained effectiveness. Furthermore, the benefits of competitive superiority far outweigh the dubious gains from attempts at collusion.

Adaptive Processes

Other writers have been more eclectic than the preceding two approaches. These writers view strategy more as an adaptive process or way of thinking. (See, for example, Ansoff, 1965; Steiner, 1979; Steiner, Miner, and Gray, 1986; Bogue and Buffa, 1986; Quinn, Mintzberg, and James, 1988.) Some writers also emphasize the uniqueness of each firm. "In essence, the concept is that a firm's competitive position is defined by a bundle of unique resources and relationships and that the task of general management is to adjust and renew these resources and relationships as time, competition, and change erode their value" (Rumelt, 1984, p. 557).

More generally the adaptive processes orientation involves matching resources to investment opportunities under environmental uncertainty compounded with uncertain competitors' actions and reactions. The methodology for dealing with these kinds of "ill-structured problems" requires an iterative solution process. Most managers in an organization have responsibilities for the inputs and studies required for the repeated "going around the loop" in the strategic planning processes outlined in Table 3.1.

In performing the iterated checklist procedures, difficult questions are encountered. For example, is the firm maximizing its potential in relation to its feasible environment? Is there a gap between the firm's goals and prospects based on its present capabilities? Should the firm attempt to alter its environment or capabilities or both? Should the firm change its missions? What will be the cost of each alternative? What are the risks and unknowns? What are the rewards of success and penalties of failure?

The methodology involves not closed-form mathematical solutions but *processes*. It involves ways of thinking which assess competitors' actions and reactions in relation to the changing environments.

EVALUATION OF THE ALTERNATIVE APPROACHES

While some approaches emphasize generalizations, all make heavy use of checklists that have evolved into expert systems. Writers who have emphasized strategy implementation have recently shifted from a list of precepts to an emphasis on flexibility.

Checklists and Iterations

The adaptive processes methodologies emphasize the use of checklists to stimulate insights, but the BCG and Porter approaches to strategy formulation also rely heavily on similar techniques. For example, in his earlier book on *Competitive Strategy* (1980), Michael Porter utilized 134 checklists and checklist-like diagrams—one about every three pages. In his later *Competitive Advantage* (1985), the number had expanded to 187 checklists and checklist-like diagrams—about one every 2.5 pages. Stryker (1986) (adaptive approach) has 174 checklists in 269 pages—one checklist per 1.5 pages. Thus, the process of strategic planning includes the art of making checklists, going around the loop iteratively, with the expectation that the thinking stimulated will lead to useful insights and sound strategies, policies, and decisions.

The BCG and Porter approaches emphasize prescriptions. But in their actual implementation, they employ checklists not limited to the generalizations each emphasizes. In practice all approaches to strategy become relatively eclectic.

With the greater use of computers in strategic planning, the different approaches appear to have more and more elements in common. Particularly in recent years, expert systems and other decision support systems have been developed. These represent a disciplined approach to strategic planning in which rules are used to guide implementation of the iterated checklist approach, making use of ideas from a wide range of philosophic perspectives (Chung and Davidson, 1987).

Some Recent Developments

Publications by writers who have popularized strategy implementation exhibit a recent change in emphasis. In their earlier book entitled, *In Search of Excellence*, Peters and Waterman (1982) asserted that the precepts for success could be reduced to a short checklist: (1) bias for action; (2) close to the customer; (3) autonomy and entrepreneurship; (4) productivity improvement; (5) hands-on, value driven; (6) stick to core businesses; (7) simple form, lean staff; and (8) loose-tight properties.

Peters and Waterman (1982) admonished their readers to learn how the best-run American companies use eight basic principles to stay "on top of the heap!" Although *In Search of Excellence* was a commercial success, it also received criticisms (Carroll, 1983; Johnson, Natarajan, and Rappaport, 1985; Ramanujam and Venkatraman, 1988). Of particular interest to business economists was the analysis in the cover story of the November 5, 1984 issue of *Business Week* entitled, "Who's Excellent Now? Some of the Best-Seller's Picks Haven't Been Doing So Well Lately." *Business Week* (p. 74) studied the 43 "excellent" companies and concluded that many had encountered difficulties. The article observed:

> Of the 14 excellent companies that had stumbled, 12 were inept in adapting to a fundamental change in their markets. Their experiences show that strict adherence to the eight commandments—which do not emphasize reacting to broad economic and business trends—may actually hurt a company.

Peters and Waterman appear to acknowledge the deficiencies in their earlier prescriptive approach by shifting their emphasis in later publications. In *The Renewal Factor,* Waterman emphasizes flexibility; he quotes with approval the executive who stated that he wanted his managers to be "Fred Astaires—intellectually quick, nimble, and ready to act." (Waterman, 1987, p. 6.) Similarly, the coauthor of the earlier book, *In Search of Excellence,* in his 1987 publication begins, "There are no excellent companies. The old saw 'If it ain't broke, don't fix it' needs revision. I propose: 'If it aint' broke, you just haven't looked hard enough.' Fix it anyway" (Peters, 1987, p. 1). Similarly, two executives associated with the Boston Consulting Group have proposed that to manage for increased competitiveness companies need to "make decisions like a fighter pilot" (Hout and Blaxhill, 1987, p. 3).

But flexibility and rapid adjustments are more the stuff of tactics, not strategy! We believe that these recent developments in the literature on implementing strategy continue to suffer from the criticism conveyed by the *Business Week* article previously quoted. They make inadequate use of perspectives offered by economic analysis. Economics is forward looking, projecting market and supply conditions and patterns. Economic analysis can help identify prospective changes in such areas as demand, product differentiation, market growth segments, and behavior of rivals. Analysis of supply conditions can help identify areas of potential cost changes and thus targets for cost control. Economic analysis can delineate critical monitoring variables to indicate when changes in economic directions are likely to occur. Given this information, tradeoff analysis (the bread and butter of economic marginal analysis) can identify and analyze alternative paths of action and their consequences. In short, economics aids in dealing with uncertainty and in anticipating change, rather than reacting to events after they have occurred.

Economics seeks an understanding of environmental developments to identify the trends and discontinuities important to strategy formulation and implementation, as well as for providing a framework within which flexibility and adjustments can be achieved efficiently. From the preceding analysis of alternative approaches to strategy, we are now in a position to develop guidelines for developing competitive strategy.

FORMULATING A COMPETITIVE STRATEGY

The literature on long-range strategic planning indicates that one of the most important elements in planning is continuing reassessment of the firm's environment. In order to determine what is happening in the environment, the firm should analyze its industry, competitors, and social and political factors.

Industry analysis allows the firm to recognize the key factors required for competitive success in the industry and the *opportunities* and *threats* present in the industry. From competitor analysis, the firm finds out the capabilities and limitations of existing and potential competitors, and their probable future moves. Through these analyses and with additional consideration of societal factors, the firm's *strengths* and *weaknesses* relative to present and future competitors can be ascertained.

The purpose of the environmental reassessment is to provide the firm with a choice among strategic alternatives. For this choice, the firm then considers whether its current goals and policies are appropriate to exploit industry opportunities and to deal with industry threats. At the same time, it is necessary for the firm to examine whether the goals and policies match the managerial, technological, and financial resources available to the firm; and whether the timing of the goals and policies appropriately reflects the ability of the organization to change.

The firm then works out feasible strategic alternatives given the results of the analyses. The current strategy (represented by its goals and policies) may or may not be included in the set of feasible alternatives. A strategic choice is made from this set such that the chosen strategy best relates the firm's situation to external opportunities and threats.

Business Goals

General goals may be formulated with respect to size, growth, stability, flexibility, and technological breadth. Size objectives are established in order to use effectively the fixed factors the firm owns or buys. Size objectives have also been expressed in terms of critical mass. Critical mass refers to the size a firm must achieve in order to attain cost levels that enable the firm to operate profitably at market prices.

Growth objectives may be expressed in terms of sales, total assets, earnings per share, or the market price of the firm's stock. These are related to two valuation objectives. One is to attain a favorable price/earnings multiple for the firm's shares. A second is to increase the ratio of the market value of a firm's common stock to its book value.

Two major forms of instability can be distinguished. The first is exemplified by the defense market, which is subject to large, erratic fluctuations in its total size and abrupt shifts in individual programs. Another form of instability is the cyclical instability that characterizes producers of both industrial and consumer durable goods.

The goal of flexibility refers to the firm's ability to operate in a wide variety of product markets. Such flexibility may require a breadth of research, manufacturing, or marketing capabilities. Of increased interest in recent years is technological breadth. With the increased pace of technological change in the U.S. economy, a firm may consider it important to possess capabilities in the rapidly advancing technologies.

Goals may be stated in general or specific terms, but both are subject to quantification. For example, growth objectives may be expressed in relationship to the growth of the economy or the firm's industry. Specific objectives may be expressed in terms of percentage of sales in specified types of markets. The quantification of goals facilitates comparisons of goals with the potential for achieving them.

Efforts to achieve multiple goals suggest a broader range of variables in the decision processes of the firm. Decisions require judgments of the nature of future environments, the policies of other firms with respect to the dimensions described, and new needs of customers, technologies, and capabilities. In short, to the requirements of operating efficiency and optimal output adjustments has been added the increased importance of the planning processes.

Aligning the Firm
to Its Changing Environments

When it is necessary to take action to close a prospective gap between the firm's objectives and its potential based on its present capabilities, difficult choices must be made. For example, should the firm attempt to change its environment or capabilities? What will be the costs of such changes? What are the risks and unknowns? What are the rewards if successful? What are the penalties of failure? Because the stakes are large, an iterative process is employed. A tentative decision is made. The process is repeated, perhaps from a different management function orientation and at some point, the total-enterprise point of view is brought to bear on the problem. At some point, decisions are made and must involve entrepreneurial judgments.

The emphasis is on the effective alignment of the firm with its environments and constituencies. Different approaches may be emphasized. One approach seeks to choose products related to the needs or wants of the customer that will provide large markets. A second approach focuses on technological bottlenecks or barriers, the solution of which may create new markets. A third strategy chooses to be at the frontiers of technological capabilities on the theory that some attractive product fallout will result from such competence. A fourth approach emphasizes economic criteria including attractive growth prospects and appropriate stability.

If it is necessary for the firm to alter its product-market mix or range of capabilities to reduce or close the strategic gap, a diversification strategy may be formulated. Thus, the key connection between planning and diversification or mergers lies in the evaluation of current managerial and technological capabilities relative to capabilities required to reach objectives.

DIVERSIFICATION STRATEGY

Other things being equal, a preferred strategy is to move into a diversification program from a base or core of existing capabilities or organizational strengths. Guidance may be obtained by answers to the following questions: Is there strength in the general management functions? Can the company provide staff expertise in a wide range of areas? Can the firm's financial planning and control effectiveness have a broad application? Are there specific capabilities such as research, marketing, and manufacturing that the firm is seeking to spread over a wider arena?

The firm should be clear on both its strengths and its limitations. To remedy weaknesses, the firm should clearly define the specific new capabilities it is seeking to obtain. If the firm does not possess a sufficient breadth of capability to use as a basis for moving into other areas, an alternative strategy may be employed. This would be to establish a beachhead of capabilities in one or more selected areas. The firm is then in a position to develop concentrically from each of these nuclei.

To understand the potential carry-over of capabilities even in pure conglomerate mergers, one needs to recognize that the nature of firms and the boundaries of industries have become much more dynamic and flexible in recent years. The emphasis of traditional economic theory, as reflected in the Census Bureau's Standard Industrial Classification, is on industry boundary delineation that is mainly product or process oriented. However, organization theory and the behavior of individual firms reflect an emphasis increasingly on missions and capabilities.

In a world of continuing change, managements must relate to *missions*, defined in terms of customer needs, wants, or problems to be solved. In addition to missions, another important dimension of the concept of industries is a *range of capabilities*. Technological capabilities embrace all processes from basic research, product design and development, and applications engineering through interrelated manufacturing methods and obtaining feedback from consumers. Managerial capabilities include competence in the *generic management functions* of planning, organizing, directing, and controlling, as well as in the *specific management functions* of research, production, personnel, marketing, and finance. Another important dimension of managerial capabilities is coordinating and achieving an effective organization system or entity.

The development of such a range of capabilities requires substantial investments in the training and experience of people. It includes investments in holding organizations together during periods of depressed sales. Market demand-and-supply forces place a high value on executive talent and staff expertise. Managerial technology and the effectiveness of management practices are key factors in the efficiency performances of firms.

Potential competition has been enlarged. Industry boundaries defined by products become less meaningful than industries defined by the ability to perform the critical functions for meeting customer needs. The ease of entry is increased because the critical factors for success in changing environments include a range of technologies, experience developed in international markets, and even the adoption of new managerial techniques.

Internal versus External Growth

Growth and diversification may be achieved both internally and externally. For some activities, internal development may be advantageous. For others, careful analysis may reveal sound business reasons for external diversification.

Factors favoring external growth and diversification through mergers and acquisitions include the following:

1 Some goals and objectives may be achieved more speedily through an external acquisition.
2 The cost of building an organization internally may exceed the cost of an acquisition.
3 There may be fewer risks, lower costs, or shorter time requirements involved in achieving an economically feasible market share by the external route.
4 The firm may be able to use securities in obtaining other companies, whereas it might not be able to finance the acquisition of equivalent assets and capabilities internally.
5 Other firms may not be utilizing their assets or managements as effectively as they could be utilized by the acquiring firm.
6 There may be tax advantages.
7 There may be opportunities to complement the capabilities of other firms.

In general, internal development is favored when the preceding advantages are minimal. Frequently the firms available for acquisition will not provide attractive opportunities for achieving the goals that have been set forth; as in make-or-buy decisions, internal development may be more feasible from an economic standpoint. Merger and acquisition activity involves very large stakes and high risks.

From a practical business standpoint, growth through mergers and diversification represents a sound alternative to be taken into account in business planning. We do not wish to imply that external growth and diversification should be the major form of growth, but experience suggests that at times external growth may contribute to opportunities for effective alignment to the firm's changing environments. Combining firms, however, does not provide an automatic basis for success. Even the combination of related activities presents formidable challenges to effective managerial planning and control performance. Concentric mergers that involve the carry-over of specific capabilities provide more direct opportunities for cost reduction and scale economies. However, even with conglomerate mergers, important social and business gains are possible.

Diversification Planning, Mergers, and the Carry-Over of Managerial Capabilities

From an economic standpoint, does any justification exist for these long-range-planning efforts of firms to achieve the regeneration of their organization systems? Particularly, does any justification exist for the use of mergers to seek continuity of firms? One justification for the continuity of firms whose performance is falling short of their competitors is the reduction in the expected present value of the costs of bankruptcy or liquidation. Whether bankruptcy is due to, for example, financial causes, operating or managerial weakness, or inappropriate balance with the environment, one of the potential areas of loss is in investment in reputation and organization capital (which represents firm-specific information embodied in employees or used in forming efficient production and management teams in the organization).

Data compiled on conglomerate mergers by the Federal Trade Commission divide them into three groups: (1) product extension, (2) market extension, and (3) others that might be called pure conglomerate mergers. Product-extension and market-extension mergers usually provide opportunities for the carry-over of industry-specific management capabilities such as research, applications engineering, production, marketing, and so on. Pure conglomerate mergers, then, would involve, at least initially, the potential carry-over only of the general management functions of planning, organizing, directing, controlling, and so on. While finance is a specific management function, its role in the generic functions of planning and control and the broad generality of its applications suggest its treatment as a general management function as well.

The motivation on the part of the diversifying or acquiring firm is an expectation that it has or will have excess capacity of general managerial capabilities in relation to its existing product-market activities. Furthermore, there is an expectation that in the processes of interacting on the generic management activities, particularly overall planning and control and financial planning and control, the diversifying firm will develop industry-specific managerial experience and firm-specific organization capital over time.

However, even this formulation is somewhat restrictive. It applies to companies such as ITT in which under Harold Geneen a high level of capability had been achieved in financial planning and control systems. But other types of carry-overs were also involved. For example, for Litton Industries the original conception was to apply advanced technologies from its defense business to industries for which such applications appeared to have a sound economic and business basis as well as to bring to organization interactions a systems approach to management (again developed out of prior experience of the top managers of Litton). A high percentage of conglomerates came out of the defense industry, not only with an objective to apply organizational capital and the desire to avoid the destruction of such organization capital, but also with a need to acquire additional critical managerial capabilities to be successful in the nondefense sector of the economy. Particularly critical for the defense firms was the establishment of a capability for performing industrial marketing. This suggests that where the desired capability requires an organizational learning and development process that involves time and uncertainties, merger enables the firm to obtain such critical capabilities at a determinate cost and to avoid the risks of extreme and uncertain outcomes.

Another capability that defense firms had was the ability to manage change. The ability to manage change as such represented an important contribution to a wide range of nondefense industries that had not developed this kind of organization knowledge. Again, even though there appeared to be no relationships between the merging firms, there was a complementarity when firms were viewed as groups of capabilities in the framework of an organization.

Four factors have contributed to increased diversification by business firms: (1) the revolution that has taken place in management technology since World War II, (2) the increased pace of technological change in the U.S. economy, (3) the higher fixed costs for management-staff services, and (4) changes in the equity markets which have reinforced these other factors.

ADVANCES IN MANAGERIAL TECHNOLOGY   Important changes in management technology include the following:

1 The developments in the theory and practice of planning.
2 The relating of long-range planning to management by financial objectives.
3 The changes in information science brought about by computers and the increased computerization of information analysis within a firm.
4 The development and use of formal decision models which may be summarized in the term *management science*.
5 The increased use of a systems-analysis approach to the firm with emphasis on viewing all aspects of the firm's operations in a dynamic process (in contrast to the static microeconomic theory of the firm).
6 The increased role of management functions in the firm's operations.
7 The increased use of balanced centralized and decentralized decision making.
8 The increased recognition of the quality and continutiy of the firm's management organization as an important economic variable.
9 The increased recognition of the value of investments in people, resulting in more extensive training programs throughout the worker and management organizations.

These nine developments in management technology have led to an emphasis on increased diversification by business firms. The increasing range of management capabilities has made it advantageous to spread these abilities over a greater number of activities. However, these management capabilities are not evenly distributed throughout industries. Consequently, opportunities have de-veloped for firms to extend their capabilities to other firms and to new areas in order to increase the returns on investments in both management and physical assets.

INCREASED TECHNOLOGICAL CHANGE   The second trend stimulating greater business diversification has been the increased rate of technological change in the U.S. economy. The increased pace of product development short-ens the life cycles of products. The growth rates in sales for individual industries and individual products begin to level off in less time, while opportunities for growth in new areas multiply at a faster pace. Thus, the opportunities for diversi-fication have increased along with the pressures for change. Technological exper-tise is spread unequally among business firms and industries, and the prospect for economic profits from supplying advanced technological capabilities to indus-tries and firms who need them provides an increased incentive to diversify.

It has been argued that diversification can be achieved as well through internal expansion as through external acquisition. This view fails to recognize the size and risks of the investments and costs involved in diversification activ-ity. For a firm with advanced technological capability, but without the requisite industrial production or marketing facilities and experience, to attempt to apply these capabilities de novo in diverse areas represents a high-risk investment. The high cost of capital associated with such risks would be prohibitive for some firms and thus some of these investments would not be made. Other invest-ments of this type would take place, but at a much slower pace than that which typifies external acquisition.

Thus, business firms hope to achieve synergistic or carry-over effects from the distinctive attributes or qualities which they bring to a merger. These gains to the individual firms are also social gains. They represent an increase in the pace at which efficiencies are spread throughout the economy. They contribute to the quality, level, and growth rate of output in the economy.

LARGER FIXED COSTS FOR STAFF SERVICES   The advances in manage-ment technology and the increased pace of technological change, coupled with more dynamic economic and cultural environments, have increased the complex-ity of business operations. Furthermore, the expanding role and requirements of government bodies have necessitated a larger complement of staff services in modern business firms. Both the need and the costs for staff services have increased. The need to maintain an effectively competitive position in the world economy has also resulted in a larger management staff with a broader range of management capabilities and has thus increased the fixed costs of business operations. Scale economies have increasingly resulted from investment in mana-gerial organizations rather than from investment in physical plants.

The economies derived from spreading the fixed costs for managerial staff and specialist functions over a wide range of activities have increased. Small firms have difficulty attracting management with a full range of abilities. Even if the small firms were able to bid successfully for such capabilities, their fixed costs would be substantially raised. Many staff and specialist functions are applicable in different types of industries. Thus, a further stimulus to diversification, both internal and external, has resulted.

DEVELOPMENTS IN THE EQUITY MARKETS   Trends in the equity markets have reinforced the influence of the foregoing factors in encouraging diversification by external acquisition. One significant influence was the discovery of the concept of growth stocks by the financial press and academic writers in the late 1950s and early 1960s. Higher valuations were placed on stocks with recognized potential for growth in earnings and dividends than on stocks with little or no expected growth in earnings or dividends. Thus, higher price/earnings (P/E) ratios resulted for growth stocks. Because of the upward drift in price/earnings ratios from the 1950s through the early 1960s, the growth rate for stock prices increased more rapidly than the growth rate for earnings or dividends during that period.

The increased interest in growth stimulated mergers in various ways. It intensified management's search for product markets with growth opportunities. Along with improved methods of financial planning and control, management had incentives to seek methods for effectively controlling costs in order to increase both average earnings and the growth rate of earnings. A wide variety of financial methods were available to contribute to favorable performance and to the growth in earnings per share of the companies' securities.

The foregoing review of the economic and financial developments that stimulated an emphasis on diversification indicates that there were both business and economic benefits to be gained from diversification efforts. The objective of achieving increased shareholder values has stimulated creativity in operating activities and in a variety of financial methods as well.

CONCLUSIONS

Evaluation of how strategy is performed by business firms depends on the particular conceptual approach to the subject. The BCG and Porter approaches argue that well-formulated principles can guide firms unerringly to the right decisions. The BCG approach emphasizes gaining market share in emerging industries to always be farther along the experience curve than your competitors. The Porter approach incorporates the tenets of the structural theory of industrial organization economics. This theory claims that firms can erect and protect monopoly advantages. The Porter approach to strategy reflects this basic ideology: Find an attractive industry or industry segment, defined as an area in which large firms can collude behind entry barriers buttressed by credible deterrence. With this clear prescription, firms should not have a high rate of product-market adjustments and changes. In this framework divestiture represents a mistake. Hence, Porter's tests of effective strategy rely on a measure of the rate of divestitures to movements into new areas.

In the process approach to strategy each firm has a set of capabilities and opportunities. The firm must seek to exploit these effectively in relation to its changing environments. It must recognize that the dynamics of competition and economic change will require continuous reassessment of its position and realignment to its new challenges and opportunities. In this view the firm is required to make strategic decisions in the face of much uncertainty and considerable risk.

In this process view of strategy, divestitures represent a form of a strategic adjustment process. Divestitures are not necessarily management mistakes. Numerous case studies demonstrate that many divestitures were planned in advance in order to retain the desired parts of an acquisition. Or divestitures can represent a method of making acquisitions and paying them off in part or sometimes entirely by the segments sold off. At a minimum this may help make the diversification effort a low-cost one. Hence, it is erroneous to conclude that divestitures represent management mistakes.

Internal and external investment programs may be successful or unsuccessful. Firms may try either or both approaches in their efforts to increase shareholder value. The generalizations of writers on strategic planning contain valuable insights for helping firms carry out strategies with a higher degree of efficiency than they otherwise would have been able to attain. The critical need is a rapid information feedback system in the firm to improve its capabilities for adapting to change, correcting errors, and seizing new opportunities.

QUESTIONS

1. What is strategy?
2. The Boston Consulting Group approach identifies three main concepts. Discuss the implications and limitations of the following three concepts:
   a. The experience curve
   b. The product life cycle
   c. Product-market portfolio balance
3. What is an attractive industry according to Porter?
4. What does Porter mean by "competitive advantage" through cost leadership? Through product differentiation?
5. What are entry barriers and what is their significance?
6. What is the adaptive approach to strategy? (Include a discussion of the role of checklists and iterative processes.)
7. Discuss different types of business goals.
8. What is meant by aligning a firm to its environment(s)?
9. Why does a firm seek to continue to exist after its main products are either obsolete or out of favor for health or other reasons?
10. What factors resulted in the conglomerate merger movement of the late 1960s?

REFERENCES

ANSOFF, H. IGOR, *Corporate Strategy,* New York: McGraw-Hill, 1965.

BOGUE, MARCUS C., III, and ELWOOD S. BUFFA, *Corporate Strategic Analysis,* New York: The Free Press, 1986.

BOSTON CONSULTING GROUP, *The Strategy Development Process,* Boston: The Boston Consulting Group, 1985.

CARROLL, D. T., "A Disappointing Search for Excellence," *Harvard Business Review,* 61, November–December 1983, pp. 78–88.

CAVES, RICHARD E., "Industrial Organization, Corporate Strategy and Structure," Chapter 5 in *Competitive Strategic Management,* R. B. Lamb, ed., Englewood Cliffs, NJ: Prentice-Hall, 1984.

———, "Economic Analysis and the Quest for Competitive Advantage," *American Economic Review,* May 1984a, pp. 127–132.

CHANDLER, ALFRED D., JR., *Strategy and Structure: Chapters in the History of the American Industrial Enterprise,* Cambridge, MA: The M.I.T. Press, 1962.

CHUNG, KWANG S., and J. FRED WESTON, "Diversification and Mergers in a Strategic Long-Range-Planning Framework," *Mergers and Acquisitions,* M. Keenan and L. J. White, eds., Lexington, MA: D. C. Heath & Co., 1982.

CHUNG, MARY, and ALISTAIR DAVIDSON, "Business Experts," *PC AI,* 1, Summer 1987, pp. 16–21.

HENDERSON, BRUCE D., *The Logic of Business Strategy,* Cambridge, MA: Ballinger, 1984.

HOUT, THOMAS M., and MARK F. BLAXILL, "Make Decisions Like a Fighter Pilot," *New York Times,* November 15, 1987, Sec. 3, p. 3.

JOHNSON, W. BRUCE, ASHOK NATARAJAN, and ALFRED RAPPAPORT, "Shareholder Returns and Corporate Excellence," *Journal of Business Strategy,* Fall 1985, pp. 52–62.

LINDBLOM, CHARLES E., "The Science of 'Muddling Through'," *Public Administration Review,* Spring 1959, pp. 79–88.

———, *The Intelligence of Democracy: Decision Making Through Mutual Adjustment,* New York: The Free Press, 1965.

PETERS, THOMAS J., *Thriving on Chaos,* New York: Alfred A. Knopf, Publishers, 1987.

———, and ROBERT H. WATERMAN, JR., *In Search of Excellence,* New York: Harper & Row, 1982.

PORTER, MICHAEL E., "How Competitive Forces Shape Strategy," *Harvard Business Review,* 57, March–April 1979, pp. 137–145.

———, *Competitive Strategy,* New York: The Free Press, 1980.

———, *Competitive Advantage,* New York: The Free Press, 1985.

———, "From Competitive Advantage to Corporate Strategy," *Harvard Business Review,* May–June 1987, pp. 43–59.

QUINN, JAMES BRIAN, "Strategic Goals: Process and Politics," *Sloan Management Review,* Fall 1977, pp. 21–37.

———, *Strategies for Change: Logical Incrementalism,* Homewood, IL: Irwin, 1980.

————, HENRY MINTZBERG, and ROBERT M. JAMES, *The Strategy Process*, Englewood Cliffs, NJ: Prentice-Hall, 1988.

RAMANUJAM, VASUDEVAN, and N. VENKATRAMAN, "Excellence, Planning, and Performance," *Interfaces*, 18, May–June 1988, pp. 23–31.

ROCK, MILTON L., *The Mergers and Acquisitions Handbook*, New York: McGraw-Hill, 1987.

RUMELT, RICHARD P., *Strategy, Structure, and Economic Performance*, Boston: Division of Research, Harvard Business School, 1974.

————, "Towards a Strategic Theory of the Firm," Chapter 26 in *Competitive Strategic Management*, R. B. Lamb, ed., Englewood Cliffs, NJ: Prentice-Hall, 1984.

STEINER, GEORGE A., *Strategic Planning*, New York: The Free Press, 1979.

————, JOHN B. MINER, and EDMUND R. GRAY, *Management Policy and Strategy*, 3rd ed., New York: Macmillan, 1986.

STRYKER, STEVEN C., *Plan to Succeed: A Guide to Strategic Planning*, Princeton, NJ: Petrocelli Books, 1986.

TEECE, DAVID J., "Economic Analysis and Strategic Management," *California Management Review*, Spring 1984, pp. 87–109.

THOMAS, LACY GLENN, III, ed., *The Economics of Strategic Planning*, Lexington, MA: Lexington Books, 1986.

————, "The Economics of Strategic Planning: A Survey of the Issues," Chapter 1 in *The Economics of Strategic Planning*, 1986a.

WATERMAN, ROBERT H., JR., *The Renewal Factor*, New York: Bantam Books, 1987.

WESTON, J. FRED, *Concentration and Efficiency: The Other Side of the Monopoly Issue*, Special Issues in the Public Interest No. 4, New York: Hudson Institute, 1978.

————, "Section 7 Enforcement: Implementation of Outmoded Theories," *Antitrust Law Journal*, 49, 1982, pp. 1411–1450.

CHAPTER **4**

Merger Types and Characteristics

The 1950 amendments to the Clayton Act tightened restrictions against horizontal and vertical mergers. The regulatory agencies and the courts vigorously enforced the new antitrust provisions of the 1950 act. As a result, few major horizontal and vertical mergers were completed, but conglomerate mergers increased especially during the decade of the 1960s. However, the changed regulatory and economic climate since 1980 produced an increase in the dollar amounts of mergers with most major mergers being the horizontal or related types.

The nature of the different types of mergers was briefly described in Chapter 1. In the present chapter we explain more fully the different kinds of mergers, then seek to develop a rigorous theoretical framework to analyze and explain their rationale. We follow general practice by not distinguishing between mergers and tender offers in the present discussion. We include all types of business combinations, referring to all as "mergers" for convenience and brevity.

ECONOMIC RATIONALES
FOR MAJOR TYPES OF MERGERS

Horizontal Mergers

A horizontal merger involves two firms operating and competing in the same kind of business activity. Thus, the acquisition in 1987 of American Motors by Chrysler represented a horizontal combination or merger. Forming a larger firm may have the benfit of economies of scale. But the argument that horizontal mergers occur to realize economies of scale is not sufficient to be a theory of horizontal mergers. Although these mergers would generally benefit from large-scale operation, not all small firms merge horizontally to achieve economies of scale. Further, why do firms decide to merge at a particular time? Why do they choose a merger rather than internal growth? Since a merger theory should have implications on these aspects, it must be more than a theory of large firm size or a theory of horizontally integrated operation.

Horizontal mergers are regulated by the government for their potential negative effect on competition. The number of firms in an industry is decreased by horizontal mergers and this may make it easier for the industry members to collude for monopoly profits. Horizontal mergers are also believed by many as potentially creating monopoly power on the part of the combined firm enabling it to engage in anticompetitive practices. Whether horizontal mergers take place to gain from collusion or to increase monopoly power of the combined firm, in the presence of continuing government scrutiny of these mergers, is an empirical question.

Vertical Mergers

Vertical mergers occur between firms in different stages of production operation. In the oil industry, for example, distinctions are made between exploration and production, refining, and marketing to the ultimate consumer. In the pharmaceutical industry one could distinguish between research and the development of new drugs, the production of drugs, and the marketing of drug products through retail drugstores.

There are many reasons why firms might want to be vertically integrated between different stages. There are technological economies such as the avoidance of reheating and transportation costs in the case of an integrated iron and steel producer. Transactions within a firm may eliminate the costs of searching for prices, contracting, payment collecting, and advertising and may also reduce the costs of communicating and of coordinating production. Planning for inventory and production may be improved due to more efficient information flow within a single firm. When assets of a firm are specialized to another firm, the latter may act opportunistically to expropriate the quasi-rents accruing to the specialized assets. Expropriation can be accomplished by demanding supply of a good or service produced from the specialized assets at a price below its average cost. To avoid the costs of haggling which arise from the expropriation attempt, the assets are owned by a single vertically integrated firm. Divergent interests of parties to a transaction will be reconciled by common ownership.

The efficiency and affirmative rationale of vertical integration rests primarily on the costliness of market exchange and contracting. The argument, for instance, that uncertainty over input supply is dissipated by backward integration reduces to the fact that contracts are difficult to write, execute, and police. This difficulty is the result of bounded rationality and opportunism, as explained in Chapter 2 on the theory of the firm. When opportunistic inclinations are coupled with limited numbers of suitable firms to transact with, market contracting is exposed to hazards. (When the market is competitive with many suitable bidders, opportunism is discouraged because of the rivalry among the bidders. Opportunistically behaving parties can be avoided at contract renewal since there are many alternative bidders.)

As in the case of horizontal mergers, the affirmative reasons for vertical integration are not sufficient as a theory of vertical mergers. They have no general implications for the timing of a merger in the life of a firm or the characteristics of vertically integrating firms. Further, firms are sometimes vertically disintegrated. A theory would be required to have implications on both integration and disintegration.

Anticompetitive effects have also been cited as both the motivation of these mergers and the result. Most conceived anticompetitive effects assume a monopoly power of the integrated firm at one stage of operation. A monopolist input supplier may be able to practice price discrimination through vertical integration, when the input is used by different industries having different elasticities of demand. The purpose in this case is to prevent the resale of the input by low-price buyers (that is, final good producers with higher demand elasticities) to high-price buyers. The input monopolist directly produces final goods whose demand elasticities are high and continues to supply input to less elastic markets at higher prices.

It has been alleged that an integrated firm having monopoly over an input may raise the input price to independent firms and engage in predatory pricing in the final good market to squeeze out those independent firms. However, it is not always correct to accept this reasoning as a valid rationale for forward integration. The input monopolist can extract all monopoly profits even in the absence of integration and its profits cannot be increased by integration. One exception occurs when input proportions for the final good production are not fixed but variable. When inputs are used in variable proportions, the final good industry will reduce the use of the monopoly-priced input, relative to the case where the input is priced at its marginal cost. Thus, the input monopolist integrates forward and squeezes out independent firms to "correct" the proportion of inputs used in the final good production. The resources saved in the process represent a social welfare gain. But the integrated input monopolist may raise the price of the final good above the preintegration level, which reduces social welfare. The net effect of the forward integration on social welfare is ambiguous and depends on demand and supply conditions.

When the market share of an integrated firm at one stage is large, nonintegrated firms at the other stage may be foreclosed from their customers or suppliers. If monopoly power exists at one stage, vertical integration can thus have anticompetitive effects. This same condition, it is suggested in the literature, can raise entry barriers because new entrants need to enter both stages of an industry unless new entrants occur simultaneously at the other stage. The difficulty of entry arises because the capital and knowledge required to operate

in both stages of production are greater than in the case of single-stage operation. Lack of experience in the other stage or incomplete investor information on
its qualifications will raise its cost of capital relative to firms already in the
industry. If the industry were not integrated, the new firm could enter only one
desired stage and rely on existing firms in the other stage to expand appropriately by acquiring capital at lower costs. Teece (1976) points out that the key issue
is a new entrant's disadvantage relative to what its position would have been
had single-stage entry been possible, and not the new entrant's disadvantage
relative to the position of existing firms at the time of entry, which will naturally
command a return on their experience, information, and competence.

Conglomerate Mergers

Conglomerate mergers involve firms engaged in unrelated types of business activity. Thus, the merger between Mobil Oil and Montgomery Ward was generally
regarded as a conglomerate merger. Among conglomerate mergers, three types
have been distinguished. Product-extension mergers broaden the product lines of
firms. These are mergers between firms in related business activities and may also
be called concentric mergers. A geographic market-extension merger involves two
firms whose operations have been conducted in nonoverlapping geographic areas. Finally, the other conglomerate mergers which are often referred to as pure
conglomerate mergers involve unrelated business activities. These would not
qualify as either product-extension or market-extension mergers.

By contrasting four categories of companies, the economic functions of
conglomerate mergers may be illuminated. Investment companies can be compared with three categories of multi-industry firms to highlight their characteristics. A fundamental economic function of investment companies is to reduce risk
by diversification. Combinations of securities whose returns are not perfectly
correlated reduce portfolio variance for a target rate of return. Because investment companies combine resources from many sources, their power to achieve a
reduction in variance through portfolio effects is greater than that of individual
investors. In addition, the managements of investment companies provide professional selection from among investment alternatives.

Conglomerate firms differ fundamentally from investment companies in
that they control the entities to which they make major financial commitments.
Two important characteristics define a conglomerate firm. First, a conglomerate
firm controls a range of activities in various industries that require different skills
in the specific managerial functions of research, applied engineering, production, marketing, and so on. Second, the diversification is achieved mainly by
external acquisitions and mergers, not by internal development.

FINANCIAL CONGLOMERATES   Within this broader category, two types
of conglomerate firms should be distinguished. Financial conglomerates provide
a flow of funds to each segment of their operations, exercise control, and are the
ultimate financial risk takers. In theory, financial conglomerates undertake strate-

gic planning but do not participate in operating decisions. Management conglomerates not only assume financial responsibility and control, but also play a role in operating decisions and provide staff expertise and staff services to the operating entities.

The characteristics of financial conglomerates may be further clarified by comparisons with investment companies. The financial conglomerate serves at least five distinct economic functions. First, like investment companies, it improves risk/return ratios through diversification. Second, it avoids "gambler's ruin" (an adverse run of losses which might cause bankruptcy). If the losses can be covered by avoiding gambler's ruin, the financial conglomerate maintains the viability of an economic activity with long-run value. Without this form of risk reduction or bankruptcy avoidance, the assets of the operating entity might be shifted to less productive uses because of a run of losses at some point in its development.

A third area of potential contributions by financial conglomerates derives from their establishing programs of financial planning and control. Often, these systems improve the quality of general and functional managerial performance, thereby resulting in more efficient operations and better resource allocation for the economy.

A fourth benefit also results from financial planning and control. If management does not perform effectively but the productivity of assets in the market is favorable, the management is changed. This reflects an effective competitive process because assets are placed under more efficient managements to assure more effective use of resources. A contribution to improved resource allocation is thereby made.

Fifth, in the financial planning and control process, distinction is made between performance based on underlying potentials in the product-market area and results related to managerial performance. Thus, adverse performance does not necessarily indicate inadequate management performance. If management is competent but product-market potentials are inadequate, executives of the financial conglomerate will seek to shift resources by diverting internal cash flows from the unfavorable areas to areas more attractive from a growth and profitability standpoint. From the standpoint of the economy as a whole, this also improves resource allocation.

MANAGERIAL CONGLOMERATES   Managerial conglomerates carry the attributes of financial conglomerates still further. By providing managerial counsel and interactions on decisions, managerial conglomerates increase the potential for improving performance. One school of management theory holds that the generic management functions of planning, organizing, directing, and controlling are readily transferable to all types of business firms. Those managers who have the experience and capability to perform general management functions can perform them in any environment.

This theory argues for management transferability across a wide variety of industries and types of organizations, including government, nonprofit institutions, and military and religious organizations. To the extent that this proposition is valid, it provides a basis for the most general theory of mergers. When any two firms of unequal management competence are combined, the performance of the combined firm will benfit from the impact of the superior management firm and the total performance of the combined firm will be greater than the sum of the individual parts. This defines *synergy* in its most general form. In the managerial conglomerate, these economic benefits are achieved through corporate headquarters that provide the individual operating entities with expertise and counsel on the generic management functions.

CONCENTRIC COMPANIES   The difference between the managerial conglomerate and the concentric company is based on the distinction between the general and specific management functions. If the activities of the segments brought together are so *related* that there is carry-over of specific management functions (research, manufacturing, finance, marketing, personnel, and so on) or complementarity in relative strengths among these specific management functions, the merger should be termed concentric rather than conglomerate. This transferability of specific management functions across individual segments has long been exemplified by the operations of large, multiproduct, multiplant firms in the American economy. The characteristic organizational structure of these firms has included senior vice presidents who perform as staff specialists to corresponding functional executives in operating departments.

Definitions are inherently arbitrary. Is there any reason to distinguish between managerial conglomerates and concentric companies? The two types have in common a basic economic characteristic. Each transfers general management functions over a variety of activities, using the principle of spreading a fixed factor over a larger number of activities to achieve scale economies and to lower the cost function for the output range. Concentric companies achieve these economic gains in specific management functions as well as in general management functions. A priori the potential economies for the concentric companies might be expected to be larger. But the magnitude of economies gained in general rather than specific management functions may vary by industry and by industry mix. Further, in the multiproduct, multiplant firms that have achieved economies of carry-over of both specific and general management functions, the interactions may be so great that it is impossible to differentiate between the two.

Similarly, a managerial conglomerate which originally provided expertise on general management functions may increasingly act on specific management functions as its executives become more familiar with the operations of the individual entities. Financial conglomerates also may increasingly provide staff service for both general and specific management functions.

Additional illustrations will clarify these concepts and their economic implications. If one company has competence in research, manufacturing, or marketing that can be applied to the product problems of another company that lacks that particular competence, a merger will provide the opportunity to lower cost functions. For example, firms seeking to diversify from advanced technology industries may be strong on research but weaker on production and marketing capabilities firms in industries with less advanced technology.

To this point we have described the different kinds of mergers and explained some of the reasons why they appear to take place. In the following section we seek to develop a rigorous theoretical framework which provides a more fundamental understanding of the processes observed.

A FRAMEWORK FOR ANALYSIS
OF MERGERS

It was observed in Chapter 2 that the distinguishing feature of the firm is its possession of organization capital. With the purpose of explaining different types of mergers, we first examine the concept of *organization capital* in greater detail. Second, a model of the firm with organization capital as a factor of production is presented, in which the firm may earn economic rents to its organization capital (or positive economic profits) under competition. *Investment opportunities* are defined in this context and mergers are hypothesized to represent a process of reallocating resources across activities or industries in the firms' efforts to internalize investment opportunities, that is, to earn rents from their organization capital. Next, two separate synergy effects, managerial and financial, are introduced to describe how the investment opportunities are captured. The hypothesis developed here is that mergers between firms in related industries involve managerial synergy and pure conglomerate mergers involve financial synergy, although in reality both effects are present in any particular merger in varying degrees.

Organization Learning
and Organization Capital

Organization capital is accumulated through experience within the organization called the firm. To avoid any confusion that may exist in the literature on the concept and role of organization capital and to sharpen the theoretical exposition, we introduce a separate concept that we call *organization learning* and define it as improvement in the skills and abilities of individual employees through learning by experience within the firm.

We distinguish three types of organization learning. Rosen (1972) in explaining what could constitute "production knowledge" suggests that one case of learning is in the area of entrepreneurial or managerial ability to organize and maintain complex production processes economically. A useful dichotomy of this managerial learning is between general and industry-specific experiences. The first form of organization learning may be termed raw managerial experience which refers to the capabilities developed in generic management functions of planning, organizing, directing, controlling, and so on as well as in financial planning and control.[1] The second form consists of industry-specific managerial experience, which refers to the development of capabilities in specific management functions related to the characteristics of production and marketing in particular industries. The third type of organization learning is in the area of nonmanagerial labor input. The level of skills of the production workers will improve over time through learning by experience.

The stock of organization learning in the three areas—generic managerial, industry specific, and nonmanagerial—has no significance by itself in the theory of the firm. This is because we identify organization learning with improvements in individual ability through experience in the firm and each individual thus will be free to move to another firm. Organization learning becomes significant, however, when it is combined with firm-specific information or organization capital and thus *cannot be transferred freely to other firms through the labor market.*

The most detailed discussion of organization capital has been provided by Rosen (1972) and by Prescott and Visscher (1980). The first type of organization capital is firm-specific information embodied in individual employees and is called *employee-embodied information.* This information is obtained when employees become familiar with the firm's particular production arrangements, management and control systems, and to other employees' skills, knowledgeability and job duties in the firm.

The second and third types of organization capital may be termed *team effects.* That is, the role of information here is to allow the firm to organize efficient managerial and production teams within the firm. The second type consists of information on employee characteristics, allowing an efficient match between workers and tasks to the extent that some tasks are better fulfilled by particular talents and skills. In the formulation of Prescott and Visscher, new employees are initially assigned to a screening job which can be performed equally well by workers with different talents. After information on characteristics is obtained, workers are assigned to jobs that can be better implemented by workers with particular characteristics. The precision of the information will depend on the length of time that workers spend on the screening job.

The third type of information is used in the matching of workers to workers, since how well the characteristics of an individual mesh with those of others performing related duties is important to the overall performance of the team.

The types of information that we have included in organization capital are likely to be firm specific. Information on workers that gives rise to team effects may be better known to the firm's owners (managers) than to the workers themselves. It would be transferred to other firms only with noise and subject to transactions costs. Employee-embodied information is firm specific by defini-

---

[1] While finance is a specific management function, its role in the generic functions of planning and control and the broad generality of its applications suggest its treatment as a general management function as well.

tion, since it is information on workers and systems that are components of the firm.

To an extent, organization capital is a joint product which does not involve extra costs in production. Greater investment and production activity in one period will therefore lead to a greater amount of organization capital in the next period. However, since it can be preserved in the firm into the future and its value in future production will be positive, it is in the firm's interest to produce the firm-specific assets at its own cost. For example, new employees often receive on-the-job training that is specialized to the firm. Also, management spends real resources to organize efficient production and managerial teams. However organization capital is obtained, the important point is that it increases and accumulates within the firm over time, at least until its depreciation becomes fast enough, if it ever does, to offset the additions.

The concepts used to this point are summarized in Table 4.1 which lists the elements of organization learning and organization capital. This provides a framework for discussing the combination of organization learning and organization capital which follows.

The final human capital resources available to the firm as inputs for production are the output resulting from the combination of organization learning and organization capital. The first of these human capital resources may be termed *generic managerial capabilities* to represent the combination of organization learning in the generic managerial functions and the relevant organization capital. The second is called *industry-specific managerial capabilities.* Finally, the third includes all others and can be called *nonmanagerial human capital.*

Given that the three types of human resources are specialized to the firm to some extent, we need to examine the implications and degrees of their specific-

TABLE 4.1

Organization Learning and Organization Capital

I. *Organization Learning*—Improvement in skills and abilities through learning within firm
  A. Generic managerial
  B. Industry-specific managerial
  C. Nonmanagerial

II. *Organizational Capital*—Firm-specific informational assets
  A. Employee-embodied
  B. Match between worker and job (team effect)
  C. Match between worker and other workers (team effect)

III. *Combination of Organization Learning and Organization Capital*
  A. Generic managerial capabilities (C_1)
  B. Industry-specific managerial capabilities (C_2)
  C. Firm-specific nonmanagerial human capital (C_3)

IV. *Transfer through Mergers*
  A. C_1 = Transferable to most other industries
  B. C_2 = Transferable only to related industries
  C. C_3 = Difficult to transfer even to other firms in the same industry

ity. The jobs of nonmanagerial production workers are specified according to the details of the production facility. Once a team of workers is organized with each worker assigned to a different job based on specific information on their characteristics, the team is specialized to the facility. Therefore, it is specialized to the firm's production establishment or can at best be transferred to a similar establishment. A merger between firms even in related industries will therefore not include the transfer of nonmanagerial human capital between the firms. Its transfer between firms is only feasible in horizontal mergers.

The industry-specific managerial capabilities can be transfered to other firms in related industries without impairing the team effect, as they are not identified with a particular establishment. The requirement that managers should be transferred as a team is met by a merger initiated to carry over industry-specific managerial capabilities. The team-effect portion of organization capital will be preserved through a merger, although the other type of organization capital (that is, employee-embodied firm-specific information) has to be reacquired for the new setting of the acquired or combined firm. Mergers between firms therefore are more efficient than the movements through the labor market of individual managers in transferring these capabilities. Mergers thus cause the supply of managerial capabilities in the market to be more elastic.

The generic managerial capabilities can, of course, be carried over through a merger with a firm even in an unrelated industry. Again, to the extent that team effects are important, a merger which can preserve these effects is more efficient than interfirm movements of managers as individuals. However, there are reasons to believe that invoking a merger to acquire or to carry over generic managerial resources will not be as compelling as in the case of industry-specific resources. First, the team size to produce generic managerial service is in general smaller than that for managerial resources related to production and marketing. Thus, the organization of a mangerial team for control, coordination, and planning requires less time than the organization of a team for other managerial capabilities. Second, information on top-level managers who perform the control and coordination functions may be more public than on lower-level managers for the production and marketing functions. This also makes team organization more expedient. Third, managers for generic functions can come from even remotely related industries, whereas managers in specific function areas should have experience in closely related industries. Thus, the supply of the former type of managers is more elastic than that of the latter. Assuming that these are empirically valid observations, the case for a merger for the purpose of transferring generic managerial resources would seem weaker than for the transfer of industry-specific resources.

Investment Opportunities

Investment (or growth) opportunities exist for a firm if the present value of an investment is positive. Given this definition, a value-maximizing firm will attempt to internalize whatever investment opportunities it can find. The literature has not been clear, however, on what factors in general give rise to investment opportunities in competitive industries. Miller and Modigliani (1961, p. 416) give only a cursory hint:

> [Investment] opportunities, frequently termed the 'good will' of the business, may arise, in practice, from any of a number of circumstances (ranging all the way from special locational advantages to patents or other monopolistic advantages).

Further insights on the nature of investment opportunities can be provided by treating organization capital as a factor of production, as in Rosen (1972). Recall that organization capital is defined as firm-specific informational assets. Then we can envisage a simple production process having organization capital and investments as the only two input variables.

Given the short-run fixity of organization capital as a factor of production and the elastic supply of capital, any adjustment in the output quantity occurs by changing the amount of capital investments. But in general as investments are increased, output is increased only at a decreasing rate. That is, investments are subject to diminishing returns in the short run. This implies that the marginal cost of output is increasing due to increasing capital input per output and the fixed factor (organization capital) will earn the Marshallian quasi-rent. Thus, any positive net present value of a project is the quasi-rent accruing to organization capital.[2] It is in this sense that the existence of investment opportunities hinges on the organization capital vested in the firm.

MANAGERIAL SYNERGY AND HORIZONTAL AND RELATED MERGERS

We next develop a hypothesis on horizontal mergers and mergers between firms in related businesses or industries. The hypothesis also has implications on vertical mergers to the extent that these mergers involve firms in related industries. The immediate theoretical questions are directed to why such mergers occur and what types of firms are involved in such mergers.

Now imagine a production process employing four factor inputs—generic managerial capabilities, industry-specific managerial capabilities, firm-specific nonmanagerial human capital, and capital investment. The firm-specific nonmanagerial human capital can only be supplied by a long-term learning effort or

[2]The quasi-rent accruing to the organization capital will normally be divided among the stakeholders of the firm including the capital owner, the employees, the suppliers, and so on. Therefore, the "value of the firm" in the ordinary usage of the term will reflect only a portion of the quasi-rent and the rest will be distributed to other stakeholders. Existence of labor unions may be at least partly explicable by the accrual of rents to organization capital, as discussed in Chapter 2. In the extreme case of a monopolist labor union and competitive firms, all rents may be captured by labor, although there will be bargaining between stakeholders on the division of the rents. However the rents are distributed, the behavior of the firm as a coalition will approximate that of maximizing the rents to organization capital as long as the coalition participants behave rationally to maximize the total "pie" available for allocation.

by merging with existing firms in the same industry. The industry-specific managerial resources can be obtained by internal learning or by merging with a firm in the same or related industries. An additional way of obtaining industry-specific resources may be to employ managers with industry-specific knowledge acquired while they were employed by other firms in the same or related industries. However, as discussed earlier, this route of obtaining industry-specific resources in large scale is inefficient and may be infeasible since they are a team product and the managers have firm-specific information whose value is appreciated only by the current firm. Generic managerial capabilities may be obtained by any of the three means and their supply in the labor market is likely to be more elastic than industry-specific resources. We assume here that generic managerial resources can be obtained through the market.

Suppose that a firm, call it B (Bidder), has "excess capacity" in industry-specific resources and that another firm in a related industry, call it T (Target), experiences "shortages" in these resources. Or more generally, suppose that the ratio of industry-specific managerial capabilities to firm-specific nonmanagerial human capital is greater for B than for T; in other words, the ratio of the two factors that are fixed in quantity in the short run is greater for Bidder relative to Target. The acquisition of T by B will make the firms realize more balanced factor proportions between industry-specific and firm-specific resources by transferring the excess capacity of B in the industry-specific capabilities to T's operation. Given the transferability of industry-specific resources through a merger between firms in related industries, efficiency in factor proportions is achieved by the merger through the equalization between B and T of the marginal rates of factor substitution in industry-specific managerial capabilities and nonmanagerial human capital. An example of the T-type firm will be an R&D oriented firm lacking marketing organizations and being acquired by a B-type firm with strong marketing capabilities in related fields of business.

Several theoretical questions need to be illuminated: (1) why B with excess capacity in industry-specific resources does not remove managers; (2) why the two firms cannot use contracting instead of merging; and (3) why T does not develop industry-specific resources internally. Question 1 (or 3) can be similarly phrased in terms on nonmanagerial human capital of T (or B). Answers to all three questions should necessarily be related to the theory of the firm and thus to the concept of organization capital.

The response to the first has already been suggested. Managers as employees typically have made investments in firm-specific knowledge. Thus, managers themselves are a part of the firm-specific assets and their value within the firm is greater than their market value. Movement of managers entails a loss of employee-embodied firm-specific information. More importantly, the excess capacity in industry-specific managerial capabilities is likely to be the result of superior team organization and not necessarily of an excessive number of managers. Therefore, dividing up the team may result in the loss of these resources. Merger provides an efficient way of transferring the services of industry-specific resources to other firms without impairing their total capacity.

With respect to the second question, note that merging as opposed to contracting amounts to a kind of vertical integration between firm-specific nonmanagerial resources (of T) and industry-specific managerial resources (of B). Rendering managerial services to T under a long-term contract will still require investment in information or knowledge specialized to T. Once B's management acquires the specialized information, it becomes subject to appropriation by T since its value to the next best use is zero in this case. If B's management refuses to make investments in T-specific knowledge in anticipation of such opportunistic behavior, its managerial service is ineffectual. With the necessity of investments in specialized knowledge, the threat of appropriability of the quasi-rent accruing to such assets leads to integration into a single organization (see Chapter 2).

For the third question, three different forces are likely to work together: economies of scale, timing, and constraints on growth. For T to develop industry-specific capabilities internally may not be feasible if their production is subject to economies of scale and if the size of T is not large enough to realize the full benefits of scale economies or, in the terminology of the management literature, to reach the "critical mass" in managerial team production. By sharing the resources of B, managerial economies of scale become available. Utilizing excess managerial capabilities of B without merger requires developing firm-specific nonmanagerial human capital for operation either in its own or in T's industry. However, accumulation of nonmanagerial human capital is a long-term process during which the excess managerial resources are underexploited and may further accumulate, keeping the factor proportions continuously unbalanced. Further, since it is imperative to keep nonmanagerial human capital resources proportional to the size of the firm, an increase in these resources requires the growth of the firm itself which should be governed by industry demand growth. Similarly, internal development of industry-specific managerial resources by T is also subject to time requirements, and inefficient performance of the firm in the meantime may jeopardize the firm's survival.

Firm and Industry Characteristics in Horizontal and Related Mergers

So far we have hypothesized that horizontal mergers or mergers between firms in related industries are characterized by carry-over of industry-specific managerial resources. Firm T experiences a shortage and B an excess of these resources. Since acquisition initiatives or programs more frequently start with the discovery of underutilized managerial resources, initiation of the merger will normally come from B rather than T. Thus, we define B, the firm with excess industry-specific managerial resources, as the acquiring firm (or bidder) and T, the one with a shortage, as the acquired firm (or target) in horizontal or related mergers.

A prediction on the characteristics of T-type firms is that their performance measures (for example, profit rates) will not be high relative to their industry averages, other things being equal. The existence of excess or underutilized managerial assets in B may imply greater efficiency than a firm with no such assets. However, this is not necessary since the contribution of the excess capacity to the firm's performance may be zero.

The excess in industry-specific managerial capabilities in B may have arisen because managerial capacity increases over time (Penrose, 1959; Rosen, 1972; Rubin, 1973). "The services available from resources (and particularly from management) grow over time, even if no new managers are hired" (Rubin, p. 939). The reason for the increasing capacity appears to be threefold. First, the ability of managers to organize production and marketing processes is increased by experience. Second, the organization of the management team is improved over time by accumulating information on individual managers and matching jobs and skills in an efficient way. Third, once an efficient production team is organized by identifying superior combinations of inputs, the demand for managerial inputs relative to firm outputs is reduced. In sum, the managerial services available from given resources grow and the relative internal demand for managerial services declines over time.

The time requirement for the development of excess managerial capacity may suggest certain industry characteristics in related mergers. No such characterization is relevant for horizontal mergers, although the following life cycle considerations yield some implications on industry characteristics in horizontal mergers. The deficiency in managerial resources of the acquired firms implies that they may have grown fast physically presumably because industry demand has grown fast—faster than the growth in managerial capacity could support. Therefore, other things being equal, the growth rates of these acquired firm industries (or lines of business) for a premerger period will be greater than the average for the economy. From the investment opportunities consideration, it is also predicted that the acquired firm industries will not be those whose demand growth is lagging relative to the economy. This is because the value of increased productivity of investment resulting from the improvement in factor proportions through the merger will be greater, the higher the growth rate of the industry. Simply put, the demand for extra resources, in particular for industry-specific managerial resources, will be greater in industries or lines of business with greater increases in product demand.

As for the acquiring firms in related mergers, their excess managerial capacity should indicate their long-time presence in industries with long histories. This would imply their product demand growth rates will generally be no greater than an average industry in related industry groups. A similar prediction would also follow from investment opportunities arguments. One motivating factor for the acquiring firms is that they find better opportunities in related than in strictly their own industries or lines of business for the utilization of excess managerial capabilities, and this will be more likely if investment opportunities in their own industries are more difficult to find. These statements are, of course, subject to the problems of defining industries and lines of business.

FINANCIAL SYNERGY
AND PURE CONGLOMERATE MERGERS

Mergers between firms in unrelated industries do not involve, by definition, the carry-over of industry-specific managerial capabilities. Therefore, any benefits related to managerial capabilities have to be in the area of generic managerial functions. Whether a merger is desirable to effect the transfer of generic managerial resources from one firm with excess capacity to another with excess demand again depends on the factors previously considered; namely, the extent that generic managerial capabilities are a team product, subject to economies of scale, and managers in these functional areas possess firm-specific information. However, the coordination of demand and supply in the managerial labor market would seem more efficient in the case of generic than industry-specific managerial resources for several reasons as discussed earlier. In any event, the case for a merger for the carry-over of generic capabilities only should be weaker than for the carry-over of both.

Besides the possible efficiency of mergers in transferring generic managerial capabilities, we formulate an alternative hypothesis on the mergers between firms in unrelated industries. The fundamental assumption is that the acquiring firms in these mergers are not motivated by the discovery of underexploited specialized resources within the firm, but by the realization that investment opportunities are limited in the areas of their existing activities. This assumption is at least consistent with the fact that these acquiring firms diversify into unrelated industries rather than related areas where the utilization of any industry-specific assets should be easier.

The hypothesis is that a pure conglomerate merger occurs when a firm in an industry with low demand growth relative to the economy acquires a firm which operates in another industry with high expected demand growth. The motive of the merger is to capture investment opportunities available in the acquired firm's industry by lowering the costs of capital of the combined firm through the merger and also utilizing lower-cost internal funds of the acquiring firm. The opportunity for utilizing the cash flows of the acquiring firm will be enhanced if the cash flow of the acquired firm is low. Thus, the hypothesis implies a process of (financial) resource reallocation in the economy from the acquiring firm's industry with low demand growth to the acquired firm's industry with high demand growth. The hypothesized differences in industry demand growth rates indicate differential investment opportunities in the two industries.

The reason why a firm needs to acquire another firm in order to internalize investment opportunities in the latter's industry is that the acquiring firm lacks the organization capital or production knowledge specific to the industry of the acquired. De novo entry by the acquiring firm may not be feasible if it does not possess any organization capital specialized to the new area. What distinguishes a merger or acquisition from the simple purchase of assets and employment of new workers is that the former involves the acquisition and preservation of organization capital. A theoretical definition of the pure conglomerate merger is provided by this consideration: When the acquiring firm completely lacks organization capital applicable to the acquired firm's industry, the merger is purely conglomerate.

The questions relating to the costs of capital are far from settled in the finance literature, and therefore the lowering of costs of capital through conglomerate mergers should properly be treated as a hypothesis in the present theory.

The cost of capital may be lowered for a number of reasons. If the cash flow streams of the two firms are not perfectly positively correlated, bankruptcy probabilities may be lowered. This will decrease the "lender's risk" and the debt capacity will be increased (Lewellen, 1971). A more rigorous treatment of this proposition has been provided by Stapleton (1982) in the option pricing model (OPM) framework, in which debt capacity is defined as the maximum amount of debt that can be raised at a given rate of interest. If bankruptcy costs are significant, the debt-capacity argument is reinforced. The decrease in bankruptcy probability may decrease the expected value of bankruptcy costs and increase the expected value of tax savings from interest payments for premerger debts, and thus increase the value of the combined firm by lowering its cost of capital. Apart from these, if the value of the firm is assumed to be unchanged, the increase in debt values as a result of the merger's co-insurance effect is at the expense of equity values, as pointed out by Higgins and Schall (1975). But this shift can be offset by increasing leverage (Galai and Masulis, 1976; Kim and McConnell, 1977). A postmerger increase in leverage will allow the firm to realize an incremental stream of tax savings from interest payments on new debt,[3] although the increased leverage can offset the other benefits of lower bankruptcy probabilities.[4]

A potentially more important source of the lower cost of capital for postmerger investments in the acquired firm's industry stems from the distinction between internal and external funds. Internal funds do not involve transaction costs of the flotation process and may have differential tax advantages over external funds.[5] Further, internal financing can have an advantage over external financing if insiders (managers) have more information on the value of the firm's assets than outside investors and act in the interest of the current shareholders (Myers and Majluf, 1984). When the firm issues risky securities, this asymmetry in information causes investors to believe that the securities are overvalued and thus to react negatively.

The potential importance of internal funds is provided by the hypothesized

---

[3] Miller (1977) shows that lower personal taxation of equity investment income than interest income will decrease and can even completely offset the benefit of corporate tax savings on interest payment. The extent that the corporate tax savings are offset by the rise in interest rate to compensate the personal tax disadvantage of debt must be determined empirically. For further discussion on this and related issues on the cost of capital, see Copeland and Weston (1988), Chapters 13, 14, and 19.

[4] For more discussion on the subject, see Scott (1977).

[5] Miller and Scholes (1978) argue that there may be no tax advantage for internal funds, but Feldstein, Green, and Sheshinski (1979) hold that the argument of Miller and Scholes does not have empirical support.

characteristics of the acquiring firms. Since their industry demands grow at lower rates than an average industry in the economy, these firms are likely to have internal cash flows in excess of current investment opportunities in their own industries. Thus, the acquiring firms may supply lower-cost internal funds to the combined firm. Further, the acquired firms will typically have low free cash flows because high expected demand growth in their industries requires greater investments. The low free cash flows of the acquired firms provide synergistic opportunities in financing. Hence, the pure conglomerate merger represents a process of redeploying capital. A similar view has been advanced by Myers and Majluf (1984) that firms rich in financial slack (defined as cash, cash equivalents, and unused capacity to raise risk-free debt) will take over slack-poor firms with investment opportunities.

Economies of scale in flotation and transaction costs of securities are another potential source of financial synergy. A part of the scale economies is presumably due to fixed costs of information production and dissemination and mergers may achieve informational economies of scale.

An important implication of the financial synergy hypothesis is that the possibility of reducing the cost of capital will be greater when the premerger cost of capital of the acquired firm is higher and in some limited sense, when the cost of capital (that is, the internal cash flow) of the acquiring firm is lower. This is likely to be true if the higher cost of capital of the acquired firm results from its (1) greater bankruptcy probability, (2) smaller amount of internal funds, and (3) smaller size. In a conglomerate merger, the three forces may operate in varying degrees to reduce the capital costs for investments in the acquired firm's industry.

To summarize the foregoing discussion, a pure conglomerate merger occurs to internalize the investment opportunities in the acquired firm's industry by initially lowering the cost of capital of the combined firm. Investment opportunities in the industry of the acquired firm are greater when the growth rate of its demand is higher. Reduction in costs of funds to be invested in the acquired firm's operations is greater when the premerger cost for the acquired firm is higher and when the acquiring firm's cost is lower because of one or more of the possibilities hypothesized. The acquiring firm is in an industry that is mature in the sense that its product demand growth rate is no greater than the growth rate of the economy as a whole. Thus, the acquiring firm finds investment opportunities in its own industry relatively less favorable and seeks them in other industries to maximize firm value.

The benefit from a pure conglomerate merger is not limited to the initial gain from a reduction in the cost of capital. A greater degree of investment activity taken in this period will lead to greater organization capital available in the following periods. Therefore, the marginal efficiency of investment (MEI) curve of the firm in the next period shifts out. This dynamic effect may constitute a major source of gains in a pure conglomerate merger in the long run. This is likely to be the expectation of the acquiring firm in a pure conglomerate merger. In particular, there will be an expectation on the part of the acquiring firm that in the processes of interacting on the generic management activities, the firm will develop (a greater amount of) industry-specific managerial resources and firm-specific human capital.

The theory presented with respect to pure conglomerate mergers is consistent with the empirical evidence reported by Markham (1973, pp. 88–89). In his sample of 30 large acquisitions, new capital outlays for the acquired companies' operations in the three-year period following acquisitions averaged 220 percent of premerger outlays for the same time span. Markham further reports that the managerial function of capital expenditure planning was in most cases relocated to the corporate headquarters after acquisitions, while such relocation was not frequent for other managerial functions. A recent study by Bruner (1988) finds that successful bidders have more financial slack than targets and a large sample of general firms, that acquired firms are more levered than a control sample, and that bidders' returns are significantly associated with leverage changes after merger. More empirical results are discussed in Chapter 13.

THE ROLE OF THE INDUSTRY LIFE CYCLE

The role of the industry life cycle is in much dispute. It has never been supported by rigorous empirical evidence. But it represents a useful concept for organizing ideas on business activity, if treated as suggestive rather than a set of fixed and established principles. In this spirit, the concept is used as a framework for indicating when different types of mergers may have an economic basis at different stages of an industry's development.

THE DEVELOPMENT STAGE   At the start of a new product or industry, an introduction period may be required. Time and money may be needed to inform consumers of the nature and uses of the new product. Product development problems may also be involved. The introduction stage of a new product may be associated with losses to the innovating producers.

THE GROWTH STAGE   When consumer acceptance has been achieved, sales may expand rapidly. In this stage a reservoir of demand can be drawn on since a new product has by now either created a new demand or is substituting for an old product for which demand already existed. The explosive growth in sales is associated with high profitability. Additional capacity is attracted into the industry. Even if the existing firms have patent protection, competitors will introduce related products to obtain a share of the market.

Entry conditions are relatively easy because of the large reservoir of demand, the substantial growth of sales, and the high prices and profits produced by the limited existing capacity. Capacity in the industry expands with increasing momentum.

At some point in this market-exploitation period, the relationship between sales and capacity may become less favorable. For example, there was a stage when the sales of the pleasure boat industry were growing at the impressive rate of 12 to 15 percent per year. But capacity was growing at 20 percent per year. Pressure on prices and profits began to develop.

THE MATURITY STAGE   Near the end of the growth stage or at the beginning of the maturity stage of development in industry, the growth rate of sales slows down. The additions to capacity, stimulated by the record of high profits, may reach their peak as the growth rate of sales begins to slow. Excess capacity in the industry may develop. Prices and profits decline.

It is at this point of the cycle that the analysis becomes particularly relevant for merger policy. The only firms that can survive are those that can reduce prices to the levels required by the adverse sales-to-capacity relations. Mergers may take place. Larger firms within the industry or from other industries are likely to be the acquirers. The existing firms may have represented the efforts of a small number of individuals with great competence in one area such as research, production, sales, or advertising. In a rapidly growing industry, possession of one strong management attribute may be sufficient for success. However, as competitive pressures increase, the need increases for a full range of management capabilities. Individual firms may sometimes extend their range of capabilities or combine with other small firms having complementary skills. But selling out to a larger firm which possesses a full range of managerial skills may be most profitable for smaller firms.

Near the end of the maturity stage, the growth rate in sales declines further. Profit margins experience greater pressures. While the growth rate in the industry slows, the absolute level of sales in the industry may be large. The critical factor for profitable operations may be effective cost control of large scale, mass-production operations. The effective coordination of research, advertising, production, and marketing may be required to reduce costs by a few cents per unit, but such a reduction may make the difference between profitable and unprofitable operations. Spreading the heavy fixed costs of the machinery, presses, dies, jigs, and fixtures associated with product developments or model improvements may constitute significant economies. If, as a consequence of these factors, the largest firm in the industry is the low-cost producer, strong motivation is exerted on the smaller firms to combine in an effort to match the efficiencies of the largest firm.

When the industry is mature, it is characterized by a small number of large firms which compete on product quality and price and which emphasize production efficiency. It also includes a large number of small firms that may be part of the supply system, the consumer distribution system, the service organization, or producers of distinctive custom items for specialized segments of the market.

THE DECLINE STAGE   The development of substitute products starts new industry life cycles for the new products. But new products substitute at least in part for existing products. As substitute products are successfully introduced, they begin to erode the sales of the older product lines and growth rates for the older firms decline.

Characteristic growth rates per annum might be 1 to 2 percent in the development stage, 8 to 20 percent in the growth stage, 4 to 6 percent in the maturity stage, and within the range of plus 2 percent to negative 10 percent in the decline stage.

In the decline stage or in the late maturity stage, pressures are created for different types of mergers: mergers for vertical integration, horizontal mergers for survival, and mergers for diversification, particularly the concentric form of conglomerate mergers. There are several reasons for these pressures. The industry has now nearly reached the maximum volume it will achieve. Profit margins have become small because of the unfavorable relationship between sales and capacity. Therefore, horizontal mergers are sought by the higher-cost producers in their efforts to match the performances of the larger, low-cost firms.

In the early stages of the industry when its volume was relatively small, specialist firms became suppliers. By supplying several firms in the industry, the supplier firms may have achieved economies not available to the end-item manufacturers. In turn, however, the end-item manufacturer was able to make a smaller initial investment. When the industry reaches the late maturity or early decline period, the characteristics of the industry create tendencies for vertical integration. The earlier mergers have resulted in a smaller number of end-item manufacturers. The industry volume is large and the sales of each individual firm are large. Profit margins have declined and the total process from raw materials to end product is reviewed to seek economies in vertical value chains.

In addition, strong pressures develop for changing the product mix of the firm. The internal cash flow of the firm can no longer be profitably invested in the declining product lines. The firm, therefore, seeks to achieve diversification in its products. The diversification may be sought through internal development or through external mergers and acquisitions. From a managerial standpoint, basic capital budgeting issues are involved. Factors such as alternative profits, risks, requirements for developing organizations, and marketing acceptance must be taken into account.

Product Life Cycle and Merger Types

In summary, the product life cycle considerations and the theoretical framework discussed above predict different types of mergers at different stages of a firm's development, as suggested in Table 4.2. In the earlier introduction and exploitation stages, new or small firms will become targets for related or conglomerate mergers initiated by larger firms in mature or declining industries. Through the merger, managerial and financial resources are provided by the latter firms. Since the industry is growing at a high rate, there will be few firms in the same industry which are strategically motivated for a merger to provide such resources. However, horizontal mergers between smaller firms may occur to pool managerial and financial resources.

Horizontal and related mergers may be undertaken in the maturity stage to match the low cost and price performance of other firms, domestic or foreign, by achieving economies of scale in research, marketing, and production. Some

TABLE 4.2
Mergers and Industry Life Cycle

STAGE OF INDUSTRY LIFE CYCLE	TYPE OF MERGER
Introduction stage	Newly created firms may sell to outside larger firms in a mature or declining industry, thereby enabling larger firms to enter a new growth industry. These result in related or conglomerate mergers. The smaller firms may wish to sell because they want to convert personal income to capital gain and because they do not want to place large investments in the hands of managers that do not have a long record of success. Horizontal mergers between smaller firms may also occur, enabling such firms to pool management and capital resources.
Exploitation stage	Mergers during the exploitation stage are similar to mergers during the introductory stage. The impetus for such mergers is reinforced by the more visible indications of prospective growth and profit and by the larger capital requirements of a higher growth rate.
Maturity stage	Mergers are undertaken to achieve economies of scale in research, production, and marketing in order to match the low cost and price performance of other firms, domestic or foreign. Some acquisition of smaller firms by larger firms takes place for the purposes of rounding out the management skills of the smaller firms and providing them with a broader financial base.
Decline stage	Horizontal mergers are undertaken to ensure survival. Vertical mergers are carried out to increase efficiency and profit margins. Concentric mergers involving firms in related industries provide opportunities for synergy and carry-over. Conglomerate acquisitions of firms in growth industries are undertaken to utilize the accumulating cash position of mature firms in declining industries whose internal flow of funds exceeds the investment requirements of their traditional lines of business.

horizontal acquisitions of smaller firms by larger firms take place to provide management skills and a broader financial base.

In the decline stage, horizontal mergers to ensure survival take place. Vertical mergers are carried out to increase efficiency and profit margins. Some firms will be engaged in concentric acquisitions to obtain opportunities for synergy and carry-over of managerial capabilities. Conglomerate acquisitions of firms in growth industries may be undertaken to utilize financial slack of mature firms in declining industries. The firms that had been acquired previously in conglomerate mergers may now be divested. The opportunity for the parent company to profitably apply management and capital resources to the acquired business no longer exists because of the slow growth, self-sufficiency in management, and the absence of major financing requirements typical in mature or declining industries. This lack of synergy opportunities coupled with the opportunity to achieve the efficiency of unitary-form organization and managerial motivation may result in restructuring activities. These may include divestiture, frequently resulting in horizontal consolidation (if acquired by another firm in its industry) or a management buy-out. Also, a divestiture leading to a horizontal acquisition can be motivated by the same forces that bring horizontal mergers for survival in the later stages of the product life cycle.

SUMMARY

In this chapter we discuss and define the various types of mergers and begin to develop a framework to explain these differences as a first step toward a theory of mergers.

The three main merger types are horizontal, vertical, and conglomerate. An affirmative rationale can be made for each. Horizontal mergers provide economies of scale. Vertical mergers internalize transactions to achieve cost efficiencies. Conglomerate mergers have the potential for improved resource allocation in financial conglomerates; managerial and concentric conglomerates have the potential for synergy and transfer of managerial capabilities.

The issue of capability transference is also fundamental to the framework developed to explain horizontal and related industry mergers. The firm is viewed as a combination of organization capital and investment opportunities. Organization capital results from team effects and organization learning, defined as the improvement in the capabilities of managers and other employees through experience. The three types of organization learning vary in their transferability. *Generic management capabilities* are generally obtainable on the open market, but it is more difficult to obtain industry-specific management capabilities this way because of development time and team effects. *Industry-specific management capabilities* are transferable only in mergers within the same or a related industry. Similarly, *firm-specific human capital* develops through a long-term learning process and is otherwise obtainable only through merger. From this basis, we can project further characteristics of bidder- and target-type firms. Target firms are likely to have high growth rates; in fact, they have grown so fast there has not been time to develop needed management capabilities. As a result performance measures may be low. Bidder firms, on the other hand, are likely to have a long history in a mature industry, and over time have developed excess capabilities which can be used to complement the needs of target firms.

In the case of pure conglomerate mergers, by definition the only possible carry-over would be in generic management capabilities. This makes a weaker case for merger for capabilities transference, however a financial rationale is made. Pure conglomerate mergers may reduce the cost of capital by the combination of imperfectly correlated cash flow streams (reduces probability of bankruptcy and increases debt capacity) and by more effective utilization of internal funds which are directed to their most efficient use via an internal capital market.

A generalized industry life cycle model is used to describe how different stages in an industry's development may lend themselves to different types of merger activity. The introductory and growth stages are characterized by attractive sales growth and ease of entry. New small firms with investment opportunities but no cash to exploit them may sell out to larger firms from mature industries where cash flows exceed investment opportunities. As products reach the maturity stage, growth slows and competitive pressures increase as excess capacity develops. This period is more likely to produce horizontal mergers in an effort to keep costs down via economies of scale. As the decline phase progresses, horizontal mergers become a matter of survival, to meet the lower-cost leadership of large firms; vertical integration is used to increase efficiency to lower costs and strengthen profit margins; and conglomerate mergers will be seen as firms attempt to diversify away from the declining industry and acquire needed capabilities in more promising areas.

QUESTIONS

1. Define horizontal mergers and give their rationale.
2. Define vertical mergers and give their rationale.
3. What are conglomerate mergers? Distinguish between the various types of conglomerate mergers.
4. Discuss the differences between financial and management conglomerates.
5. How could a conglomerate merger lower capital costs?
6. What is organization capital and what is its significance?
7. What role might organization capital play in mergers or tender offers?

REFERENCES

BRUNER, R., "The Use of Excess Cash and Debt Capacity as a Motive for Merger," *Journal of Financial and Quantitative Analysis*, June 1988, pp. 199–217.

COPELAND, T. E., and J. F. WESTON, *Financial Theory and Corporate Policy*, 3rd ed., New York: Addison-Wesley, 1988.

FELDSTEIN, MARTIN, JERRY GREEN, and EYTAN SHESHINSKI, "Corporate Financial Policy and Taxation in a Growing Economy," *Quarterly Journal of Economics*, August 1979, pp. 411–432.

GALAI, D., and R. W. MASULIS, "The Option Pricing Model and the Risk Factor of Stock," *Journal of Financial Economics*, 3, January/March 1976, pp. 53–81.

HIGGINS, R. C., and L. D. SCHALL, "Corporate Bankruptcy and Conglomerate Merger," *Journal of Finance*, 30, March 1975, pp. 93–113.

KIM, E. H., and J. J. MCCONNELL, "Corporate Mergers and the Co-insurance of Corporate Debt," *Journal of Finance*, May 1977, pp. 349–370.

LEWELLEN, W. G., "A Pure Financial Rationale for the Conglomerate Merger," *Journal of Finance*, May 1971, pp. 521–545.

MARKHAM, JESSE W., *Conglomerate Enterprise and Public Policy*, Boston, MA.: Harvard University, 1973.

MILLER, M., "Debt and Taxes," *Journal of Finance*, May 1977, pp. 261–275.

———, and F. MODIGLIANI, "Dividend Policy, Growth and the Valuation of Shares," *Journal of Business*, October 1961, pp. 411–433.

MILLER, M., and M. SCHOLES, "Dividends and Taxes," *Journal of Financial Economics*, December 1978, pp. 333–364.

MYERS, S., and N. MAJLUF, "Corporate Financing and Investment Decisions when Firms have Information that Investors Do Not Have," *Journal of Financial Economics*, June 1984, pp. 187–221.

PENROSE, EDITH T., *The Theory of the Growth of the Firm*, New York: John Wiley & Sons, Inc., 1959.

PRESCOTT, E., and M. VISSCHER, "Organization Capital," *Journal of Political Economy*, June 1980, pp. 446–461.

ROSEN, SHERWIN, "Learning by Experience as Joint Production," *Quarterly Journal of Economics*, August 1972, pp. 366–382.

RUBIN, PAUL H., "The Expansion of Firms," *Journal of Political Economy*, July/August 1973, pp. 936–949.

SCOTT, J. H., JR., "On the Theory of Conglomerate Mergers," *Journal of Finance*, September 1977, pp. 1235–1250.

STAPLETON, R. C., "Mergers, Debt Capacity, and the Valuation of Corporate Loans," *Mergers and Acquisitions*, M. Keenan and L. J. White, eds., Lexington, MA: Lexington Books, 1982.

TEECE, D., *Vertical Integration and Vertical Divestiture in the U.S. Oil Industry*, Stanford University Institute for Energy Studies, 1976.

CHAPTER **5**

Corporate Finance Framework

The restructuring and ownership changes involved in merger and tender offer activity often affect and are influenced by the financial structures of firms. To separate the effects of purely financial policy changes from other forms of restructuring, this chapter seeks to provide some perspectives on corporate financial policies and decisions.

THEORY OF THE FIRM AND CORPORATE FINANCE

The theory of the firm has a number of implications for the financial behavior of the firm. We discuss its relevance to the central issues of finance theory: corporate capital structure decisions and dividend policy.

Capital Structure Decisions

Agency costs have been recognized to be a potential explanatory factor in capital structure decisions of firms. Jensen and Meckling (1976) argue that the probability distribution of cash flows of the firm is not independent of its ownership structure because of agency costs. If so, the existence of optimal capital structure can be demonstrated.

First, an increase in debt is likely to increase agency costs. When the firm uses a greater amount of debt, it has more opportunities to shift wealth from bondholders to shareholders. This transfer of wealth can be accomplished, for example, by undertaking riskier projects than promised to the bondholders. Since shareholders have limited liability, their potential losses are finite; however, their potential gains are limitless. Bondholders have both limited liability and fixed rewards. Therefore, shareholders have the incentive to increase the riskiness of the firm's investments if the firm's value does not decline too much as a result.

Consider, for example, two projects, both having the same systematic risk and net present values but different total risks (variances). Project 1 has a 50/50 chance of achieving an end-of-period cash flow of $40 or $60. Project 2 has a 50/50 chance of returning $20 or $80. Both have the same expected return of $50 and are assumed to cost $40. If the firm borrows $30 by promising to undertake Project 1, then the debt is riskless, assuming an interest payment of less than $10. However, if the firm undertakes Project 2 instead of Project 1, the debt becomes risky. The value of the debt will decline, but the value of shares will increase. This example shows one way of transferring wealth from the bondholders to the shareholders. Therefore, bondholders require various types of agreements (covenants) in the bond contract to protect their position. However, the costs of writing and enforcing such agreements, an agency cost, may be large. These costs will rise as the amount of debt increases, because the incentives of shareholders to behave opportunistically increase with the increase in debt. In the preceding example, the firm would have no incentive to switch from Project 1 to Project 2 if it borrowed, say, only $10.

If the firm raises funds by issuing outside equity instead of debt, this increases another kind of agency costs. Starting with a 100 percent ownership by an individual, the owner-manager, his or her equity ownership decreases as new shares are sold to outside investors. Any consumption of the firm's resources by the original owner-manager is now paid for in part by the new shareholders. Since he or she has greater incentives to indulge in perquisites (luxurious office, company car, paid club memberships), the new shareholders will have to incur monitoring costs to ensure that the original owner-manager acts in their interest.

In sum, if the firm uses debt instead of external equity, the agency costs of using debt will increase, but the agency costs of using external equity will decrease. This kind of tradeoff gives rise to an optimal capital structure as shown in Figure 5.1. At the optimal combination of outside debt and outside equity, the total agency costs are minimized. Jensen and Meckling thus argue that agency costs will influence the ownership and capital structures of a firm.

The concept of plasticity is used by Alchian and Woodward (1987, 1988) to explain when the moral hazard costs (or agency costs) of debt are likely to be large and thus the debt/equity ratio low. As discussed earlier, assets are called plastic when a wide range of legitimate choices can be made on their use. For example, a drug company's assets are typically more plastic than the assets of a steel mill and also the activities of the former are more difficult to monitor than the latter's. Moral hazard opportunism of equity holders includes increasing the

FIGURE 5.1   Optimal Capital Structure with Agency Costs of Equity and Debt

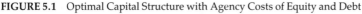

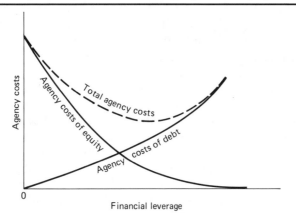

riskiness of the assets by redeploying them and also increasing the size of dividends. Control of this opportunism through contracts is more difficult for assets that are both plastic and costly to monitor. Therefore, given that there are benefits to the use of debt, Alchian and Woodward predict firms with less plastic assets will have higher debt/equity ratios than firms with more plastic assets.

There are other considerations that also may be regarded as agency costs with implications for capital structure. Titman (1984) points out that customers who buy durable products such as automobiles, washing machines, or refrigerators need to have future services such as parts and repair. When a customer buys a durable good, he or she is paying for the product itself and also for the availability of follow-up parts and repair services. If a firm goes bankrupt and is liquidated, customers are unable to obtain the parts and services they had expected. Hence, the agency problem in this relationship is the assurance that the future required parts and services will be forthcoming. Consumers must judge the probability that a seller of durable goods may fail and be liquidated. Hence, firms that produce and sell durable goods run the risk that if they use higher leverage which will increase their probability of bankruptcy, it may reduce the demand for their products. Therefore, we would expect, other things being equal, that durable goods producers would carry less debt than producers of nondurable goods such as food.

In a similar study, Chung and Smith (1987) argue that firms with larger investments in reputation to guarantee product quality (that is, the brand-name capital of Klein and Leffler explained earlier) will employ lower financial leverage. Firms use investments in nonsalvageable capital to signal commitment not to depreciate quality for opportunistic gain. The credibility of these investments in reputation is diminished by financial leverage, since the shareholders of a more highly levered firm will find it in their interest to depreciate quality and cash in on the firm's reputation with a greater probability (in a greater number of states of the world). If quality depreciation occurs under financial distress, part of the resulting decline in firm value accrues to creditors, whereas the entire gain (current income) from cheating may be realized by equity holders. The increased incentive of equity holders to depreciate quality resulting from increased leverage causes a decline in the value of reputation. Therefore, firms with larger investments in reputation will maintain a lower level of debt financing.

Organization capital is also relevant in the determination of capital structure. Workers acquire specialized skills and information which cannot be used easily in other employment. These workers bear nontrivial costs if the firm goes bankrupt. (Bankruptcy often results in changes in ownership and in organizational structure and composition, increasing the probability of discontinuation of employment.) The bankrupt firm does not compensate workers for this loss. Under competitive labor markets, workers will charge lower wages to work for firms that have a lower probability of bankruptcy. Thus, firms that involve the development of a considerable amount of organization capital tend to carry less debt than firms with smaller organization capital.

As already indicated, Cornell and Shapiro attribute capital structure to the fraction of firm value attributable to the net present value of future implicit claims which the firm hopes to sell. The value of implicit claims is dependent on a firm's ability and willingness to honor those claims. Thus, firms have an incentive to bond themselves in order to sell those claims at high prices today. One way for a firm to back its promise of high payouts or implicit claims is to alter the firm's financial structure so as to reduce the future opportunity costs of making such payments. Thus, the firm may want to hold excess cash and marketable securities. Also, the firm would rather issue equity than debt in the current period and hold the funds as cash. This will cause current costs to be high, but it will represent a cheap source of funds (that is, internal funds held as cash) in the future. For this reason, firms that have large amounts of net organization capital (in the Cornell and Shapiro definition, the net present value of implicit claims to be sold in the future) will predominantly be equity financed and hold relatively large cash balances.

Fama (1985) uses contract costs as an explanation for financing decisions. He argues that equity is used as the primary risk-bearing claim, while loans and bonds are used to reduce contracting costs for the firm in its dealings with other claim holders, mainly the firm's suppliers of goods and services. These claimants are not financial experts, but specialize in providing goods and services; for each of them to make detailed analyses of the firm's prospects would be both more costly and less accurate than if financial specialists (lenders and bondholders) were to evaluate the firm's default risk. The firm, therefore, takes on debt, subjecting itself to the scrutiny of the market to assure these other claimants that their own claims will be honored, freeing them to concentrate on supplying the goods and services needed by the firm in the most efficient way possible.

A similar argument can be made that debt is issued because monitoring done by bondholders reduces the need for equity holders to monitor managers. This "enlist the bondholders" theory implies that firms with more plastic assets will issue bonds because these firms have more shareholder/manager conflicts of interest. Thus, the theory runs counter to the Alchian and Woodward proposition that less debt will be used with more plastic assets. However, Alchian and Woodward (1987) believe that asset plasticity increases both shareholder/manager conflicts and shareholder/creditor conflicts and issuing debt to allay the former type of conflicts merely creates the latter type of conflicts. The "enlist the bondholders" theory can be valid if financial specialists (bondholders) have expertise that equity holders lack in monitoring managers or if some assets are more vulnerable to shareholder/manager conflicts than to shareholder/creditor conflicts.

Debt is also viewed as a device to avoid holdup and moral hazard problems. Whenever a firm has larger flows of quasi-rents arising from sunk costs or a windfall gain, they are vulnerable to expropriation either by unions or by managers. Ippolito (1985) suggests that committing the quasi-rent to debt payment keeps strong unions from expropriating the rents, especially in heavy manufacturing industries with large sunk costs. Underfunded pension plans are also seen as a device to increase debt and at the same time to make unions the debt holder. Jensen (1986) argues that the discretionary power of managers with respect to the use of large cash flows of quasi-rents or profits is limited if the cash flows are committed to bondholders. This version of the "commit the quasi-rent" view relies on the presence of high monitoring costs and thus appears internally inconsistent because of the additional monitoring problems brought about by the issue of debt.

Dividend Policy

In the same spirit as the discussion of the impacts of concepts from the theory of the firm on capital structure, agency cost explanations of dividends have also been formulated (Easterbrook, 1984). In this view, dividends exist because they induce firms to issue new securities. By requiring that firms make repeated trips to the capital markets, efficient mechanisms for reducing agency problems are brought into operation. One agency problem is to monitor managers. But with common stock ownership widely diffused, it does not pay individual shareholders to bear the full costs of monitoring, since any one shareholder receives only a small fraction of the gains.

Conflicts of interest arise between managers and shareholders and between shareholders and bondholders. Since large percentages of the wealth and reputation of managers are related to their firms, managers are concerned with total risk, not just undiversifiable risk. Risk-averse managers may favor safer investments with lower expected returns than risky investments. Shareholders prefer that the firm take on greater risk since they have limited liability, but after payment of fixed returns to debt holders, receive all the gains from successful risky ventures.

Debt holders seek to control their risk exposure by bond indentures and related instruments. The interest rate they are willing to accept is based on their expected level of risk exposure. Dividend policy has a role to play in controlling managers and shareholders. Lower dividends mean more financing of investments from retained earnings which provides more protection to debt holders. A higher dividend rate benefits shareholders once a rate of interest has been set on debt, but higher dividends may also mean successful investment programs which benefit debt holders as well. The need is for efficient mechanisms to convey information. Continuing dividends force companies to obtain additional funds for expanding their investments. Dividends thus create a need to go to the external capital markets where investment bankers and other financial intermediaries perform monitoring and certification functions as described earlier. The new financing can also be used to adjust the debt/equity ratio which keeps in balance the leverage risk exposure of debt holders. Successful investments whose earnings are retained reduce the debt/equity ratio and thereby afford greater protection to debt holders. They are receiving a windfall in relation to the interest contract based on a higher expected leverage ratio.

Easterbrook (1984) who has set forth most fully the monitoring and leverage adjustment functions of dividends acknowledges that information or other signaling explanations are also involved in dividend patterns [p. 655]. He observes, however, that the monitoring and certification provided by financial intermediaries help explain how dividends convey information that earnings announcements would not convey. Easterbrook also recognizes that other mechanisms could accomplish results similar to those achieved by continuing dividends. Share repurchases, for example, or the issuance of debt instruments in series resulting in continuous offsetting payments and refinancings would also accomplish similar results.

Anecdotal evidence in support of the agency cost explanations of dividends is the recognized pattern that low dividend policies are associated with growth companies which need to be in the capital markets on a regular basis. More mature firms with less pressures for financing growth are likely to have higher dividend payouts.

Easterbrook also argues that the stability of dividends is implied by agency cost explanations. Commitment to a fixed pattern of dividends irrespective of profit fluctuations is likely to push the company to the capital markets for financing investments.

Easterbrook also predicts substitution among agency-cost control devices. The higher the share ownership by managers, the better are shareholder and manager interests balanced and the less need for dividends to serve a monitoring function on behalf of shareholders.

THEORIES OF CAPITAL STRUCTURE

The implications of the theory of the firm for corporate finance provide a useful background discussion of a more general discussion of theories of capital structure and dividend policy decisions. The developments in the theory of capital structure are set forth in Table 5.1. We limit ourselves to only a brief summary of

TABLE 5.1
Theories of Capital Structure

---

1 Modigliani and Miller (1958): Leverage irrelevance with no taxes.

2 Modigliani and Miller (1963): Tax advantage of debt equal to T_cB.

3 Miller (1977): Tax advantage based on marginal tax rates, including personal taxes.

4 Feldstein, Green, & Sheshinski (1979): Leverage is influenced by the full structure of tax effects and changes in the debt/equity ratio are influenced by risk premium effects as well.

5 Modigliani (1982): Leverage influenced by average tax rates and uncertainty.

6 Jensen and Meckling (1976): Optimal capital structure minimizes total agency costs.

7 DeAngelo and Masulis (1980): Optimal tradeoff between the marginal expected benefit of interest deductions plus other tax shields and the marginal expected cost of bankruptcy.

8 Ross (1977): Financial leverage and dividend policy used to signal future financial performance.

9 Myers and Majluf (1984): Information asymmetry and rational expectations signaling.

10 Ross (1985): With tax effects of DeAngelo and Masulis, a relationship between capital structure and beta measures of risk.

11 Jensen (1986): High debt ratios bond future cash payouts.

12 C. Smith (1986); Booth and R. Smith (1986): Certification role of investment bankers.

---

each of these developments. More complete treatments are found in standard textbooks on corporate finance.

In Modigliani and Miller (1958), the conditions of leverage irrelevance were established by postulating perfect markets, no taxes; risk or uncertainty is finessed by comparing firms in the same risk class. In their tax correction article, Modigliani and Miller (1963) included corporate income taxes in the analysis. The tax advantage of debt was shown to be T_cB where the symbols used here and throughout this chapter are defined in Table 5.2.

In Miller (1977) personal taxes are considered as well as corporate taxes. In equilibrium, the aggregate amount of debt in the economy is determined by the requirement that the before-tax cost of corporate debt must equal the tax-free rate grossed up by the corporate tax rate. The capital structure for the individual firm is irrelevant because the marginal cost of debt is equal to the marginal cost of equity. Miller also develops a model to measure the gains from leverage including the effect of personal taxes. The Miller relations are shown in Table 5.3. Part A of the table sets forth the Miller model as equation (5.1) with an explanation of his symbols. Part B shows that using the marginal tax rate before the Tax Reform Act of 1986 (TRA), there appears to be no gain from the use of leverage. However, in Part C of the table the new marginal tax rates post-TRA are shown. It will be noted that the relevant tax rate for income from common stock is shown to rise from .07 to .20. This is because TRA eliminated the preferentially lower tax rate on capital gains. The rate is shown somewhat below the personal tax rate of 28 percent, since retained income which is taken ultimately in the form of capital gains still has the benefit of tax deferment.

Feldstein, Green and Sheshinski (1979) generalize the Miller debt and taxes

TABLE 5.2

Explanation of Symbols Used in Capital Structure and Dividend Theories

X = relevant cash flow
B = market value of debt
D = book value of debt
S = market value of equity
V_u = value of unlevered firm
V = value of levered firm
k = weighted marginal cost of capital
k_b = cost of debt
k_s = cost of equity
T_c = corporate tax rate = T
T_p = personal income tax rate
μ = tax reduction rate due to captial gains effects
b = investment requirements ratio or retention ratio
ϕ = corporate bond risk premium factor
ψ = corporate equity risk premium factor
G = gain from use of leverage
Z = relevant discount factor for capitalizing G
β_j = levered beta for firm j
β_u = unlevered beta

model somewhat further. Their discussion suggests that the relationship is as shown in equation (5.2), where the symbols are as defined in Table 5.2. When debt/equity ratios are changed, the marginal risk relations should be considered as in equation (5.3).

$$\phi(1 - T_p)k_b = \psi k_s(1 - T_c)[b(1 - T_p) + (1 - b)(1 - \mu T_p)] \qquad (5.2)$$

$$\phi'(1 - T_p)k_b = \psi' k_s(1 - T_c)[b(1 - T_p) + (1 - b)(1 - \mu T_p)] \qquad (5.3)$$

In the Feldstein, Green, and Sheshinski equation, the cost of debt (k_b) and the cost of equity (k_s) may be different. In addition, the risk premium factors ϕ for debt and ψ for equity may also be different. It will be noted also that the tax on retained earnings is the personal income tax rate modified by a reduction factor. Aside from the tax deferment benefits of capital gains, the TRA86 would make μ equal to one. Feldstein, Green, and Sheshinski also argue that changes in the debt/equity ratio will cause the marginal risk premiums applicable to the cost of debt and to the cost of equity to change as well.

In Modigliani (1982) the benefits of leverage are based on average tax rates rather than on marginal tax rates, as in Miller (1977). In addition, the value of the benefits of leverage are capitalized at a risky capitalization rate rather than the risk-free or cost-of-debt rate.

TABLE 5.3

Analysis of the Gains from Leverage

A Miller's Debt and Taxes Model

$$G = \left[1 - \frac{(1 - T_c)(1 - T_s)}{(1 - T_b)} \right] B \tag{5.1}$$

where:

G = the gain from leverage

T_c = marginal corporate tax rate

T_b = marginal ordinary personal income tax rate (paid on debt interest)

T_s = marginal tax rate paid by persons who receive income or capital gains from stock. It is an "average" of the capital gains tax rate and the ordinary rate on dividends received and is less than T_b

B = market value of debt

B Illustrative relations pre-TRA86

$$T_c = .46 \qquad T_b = .5 \qquad T_s = .07$$

$$G = \left[1 - \frac{(.54)(.93)}{.5} \right] B = \left(1 - \frac{.5}{.5} \right) B = 0$$

C Illustrative relations post-TRA86

$$T_c = .34 \qquad T_b = .28 \qquad T_s = .20$$

$$G = \left[1 - \frac{(.66)(.8)}{.72} \right] B = .27B$$

Jensen and Meckling (1976) introduced the concept of agency costs. Agency costs increase with higher proportions of debt to equity. An optimum combination minimizes total agency costs. If the agency costs of external equity are low, there may be an optimal capital structure from the tax shelter benefit of debt and its agency costs, as described in the first section of this chapter.

DeAngelo and Masulis (1980) developed a model in which the optimal use of debt (in the absence of bankruptcy and agency costs) is negatively related to the level of available tax shields (for example, accelerated depreciation). In their model there is an optimal tradeoff between the marginal expected benefit of interest deductions plus other tax shields and the marginal expected cost of bankruptcy.

In Ross (1977) an information asymmetry and signaling model is developed. Financial leverage or dividend policy may be used to signal favorable future performance. Firms with an unfavorable outlook cannot mimic firms with a favorable outlook. This is because they lack sufficient cash flow to back up the false signal, and managers would suffer penalties if they send false signals.

Myers and Majluf (1984) developed more extensively a model of information asymmetry with rational expectations signaling. In their model, a firm issues new equity shares only when managers expect unfavorable future states to occur. The firm holds excess liquid assets to finance future positive net present value projects. They observe that debt financing has future payoffs less correlated with future states than does equity financing.

In Ross (1985) the role of uncertainty becomes more important. With the tax effects of DeAngelo and Masulis, Ross obtains a relationship between capital structure and beta measure of risk. He also observes that mergers and spin-offs make tax credits marketable and thereby avoid leverage-related costs.

A free cash flow theory of capital structure is developed in Jensen (1986). Jensen holds that excess cash is likely to be used unwisely by managers. He proposes high dividend payouts and would have companies incur high debt ratios in order to bond managers to make future cash payouts.

Finally, in C. W. Smith (1986) and in Booth and R. Smith (1986), the certification role of investment bankers is described. Because of the high uncertainty associated particularly with new issues and with other new financing, there is a need for monitoring. The reputation of the investment banker is used to reduce the credibility problem of the managers of firms issuing additional securities.

Financial Leverage Policy in Practice

From a practical standpoint, the preceding theories provide a basis for some generalizations. The greater the debt the greater the financial risk. This is because the higher the leverage ratio, the more bankruptcy risk is increased due to increased vulnerability to the fluctuations in operating income.

With regard to setting target leverage ratios, in theory managers should seek to maximize tax benefits and to minimize the cost of capital, taking risk into account. The theoretical recommendations are difficult to implement in practice. One method is to have a target beta measure. Since beta is composed of both business and financial risks, leverage will increase the observed beta by the relationship shown in equation (5.4).

$$\beta_j = \beta_u + \beta_u \left[\frac{B(1 - T)}{S} \right] \tag{5.4}$$

Thus, if a firm has a target beta in mind, it can do the following. It takes its observed beta, it can use equation (5.4) to solve for the unlevered beta. It can then relever its beta to the desired target level.

Another practical approach is a balance sheet analysis of the ratio of debt to the book value of equity and to the market value of equity. What is likely to dominate here is the customary practice of the industry. This is the so-called "investment banker" approach in which six to ten firms are selected as closely comparable as possible to the firm under analysis. The ratios of total debt-to-equity at both book and market are calculated. By comparison with similar firms, an acceptable leverage ratio may be developed on a judgmental basis.

A final measure would be to use fixed-charge coverage. Fixed charges should be covered more than one time. The literature provides no standard. Whether the fixed-charge coverage should be two, three, or four or more times is a judgmental matter. Again, it would be greatly influenced by comparison to other firms in similar lines of business. Analytically, however, the target fixed-charge coverage should be related to the stability of sales and operating income of the firm. In addition, manager and shareholder attitudes toward risk need to be taken into account.

THEORIES OF DIVIDEND POLICY

Dividend policy has come to be viewed as the issue of choosing between alternative methods of returning cash to shareholders. Table 5.4 shows that during the last decade cash dividends have declined from 86 percent of corporate cash distributions to less than 50 percent. Share repurchases have risen to over 20 percent of cash distributions. Cash paid out to shareholders via acquisitions appears to be approaching a level almost as high as cash dividends.

While corporate profits in the aggregate are subject to substantial swings, Table 5.5 demonstrates that dividends since 1960 have never declined substantially from their previous year's level. Dividends appear to be a stable percentage of future expected smoothed earnings. The percentage has been relatively stable

TABLE 5.4
Corporate Cash Distributions, 1976–1985 ($ Billion)

| YEAR | CASH DIVIDENDS | | SHARE REPURCHASES | | ACQUISITIONS | | TOTAL |
	AMOUNT	PERCENT	AMOUNT	PERCENT	AMOUNT	PERCENT	
1976	$36.4	85.6	$ 1.8	4.2	$ 4.3	10.1	$ 42.5
1977	42.1	79.3	3.9	7.3	7.1	13.4	53.1
1978	47.0	76.7	4.3	7.0	10.0	16.3	61.3
1979	54.8	67.6	5.6	6.9	20.7	25.5	81.1
1980	60.9	71.3	6.6	7.7	17.9	21.0	85.4
1981	71.2	63.6	6.2	5.5	34.6	30.9	112.0
1982	76.0	65.3	10.6	9.1	29.7	25.5	116.3
1983	82.3	70.8	9.8	8.4	24.2	20.8	116.3
1984	86.4	48.2	30.3	16.9	62.6	34.9	179.3
1985	85.8	42.2	43.0	21.2	74.5	36.6	203.3

SOURCE: Basic data from J. Poterba, "Tax Policy and Corporate Saving," *Brookings Papers on Economic Activity,* 2, 1987, p. 471.

TABLE 5.5
Dividend Payout Patterns ($ Billion)

	(1)	(2)	(3)	(4)	(5)
		CORPORATE PROFITS	CAPITAL CONSUMPTION ALLOWANCE	DIVIS AS	DIVIS AS % OF PROFITS
	DIVIS	(AFTER-TAX)	(CCA)	% OF PROFITS	+ CCA
1960	12.9	26.8	25.3	48.1	24.8
1961	13.3	27.6	26.0	48.2	24.8
1962	14.4	34.3	27.0	42.0	23.5
1963	15.5	37.4	28.2	41.4	23.6
1964	17.3	42.7	29.6	40.5	23.9
1965	19.1	50.4	31.6	37.9	23.3
1966	19.4	52.9	34.5	36.7	22.2
1967	20.2	51.4	37.8	39.3	22.6
1968	22.0	51.4	41.7	42.8	23.6
1969	22.5	47.7	45.7	47.2	24.1
1970	22.5	40.3	50.2	55.8	24.9
1971	22.9	49.3	55.1	46.5	21.9
1972	24.4	58.8	60.5	41.5	20.5
1973	27.0	64.1	65.6	42.1	20.8
1974	29.7	49.9	76.8	59.5	23.4
1975	29.6	66.7	92.5	44.4	18.6
1976	34.6	81.0	103.0	42.7	18.8
1977	39.5	101.8	115.1	38.8	18.2
1978	44.7	113.7	130.8	39.3	18.3
1979	50.1	112.1	150.7	44.7	19.1
1980	54.7	92.4	172.5	59.2	20.6
1981	63.6	106.8	200.2	59.6	20.7
1982	66.9	86.9	223.0	77.0	21.6
1983	71.5	136.5	229.8	52.4	19.5
1984	79.0	173.0	240.1	45.7	19.1
1985	81.3	189.9	252.8	42.8	18.4
1986	86.8	179.4	264.4	48.4	19.6
1987	93.8	167.8	275.9	55.9	21.1

SOURCE: *Economic Report of the President*, 1988, Tables B-12 and B-87.

at about 50 percent of earnings, as shown in Table 5.5. In relation to cash flows—corporate profits plus capital consumption allowances—dividends have long been relatively stable at 20 percent.

The Dividend Paradox

It has long been puzzling why corporations which need to raise funds would pay out dividends. Why pay out dividends subject to personal taxes and then seek to raise additional funds? In terms of equation (5.2) presented in connection with the discussion of capital structure decisions, it can be seen that before TRA86 when the top bracket marginal tax rate on personal income was 50 percent, there was a substantial tax advantage of retained earnings that would ultimately be returned to shareholders as capital gains. It has been estimated that retained corporate profits benefited from a lower capital gains rate as well as deferment of the taxes paid. A reasonable estimate of μ would be in the range of .2 so that the effective tax rate on the $(1 - b)$ fraction of corporate profits retained was about 10 percent at the top bracket rate and even lower if the average effective personal income tax rates were applicable.

Possible Explanations for Dividends

In spite of the apparent substantial tax disadvantages of paying out cash dividends in the pre-TRA86 era, about one half of pretax profits were paid out. Five possible explanations are: (1) no tax disadvantage in practice, (2) need to balance present and future consumption in an aggregate sense, (3) information-signaling role of dividends, (4) role in controlling agency costs, and (5) high discount rate for determining the value of tax disadvantages.

Miller and Scholes (1978) described how the receipt of cash dividends could be offset from a tax standpoint. They showed how personal leverage could be used to generate tax savings to offset the income from dividends. In addition, the leverage effect could be neutralized by tax-deferred investments such as single-payment deferred annuities. The methods involve some financial sophistication and other transactions costs would be incurred. Empirical tests based on actual individual income tax returns find that individuals do not offset their dividend income by borrowing and tax-deferred investments (Feenberg, 1981).

Another possible explanation is that dividends perform an important role in balancing current consumption and future consumption (DeAngelo, 1989). This position holds that if dividends did not perform a role in providing for current consumption, yields on equities would be required to be higher. Dividends have a role in equating the marginal rates of substitution between present and future consumption.

A third explanation for dividends is that they perform an information-signaling role (Miller and Rock, 1985). Miller and Rock start with the assumption of asymmetric information in which "managers know more than outside investors about the true state of the firm's current earnings" (p. 1031). The market's estimate of current earnings is said to contribute to the estimate of the expected future earnings which determines the firms's market value. But with information asymmetry, "temptations arise to run up the price by paying out more dividends (or engaging in less outside financing) than the market was expecting, even if that means cutting back on investment" (p. 1032). The problem is solved by a signaling equilibrium. The Miller-Rock equilibrium-signaling model holds that investors anticipate such behavior by managers, who in turn expect the market to allow for this departure. The announcement effects of earnings surprises, unexpected dividend changes, and unexpected external financing emerge as implications of a basic valuation model.

A fourth model to explain dividends is control of agency costs, as discussed in the first section of this chapter. Dividends push the firm to use the external markets for financing. As a consequence, financial intermediaries will provide monitoring services and the firm will adjust more promptly to leverage ratios upon which financial contracts were priced.

A fifth explanation is that the value of any tax differential on dividends versus capital gains must be capitalized at the rate applicable to an uncertain stream. This risk-adjusted discount rate takes into account uncertain earnings, uncertain dividend payout policies, and uncertain tax regimes (Modigliani, 1982). As a result, the impact of a change in dividend payout on value is attenuated. Modigliani (1982, p. 156) estimates that a 10 percent change in the dividend payout policy would change market value by only 3 percent. Thus, the effect of dividend policy on value could easily be swamped by other considerations.

We have reviewed five reasons why dividends would be paid despite tax disadvantages. These considerations lead to a model which simultaneously takes into account investment opportunities, effects on cost of capital, clientele effects, and dividends as a residual payout.

INVESTMENT, DIVIDENDS, AND TAXES

Corporate finance has long postulated that internal funds are cheaper than external funds. This was presented as a pecking order sequence of financing by Myers (1984). A more formal model is set forth by Masulis and Trueman (1988). This presentation provides a numerical and graphical exposition of their materials. Some key assumptions and illustrative values are:

1 Corporations pay an effective marginal tax rate, $T_c = 40$ percent.
2 Individuals pay different personal tax rates on dividend income; high tax rate shareholders pay a personal tax rate, T_{ph} of 50 percent, while low tax rate shareholders pay a personal tax rate, T_{pw} of 20 percent.
3 There are no capital gains taxes, $T_g = 0$.
4 The IRS taxes regular corporate repurchases and equity in the same way as dividend payments.
5 There is an 80 percent dividend exclusion from taxes on all dividends paid by one corporation to another.
6 No debt.
7 Investments in real assets earn a before-tax rate of return of $R = 18$ percent.
8 Investments in securities of other firms earn a before-tax rate of return of $R_s = 10$ percent.

For the high tax rate shareholder, the after-tax rate of return on dividends received is:

$$R(1 - T_c)(1 - T_{ph}) = .18(.6)(.5) = .054$$

If the funds are retained by the firm; the before-tax return required to earn the same after-tax yield is:

$$R(1 - T_c) = .054$$

$$R = .09$$

For the low tax rate shareholder, the after-tax rate of return on dividends received is:

$$R(1 - T_c)(1 - T_{pw}) = .18 (.6)(.8) = .0864$$

If the funds are retained by the firm, the before-tax return required to earn the same after-tax yield is:

$$R(1 - T_c) = .0864$$

$$R \doteq .144$$

For the high tax rate shareholder, an 18 percent pretax return by the firm will net 5.4 percent after corporate and personal income taxes. Under the pre-TRA capital gains tax provisions, the retained earnings are paid to the high tax rate shareholder in the form of capital gains subject essentially to no tax. Under the preceding assumptions, to yield the high tax rate shareholder the same return of 5.4 percent after all taxes requires a 9 percent cost of retained earnings and an 18 percent cost when funds are paid out and subject to personal taxes as well as the corporate tax. By the same reasoning, the cost of retained earnings when the shareholder pays only a 20 percent personal tax is 14.4 percent. The low tax bracket shareholder receives a higher after-tax return on dividends than the high tax bracket shareholder, and thus has a greater preference for dividends. The high tax bracket shareholder would let the firm retain earnings to invest until the pretax return fell below 9 percent; the low tax bracket shareholder would require a pretax earnings rate of 14.4 percent or more.

One final piece of information enables us to explain Figure 5.2. When the firm invests in other companies, it earns R_s on which it pays the corporate income tax T_c on 20 percent of the income after the 80 percent exclusion. The applicable tax is $.2T_c$; with T_c equal to 40 percent, the effective tax rate on dividends received from other firms is 8 percent. If the pretax R_s is 10 percent, the after-tax R_s will be $R_s(1 - .2T_c)$ which equals 9.2 percent.

As shown in Figure 5.2, for a firm whose shares are held by the high tax rate shareholder, the cost of retained earnings on a pretax basis is 9 percent. It will pay no dividends and invest I_aI^* in other firms. Firms whose shareholders are in low tax brackets would invest I^* equal to I_a and pay dividends equal to the residual amount of its internal funds, as shown in Figure 5.2.

Masulis and Trueman suggest that their model yields testable predictions. Mergers are predicted between firms that finance their investment projects from

FIGURE 5.2   Corporate Investment and Dividend Decisions with Differing Personal Tax Rates

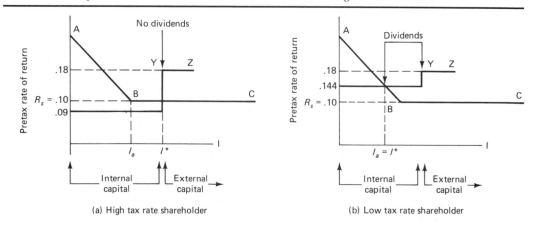

(a) High tax rate shareholder   (b) Low tax rate shareholder

internal funds and firms that finance their investment projects from external funds. Such mergers could achieve gains by shifting funds from the firms with internal financing to the high-yielding projects of firms using external financing. It further predicts that purchases of securities for investment purposes will be made only from internal funds, since external funds will cost the firm more than the yields of the securities. In addition, potential disagreements are likely to occur among shareholders in different tax brackets over desired investment and dividend levels.

If this type of model has validity, clientele effects of taxes are likely to be observed. High tax bracket individuals will prefer firms which have low dividend payouts. Low tax bracket individuals will prefer firms with high dividend payouts. Tests for dividend-clientele effects have been made in a number of ways. Elton and Gruber (1970) developed a model in which the decline in stock price on the ex-dividend date in relation to the dividend paid is used to estimate the marginal tax rate of the investor by dividend yields. Their evidence supports a tax-induced clientele effect. Other studies also support a similar conclusion (Eades, Hess, and Kim, 1984; Lakonishok and Vermaelen, 1986; Pettit, 1977). However, a study by Lewellen, Stanley, Lease, and Schlarbaum (1978) finds only very weak relationships. A 10 percent increase in an investor's marginal (imputed) tax bracket was associated with only a .1 percent decline in the yield of securities held. With the TRA86 elimination of a preferential capital gains tax rate, a dividend tax-induced clientele effect is likely to be even weaker.

DIVIDEND POLICY IN PRACTICE

With the benefit of the survey of models from the literature, we are able to make recommendations for dividend policies by business firms. Managements should seek to communicate their policies with respect to dividends in the clearest possible manner to their shareholders and to the marketplace. If the firm is a high-growth firm which must periodically go to external markets for financing, a policy of paying no dividends will be understood by the market and no penalty imposed. The agency-cost rationale for paying dividends will have been met by periodically raising funds externally. In view of the possible dividend-clientele relationships, investors for whom continuing dividend cash flows are not important would be attracted to such a firm.

Firms with somewhat lower growth rates are more likely to attract investor clienteles seeking income in the form of dividends. For such firms dividends will lag behind earnings increases. Dividend increases can plausibly be taken as signals that management's true expectation of future earnings levels have been increased. Management should not falsely signal future earnings by dividend increases because internal cash balances may be depleted, and when the market realizes it has been fooled, a severe drop in the firm's stock prices will take place. The evidence appears to suggest that instead of paying a quarterly extra dividend when earnings are favorable, it is better to build up the firm's cash balances. Only when the firm's earnings prospects and cash balances provide a sufficient margin of safety to make a dividend increase that will be subject to low risk of subsequent reversal, should a dividend adjustment upward and its attendant signal be announced.

With this general background on corporate financial policy, we next turn to trends in the financial position of business corporations.

TRENDS IN FINANCIAL POSITION

It is easy enough to trace the patterns in the financial position of corporations over time. One can readily compile trends in financing practices as well. But some subtleties and interpretations are also involved. We begin with the basic facts and then attempt to look behind them.

The basic data on year-end balance sheets of all manufacturing corporations for selected years since 1970 are set forth along with some key ratios in Table 5.6. Total liabilities as a percentage of total assets have risen by about 10 percentage points from 46 percent to 56 percent. As a result, total stockholders' equity has declined from 116 percent of total liabilities to 79 percent.

Another measure can be derived from Table 5.6 to facilitate other comparisons. In Table 5.7, total liabilities are separated into interest-bearing debt [total debt, column (4)] and noninterest-bearing liabilities [NIBL, column (5)]. Total debt has risen only slightly from 24 percent of total assets (or total claims) to 26 percent. The large rise has been in noninterest-bearing liabilities—from 22.2 percent to 30 percent of total claims. The amount of shareholders' equity at book has declined by almost the same number of percentage points as the increase in noninterest-bearing liabilities. Thus interest-bearing debt has not increased, but rather noninterest-bearing liabilities have increased as shareholders' equity has

TABLE 5.6
Balance Sheet Trends, 1970–1986

RATIOS (AS A PERCENT OF TOTAL ASSETS)	4TH QUARTER		
	1986	1980	1970
Total cash, U.S. government and other securities	6.40%	5.30%	5.00%
Trade accounts, and trade notes receivable	14.30	16.80	17.30
Inventories	15.60	19.70	23.00
Total current assets	39.80	44.50	48.70
Net property, plant and equipment	36.60	36.50	40.30
Short-term debt, including installments on long-term debt	5.50	4.90	6.30
Total current liabilities	26.10	26.80	24.60
Long-term debt	20.50	16.60	17.70
Total liabilities	56.00	50.40	46.20
Stockholders' equity	44.00	49.60	53.80
Other ratios			
Total current assets to current liabilities	1.53	1.66	1.98
Total cash, U.S. government and other securities to total current liabilities	.24	.20	.20
Total stockholders' equity to total debt	1.70	2.31	2.25
Total stockholders' equity to total liabilities	.79	.98	1.16

SOURCE: Department of Commerce, *Quarterly Financial Report*, First Quarter, 1987 and earlier issues.

declined. The decline in equity is at least in part due to the large equity retirements associated with mergers, acquisitions, leveraged buy-outs, and stock repurchase programs. These activities resulted in the retirement of about $110
billion in equity for each of the years 1984 and 1985. The total of $220 billion
represented nearly 10 percent of the market value of equity outstanding (Henry
Kaufman, *Comments on Credit*, January 3, 1986, Salomon Brothers Inc., pp. 3–4).
These data on all manufacturing corporations suggest that the rise in the book
ratios of debt to equity result more from equity retirements and from the rise of

TABLE 5.7
Debt to Assets, 1970, 1986

	(1)	(2)	(3)	(4) (2) + (3)	(5) (1) − (4)	(6)	(7) (4) + (6)	(8) (4) − (7)
			DEBT					DEBT-
	TOTAL LIABILITIES	SHORT-TERM	LONG-TERM	TOTAL	NIBL*	SHARE-HOLDERS' EQUITY	TOTAL CAPITAL	TO-TOTAL CAPITAL (%)
1970	46.2	6.3	17.7	24.0	22.2	53.8	77.8	30.8
1986	56.0	5.5	20.5	26.0	30.0	44.0	70.0	37.1

*NIBL—Noninterest-bearing liabilities
SOURCE: Table 5.6.

noninterest-bearing debt such as accrued tax obligations and tax deferments from the use of accelerated depreciation than from the modest increase in interest-bearing debt.

Other data provide further perspectives on financial patterns. In his National Bureau of Economic Research study of "Secular Patterns in the Financing of U.S. Corporations," Professor Taggart (1985) summarizes studies of debt ratios taking market values into account. For all nonfinancial corporations, the ratio of total debt to total capitalization (adding preferred stock and equity to total debt) fluctuates in the .21 to .40 range for recent years. Similarly, the ratio of the market value of total debt to the market value of total assets has risen from about .17 in the early 1950s to .25 to .28 in more recent years. This is evidence of a rise in debt ratios, but the ratio levels are much below those measured at book values. The market value estimates vary greatly among the different studies, suggesting they are subject to a relatively wide margin of error.

To this point the evidence has used balance sheet data based on book values and on market values. We next turn to the data on flows. Here we focus on total debt as a ratio of total funds sources and also on the role of gross internal funds (retained earnings plus depreciation). The data cover the period from 1901–1984 (Taggart, 1986, p. 38). On an unadjusted basis, the ratios of total debt to total sources have fluctuated but exhibit a rising trend in recent years. The ratios of gross internal funds to total sources of funds show no strong trend. Professor Taggart makes an adjustment calculation as well. The percentage change in the price level is applied to the total beginning-of-period debt outstanding to measure the decline in the real value of debt during the period. This decline is subtracted from total debt and added to gross internal funds for the period. After adjustment, total debt as a fraction of total sources of funds appears to show no strong trend and to have fluctuated mostly in the 25 to 30 percent range. Gross internal funds appear to have fluctuated mainly in the range of 65 to 75 percent of total sources of funds.

Thus, Taggart in the most exhaustive study made of the issues (1985, 1986, 1986a) concludes that corporate debt financing does not exhibit an upward trend in recent years. Rather he finds that corporate financing patterns reflect more fundamental economic influences superimposed on cyclical factors. The basic economic variables are the inflation rate, tax incentives, risk, and competition for raising funds in the capital markets. The inflation rate is measured by the average annual percentage change in the implicit GNP deflator. The debt incentive tax ratio is the personal tax rate minus the corporate tax rate all divided by one minus the personal tax rate. These two variables are positively associated with the use of debt financing. Perceived risk is measured as the average annual standard deviation of monthly changes in the S&P 500 composite stock index. Competition for borrowing is measured by federal borrowing as a fraction of total borrowing by domestic nonfinancial sectors. The latter two variables are said to be negatively associated with incentives for debt financing. [The use of junk bonds is discussed in Chapter 13 which deals with financing M&As.]

Typical cyclical corporate financing patterns have also been widely recognized. Toward the end of an economic expansion, capital outlays and investment in inventory tend to exceed the availability of internal financing. Debt financing increases, mostly in the form of short-term financing since interest rates are relatively high. As an economic downturn develops, internal financing available exceeds investment needs. Internal funds are available to reduce debt and in addition, longer-term debt at lower long-term interest rates is substituted for shorter-term liabilities. These cyclical patterns need to be considered in appraising year-to-year changes in corporate financial structures.

THE MARKET IMPACT
OF NEW FINANCING

Despite the large volume of gross public financing, probably in the region of $500 billion between 1980 and 1986, on average the market has registered a negative reaction to security offer announcements. In summary, the findings of a large number of studies indicate the following results:

1 Market reactions were negative or zero for common equity, preferred equity, convertible preferred equity, convertible debt, and straight debt.
2 Returns were more negative for common equity (-3.0 percent) offering announcements than for straight preferred or debt issues (-0.2 percent).
3 Returns were more negative for convertible issue announcements (-2.0 percent) than for nonconvertibles (-0.2 percent).
4 Returns were more negative for industrials than for utilities.

In general, the stock market response to announcements of security offerings is negative in varying degrees. The reasons for these negative reactions may be considered (C. W. Smith, 1986, 1986a). Among the explanations suggested for the market's reaction to announcements of security offerings are the following:

1 Earnings per share (EPS) dilution
2 Price pressure
3 Departures from optimal capital structure
4 Tax effects
5 Information disparity
6 Signaling
7 Investment opportunities

Each of these is considered in turn.

EPS Dilution

This view argues that since equity and convertible offerings increase the number of common stock shares outstanding, reported earnings per share (EPS) will decline with unfavorable effects on stock prices. This view fails to take into account that the funds raised may produce additional earnings. If the new funds received earn more than their cost, the issue or stock price should not decline. Furthermore, considerable evidence demonstrates that stock market prices are based on expectations of future cash flows, not on accounting-based changes in numbers such as earnings per share.

Price Pressure

The price pressure argument is based on the premise that the demand curve for the securities of an individual company is downward sloping. However, modern portfolio theory has established that the risk-return profile for any given security can be duplicated by other individual securities or through a combination of other securities. Thus, the demand curve for the equity securities of any individual firm should be close to a horizontal line.

Studies of the sales of large blocks of common stock indicate a negative price effect. But if price pressure exists, the price changes accompanying such offers should be positively related to the size of the block of shares offered. Such a relationship has not been observed in the empirical studies. Thus, both theory and evidence contradict the price pressure explanation.

Departures from Optimal Capital Structure

If business firms have an optimal capital structure, new offerings might either move the firm toward its target capital structure or away from it. If new offerings move the firm toward its target capital structure, the market response should be positive. But the facts are the opposite.

The negative market response to new security offerings might also be interpreted as evidence that the firm is moving away from its optimal capital structure. This would appear to be irrational behavior on the part of financial managers, so this explanation should also be discarded. The negative responses suggest that either firms do not have target capital structures or that other factors explain the negative market reaction.

Tax Effects

Related to the target capital structure argument is the tax explanation. Interest on debt is a deductible expense for tax purposes while dividends on common stock are not. Thus, there is in some sense a tax subsidy to the use of debt. C. W. Smith (1986, 1986a) summarizes data to show that pure financial structure changes that increase leverage are associated with a positive stock market response. He finds also that leverage-reducing transactions are associated with negative returns. He finds also that exchange offers of debt for debt have no statistically significant effect on common stock prices.

Thus, the tax effect appears to have explanatory value. However, some matters are still unsettled. A basic question is, why is it that firms do not immediately move to obtain the maximum tax advantages by issuing the greatest possible amount of debt? Why do we observe individual firms with virtually no debt in their financial structures? (If marketable securities are treated as offsets to debt, why do some firms even have negative leverage?) While there may be a positive benefit to more debt, it is not clear why new debt offerings have a negative market response when debt is not substituted for other more junior securities. The effect is the same; leverage is increased. Yet in offerings where debt is exchanged for more junior securities, the market response is positive. In straight-debt offerings that do not involve an exchange, the market response is negative.

Information Disparity

The information disparity view argues that management possesses more information about the firm's prospects than outside investors. This theory suggests that firms time their offerings of new equity securities when management believes them to be overvalued. Investors through experience will then come to discount the stock prices of companies announcing new common stock offerings. This would explain the negative response to equity offerings but would not explain the negative response to debt offerings. Hence, the information disparity argument is at best an incomplete explanation of empirical data.

Signaling

The signaling hypothesis argues that when a firm raises additional external financing, this is a signal that unfavorable changes in future cash flows are in prospect. This argument is made by analogy to other changes in financial policy. For example, dividend initiation or a dividend increase implies an increase in future corporate cash flows and the market has a positive response to such announcements. Common stock repurchases are also regarded by some as an indication of an implied increase in future corporate cash flows, and carry a very strong positive stock market reaction. The two-day announcement period return on common stock repurchases is a positive 16 percent. However, this result is also consistent with the information disparity argument. It could be argued that the repurchase of common stock by the firm conveys information that the managers judge the common stock to be undervalued. Perhaps both influences are operating simultaneously: the information effect and the signaling effect. In a sense the information effect and the signaling effect may be difficult to separate.

Most of the preceding explanations for the stock market response to public security offerings are incomplete at best. And even those which appear to have some validity—the information and signaling theories—do not explain why the firm's future prospects are likely to be favorable or unfavorable.

Investment Opportunities

Basic economic principles would argue that the value of the firm's common stock ought to be dominated by the quality and quantity of the firm's existing and prospective investment opportunities. Consistent with this theory is the finding that announcements of investment increases have a positive two-day announcement period return, while announcements of investment decreases elicit a negative stock market response (McConnell and Muscarella, 1985). The response to investment increases or decreases is relatively small—about a 1 percent two-day announcement period return. The effect of common stock repurchases is 16 times larger. However, it is of the same order of magnitude as the negative impact of announcements of security sales.

Studies to date of the effect of investment increases or decreases may understate the impact of investment changes. The studies have looked at periodic announcements of revisions in investment programs. It is plausible that the announcement of major new investment projects or product programs could have a much larger impact. However, it is not likely that firms will publicize major strategic changes in product-market plans. Such announcements would provide valuable information to competitors. Thus, it would not be expected that firms will trumpet with loud fanfare major changes in strategic policies and directions of the firm. Hence, the difficulty of providing full explanations for the generally negative market response to the announcements of security sales may be because tests are getting at only a partial aspect of what is really important. Surely the prospects for existing and future investment opportunities must be overriding in determining the current value of a firm's common stock. Until the empirical evidence can link changes in current and prospective investment opportunities to security price changes, attempted explanations are likely to be incomplete.

FINAL COMMENTS

Debt ratios measured at book values have been rising in recent years. In a longer-term perspective, the recent rises in debt may represent only a readjustment from the abnormally low debt levels of the immediate post-World War II period. Also the data suggest not so much a rise in the use of debt as a decline in the amount of equity reflecting retirements associated with mergers, acquisitions, leveraged buy-outs and stock repurchase programs plus a rise in noninterest-bearing debt. When measured at market values, overall debt ratios have been rising moderately. In some individual companies debt ratios are unusually high as compared to historical standards. At book values, debt ratios have risen substantially since 1983, especially in those industries in which the incidence of LBOs is relatively high.

The use of debt appears to be influenced by underlying economic factors such as the rate of inflation, relative tax incentives, risk, and the competition from the federal government in raising funds in the capital markets. Cyclical corporate financing patterns highlight the interaction of investment opportunities and the availability of internal funds. During a business upturn, investment requirements outpace the availability of internal financing, leading to an increase in the use of external financing, particularly short-term debt. During business downturns, internal funds exceed investment opportunities so that less external financing is required and facilitate the reduction in debt and/or the substitution of long-term debt for short-term debt.

QUESTIONS

1. What are the advantages of internal funds compared with external funds?
2. What developments could cause higher leverage ratios to be observed in industry generally?
3. Explain why the immediate stock market reaction to new external financing by either straight debt or by common stock is negative.
4. List and briefly explain alternative methods of paying out cash.
5. Discuss the influences on dividends and present a recommendation for policy by managements.
6. a. What tests would you apply to determine whether leverage ratios in the economy were too high?
   b. What tests would you use to determine whether leverage in an individual firm is too high or too low?
7. How would you respond to concerns about "alarming increases" in corporate debt financing?

REFERENCES

ALCHIAN, A., and S. WOODWARD, "Reflections on the Theory of the Firm," *Journal of Institutional and Theoretical Economics*, March 1987, pp. 110–136.

———, "The Firm is Dead; Long Live the Firm: A Review of Oliver E. Williamson's *The Economic Institutions of Capitalism*," *Journal of Economic Literature*, March 1988, pp. 65–79.

BOOTH, J., and R. SMITH, "Capital Raising, Underwriting and the Certification Hypothesis," *Journal of Financial Economics*, 15, 1986, pp. 261–281.

CHUNG, K. S., and R. L. SMITH, "Product Quality, Nonsalvageable Capital Investment, and the Cost of Financial Leverage," in T. E. Copeland, ed., *Modern Finance and Industrial Economics*, New York: Basil Blackwell, 1987, pp. 146–167.

DEANGELO, H., "Dividend Policy and Personal Taxes," Working Paper, January 1989.

————, and R. Masulis, "Optimal Capital Structure Under Corporate and Personal Taxation," *Journal of Financial Economics*, March 1980, pp. 3–30.

Eades, K., P. Hess, and E. H. Kim, "On Interpreting Security Returns during the Ex-Dividend Period," *Journal of Financial Economics*, March 1984, pp. 3–34.

Easterbrook, F., "Two Agency-Cost Explanations of Dividends," *American Economic Review*, 74, 1984, pp. 650–659.

Economic Report of the President, 1988, Tables B-12 and B-87.

Elton, E. J., and M. J. Gruber, "Marginal Stockholders' Tax Rates and the Clientele Effect," *Review of Economics and Statistics*, February 1970, pp. 68–74.

Fama, E., "Contract Costs and Financing Decisions," ms., 1985.

Feenberg, D., "Does the Investment Interest Limitation Explain the Existence of Dividends?" *Journal of Financial Economics*, 9, 1981, pp. 265–269.

Feldstein, M., J. Green, and E. Sheshinski, "Corporate Financial Policy and Taxation in a Growing Economy," *Quarterly Journal of Economics*, 93, 1979, pp. 411–431.

Ippolito, R. A., "The Labor Contract and True Economic Pension Liabilities," *American Economic Review*, December 1985, pp. 1031–1043.

Jensen, Michael C., "Agency Costs of Free Cash Flow, Corporate Finance, and Takeovers," *American Economic Review*, December 1986, pp. 323–329.

————, and William H. Meckling, "Theory of the Firm: Managerial Behavior, Agency Costs and Ownership Structure," *Journal of Financial Economics*, October 1976, pp. 305–360.

Kaufman, Henry, *Comments on Credit*, Salomon Brothers Inc., January 3, 1986, pp. 3–4.

Lakonishok, J., and T. Vermaelen, "Tax-Induced Trading around Ex-Dividend Days," *Journal of Financial Economics*, July 1986, pp. 287–320.

Lewellen, W., K. Stanley, R. Lease, and G. Schlarbaum, "Some Direct Evidence on the Dividend Clientele Phenomenon," *Journal of Finance*, December 1978, pp. 1385–1399.

Masulis, Ronald W., and Brett Trueman, "Corporate Investment and Dividend Decisions under Differential Personal Taxation," *Journal of Financial and Quantitative Analysis*, 23, December 1988, pp. 369–385.

McConnell, John J., and Chris J. Muscarella, "Corporate Capital Expenditure Decisions and the Market Value of the Firm," *Journal of Financial Economics*, 14, 1985, pp. 399–422.

Miller, M., "Debt and Taxes," *Journal of Finance*, 32, 1977, pp. 261–275.

————, and K. Rock, "Dividend Policy Under Asymmetric Information," *Journal of Finance*, September 1985, pp. 1031–1051.

Miller, M., and M. Scholes, "Dividends and Taxes," *Journal of Financial Economics*, 6, 1978, pp. 333–364.

Modigliani, F., "Debt, Dividend Policy, Taxes, Inflation and Market Valuation," *Journal of Finance*, 37, 1982, pp. 255–273.

————, and M. Miller, "The Cost of Capital, Corporation Finance and the Theory of Investment," *American Economic Review*, 48, 1958, pp. 261–297.

————, "Corporate Income Taxes and the Cost of Capital: A Correction," *American Economic Review*, 53, 1963, pp. 433–443.

Myers, S. C., "The Capital Structure Puzzle," *Journal of Finance*, July 1984, pp. 575–592.

———, and N. MAJLUF, "Corporate Financing and Investment Decisions When Firms Have Information That Investors Do Not Have," *Journal of Financial Economics*, June 1984, pp. 187–221.

PETTIT, R. R., "Taxes, Transactions Costs and Clientele Effects of Dividends," *Journal of Financial Economics*, December 1977, pp. 419–436.

POTERBA, J., "Tax Policy and Corporate Saving," *Brookings Papers on Economic Activity*, 2, 1987, pp. 455–515.

ROSS, S., "The Determination of Financial Structures: The Incentive Signalling Approach," *Bell Journal of Economics*, 8, 1977, pp. 23–40.

———, "Debt and Taxes and Uncertainty," *Journal of Finance*, 60, 1985, pp. 637–658.

SMITH, CLIFFORD W., JR., "Investment Banking and the Capital Acquisition Process," *Journal of Financial Economics*, January/February 1986, pp. 3–29.

———, "Raising Capital: Theory and Evidence," *Midland Corporate Finance Journal*, Spring 1986a, pp. 6–22.

TAGGART, ROBERT A., JR., "Secular Patterns in the Financing of U.S. Corporations," *Corporate Capital Structures in the United States*, Benjamin M. Friedman, ed., National Bureau of Economic Research, Chicago, IL: The University of Chicago Press, 1985, pp. 13–80.

———, "Corporate Financing: Too Much Debt?" *Financial Analysts Journal*, May–June 1986, pp. 35–42.

———, "Have U.S. Corporations Grown Financially Weak?" *Financing Corporate Capital Formation*, Benjamin M. Friedman, ed., National Bureau of Economic Research, Chicago, IL: The University of Chicago Press, 1986a, pp. 13–33.

TITMAN, S., "The Effect of Capital Structure on a Firm's Liquidation Decision," *Journal of Financial Economics*, March 1984, pp. 137–152.

U.S. Department of Commerce, Bureau of the Census, *Quarterly Financial Report for Manufacturing, Mining, and Trade Corporations*, Superintendent of Documents, U.S. Government Printing Office, selected issues.

CHAPTER **6**

Principles of Valuation

This book is concerned with M&As, restructuring, and corporate control. In their proper perspective, these are all forms of capital budgeting activities—the heart of financial theory. Capital budgeting is a form of cost-benefit analysis, a method of determining whether benefits exceed costs when both are properly measured and evaluated. Therefore, we begin with some basics on capital budgeting. From these foundations, we then show how the important valuation models can be developed.

CAPITAL BUDGETING DECISIONS

Capital budgeting represents the process of planning expenditures whose returns extend over a period of time. Examples of capital outlays for tangible or physical items are expenditures for land, building, and equipment. Outlays for research and development, advertising, or promotion efforts may also be regarded as investment outlays when their benefits extend over a period of years. While capital budgeting criteria are generally discussed in relation to investment in fixed assets, the concepts are equally applicable to investment in cash, receivables, or inventory, as well as M&As and other restructuring activities.

Administrative Aspects

Investment decisions and their evaluation by capital budgeting analysis are important for a number of reasons. (1) The consequences of the decision continue for a number of years. Thus, after making an investment decision, some flexibility for the future is reduced. (2) Capital budgeting requires effective planning, including accurate sales forecasts, to assure the proper timing of asset acquisitions. This means that capital assets should be available when needed, and yet not too early to avoid the extra cost of having them idle until required. (3) Since asset expansion involves substantial outlays, the required financing must be arranged in advance. (4) Since the dollar amounts of outlays on investments are large, the success or failure of an enterprise may result from excessive investments, inadequate amounts of investment, or undue delay in replacing obsolete assets.

Individual firms usually have formal administrative procedures for reviewing capital budgeting requests. Small items can be approved by individual department heads, while larger dollar amounts require approval from officers at higher levels in the organizational structure. Major investment outlays require the review and approval of the company's finance committee or, in some instances, the board of directors.

The finance department generally coordinates its activities with other departments to develop systematic records on the use of investment funds. Records are also compiled on revenues and savings from equipment purchased. An important aspect of the recordkeeping is postaudits, which provide a comparison between the initial estimates and the actual results. The postaudits review past decisions to aid in improving decisions on new investment outlays.

Evaluation and Ranking Criteria

Several major methods for evaluating projects have been developed. The net present value methodology is widely agreed to be the superior method for evaluation and ranking of investment proposals. The net present value (NPV) method is the present value of all future cash flows discounted at the cost of capital, minus the cost of the investment also discounted at the cost of capital. Its main competitor is the internal rate of return method (IRR). The IRR represents the discount rate at which the net present value or net terminal value of all cash flows is zero. We illustrate each by a case problem example.

A firm can invest $180,000 now to receive $40,000 per year for ten years. The cost of capital for this project is 14 percent. What is the NPV of the project? The formula for calculating the NPV is:

$$\text{NPV} = \sum_{t=1}^{n} \frac{CF_t}{(1+k)^t} - I_0$$

$$NPV = \sum_{t=1}^{10} \frac{\$40{,}000}{(1.14)^t} - \$180{,}000$$

where:

NPV = net present value

CF_t = net cash flow in year t (after taxes)

k = marginal cost of capital

n = number of years, investment horizon

I_0 = investment outlay in year zero

We can now calculate the NPV by using the information from the problem statement.[1]

$$NPV = 40{,}000 \, [\text{PVIFA} \, (14\%, \, 10 \text{ yrs.})] - 180{,}000$$

$$= 40{,}000 \, (5.2161) - \$180{,}000$$

$$= \$208{,}644 - \$180{,}000$$

$$NPV = GPV - I_0$$

$$= \$28{,}644$$

The present value of the cash inflows is the gross present value of the project (GPV). From this figure, the present value of the investment outlays is deducted to obtain the NPV of the project. The discount rate is the applicable marginal cost of capital for this project.

From the same data we can also readily calculate the IRR of the project. It is the discount rate which makes the NPV in the preceding equation equal to zero. We set the NPV equal to zero and solve for the interest rate as follows.

$$0 = \$40{,}000 \, [\text{PVIFA}(\text{IRR}, \, 10 \text{ yrs.})] - \$180{,}000$$

$$\text{PVIFA}(\text{IRR}, \, 10 \text{ yrs.}) = \$180{,}000/40{,}000 = 4.5000 = \text{PVIFA} \, (18\%, \, 10 \text{ yrs.})$$

The interest factor of 4.5000 tells us that the IRR is equal to 18 percent. For the preceding illustrative problem, both the NPV and IRR procedures give us the same selection result. With the NPV method, with the cost of capital at 14 percent, the project has a positive NPV and should be accepted. The IRR of 18 percent exceeds the cost of capital at 14 percent, so by the IRR criterion, the project again passes the acceptability test.

A major difference between the NPV and the IRR methods is that the NPV method assumes reinvestment at the cost of capital, while the IRR assumes

---

[1] PVIFA is the present value interest factor of an annuity whose value is widely available in interest tables or calculated from $[1 - (1 + k)^{-n}]/k$.

reinvestment at the IRR rate. The reinvestment-rate assumption is a misnomer for what should be called the opportunity-cost assumption. All investment projects of equal risk will have the same opportunity cost from the point of view of all investors. The real issue is, given the risk of the project, the rate at which funds can be invested (or reinvested) somewhere else for the same level of risk.

A major advantage of the NPV method is that it satisfies the value additivity principle (VAP). The VAP permits managers to consider each project independently of all others. Also, important from the point of view of this book, the NPV from each project represents the amount which the investment in that project adds to the value of the firm. Thus, NPV is the basis for increases in the value of the firm. Hence, from the standpoint of creating value for the firm (and adding value to the economy as a whole), maximizing NPVs is the correct goal for decision makers.

It is useful to understand both the NPV and IRR methods of capital budgeting. Both provide useful insights. But in developing concepts of valuation for use in M&A and related analysis, the NPV provides us with the necessary foundation for the further analysis undertaken next.

DEFINITION AND MEASUREMENT OF CASH FLOWS

The critical variables in the expressions for calculating the NPV and the IRR are the cash flows (CF_t) and the cost of capital (k). We have explained the cost of capital as the relevant marginal (opportunity) cost of capital commensurate with the risk of the project. We describe the methods of calculating the marginal cost of capital in the following chapter. Here we need to make clear the nature of the annual cash flows (CF_t). We do this in the context of the valuation models required for M&A analysis.

When we move to the level of the firm, we add up all the investment projects undertaken. The analysis then utilizes the basic financial statements of the firm, the income statement and the balance sheets. These can be used to explain what elements are contained in the annual cash flow figures to be capitalized.

We begin with an illustrative income statement, as shown in Table 6.1. In the illustrative income statement, the focus is on the elements below "Earnings before depreciation, interest, and taxes (EBDIT)." These are the components to be considered in defining the relevant cash flows. It is assumed that the firm does not have any nonoperating income or expenses that would cause net operating income (NOI) to differ from earnings before interest and taxes (EBIT). Note that the abbreviations that we use in the following models are defined in the illustrative income statement.

In the related balance sheets, it is assumed that the firm has no plant and equipment retirements between the two years so that the reserve for depreciation between year 1 and year 2 is the $20,000 amount in the income statement.

TABLE 6.1
Financial Statements

Illustrative Income Statement

	YEAR 2
Sales	$145,000
Operating costs excluding depreciation	95,000
Earnings before depreciation, interest, and taxes (EBDIT)	50,000
Depreciation expense (Dep)	20,000
Earnings before interest and taxes (EBIT = NOI = X)	30,000
Interest expense (f)	5,000
Earnings before taxes (EBT)	25,000
Taxes @ 40 percent (T = tax rate)	10,000
Net income (Y) (NI)	$ 15,000

Related Balance Sheets (in thousands) [end-of-year (EOY) amounts]

	YEAR 1	YEAR 2		YEAR 1	YEAR 2
Current assets	40	70	Interest-bearing debt	30	45
Gross fixed assets	70	100	Noninterest-bearing debt	20	30
Reserve for Dep.	10	30	Shareholders' equity	50	65
Net fixed assets	60	70			
Total assets (net)	100	140	Claims on assets	100	140

Also, gross fixed assets increase by $30,000 between the two years, representing the amount of gross investment made by the firm during year 2. It is further assumed that the firm pays no dividends, so that shareholders' equity in year 2 increases by $15,000, the net income shown in the income statement.

Utilizing the information in the income statement and related balance sheets, we can measure key components of the firm's cash flows. These are first defined on a gross basis as follows:

Free Cash Flow (FCF)—Gross Basis

	YEAR 2
Net Income	$15,000
+ Depreciation	20,000
= *Cash flow from operations*	35,000
+ After-tax interest [$f(1 - T)$]	3,000
= *Cash operating income* (gross)	38,000
− Investment (G)	30,000
= *Free cash flow (FCF)*	8,000

On a gross basis, depreciation is added to net income to obtain *cash flow from operations*. This is consistent with the writings of financial analysts in evaluating common stock who measure cash flow in this same way. After-tax interest expenses (or more generally, financial charges) are added to cash flow from operations to obtain *cash operating income*. The firm pays $5,000 interest expense, but with a 40 percent tax rate, this saves $2,000 in taxes. Hence, the cash operating income (the cash flow, CF_t, used in evaluating investment projects) would include only the after-tax interest expenses. This item is used in the basic capital budgeting equation to calculate the NPV or IRR on a gross basis.

Cash flows (CF_t) or cash operating income can be calculated either on a top-down or a bottom-up basis, as follows:

Return to Capital Investments (Cash Operating Income)

1   EBDIT $(1 - T) + T(\text{Dep}) = 50,000\,(.6) + .4\,(20,000) = \$38,000$
1a $(X + \text{Dep})\,(1 - T) + T\,(\text{Dep}) = \$38,000$
2   $X(1 - T) + \text{Dep} = 30,000\,(.6) + 20,000 = \$38,000$
2a $(\text{EBT} + f)\,(1 - T) + \text{Dep} = \$38,000$
3   $\text{NI} + \text{Dep} + f(1 - T) = 15,000 + 20,000 + 5,000\,(.6) = \$38,000$

Measuring from the top down, the relevant cash flows on a gross basis for capital budgeting in line 1 start with earnings before depreciation, interest, and taxes (EBDIT) on an after-tax basis to which is added the tax shelter from depreciation [$T(\text{Dep})$]. Line 1a is the same except that EBDIT is broken into its component parts of NOI and Dep. In line 2, the same result of $38,000 is obtained by adding after-tax NOI to the full amount of depreciation. Line 2a breaks NOI into earnings before tax (EBT) and financial charges (f). Line 3 (a bottom-up method) begins with the financial analysts' measure of cash flow consisting of net income (NI) plus depreciation (Dep) to which is added after-tax financial charges [$f(1-T)$]. Thus, we can obtain cash operating income (CF_t) by a number of alternative methods which are equivalent and give the same numerical result, in this case— $38,000. Note that in lines 1 and 2, we do not need the data for interest expenses. This implies that in measuring the free cash flow, financial leverage need not be considered.

As in our simple example of capital budgeting for a project, we next deduct the amount of investment required for the period to finally arrive at the free cash flow (FCF) of the firm. Since we are measuring cash operating income gross of (adding back) depreciation, the investment figure that is deducted is also on a gross basis (before deducting depreciation). The result is a free cash flow (FCF) of $8,000.

We next set forth the calculation of the free cash flow on a net basis:

Free Cash Flow (FCF)—Net Basis

	YEAR 2
Net income (NI)	$15,000
+ After-tax interest [$f(1 - T)$]	3,000
= Cash operating income [$X(1 - T)$]	18,000
− Investment (I)	10,000
= Free cash flow (FCF)	8,000

On a net basis, we simply omit the same depreciation figure in the cash operating income item and in the investment measure. Both are net of depreciation. Cash operating income is now [$X(1 - T)$] which is net operating income after taxes, or $18,000 in our example. The same result is obtained by adding NI + $f(1 - T)$ which is $15,000 + $3,000 = $18,000. It is more convenient in practice and simpler from an analytical standpoint to do the analysis on a net basis. Hence, we use this general procedure in the materials which follow.

CAPITAL BUDGETING BASIS
FOR FIRM VALUATION

We now have all the elements to move the analysis to the level of firm valuation. We simply build upon the net-basis relationships just observed. We do this on a yearly basis. The sum of each year's cash flows less the investment requirements, appropriately discounted, is the value of the firm.

$$V_0 = \frac{X_1(1 - T_1) - I_1}{(1 + k_1)} + \frac{X_2(1 - T_2) - I_2}{(1 + k_1)(1 + k_2)} + \frac{X_3(1 - T_3) - I_3}{(1 + k_1)(1 + k_2)(1 + k_3)} +$$

$$\ldots \frac{X_{n-1}(1 - T_{n-1}) - I_{n-1}}{(1 + k_1)(1 + k_2)\ldots(1 + k_{n-1})} + \frac{X_n(1 - T_n)}{(1 + k_1)(1 + k_2)\ldots(1 + k_n)}$$

(6.1)

Each term on the right-hand side of equation (6.1) represents the [$X(1 - T)$], or after-tax net operating income less the investment for that year, discounted back to the present. The investment outlays result in inflows beginning one period after the investment outlays. In this most general statement of valuation, all of the key factors could be different for each year, namely cash inflows (X_t), investment outlays (I_t), the cost of capital (k_t), and the tax rate (T_t).

To help give meaning to this equation, we present a numerical example. We assume that the firm comes to an end after period 4. Since investment would produce additional income during the next period, the firm will make no investment in period 4. If we then assume data for each of the four periods for X, T, I, and k (with the dollar amounts in millions), the value of the firm is:

$$V_0 = \frac{\$200(.6) - \$100}{1.1} + \frac{\$240(.7) - \$120}{(1.1)(1.12)} + \frac{\$300(.5) - \$150}{(1.1)(1.12)(1.11)}$$

$$+ \frac{\$350(.6)}{(1.1)(1.12)(1.11)(1.08)}$$

$$V_0 = \$18.18 + \$38.96 + 0 + \$142.19 = \$199.33$$

The calculation for each term is made and summed to arrive at a value of the firm of $199.33 million.

The valuation for any firm under any set of data assumptions or circumstances could be performed using the very general expression in equation (6.1). The number of periods could be considered to go on indefinitely or the analysis could be performed for a shorter period of time as illustrated in our example for four periods. Each of the variables could be different for each time period and no relationship need exist between one time period and another. Large-scale computer programs can readily handle a problem of this type no matter how complex. However, the programs would have to represent very large-scale systems and would be very expensive in their use of computer time.

Since valuation is based on net cash flows for future periods, projections or forecasts for the future are required. These will necessarily involve judgments. Most practitioners assume some systematic relations between the time periods. Specifically, it is usually postulated that sales and the free cash flow will grow at some rate. Also fixed relationships are implicitly assumed for the key performance variables of the firm. For these reasons it is useful to reformulate the most general capital budgeting valuation expression, equation (6.1), into more compact expressions (formulas). This can be done by postulating patterns of relationships in the behavior of the underlying variables from period to period. First, we set forth some numerical illustrations and definitional relationships to make the analysis more concrete.

Illustrative Data and Definitions for Valuation Analysis

In Table 6.2 we set forth illustrative data over five time periods starting with period 0. These data are used in numerical illustrations to help explain the new definitions and relationships that will be employed. The advantage of this procedure is that it gives us an unambiguous language to use in the subsequent analysis. Furthermore, the financial models that we develop give us insights on the fundamental relationships between the key parameters that determine the

TABLE 6.2

Illustrative Data with Definitions

	YEARS				
	0	1	2	3	4
1 ªSales $(S_t) = 2A_{t-1}$	1,000	1,200	1,440	1,728	2,074
2 Total capital $(A_t) = A_{t-1} + I_t$	600	720	864	1,037	1,244
3 ᵇInvestment $(I_t) = A_t - A_{t-1}$	100	120	144	173	
$= 0.8333X_t(1 - T)$					
4 Net operating income	200	240	288	346	415
$(X_t) = .4A_{t-1}$					
5 Net operating income after taxes $[X_t(1 - T)] = .24A_{t-1}$	120	144	173	208	249
(when $T = .4$)					

6 Profitability rate before tax (R_t) $= \dfrac{X_t - X_{t-1}}{I_{t-1}}$ or $X_t = R_t I_{t-1} + X_{t-1}$

$$R_t = .4$$

Note: This definition of R_t implies that I_{t-1} produces an increase in X_t and that an investment generates the same net operating income in all future periods.

7 Profitability rate after tax (r_t) $= R_t(1 - T)$ or $r_t = \dfrac{X_t(1 - T) - X_{t-1}(1 - T)}{I_{t-1}}$

It is assumed that r_t is constant so that $r = X_t(1 - T)/A_{t-1} = .24$

8 Investment requirements (opportunities) per dollar of after-tax cash flows:

$$b_t = \frac{I_t}{X_t(1 - T)} = 0.8333$$

9 Growth is measured by rate of increase in after-tax cash flows.

9a $g_t = \dfrac{X_t(1-T) - X_{t-1}(1-T)}{X_{t-1}(1-T)} = \left[\dfrac{X_t(1-T)}{X_{t-1}(1-T)} - 1 \right] = \left[\dfrac{X_t}{X_{t-1}} - 1 \right]$

9b $g_t = \dfrac{X_t(1-T) - X_{t-1}(1-T)}{X_{t-1}(1-T)} \cdot \dfrac{I_{t-1}}{I_{t-1}} = \dfrac{I_{t-1}}{X_{t-1}(1-T)} \cdot \dfrac{X_t(1-T) - X_{t-1}(1-T)}{I_{t-1}} = b_{t-1} r_t$

When r, b, and g are assumed constant, $g = br$

ªEA$_{t-1}$ generates sales in time t.
ᵇInvestments in t are included in assets at time t. Assume no investment after year 3.

value of a firm. Many widely-quoted authors and practitioners in the valuation field use more verbal or more complicated financial explanations. The related models even for the personal computer are unnecessarily complex and expensive. Furthermore, these other models obscure the fundamental relationships among the variables. As a consequence, the resulting analysis often contains inconsistencies in these key relationships.

We therefore proceed to explain the relations in Table 6.2. The first line is sales or net revenues. The second line is total capital or (net) total assets as usually presented in the balance sheets of the published financial statements of business firms.

Line 3 is investment (I_t). It is defined as the change in total capital or in net total assets. It is this year's total capital less last year's total capital. Throughout our analysis, investment is postulated to produce a constant amount of increase in earnings in all following periods. The increase in earnings starts one period after the investment, since some time is required before the investment is put in place and before it will generate additional revenues. This is also the assumption followed by Miller and Modigliani in their seminal paper on valuation (1961).

Line 4 is net operating income (X_t). In most of the analysis which follows, we assume that the firm does not have nonoperating income or expenses, so that net operating income is equal to earnings before interest and taxes (EBIT). This is another justifiable assumption because we are emphasizing the fundamental operating decisions of the firm. Furthermore, in most normal circumstances the amount of nonoperating income or nonoperating expense is relatively small and would not affect the valuation analysis in a material way.

Line 5 is net operating income after taxes [$X_t(1 - T)$]. It is shown for an assumed tax rate of 40 percent. If leverage were present, it would be equal to net income plus after-tax financial charges.

Line 6 sets forth the definition of the profitability rate before tax (R_t). In other words, the profitability rate before tax is the change in net operating income produced in period t by the investment made in period $t - 1$. It should be emphasized that the investment in the previous period is responsible for the increase in net operating income in the current and following periods. Analytically, it is convenient to assume that a given investment generates the same amount of net operating income in all future periods. Further, it may be assumed that investments in each period have the same profitability rate ($R_t = R$ for all periods). If we make these two assumptions, then the profitability rate before tax represents net operating income in period t divided by total capital in period $t - 1$ ($R_t = X_t/A_{t-1} = R$ for all periods). In fact, the data in Table 6.2 are generated under these assumptions. In the following discussion, we continue to assume constant profitability of investments made in each period and constant returns over time to a given investment.

Line 7 defines the profitability rate after tax (r_t). It is simply the relationships in line 6 multiplied by the ($1 - T$) factor. Some authors and practitioners define profitability in relation to sales rather than to investment. There are two things wrong in this approach. First, since capital intensity varies among industries and firms, profitability measured as a ratio of sales is simply not very meaningful in setting control standards or for planning purposes. For example, profit in relation to sales for capital-intensive industries such as steel or chemicals would have to be much higher than the required profitability ratio for wholesale or even retail establishments where profitability in relation to sales can be a fraction of 1 percent. Second, it fails to recognize that sales cannot be made without making investments representing the accumulation of a stock of working capital and net fixed assets by the firm.

Similarly in line 8, investment requirements (opportunities) (b_t), are defined per dollar of after-tax cash flows. These are the same two variables that define free cash flow in dollars. The same logic for defining free cash flow in dollars applies to defining investment requirements as the ratio of investment to after-tax cash flows.

Some authors and practitioners define investment requirements in relation to sales. Sales are fundamental in that investments are made in the expectation of future sales. Sales growth requires investment growth. Investment represents the resources required to produce the goods and services that result in sales. Sales and investment together provide information on capital intensity which is a determinant of the economic nature of production operations. But relating investment to sales has limitations similar to the definition of profitability in relation to sales. Since the focus is on free cash flows, a definition of investment requirements related to sales does not provide any information or insights. Hence, definition of investment requirements by the two elements that determine free cash flow makes much more sense. This is also the definition employed in the classic work on valuation (Miller and Modigliani, 1961). An additional benefit is that a tractable analytic model can thereby be developed. This is useful for checking more complex computer models and for insights into the underlying economic and business relations.

Finally, in line 9a of Table 6.2 we have a logical basis for measuring growth. The relevant measure of growth (g_t) is the rate of change in after-tax cash flows or net operating income after taxes. Other authors and practitioners often define growth in relation to sales (revenues) or total assets or what we have defined as total capital. But these measure input variables rather than final results. It is final results that count. Final results are best measured by net operating income after taxes. In this and most other models in the literature and in practice, sales and total assets grow at the same rate as net operating income after taxes because of simplifying assumptions on profitability, investment requirements, and other relationships.

In line 9b we begin to see some of the benefits of the analytical framework that is being developed. Starting with the measure of growth defined in line 9a, we multiply the numerator and denominator by the same item, last year's investment. Rearranging the terms, we find that growth can be expressed simply as the product of the (constant) investment requirement rate times the (constant) profitability rate ($g = br$).

We can develop another relationship from the definition of growth. This is shown in the following pattern which reflects the two constancy assumptions previously indicated.

$$X_t (1 - T) = rI_{t-1} + X_{t-1}(1-T). \quad \text{But } I_{t-1} = b\, X_{t-1} (1 - T)$$

$$X_t(1 - T) = rb\, X_{t-1}(1 - T) + X_{t-1}(1 - T)$$

$$= (1 + rb)X_{t-1}(1 - T). \quad \text{Since } g = br,$$

$$X_t(1 - T) = (1 + g)X_{t-1}(1 - T)$$

TABLE 6.3

Illustrative Numerical Values from Table 6.2

1 Turnover $= S_t/A_{t-1} = 2$

2 Profitability rate before tax R_1 $= \dfrac{240 - 200}{100} = .4 = R$

3 Profitability rate after tax $r_1 = R_1(1 - T)$ $= \dfrac{144 - 120}{100} = .24 = r$

   Investment requirements b_1 $= \dfrac{120}{144} = .8333 = b$

   Growth $g_1 = \dfrac{120 - 100}{100} = 1.2 - 1.0 = .20 = 20\% = g$

   $g = br = .8333(.24) = .20 = 20\%$

   $X_t(1 - T) = (1 + g)X_{t-1}(1 - T)$

   $X_1(1 - T) = (1 + g)X_0(1 - T) = (1.2)\,(120) = 144$

The preceding pattern states that net operating income after taxes in the current time period is equal to its amount in the previous period plus the current return on investment made in the previous period. From the definition of investment, we then see that the net operating income after taxes in any period is one plus the growth rate times net operating income after taxes of the previous period.

Based on the patterns set forth in Table 6.2 we can obtain numerical values for the key parameters that affect the valuation of the firm. In Table 6.3, turnover (or capital intensity) is defined as sales divided by total capital which is two for the data of our example. The before-tax profitability rate is 40 percent. The profitability rate after tax is 24 percent. The investment requirement is .8333 for each period. Finally, the growth for each period is 20 percent. Thus, net operating income after taxes in period 1 will be 1.2 times the net operating income after taxes in period 0.

Application of Capital Budgeting Basis to Four-Period Case

We may now draw on the data and relationships in Tables 6.2 and 6.3 to present illustrative calculations of valuation. We start with some simple cases which provide a foundation for developing more powerful and useful valuation models. A widely used valuation model is for a period of supernormal growth followed by no growth. We illustrate this by a numerical example using the form of equation (6.1). We utilize the data from Table 6.2 and assume that the cost of capital is constant at 16 percent. The expression becomes that set forth below in equation (6.2).

$$V_0 = \frac{X_1(1-T)-I_1}{(1+k)} + \frac{X_2(1-T)-I_2}{(1+k)^2} + \frac{X_3(1-T)-I_3}{(1+k)^3} + \frac{X_4(1-T)}{k(1+k)^3} \quad (6.2)$$

Equation (6.2) assumes three periods of growth. It postulates that future cash flows after period 3 remain constant. Thus, future cash flows after period 3 remain the same as $[X_4(1-T)]$. We insert the appropriate data and make the calculations to arrive at a value of $1,061.60$ at the end of period 0 (but after the cash flow in period 0).

$$V_0 = \frac{240(.6)-120}{(1.16)} + \frac{288(.6)-144}{(1.16)^2} + \frac{346(.6)-173}{(1.16)^3} + \left[\frac{415(.6)}{.16}\right] \Big/ (1.16)^3$$
$$= 20.7 + 21.6 + 22.4 + 1556/(1.16)^3 \quad (6.2a)$$
$$V_0 = 64.7 + 996.9 = \$1,061.60$$

Note that in this example we are showing the dollar amount of investment each period as a deduction from the after-tax cash flows for the corresponding period. Note that for the after-tax cash flows beginning in period 4 and continuing at that same constant level to infinity, there is no deduction for investment. Investment is justified only if it produces growth. If no growth is assumed, then no investment would be required.

THE FREE CASH FLOW (FCF) BASIS FOR VALUATION

We have now developed the background for a rigorous derivation of the free cash flow basis for valuation. We have demonstrated that it has its roots in a generalization of the basic capital budgeting equation. We develop four basic models, but we could easily derive many other variants reflecting any range of assumptions postulated for analysis. The four basic models are:

1 No growth
2 Constant growth
3 Supernormal growth followed by no growth
4 Supernormal growth followed by constant growth

Observe that the relatively simple models that we derive for no growth and constant growth are simply appended to a term for temporary supernormal growth to obtain the third and fourth models.

Before we consider each case separately, we develop a general methodology which can be efficiently applied to all the cases. We start with a modified equation (6.1m):

$$V_0 = \frac{X_1(1 - T) - I_1}{(1 + k)} + \frac{X_2(1 - T) - I_2}{(1 + k)^2} + \ldots + \frac{X_n(1 - T) - I_n}{(1 + k)^n} \quad (6.1m)$$

Recall that equation (6.1m) is a very general capital budgeting expression. Now we are going to let n go for an infinitely large number of periods. Therefore, since there will always be another period, investment takes place in the nth period, as shown in (6.1m).

We had defined b as $I_t/X_t(1 - T)$; hence, we can write $I_t = bX_t(1 - T)$. We can then substitute this expression into (6.1m) to obtain (6.1a):

$$V_0 = \frac{X_1(1 - T) - bX_1(1 - T)}{(1 + k)} + \frac{X_2(1 - T) - bX_2(1 - T)}{(1 + k)^2} + \ldots +$$

$$\frac{X_n(1 - T) - bX_n(1 - T)}{(1 + k)^n} \quad (6.1a)$$

Next we make an assumption with regard to the pattern of the after-tax cash flows, $[X_t(1 - T)]$. In equation (6.1m), we made no assumptions whatsoever. The after-tax cash flows could go up, down, sideways, move erratically—any pattern. Now we make an assumption that is widely made (but usually not explicitly). We assume that the initial X_0 grows at some rate, g. It is a modest assumption; g can be positive, negative or zero. We can then replace all of the X_t values in (6.1a) by $X_0(1 - T)(1 + g)^t$ as in (6.1b).

$$V_0 = \frac{X_0(1 - T)(1 + g) - bX_0(1 - T)(1 + g)}{(1 + k)} + \frac{X_0(1 - T)(1 + g)^2 - bX_0(1 - T)(1 + g)^2}{(1 + k)^2}$$

$$\quad (6.1b)$$

$$+ \ldots + \frac{X_0(1 - T)(1 + g)^n - bX_0(1 - T)(1 + g)^n}{(1 + k)^n}$$

For simplification, we next factor the common expression $X_0(1 - T)(1 + g)^t$ from each term in the numerator to obtain (6.1c).

$$V_0 = \frac{X_0(1 - T)(1 + g)(1-b)}{(1 + k)} + \frac{X_0(1 - T)(1 + g)^2(1 - b)}{(1 + k)^2} + \ldots +$$

$$\frac{X_0(1 - T)(1 + g)^n(1 - b)}{(1 + k)^n} \quad (6.1c)$$

Further simplification suggests itself. We can factor from each term in (6.1c), a common expression:

$$X_0(1 - T)(1 + g)(1 - b)/(1 + k).$$

We then have equation (6.1d):

$$V_0 = \frac{X_0(1-T)(1-b)(1+g)}{(1+k)}\left[1 + \frac{(1+g)}{(1+k)} + \frac{(1+g)^2}{(1+k)^2} + \ldots + \frac{(1+g)^{n-1}}{(1+k)^{n-1}}\right] \quad (6.1d)$$

From the expression in (6.1d), we can now readily obtain all the valuation formulas by specifying how g, the growth rate, behaves.

The No-Growth Case

First let us assume no growth, so that $g = 0$. If $g = 0$, the firm will be making no investment, so $b = 0$ as well. Equation (6.1d) then becomes (6.1e) as follows:

$$V_0 = \frac{X_0(1-T)}{(1+k)}\left[1 + \left(\frac{1}{1+k}\right) + \left(\frac{1}{1+k}\right)^2 + \ldots + \left(\frac{1}{1+k}\right)^{n-1}\right] \quad (6.1e)$$

The term in front of the brackets has parameters that are all constants. The terms inside the brackets form a geometrical progression which starts with the constant term 1 and increases by the ratio $1/(1 + k)$. A standard geometric progression in abstract terms can be written as follows:

$$a + ar + ar^2 + ar^3 + \ldots + ar^{n-1} = a[1 + r + r^2 + r^3 + \ldots + r^{n-1}]$$

Note that the constant term, a, can be factored out and the form of the standard geometric progression is exactly as in equation (6.1e). When there is a finite number of terms, n, the sum of these terms is:

$$S^n = a(r^n - 1)/(r - 1)$$

When n goes to infinity the sum of this geometric progression is equal to: $S^\infty = \frac{a}{1-r}$ when $(r < 1)$. We use both of these summation formulas subsequently.

In equation (6.1e) the constant is the term outside the brackets. We have already identified the ratio in the geometric expression as:

$$r = 1/(1 + k).$$

We can therefore write (when $k > 0$ and $r < 1$ and as n goes to infinity):

$$V_0 = \frac{X_0(1-T)}{(1+k)}\left[\frac{1}{1 - \frac{1}{1+k}}\right] = \frac{X_0(1-T)}{(1+k)}\left[\frac{1}{\frac{1+k-1}{1+k}}\right] = \frac{X_0(1-T)(1+k)}{k(1+k)}$$

Cancel the $(1 + k)$ in the numerator and denominator to obtain:

$$V_0 = \frac{X_0(1-T)}{k} \quad \text{for } k > 0. \quad (6.3)$$

The result in equation (6.3) is the familiar formula for the valuation of a stream of receipts or cash flows that continues at a constant level to infinity. This is the standard valuation expression for a perpetuity or a bond that has no maturity, often called a consol.

Constant Growth

For the second basic case, assume that g is not zero but a constant rate. This is another standard assumption in the development of valuation expressions. To develop the formula we return to equation (6.1d). In that equation we recognize that the constant ratio of increase is equal to $(1 + g)/(1 + k)$. Again we use the expression for the summation of a geometric progression that continues to infinity which is $a/(1 - r)$ when $r = (1 + g)/(1 + k) < 1$. Using this formula, equation (6.1d) can be written as:

$$V_0 = \frac{X_0(1-T)(1-b)(1+g)}{(1+k)} \left[\frac{1}{1 - \frac{1+g}{1+k}} \right]$$

Simplifying we obtain equation (6.4).

$$V_0 = \frac{X_0(1-T)(1-b)(1+g)}{(k-g)} \quad \text{for } g < k. \tag{6.4}$$

Equation (6.4) is the valuation expression in general terms when k is larger than g. It is for cash flows that grow at a constant rate, g, to perpetuity.

Supernormal Growth Followed by No Growth

The third basic case is temporary supernormal growth followed by no growth. The fourth will be constant growth during the second phase. So we need to develop an expression for the first term of temporary supernormal growth to which we will add a second term representing either no growth or constant growth.

For the derivation, we return to equation (6.1d) from which we stated all valuation formulas could be derived by specifying the behavior of g. Hence, we rewrite it as (6.1ds) in which both g and its associated investment rate b with the s subscripts are for the supernormal growth phase lasting n periods. We also change V_0 to S^n to signify that it now represents the present value of n-period cash flows only.

$$S^n = \frac{X_0(1-T)(1-b_s)(1+g_s)}{(1+k)} \left[1 + \frac{(1+g_s)}{(1+k)} + \frac{(1+g_s)^2}{(1+k)^2} + \cdots + \frac{(1+g_s)^{n-1}}{(1+k)^{n-1}} \right] \tag{6.1ds}$$

This can be rewritten as:

$$S_n = \frac{X_0 (1 - T) (1 - b_s) (1 + g_s)}{1 + k} \sum_{t=1}^{n} \frac{(1 + g_s)^{t-1}}{(1 + k)^{t-1}}$$

Or we can move the $(1 + g_s)/(1 + k)$ into the summation expression to obtain:

$$S_n = X_0 (1 - T) (1 - b_s) \sum_{t=1}^{n} \frac{(1 + g_s)^t}{(1 + k)^t} \tag{6.1ds}$$

The formula for our third case of temporary supernormal growth followed by zero growth combines the preceding sum and equation (6.3) as follows:

$$V_0 = X_0 (1 - T) (1 - b_s) \sum_{t=1}^{n} \frac{(1 + g_s)^t}{(1 + k)^t} + \frac{X_0(1 - T) (1 + g_s)^{n+1}}{k(1 + k)^n} \tag{6.5}$$

The second term represents the present value of constant cash flows of $X_0(1- T) (1 + g_s)^{n+1}$ starting in period $n + 1$, discounted back to the present; that is, we grow $X_0(1 - T)$ for $(n + 1)$ periods and capitalize it at k to obtain its value at the end of n periods. We then discount it back to the present by $1/(1 + k)^n$ to obtain the present value of the second term. Adding the two terms gives us V_0.

Supernormal Growth Followed by Constant Growth

By the same logic, we can readily develop the expression for the fourth case by combining what we already have. We use the first term of equation (6.5) and use equation (6.4) as the basis for the second term. Recall that for the second term we have to grow X_0 for $(n + 1)$ periods at the rate of g_s and then discount back for n periods the cash flows growing at a constant rate g_c. Also note that the constant growth period will have a different investment rate, here designated as b_c. Thus we have equation (6.6) for the fourth case:

$$V_0 = X_0(1 - T) (1 - b_s) \sum_{t=1}^{n} \frac{(1 + g_s)^t}{(1 + k)^t} + \frac{X_0 (1 - T) (1 - b_c)}{k - g_c} \times \frac{(1 + g_s)^{n+1}}{(1 + k)^n} \tag{6.6}$$

This completes the four basic cases of growth patterns which adapt the general capital budgeting equation for valuation into relatively compact expressions. We can now summarize all of the valuation expressions for the free cash flow formulation in Table 6.4.

TABLE 6.4

Free Cash Flow Valuation of the Firm

No growth:

$$V_0 = \frac{X_0(1 - T)}{k}$$ (6.3)

Constant growth:

$$V_0 = \frac{X_0(1 - T)(1 - b)(1 + g)}{k - g}$$ (6.4)

Temporary supernormal growth, then no growth:

$$V_0 = X_0(1 - T)(1 - b_s) \sum_{t=1}^{n} \frac{(1 + g_s)^t}{(1 + k)^t} + \frac{X_0(1 - T)(1 + g_s)^{n+1}}{k(1 + k)^n}$$ (6.5)

Temporary supernormal growth, then constant growth:

$$V_0 = X_0(1 - T)(1 - b_s) \sum_{t=1}^{n} \frac{(1 + g_s)^t}{(1 + k)^t} + \frac{X_0(1 - T)(1 - b_c)}{k - g_c} \times \frac{(1 + g_s)^{n+1}}{(1 + k)^n}$$ (6.6)

Numerical Illustration

The preceding derivations have been somewhat abstract. To aid in understanding their use, we set forth a numerical illustration for the most widely used formula, which is the free cash flow formula for temporary supernormal growth followed by zero growth. We therefore use equation (6.5) which we repeat here:

$$V_0 = X_0(1 - T)(1 - b_s) \sum_{t=1}^{n} \frac{(1 + g_s)^t}{(1 + k)^t} + \frac{X_0(1 - T)(1 + g_s)^{n+1}}{k(1 + k)^n}$$ (6.5)

If we let $(1 + h) = (1 + g_s)/(1 + k)$, then this can be rewritten as:

$$V_0 = X_0(1 - T)(1 - b_s)(1 + h) \sum_{t=1}^{n} (1 + h)^{t-1} + \frac{X_0(1 - T)}{k}(1 + h)^n(1 + g_s)$$

The following numerical parameters can be obtained from Table 6.2 plus assumptions for n and k.

$$X_0 = 200 \qquad g_s = .20 \qquad (1 + h) = (1 + g)/(1 + k)$$

$$(1 - T) = .6 \qquad n = 3 \qquad (1 + h) = (1.20)/(1.16) = 1.0345$$

$$b = .833 \qquad k = .16 \qquad h = .0345 = 3.45\%$$

We substitute these values into equation (6.5) to obtain the following:

$$V_0 = 200(.6)(.167) \sum_{t=1}^{3} \left(\frac{1.20}{1.16}\right)^t + \frac{200(.6)}{.16}\left(\frac{1.20}{1.16}\right)^3 (1.20)$$

$$= 200(.6)(.167)(1.0345) \text{ FVIFA } (3.45\%, 3 \text{ yrs.}) + \frac{200(.6)}{.16} \text{ FVIF } (3.45\%, 3 \text{ yrs.})$$

In the preceding equation the term FVIFA ($h\%$, 3 yrs.) represents the future value of a deferred annuity of $1 at h percent for three years. This expression is also equal to the following:

$$\text{FVIFA}(h\%, 3 \text{ yrs.}) = 1 + (1 + h) + (1 + h)^2$$

In the second term on the right-hand side, the expression FVIF ($h\%$, 3 yrs.) represents a compound sum of a dollar invested now which grows at h percent for three years. This could also be written as:

$$\text{FVIF}(h\%, 3 \text{ yrs.}) = (1 + h)^3$$

Performing the indicated numerical computations, we finally obtain the following:

$$V_0 = 20.0(1.0345)\text{FVIFA}(3.45\%, 3 \text{ yrs.}) + 996.4$$

$$V_0 = 20.7(3.105) + 996.4 = 64.3 + 996.4 =$$
$$\$1,060.7 \approx \$1,061.6.$$

Note that this result is exactly the same as we obtained in equation (6.2a) when investment requirements as expressed by I_t were deducted each year. This illustrates that the compact formulas give the same result as the original basic capital budgeting expression with which we started.

DIVIDEND GROWTH VALUATION MODEL

Under appropriate assumptions, we can also treat dividends as the cash flows to obtain the valuation of the equity of a firm (Cf., Malkiel, 1963). We could go through the same derivation process to obtain valuations of the equity for alternative assumptions about the growth rate in dividends. The results are summarized in Table 6.5.

When g is zero we have the result for the no-growth model which is similar to the first formula presented in Table 6.4. In Table 6.5, we call it equation (6.3a). The cost of capital for equity is denoted k_e and D_0 represents dividends paid at

TABLE 6.5
Equity Valuation in Dividend Form

No growth:

$$S_0 = \frac{D_0}{k_e} \qquad\qquad (6.3a)$$

Constant growth:

$$S_0 = \frac{D_1}{k_e - g} \qquad\qquad (6.4a)$$

Temporary supernormal growth, then no growth:

$$S_0 = \sum_{t=1}^{n} \frac{D_0(1 + g_s)^t}{(1 + k_e)^t} + \frac{Y_0(1 + g_s)^{n+1}}{k_e(1 + k_e)^n} \qquad\qquad (6.5a)$$

Temporary supernormal growth, then constant growth:

$$S_0 = \sum_{t=1}^{n} \frac{D_0(1 + g_s)^t}{(1 + k_e)^t} + \frac{Y_0(1 - b_c)(1 + g_s)^{n+1}}{(k_e - g_c)(1 + k_e)^n} \qquad\qquad (6.6a)$$

Note: D_0 in (6.5a) and (6.6a) equals $Y_0(1 - b_s)$.

Where the new symbols are defined as:

S_0 = value of equity of the firm
D_t = dividends of the firm per period
Y_t = net income of the firm per period
k_e = cost of equity of the firm
b = retention rate relative to net income

the end of the last period (period 0). The familiar constant-dividend growth valuation model is equation (6.4a).

$$S_0 = \frac{D_0(1 + g)}{(k_e - g)} = \frac{D_1}{(k_e - g)} \qquad\qquad (6.4a)$$

By symmetry the parallel to equation (6.5) is equation (6.5a), where Y_0 denotes net income in the last period. In the second term, since no further net retention of net income takes place with zero growth, dividends equal net income: $D_t = Y_t = Y_0(1 + g_s)^t$ for $t > n + 1$. Similarly, equation (6.6) is converted to equation (6.6a) in Table 6.5. In the second term $Y_0(1 - b_c)$ takes the place of D_0 which appears in the first term where it equals $Y_0(1 - b_s)$. Note that b is now the retention rate relative to net income: $b = (Y - D)/Y$.

Thus, Tables 6.4 and 6.5 present in compact form the most widely used

valuation models for the firm and for the equity value of the firm. In our judgment the free cash flow formulations are more general and more flexible to use.
However, because of the widespread use of valuation in dividend form, we have
also summarized those equations in Table 6.5.

ILLUSTRATIVE PROBLEM EXAMPLES

To illustrate and reinforce the use of the valuation formulas developed thus far,
three problem examples are presented. The statement of each case is quite compact. The emphasis is on illustrating how the formulas developed to this point
can be employed.

Use of the Free Cash Flow Valuation Models

This first example illustrates the application of equations (6.5) and (6.6) that were
set forth in Table 6.4.

The Pelman Company has a required return of 15 percent. Its net operating
income, now $4 million, is expected to grow at a rate of 26.5 percent for $n = 8$
years, with a ratio of investment to after-tax net operating income of 0.20. The
applicable tax rate is 40 percent.

1 If, after the period of supernormal growth, the net operating income of Pelman has zero
  growth, what is the current value of the firm?
2 If, after the period of supernormal growth, the net operating income of Pelman grows at
  10 percent per year, with the investment to after-tax NOI ratio still being 0.20, what is the
  current value of the firm?
3 Compare the value to after-tax earnings ratios for the two alternative assumptions with
  respect to the growth of net operating earnings after the period of supernormal growth.

The solutions to each part of the Pelman Company problem follow.

$$1 \quad V_0 = X_0 (1 - T) (1 - b_s) \sum_{t=1}^{n} \frac{(1 + g_s)^t}{(1 + k)^t} + \frac{X_0(1 - T) (1 + g_s)^{n+1}}{k(1 + k)^n} \tag{6.5}$$

$$= (\$4) (1-.40) (1-.20) \sum_{t=1}^{8} \frac{(1+.265)^t}{(1+.15)^t} + \frac{(\$4) (1-.40) (1+.265)^9}{(.15) (1+.15)^8}$$

$$V_0 = (\$4) (.6) (.8) (12.5785) + \frac{(\$4) (.6) (8.2950)}{(.15) (3.0590)}$$

$$= \$24.1507 + \$43.3866$$

$$= \$67.5373$$

$$2 \; V_0 = X_0(1 - T)(1 - b_s) \sum_{t=1}^{n} \frac{(1 + g_s)^t}{(1 + k)^t} + \frac{X_0(1 - T)(1 - b_c)}{(k - g_c)} \times \frac{(1 + g_s)^{n+1}}{(1 + k)^n} \quad (6.6)$$

$$V_0 = \$24.1507 + \frac{(\$4)(1-.40)(1-.20)}{(.15-.10)} \times \frac{(1+.265)^8(1.265)}{(1+.15)^8}$$

$$= \$24.1507 + \frac{\$1.92}{.05} \times (1.1)^8(1.265)$$

$$= \$128.28$$

3 No growth after supernormal growth:

$$V_0/X_0(1 - T) = 67.5373/[(4)(1-.40)] = 28.1$$

10 percent growth after supernormal growth:

$$V_0/X_0(1 - T) = 128.28/[(4)(1-.40)] = 53.45$$

It can be seen from the preceding solution that, for this example, the second term in the valuation models is a more powerful builder of value than the first term. This is true even though the first term is the one that embodies the period of supernormal growth. Since the period of supernormal growth is relatively short and the second term goes to infinity either with zero growth or with constant growth, the latter constitutes the greater portion of the total value of the firm. Expressed in the form of a value to after-tax earnings ratio, it can be seen that the assumption of constant nonzero growth after the period of supernormal growth has a powerful influence on value. This example is for the purpose not only of learning to understand better the financial models but also to provide perspective in their implications. We apply these models to an actual company in the following chapter which deals with enhancing shareholder value. However, our experience has been that in actual application of these financial models, it is important to keep in perspective how the key valuation parameters interact and how they affect final value. Other writers who employ more verbal and more detailed models are often overwhelmed by the complexity resulting from detail that does not greatly affect the final valuation. Also we observe that many other writers using more verbal and detailed models (often computer assisted) make assumptions and judgments that are often mutually inconsistent or contradictory.

The Use of the Dividend Growth Valuation Model

In this example we use the most complex of the dividend growth valuation models. This is equation (6.6a).

$$S_0 = \sum_{t=1}^{n} \frac{D_0(1 + g_s)^t}{(1 + k_e)^t} + \frac{Y_0(1 - b_c)(1 + g_s)^{n+1}}{(k_e - g_c)(1 + k_e)^n} \qquad (6.6a)$$

We place the example in the setting of a merger and acquisition analysis.

The Rowe Company is contemplating the purchase of the Colima Company. During the most recent year, Colima had net income of $2 million and paid dividends of $1 million. The earnings and dividends of Colima are expected to grow at an annual rate of 30 percent for $n = 5$ years, after which they will grow at an 8 percent rate per year with annual retention continuing at 50 percent of net income. The required return on an investment with the risk characteristics of the Colima Company stock is 16 percent.

What is the maximum that the Rowe Company could pay for the Colima Company to earn at least a 16 percent return on its investment? (Assume no synergy effect.)

The solution proceeds as follows. We begin with equation (6.6a). $[D_0 = Y_0(1 - .5)$ for both growth segments].

$$S_0 = \sum_{t=1}^{n} \frac{D_0(1 + g_s)^t}{(1 + k_e)^t} + \frac{D_0(1 + g_s)^{n+1}}{(k_e - g_c)(1 + k_e)^n} \qquad (6.6a)$$

Using formula (6.6a) we insert the data from the problem to obtain the following result:

$$S_0 = \sum_{t=1}^{5} \frac{1(1.30)^t}{(1.16)^t} + \frac{1(1.30)^6}{(.16 - .08)(1.16)^5}$$

$$= (1.1207) \left[\frac{(1.1207)^5 - 1}{.1207} \right] + \frac{(4.827)}{(.08)(2.10)}$$

$$= (1.1207)(6.3617) + \frac{4.827}{.168}$$

$$= 7.13 + 28.73$$

$$S_0 = \$35.86 \approx \$36 \text{ million.}$$

This problem illustrates how a valuation model can be employed in merger and acquisition analysis. We see from the preceding example that the Rowe Company could pay (up to) $36 million for Colima and earn the applicable cost of capital of 16 percent (or more) if the projected growth rates are realized.

Free Cash Flow Valuation Model
Sensitivity Analysis

In order to avoid making inconsistent assumptions, it is useful to see the relationships among the key parameters that determine value. Here we keep the problem statement as simple as possible. You are given the following information on the key input parameters that determine the value of a firm:

$$X_0 = \$600{,}000 = \text{NOI}$$
$$T = .40 = \text{tax rate}$$
$$b_s = .50 = \text{ratio of net investment to after-tax NOI}$$
$$g_s = .30 = \text{rate of supernormal growth}$$
$$k = .15 = \text{cost of capital}$$

We next consider the following two sets of cases. (In the solution, we show the internal profitability rate implied by the given values of b_s and g_s.)

1 Assuming that the firm experiences zero growth following the $n = 5$ supernormal growth period.
2 Instead of zero growth after the supernormal growth, constant growth is illustrated under alternative assumptions.

We utilize the most widely used free cash flow valuation model. This is equation (6.5).

$$V = X_0(1 - T)(1 - b_s) \sum_{t=1}^{n} \frac{(1 + g_s)^t}{(1 + k)^t} + \frac{X_0(1 - T)(1 + g_s)^{n+1}}{k(1 + k)^n} \tag{6.5}$$

Using equation (6.5) and the data given in the problem statement, we present the following results for the initial case plus the effects of varying three of the key valuation input parameters.

PART A

	k	b_s	r_s	g_s	N	T	VALUATION	2ND TERM AS % OF TOTAL
Initial Case								
1)	.15	.50	.20	.10	5	.40	2,903,065	73
Change b, g, and r:								
2)	.15	1.0	.20	.20	5	.40	3,562,948	100
3)	.15	1.0	.30	.30	5	.40	5,759,465	100
4)	.15	1.5	.20	.30	5	.40	4,439,733	130
Back to initial case, but vary k:								
5)	.13	.50	.20	.10	5	.40	3,493,511	76
6)	.17	.50	.20	.10	5	.40	2,461,903	70
Back to initial case, but vary n:								
7)	.15	.50	.20	.10	4	.40	2,855,023	77
8)	.15	.50	.20	.10	6	.40	2,949,019	69
Back to initial case, but vary T:								
9)	.15	.50	.20	.10	5	.38	2,999,834	73
10)	.15	.50	.20	.10	5	.42	2,806,296	73

From the preceding table, we can see that when r_s exceeds k an increase in investment requirements or opportunities will greatly increase value. Line 1 is the initial case. While the value of profitability, r_s, was not given, since $g_s = br$ the value of r_s can be obtained by dividing g_s by b_s. In the base case shown in line 1 of the solution, the valuation is $2.9 million. In line 2 we observe that the investment requirements or opportunities have doubled. Since profitability exceeds the cost of capital, this causes the valuation to increase and it moves up to $3.6 million. Note that in line 2 the $(1 - b_s)$ expression in the first term of equation (6.5) becomes zero so that the entire first term becomes zero. Nevertheless, the valuation increases by a substantial amount. This is because the higher b_s results in a higher g_s. Hence, the level of free cash flow at the beginning of the no further growth period is much higher than in the initial case. In line 3 profitability increases. This causes growth to increase as well. The valuation rises to $5.8 million. In line 4 profitability returns to its previous level but investment requirements increase further. Hence, growth in line 4 is greater than in line 2 and valuation increases from $3.6 million to $4.4 million. In lines 5 and 6 we return to the initial case but vary k, the cost of capital. When we reduce the cost of capital, valuation rises from $2.9 million to $3.5 million (line 5). When we increase the cost of capital, the valuation falls (line 6). Valuation is found to be very sensitive to variations in the cost of capital.

We then again return to the initial case but vary n, the number of periods of growth. We obtain the readily predictable results in lines 7 and 8. When the period of supernormal growth is reduced, valuation is reduced. When the period of supernormal growth is increased, valuation increases.

In lines 9 and 10 we vary the tax rate. Again the results are readily predictable. When the tax rate is reduced, valuation is increased. When the tax rate is increased, the valuation is reduced.

Next we consider the effects of making alternative assumptions about what happens to free cash flow after the period of supernormal growth. In Part B we assume that constant growth takes place under a number of alternative assumptions. We vary both the investment requirements rate and the profitability rate after the period of supernormal growth. As a consequence the level of constant growth is determined. The results follow.

PART B
Temporary Supernormal Growth, then Constant Growth

	b_c	r_c	g_c	VALUATION	2ND TERM AS % OF TOTAL
11)	.20	.17	.034	2,975,957	73
12)	.10	.16	.016	2,918,840	73
13)	.30	.17	.051	3,031,179	74
14)	.40	.18	.072	3,228,276	76
15)	.50	.17	.085	3,228,276	76
16)	.60	.17	.102	3,431,533	77

All inputs same as initial case in Part A, plus new inputs, b_c, r_c, and g_c.

Lines 11 to 16 illustrate that combining different levels of investment requirements with different levels of profitability produces a resulting range of constant growth factors. It is clear from the results that the higher the constant rate of growth the higher the resulting valuation.

It will be noted that in both Parts A and B, the second term in the valuation model represents the higher proportion of the valuation. This is true in many practical cases. This should alert those who are performing the valuation to be quite careful as to the assumptions made about the factors which affect so-called exit or terminal values.

COMPARISONS OF VALUATION MODELS

The purpose of background materials for the development of valuation models and formulas is to improve understanding of how they may be effectively utilized. In this section further materials are presented with the same objective in mind.

Comparison with the Miller-Modigliani Model

The intellectual source of modern valuation models is the classic article by Miller and Modigliani (1961). They demonstrate that the same basic valuation model can be derived using four different approaches. The discounted cash flow approach is essentially the basic capital budgeting approach set forth in equation (6.2). The stream of dividends approach is a modified version of the dividend growth valuation model in Table 6.5. Their stream of earnings approach is equivalent to their current earnings plus future investment opportunities approach. These latter two methods are equivalent to the free cash flow models which are the emphasis of our presentation and summarized in Table 6.4.

In addition to representing the intellectual foundation of the best valuation models in use, the Miller-Modigliani approach contains some useful insights. To show this we employ a variant of their equation (22a) (page 352, footnote 15) developed by them "assuming that the special investment opportunities are available not in perpetuity but only over some finite interval. . . ." We present this as equation (6.7).

$$V_0 = \frac{X(1-T)}{k} \left\{ 1 + \frac{b(r-k)}{g-k} \left[\left(\frac{1+g}{1+k} \right)^n - 1 \right] \right\} (1+g) \qquad (6.7)$$

We can illustrate the use of the Miller-Modigliani model using the following inputs:

$g = 9.0\%$
$k = 10\%$
$b = 60\%$
$n = 15$

$X(1 - T) = \$100,000$

$r = 15\%$

Using this information in equation (6.7) we obtain:

$$V_0 = \$100,000 \times 1.09/0.1 \times [1 + (-3.000) \times (-0.128)]$$

$$V_0 = \$1,508,621$$

This result can be compared with the use of our free cash flow model, for temporary supernormal growth, followed by no growth, which is our equation (6.5).

$$V = X_0(1 - T)(1 - b_s) \sum_{t=1}^{n} \frac{(1 + g_s)^t}{(1 + k)^t} + \frac{X_0(1 - T)(1 + g_s)^{n+1}}{k(1 + k)^n} \qquad (6.5)$$

We then insert the numbers from the example.

$$V_0 = \$100,000 \times 0.40 \times \frac{1.09}{1.10} \times 14.08205 + \$100,000/0.10 \times 0.8719813 \times 1.09$$

$$= \$558,161 + \$950,460$$

$$= \$1,508,621$$

We see that we obtain the same result. What is the value of the Miller-Modigliani formulation since it gives the same result? A number of insights can be derived from the Miller-Modigliani model. First, it highlights the critical relation between profitability, r, and the cost of capital, k. This relationship appears only one place. It is in the numerator of the expression in their formula which determines the degree to which value will be increased beyond that of a no-growth firm. If r were exactly equal to k, the whole expression in brackets would simply become 1 and we would have a no-growth firm. If the firm can earn no more than its cost of capital, then it will not be a growth firm. This gives us the definition of a growth firm. The growth firm is one which is able to attain at least for a limited period of time a profitability rate which exceeds its cost of capital. Second, the Miller-Modigliani formulation emphasizes that each firm is indeed a no-growth firm unless it has favorable investment opportunities.

For these reasons the Miller-Modigliani (1961) article is not only the classic writing on the subject but continues to be as applicable and modern today as it was when first published. Hence, it is appropriate to acknowledge the source of all current rigorous formulations of valuation analysis.

Comparison with Stern's Approach

In two important writings Joel Stern (1974, 1977) shows how the Miller-Modigliani article provides the foundations for analytic approaches to financial planning. He argues that their valuation approach provides the basic themework for planning most types of fundamental financial policy decisions.

In Stern's extended explanation of the correct procedures for valuation, he builds on the original Miller-Modigliani (1961) article. However, in his numerical calculations, he sets forth two tables which have multiplier or interest factors. While the verbal discussion is all Miller and Modigliani (and properly so), his numerical methods are based on our basic equation (6.5) the free cash flow model for temporary supernormal growth. The Stern model can be summarized as follows:

$$V_0 = \text{FCF}_1 \text{ (Table 1 Interest Factor)} \qquad + \text{ NOPAT}_1 \text{ (Table 2 Interest Factor)}$$

$$= \text{value of supernormal growth period} \quad + \quad \text{value at end of growth period discounted to present}$$

where:

$$\text{FCF} = X_1 (1 - T)(1 - b)$$

$$\text{NOPAT} = X_1 (1 - T)$$

$$\text{Table 1 Interest Factor} = \frac{\text{FVIFA }(h\%, n \text{ yrs.})}{1 + k}$$

$$\text{Table 2 Interest Factor} = \frac{\text{FVIF}(h\%, n \text{ yrs.})}{k}$$

The Stern model will, of course, give exactly the same result for any set of facts as the MM model in equation (6.7) or our free cash flow formulation in Table 6.4. One great value of the Stern presentations is that they make clear the critical role that a sound valuation model has for all aspects of financial planning.

Comparison with
the Rappaport Approach

In a number of articles and in his book, *Creating Shareholder Value* (1986), Alfred Rappaport develops materials which he elaborates into a model for use on the personal computer for valuing a firm. Again one of the strengths of Rappaport's approach is that he demonstrates how the use of a financial model can be helpful in strategic planning and in improving returns for shareholders.

The Rappaport approach, however, does have some defects. Profitability is measured by the profit margin on sales. But as indicated earlier, it is generally recognized that profit margin on sales is not a good index for comparing profitability among firms in different industries. Because of different degrees of capital intensity, the normal profit margin in a highly capital-intensive industry should be relatively high. But in an industry where turnover is relatively high as in wholesale and retail trade, the expected profit margin on sales should be relatively low. Thus, profit margin on sales does not facilitate good planning in terms of a target or standard for profitability.

Another limitation of the Rappaport approach is that it is unnecessarily cumbersome. Because the model is essentially verbal in nature, it requires a relatively complex computer program to work through to solutions. However, by recasting some of his variables in a modest way his model is seen to be readily simplified to the cash flow models we have employed.

To illustrate this point we can utilize the example which he presents in his 1986 book (p. 64). He presents a measurement of cash flow which embodies verbally all of the key input assumptions as follows.

[(Sales in prior year) (1 + Sales growth rate) (Operating profit margin) (1 − Cash income tax rate)] − [(Sales in prior year) (Sales growth rate) (Incremental fixed plus working capital investment rate)]

$$= [(100) (1 + .16) (.13) (1 - .50)] - [(100) (.16) (.21 + .15)]$$
$$= 7.54 - 5.76$$

$$= \$1.78 \text{ million.}$$

Defining the words used in the preceding expression in our symbols, we can write a number of relationships and derive the value for the expression which is called investment requirements, b, in the free cash flow formulation. This can be done as follows:

$$I_t = .36\Delta S = .36 (S_t - S_{t-1}) = .36(1.16S_{t-1} - S_{t-1})$$

$$= .36(.16S_{t-1})$$

$$I_t = .0576S_{t-1} = (.0576S_t)/(1.16) = .04966S_t$$

$$X_t(1 - T) = .065S_t \quad S_t = 15.385X_t(1 - T)$$

$$I_t = .04966 (15.385)X_t(1 - T)$$

$$I_t = .764X_t(1 - T)$$

$$\therefore b = .764$$

We can now put the Rappaport material into our basic free cash flow model for temporary supernormal growth followed by no growth. This is our equation (6.5).[1]

$$V_0 = X_0(1-T)(1-b_s) \sum_{t=1}^{n} \left(\frac{1+g_s}{1+k}\right)^t + \frac{X_0(1-T)}{k} \left(\frac{1+g_s}{1+k}\right)^n \qquad (6.5)$$

We can then insert the Rappaport numbers for each of the terms. Rappaport defined the operating profit margin as 13 percent on sales of 100. Hence, initial net operating income would be $13. This is the first term in equation (6.5). He assumes the tax rate to be 50 percent so $(1 - T)$ would be .5. He has assumed an implicit b of .764 so the $(1 - b)$ term would be .236. He assumes a growth rate of 16 percent for $n = 5$ years and a k of 20 percent. We can, therefore, write his valuation expression as follows.

$$V_0 = 13(.5)(.236) \sum_{t=1}^{n} \left(\frac{1.16}{1.20}\right)^t + \frac{13(.5)}{.2} \left(\frac{1.16}{1.20}\right)^n$$

$$V_0 = 1.534 \sum_{t=1}^{5} (.967)^t + 32.5(.844)$$

$$= 1.534(.967) \left(\frac{.844 - 1}{-.033}\right) + 27.43$$

$$= 1.483 \left(\frac{-.156}{-.033}\right) + 27.43$$

$$= 1.483(4.7) + 27.43$$

$$= \$6.97 + 27.43 = \$34.40$$

We can then proceed to evaluate our standard free cash flow model to obtain a result of $34.40 million. This is the same result that Rappaport obtains in his Table 3-1 on page 66 where he makes the calculation on a yearly basis. The $34.40 million is equivalent to the $34.371 which he obtains before adding marketable securities and investments and deducting the market value of debt and other obligations.

No elaborate computer program is required to obtain Rappaport's results if the problem formulation is slightly modified to tighten its analytics. Making the calculations amenable to solution by the use of compact formulas greatly facilitates a sensitivity analysis and improves insights on related plans and strategies.

---

[1] Because of different assumptions, the last exponent is n, not $(n + 1)$ as in our equation (6.5).

CONCLUDING COMMENTS

The comparison with other approaches to valuation suggests that the more that some things appear different the more they are really the same. The correct valuation models are summarized in this chapter in Table 6.4 which employs the free cash flow approach and in Table 6.5 which uses the dividend growth valuation models. The methodology proposed in this chapter seeks to apply the principles enunciated in the two classic articles.

While alternative approaches may arrive at similar results, their procedures are more cumbersome. Because the analytics are not clear, the other approaches may be impaired by internal inconsistencies.

We believe that the rigorous models first enunciated by Miller and Modigliani (1961) and subsequently expressed in an alternative form by Malkiel (1963) have a number of superiorities. Our models seek to implement the logic of their formulations. The resulting formulations have a number of advantages. First, there is a relatively simple basis for their derivation from basic capital budgeting models. Second, the resulting valuation models are easy to utilize. They can be solved on a hand calculator or are readily programmable for use on a personal computer to facilitate a sensitivity analysis. For a basic personal computer programming of valuation and cost of capital models, see topics 16 and 17 in Smith and Weston (*PC Self-Study Manual for Finance*, 1987).

A third advantage of the straightforward analytical approach to valuation presented in this chapter is that analysts can be sure that their projections and assumptions with regard to the key parameters which determine value can be checked for internal consistency. For example, in other valuation studies assumptions are made about the value of b, financing requirements, and g, the growth rate of what would be equivalent to what we have called free cash flows. But setting values of b and g necessarily determines the value of r.

Some studies we have analyzed have values, for example, of .5 for b and a value of 10 percent for the growth rate. This implies a marginal after-tax profitability rate of 20 percent. This is plausible enough. Then these other analysts may change the growth rate to 20 percent, keeping r at 20 percent or perhaps raising it to 25 or 30 percent. But given an analytical framework in which $(br = g)$ if g is 20 percent and b remains at .5, then r must be 40 percent. If any other assumption is made for r there is an internal contradiction in the formulation of the problem. Further, failure to recognize that the assumed values of g and b require a profitability rate, r, of 40 percent may represent an unintended related assumption. It might be implausible for the industry or firm to have a marginal after-tax profit rate of 40 percent. But without seeing the fundamental relationships among the key valuation models, such implausible assumptions may be made.

For the preceding three reasons we feel that the compact straightforward approach to valuation developed in this chapter is more useful in enhancing the value of the firm and the position of each of its stakeholders than some other valuation models in other writings used by practitioners. To demonstrate further how the use of this valuation framework can be used in enhancing values, we apply it to actual company examples in the following chapter.

QUESTIONS

1. How are mergers and acquisitions related to capital budgeting?
2. List four methods of valuation (capital budgeting) and briefly set forth the advantages and limitations of each.
3. What is the difference between gross basis and net basis cash flows?
4. How are the following valuation parameters related to each other? How do they affect the general free cash flow valuation model?
   Sales
   Total capital
   Investment
   Net operating income
   Profitability rate
   Growth rate
5. Compare the free cash flow valuation model and analysis with the approaches of: (a) Miller and Modigliani; (b) Joel Stern; and (c) Rappaport. What are the advantages and limitations of each?

REFERENCES

MALKIEL, BURTON G., "Equity Yields, Growth, and the Structure of Share Prices," *American Economic Review*, 53, December 1963, pp. 1004–1031.

MILLER, MERTON H., and FRANCO MODIGLIANI, "Dividend Policy, Growth, and the Valuation of Shares," *Journal of Business*, 34, 4, October 1961, pp. 411–433.

RAPPAPORT, ALFRED, *Creating Shareholder Value*, New York: The Free Press, 1986.

SMITH, JAMES H., and J. FRED WESTON, (assisted by Susan Hoag), *PC Self-Study Manual for Finance*, Chicago, IL: The Dryden Press, 1987.

STERN, JOEL M., "Earnings Per Share Don't Count," *Financial Analysts Journal*, July–August 1974, pp. 39–40, 42–43, 67–75.

———, *Analytical Methods in Financial Planning*, The Chase Manhattan Bank, N.A., November 1977.

WESTON, J. FRED, and THOMAS E. COPELAND, *Managerial Finance*, 8th ed., Chicago, IL: The Dryden Press, 1986.

CHAPTER **7**

Increasing the Value
of the Organization

The preceding chapter developed the fundamental principles of valuation. They are technical and complex. In this chapter we seek to show how these principles can be applied in practice. Hopefully this will make the meaning of the concepts come alive. In addition, we hope to illustrate how valuation principles provide a powerful and valuable planning framework for the firm. Indeed, as the title of this chapter suggests, the principles are applicable to all types of organizations. The interactions between strategy discussed in Chapter 3 and valuation discussed in Chapter 6 are also important to the analysis.

The principles are most meaningful when applied to an actual company. The company used for this example is Eli Lilly and Company (Lilly), a leading pharmaceutical company. We have two main reasons for choosing Lilly. First, in order to do a valuation of a company the basic industrial economics of the industry must be understood. The pharmaceutical industry is one among a number of industries which the authors have studied on a continuing basis. Second, the dynamics of the pharmaceutical industry provide a rich setting for describing the interaction between valuation models, strategy, and the underlying business economics or industrial organization economics of the industry. The financial models provide a guide to valuation results based on numbers that are used as inputs. But the subjects of business economics and strategy are the materials that guide us to improve the key input parameters so that the value of an organization may be increased. The objective is not to grind numbers through valuation models. One can readily develop computer models to do this. The objective is to elucidate the interaction between financial valuation and the concepts of business economics and strategic planning.

Procedurally what we need to do is to obtain the basic financial information required to calculate the key input parameters that determine value. That is the first stage. In the second stage we go behind these numbers to look at elements of business economics and strategic planning to build and increase value. But we have to start with the numbers needed to calculate the key valuation input parameters.

ALTERNATIVE MEASURES
OF THE INVESTMENT RATE

We first consider the issue of how to measure the changes in total capital requirements of the firm, and to measure the rate of investments. We can illustrate the issues by reference to the material presented in the illustrative balance sheets from the previous chapter in Table 6.1. Our aim is to obtain a measure of the amount of investment in assets that the firm will have to finance. Utilizing the format of the balance sheets in Table 6.1, total capital requirements or total financing requirements equal (current assets less noninterest-bearing debt) plus (net fixed assets). Using the data from Table 6.1 by this measure total capital for year 2 would be:

$$\text{Current assets (70)} - \text{noninterest-bearing debt (30)}$$
$$+ \text{ net fixed assets (70)} = 110$$

This measure has also been referred to as net working capital (NWC) requirements plus net fixed investment (NFA) requirements. Some authors and practitioners measure working capital requirements as current assets minus current liabilities. But current liabilities often contain interest-bearing debt such as notes payable as well as the current portion of long-term debt payable. Since the objective is to measure financing requirements, it is logical to net out "spontaneous financing," but not important elements of financing.

An alternative procedure for calculating total capital is to add interest-bearing debt and shareholders' equity. For year 2 from Table 6.1 this would be:

$$\text{Interest-bearing debt (45)} + \text{Shareholders' equity (65)} = \$110$$

We get the same result. The sum of interest-bearing debt and shareholders' equity is also often referred to as total capitalization. It represents the total outside funding required for financing the economic resources employed by the firm.

Investment is the change in total resources. We can show the equality of both approaches on an incremental basis as well. The changes in the major accounts in Table 6.1 are as follows:

Change in current assets	$30	Change in interest-bearing debt	$15
Change in net fixed assets	10	Change in shareholders' equity	15
Total	$40	Investment (liability side)	$30
Less: Change in noninterest-bearing debt	10		
Investment (Asset side or NWC + NFA)	$30		

Thus, again we observe that there is no change whether investments are measured from the changes on the asset side or from changes on the sources of financing shown on the right-hand side of the balance sheet.

But when the firm has marketable securities (MS) and investments (in other companies), then the equality relationships discussed above will usually not hold. This is because both the balance sheet and income statements will be augmented by additional accounts as shown in Table 7.1, based on Table 6.1. The asset side of the balance sheet is augmented by the marketable securities and investment accounts. The debt and equity accounts are increased to provide financing for the increased assets. In the illustrative income statement, net operating income is unchanged at $30,000. But an account which reflects the income from marketable securities and investments is now added. The amount is assumed to be $6,000. The next account is "earnings before interest and taxes (EBIT)," seen to be larger than NOI. Since interest-bearing debt was increased as a partial source of financing the increased assets, interest expense is also increased.

The main consequence of adding the marketable securities and investments to the analysis is that NOI and EBIT are now different in concept and in dollar amounts. This makes it desirable to recognize two alternative approaches to measuring investment requirements: (1) *Total Capitalization—EBIT Measure,* and (2) *Operating Assets—NOI Measure.* Each is described.

Total Capitalization—EBIT Measure (Method 1)

Investment requirements are measured by the changes in financing required, that is, the sum of changes in interest-bearing debt (IBD) plus shareholders' equity (SHE). From Table 7.1 this would be:

$$\Delta IBD(15) + \Delta SHE(20) = \$35$$

It is likely that the asset side of the balance sheet that is being financed will include marketable securities and investments in other companies. These investments will generate income designated as "interest earned" or "other income" in the income statement. The related measure of (before-tax) cash flows should be

TABLE 7.1
Financial Statements

ILLUSTRATIVE INCOME STATEMENT

	YEAR 2
Sales	$145,000
Operating costs excluding depreciation	95,000
Income before depreciation, interest and taxes	50,000
Depreciation expense (Dep)	20,000
Net operating income (NOI)	30,000
Other income less income deductions	6,000
Earnings before interest and taxes (EBIT)	36,000
Interest expense (f)	6,000
Income before taxes (IBT)	30,000
Taxes @ 40 percent (T = tax rate)	12,000
Net income (Y) (NI)	$ 18,000

RELATED BALANCE SHEETS (in thousands) [end-of-year (EOY) amounts]

	YEAR 1	YEAR 2		YEAR 1	YEAR 2
Marketable securities	10	15	Interest-bearing debt	40	55
Other current assets	40	60	Noninterest-bearing debt	30	35
Total current assets	50	75			
Investments in other firms	20	25	Shareholders' equity	60	80
Fixed assets gross	70	100			
Reserve for Dep	10	30			
Net fixed assets	60	70			
Total assets (net)	130	170	Claims on assets	130	170

earnings before interest and taxes (EBIT). The measure of investment will include marketable securities and investments which are not included in the second (NOI) measure of investment. The measure of investment requirements rates (the rates of investment to net cash flows—what we have labeled, b) would be higher than in the second method if cash flows were measured identically under the two alternative methods. When total valuation of the firm is calculated by this method, it is not necessary to add the value of marketable securities (MS) plus investments since they have already been included in the calculations.

Operating Assets—NOI Measure (Method 2)

Investment is measured as changes in net current assets ($\Delta CA - \Delta MS - \Delta NIBCL$) plus changes in net fixed assets (ΔNFA). Marketable securities should not be included in current assets for this measure unless they are held as a form of cash or working capital, that is, for transactions purposes. From Table 7.1 investment in year 2 would be $\Delta CA(25) - \Delta MS(5) - \Delta NIBCL(5) + \Delta NFA(10) = \$25$. This is smaller than in Method 1 because investments in marketable securities and in other companies are not considered investments in operating assets. If investment is measured this way, the NOI should be the measure of cash flows. After the valuation of the firm has been calculated, we add back the value of marketable securities plus investments.

To reiterate, under the NOI method of calculating investment requirements we work from the asset side. We sum net working capital requirements plus the net fixed assets. Net working capital is measured by current assets excluding marketable securities less noninterest-bearing current liabilities (NIBCL). Thus, cash required for transactions purposes is included. NIBCL is obtained by deducting from current liabilities all interest-bearing short-term debt (notes payable and the current portion of long-term debt due during the year). Accrued taxes are in NIBCL, but deferred taxes are not. Deferred taxes are already taken into account by using actual taxes currently paid rather than current plus deferred taxes in adjusting the income statement data to a cash flow basis.

In theory, when investment is measured on an incremental basis in the underlying accounts, and during the period of analysis the firm does not add to its marketable securities or investments in other companies, both methods will give the same results. The firm initially may have a large investment in marketable securities and a large investment account in other companies. However, if these items do not change during the period under analysis, they will not show up in an incremental measure of investment. But even when the firm changes its investment in marketable securities and in other companies and the measures differ, the valuation result may not be materially affected.

AN EXAMPLE:
MEASURING INPUT PARAMETERS FOR LILLY

We first organize the data for the use of the EBIT method. Next we develop the data for the NOI method. We can then use each in the valuation computations in order to compare the results.

The EBIT Method

The basic data for the EBIT method are summarized in Table 7.2. Only five columns of input data are required for our calculations. Column (1) is shareholders' equity and column (2) is interest-bearing debt. These are added to obtain total capital shown in column (3). Changes in capital from year to year represent investment, calculated in column (4). The third element of basic input information is earnings before taxes (EBT) shown in column (5).

Column (6) is current taxes. Total income taxes are composed of taxes

TABLE 7.2

Basic Input Data for EBIT Method, Lilly

t	YEAR	(1) SHE	(2) IBD	(3) TOTCAP (A)	(4) INVEST (I)	(5) EBT	(6) CURRENT TAXES	(7) TAX RATE	(8) EBIT (X)	(9) EBIT(1 − T)	(10) r	(11) b
1	1974	$ 848	$158	$1,006		$303	$120	0.400	$317	$209		0.820
2	1975	958	221	1,179	$173	299	113	0.380	319	211	0.156	0.420
3	1976	1,079	200	1,279	100	341	136	0.400	361	238	0.280	0.583
4	1977	1,209	225	1,434	155	395	151	0.380	403	266	0.413	0.467
5	1978	1,384	204	1,588	154	483	201	0.420	500	330	0.273	0.231
6	1979	1,570	104	1,674	86	559	216	0.390	563	372	0.477	0.680
7	1980	1,737	218	1,955	281	590	239	0.405	626	413	0.153	0.430
8	1981	1,888	263	2,151	196	646	250	0.387	691	456	0.112	0.416
9	1982	2,055	295	2,350	199	684	243	0.355	724	478	0.241	0.319
10	1983	2,121	397	2,518	168	755	242	0.321	797	526	0.089	0.299
11	1984	2,221	459	2,680	162	771	92	0.119	820	541	0.123	0.444
12	1985	2,388	541	2,929	249	797	224	0.281	850	561	0.253	0.700
13	1986	2,740	626	3,366	437	876	282	0.322	946	624		
	Sum or Weighted Average:			$26,109	$2,360	$7,499	$2,509	0.335	$7,917	$5,225	0.215	0.470
	Unweighted Average:							0.351			0.234	0.484
	Growth rates:											
	d	10.3%	12.2%	10.6%		9.3%			9.5%	9.5%		
	c	9.4%	10.7%	9.6%		9.5%			9.4%	9.4%		
	d = e^c − 1	9.9%	11.3%	10.1%		10.0%			9.9%	9.9%		

currently paid and taxes that are deferred. Since we use a cash flow model, only taxes that involve cash outflows in the years under analysis should be included. This is standard practice by most writers and practitioners. Current taxes (6) divided by EBT (5) gives the tax rate in column (7). Both the weighted and unweighted tax rates approximate 34 percent, which is the marginal corporate tax rate under the Tax Reform Act of 1986. We employ 34 percent as the measure of the tax rate, T, in the Lilly valuation analysis.

Earnings before interest and taxes (EBIT) is shown in column (8). To calculate EBIT we start with EBT in (5). To EBT we add all pretax financial charges—interest, amortization of bond discounts (less amortization of bond premiums) plus an estimate of the interest expense in lease payments related to capital leases included in equipment in the consolidated balance sheet. We do not list these amounts since they are the difference between columns (8) and (5).

Column (9) is EBIT $(1 - T)$. As noted T is equal to 34 percent in our valuation of Lilly. Hence, column (9) is column (8) multiplied by the .66 factor.

In column (10), we calculate the profitability rate. It is the increase in column (9) for a given year divided by the investment made in the previous year, as defined in Chapter 6.

The last column in Table 7.2 is the investment requirements rate. This is the amount of investment in a given year, column (4), divided by the after-tax EBIT from column (9).

Because of the crucial role that the growth rate performs in the valuation formulas, we calculate growth rates in a number of ways to obtain a better basis for a judgment about which growth rates should be employed. Accordingly in Table 7.3, growth rates are calculated in three ways. What we designate as d stands for a discrete growth rate. It is simply the final year divided by the initial year to the twelfth root to obtain a geometric average based on the end points. What we have designated as c is a continuously compounded growth rate. It is (most efficiently) calculated by determining the slope of the regression line of the

TABLE 7.3
Alternative Estimates of Growth Rates for Lilly

GROWTH RATES[a]	(1) SHE (%)	(2) IBD (%)	(3) TOTCAP (%)	(4) CURRENT TAXES (%)	(5) EBIT $(1 - T)$ (%)
d	10.3	12.2	10.6	9.3	9.6
c	9.4	10.7	9.6	9.5	9.4
$d = e^c - 1$	9.9	11.3	10.1	10.0	9.9

[a]Growth rates:

$d = (1986/1974)^{1/12} - 1 =$ end-point growth rate

$c =$ continuously compounded growth rate (measured by the slope of the regression line of the natural logarithm of the variable against years)

$d = e^c - 1 =$ discrete rate converted from continuously compounded growth rate natural logarithm of the variable for which growth is being measured against years over the time period of the analysis. An alternative estimate of the discrete growth rate is to use a standard formula to convert from a continuously compounded growth rate. Here $d = e^c - 1$.

In addition to calculating growth rates, we need to develop other measures. Valuation involves capitalizing future cash flow streams. Ideally we need forecasts. An initial step in developing forecasts is to see what has transpired historically. But this is a basis only for developing forecasts in conjunction with a review of the economic and strategic factors affecting the future of the firm. Accordingly our next step is to develop relationships that will further guide us from a numerical standpoint before applying the economic and strategic analysis. We therefore proceed to calculate some average relationships.

The calculations of the average values of the key valuation parameters are shown in Table 7.4. Line 1 is the tax rate calculated as a weighted average over the period 1974–1986. As we have observed, the result of approximately 34 percent is the applicable tax rate for large corporations under the Tax Reform Act of 1986.

In line 2, we calculate the profitability rate as defined in Chapter 6. An average of the profitability rates for each year from Table 7.2 provides an unweighted average of 23.4 percent. A weighted average over the period of data is somewhat lower, 21.5 percent. The unusually high values for some individual years, shown in column (10) of Table 7.2, cause the unweighted average to be higher.

The investment rate is calculated in line 3. The unweighted average is 48.4 percent. The weighted average is 47 percent. The high b values for individual years, shown in column (11) of Table 7.2, push up the unweighted average.

In line 4, we calculate a growth rate based on a weighted average b and a weighted average r. This gives a growth rate of 10.1 percent, based on historical data taking the entire period 1974–1986 into account.

The NOI Method

Table 7.5 shows the measurement of total resources using the NOI method. It illustrates the calculation of the annual investment in the final column (9) as the change in A_t.

In Table 7.6, the profitability rate and investment rate are calculated by the NOI method. Using a measure of investment based on net working capital and net fixed assets, we relate that to net operating income to calculate r and b values.

In Table 7.7, the weighted averages of profitability and investment rate are calculated. The weighted averages are more reliable than the average of the yearly rates because unweighted averages always exaggerate unusual individual calculations. Part A of Table 7.7 repeats the results from Table 7.4 which calculated profitability using EBIT because capital requirements were measured by

TABLE 7.4

Calculation of Averages for Key Valuation Parameters

1. *Tax Rate*

$$T = \sum_{t=1}^{n} \frac{(\text{Taxes Paid})_t}{\sum\limits_{t=1}^{n} \text{EBT}_t} = \frac{\sum\limits_{t=74}^{86} \text{Taxes}}{\sum\limits_{t=74}^{86} (\text{EBT})_t} = \frac{\$2,509}{\$7,499} = .335 \approx .34$$

2. *Profitability*

$$r_t = \frac{X_t(1-T) - X_{t-1}(1-T)}{I_{t-1}} \qquad \bar{r}_t = \frac{\sum\limits_{t=3}^{n} r_t}{n-2} = \frac{2.57}{11} = .234 \text{ unweighted}$$

$$\bar{r} = \frac{\begin{array}{c}X_n(1-T) - \\ X_2(1-T)\end{array}}{A_{n-1} - A_1 \equiv \sum\limits_{t=2}^{n-1} I_t} = \frac{\begin{array}{c}X_{86}(1-T) - \\ X_{75}(1-T)\end{array}}{A_{85} - A_{74} \equiv \sum\limits_{t=75}^{85} I_t} = \frac{624-211}{2,929-1,006} = \frac{413}{1,923} = .215 \text{ weighted}$$

3. *Investment Rate*

$$b = \frac{\sum\limits_{t=2}^{n} b_t}{n-1} = \frac{5.809}{12} = .484 \text{ unweighted}$$

$$b = \frac{\sum\limits_{t=2}^{n} I_t}{\sum\limits_{t=2}^{n} X_t(1-T)} = \frac{\sum\limits_{t=75}^{86} I_t}{\sum\limits_{t=75}^{86} X_t(1-T)} = \frac{\$2,360}{\$5,225-209} = \frac{\$2,360}{\$5,016} = .470 \text{ weighted}$$

4. *Growth Rate*

$$g = b\,\bar{r} = (.470)(.215) = .101 = 10.1\%$$

TABLE 7.5

Calculation of I_t by NOI Method, Lilly

	(1) CA	(2) MS	(3) CL*	(4) NP	(5) NIBCL	(6) NWC	(7) NPPE	(8) (NWC + NPPE)=A_t	(9) Change in (NWC + NPPE)=I_t
1974	$ 849	$235	$ 387	$153	$234	$380	$ 371	$ 751	
1975	949	304	432	209	223	422	444	866	$ 115
1976	1,072	364	451	180	271	437	474	911	45
1977	1,219	405	495	225	270	544	513	1,057	146
1978	1,318	347	594	199	395	576	556	1,132	75
1979	1,317	147	533	100	433	737	680	1,417	285
1980	1,538	171	739	185	554	813	849	1,662	245
1981	1,665	219	818	209	609	837	1,006	1,843	181
1982	1,681	268	874	246	628	785	1,136	1,921	78
1983	1,830	457	988	307	681	692	1,213	1,905	(−16)
1984	1,828	392	953	343	610	826	1,280	2,106	201
1985	1,940	369	919	302	617	954	1,374	2,328	222
1986	2,072	453	1,017	231	786	833	1,528	2,361	33
								Sum	$1,610

CA = Current assets.
MS = Marketable securities.
CL* = Current liabilities less deferred income taxes in current liabilities (to avoid double counting since current taxes, not deferred taxes, are used).
NP = Notes payable.
NIBCL = Noninterest-bearing current liabilities = (CL*−NP).
NWC = Net working capital = CA−MS−NIBCL.
NPPE = Net property, plant, and equipment.
A_t = Assets in period t.
I_t = Investment in period t.

TABLE 7.6

Calculation of r and b by Method 2, Lilly

YEAR	(1) INVEST	(2) NOI(X)	(3) X(1 − T)	(4) r	(5) b
1974		$288	$190		
1975	$115	293	193		0.596
1976	45	340	224	0.270	0.201
1977	146	398	262	0.844	0.557
1978	75	472	311	0.336	0.241
1979	285	542	357	0.613	0.798
1980	245	565	373	0.056	0.657
1981	181	617	407	0.139	0.445
1982	78	671	443	0.199	0.176
1983	(−16)	725	478	0.449	(−0.033)[a]
1984	201	744	491	(−0.813)[a]	0.409
1985	222	764	505	0.070	0.440
1986	33	860	568	0.284	0.058
Sum or Weighted Average:	$1,610	$7,278	$4,802	0.238	0.349
Unweighted Average:				0.326	0.379
Growth rates:					
d		9.6%	9.6%		
c		9.4%	9.4%		
$d = e^c - 1$		9.9%	9.9%		

[a] When investments are negative and changes in income are positive, r and b are not defined.

interest-bearing debt plus shareholders' equity. The weighted profitability rate is 21.5 percent and the investment rate on the same basis is 47 percent.

In Part B of Table 7.7, where capital requirements are calculated using net working capital plus net fixed assets, net operating income is used as a measure of free cash flow. The weighted profitability rate is 23.8 percent and the investment rate is about 35 percent.

We now have all of the input parameters for calculating the valuation of Lilly except its cost of capital to which we now turn.

CALCULATING THE COST OF CAPITAL FOR LILLY

To calculate the cost of capital, we make a number of alternative estimates of the cost of equity capital. We also calculate the cost of debt. Next, we use an appropriate estimate of financial structure or financial proportions for the firm. We apply the appropriate financial proportions to the cost of equity capital and to the cost of debt. We are thereby enabled to calculate a weighted cost of capital. This

TABLE 7.7
Calculation of r and b by Two Alternatives

A. Capital requirements measured by (IBD + SHE) and EBIT used
   1. Profitability

$$\bar{r} = \frac{X_n(1-T) - X_2(1-T)}{A_{n-1} - A_1 \equiv \sum\limits_{t=2}^{n-1} I_t} = \frac{X_{86}(1-T) - X_{75}(1-T)}{A_{85} - A_{74} \equiv \sum\limits_{t=75}^{85} I_t} = \frac{624 - 211}{2,929 - 1,006} = \frac{413}{1,923} = .215$$

   2. Investment Rate

$$\bar{b} = \frac{\sum\limits_{t=2}^{n} I_t}{\sum\limits_{t=2}^{n} X_t(1-T)} = \frac{\sum\limits_{t=75}^{86} I_t}{\sum\limits_{t=75}^{86} X_t(1-T)} = \frac{2,360}{5,225 - 209} = \frac{2,360}{5,016} = .470$$

B. Capital requirements measured by (NWC + NPPE) and NOI used; add back marketable securities
   and investments
   1. Profitability

$$\bar{r} = \frac{X_n(1-T) - X_2(1-T)}{A_{n-1} - A_1 \equiv \sum\limits_{t=2}^{n-1} I_t} = \frac{X_{86}(1-T) - X_{75}(1-T)}{A_{85} - A_{74} \equiv \sum\limits_{t=75}^{85} I_t} = \frac{568 - 193}{1,577} = \frac{375}{1,577} = .238$$

   2. Investment Rate

$$\bar{b} = \frac{\sum\limits_{t=2}^{n} I_t}{\sum\limits_{t=2}^{n} X_t(1-T)} = \frac{\sum\limits_{t=75}^{86} I_t}{\sum\limits_{t=75}^{86} X_t(1-T)} = \frac{1,610}{4,802 - 190} = \frac{1,610}{4,612} = .349$$

weighted cost is a weighted marginal cost of capital because of the method
utilized. We do not use book or historical cost. What is relevant are current
market opportunity costs of both equity and debt capital. As we shall see, the
correct proportions to use are neither book nor market, although each of these
can provide guidelines.

The cost of equity capital is generally estimated employing four different
methodologies. These are:

1 CAPM
2 Bond yield plus equity risk premium
3 Average investor's realized yield
4 Dividend growth model

Each will be discussed in turn.

Capital Asset Pricing Model (CAPM)

The basic CAPM equation is

$$k_e = R_f + [\bar{R}_M - R_f]\beta_j \tag{7.1}$$

where:

R_f = risk-free rate

$\bar{R}_M - R_f$ = long-term average market price of risk

β_j = the systematic risk of the individual asset or firm

k_e = the cost of equity capital

We need to obtain estimates for each term on the right-hand side of the equation.

Many alternative approaches can be used to estimate the risk-free rate. The general practice now is to use the yield to maturity on ten-year government securities. The advantage of this is that with government securities default risk is relatively low. Using the medium-term maturity avoids the sharp fluctuations in shorter-term government securities. In addition, ten years is a reasonable time horizon for which to make estimates of the cost of equity capital. For this analysis in the autumn of 1987 we used 9 percent.

The next parameter we need to estimate is $(\bar{R}_M - R_f)$. This difference between the return on the market and the risk-free rate represents the average market price of risk. A number of sources have estimated this parameter on average over a period of years to be in the range of 6.5 to 8.5 percentage points. For our analysis it is reasonable to use the midpoint of this range of 7.0 percent.

A number of financial services supply estimates of beta for individual companies. Most sources set a beta of something over 1 for Lilly in the time period under analysis. We employ a beta of 1.05.

Utilizing the numerical values for each of the terms on the right-hand side of equation (7.1), we obtain a numerical value shown in equation (7.1a).

$$k_e = 9\% + 7.0(1.05) = 16.4\% \tag{7.1a}$$

This gives an estimate of the cost of equity for Lilly of 16.4 percent.

The arbitrage pricing theory (APT) holds that security returns depend not directly on the market return, but on other fundamental factors. The APT has also been used to estimate the cost of capital. Four macroeconomic factors have been found to be correlated with returns on portfolios that mimic the underlying factors. They are: (1) the growth rate of industrial production, (2) a default risk premium measured by the differences in promised yields on long-term government bonds versus Baa corporate bonds, (3) the slope of the yield curve as measured by differences in promised yields on long-term versus short-term government bonds, and (4) the rate of unanticipated inflation. These four factors represent plausible economic influences. Stock prices are the present values of expected future cash flows. The first variable is related to profitability; the other three are related to the discount rate.

Several consulting firms provide estimates of the cost of capital based on the APT rather than on the CAPM. This is an additional useful information input. But the cost of capital cannot usually be determined by quantitative procedures alone. An understanding of the underlying business economics of the industry and firm is required to develop an informed judgment of the applicable cost of capital for equity funds.

Bond Yield Plus Equity Risk Premium

The logic of this estimate is that on average the cost of equity should exceed the cost of debt, since equity is junior in priority to debt. The procedure is to analyze historically the yield shareholders require for equity as compared with the average yield to maturity on the firm's bonds. Since Lilly is of triple-A level of financial strength, we can use the triple-A yield to maturity (10.1 percent in the autumn of 1987) as an estimate of the cost of debt for Lilly. Historical data suggest that the average equity risk premium for Lilly is 3.5 percent. These numerical values can be used in equation (7.2) to obtain an estimate of the cost of equity for Lilly of 13.6 percent.

$$k_e = 10.1 + 3.5\% = 13.6\% \tag{7.2}$$

Average Investor's Realized Yield

Another approach is to use what investors historically have required as their return on investment in this company or in this industry. This yield can be calculated on a market basis or on accounting returns. Data for both these measures are shown for Lilly in Table 7.8.

The accounting return to shareholders has been stable at about 20 percent. It has exhibited no clear trend over the 17-year period. The market returns to shareholders have fluctuated greatly. Sharp negative returns have been recorded in some years. High yields were achieved during the years 1985 and 1986 with substantial increases in the price of Lilly common stock. Despite these large increases, the average total yield to shareholders measured on a market return basis was 11.7 percent. This may be taken as a measure of the cost of equity, but is clearly on the low side. It is probable that investor expectations were higher.

Dividend Growth Model

This approach estimates the cost of capital by using the constant-growth dividend valuation model we developed in Chapter 6 as equation (6.4a).

$$S_0 = \frac{D_1}{k_e - g} \tag{6.4a}$$

TABLE 7.8

Shareholder Realized Returns—Lilly

		Market Returns			Accounting Returns		
	AVERAGE PRICE	% Δ PRICE	DIVIDEND YIELD(%)	TOTAL YIELD	NET INCOME	($Million) SHE	% RETURN
1970	45.69	6.4	1.4	7.8	94.4	455.4	20.73
1971	57.56	26.0	1.2	27.2	96.1	513.2	18.73
1972	67.44	17.2	1.1	18.3	126.3	618.2	20.43
1973	81.13	20.3	1.0	21.3	155.5	730.2	21.20
1974	69.25	(14.6)	1.4	(13.2)	178.8	848.5	21.07
1975	63.63	(8.1)	1.7	(6.4)	181.3	958.0	18.92
1976	51.50	(19.1)	2.4	(16.7)	200.2	1,078.6	18.56
1977	40.44	(21.5)	3.5	(18.0)	218.7	1,208.7	18.09
1978	45.31	12.0	3.6	15.6	277.5	1,384.1	20.05
1979	55.50	22.5	3.5	26.0	329.5	1,570.4	20.98
1980	54.50	(1.8)	4.0	2.2	342.0	1,736.7	19.69
1981[a]	26.00	(4.6)	4.0	(.6)	374.5	1,888.3	19.83
1982	27.56	6.0	4.8	10.8	411.8	2,055.5	20.03
1983	31.19	13.2	4.4	17.6	457.4	2,121.0	21.56
1984	30.19	(3.2)	4.9	1.7	490.2	2,221.2	22.07
1985	44.13	46.2	3.6	49.8	517.6	2,387.7	21.68
1986	67.06	52.0	2.7	54.7	558.2	2,739.6	20.38
Average		8.8	2.9	11.7			20.24

[a] 2-for-1 stock split.

A number of assumptions underlying the dividend valuation model should be noted to understand how it may be used to estimate the required return on equity for a firm. The growth rate, g, refers to the growth in dividends. The model requires constant growth which continues through infinity.

The logic of the model indicates that the g refers to the growth rate in dividends, but under the assumptions of the model everything else also grows at the same rate. If dividends grow at 10 percent, and the payout ratio (or equivalently the retention rate) and financial leverage ratio are constant, earnings and total assets of the firm must also be growing 10 percent. And over time, the value of the firm and the price of its common stock will be growing at a rate of 10 percent as well. There are interdependencies between S_0, the value of the equity, and the growth rate in earnings, dividends, and the total assets of the firm. Thus, the model does not provide an unambiguous basis for estimating k_e.

Nevertheless, the dividend valuation model is widely used in practice, both for valuing common stock and for estimating the cost of equity capital. In estimating the cost of equity capital for Lilly, the valuation expression is solved for k_e as shown in equation (7.3).

$$k_e = \frac{D_1}{S_0} + g \qquad (7.3)$$

Equation (7.3) states that the required return on equity is the expected dividend yield plus the expected growth rate in dividends. The expected dividend is obtained by taking the current dividend, D_0, and applying the expected growth rate. It is difficult to arrive at a reliable figure for the expected growth rate. One approach is to begin with the growth over a previous period. But the position of the firm is likely to be affected by developments in the economy as a whole as well as in its own industry. One intractable problem is that the model calls for the growth rate to infinity. But no growth rate to infinity for an individual firm can exceed the growth rate of the economy as a whole or the firm would exceed the size of the economy at some point in the future. Thus, the most plausible valuation formula has a period of supernormal growth followed by no growth in excess of normal growth in the economy reflected in the discount rate.

Nevertheless, various financial services provide estimates of expected growth in earnings and dividends for individual firms. In particular, we have found the earnings and dividend forecasts compiled by Lynch, Jones & Ryan in their Institutional Brokers Estimate System (I/B/E/S) to be a useful data source. In addition, an independent analysis can be made by the analyst attempting to make a calculation of the cost of capital for the firm. Suppose that by a combination of all of these methods we arrive at an expected growth rate in dividends for Lilly of 10 percent. Then we estimate the expected dividend yield for the year at 3 percent. When this is added to the 10 percent expected growth rate, we obtain a 13 percent estimate of the required return on equity.

Summarizing thus far, we have the following results for the four methods:

1 CAPM—16.4 percent
2 Bond yield plus equity risk premium—13.6 percent
3 Realized investor yield—11.7 percent
4 Dividend growth model—13 percent

The level of general equity market uncertainty will also affect the cost of equity capital. The sharp stock market decline of October 1987 represented a readjustment of general market expectations. The shift from optimism to pessimism added from 1 to 3 percentage points to the market-required cost of equity capital. Thus, the level of the general equity market uncertainty is another variable that must be taken into account.

Averaging the four measures of the cost of equity capital gives 13.8 percent. The changes in general equity market uncertainty must also be taken into account. Comparisons with the cost of equity capital estimates for other firms in the pharmaceutical industry must also be made. Taking all of these factors into account leads us to believe that we may appropriately use a figure of 13 to 13.5 percent.

Cost of Debt

The cost of debt should be on an after-tax basis because interest payments are tax deductible. Therefore, the cost of debt capital is calculated as follows:

$$k_b(1 - T) = \text{after-tax cost of debt}$$

Here T is the corporate tax rate as used previously. Thus, if the before-tax cost of debt were 10 percent and the firm's effective corporate tax rate were 34 percent, the after-tax cost of debt would be 6.6 percent.

We start with the firm's before-tax cost of debt and multiply it by the $(1 - T)$ factor to obtain the relevant after-tax cost. How do we obtain the before-tax cost of debt in practice for an actual firm? Two main procedures may be used. We can look in any of the investment manuals to determine the rating of the firm's outstanding publicly-held bonds. Various government agencies and investment banking firms periodically publish promised yields to maturity of debt issues by rating categories.

Lilly's bonds would be rated AAA. In the publications of Salomon Brothers at the time, we find that seasoned AAA industrial debt issues of mid-range maturity (the remaining years to maturity of most of Lilly's debt) are slightly over 10.0 percent. We can check this by calculating the promised yield to maturity on the cash flow from Lilly's long-term debt in relation to its current price. Again we obtain about 10 percent. Since k_b should be expected yield to maturity rather than promised yield, k_b could be a smaller number. But it will not be materially different from the calculated promised yield since Lilly's bankruptcy risk is very low.

Cost of Preferred Stock

Lilly has no preferred stock outstanding. We shall indicate the procedure for completeness. Preferred stock is a hybrid between debt and common stock. Like debt, preferred stock carries a fixed commitment on the part of the corporation to make periodic payments; in liquidation, the claims of the preferred stockholders take precedence over those of the common stockholders. However, failure to make the preferred dividend payments does not result in bankruptcy as nonpayment of interest on bonds does. Thus, to the firm, preferred stock is somewhat less risky than common stock but riskier than bonds. To the investor, preferred stock is also less risky than common but riskier than bonds.

From the standpoint of the issuing firm, preferred stock has the disadvantage that its dividend is not deductible for tax purposes. On the other hand, the tax law provides that a high percent of all dividends received by one corporation from another is not taxable. This dividend exclusion makes preferred stock a potentially attractive investment to other corporations. This attractiveness on the demand side pushes the yields on preferred stock to slightly below yields on bonds of similar companies. Although preferred issues may be callable and may be retired, most are perpetuities. If the preferred issue is a perpetuity, then its yield is calculated as follows:

$$\text{Preferred yield} = \frac{\text{Preferred dividend}}{\text{Price of preferred stock}} = \frac{d_{ps}}{p_{ps}} \qquad (7.5)$$

The Marginal Cost of Capital

We now have estimates of all of the costs of the individual components in financing. We next consider how we can pull all of this information together to calculate the weighted average marginal cost of capital for Lilly as a whole, an expression that is referred to as WACC or MCC.

The formula to calculate the weighted cost of capital, k, is the following:

$$k = k_b(1 - T)\,(B/V) + k_e(S/V) \tag{7.6}$$

Recall that:

B = market value of debt
S = market value of shareholders' equity
V = total market value of the firm

To utilize the formula requires that we have the weights to apply to the debt and equity proportions. We can start with the proportions based on book values, as shown in Table 7.9.

We observe about 20 percent debt and 80 percent equity as the financing proportions from Table 7.9. We do not believe this to be an appropriate measure of the financing proportions since market values are more relevant. When we use market values the debt ratio is even lower because the market-to-book ratio for Lilly common stock is 4 to 1. The market value of debt is not greatly different from its book value, so the financing proportions would weight equity even more heavily if market values were employed. But since equity costs are higher than debt costs, increasing the proportion would raise Lilly's cost of capital.

Opposing forces are involved. Pharmaceutical companies such as Lilly face a number of special risk factors. Their future depends on a stream of important new drug discoveries over the years. Some firms succeed in doing this; others do not. The earnings and stock prices of drug firms are directly related to their performance in bringing high-sales volume new drugs to the market. This is a high-risk activity.

Another special risk is that pharmaceutical companies have a large investment in scientific and investigating personnel. This represents a large fixed

TABLE 7.9.
Book Financial Proportions

	AMOUNT	PERCENT
Total interest-bearing debt (231 + 395)	626	19
Shareholders' equity	2,740	81
Total	3,366	100

TABLE 7.10

Lilly Cost of Capital with Target Proportions

	TARGET FINANCIAL PROPORTIONS	BEFORE-TAX COST	AFTER-TAX COST	WEIGHTED COST
Debt	30%	.100	.066	.020
Equity	70%	.135		.094
Cost of Capital				.114

investment with a large annual fixed commitment to fund research. These out-lays may or may not pay off. The market looks to the firm's track record of effectiveness in developing new drug products and marketing them. While the inherent risks are high they do not appear so high to financial analysts if the firm has a favorable record of past performance and good prospects for the future.

Taking all these factors into account, we have formulated an estimate of the representative or target financial proportions for Lilly, as shown in Table 7.10. Since these target proportions are not greatly different from the past actual proportions, the estimated component costs of each form of financing would not change much even if Lilly moved to the target proportions.

Using the component costs for each form of financing already computed, we obtain a cost of capital for Lilly of 11.4 percent. Based on the assessments of the economic factors already discussed, our judgment is that a weighted cost of capital in the range of 10 to 11 percent would be reasonable in the subsequent valuation analysis to which we now turn.

VALUATION OF LILLY

The valuation of Lilly uses the most widely accepted model of valuation, which is the free cash flow formula for a period of supernormal growth followed by a period of no growth. This is equation (6.5) from the previous chapter:

$$V_0 = X_0(1-T)(1-b) \sum_{t=1}^{n} \left(\frac{1+g}{1+k}\right)^t + \frac{X_0(1-T)}{k} \left(\frac{1+g}{1+k}\right)^n (1+g) \qquad (6.5)$$

where:

V_0 = Total firm value [value of equity (S) plus debt (B)]
X_0 = EBIT or NOI
T = Tax rate
b = Investment rate
r = Profit rate

g = Growth rate
N = Growth period
k = Cost of capital

In the previous discussion we have developed historical numbers for the key valuation parameters. But valuation is based on estimates of the future. The forward-looking valuation performs an economic analysis of developments in the pharmaceutical industry and particularly the outlook for Lilly. The pharmaceutical industry as a whole goes through fluctuations in its ability to develop new important drugs that will receive approval of government regulatory agencies such as the Food and Drug Administration (FDA). During the period between 1980 and 1985, there was a slump in FDA drug approvals. In addition foreign currency exchange rates were unfavorable in that the dollar was appreciating in relation to foreign currencies. Many large pharmaceutical companies sell 40 to 50 percent of their sales volume abroad. Thus, they are highly sensitive to currency exchange rates. The entire industry now seems to be in a more favorable trend with regard to the development of new products. Much basic research that required investment in the earlier years with relatively small returns is now bearing fruit. In addition foreign exchange rate movements which were unfavorable to the drug companies through 1985 have been more favorable in recent years with the relative decline of the dollar in relation to foreign currencies.

For Lilly in particular some negative and positive economic factors are applicable. There is increasing competition from generic products to the relatively mature injectable antibiotic line of Lilly. But there are also strong pluses. Strong sales gains are projected for Ceclor, an oral antibiotic. Also the outlook for Humulin, a human insulin product, is favorable. In early September the FDA approved Lilly's new antidepressant drug Prozac. In addition to being an antidepressant, Prozac appears to have important potential for treating obesity as well. Others view it as having additional potential for the treatment of alcoholism. Some analysts forecast an annual rate of sales of Prozac in excess of $200 million by the early 1990s.

These favorable projections are reflected in the optimistic estimates of the key input parameters for estimating value used in Table 7.11. Both our data and the projections made by financial analysts support a growth rate in EBIT and NOI of 15 percent per year. The pattern of the relationships between the EBIT and NOI methods indicates an investment rate, b, of .50 for the EBIT method and .43 for the NOI method. Postulating that the growth rates of EBIT and NOI would be the same, we can infer the profitability rates from the estimates of the investment rates we have already made. They are 30 percent for the EBIT method and 35 percent for the NOI method. Utilizing the other input valuation parameters developed earlier, the resulting total company values are shown to be somewhat over $15 billion. After deducting the debt of $626 million, the value of equity is about $14.5 billion. The indicated market price per share is about $104—Lilly's precrash market price.

Note that the two alternative valuation methods produced about the same

TABLE 7.11
Lilly Valuation: Optimistic

VALUATION PARAMETERS	EBIT METHOD	NOI METHOD
X_0 = EBIT or NOI	$946	$860
T = Tax rate	.34	.34
b = Investment rate	.50	.43
r = Profit rate	.30	.35
g = Growth rate	.15	.15
N = Growth period	10	10
k = Cost of capital	.10	.10
Results:		
First term	$4,019	$ 4,176
Second term	11,199	10,230
Value	$15,218	$14,406
Plus marketable securities		453
Plus investment		$274
Value of firm	$15,218	$15,133
Less total debt	626	626
Value of equity	$14,592	$14,507
Number of shares	140	140
Value per share	$104.23	$103.62

TABLE 7.12
Lilly Valuation: Less Optimistic

VALUATION PARAMETERS	EBIT METHOD	NOI METHOD
X_0 = EBIT or NOI	$946	$860
T = Tax rate	.34	.34
b = Investment rate	.50	.43
r = Profit rate	.26	.30
g = Growth rate	.13	.13
N = Growth period	10	10
k = Cost of capital	.11	.11
Results:		
First term	$ 3,449	$ 3,556
Second term	7,668	6,903
Value	$11,116	$10,459
Plus marketable securities		453
Plus investment		$274
Value of firm	$11,116	$11,186
Less total debt	626	626
Value of equity	$10,490	$10,560
Number of shares	140	140
Value per share	$74.93	$75.43

results. While the assumptions are different, offsetting numerical relationships can produce the same results. There is no conflict between the two methods, but the methodologies should not be mixed.

In Table 7.12, we consider some slightly less optimistic forecasts for Lilly. The growth rate in earnings is lowered from 15 to 13 percent. Holding the same levels for investment rates implies profitability rates of 26 percent for the EBIT method and 30 percent for the NOI method. To reflect the higher equity market uncertainty, the cost of capital is raised from 10 to 11 percent. The resulting market price is about $75 per share by each method, which approximates the Lilly equity price per share in late January 1988.

SENSITIVITY ANALYSIS

We observe that valuations are highly sensitive to the key input parameters. Valuation results are particularly sensitive to the profitability rate and the investment rate along with the applicable cost of capital. Small changes in any of these produce a substantial change in the resulting value of the firm.

In the next four tables, we present a sensitivity analysis of the value of Lilly based on variations in the key input parameters, using the EBIT method. In Table 7.13, we vary the cost of capital, k, around the range of 10 percent, our base estimate. The indicated value is highly sensitive to changes in the cost of capital.

TABLE 7.13
Effect on Valuation of Varying the Cost of Capital

VALUATION PARAMETERS	BASE CASE	$k = .08$	$k = .09$	$k = .11$	$k = .12$
X_0 = EBIT	$946	$946	$946	$946	$946
T = Tax rate	.34	.34	.34	.34	.34
b = Investment rate	.50	.50	.50	.50	.50
r = Profit rate	.24	.24	.24	.24	.24
g = Growth rate	.12	.12	.12	.12	.12
N = Growth period	10	10	10	10	10
k = Cost of capital	.10	.08	.09	.11	.12
Results:					
First term	$3,452	$ 3,834	$ 3,636	$3,281	$3,122
Second term	8,373	12,575	10,194	6,954	5,827
Value of firm	$11,825	$16,409	$13,829	$10,234	$8,949
Less total debt	626	626	626	626	626
Value of equity	$11,199	$15,783	$13,203	$ 9,608	$8,323
Number of shares	140	140	140	140	140
Value per share	$79.99	$112.73	$94.31	$68.63	$59.45

TABLE 7.14

Effects of Expected Profitability Rate on Valuation

VALUATION PARAMETERS	BASE CASE	$r = .18$ $g = .09$	$r = .20$ $g = .10$	$r = .22$ $g = .11$	$r = .26$ $g = .13$	$r = .28$ $g = .14$
X_0 = EBIT	$946	$946	$946	$946	$946	$946
T = Tax rate	.34	.34	.34	.34	.34	.34
b = Investment rate	.50	.50	.50	.50	.50	.50
r = Profit rate	.24	.18	.20	.22	.26	.28
g = Growth rate	.12	.09	.10	.11	.13	.14
N = Growth period	10	10	10	10	10	10
k = Cost of capital	.10	.10	.10	.10	.10	.10
Results:						
First term	$3,452	$2,970	$3,122	$3,282	$3,631	$ 3,819
Second term	8,373	6,212	6,868	7,587	9,234	10,173
Value of firm	$11,825	$9,181	$9,990	$10,869	$12,864	$13,993
Less total debt	626	626	626	626	626	626
Value of equity	$11,199	$8,555	$9,364	$10,243	$12,238	$13,367
Number of shares	140	140	140	140	140	140
Value per share	$79.99	$61.11	$66.88	$73.16	$87.42	$95.48

Starting at a cost of capital of 12 percent, a one percentage point decrease, increases the indicated value of the common stock of Lilly by about $10. As the indicated cost of capital reaches the 9 percent level, a further one percentage point decline results in an increase in price of $19. Thus, a powerful effect can be induced by changes in the cost of capital.

In Table 7.14, the indicated profitability rate of Lilly is changed. Here we have to remember that the growth rate is br or investment requirements times the profit rate. We do not change b, the investment rate. So as we increase r, the profitability rate, corresponding increases in g also occur. Here we assume that r increases due to improved performance such as more good products. If so, the effect of the rising r is to increase the value of equity per share.

In Table 7.15, the investment rate is changed. The issue is raised, what will be the effect on r, the profitability rate. If investment increases because the investment hurdle rate is lowered, r will also decline. But if r is greater than k, more investment will increase value. A rising b will then increase the value of the firm, with a stronger effect as b rises above the base case of .5.

Value is also sensitive to the number of years of supernormal growth and to income tax rates, as shown in Table 7.16. These also have very powerful effects in directions that are predictable.

TABLE 7.15
Effects of Expected Investment Rate on Valuation

VALUATION PARAMETERS	BASE CASE	b = .30 g = .07	b = .40 g = .10	b = .60 g = .14	b = .70 g = .17
X_0 = EBIT	$946	$946	$946	$946	$946
T = Tax rate	.34	.34	.34	.34	.34
b = Investment rate	.50	.30	.40	.60	.70
r = Profit rate	.24	.24	.24	.24	.24
g = Growth rate	.12	.07	.10	.14	.17
N = Growth period	10	10	10	10	10
k = Cost of capital	.10	.10	.10	.10	.10
Results:					
First term	$3,452	$3,803	$3,672	$ 3,118	$ 2,644
Second term	8,373	5,172	6,598	10,573	13,286
Value of firm	$11,825	$8,975	$10,270	$13,691	$15,930
Less total debt	626	626	626	626	626
Value of equity	$11,199	$8,349	$ 9,644	$13,065	$15,304
Number of shares	140	140	140	140	140
Value per share	$79.99	$59.64	$68.89	$93.32	$109.31

TABLE 7.16
Effects of Planning Horizon and Expected Tax Rate on Valuation

VALUATION PARAMETERS	BASE CASE	N = 5	N = 15	T = .3	T = .4
X_0 = EBIT	$946	$946	$946	$946	$946
T = Tax rate	.34	.34	.34	.30	.40
b = Investment rate	.50	.50	.50	.50	.50
r = Profit rate	.24	.24	.24	.24	.24
g = Growth rate	.12	.12	.12	.12	.12
N = Growth period	10	5	15	10	10
k = Cost of capital	.10	.10	.10	.10	.10
Results:					
First term	$3,452	$1,648	$5,425	$3,661	$3,138
Second term	8,373	7,652	9,163	8,881	7,612
Value of firm	$11,825	$9,300	$14,588	$12,542	$10,750
Less total debt	626	626	626	626	626
Value of equity	$11,199	$8,674	$13,962	$11,916	$10,124
Number of shares	140	140	140	140	140
Value per share	$79.99	$61.96	$99.73	$85.11	$72.32

CONCLUSIONS

The evidence of the sensitivity of valuation to the key input parameters has both negative and positive implications. On the negative side it indicates how subjective valuations can be. Slight changes in estimates of the key input parameters result in wide fluctuations in estimated values. Thus, arriving at valuations is an art requiring much judgment. It is not an objective procedure.

Nevertheless, this provides a basis for insights as well. A useful analysis is to start with the current market price of the common stock of a company. Using the basic valuation models presented, we can determine the key input valuation factors required to produce such values. Having determined the combination of input valuation factors that would be consistent with the observed market price of the stock, we can raise questions whether the required levels of the key input valuation parameters can plausibly be achieved by the company.

One possibility is that the analyst concludes that the levels of the input parameters are not plausible to support current market values. The conclusion would follow that the stock was overvalued. Alternatively, the analysis might pose challenging targets for the company to work toward accomplishing.

Thus, on the positive side our analysis shows that valuation is highly sensitive to the performance of the firm. The key valuation parameters can provide a very powerful set of instruments for general and financial strategic planning by the firm. Making even a slight improvement in any of the key inputs can yield very substantial increases in the value of the firm. These improvements in the value of the firm can benefit greatly not only the shareholders but the other stakeholders of the firm including customers, employees, government, and various elements in the distribution process. Particularly in the pharmaceutical industry improved performance which in turn reflects and stimulates the development of further advances in pharmaceutical products is of great benefit to customers and society as a whole.

QUESTIONS

1. What is the difference between the EBIT and NOI methods of measuring the change in total resources (investment)? Does it matter?
2. Discuss the four methods of calculating the cost of equity capital and how they are used in the valuation model.
3. What are three methods of calculating the weighted average cost of capital?
4. The Smith Company has free cash flows (X) of $19 million, and is expected to grow at a rate of 26.5 percent for the next five years. Its ratio of investment to after-tax NOI (b) is 0.5. The applicable tax rate is 30 percent; Smith's cost

of capital is 10 percent. After the period of supernormal growth, Smith Company is not expected to grow any further.
   a. What is the value of Smith Company?
   b. What is the implied profitability rate (r)?
   c. If Smith has $110 in interest-bearing debt, what is the value of Smith's equity?

5. The Jones Company has the same parameters as the Smith Company in question 4, except that its investment rate (b) is 1.0, and its profit rate is 26.5 percent.
   a. What is the value of Jones Company?
   b. If Jones Company has $68 million in interest-bearing debt, what is the value of Jones's equity?

6. Given the following information on the Paul Company and the Rick Company, as well as the Smith and Jones Companies, use the investment banker comparables method to value the equity of Smith and Jones. All four firms are roughly similar in size and have similar product-market mix characteristics. In performing the comparables analysis, use the following ratios:
   a. Market to book value
   b. Market to replacement cost
   c. Market to sales
   d. Price to earnings (P/E)
   e. Market to after-tax EBIT   [EBIT $(1 - T)$]

	PAUL CO.	RICK CO.	SMITH CO.	JONES CO.
Revenues	$600	$400	$500	$400
EBDIT	40	40	33	40
Depreciation	6	8	7	13
EBIT	34	32	26	27
Interest expense	10	10	8	8
EBT	24	22	18	19
Current taxes	7	6	5	6
Net income	17	16	13	13
Current ratio	2/1	2/1	2/1	2/1
Interest-bearing debt/NW	50%	50%	55%	45%
Fixed-charge coverage	3X	3X	3X	3X
Revenue growth	25%	30%	24%	31%
EBIT growth	30%	30%	26.5%	26.5%
Net income growth	30%	30%	28%	28%
Marginal free cash flow to total investment capital, net (r)	50%	25%	53%	26.5%
Marginal investment requirements to free cash flow, net (b)	0.6	1.2	0.5	1.0
Market value	$400	$350		
Book value	300	200	150	100
Replacement cost	500	400	300	300

CHAPTER **8**

Theories of Mergers and Tender Offers

Redeployment of corporate assets is accomplished through many forms—mergers, tender offers, joint ventures, divestitures, and spin-offs. *Reverse mergers,* which refer to divestitures and spin-offs, represent to some degree a mirror image of the combining of assets. Thus, we will mainly consider the explanations for mergers, tender offers, and joint ventures and then take up reverse mergers in later chapters. The explanations are summarized in Table 8.1.

EFFICIENCY THEORIES

These theories hold that mergers and other forms of asset redeployment have potential for social benefits. They generally involve improving the performance of incumbent management or achieving a form of synergy. Unfortunately, during the heyday of the conglomerate merger activities of the late 1960s, exaggerated claims were made for synergy which came to be referred to as the "2 + 2 = 5" effect. But, while the claims for synergy achieved through asset redeployment were exaggerated, there is a solid basis for achieving positive net present value investments by recombining the activities of business operations.

Most or all of the efficiency theories have been incorporated in the model of conglomerate mergers in Chapter 3. However, we now present each of these theories separately in order to clearly differentiate them, and because each by itself may explain certain classes of mergers.

TABLE 8.1
Theories of Mergers and Tender Offers

I. Efficiency theories
    A. Differential managerial efficiency
    B. Inefficient management
    C. Operating synergy
    D. Pure diversification
    E. Strategic realignment to changing environments
    F. Undervaluation
II. Information and signaling
III. Agency problems and managerialism
IV. Free cash flow hypothesis
V. Market power
VI. Taxes
VII. Redistribution

Differential Efficiency

The most general theory of mergers that can be formulated involves differential efficiency. In everyday language, if the management of firm A is more efficient than the management of firm B and if after firm A acquires firm B, the efficiency of firm B is brought up to the level of efficiency of firm A, efficiency is increased by merger. Note that this would be a social gain as well as a private gain. The level of efficiency in the economy would be raised by such mergers.

One difficulty in the differential efficiency theory is that if carried to its extreme, it would result in only one firm in the economy, indeed in the world—the firm with the greatest managerial efficiency. Clearly, problems of coordination in the firm or of managerial capacity limit would arise before that result was reached.

The theory suggests that there are firms with below average efficiency or that are not operating up to their potential, however defined. It is further suggested that firms operating in similar kinds of business activity would be most likely to be the potential acquirers. They would have the background for detecting below-average or less-than-full-potential performance and have the managerial know-how for improving the performance of the acquired firm. The latter scenario is plausible, but in practice the acquiring firms may be overoptimistic in their judgments of their impact on the performance of the acquired firms. As a consequence, they may either pay too much for the acquired firm or fail to improve its performance to the degree reflected in the acquisition value placed upon it.

The differential efficiency explanation can be formulated more vigorously and may be called a *managerial synergy* hypothesis. If a firm has an efficient management team whose capacity is in excess of its current managerial input demand, the firm may be able to utilize the extra managerial resources by acquiring a firm that is inefficiently managed due to shortages of such resources. This hypothesis involves some theoretical assumptions.

For the acquiring firm with excess managerial resources, a merger will not be necessary if it can simply release its excess resources. However, if a management is efficient as a team and is subject to indivisibilities or economies of scale, the disemployment of excess resources will not be feasible. Given this condition and assuming that capacity expansion in its own industry is not possible due to industry demand conditions, the acquiring firm could still utilize its excess managerial capacity by making de novo entry into the acquired firm industry. But de novo entry by the acquiring firm may not be profitable (or competitive) if the firm does not possess technological learning-by-doing (or nonmanagerial organization capital) specific to the acquired firm industry. Thus, this firm will attempt a "toehold entry" through acquisition of an incumbent firm with the requisite organization capital, thereby utilizing its excess managerial capabilities.

The inefficiently managed or underperforming firm could improve its managerial performance by employing additional managerial input through direct employment of managers or contracting with outside managers. Direct employment of managers may be inadequate, since it does not guarantee the organization of an efficient management team within a relevant period of time. The contracting solution will not in general be adopted since management of a firm requires investment in firm-specific knowledge and the anticipated appropriation by the firm of the quasi-rents accruing to this firm-specific asset will lead to the "ownership" of the management by the firm.[1] Further, if efficient management requires a critical mass of managerial talents, its attainment by the smaller, underperforming firm may not be feasible.

Under the conditions just described, a merger between the two firms will be synergistic since it combines the nonmanagerial organization capital of the acquired firm with the excess managerial resources of the acquiring firm.

Inefficient Management

The inefficient-management theory may be difficult to distinguish from the differential efficiency theory previously discussed or the following agency problem theory. In one sense, inefficient management is simply not performing up to its potential. Another control group might be able to manage the assets of this area of activity more effectively. Or inefficient management may simply represent management that is inept in an absolute sense. Almost anyone could do better. If so, this would provide a rationale for conglomerate mergers. In the differential efficiency (or managerial synergy) theory, the acquiring firm's management seeks to complement the management of the acquired firm and has experience in the particular line of business activity of the acquired firm. Thus, the differential

---

[1] This argument is borrowed from the theory of vertical integration by Williamson (1975) and Klein, Crawford, and Alchian (1978).

efficiency theory is more likely to be a basis for horizontal mergers. In contrast, the inefficient management theory could be a basis even for mergers between firms with unrelated businesses.

Several observations can be made on the theory. First, the theory assumes that owners (or shareholders) of acquired firms are unable to replace their own managers, and thus it is necessary to invoke costly mergers to replace inefficient managers. In advancing his thesis of efficient managerial labor market, Fama (1980, p. 295) cast doubt on the theory:

> . . . Manne's (1965, 1967) approach, in which the control of management relies primarily on the expensive mechanism of an outside takeover, offers little comfort. The viability of the large corporation with diffuse security ownership is better explained in terms of a model where the primary disciplining of managers comes through managerial labor markets, both within and outside of the firm, with assistance from the panoply of internal and external monitoring devices that evolve to stimulate the ongoing efficiency of the corporate form, and with the market for outside takeovers providing discipline of last resort.

It does not seem convincing that merger activity in general is a result of invoking the disciplinary means of last resort. It should be noted that Manne (1965), as an original inspirer of this theory, suggested that mergers for corporate control will principally be of the horizontal and vertical types in which the acquiring firm's management is familiar with the environment of the acquired firm's activities. Proponents of the theory may argue that mergers do not imply the inability of the owners to replace their inefficient managers but the scarcity of able managers in the market. They may continue that mergers with other firms can provide the necessary supply of managerial capabilities. If so, then the theory becomes almost indistinguishable from the differential efficiency theory.

Second, if the replacement of incompetent managers were the sole motive for mergers, it should be sufficient to operate the acquired firm as a subsidiary rather than to merge it into the acquirer. We should frequently observe the undoing of the merger after the inefficient management had been replaced, if merged operation involved costs but no benefits. However, this does not seem to be true for the majority of mergers.

Third, one clear prediction made by the theory is that the managers of the acquiring firm will be replaced after the merger. Empirical evidence suggests that this is not the case at least in conglomerate mergers. Based on his dissertation study of 28 conglomerate firms, Lynch (1971) concludes that these firms tried to acquire companies with capable managements that could be retained. Similarly, Markham (1973, pp. 85–86) finds from his survey of 30 large acquisitions by conglomerate firms that in only 16 percent of the acquisitions were two or more members of top management replaced, and in 60 percent of the cases all top managers were retained. (The rest, or 24 percent of those surveyed, did not respond to the question.) These results are in accord with the expectation that a firm making multiple acquisitions in a relatively short period of time would face difficulties in managing the acquired firms efficiently if it used its own premerger managerial resources only or if it employed new managers after displacing the acquired firms' managers. Thus, if the replacement of inefficient managers had been the main motive, acquisitions could not have been concentrated on a few multiple-acquiring firms, and probably we could not have seen such a rapid rise in conglomerate firms as in the 1960s.

In view of the preceding discussion, it is difficult to accept the inefficient management hypothesis as a general explanation of mergers, although it may seem evident that some mergers or tender offers occur to displace less able incumbent managers.

Operating Synergy

Operating synergy or operating economies may be achieved in horizontal, vertical, and even in conglomerate mergers. The theory based on operating synergy assumes that economies of scale do exist in the industry and that prior to the merger, the firms are operating at levels of activity that fall short of achieving the potentials for economies of scale.

Economies of scale arise because of indivisibilities, such as people, equipment, and overhead, which provide increasing returns if spread over a large number of units of output. Thus, in manufacturing operations, heavy investments in plant and equipment typically produce such economies. For example, costly machinery such as the large presses used to produce automobile bodies requires optimal utilization. The research and development departments of chemical and pharmaceutical companies often must have a large staff of highly competent scientists who, if given the opportunity, could develop and oversee a larger number of product areas. In marketing, having one organization cover the entire United States may yield economies of scale because of the increase in the ratio of calling-on-customer time to traveling time, which in turn is due to the higher density of customers who can be called on by the same number of salespeople.

One potential problem in merging firms with existing organizations is the question of how to combine and coordinate the good parts of the organizations and eliminate what is not required. Often the merger announcement will say that firm A is strong in research and development but weak in marketing, while firm B is strong in marketing but weak in research and development, and the two firms combined will complement each other. Analytically, this implies underutilization of some existing factors and inadequate investment in other factors of production. (Since the economies are jointly achieved, the assignment of the contributions of each firm to the merger is difficult both in theory and in practice.)

Managerial economies in production, research, marketing, or finance are sometimes referred to as economies in the specific management functions. It has also been suggested that economies may be achieved in generic management activity such as the planning and control functions of the firm. It is argued that firms of even moderate size need at least a minimum number of corporate officers. The corporate staff with capabilities for planning and control is therefore assumed to be underutilized to some degree. Acquisitions of firms just approaching the size where they need to add corporate staff would provide for fuller utilization of the corporate staff of the acquiring firm and avoid the necessity of adding such staff for the other firm.

Another area in which operating economies may be achieved is in vertical integration. Combining firms at different stages of an industry may achieve more efficient coordination of the different levels. The argument here is that costs of communication and various forms of bargaining can be avoided by vertical integration (Williamson, 1975; Arrow, 1975; Klein, Crawford, and Alchian, 1978).[2]

Pure Diversification

Diversification per se may have value for many reasons, including demand for diversification by managers and other employees, preservation of organizational and reputational capital, and financial and tax advantages.

First, in contrast to the position of shareholders who can diversify across firms in the capital market, employees of the firm have only a limited opportunity to diversify their labor income sources. In general, employees need to make firm-specific investments. Most of their knowledge acquired while working for the firm may be valuable to the firm but not to others. Typically employees are more productive in their current job than in other firms because of their specialized knowledge. They are compensated for these firm-specific investments. Thus, they value stability in their job and greater opportunity to acquire specialized knowledge and to get higher pay. This latter opportunity normally comes with promotion in the firm. Diversification of the firm can provide managers and other employees with job security and opportunities for promotion and, other things being equal, results in lower labor costs.

This diversification argument also applies to an owner-manager whose wealth is concentrated in his or her firm. The owner-manager may not want to sell ownership shares in the firm for reasons of corporate control. An undiversified owner will require a higher risk premium in investments and make smaller investments than otherwise optimal (Fama and Jensen, 1985). Thus, diversification at the firm level (that is, diversification of the firm itself) is valuable for such an owner-manager or, in general, for shareholders who hold a controlling interest and are undiversified.

Second, in the modern theory of the firm, information on employees is accumulated within the firm over time. This information is firm specific to the extent that its transfer to outside firms or the market is not feasible or is done with noise. The information is used for efficient matching of employees and jobs or of employees themselves for a particular job. This implies that managerial and other teams are formed in the firm. When a firm is liquidated, these teams are destroyed and the value of the organization is lost. If the firm is diversified, these teams can be transferred from unprofitable business activities to growing and profitable activities. Diversification may ensure smooth and efficient transition of the firm's activities and the continuity of the teams and the organization.

Third, firms have reputational capital which customers, suppliers, and

---

[2] For more details, see Chapter 2.

employees utilize in establishing their relationships with the firm. Reputation is acquired over time through firm-specific (and thus nonsalvageable) investments in advertising, research and development, fixed assets, personnel training, organizational development, and so on. Diversification can help preserve the firm's reputational capital which will cease to exist if the firm is liquidated.

Fourth, as is discussed later with regard to financial synergy and tax effects, diversification can increase corporate debt capacity and decrease the present value of future tax liability. These effects are a result of the decrease in cash flow variability due to the merger.

Diversification can be achieved through internal growth as well as mergers. However, mergers may be preferred to the internal growth avenue to diversification under certain circumstances. The firm may simply lack internal growth opportunities for lack of requisite resources or due to potential excess capacity in the industry. Timing may be important and mergers can provide diversification more quickly. There may exist many firms in pursuit of diversification at any time.

Financial Synergy

The rapid rise of acquisitive conglomerate firms in the 1960s casts considerable doubt on the applicability of the managerial synergy hypothesis to the pure conglomerate type of merger. One reason is that managerial capacity of a firm presumably will not grow so rapidly as to allow multiple acquisitions in a few years with the purpose of extending the acquirer's managerial efficiency. Such a limitation on firm growth is obvious in discussions of organization capital and optimal growth of firms (Prescott and Visscher, 1980). Another is that while most conglomerate firms made acquisitions mainly in dissimilar operating areas, managerial synergy is more relevant in mergers between firms in similar businesses, since carry-over of managerial capabilities is easier in the latter cases or applicable only in such cases.

For empirical evidence, Markham (1973) reports that the managerial function of capital expenditure planning was in most cases relocated to the corporate headquarters after conglomerate acquisitions, whereas such relocation was not frequent for other managerial functions.

Casual observations also suggest that there should be more than managerial synergy in many mergers. For example, the mergers and acquisitions (or attempts) of large mining firms by firms in other industries in the late 1970s and early 1980s do not appear to be explainable by managerial synergy.[3] Have all

---

[3] The many mining industry acquisitions or such attempts include the bid for St. Joe Minerals Corporation by Seagram Company and the subsequent acquisition of the former by Fluor Corporation; the acquisition of the Kennecott Corporation by Standard Oil Company (Ohio); the bid for Amax, Inc., by Standard Oil Company of California. It is said that Phelps Dodge Corporation and Newmont Mining Corporation have been on the "takeover list" (*The Wall Street Journal*, March 13, 1981). It has been also conjectured in the press that the real interest of Seagram in bidding for Conoco was in the coal reserves of the latter.

these mining firms been managed inefficiently? The only "well-known" characteristics of the mining (especially coal) industry are that its profitability has been depressed for a substantial period for one reason or another and that its demand is expected to increase faster than before. Another casual example is provided by the acquisitions of the largest firms in the cable TV industry since 1978.[4] Have these acquired firms been managed less efficiently? Again, the obvious characteristics of this industry are that it is highly capital intensive and that its demand growth prospect has been rediscovered in the capital market during the last years of the 1970s.

Paralleling the increases in pure conglomerate mergers, there have appeared a number of financial theoretical propositions on conglomerate mergers in the relevant literature. The potentially most important proposition is based on the distinction between internal and external funds. The nontrivial transactions costs associated with raising capital externally and the differential tax treatment of dividends may constitute the condition for more efficient allocation of capital through mergers from low to high marginal returns production activities and provide a rationale for the existence of conglomerate firms (Weston, 1970; Williamson, 1970, pp. 142–145). Williamson (p. 143) elaborates on this point.

> If . . . an earnings retention bias exists, and since assigning cash flows to their sources constitutes what may often be a serious investment restraint, the economy organized along conglomerate lines might well enjoy an advantage over the specialized firm economy. The earmarking of funds in the latter would result in what would frequently be delayed responses to market signals and otherwise arbitrary allocations of investment. In the conglomerate firm economy, by contrast, cash flows, from whatever source, are not automatically retained by the sectors from which these funds originate but are (ideally) assigned on the basis of prospective yields instead. The conglomerate acts in this respect as a miniature capital market; it internalizes the funds metering function normally imputed to the capital market—a function which Baumol's (1965) analysis of the traditional mechanisms found to be defective.

Previous empirical findings appear to support this internal funds effect. Nielsen and Melicher (1973) find that the rate of premium paid to the acquired firm as an approximation to the merger gain is greater when the cash flow rate of the acquiring firm is greater and that of the acquired firm is smaller. This implies that there is redeployment of capital from the acquiring to the acquired firm's industry. The investment literature also indicates that internal cash flows affect at least the rate of investment of firms.[5] Thus, if unexpected investment opportunities in growing industries are captured *sequentially* by competing firms, it is plausible that the total investment made by a firm in such an industry will be

---

[4] Time, Inc., acquired American Television and Communications Corporation in 1978. American Express Company bought a 50 percent interest in Warner Communications' cable TV division in 1979. And Westinghouse acquired Teleprompter Corporation in 1980. Some of these mergers may involve aspects of vertical mergers, although they appear to be predominantly pure conglomerate mergers.

[5] See the theoretical exposition and review of the literature by Nickell (1978), Chapters 8, 9, 11 and 12.

related to the magnitude of internal funds. This argument is consistent with the theory emphasized by Duesenberry (1958, pp. 87–112).

Another widely discussed proposition is that the debt capacity of the combined firm can be greater than the sum of the two firms' capacities before their merger, and this provides tax savings on investment income. There now exists a considerable body of empirical literature which documents significant post-merger increases in leverage.[6] Still another possible dimension is economies of scale in flotation and transaction costs of securities.

The financial synergy proposition is consistent with the empirical evidence reported by Markham (1973, pp. 88–89). In his sample of 30 large acquisitions, new capital outlays for the acquired companies' operations in the three-year period following acquisitions averaged 220 percent of the premerger outlays for the same time span. This evidence suggests that investment opportunities are improved.

Strategic Realignment to Changing Environments

One part of the literature on long-range strategic planning is devoted to diversification through mergers. Strategic planning is concerned with the firm's environments and constituencies, not just operating decisions. The strategic planning approach to mergers implies either the possibilities of economies of scale or tapping an underused capacity in the firm's present managerial capabilities.

Another rationale is that by external diversification the firm acquires management skills for needed augmentation of its present capabilities. This still leaves some questions unanswered. After all, new capabilities and new markets could be developed internally. But it may be that timing is important in capturing growth opportunities. The speed of adjustment through merger would be quicker than internal development. There may be opportunities to realize synergies in managerial capabilities. On the other hand, a competitive market for acquisitions implies that the net present value from merger and acquisition investments is likely to be small. Nonetheless, if these investments exploit synergy opportunities and can be used as a base for still additional investments with positive net present values, the strategy may succeed.

Undervaluation

Some studies attribute merger motives to the undervaluation of target companies. One cause of undervaluation may be that management is not operating the company up to its potential. This is then an aspect of the inefficient management theory. A second possibility is that the acquirers have inside information. How they acquired this special information may vary with circumstances, but if the

---

[6] Results of tests of the "increased debt capacity" hypothesis are found in Chapter 10.

bidders possess information which the general market does not have, they may place a higher value on the shares than currently prevails in the market.

Another aspect of the undervaluation theory is the difference between the market value of assets and their replacement costs. One frequently discussed reason that firms stepped up acquisition programs in the late 1970s is that entry into new product market areas could be accomplished on a bargain basis. Inflation had a double-barreled impact. For various reasons supposedly including inflation, stock prices were depressed during the 1970s and did not recover until the latter part of 1982 as the level of inflation dropped and business prospects improved. The second impact of inflation was to cause current replacement costs of assets to be substantially higher than their recorded historical book values. These twin effects resulted in a decline of the q-ratio, defined as the ratio of the market value of the firm shares to the replacement costs of the assets represented by these shares.

In the late 1970s and early 1980s the q-ratio had been running between 0.5 and 0.6. If a company wished to add to capacity in producing a particular product, it could acquire the additional capacity more cheaply by buying a company that produces the product rather than building brick-and-mortar from scratch. If firm A seeks to add capacity, this activity implies that its marginal q-ratio is greater than 1. But if other firms in its industry have average q-ratios of less than 1, it is efficient for firm A to add capacity by the purchase of other firms. For example, if the q-ratio is 0.6 and if in a merger the premium paid over market value is 50 percent (which is the average figure for the late 1970s), the resulting purchase price is 0.6 times 1.5 which equals 0.9. This means that the average purchase price would still be 10 percent below the current replacement costs of the assets acquired. This potential advantage would provide a broad basis for the operation of the undervaluation theory in recent years when the q-ratio was low.

The undervaluation theory even in this account is not much different from the inefficient management or differential efficiency theory. Why would a firm add to its capacity at a time when corporate assets on average sell below their replacement costs? It must be true that the acquiring firm is more efficient than an average firm or at least than the acquired firm. Thus, the undervaluation theory cannot stand alone and requires an efficiency rationale.

INFORMATION AND SIGNALING

It has been suggested in the literature that the shares of the target firm in a tender offer experience upward revaluation even if the offer turns out to be unsuccessful (Dodd and Ruback, 1977; Bradley, 1980). A hypothesis based on this empirical observation posits that new information is generated as a result of the tender offer and the revaluation is permanent. Two forms of this information hypothesis can be distinguished. One is that the tender offer disseminates information that the target shares are undervalued and the offer prompts the market to revalue those shares. No particular action by the target firm or any others is necessary to cause the revaluation. This has been called the "sitting on a gold mine" explanation (Bradley, Desai, and Kim, 1983). The other is that the offer inspires target firm management to implement a more efficient business strategy on its own. This is the "kick in the pants" explanation. No outside input other than the offer itself is required for the upward revaluation.

An opposing view holds that the increase in share value of the target firm involved in an unsuccessful offer is due to the expectation that the target firm will subsequently be acquired by another firm. The latter would have some specialized resources to apply to the target resources. Bradley, Desai, and Kim (1983, 1988) examine the data to determine whether the information hypothesis or the latter (synergy) explanation is acceptable. According to their results, the share prices of the target firms that do not subsequently receive acquisition offers within five years of the initial unsuccessful offer fall back to their preoffer level. The share prices of those targets that receive a subsequent bid increase further. They interpret this result as indicating that the information hypothesis is not valid. A permanent revaluation of the target shares occurs when the target resources are combined with the resources of an acquiring firm, or at least when the control of the target resources is transferred to the acquiring firm. According to Bradley, Desai, and Kim, the empirical evidence is consistent with the synergy explanation. They hold that tender offer does not automatically imply that the target shares are undervalued in the market or that the target firm can improve its operation on its own.

An important variant of the information hypothesis is signaling theory. The theory of signaling states that particular actions may convey other significant forms of information. Spence (1973, 1974) originally developed the theory in connection with labor markets. His theory was that it was less expensive in terms of outlays and effort for higher-quality labor (in terms of intelligence, aptitudes, or ease of developing skills) to spend more on education and other forms of self-development than lower-quality labor. Hence, the level of education of a laborer was a signal not only of more training but of higher innate abilities as well. Lower-quality labor could not attempt to fool the market by substantial outlays for obtaining more education and training. The outlays required would be so high that they would have negative returns on their investments. This illustrates the fundamental nature of signaling in that it is advantageous for some to signal, but disadvantageous for others. Hence, using the signal conveys meaningful and correct information.

The signaling concept was used by Ross (1977) in connection with capital structure decisions. Ross describes how signaling and managerial compensation arrangements can be used to deal with information asymmetry. Ross postulates that managers-insiders have information about their own firms not possessed by outsiders. When this occurs, Ross shows that the capital structure decision is not irrelevant and an optimal capital structure may exist if (1) the nature of the firm's investment policy is signaled to the market through its capital structure decision and (2) the manager's compensation is tied to the truth or falsity of the capital structure signal.

In Ross's model a manager may not trade in the financial instruments of his own firm. This avoids the moral hazard problem as well as violation of the incentives structure that he develops. Investors use the face amount of the debt (or dividends) the manager decides to issue as a signal of the firm's probable performance. Ross analyzes two types of firms. Type A is a firm that will be successful, whereas Type B is a firm that will be unsuccessful. With reference to a critical level of debt, D^*, the market perceives the firm to be Type A if it issues debt greater than this amount and Type B if it issues debt less than this amount. In order for the management of a Type B firm to have the incentive to signal that the firm will be unsuccessful, the payoff from telling the truth must be greater than that produced by telling lies. This is achieved by assessing a substantial penalty against the manager if his or her firm experiences bankruptcy.

A signaling equilibrium is achieved if "A" managers choose debt financing levels above the critical amount and "B" managers choose debt levels below that amount. An "A" manager will have no incentive to change because the compensation system maximizes his or her return under the true signal. The "B" manager will not have an incentive to signal falsely because the penalty built into the incentive structure would reduce the compensation.

Signaling may be involved in mergers and tender offers in a number of ways. The fact that a firm has received a tender offer may signal to the market that hitherto unrecognized extra values are possessed by the firm or that future cash flow streams are likely to rise. When a bidder firm uses common stock in buying another firm, this may be taken as a signal by the target and others that the common stock of the bidder firm is overvalued ("funny money" to some degree). When business firms repurchase their shares, the market may take this as a signal that management has information that its shares are undervalued and that favorable new growth opportunities will be achieved.

AGENCY PROBLEMS AND MANAGERIALISM

In their seminal paper, Jensen and Meckling (1976) formulated the implications of agency problems. An agency problem arises when managers own only a fraction of the ownership shares of the firm. This partial ownership may cause managers to work less vigorously than otherwise and/or to consume more perquisites (luxurious offices, company cars, memberships in clubs) because the majority owners bear most of the cost. Furthermore, the argument goes, in large corporations with widely dispersed ownership, there is not sufficient incentive for individual owners to expend the substantial resources required to monitor the behavior of managers.

Agency problems arise basically because contracts between managers (decision or control agents) and owners (risk bearers) cannot be costlessly written and enforced. Resulting (agency) costs include (1) costs of structuring a set of contracts, (2) costs of monitoring and controlling the behavior of agents by principals, (3) costs of bonding to guarantee that agents will make optimal decisions or principals will be compensated for the consequences of suboptimal decisions, and (4) the residual loss, that is, the welfare loss experienced by principals, arising from the divergence between agents' decisions and decisions to maximize principals' welfare. This residual loss can arise because the costs of full enforcement of contracts exceed the benefits.

Takeovers as a Solution to Agency Problems

The agency problems may be efficiently controlled by some organizational and market mechanisms. Fama and Jensen (1983) hypothesize that, when a firm is characterized by separation of ownership and control, decision systems of the firm separate decision management (initiation and implementation) from decision control (ratification and monitoring) in order to limit the power of individual decision agents to expropriate shareholders' interests. Control functions are delegated to a board of directors by the shareholders who retain approval rights on important matters including board membership, mergers, and new stock issues.

A number of compensation arrangements and the market for managers may mitigate the agency problem (Fama, 1980). Compensation can be tied to performance through such devices as bonuses and executive stock options. Managers carry their own reputation and the labor market sets their wage levels based on performance reputation.

The stock market gives rise to an external monitoring device because stock prices summarize the implications of decisions made by managers. Low stock prices exert pressure on managers to change their behavior and to stay in line with the interests of shareholders (Fama and Jensen, 1983).

When these mechanisms are not sufficient to control agency problems, the market for takeovers provides an external control device of last resort (Manne, 1965). A takeover through a tender offer or a proxy fight enables outside managers to gain control of the decision processes of the target while circumventing existing managers and the board of directors. Manne emphasized mergers as a threat of takeover if a firm's management lagged in performance either because of inefficiency or because of agency problems.

Managerialism

In contrast to the view that mergers occur to control agency problems, some observers consider mergers as a manifestation of agency problems rather than as a solution. The managerialism explanation for conglomerate mergers was set forth most fully by Mueller (1969). Mueller hypothesizes that managers are motivated to increase the size of their firms. He assumes that the compensation to managers is a function of the size of the firm, and he argues, therefore, that managers adopt a lower investment hurdle rate. But in a study critical of earlier evidence, Lewellen and Huntsman (1970) present findings that managers' compensation is significantly correlated with the firm's profit rate, not its level of sales. Thus, the basic premise of the Mueller theory is doubtful.

As discussed earlier, agency theory suggests that when the market for managers does not solve the agency problem, the market for firms or merger activity will come into play. This theory suggests, therefore, that merger activity is a method of dealing with the agency problem. The managerialism theory argues that the agency problem is not solved, and the merger activity is a manifestation of the agency problems of inefficient, external investments by managers.

Hubris Hypothesis

Roll (1986) hypothesizes that managers commit errors of overoptimism in evaluating merger opportunities due to excessive pride, animal spirits, or hubris.

In a takeover, the bidding firm identifies a potential target firm and values its assets (stock). When the valuation turns out to be below the market price (of the stock), no offer is made. Only when the valuation exceeds the current market price, a bid is made and enters the takeover sample. If there are no synergy or other takeover gains, the mean of the valuations will be the current market price. Offers are made only when the valuation is too high. The takeover premium is a random error, a mistake made by the bidder.

Roll (1986, p. 199) poses the question: "If there were no value at all in all takeovers, why would firms make bids in the first place?" He suggests that a particular individual bidder may not learn from his or her own past errors and may be convinced that the valuation is correct. Therefore, the takeover phenomenon is a result of hubris on the part of bidders, the overbearing presumption that their valuations are right. If there are no gains in takeovers, hubris can explain why managers make bids even though past experience would suggest that bids represent positive valuation errors.

If gains exist but are small, some valuations will be below the current market price. No bids are made in these cases and, therefore, fewer negative errors will be observed than positive errors. At least part of the average observer takeover premium could still be the result of valuation error and hubris.

The hubris hypothesis assumes strong-form efficiency of markets. Stock prices reflect all (public and nonpublic) information; redeployment of productive resources cannot bring gains, and management cannot be improved through reshuffling or combinations across firms. On the other hand, the efficiency theories of takeovers are based on some form of market inefficiency. Roll claims that the hubris hypothesis thus serves the role of benchmark for comparison and is the null against which other hypotheses should be compared. Further, the hypothesis does not require conscious pursuit of self-interest by managers. Managers may have good intentions but can make mistakes in judgment.

The hubris hypothesis may have its role as the null, but as an actual explanation of merger phenomena, its basic premise has difficulty with respect to strong-form market efficiency. The modern theory of the firm suggests that firms exist because the market is not frictionless. Economies of scale arise out of indivisibilities. Managements are organized as teams based on firm-specific information on individual characteristics. Firm reputation is valuable because information is costly. Certain transaction costs lead to integration of operations. The existence of these imperfections (indivisibilities, information costs, and transaction costs) may make it inefficient to have individual productive inputs move individually and separately across firms. Takeovers and mergers may be one means of efficiently redeploying corporate resources across firms while minimizing transaction costs and preserving organizational values. Product and labor market efficiency would not automatically obtain in changing market conditions and would require reallocation of resources across economic activities. Mergers and takeovers may well represent one of the very processes to maintain or restore efficiency at the minimum cost.

THE FREE CASH FLOW HYPOTHESIS
(FCFH)

The problem of agency costs discussed in the preceding section also gives rise to the free cash flow hypothesis. Michael Jensen (1986, 1988) observes that among more than a dozen separate forces involved in takeover activity in the last decade, inadequate attention has been given to the payout of free cash flow. He considers the agency costs associated with conflicts between managers and shareholders over the payout of free cash flow to be a major cause of takeover activity. According to Jensen, shareholders and managers (who are their agents) have serious conflicts of interest over the choice of corporate strategy. Agency costs result from these conflicts of interest that can never be resolved perfectly. (The kinds of agency costs were described in the previous section.) When these costs are large, takeovers can help reduce them, according to Jensen.

Statement of the Hypothesis

Jensen argues that the payout of free cash flow can serve an important role in dealing with the conflict between managers and shareholders. Jensen defines free cash flow as cash flow in excess of the amounts required to fund all projects that have positive net present values when discounted at the applicable cost of capital. He states that such free cash flow must be paid out to shareholders if the firm is to be efficient and to maximize share price. The payout of free cash flow (FCF) reduces the amount of resources under the control of managers and thereby reduces their power. In addition, they are then more likely to be subject to monitoring by the capital markets when they seek to finance additional investments with new capital.

In addition to paying out the current amount of excess cash, Jensen considers it important that managers bond their promise to pay out future cash flows. An effective way to do this is by debt creation without retention of the proceeds of the issue. Jensen argues that by issuing debt in exchange for stock, for example, managers bond their promise to pay out future cash flows more effectively than any announced dividend policy could achieve. Jensen emphasizes that the control function of debt is most important in organizations that generate large cash flows, but whose outlook involves low growth or an actual reduction in size.

He recognizes that increased leverage involves costs. It increases the risks of bankruptcy costs. There are agency costs of debt as well. One is for the firm to take on highly risky projects which benefit shareholders at the expense of bondholders. He defines an optimal debt/equity ratio where the marginal costs of debt equal the marginal benefits of debt.

Evidence on the FCFH

For evidence Jensen begins with a review of a wide range of financial transactions. He cites an earlier study by Smith (1986a, 1986b) of 20 studies of stock price changes at announcements of transactions that involve a change of capital structure or dividend behavior. In a preliminary to a review of the evidence, he restates the prediction of the FCFH. For firms with positive FCF, stock prices will increase with unexpected increases in payouts and decrease with unexpected decreases in payouts to shareholders. The hypothesis predicts further that increasing tightness of the constraints requiring the payout of future FCF will behave in a similar fashion.

Jensen considers eight types of financial transactions. He argues that in virtually all of the 32 cases he summarizes, the direction of the effect on share price agrees with the predictions of the free cash flow hypothesis. We believe he claims too much. Jensen states that his predictions do not apply to firms with more profitable projects than cash flow to fund them. He states that the theory does not apply to growth firms, only to firms that should be exiting some of their activities. But the studies to which he refers are of groups of firms not identified as to whether they are firms with zero or negative free cash flow (growth firms) or firms with positive free cash flows (exit firms). Furthermore, an alternative hypothesis, the signaling hypothesis set forth by Ross (1977) yields the same predictions as the free cash flow theory and would be equally supported by the evidence. In the mainstream of the signaling literature, transactions which carry implications for increased future cash flows cause share prices to increase in value, and conversely. A more careful partitioning of the evidence is required to test the free cash flow theory versus the signaling theory since their predictions are similar.

Such an analysis was performed by Copeland and Lee (1988) in their study of exchange offers and stock swaps. This is one of the types of transactions that Jensen argued provided evidence in support of the free cash flow theory. Copeland and Lee study the expected and unexpected changes in fully diluted earnings, sales, capital expenditures, and assets per share for 59 leverage-increasing and 102 leverage-decreasing transactions involving exchange offers and stock swaps for the period 1962–1984. The leverage-increasing transactions were associated with positive future changes in earnings per share, capital expenditures per share, sales per share, and total assets per share. The opposite was true for the leverage-decreasing transactions. The pre-event insider ownership was about 21 percent for the leverage-increasing transactions and only about 9 percent for the leverage-decreasing transactions. In addition, the leverage-increasing firms were about one tenth the size of the leverage-decreasing firms. The other vital piece of information noted by Copeland and Lee (earlier pointed out by Masulis, 1980, p. 308) is that insiders do not exchange their common shares in leverage-increasing transactions. Thus, Copeland and Lee (1988, p. 13) conclude that their evidence "is consistent with the interpretation that exchange offers are really non-cash share repurchases designed to increase the concentration of ownership in small firms with good future prospects (the signaling hypothesis). . . ."

The Copeland and Lee (1988) evidence directly contradicts Jensen's free cash flow theory. The firms which exchange debt for stock to increase leverage are growth firms; but Jensen states that such firms do not need to use increased debt to bond future cash payouts because they have positive net present value projects to use their retained cash flows efficiently. The firms which engaged in leverage-decreasing activities were what Jensen calls the "exit-type" firms which the FCFH predicts should be increasing leverage. Thus, a partitioning of the sample of firms engaged in exchange offers provides evidence that is inconsistent with Jensen's FCFH, but is consistent with the signaling theory. Without more detailed analysis of the firms engaging in the many other types of dividend and capital structure transactions cited by Jensen in support of his FCFH, we cannot know whether the evidence will actually support or contradict his hypothesis.

Similarly, Jensen argues that in leveraged buy-outs the high debt ratios undertaken cause the increase in share price. But the high debt ratios in LBOs provide tax advantages and shift risks to the creditors. Also, in LBOs the executive group is provided with a large ownership stake in the company which will have substantial value if the LBO succeeds. It is possible that the incentives provided by the strong ownership stake and other characteristics of LBO situations account for the rise in value rather than the bonding effect of the high debt ratios.

Much more detailed analysis of the other financial transactions cited by Jensen in support of the free cash flow theory is required before they can be taken as evidence consistent with his theory. More detailed analysis may reveal that the evidence, as in the cases of exchange offers and LBOs, is consistent with other theories rather than with the free cash flow theory.

On a priori grounds there is a basis for skepticism of the free cash flow theory. It is implausible that the conflict of interest between managers and shareholders could not be resolved by more efficient, less risky devices than by loading a firm up with debt. For example, management compensation packages that include giving managers a stake in improving share price and, therefore, aligning their interests with shareholders, would provide stronger and more healthy incentives. If this represents dividing management compensation into multiple forms, it would not be costly to the shareholders.

Furthermore, the free cash flow theory is inconsistent with the writings of Fama and Jensen on the theory of the firm (1983, 1985). In their articles on the theory of the firm, they argue that the widespread use of large corporations with diffused ownership among a large number of relatively small shareholders takes place because it is the most efficient form of business organization for large-enterprise activity. They argue that there are advantages to this form of organization, particularly that it enables small shareholders to diversify their risks efficiently. They go on to claim that effective control is achieved by the managerial labor market, through compensation arrangements, through the board of directors, and by the threat of takeovers. If separation of ownership and control is efficient despite conflicts of interest and if mechanisms are already in place to deal with the agency problems of managers versus shareholders, the use of high debt ratios as a bonding vehicle is not necessary.

MARKET POWER

One reason often given for a merger is that it will increase a firm's market share, but it is not clear how increasing the market share will achieve economies or synergies. If increasing the firm's market share simply means that the firm will be larger, then we are essentially talking about economies of scale, which we have already discussed. Increasing market share really means increasing the size of the firm *relative* to other firms in an industry. But it is not made clear why increasing the firm's relative size will provide economies or other social gains.

Indeed, this poses a challenge to the arguments for merger emphasizing economies of scale and vertical integration. These could also be achieved by the internal expansion of the firm. Why is the external acquisition of another firm necessary to achieve these economies if indeed they do exist? A number of possible explanations may be offered such as acquiring a larger volume of operations sooner. But it is not clear whether the price required by the selling firm (the firm to be acquired) will really make the acquisition route the more economical method of expanding a firm's capacity either horizontally or vertically.

An objection that is often raised against permitting a firm to increase its market share by merger is that the result will be "undue concentration" in the industry. Indeed, public policy in the United States holds that when four or fewer firms account for 40 percent or more of the sales in a given market or line of business, an undesirable market structure or undue concentration exists. The argument in brief is that if four or fewer firms account for a substantial percentage of an industry's sales, these firms will recognize the impact of their actions and policies upon one another. This recognized interdependence will lead to a consideration of actions and reactions to changes in policy that will tend toward "tacit collusion." As a result, the prices and profits of the firms will contain monopoly elements. Thus, if economies from mergers cannot be established, it is assumed that the resulting increases in concentration may lead to monopoly returns. If economies of scale can be demonstrated, then a comparison of efficiencies versus the effects of increased concentration must be made.

In 1982 and 1984, the Department of Justice announced new merger guidelines to supersede those which had been issued in 1968. The new merger guidelines adopt the Herfindahl index (H index) which takes into consideration the market shares of all of the firms in the industry. The theory behind the use of the Herfindahl index is that if one or more firms have relatively high market shares, this is of even greater concern than the share of the largest four firms. An example presented with the announcement of the new merger guidelines illustrates this point. In one market four firms each hold a 15 percent market share and the remaining 40 percent is held by 40 firms, each with a 1 percent market share. Its H index would be:

$$H = 4(15)^2 + 40(1)^2 = 940$$

In another market one firm has a 57 percent market share and the remaining 43 percent is held by 43 firms, each with a 1 percent market share. Like the first market, the four-firm concentration ratio here would be the same 60 percent. However, the H index would be:

$$H = (57)^2 + 43(1)^2 = 3,292$$

Thus, the H index registers a concern about inequality of firms as well as the degree of concentration of industry sales. The economic basis for either concern has not been well established.

While some economists hold that high concentration, however measured, causes some degree of monopoly, other economists hold that increased concentration is generally the *result* of active and intense competition. They argue further that the intense competition continues among large firms in concentrated industries because the dimensions of decision making over prices, outputs, types of product, quality of product, service, and so on are so numerous and of so many gradations that collusion simply is not feasible. This is an area where the issues continue to be unresolved.

TAX CONSIDERATIONS

Some mergers may be motivated by tax-minimizing opportunities. Whether tax considerations induce mergers, however, depends on whether there are alternative methods of achieving equivalent tax benefits. For example, the Economic

Recovery Tax Act of 1981 provided for the "sale of tax credits" generated from the use of accelerated depreciation. Sale and lease-back arrangements of corporate assets effect this transfer of tax credits between separate corporations. These opportunities mitigate the tax incentives for merger.

Mergers for tax benefits have often been regarded as zero-sum games against the Treasury. If these mergers involved use of real resources or caused distortions in the tax system by increasing taxes on others in the economy, they would be socially undesirable. However, mergers for tax reasons may also facilitate more efficient behavior by wiping out tax losses (Auerbach and Reishus, 1986).

Taxes affect the merger process as well as merger incentives (Smirlock, Beatty, and Majd, 1986). Depending on the method of reorganization (merger) and the medium of exchange, the tax attributes of the acquired firm may be transferred to the acquiring and shareholders of the acquired may be able to defer capital gains taxes. The price paid to the shareholders of the acquired firm would have to be different (that is, larger) if they became subject to immediate capital gains taxes.

Carry-over of Net Operating Losses and Tax Credits

A firm with accumulated tax losses and tax credits can shelter the positive earnings of another firm with which it is joined. For the acquired firm to be able to inherit desirable tax attributes requires "continuity of interest." This continuity is achieved when two conditions are met. First, the majority of the target corporation should be acquired in exchange for the stock of the acquiring firm. This ensures investor continuity in which the target shareholders have an ownership interest in the merged firm. Second, the acquisition should have legitimate business purposes. This requirement is fulfilled when the target's operations are continued. This amounts to corporate continuity. When continuity of interest is established, a merger becomes a tax-free reorganization in which the target shareholders' capital gains or losses can be deferred and the target's tax attributes are inherited.[7]

Net operating losses can be carried back three years and forward fifteen years. That is, the firm may deduct its losses up to the sum of taxes paid during the past three years. Any remaining losses can be taken against future profits, up to a limit of fifteen years. If the target cannot utilize this provision now or in the near future, the present value of this provision is small. But if the losses are transferred to an acquiring firm with sufficient profits to use the carry-over now or in the near future, then the value of the carry-over is increased. Tax credits for investments and increased research and development expenditures can also be transferred when the merger meets the tests of continuity of interest.

---

[7] For details of conditions for tax-free and taxable reorganizations, see Smirlock, Beatty, and Majd (1986).

Stepped-Up Asset Basis

Transactions between corporations which involve cash and nonstock securities exceeding 50 percent of the total purchase price do not allow for continuity of interest. These are treated as taxable transactions. Following sale of its assets or stock to the buying corporation, the selling corporation distributes, within a 12-month period, all of its assets to its shareholders in complete liquidation. The shareholders of the seller are liable for the tax on any gain. The shareholders' gain (or loss) equals the difference between the fair market value of the distribution received and the adjusted basis of their stock.

The acquiring firm can increase or step-up the tax basis of the acquired firm's assets to their fair market value and take depreciation charges on this new basis. Thus, the increase in the tax basis of the acquired firm's assets results in greater cash flows and may also reduce any gains realized on a premature disposition of assets.

A factor which mitigates this tax incentive is that the selling company (and, therefore, its new parent) may pay some taxes due to the recapture of depreciation (Internal Revenue Code Sections 1245 and 1250). However, recapture is very limited in the case of structures relative to other assets such as equipment (Auerbach and Reishus, 1986). Another factor is that any excess of the purchase price paid over the fair market value of the acquired's assets is recorded as good will on the acquirer's balance sheets. Good will is amortized over a period not to exceed 40 years. This amortization is not tax deductible.

Substitution of Capital Gains for Ordinary Income

A mature firm with few internal investment opportunities can acquire a growth firm in order to substitute capital gains taxes for ordinary income taxes. The growth firm has no or a small dividend payout and requires continued capital and noncapital expenditures. The acquiring firm provides the necessary funds which otherwise would have to be paid out as dividends taxable as ordinary income. Later, the acquiring firm may sell the acquired firm to realize capital gains.

Similarly, when the growth of a firm has slowed so that earnings retention cannot be justified to the Internal Revenue Service, an incentive for sale to another firm is created. Rather than paying out future earnings as dividends subject to the ordinary personal income tax, an owner can capitalize future earnings in a sale to another firm. The buyer will be a firm which welcomes additions to its internal cash flow for investment purposes. Usually the transaction is a tax-free exchange of securities. The owner of the selling firm is not subject to taxes until he or she sells off the securities received; it will be a capital gain, and the owner can choose the time at which to recognize the gain. One often finds a small proprietor who develops an ongoing business (say, Company

A) and begins to have a significant flow of net income. His or her incentive to sell the firm is often reinforced by consideration of potential competition from other firms. The ability of Company A to earn income in the future is uncertain from the owner's standpoint. The certainty of that income flow would be increased if Company A were part of a larger firm which had the necessary full complement of management capabilities. By selling out, the owner of Company A converts a nonmarketable ownership claim to a marketable one.

Still other tax effects are associated with inheritance taxes. A closely-held firm may be sold as the owners become older because of the uncertainty of the value placed on the firm in connection with estate taxes. Or a sale may be made to provide greater liquidity for the payment of estate taxes.

Other Tax Incentives

As seen earlier, if a firm has current operating losses, its merger with another firm with current taxable profits can result in a net gain at the expense of the government. In the merger, the losses are used to reduce the taxes owed. However, Majd and Myers (1984) show that even if both firms have current profits, their merger can reduce future tax liability as the variability of cash flows is lowered following the merger. In future periods, one firm's profits will be offset or reduced by the other's losses, which results in tax savings. Thus, the present value of the combined firm's tax liability is reduced. This effect will be larger if the correlation between the two firms' cash flows is smaller. Diversification of a firm's cash flow can impact the value of the firm through this tax effect. Majd and Myers note that this is the result of asymmetric taxation by which the government shares in operating gains but does not share in operating losses. The government's tax claim is equivalent to a portfolio of call options, one on each year's operating cash flow.[8] When the firm has a gain, the government exercises its option to collect taxes. Otherwise, the government lets the option expire unexercised. It is well known in the option pricing theory that a decrease in the variability of cash flows causes a decline in the value of a call option on the cash flows.

Jones and Taggart (1984) present a life cycle model of firm ownership. When an asset (a firm) is young, its depreciation charges and other tax deductions may exceed its pretax cash flows. In this stage, the firm should be owned by high tax bracket investors in partnership form. When the firm reaches the stage in which its depreciation tax shield is small enough to leave a positive but

---

[8] Consider the cash flow of a firm in year t in the absence of tax loss carry-backs and carry-forwards:

$$C_t = Y_t - \tau \text{MAX}[Y_t - d_t, 0]$$

where C_t is the after-tax cash flow, Y_t is the pretax cash flow, d_t is the depreciation charge, and τ is the corporate tax rate. If Y_t is greater than d_t, the government exercises its option to collect taxes on the difference at the rate of τ. If Y_t is less than d_t, the government does not exercise the option. Thus, the government's tax claim is equivalent to τ European call options whose exercise price is d_t. For more detailed analysis, see Majd and Myers (1984).

small operating profit after depreciation, corporate ownership may be optimal if the corporate tax rate is lower than the rate of high tax bracket investors. The change in ownership can be accomplished by selling the firm to a corporation. When the firm becomes old, depreciation declines further and pretax cash flows increase. The firm is taxed heavily. Now the firm can be owned by investors with low tax rates such as a royalty trust. Alternatively, the firm can merge with another firm to effect a step-up in the tax basis of assets. (A part of the step-up will be taxed at ordinary income tax rates for recapture of excess depreciation.)

VALUE INCREASES BY REDISTRIBUTION?

Another theory of M&A activity encountered in the literature is that the source of the value increases in mergers is redistribution among the stakeholders of the firm. Possible shifts are from bondholders to stockholders and from labor to stockholders and/or consumers.

Most of the studies find no evidence that shareholders gain in mergers and tender offers at the expense of bondholders (Asquith and Kim, 1982; Dennis and McConnell, 1986; Kim and McConnell, 1977). Even in debt for common stock exchanges, most of the evidence indicates that there is no negative impact on bondholders even though leverage has been increased. However, in leveraged buy-outs in which debt is increased by very high orders of magnitude, there is evidence of negative impacts on bondholders (McDaniel, 1986). There is also dramatic evidence of negative effects on bondholders in individual cases and in patterns of downgrading (*The Wall Street Journal*, October 25, 1988).

To the extent that taxes are part of the explanation for mergers, redistribution is involved. As the previous section shows, taxes may play a role in motivating mergers but generally are not the major explanatory factor. To the extent that taxes perform a role, they represent redistribution from the government tax collector (really the general public) to the firm.

Redistribution from labor to shareholders has also received attention (Shleifer and Summers, 1988). The problem has been formalized by Williamson (1988). The issues can be delineated by a case example based on the TWA-Icahn study outlined by Shleifer and Summers (1988) and covered in some detail in the press. The stylized facts can be summarized as shown in Table 8.2.

The original annual salary levels of the pilots, machinists, and flight attendants are shown in column (3). When these are multiplied by the number of employees shown in column (2) we obtain the total annual wage bill shown in column (4). Column (5) is a stylized estimate of the salary cuts achieved by Icahn after he obtained control of TWA. They represent the percentage rate reductions in the annual compensation rates shown in column (3). Applying the rate reductions to the total annual wage bill yields the annual savings shown in column (6). The total annual savings appear to be roughly $200 million per year. The gains from the savings are shown in Table 8.3.

TABLE 8.2
Labor Cost Savings in the TWA Takeover
(M = $ Million)

(1) CATEGORY	(2) NUMBER OF EMPLOYEES	(3) ANNUAL WAGE RATES	(4) TOTAL ANNUAL WAGE BILL	(5) RATE REDUCTIONS	(6) ANNUAL SAVINGS
Pilots	3,000 @	$90,000 =	$270M	33%	$ 90M
Machinists	9,000 @	38,000 =	342M	15%	50M
Flight Attendants	6,000 @	35,000 =	210M	28.5%	60M
				Total Savings	$200M

Before the takeover, TWA had 33 million shares of common stock outstanding, whose market price was $8 per share giving a total market value of $264 million. The final block of shares obtained in the takeover were priced at $24. The gains to the participants can, therefore, be calculated. For the roughly 6.5 million shares Icahn purchased at an average price of $12, his gain would be the difference between $24 and $12, or $12 per share. For the 6.5 million shares Ichan purchased at $18, his gain would be $6 per share. The total gains to Icahn would, therefore, be $117 million. Similarly, the gains to the original shareholders are shown in column (3). The gains per share represent the difference between the $8 price and the Icahn purchase price. The gains to the original shareholders total $411 million. When these gains are added to the original value of the company, we obtain a total value for TWA after the takeover of $792 million.

TABLE 8.3
Gain from Savings
(M = $ Million)

(1) ICAHN PURCHASES	(2) GAINS TO ICAHN	(3) TO ORIGINAL SHAREHOLDERS
6.5 @ $12	$12 × 6.5 = $ 78M	$ 4 × 6.5 = $ 26M
6.5 @ 18	6 × 6.5 = 39M	10 × 6.5 = 65M
20.0 @ 24	0M	16 × 20 = 320M
	$117M	$411M
		117M
Total		$528M
	Original Value	264M
	Total Value	$792M

TABLE 8.4
Alternative Sources of Increases in Value

LABOR COSTS	PRODUCT MARKET	PRODUCT QUALITY
Union power	Regulated	Down
Firm-specific productivity	Monopoly	Same
Management inefficiency	Competitive	Up

Now the issue of redistribution and the possible sources of the gain are considered. A number of variables are involved. These are set forth in Table 8.4. The labor costs that were subsequently reduced could have reflected union power, the firm-specific productivity of the employees, or a form of management inefficiency. Another set of variables which influences the interpretation of the case is whether the product markets in which airline services were being sold were competitive, monopolized, or operated under government regulation. A third set of variables to consider is whether, as a consequence of the takeover, the quality of the product-services sold went down, up, or remained the same.

In their analysis of the case, Shleifer and Summers (1988) give emphasis to the interpretation that the high labor costs may have reflected the firm-specific productivity developed by the employees. With deregulation, new airline entrants hired employees at much lower rates than unionized airlines such as TWA were paying. But if the unionized employees at TWA were more efficient because of their firm-specific skills, the real cost of labor would not necessarily be any higher in TWA than in its nonunionized rivals. Under this scenario, Shleifer and Summers observed that a breach of trust is involved. This says that as a consequence of the takeover, investments made by employees to develop firm-specific skills are not paid their full value when previous labor contracts are broken by the new control group. If breach of trust is involved, then employees will take this into account in writing contracts in the future. It will affect their supply price. The consequence would be that labor costs in the airline industry would rise and prices to airline passengers and other users would be increased in the long run.

Another possible scenario is that the higher union wages at TWA reflect the previous period of regulation. One theory holds that in a regulated industry, employees whether unionized or not are able to extract wage increases. It is argued that either management will be soft on wage demands or that the pressure of regulatory bodies will cause managements to accept higher wages which, in turn, the regulator permits to be passed on in higher prices. With subsequent deregulation, the competition of new entrants with lower costs will result in lower product and service prices. The lower prices of competitors pressure firms with high-wage unionized employees to force wage reductions if they are to stay in business. To meet the lower prices of competitors requires a reduction of monopoly rents that formerly had been paid to unionized labor. Lower employee compensation rates in this scenario do not represent a breach of trust but a restoration of more competitive conditions. It could be argued that the rise in share prices then simply enables shareholders to earn competitive returns on their investments. Consumers benefit from the lower competitive prices. The degree of the benefit to consumers and the extent to which the returns to shareholders are competitive, depend on whether full competitive conditions are achieved in the airline industry. There appear to be some elements of regulation and supply restriction in space allocations at airport terminals. This would prevent the full realization of the competitive assumptions of the present scenario.

Still a third scenario in addition to the "breach of trust" and the "end of regulation" theories is the management inefficiency explanation. In this scenario the problem is that one of the manifestations of managerial inefficiency is the failure to bargain effectively with labor. The new competition with deregulation stimulates takeovers to provide new and efficient management. If the new management efficiencies include bargaining employee compensation down to competitive levels, shareholders should earn competitive rates of return and prices to consumers should be reduced to competitive levels. The price reductions might be expressed to some degree in the form of improved product quality.

Thus, whether the value increases associated with mergers and takeovers represent redistribution, particularly from labor, depends on which scenario is correct. If union power is reflected in monopoly rents to employees, then the employee cost reductions do not represent a breach of trust. They represent a movement from monopoly elements to competitive elements in the industry. If management inefficiency is involved, the introduction of efficient managers moves the industry from inefficiency to efficiency gains. Thus whether breach of contract or other forms of expropriation are involved depends on the facts of individual industry circumstances. In this connection, Carl Icahn broke off negotiations for TWA to acquire Eastern Airlines from Texas Air when he failed in his efforts to obtain wage and work-rule concessions from Eastern's pilots, machinists, and flight attendants (Valente and O'Brian, 1988, p. A6).

SUMMARY

Many theories have been advanced to explain why mergers and other forms of restructuring take place. Efficiency theories imply social gains from M&A activity in addition to the gains for participants. The *differential efficiency* theory says that more efficient firms will acquire less efficient firms and realize gains by improving their efficiency; this implies excess managerial capabilities in the acquiring firm. Differential efficiency would be most likely to be a factor in mergers between firms in related industries where the need for improvement could be more easily identified. The related *inefficient management* theory suggests that target management is so inept that virtually any management could do better, and thus could be an explanation for mergers between firms in unrelated industries. The theory's main limitation is its implication that agency costs are so high that shareholders have no way to discipline managers short of costly merger.

The *operating synergy* theory postulates economies of scale or of scope and that mergers help achieve levels of activities at which they can be obtained. It includes the concept of complementarity of capabilities. For example, one firm might be strong in R&D but weak in marketing while another has a strong marketing department without the R&D capability. Merging the two firms would result in operating synergy. The *financial synergy* theory hypothesizes complementarities between merging firms, not in management capabilities, but in the availability of investment opportunities and internal cash flows. A firm in a declining industry will produce large cash flows since there are few attractive investment opportunities. A growth industry has more investment opportunities than cash with which to finance them. The merged firm will have a lower cost of capital due to the lower cost of internal funds as well as possible risk reduction, savings in flotation costs, and improvements in capital allocation.

Pure diversification as a theory of mergers differs from shareholder portfolio diversification. Shareholders can efficiently spread their investments and risk among industries, so there is no need for firms to diversify for the sake of their shareholders. Managers and other employees, however, are at greater risk if the single industry in which their firm operates should fail; their firm-specific human capital is not transferable. Therefore, firms may diversify to encourage firm-specific human capital investments which make their employees more valuable and productive, and to increase the probability that the organization and reputation capital of the firm will be preserved by transfer to another line of business owned by the firm in the event its initial industry declines.

The theory of *strategic alignment to changing environments* says that mergers take place in response to environmental changes. External acquisitions of needed capabilities allow firms to adapt more quickly and with less risk than developing capabilities internally.

The *undervaluation* theory states that mergers occur when the market value of target firm stock for some reason does not reflect its true or potential value or its value in the hands of an alternative management. The q-ratio is also related to the undervaluation theory. Firms can acquire assets for expansion more cheaply by buying the stock of existing firms than by buying or building the assets when the target's stock price is below the replacement cost of its assets.

Theories other than efficiency include information and signaling, agency problems and managerialism, free cash flow, market power, taxes, and redistribution. The *information or signaling* theory attempts to explain why target shares seem to be permanently revalued upward in a tender offer whether or not it is successful. The information hypothesis says that the tender offer sends a signal to the market that the target shares are undervalued, or alternatively, the offer signals information to target management which inspires them to implement a more efficient strategy on their own. Another school holds that the revaluation is not really permanent, but only reflects the likelihood that another acquirer will materialize for a synergistic combination. Other aspects of takeovers may also be interpreted as signals of value, including the means of payment and target management's response to the offer.

Agency problems may result from a conflict of interest between managers and shareholders or between shareholders and debt holders. A number of organization and market mechanisms serve to discipline self-serving managers, and takeovers are viewed as the discipline of last resort. *Managerialism*, on the other hand, views takeovers as a manifestation of the agency problem rather than its solution. It suggests that self-serving managers make ill-conceived combinations solely to increase firm size and their own compensation. The hubris theory is another variant on the agency cost theory; it implies acquiring firm managers commit errors of overoptimism (winner's curse) in bidding for targets.

Jensen's *free cash flow* hypothesis says that takeovers take place because of the conflicts between managers and shareholders over the payout of free cash flows. The hypothesis posits that free cash flows (that is, in excess of investment needs) should be paid out to shareholders, reducing the power of management and subjecting managers to the scrutiny of the public capital markets more frequently. Debt-for-stock exchange offers are viewed as a means of bonding the managers' promise to pay out future cash flows to shareholders.

Market power advocates claim that merger gains are the result of increased concentration leading to collusion and monopoly effects. Empirical evidence on whether industry concentration causes reduced competition is not conclusive. There is much evidence that concentration is the result of vigorous and continuing competition which causes the composition of the leading firms to change over time.

Tax effects can be important in mergers, although they do not play a major role in explaining M&A activity overall. Carry-over of net operating losses and tax credits, stepped-up asset basis, and the substitution of capital gains for ordinary income (less important after the Tax Reform Act of 1986) are among the tax motivations for mergers. Looming inheritance taxes may also motivate the sale of privately-held firms with aging owners.

A final theory of the value increases to shareholders in takeovers is that the gains come at the expense of other stakeholders in the firm. Expropriated stakeholders under the *redistribution* hypothesis may include bondholders, the government (in the case of tax savings), and organized labor.

APPENDIX:
MEASUREMENT OF ABNORMAL RETURNS[9]

The first step in measuring the effect on stock value of an "event" (announcement of a tender offer, share repurchase, and so on) is to define an event period. Usually this is centered on the announcement date, which is designated day 0 in

[9] Written by Daniel Asquith with editorial assistance from James Brandon.

event time. The purpose of the event period is to capture all the effects on stock price of the event. Longer periods will make sure all the effects are captured, but the estimate is subject to more noise in the data. Many studies choose a period like days -40 to $+40$, that is from 40 days before the announcement to 40 days after the announcement. Note, day 0 is the date the announcement is made for a particular firm and will be different calendar dates for different firms.

The next step is to calculate a predicted (or normal) return, $\hat{R}_{jt}$, for each day in the event period for each firm. The predicted return represents the return that would be expected if no event took place. There are basically three methods of calculating this predicted return. These are the mean adjusted return method, the market model method, and the market adjusted return method. For most cases the three methods yield similar results. Next the residual, r_{jt}, is calculated for each day for each firm. The residual is the actual return for that day for the firm minus the predicted return, $r_{jt} = R_{jt} - \hat{R}_{jt}$. The residual represents the abnormal return, that is, the part of the return that is not predicted and is therefore an estimate of the change in firm value on that day which is caused by the event. For each day in event time the residuals are averaged across firms to produce the average residual for that day, AR_t, where $AR_t = \dfrac{\sum_j r_{jt}}{N}$ and N is the number of firms in the sample. The reason for averaging across firms is that stock returns are noisy, but the noise tends to cancel out when averaged across a large number of firms. Therefore, the more firms in the sample the better the ability to distinguish the effect of an event. The final step is to cumulate the average residual for each day over the entire event period to produce the cumulative average residual, CAR, where $CAR = \sum_{t=-40}^{40} AR_t$. The cumulative average residual represents the average total effect of the event across all firms.

The Mean Adjusted Return Method

In the mean adjusted return method a "clean" period is chosen and the average daily return for the firm is estimated for this period. The clean period may be before the event period, after the event period, or both, but never includes the event period. The clean period includes days on which no information related to the event is released, for example days -240 to -41. The predicted return for a firm for each day in the event period, using the mean adjusted return method, is just the mean daily return for the clean period for the firm. That is:

$$\hat{R}_{jt} = \overline{R}_j = \frac{\sum_{t=-240}^{-41} R_{jt}}{200}$$

This predicted return is then used to calculate the residuals, average residuals, and cumulative average residual as explained above.

The Market Model Method

To use the market model a clean period is chosen and the market model is estimated by running a regression for the days in this period. The market model is:

$$R_{jt} = \alpha_j + \beta_j R_{mt} + \epsilon_{jt}$$

where R_{mt} is the return on a market index (for example, the S&P 500) for day t, β_j measures the sensitivity of firm j to the market—this is a measure of risk, α_j measures the mean return over the period not explained by the market, and ϵ_{jt} is a statistical error term $\Sigma\epsilon_{jt} = 0$. The regression produces estimates of α_j and β_j; call these $\hat{\alpha}_j$ and $\hat{\beta}_j$. The predicted return for a firm for a day in the event period is the return given by the market model on that day using these estimates. That is:

$$\hat{R}_{jt} = \hat{\alpha}_j + \hat{\beta}_j R_{mt}$$

where now R_{mt} is the return on the market index for the actual day in the event period. Since the market model takes explicit account of both the risk associated with the market and mean returns, it is the most widely used method.

The Market Adjusted Return Method

The market adjusted return method is the simplest of the methods. The predicted return for a firm for a day in the event period is just the return on the market index for that day. That is:

$$\hat{R}_{jt} = R_{mt}$$

The market adjusted return method can be thought of as an approximation to the market model where $\hat{\alpha}_j = 0$ and $\hat{\beta}_j = 1$ for all firms. Since $\hat{\alpha}_j$ is usually small and the average β_j over all firms is 1, this approximation usually produces acceptable results.

QUESTIONS

1. Briefly explain how the various efficiency theories of mergers differ and how they are alike.
2. Explain the differences between managerial synergy, operating synergy, and financial synergy and their relationships to different types of mergers.

3. How are agency problems and managerialism related? What is the hypothesized effect of each on merger activity?

4. Discuss the hubris hypothesis in terms of efficiency theories of mergers.

5. What is the rationale for the use of such measures as the four-firm concentration ratio and the Herfindahl index?

6. How do tax considerations affect mergers and their structuring?

REFERENCES

Arrow, K. J., "Vertical Integration and Communication, " Bell Journal of Economics, 6, Spring 1975, pp. 173–183.

Asquith, P., and E. H. Kim, "The Impact of Merger Bids on the Participating Firms' Security Holders," Journal of Finance, 37, 1982, pp. 1209–1228.

Auerbach, A. J., and D. Reishus, "Taxes and Merger Decision: An Empirical Analysis," Working Paper No. 1855, Cambridge, MA: National Bureau of Economic Research, March 1986.

Baumol, W. J., The Stock Market and Economic Efficiency, New York: Fordham University Press, 1965.

Bradley, M., "Interfirm Tender Offers and the Market for Corporate Control," Journal of Business, 53, October 1980, pp. 345–376.

———, A. Desai, and E. H. Kim, "The Rationale Behind Interfirm Tender Offers: Information or Synergy?" Journal of Financial Economics, 11, April 1983, pp. 183–206.

———, "Synergistic Gains from Corporate Acquisitions and Their Division Between the Stockholders of Target and Acquiring Firms," Journal of Financial Economics, 21, 1988, pp. 3–40.

Copeland, Thomas E., and Won Heum Lee, "Exchange Offers and Stock Swaps—A Signalling Approach: Theory and Evidence," ms., August 1988.

Dennis, Debra K., and John J. McConnell, "Corporate Mergers and Security Returns," Journal of Financial Economics, 16, 1986, pp. 143–187.

Dodd, P., and R. Ruback, "Tender Offers and Stockholder Returns: An Empirical Analysis," Journal of Financial Economics, 5, December 1977, pp. 351–374.

Duesenberry, J. S., Business Cycles and Economic Growth, New York: McGraw-Hill, 1958.

Fama, E. F., "Agency Problems and the Theory of the Firm," Journal of Political Economy, 88, April 1980, pp. 288–307.

———, and M. C. Jensen, "Separation of Ownership and Control," Journal of Law and Economics, 26, 1983, pp. 301–325.

———, "Organizational Forms and Investment Decisions," Journal of Financial Economics, 14, 1985, pp. 101–119.

Haugen, R. A., and L. W. Senbet, "New Perspectives on Informational Asymmetry," Journal of Financial and Quantitative Analysis, 14, November 1979, pp. 671–694.

Jensen, M. C., "Agency Costs of Free Cash Flow, Corporate Finance and Takeovers," American Economic Review, 76, May 1986, pp. 323–329.

———, "The Takeover Controversy: Analysis and Evidence," Chapter 20 in Knights,

Raiders, and Targets, J. C. Coffee, Jr., L. Lowenstein, and S. Rose-Ackerman, eds., New York: Oxford University Press, 1988.

————, and W. MECKLING, "Theory of the Firm: Managerial Behavior, Agency Costs and Ownership Structure," *Journal of Financial Economics,* 3, October 1976, pp. 305–360.

JONES, E., and R. TAGGART, "Taxes and Ownership Structure: Corporations, Partnerships and Royalty Trusts," Working Paper No. 1441, Cambridge, MA: National Bureau of Economic Research, September 1984.

KIM, E. H., and J. MCCONNELL, "Corporate Merger and the Coinsurance of Corporate Debt," *Journal of Finance,* 32, 1977, pp. 349–365.

KLEIN, B., R. CRAWFORD, and A. ALCHIAN, "Vertical Integration, Appropriable Rents, and the Competitive Contracting Process," *Journal of Law and Economics,* 21, October 1978, pp. 297–326.

LELAND, H. E., and D. G. PYLE, "Informational Asymmetries, Financial Structure, and Financial Intermediation," *Journal of Finance,* 32, May 1977, pp. 371–387.

LEWELLEN, W. G., and B. HUNTSMAN, "Managerial Pay and Corporate Performance," *American Economic Review,* 60, September 1970, pp. 710–720.

LYNCH, H. H., *Financial Performance of Conglomerates,* Boston, MA: Harvard Graduate School of Business Administration, 1971.

MAJD, S., and S. MYERS, "Valuing the Government's Tax Claim on Risky Assets," Working Paper, M.I.T., November 1984.

MANNE, H. G., "Mergers and the Market for Corporate Control," *Journal of Political Economy,* 73, April 1965, pp. 110–120.

————, "Our Two Corporate Systems: Law and Economics," *Virginia Law Review,* 53, March 1967, pp. 259–285.

MARKHAM, J. W., *Conglomerate Enterprises and Public Policy,* Boston, MA: Harvard Graduate School of Business Administration, 1973.

MASULIS, R. W., "The Effects of Capital Structure Change on Security Prices: A Study of Exchange Offers," *Journal of Financial Economics,* 8, 1980, pp. 139–178.

————, "The Impact of Capital Structure Change on Firm Value: Some Estimates," *Journal of Finance,* 38, 1983, pp. 107–126.

MCDANIEL, MOREY W., "Bondholders and Corporate Governance," *The Business Lawyer,* 41, February 1986, pp. 413–460.

MUELLER, D. C., "A Theory of Conglomerate Mergers," *Quarterly Journal of Economics,* 83, 1969, pp. 643–659.

NICKELL, S. J., *The Investment Decisions of Firms,* Oxford, England: Cambridge University Press, 1978.

NIELSEN, J. F., and R. W. MELICHER, "A Financial Analysis of Acquisition and Merger Premiums," *Journal of Financial and Quantitative Analysis,* 8, March 1973, pp. 139–162.

PRESCOTT, E. C., and M. VISSCHER, "Organization Capital," *Journal of Political Economy,* 88, June 1980, pp. 446–461.

ROLL, R., "The Hubris Hypothesis of Corporate Takeovers," *Journal of Business,* 59, 1986, pp. 197–216.

ROSS, S. A., "The Determination of Financial Structure: The Incentive-Signalling Approach," *Bell Journal of Economics,* 8, 1977, pp. 23–40.

Shleifer, A., and L. W. Summers, "Breach of Trust in Hostile Takeovers," Chapter 2 in *Corporate Takeovers: Causes and Consequences*, A. J. Auerbach, ed., Chicago: University of Chicago Press, 1988.

Smirlock, M., R. Beatty, and S. Majd, *Taxes and Mergers: A Survey*, Monograph 1985–3, New York: Graduate School of Business Administration, New York University, June 1986.

Smith, Clifford W., Jr., "Investment Banking and the Capital Acquisition Process," *Journal of Financial Economics*, 15, January/February 1986a, pp. 3–29.

———, "Raising Capital: Theory and Evidence," *Midland Corporate Finance Journal*, Spring 1986b, pp. 6–22.

Spence, A. Michael, "Job Market Signalling," *Quarterly Journal of Economics*, 87, August 1973, pp. 355–379.

———, "Competitive and Optimal Responses to Signals: Analysis of Efficiency and Distribution," *Journal of Economic Theory*, March 1974, pp. 296–332.

Valente, Judith, and Bridget O'Brian, "TWA Chairman Icahn Breaks Off Effort to Acquire Eastern Unit of Texas Air," *The Wall Street Journal*, October 18, 1988, p. A6.

Vermaelen, T., "Common Stock Repurchases and Market Signalling: An Empirical Study," *Journal of Financial Economics*, 9, 1981, pp. 139–183.

The Wall Street Journal, October 25, 1988, p. C1.

Weston, J. F., "The Nature and Significance of Conglomerate Firms," *St. John's Law Review Special Edition*, 44, Spring 1970, pp. 66–80.

Williamson, O. E., *Corporate Control and Business Behavior*, Englewood Cliffs, NJ: Prentice-Hall; 1970.

———, *Markets and Hierarchies: Analysis and Antitrust Implications*, New York: Free Press, 1975.

———, "Comment," in *Corporate Takeovers: Causes and Consequences*, A. J. Auerbach, ed., Chicago: The University of Chicago Press, 1988, pp. 61–67.

CHAPTER **9**

Sell-offs and Divestitures

Sell-offs and divestitures are a part of what is called the restructuring of corporate America. But in addition to sell-offs and divestitures, many other forms of restructuring can also be identified. These include liquidations, leveraged buy-outs, management buy-outs, master limited partnerships, royalty trusts, as well as employee stock ownership plans (ESOPs). Because of their similarity to sell-offs and divestitures, liquidations are discussed in this chapter, but the other forms of corporate restructuring have distinctive characteristics that are covered in subsequent chapters.

The restructuring of business firms stems from a number of basic forces. One objective addresses the agency problem of the conflict of interest between managers and shareholders. A central purpose of restructuring is to align better the interests of managers and shareholders. A second function of restructuring is to move assets to owners who can utilize them more effectively. This helps the economic system move assets to their highest valued uses.

A third general reason given for the restructuring of the 1980s is to reverse the conglomerate merger movement of the 1960s. Some argue that it was unsound to combine many diverse activities into conglomerates as occurred in the 1960s. Conglomeration appeared to be the result of management theories which held that at the level of general management functions particularly, executives could effectively manage a wide range of business types. Another factor involved in conglomeration was that firms in industries with depleting resources such as forestry and a range of mining industries, or industries with narrow or specialized product lines or with uncertain outlooks such as defense industries, sought defensive diversification. In addition, horizontal and vertical mergers were effectively prohibited by the administration of the antitrust laws in the United States. Some ascribe the need to break up conglomerates as a consequence of the intensification of competition in the U.S. economy, particularly increased international competition. Others view the conglomeration as a result of a learning process and an emphasis on developing new core businesses with more favorable outlooks or better suited to the capabilities possessed by the managements of individual conglomerate firms. Voluntary liquidations and "bust-up" takeovers reflect the judgment that the sale of individual parts of some firms could realize greater values than the combination of the parts in one corporate enterprise. Thus, the subject matter of this chapter deals with a fundamental new force in the economy—the restructuring of corporate America.

DEFINITIONS AND EXAMPLES

Most studies have focused on divestitures and spin-offs as a means of eliminating or separating a product line, division, or subsidiary. Divestitures represent the sale of a segment of a company to a third party. Assets, product lines, subsidiaries, or divisions are sold for cash or securities or some combination thereof. The compensation received, net of capital gains taxation, may be used however the seller's management sees fit. The assets are revalued by the sale for purposes of future depreciation by the buyer. Dun and Bradstreet's 1983 sale of its television stations is an example of a divestiture. Divestitures are related to merger and acquisition (M&A) transactions in that in recent years about 40 percent of acquisition activities represented divestitures by other firms. This percentage has fluctuated in the 35 percent to 40 percent range during the 1980s, down from a peak of 53 percent to 54 percent during 1976 and 1975, respectively (W. T. Grimm, 1987, pp. 2, 63). Purchase prices are available on only about half of the transactions, with divestitures in recent years running at about 35 percent of the dollar value of transactions (W. T. Grimm, 1987, p. 9).

Spin-offs are more often associated with controlled subsidiaries. In a spin-off, a company distributes on a pro rata basis all the shares it owns in a subsidiary to its own shareholders. Two separate public corporations with (initially) the same proportional equity ownership now exist where only one existed before. No money changes hands, and the subsidiary's assets are not revalued. The transaction is treated as a stock dividend and a tax-free exchange. AT&T's recent reorganization represented a massive (albeit involuntary) spin-off of its operating subsidiaries.

Spin-offs are distinguished from *equity carve-outs*, in which some of a subsidiary's shares are offered for sale to the general public, bringing an infusion of cash to the parent firm without loss of control. In 1983–1984, Trans World Corporation initially sold 15 to 20 percent of its stock in TWA (its airline subsidiary) to the general public in an equity carve-out. (This transaction was followed by a spin-off in which the remaining controlling interest in TWA was spun off, that is, distributed on a pro rata basis to Trans World Corporation's shareholders.)

Other types of sell-offs include *split-offs* in which some, but not all, parent company shareholders receive the subsidiary's shares in return for which they must relinquish their parent company shares. Dome Petroleum purchased an equity interest in Conoco, which they subsequently traded for ownership of Conoco's Hudson Bay oil and gas fields. And finally there are *split-ups*, in which all of a firm's subsidiaries are spun off and the parent firm ceases to exist.

If all of the above is not confusing enough, these terms are often used in different ways by different writers. However, because of the potential for confusion, most writers are careful to describe exactly the type of transaction they mean by each term.

In the following sections of this chapter we discuss successively various aspects of divestitures, spin-offs, equity carve-outs, their rationale and case studies. We then present several aspects of liquidations.

DIVESTITURES

We first discuss divestitures because of the major role they perform in M&A activity. Like M&A activity in general, the explanations for divestitures are multiple and diverse.

Background Materials on Divestitures

First, both acquisition and divestiture activity may represent efforts by business firms to adjust to their changing economic environments. After the post-World War II adjustments appeared to have been made, the war in Korea caused new shifts in the U.S. economy. Major post-Korean War adjustments took place in the latter half of the 1950s. These abrupt changes stimulated the development of the literature on long-range planning and corporate strategy. The 1960s included the involvement in the war in Vietnam. This was the period of the conglomerate merger movement in which about half the firms actively involved were from the defense industry or natural resource industries with depleting resources. The decade of the 1970s marked a change in international currency standards, floating exchange rates, oil shocks, and relatively high rates of inflation throughout the world. The 1980s were initiated by tight monetary policy in the United States followed by an easing in part to control the debt service costs of the huge indebtedness incurred by many of the less developed nations. It was a period of deregulation in a number of major industries in the United States.

M&A activity as well as divestitures represented one set among strategies by business firms in attempting to adjust to these successive changes in their economic and political environments. Some firms succeeded better than others in these efforts.

Second, in the effort to deal with the changing economic environments discussed earlier, many firms used M&As as well as internal start-ups to probe opportunities in other product-market areas. Some firms sought to utilize the strengths in their existing product-market areas to combine with new capabilities in new environments. (The strategy literature urged them to attempt to do so; see the pioneering book by Ansoff, 1965.) A related strategy was to seek at least a toehold in new product-market areas. The hope was that initial entry could be a beachhead for further growth and development. Much M&A activity involved moving from industries with unfavorable outlooks to industries with more favorable opportunities. Sometimes firms did not have the capabilities to effectively exploit the possible opportunities. Divestitures enabled selling firms to salvage a portion of their investments by selling to other firms who could exploit the opportunities more effectively.

Third, some divestitures undoubtedly were attempts to correct previous investment decisions. The mistakes may have occurred in connection with either internal or external investments. Mistakes that subsequently caused divestitures are particularly likely to occur when companies engage in efforts to diversify. This is because they are moving into product-market areas with which they have less familiarity than their existing activities.

Fourth, some divestitures of the type that involved selling to a value-increasing buyer were planned at the time of prior M&A activity. Such divestitures may have been preplanned because they represented a poor fit to the acquiring firm. Sometimes such divestitures could be turned at a profit; sometimes they involved a loss which might have been more than offset by the good segments retained. In many cases the financial results of the acquisition-divestiture were interdependent with other strategies so its effects could not be ascertained. Related preplanned divestitures were for the purpose to help finance an individual acquisition or acquisition program.

Fifth, some acquisitions represented undervalued investments or acquiring firms where managements were underperforming. After increasing the value of the segment acquired, divestitures may be used to realize the gains achieved. The firm could then repeat the process.

Sixth, some divestitures represented harvesting other types of successful investments. Here the purpose was to make financial and managerial resources available for developing other opportunities. Such divestitures represented successes rather than failures (mistakes).

Seventh, unit management buy-outs are classified as divestitures by W. T. Grimm (1987, p. 70). They represent "a consistent 11 percent of total divestitures" (W. T. Grimm, 1987, p. 70). It would be expected that the MBOs occurred in those industries or firms in which managers needed to develop activity-specific investments. Particularly, if the industry or firm reached a stage where the activity needed to be isolated to motivate management, this kind of divestiture would be stimulated.

Porter (1987, p. 49) gives a number of examples of how divestment can perform a very valuable role in the strategic activities of a firm: "Once the results of the one-time improvement are clear, the diversified company no longer adds value to offset the inevitable costs imposed on the unit. It is best to sell the unit and free up corporate resources." Another example (p. 52): "The restructuring strategy seeks out undeveloped, sick, or threatened organizations or industries on the threshold of significant change . . . Then it may make follow-up acquisitions to build a critical mass and sell off unneeded or unconnected parts and thereby reduce the effective acquisition cost . . . As a coda, the parent sells off the stronger unit . . ."

And Porter again (p. 55): "If the company exhausts opportunities to infuse new expertise into a unit after the initial post-acquisition period, the unit should ultimately be sold." Then in a highlighted inset on the British Hanson Trust, Porter (p. 55) observes, "It's too early to tell whether Hanson will adhere to the last tenet of restructuring—selling turned-around units once the results are clear."

The preceding observations are clear examples of the useful functions that divestitures may perform in a company's evolving planning process.

A number of general observations may be made in connection with the preceding brief descriptions of reasons for divestitures. The list is not exhaustive and could be extended. But even a sample of reasons surveyed is sufficient to establish that numerous influences are operating. Given the many forces producing divestitures, it is often difficult to assess whether divestitures represent successes or failures for the divesting firm.

Another general observation is that the use of acquisitions to achieve diversification was severely restricted during the period 1950 through 1980 by government antitrust policies. The 1950 Celler-Kefauver Amendment to the 1914 Clayton Act effectively gave the government the power to stop horizontal and vertical mergers or acquisitions, and the government vigorously exercised its expanded powers. The legal and regulatory environment caused most large mergers during 1950–1980 to be the conglomerate form.

Finally, some firms had less pressure to diversify outside their core fields and industries than others. Sometimes this represented good prior strategic planning. Sometimes it represented shifts in the external economic and financial environment that turned out to be favorable for particular industries and firms. But the pressures for overcoming a firm's "strategic planning gap" or "aligning more effectively to the firm's changing environments" varied from industry to industry and during different time periods.

With this background on the economic and political setting of acquisition-divestiture activity, the evidence on the results is now examined.

Financial Effects of Divestitures

Studies on divestitures have found significant positive abnormal two-day announcement-period returns of between 1 and 2 percent for selling firm shareholders. The announcement effects on returns to buyers did not appear to be statistically significant (Alexander, Benson, and Kampmeyer, 1984; Jain, 1985;

Linn and Rozeff, 1984). A later study by Klein (1986) looks at divestitures in greater depth. Klein analyzes the announcement date effects by whether the selling firms initially announced the price of the sell-off or whether no price was initially announced. When no price was announced, there was no statistically significant effect on share price for the seller. When firms initially announced the price, the size of effects depends on the percentage of the firm being sold as measured by the announced price of the sell-off divided by the market value of the equity on the last day of the month prior to the announcement period. There is no significant price effect when the percentage of the equity sold is less than 10 percent. When the percentage of equity sold is between 10 and 50 percent, the abnormal returns to the seller average a positive 2.53 percent. When the percentage of the equity sold is greater than 50 percent, the percentage abnormal return is 8.09 percent.

When the abnormal gains to sellers from divestitures are aggregated, the totals represent substantial dollar amounts. Black and Grundfest (1988) estimate that for the period 1981 to 1986, the abnormal value increases to sellers in corporate divestitures could be conservatively placed at $27.6 billion.

Analysis of Divestiture/Acquisition Percentages

Some hold that the high rate of divestiture activity is evidence of the failure of acquisition and diversification efforts. This view has been expressed by Michael Porter (1987, p. 43) as follows: "The track record of corporate strategies has been dismal. I studied the diversification records of 33 large, prestigious U.S. companies over the 1950–1986 period and found that most of them had divested many more acquisitions than they had kept. The corporate strategies of most companies have dissipated instead of created shareholder value."

Porter compiled data on a sample of 33 companies over the period 1950–1986. Each company on average entered 27 new fields (for example, financial services) and 80 new industries (for instance, insurance), with about 70 percent of each by acquisitions. He computed the ratios of divestitures to acquisitions. On average the firms divested 53.4 percent of acquisitions in new industries and 60.0 percent of acquisitions in new fields. When the acquisitions were in fields unrelated to the companies' existing fields, the rate of divestitures was 74.0 percent. Companies are ranked by divestiture ratios. A key ranking is by the percent of acquisitions in new industries made by 1980 and then divested. The range is between 17 percent for the "highest" and 87 percent for the "lowest," with 39 percent of the firms divesting fewer acquisitions than they kept, and 61 percent divesting more acquisitions than they kept.

Porter characterizes these results as "startling" and "sobering." But Porter's results are not surprising in view of the W. T. Grimm data series on divestitures which show them ranging from 35 percent to 54 percent over the years 1975 to 1987. Porter's data are for entries into new fields and industries, more difficult than expansion programs. Given the overall acquisition-divestiture patterns observed, his results are not unexpected.

The Porter findings could also be interpreted as depicting strong and continuing entrepreneurial activities in U.S. corporations. His sample of 33 large, relatively mature corporations made an average of 115 new entries during the 1950–1986 period, constituting somewhat over three new entries per year. They were not passive or inactive in relation to their turbulent economic environments during the 37 years encompassed. Hence, the data could be regarded as evidence of vigorous dynamism rather than a "stark indication of failure."

The Porter Methodology

Apart from alternative implications of Porter's data, the divestiture/acquisition percentages employed by Porter have certain ambiguities and weaknesses. First, all acquisitions and divestitures are given equal weight. A billion dollar transaction is given no more weight than a thousand dollar one. What if most of the divestitures that enter into Porter's calculations were small and the acquisitions not divested were the larger ones? Would this affect the interpretation of his divestiture/acquisition ratios? Or what if a large acquisition motivated to acquire a valuable segment was followed by divesting several segments judged in advance to be unattractive? The resulting divestiture to acquisition percentage would be over 100 percent, but by any reasonable financial or strategic tests the divestitures added to the strength of the firm and hence were desirable.

A second area of ambiguity in Porter's procedures is that he does not give criteria for defining "fields" or "industries." To replicate the study as a scientific test or to understand what Porter actually did and what his data really mean, we would need to have some objective criteria. The U.S. government *Standard Industrial Classification Manual* (SIC) (1987) would be a helpful referent. Porter's illustration of "field" seems related to the SIC code at the "division" level (for instance, D. Manufacturing); his designation of "industry" could be at the two-digit level (for instance, Major Group 20 —Food and Kindred Products); or at the three-digit level (for instance, 201 Meat Products); or at the four-digit level (for instance, 2015 Poultry Slaughtering and Processing). But without linking to a systematic classification system, Porter's groupings involve considerable subjectivity which could influence his results and make scientific retesting impossible.

Third, Porter himself recognizes that divestitures may have a useful role in implementing successful concepts of strategy. For example, he cautions firms against postponing divestitures after they have improved an acquisition to the level where financing and managerial resources could better be shifted to new activities where the potential for further improvements are greater. Many other types of divestitures also represent successes rather than mistakes or failures. Several were listed earlier in the survey of the reasons for divestitures. Some divestitures occur after purchases of underperforming firms, undervalued firms, or after probing new product-market areas with controlled investments. Some divestitures were planned at the time of acquisition because of poor fit or because they could contribute to financing. Therefore, divestiture rates cannot be unambiguously interpreted as failure rates.

Because of these problems with the divestiture/acquisition ratios, their implications are uncertain and it is therefore difficult to draw conclusions from them. An even more serious weakness of the Porter methodology is that he does not set forth a theory or model which provides a criterion to determine which companies performed satisfactorily and which did not. How should his numbers be interpreted even if they were free of infirmities? Porter presents only three relatively brief paragraphs of discussion of his data in his 16-page paper which conveys no basis for determining critical levels for his rankings of divestiture/ acquisition percentages. Porter simply calls the performance of all "dismal." He concludes, "My data give a stark indication of the failure of corporate strategies . . . Only the lawyers, investment bankers, and original sellers have prospered in most of these acquisitions, not the shareholders" (Porter, 1987, p. 46). (Porter does not recognize that the "original sellers" also have shareholders.) From the first statement in Porter's conclusion, it appears that even the firms at the top of his list have had "failed" corporate strategies. With regard to the final sentence quoted from his conclusions, the data he presents provide no basis for his generalizations.

Measurement of Effects on Shareholder Values

Porter's conclusions imply that most of the companies in his sample would have had stockholder returns that were below average in some sense. But he admonishes that data on returns to shareholders are uninformative. First, Porter rejects the evidence from event studies which show positive gains to selling firms on the announcement of divestitures. He states, "Yet the short-term market reaction is a highly imperfect measure of the long-term success of diversification, and no self-respecting executive would judge a corporate strategy this way" (Porter, 1987, p. 45). This view flies in the face of a vast body of research in financial economics during recent decades and stems from a misunderstanding. It is inappropriate to characterize event studies as measuring "short-term market reactions." The methodology measures stock price changes in relation to total market movements for samples of firms at different calendar time periods but centered with reference to the event measured. The measurement of the impact of the event in relation to the total market movements is an estimate of the market's assessment of the long-term effects of the "unusual" event being studied. Random influences are averaged out by the use of relatively large samples. Consistent results are obtained in a large number of studies.

Porter (1987, pp. 45–46) also argues that testing the success of diversification by effects on shareholder value "only works if you compare the shareholder value that is with the shareholder value that might have been without diversification." One could add the even stronger requirement that all other influences would have to be held constant as well. But many factors go into corporate strategic planning processes. Diversification is only one dimension and is interdependent with many others. Porter's own writings convey the many dimensions of corporate strategies.

Given the many dimensions of corporate strategy, it is neither necessary nor informative to attempt to determine the impact on shareholder value of individual segments of corporate strategy such as diversification alone. Hence, analysis of shareholder returns over a long period is a meaningful and informative exercise to which we now turn.

Porter reports that he measured shareholder returns over the period of his study and compared them with divestment rates. He states, "While companies near the top of the list have above-average shareholder returns, returns are not a reliable measure of diversification success" [Porter, 1987, p. 45]. This treatment is misleading because "above-average shareholder returns" are achieved by most firms in his rankings. In Table 9.1, shareholder returns for Porter's sample of firms are listed. The shareholder returns to 64 percent of the companies in his sample exceeded the market return. Another 24 percent were within three percentage points of the market return. Only 12 percent performed poorly in relation to the market return. These results controvert Porter's conclusion (1987, p. 43) that, "The track record of corporate strategies has been dismal." Porter (1987, p. 43) does not present any systematic evidence relevant to his other conclusion that, "The corporate strategies of most companies have dissipated instead of created shareholder value."

Returns to shareholders over longer time periods have been above the market return for a large fraction of companies that have experienced high rates of divestitures. This evidence does not prove that acquisition/divestiture programs have increased shareholder value but is inconsistent with the conclusion that diversification strategies have produced "dismal" results.

The data on divestiture/acquisition rates portray a continued healthy dynamism among U.S. firms. Divestitures perform vital economic functions. Resources are being moved from less-valued uses to higher-valued uses. Whether or not sell-offs by one firm to another may sometimes represent efforts to correct previous mistakes, they are evidence that the market system is working. Irrespective of their implications for individual company strategies, sell-offs contribute to the resource mobility essential to the effective operation of an enterprise economy.

SPIN-OFFS

Schipper and Smith (1983) found a positive 2.84 percent abnormal return to the parent (statistically significant) on the spin-off announcement date. The size of the announcement effect is positively related to the size of the spin-off relative to parent size (the average size of the spin-off is about 20 percent of the original parent). Spin-offs motivated by avoidance of regulation experienced an abnormal return of 5.07 percent as compared to 2.29 percent for the remainder of the sample. Examples of regulation avoidance include separating a regulated utility

TABLE 9.1

Shareholder Returns for Porter's Sample, 1950–1986[a]

	COMPOUND AVERAGE ANNUAL RETURN [DIVIDEND YIELD PLUS CAPITAL GAINS (OR LOSSES) TO SHAREHOLDERS 1950–1986] (%)
Beatrice (1950–1985)	28.91
Gulf & Western (1965–1986)	18.96
Rockwell	17.36
Sara Lee	16.13
IBM	15.67
Exxon	15.56
Mobil	15.11
IC Industries (1964–1986)	14.80
CBS	14.79
Raytheon (1953–1986)	14.79
Johnson & Johnson	14.78
United Technologies	14.38
TRW	14.22
3M	14.20
ITT	13.87
Alco Standard (1970–1986)	13.31
GE	13.01
General Mills	12.49
RCA (1950–1985)	12.46
Procter & Gamble	12.26
Borden	12.05
MARKET RETURN	11.96
Westinghouse	11.61
Continental Group (1950–1983)	11.23
General Foods	11.21
Signal (1969–1984)	10.62
Scovill (1951–1984)	10.61
Xerox (1962–1986)	10.11
Du Pont	9.59
Grace, W. R. (1954–1986)	9.42
Tenneco (1959–1986)	7.99
Allied (1950–1984)	6.86
Cummins Engine (1965–1986)	5.66
Wickes[b]	—

[a]Based on CRSP monthly geometric returns converted to an annual basis. When data for the full period were not available from the CRSP tapes, the years provided are shown in parentheses following the company name.

[b]Wickes was not included because data were available on the CRSP tapes for only one year.

subsidiary from nonutility businesses and spinning off a foreign subsidiary to avoid restrictions by the U.S. Congress.

Hite and Owers (1983) find abnormal returns of 3.8 percent, somewhat higher than for the full sample of Schipper and Smith. They also find a positive relation between the relative size of the spin-off and the announcement effect. Neither study found an adverse effect on bondholders.

The Copeland, Lemgruber, and Mayers (1987) study extends the earlier studies in a number of dimensions. Particularly, they test for postselection bias. In their first sample, they do this by including announced spin-offs that are not completed (11 percent of the sample). This leads them to study the effects of successive announcements. A second expanded sample, subject to postselection bias, confirms the impact of successive announcements. They also study ex-date effects which they also find to have positive abnormal performance. They find that taxable spin-offs do not have positive abnormal returns, while nontaxable spin-offs do. However, when they control for the size of the spin-off, the difference between the two tax categories disappears.

For their small sample with no postselection bias, the two-day abnormal return from the first announcement is 2.49 percent; for the larger sample it is 3.03 percent. Both results are highly significant from a statistical standpoint. Thus, avoiding the postselection bias makes a difference; the return is lower for the sample which includes firms with announced spin-offs never consummated. For the eight firms with announced spin-offs which never were made, the two-day average return was a negative (but insignificant) 0.15 percent.

Copeland, Lemgruber, and Mayers (1987) also calculate the effects of announcements subsequent to the first (most firms had at least three or four announcements; one had thirteen). They find that, excluding the ex-date from the estimate, the abnormal return for a firm which actually completes spin-off is 5.02 percent. They conclude that the first announcement return is not a good estimate of the effect of a completed spin-off because not all spin-offs are completed and that earlier studies had underestimated the wealth effect of a completed spin-off.

In terms of dollar value, overall company gains are roughly equal to the value of the subsidiary spun off. The parent's value is virtually unchanged by the restructuring, while the subsidiary has a new independent market value of its own. For example, if the original firm prespin-off value is 5, and the subsidiary's value becomes 1, the postspin-off value of the parent remains at 5. Thus, the total value would be 6.

EQUITY CARVE-OUTS

An equity carve-out is the initial public offering (IPO) of some portion of the common stock of a wholly-owned subsidiary. These are also referred to as "split-off IPOs." An IPO of the equity of a subsidiary resembles a seasoned equity offering of the parent in that cash is received from a public sale of equity securities. But there are also differences. The IPO of the common stock of the subsidiary initiates public trading in a new and distinct set of equity claims on the assets of the subsidiary.

Other changes often take place as well when the subsidiary equity is "carved out" from the consolidated entity of the parent. The management system for operating the assets is likely to be restructured in this new public entity. A public market value for the operations of the subsidiary becomes established. Financial reports are issued on the subsidiary operations and are studied by financial analysts as a separate entity. Ongoing public information on the value of the subsidiary may have a positive influence on performance in the subsidiary. In addition, as an entity now separate from the parent, evaluation of performance may be facilitated. Incentives may be strengthened by relating the compensation of the executives in the subsidiary to the performance of the publicly-traded stock. If the parent should decide to sell the subsidiary, having established a public market for the stock may facilitate reaching an agreement with a buyer on a sales price.

An equity carve-out or split-off IPO is similar to a voluntary spin-off in that both result in subsidiary's equity claims that are traded separately from the equity claims on the parent entity. The equity carve-out differs from a spin-off in two respects. In a spin-off a distribution is made pro rata to the shareholders of the parent firm as a dividend—a form of noncash payment to the shareholders. In an equity carve-out, the stock of the subsidiary is sold in the public markets for cash which is received by the parent. A second distinction is that in a spin-off, the parent firm no longer has control over the subsidiary assets. In a carve-out, the parent generally sells only a minority interest in the subsidiary and maintains control over subsidiary assets and operations.

As compared with a divestiture, the split-off IPO is similar in that cash is received. But a divestiture is usually to another company. Hence, control over the assets sold is relinquished by the parent-seller and the trading of subsidiary stock is not initiated.

Spin-offs generally result in abnormal returns to the parent firm of 2 to 3 percent on average. Divestitures result in gains of 1 to 2 percent to selling firms on average. New seasoned equity issues are associated with announcement period negative residuals of about 2 to 3 percent. Since equity carve-outs have characteristics in common with each of the three types of transactions, it is not readily predictable what the announcement-period market reactions will be.

Schipper and Smith (1986) studied the performance of a usable sample of 81 equity carve-outs announced between 1965–1983. Underwritten offerings represented about 73 percent of the sample. This is lower than the 93 percent underwriting used in common stock issues of exchange-listed firms for the period 1971–1975 reported by Smith (1977). Less than 50 percent of the subsidiary shares were sold in 81 percent of the cases. The parent took a minority position in about 9 percent of the issues and data were not available on the other 10 percent. The dollar amount sold ranged widely from $300,000 to as high as $112 million. About 30 percent were below $10 million in size, but 26 percent were over $30 million. The proceeds represented a relatively small percentage of parent common equity value measured at the end of the month preceding the carve-out announcement. Data were not available on 20 percent of the sample. Of the 65 offerings for which data were available, 62 percent represented an amount less than 10 percent of the size of the parent common equity. Another 15 percent were in the 10 percent to under 15 percent range.

The initial percentage return on the stock of the new subsidiaries was calculated (Schipper and Smith, 1986) by relating the closing bid price on the first day of trading for which a price could be obtained (within ten trading days of the offering) to the offering price. The average initial return was 4.9 percent, while the median was 2.1 percent. When an outlier is removed, the average initial return drops to 1.7 percent. These returns are much lower than those observed in studies of public offerings generally. Ibbotson (1975) found average initial returns of 11.4 percent for 120 IPOs for the period 1960–1969. For the period 1977–1982, Ritter (1984) observed average initial returns of 26.5 percent for 1,028 initial public offerings, but these results were greatly influenced by the high initial returns on natural resource stocks during 1980–1981, probably related to the oil price increases in 1979 by OPEC.

While the large initial returns on IPOs generally were not matched by these split-off IPOs, substantial returns were observed in a small sample reported by *Corporate Restructuring* (1988) for the period between 1986 and the first half of 1988, which includes the major market decline of October 1987. The postoffering performance of the IPOs was related to the trends of the industries in which the firms were situated. The best performance was achieved by three split-off IPOs in the chemicals industry. During the period of the study, profits in this segment of industry had risen because of increased demand for their output while raw materials prices remained stable. USX Corporation in late 1986 took public an entity named Aristech Chemical Corp. Its offering price of 17¾ on November 26, 1987 rose to 35¼ by July 6, 1988, a gain of almost 100 percent. Similar gains were achieved by Borden Chemicals & Plastics which was taken public by its parent, Borden Inc., on November 20, 1987 and by IMC Fertilizer Group taken public by International Minerals & Chemicals on January 26, 1988. Five other companies achieved large positive gains that averaged 38 percent. The stock prices of two were unchanged. Three carve-outs by firms in financial services declined an average 32 percent. The latter firms were greatly affected by the decline in public trading following the market drop in October 1987. The other split-off IPOs provided excellent returns for the difficult time period involved.

Equity carve-outs on average are associated with positive abnormal returns of almost 2 percent over a five-day announcement period (Schipper and Smith, 1986). This is in contrast to findings of significant negative returns of about 2 to 3 percent when parent companies publicly offer additional shares of their own (as opposed to their subsidiary's) stock (Smith, 1986, 1986a).

EXPLANATIONS AND RATIONALE
FOR GAINS TO SELL-OFFS

A number of hypotheses have been advanced to explain the positive returns found in spin-offs and, to a lesser degree, in divestitures and equity carve-outs.

Information

The information hypothesis holds that the true value of subsidiary assets is obscured by the complexity of the business structure in which they are embedded. The supposed stock market preference for "pure-play" or single-industry securities is cited in support of this hypothesis. Given the disclosure requirements of public corporations and the nature and extent of the securities analysis industry, it might seem unlikely that parts of a firm would be undervalued. But security analysts tend to specialize. An oil industry analyst may undervalue an oil company's chemical and real estate businesses because he or she does not follow these industries. Also to the extent that spin-offs and equity carve-outs enhance the incentive to gather and analyze a greater amount of publicly available information through their creation of new publicly-traded securities, the information effect may explain at least part of the gains.

Managerial Efficiency

The managerial efficiency hypothesis suggests that the preference (if any) for pure-play securities stems not from lack of confidence in the market's ability to value complex organizations, but from the perceived inability of managers to manage them effectively. Even the best management team may reach a point of diminishing returns as the size and diversity of assets under their control increases. Part of the problem is that top management may be unaware of the unique problems and opportunities of a subsidiary in a different line of business. An announced motive in many sell-offs is to sharpen the corporate focus by spinning off (or divesting) units which are a poor fit (anergy) with the remainder of the parent company's operations. Writers on corporate strategy have long emphasized the principle of relatedness to guide business planning. Equity carve-outs are often preceded by asset regroupings in the effort to achieve greater efficiency (and are often followed by spin-offs or divestitures). Warner-Lambert's sale of its Entenmann's bakery subsidiary to General Foods is an example of the efficiency source of sell-off gains.

Both Entenmann's and Warner-Lambert stood to benefit from the transaction: Warner-Lambert management could now focus attention in their area of comparative advantage, pharmaceuticals; and Entenmann's would be controlled by managers more experienced with a food company's operations. The managerial efficiency hypothesis is supported by evidence of acquisition activity in the prespin-off period as well as dissimilarities between the business lines of the parent firms and spun-off subsidiaries.

Management Incentives

The issues of management incentives and accountability are related to management efficiency. Bureaucratization of management and consolidation of financial statements can stifle entrepreneurial spirit and result in good (bad) performance going unrewarded (unpunished). The problem is compounded when the subsidiary's outlook and objectives are not the same as the parent's, for example, a high-growth subsidiary of a parent in a mature industry, or a regulated subsidiary of a nonregulated parent. Incentive compensation plans tied to parent company stock options may be meaningless or even counterproductive. A spun-off subsidiary has the advantage of an independent stock price directly reflecting the market's response to management actions, and more closely linking compensation to performance.

Tax and/or Regulatory Factors

Another important source of gains available in some sell-offs is tax and/or regulatory advantages. Subsamples of spin-offs citing these motives exhibited higher abnormal returns than the more inclusive samples. Tax advantages can be achieved by the creation and spin-off into natural resource royalty trusts or real estate investment trusts; as long as these entities pay out 90 percent of their income to their shareholders, they pay no income tax. Thus, the parent company can shelter income from taxes and benefit the spun-off subsidiary's shareholders, who are the same (initially) as the parent's shareholders.

Regulated subsidiaries are sometimes penalized by their association with profitable parents if regulators look to parent company earnings when considering rate increases. The spun-off subsidiary might have a greater chance of being granted rate increases, and the nonregulated operations of the parent would be freed from regulatory scrutiny. Some parent firms have spun-off foreign subsidiaries so that they will not be subject to the laws and regulations of the home country of the parent.

Bondholder Expropriation

Agency costs are involved in the hypothesis that the gains to shareholders are the result of bondholder expropriation. A spin-off reduces (and a divestiture changes the nature of) the collateral initially relied on by bondholders. However, this argument assumes that sell-offs are unanticipated (and unanticipatable) events. In fact, most, if not all, bond covenants contain dividend restrictions (limiting stock dividends, including spin-offs) and restrictions on asset disposition (limiting divestitures).

Furthermore, many subsidiaries already have their own debt, and many are assigned a pro rata share of parent debt when they are spun off. Bondholders may actually benefit if hitherto junior claims on the parent become senior claims on the spun-off subsidiary. Studies by Hite and Owers (1983) and Schipper and Smith (1983) have found little evidence of bond prices or ratings decline to support the bondholder expropriation hypothesis.

Changing Economic Environment

Yet another rationale advanced for the positive price effects is that there has been a major shift in the economic environment affecting the firm. Thus, the opportunity sets of both parent and subsidiaries may be altered. While joint operations may have been optimal in the past, separate operations may have become more appropriate.

Option Creation

A more esoteric explanation of the value creation is based on options theory and the state preference model. The idea is that since incorporating limits the stockholders' liability, spin-offs multiply the protection. If common stock is viewed as an option on the underlying technologies of the firm, then a spin-off creates two options on the same assets. Two options will be more valuable than only one (Sarig, 1985).

Increase Market Spanning

Another theoretical benefit of sell-offs is related to financial market spanning or whether financial markets are complete. (For further explanation see Copeland and Weston, 1988, Chapter 5.) John Lintner (1971) had made a similar argument for conglomerate mergers. To the extent that financial markets may be incomplete, spin-offs increase the number of securities for a given number of possible states of the world. In addition, the opportunity set with respect to investment and financial policies of the parent and its divisions will be expanded. For example, the parent and the spun-off subsidiaries may provide investors with a wider range of different investment policies and financial policies. The parent and the new entities may package dividends, retained earnings, and capital gains possibilities in different proportions to appeal to different investor clienteles.

Enable More Focused Mergers

Spin-offs are also used to facilitate mergers when the bidder is interested in only a subset of the target's operations. That is, there may be some segments of the target that the bidder does not want to acquire. If for some reason the target/parent firm does not want to sell these segments outright before the merger (for instance, for tax reasons), a future spin-off may be included in the merger planning. At the time of the spin-off, the acquiring (bidder) firm is the parent of the subsidiary. Abnormal positive returns at the spin-off announcement may represent the market realization to the parent's (acquiring firm) shareholders of the increased value reflected in the premium paid earlier to the target shareholders.

Thus, a wide range of plausible reasons may account for the positive gains from sell-offs. Any one factor could contribute to the 3 percent to 5 percent abnormal positive gain to shareholders when a spin-off takes place.

MOTIVES FOR DIVESTITURES

Linn and Rozeff (1984) analyze the various motives given for divestitures. Among the reasons given for selling assets are to raise working capital and to pay off debt. However, these are financing decisions and can potentially be accomplished by actions that do not include divestitures. Furthermore, financing as such should not be expected to significantly increase the seller's share price (Smith, 1986, 1986a).

Linn and Rozeff (1984) argue that there are only two valid reasons for divestitures:

1 The assets are worth more as part of the buyer's organization than as part of the seller's.
2 The assets are actively interfering with other profitable operations of the seller.

For example, it is sometimes said that the reason for a divestiture is that the subsidiary is losing money. However, the present value of the subsidiary's future cash flows is already reflected in the seller's stock price. Unless the subsidiary is sold for more than this present value (that is, it is worth more to the buyer), no gain will result from the divestiture. However, if the subsidiary is actually preventing other operations from realizing their potentials, the removal of this negative synergy could cause a positive price impact even if no more than the present value of the subsidiary were received.

The fact that gains to divestitures (1 to 2 percent) are on average smaller than for spin-offs (3 to 5 percent) may reflect poor performance prior to the divestiture. Information about worse-than-expected performance may be revealed to the market simultaneously with the divestiture announcement, offsetting to an extent any positive price effect that might otherwise occur. The seller may have to dispose of assets quickly to avert a liquidity crisis, and may not be able to wait for a "fair price" (Linn and Rozeff rejected this rationale).

The smaller gains from divestitures may reflect their smaller relative scale. On average, divestitures may be smaller in relative magnitude than spin-offs. The managerial incentive factor may also perform a role. Spun-off subsidiaries become free-standing independent firms with their own common stock. But divested segments become part of another company.

CASE ILLUSTRATIONS
OF SPIN-OFFS AND DIVESTITURES

In addition to the positive average gains noted for samples of sell-offs, several individual cases of dramatic value increases have been documented. Hite and Owers (1984) describe the Dillingham case which is a virtual textbook illustration of restructuring. Over the period 1978–1983, Dillingham was involved in divestitures, a spin-off, partial liquidations and suspended operations, proxy contests, antitakeover amendments, a tender offer buy-back from small shareholders, a premium buy-back with standstill agreement to thwart a takeover, and finally a leveraged buy-out to take the company private. Although a few of these moves had immediate adverse effects, over a four-year period Dillingham's shareholders experienced abnormal positive returns of 185 percent, over 85 percent of which occurred before the LBO announcement. While these returns may not be typical, they do illustrate the potential for gains from restructuring in a dynamic setting.

Linn and Rozeff (1984) analyze the specific returns in two divestitures. In 1982, Warner-Lambert announced the sale of its Entenmann's bakery subsidiary to General Foods; the general rationale for gains was discussed earlier, here we look at the numbers involved. The sale price for Entenmann's was $315 million. Upon announcement of the sale, the value of Warner-Lambert stock increased by $101 million and the value of General Foods stock increased by about $44 million (both adjusted for market effects). Both parties benefited from the transaction. From the point of view of Warner-Lambert shareholders, we have:

Sale price of Entenmann's received	$315 million
Less: Stock value increase	101 million
Implied value of Entenmann's as part of W-L	$214 million

From the point of view of General Foods shareholders, we have:

Purchase price of Entenmann's paid	$315 million
Plus: Stock value increase	44 million
Implied value of Entenmann's as part of G.F.	$359 million

Warner-Lambert's shareholders received a premium over what they perceived to be the value of Entenmann's to them; General Foods' shareholders could expect that they would receive benefits from Entenmann's in excess of costs. The total value increase as a result of the divestiture amounted to $145 million, distributed approximately 70/30 between seller and buyer. That the seller received the larger proportion of the gain is not inconsistent with merger studies.

Another case involved the sale of Hospital Affiliates International (HAI) by INA Corporation to Hospital Corporation of America (HCA) for $650 million in 1981. INA was primarily in the insurance business, and the economic rationale for the divestiture seemed to have been that while HAI was a "poor fit" with INA's other operations, HCA would be able to realize operating economies as a result of the acquisition. INA shareholders realized a $75 million abnormal gain upon announcement of the sale, and shareholders of HCA realized $126 million. In this case the total value increase was $201 million, divided approximately 40/60 between seller and buyer respectively.

VOLUNTARY LIQUIDATIONS AND TAKEOVER BUST-UPS

Corporate liquidations are often associated with bankruptcy proceedings, but these are generally involuntary. The general rule is that a liquidation in bankruptcy will preserve values to a greater degree than continuing to attempt to operate an unsuccessful firm. But voluntary liquidations have a much more positive motivation. When a firm can be sold for an amount that exceeds the existing market value of the firm's outstanding securities, liquidation is in the best interest of the security holders. One factor stimulating managers to take such actions is the threat that outsiders will mount a proxy contest for control and conduct the liquidation themselves.

Empirical Studies

Skantz and Marchesini (1987) study a sample of 37 firms announcing liquidation between 1970–1982. They found that the announcement-month average excess return is +21.4 percent. Interestingly, they found that their sample firms were "not highly dissimilar to their industry members" (p. 71) in profitability prior to the liquidation decision.

Of the possible reasons for the positive abnormal return, Skantz and Marchesini found only one to be applicable. While divestitures had been generally subject to capital gains taxes, voluntary liquidations could be structured to qualify for preferential tax treatment on a major portion of the gains. This does not explain the much higher positive gains to liquidations (21.4 percent for the announcement with a cumulative average excess return of 41.3 percent) than for spin-offs which are also treated as tax-free exchanges. The reason may be that spin-offs average only 20 percent of the original parent; if the abnormal returns found by Copeland, Lemgruber, and Mayers (1987) of 5.02 percent are multiplied by 5 for comparable sizing of investment, the gains are similar.

An analysis of total liquidations was included in their study on the market for interfirm asset sales by Hite, Owers, and Rogers (1987). They analyzed 49 voluntary liquidations during the period 1963–1983. The median market value of equity was $41 million. The median book value of total assets was about $72 million. Although mergers were eliminated, they found that 21 of the 49 firms had been targets in earlier merger, tender offer or leveraged buy-out bids in the 24 months preceding the liquidation proposal. An additional three firms had been involved in proxy solicitation control contests.

Hite, Owers, and Rogers (1987) observed a two-day announcement period average abnormal return of 12.24 percent for total liquidations and more than 80 percent of the sample observations were positive. They estimated that for the seven liquidating firms which had senior securities, an equally weighted portfolio yielded a two-day holding period average return of 8.57 percent. Their analysis of the source of the positive returns to both the shareholders and senior claimants is that assets are being moved to higher-valued uses.

The study of voluntary liquidations by Kim and Schatzberg (1987, 1988) covered a sample of 73 liquidating firms over the period 1963–1981. They observed that their sample is composed of relatively small firms. The median market value of equity was $23 million. The median ratio of the market value of equity of the liquidating firm to the market value of equity of the acquiring firm was .28.

Kim and Schatzberg (1987, 1988) found that the liquidation announcement was associated with an average three-day market adjusted return of 14 percent to the shareholders of liquidating firms. An additional 3 percent abnormal return took place at shareholder confirmation. Acquiring shareholders experienced a small positive return at the liquidation announcement and a small negative return at confirmation, but these returns were not statistically significant.

As in the Hite, Owers, and Rogers (1987) study, the liquidation announcements were often associated with prior news relating to mergers, tender offers or partial sell-offs. At the time of the prior announcements, an abnormal return of 9 percent was realized. When Kim and Schatzberg take into effect all public announcements, they obtain even higher returns. They measure the abnormal returns for shareholders from two days before the earliest announcement date until two days after the last announcement date, obtaining total gains of 30 percent for firms without prior announcements and 34 percent for firms with prior announcements. The average gain to the shareholders of acquiring firms is not statistically significant.

The Kim and Schatzberg (1987, 1988) study confirms the beneficial effect on senior claimants found by Hite, Owers, and Rogers (1987). The majority of the firms in their sample retired debt that had a market value less than the face value.

Kim and Schatzberg (1987, 1988) analyze the question of why liquidations increase market values. They observe that one advantage to liquidations is that there may be several purchasers, whereas in a merger there is likely to be only one. This enables the selling firm to move its assets to the individual purchasers from whom the greatest value can be realized.

They also compare the tax effects of liquidations as compared with nontaxable mergers and discuss the impact of the Tax Reform Act of 1986. In general, a nontaxable merger had the advantage of deferring the recognition of a gain to the stockholders of the selling firm until a subsequent sale of the securities involved. First, in a liquidation, the selling stockholders must recognize the gain immediately. Second, unused tax credits and losses belonging to either of the premerger firms are carried over in a nontaxable merger, but those of the selling firm are lost at liquidation. Third, a liquidation permits the acquiring firm to step up the tax basis of the assets acquired, but this cannot be done in a nontaxable merger.

An important tax advantage to liquidations was removed by the Tax Reform Act of 1986. Under the General Utilities Doctrine, the corporate capital gains to the selling firm were not taxable if it adopted a plan of complete liquidation and all liquidating dividends were paid to shareholders within 12 months after the plan was adopted. One effect of the repeal of the General Utilities Doctrine by the Tax Reform Act of 1986 was to eliminate the tax incentive for firms to liquidate voluntarily after partial sell-offs. The 1986 act also eliminated the preferential personal capital gains tax rate which makes the deferral of realization in nontaxable mergers more attractive. It appears that the Tax Reform Act of 1986 reduced the tax advantages of liquidations compared to nontaxable mergers.

Case Studies of Liquidation

Liquidating for profit is discussed from the standpoint of case studies plus the analytics of what is going on. The first point we seek to emphasize is that when a firm "liquidates," this does not necessarily mean that the economic resources have been destroyed. Indeed even though an individual firm may cease to exist, it typically sells some or most of its assets to other ongoing firms. In the hands of the buying companies, the assets may be put to a higher economic use than when they were held by the seller.

The case study of Management Assistance illustrates a number of the concepts involved in liquidating a company (Rosenberg, 1985). Management Assistance had started as a company leasing punch card equipment and then later became a computer leasing company in the late 1950s. It was somewhat unique as a leasing company in that it emphasized having a strong organization in marketing and customer engineering. Particularly, it emphasized customer engineering as a method of assuring customers that the products it leased would receive prompt and effective attention to maintain their serviceability. In the 1970s it was a leader in the development of personal computers with its Basic Four Information Systems. This enabled Management Assistance to record a $19 million profit in 1979. With increased competition in personal computers, the company recorded a $17 million loss in fiscal 1984. The reported losses caused the price of its stock to decline substantially. Management Assistance caught the attention of Asher Adelman early in his career in corporate takeovers. "But where others saw only red ink, Adelman discerned hidden value" (Rosenberg, 1985, p. 9). The customer engineering and service activity of Management Assistance had been placed in a corporate subsidiary named Sorbus Service. Adelman says that he judged that this activity alone would sell for more than two times the then current market price of the common stock of Management Assistance as a whole. The personal computer business of Management Assistance had been placed in a corporate subsidiary with the name Basic Four Information Systems. The division was experiencing losses but Adelman saw potential in the strong marketing organization as a distribution operation selling not only the products of Management Assistance but the products of other companies as well. By January 1985 Adelman had won control of the board of directors and sold off Sorbus and Basic Four. In February 1985, Management Assistance began to distribute liquidating dividends of about $26 a share to stockholders. It is said that Adelman made a profit of $11 million on his investment of $15 million, a gain of 73 percent.

This case study is of interest from a number of standpoints. Note that the main assets of Management Assistance were not destroyed. They were sold to willing buyers at favorable prices. Another issue is why the previous control group in Management Assistance did not do what Adelman did. The previous control group at Management Assistance had seen the company through a number of ups and downs. Their judgment was that the company did indeed possess some valuable "crown jewels," and that in the long run the company's strength in service and in marketing would enable them to realize values greater than the $26 per share that Adelman had garnered in the short run.

Another area is represented by the restructuring which took place in the petroleum industry. An interview in *Barron's* with a security analyst on the oil industry describes the kind of thinking involved (Welling, 1985). The *Barron's* story represents an interview by Kathryn M. Welling of security analyst, Kurt Wulff. In response to questions on the need for restructuring in the oil industry, Mr. Wulff responded along the following lines. He argued that the price increases in oil that occurred during the 1970s had increased the profitability and financial resources of the oil companies. However, Mr. Wulff argued that the companies had misused the funds by investing too much in refining and marketing ("a low return business") and into diversification ("another indicator of poor investment"). Mr. Wulff argued that the market values of the common stock and debt of the U.S. oil companies were generally far below the value of the underlying assets if used properly. He argued that the real value of the oil companies was the present value of their expected future cash flow in excess of current liabilities.

Thus, we have another illustration of a situation in a broad industry where it was argued that takeovers and restructuring are called for. Again in the takeover activity the identity of the previous independent oil company could be eliminated—in a sense a form of liquidation. But again the economic resources would not be lost, rather they would be managed by another company.

Some of the issues posed persist as continuing challenges to companies today. It has been asserted that many of the large oil companies would be worth more than their current stock market value if they were purchased, broken up, and sold. It is argued that these companies are vulnerable unless they do their own restructuring. The restructuring called for involves substantially increasing leverage ratios. To do so means that the companies would cause the ratings of their debt to be downgraded. Also, it is sometimes argued by critics that the oil companies should dispose of their chemical and real estate investments. Again these are areas of management judgment. Oil companies respond that financial analysts are too narrowly focused and ignore the true long-run value of the chemical, real estate, and other investments of the oil companies. Management argues that while the payoffs may be farther into the future, they represent a necessary kind of investment commitment because oil reserves are a depleting asset.

The preceding two case studies illustrate why there are opportunities to liquidate for profit. But it is also argued that this represents taking a short-run viewpoint that will diminish the long-run economic strength of the U. S. economy. The critics argue that these actions simply redress the misuse of assets by the managements presently in control of their companies.

CONCLUSIONS

Since the sell-offs we have been considering are voluntary decisions by management, we would expect them to represent positive NPV strategies toward the goal of maximizing shareholder wealth. Several principles form the basis for the value increase observed in sell-offs. In some cases the underlying cause is clear; in others it may be impossible to distinguish between two or more possible sources.

Tax and/or Regulatory Effects

These are clearly identifiable as the source of gains in many sell-offs. They are, however, just as clearly not available in all situations.

Poor Fit

There are at least two aspects involved. The parent firm's management may lack the expertise to manage dissimilar assets. The assets may be creating negative synergy, that is, actively interfering with other profitable operations of the parent. The high incidence of sell-offs after a period of acquisitions and rapid growth may reflect this motive.

Information Effects

In sell-offs, the transaction is initiated by the seller who has discovered a higher-valued use for a subset of business assets elsewhere. However, gains which take place at the sell-off announcement dissipate if the sell-off is cancelled. This may indicate that no new information has been uncovered. Alternatively, it is possible that the new information cannot be exploited in cancelled sell-offs. It is possible that another organization is required to have the knowledge or capabilities to develop the potential of the business segment involved.

Management Efficiency and Incentives

This theory holds that more homogeneous organizations may be managed more effectively and evaluated more accurately by financial analysts. In addition, managers may receive incentives and rewards more closely related to actual performance than when the quality of performance may be obscured in consolidated financial statements, or monitored by superiors unfamiliar with the unique problems of a disparate subsidiary. In spin-offs, the creation of a free-standing stock price, reflecting the market's assessment of management's performance on a continual basis, may help assure that management compensation plans based on stock options will more directly measure and reward performance.

Divestitures and sell-offs represent mistakes in a sense because previous investment decisions are altered. However, they may also represent the harvesting of sound investments made earlier. Some sell-offs were planned at the time of earlier acquisitions, sometimes to help finance the larger transactions. Sell-offs may also reflect organization learning or reorientation of business strategies. To some degree at least, divestitures represent the movement of business resources to higher-valued uses.

Voluntary liquidations have characteristics and motives similar to divestitures but involve the sale of the total firm, usually by parts. In moving assets to different buyers, the seller can often realize higher prices than if the firm as a whole were sold to one buyer. A firm is not likely to be liquidated voluntarily unless the parts can be sold for an amount that exceeds the existing market value of the firm's outstanding securities.

QUESTIONS

1. What are the magnitude of gains in divestitures, sell-offs and voluntary liquidations? Explain the differences.
2. How does the information hypothesis explain gains resulting from spin-offs?
3. What are pure-play securities and what is their role in the information and managerial efficiency hypothesis of divestitures?
4. According to Linn and Rozeff, what are the only two valid reasons for divestitures?
5. How do tax and/or regulatory factors affect returns to spin-offs and divestitures?
6. What is the magnitude of divestiture activity in relation to merger and acquisitions activity generally?

REFERENCES

ALEXANDER, GORDON J., P. GEORGE BENSON, and JOAN M. KAMPMEYER, "Investigating the Valuation Effects of Announcements of Voluntary Corporate Selloffs," *Journal of Finance*, June 1984, pp. 503–517.

ANSOFF, H. IGOR, *Corporate Strategy*, New York: McGraw-Hill, 1965.

BLACK, BERNARD S., and JOSEPH A. GRUNDFEST, "Shareholder Gains from Takeovers and Restructurings Between 1981 and 1986: $162 Billion is a Lot of Money," *Journal of Applied Corporate Finance*, 1, Spring 1988, pp. 5–15.

COPELAND, THOMAS E., and J. FRED WESTON, *Financial Theory and Corporate Policy*, 3rd ed., Reading, MA: Addison-Wesley Publishing Company, 1988.

COPELAND, THOMAS E., E. F. LEMGRUBER, and D. MAYERS, "Corporate Spinoffs: Multiple Announcement and Ex-Date Abnormal Performance," Chapter 7 in *Modern Finance and Industrial Economics*, T. E. Copeland, ed., New York: Basil Blackwell, 1987.

Corporate Restructuring, Mergers & Acquisitions Magazine, August 1988.

HITE, GAILEN, and JAMES E. OWERS, "Security Price Reactions around Corporate Spin-off Announcements," *Journal of Financial Economics*, 1983, pp. 409–436.

———, "The Restructuring of Corporate America: An Overview," *Midland Corporate Finance Journal*, Summer 1984, pp. 6–16.

———, and R. C. ROGERS, "The Market for Interfirm Asset Sales: Partial Sell-offs and Total Liquidations," *Journal of Financial Economics*, 18, 1987, pp. 229–252.

IBBOTSON, R., "Price Performance of Common Stock New Issues," *Journal of Financial Economics*, September 1975, pp. 235–272.

JAIN, PREM C., "The Effect of Voluntary Sell-Off Announcements on Shareholder Wealth," *Journal of Finance*, March 1985, pp. 209–224.

KIM, E. H., and J. D. SCHATZBERG, "Voluntary Corporate Liquidations," *Journal of Financial Economics*, 19, 1987, pp. 311–328.

———, "Voluntary Liquidations: Causes and Consequences," *Midland Corporate Finance Journal*, Winter 1988, pp. 30–35.

KLEIN, A., "The Timing and Substance of Divestiture Announcements: Individual, Simultaneous and Cumulative Effects," *Journal of Finance*, 41, 1986, pp. 685–697.

LINN, SCOTT C., and MICHAEL S. ROZEFF, "The Corporate Sell-off," *Midland Corporate Finance Journal*, Summer 1984, pp. 17–26.

LINTNER, JOHN, "Expectations, Mergers and Equilibrium in Purely Competitive Securities Markets," *American Economic Review*, 61, May 1971, pp. 101–111.

MILES, JAMES A., and JAMES D. ROSENFELD, "The Effect of Voluntary Spin-off Announcements on Shareholder Wealth," *Journal of Finance*, December 1983, pp. 1597–1606.

PORTER, MICHAEL E., "From Competitive Advantage to Corporate Strategy," *Harvard Business Review*, May-June 1987, pp. 43–59.

RITTER, J., "The 'Hot Issue Market' of 1980," *Journal of Business*, 57, 1984, pp. 215–240.

ROSENBERG, HILARY, "Newest Kid on the Takeover Block," *Barron's*, March 11, 1985, pp. 8–9, 11.

SARIG, ODED H., "On Mergers, Divestments, and Options: A Note," *Journal of Financial and Quantitative Analysis*, September 1985, pp. 385–389.

SCHIPPER, KATHERINE, and ABBIE SMITH, "Effects of Recontracting on Shareholder Wealth," *Journal of Financial Economics*, 1983, pp. 437–467.

——, "The Corporate Spin-off Phenomenon," *Midland Corporate Finance Journal*, Summer 1984, pp. 27–34.

——, "A Comparison of Equity Carve-Outs and Equity Offerings: Share Price Effects and Corporate Restructuring," *Journal of Financial Economics*, 15, 1986, pp. 153–186.

SKANTZ, TERRANCE R., and ROBERTO MARCHESINI, "The Effect of Voluntary Corporate Liquidation on Shareholder Wealth," *The Journal of Financial Research*, 10, Spring 1987, pp. 65–75.

SMITH, CLIFFORD W., JR., "Alternative Methods for Raising Capital: Rights Versus Underwritten Offerings," *Journal of Financial Economics*, 5, December 1977, pp. 273–307.

——, "Investment Banking and the Capital Acquisition Process," *Journal of Financial Economics*, 15, January/February 1986, pp. 3–29.

——, "Raising Capital: Theory and Evidence," *Midland Corporation Finance Journal*, Spring 1986a, pp. 6–22.

United States Executive Office of the President, Office of Management and Budget, *Standard Industrial Classification Manual, 1987*, for sale by: National Technical Information Service, Springfield, Virginia 22161.

W. T. GRIMM & Co., *Mergerstat Review, 1987*.

WELLING, KATHRYN M., "Thank You, Arco, Who's Next?" *Barron's*, May 6, 1985, pp. 8–9, 24, 26, 28, 32.

CHAPTER 10

Empirical Tests of Alternative Theories

Previous chapters have discussed alternative theories of why mergers and tender offers occur. In this present chapter, we seek to review the relevant empirical tests. First we review the alternative theories to have a brief reference framework for the tests.

THEORIES OF MERGERS

Alternative theories of mergers are summarized in Table 10.1. Including the subcategories, 13 distinct theories are presented. The list could easily be expanded. The large number of alternative merger theories makes the task of conducting empirical tests to distinguish among alternative theories extremely difficult. In addition, the changing economic and financial environments may encourage some types of mergers during certain time periods and stimulate other types of mergers under different circumstances. If so, generalizations will be difficult.

Each type of theory is briefly summarized to provide a foundation for review of the empirical studies.

Inefficient Management

The removal of inefficient management by a merger or tender offer would represent a gain in efficiency. There are at least two aspects involved.

TABLE 10.1
Theories of Mergers

    I. Inefficient management
   II. Operating synergy
  III. Financial synergy
  IV. Strategic realignment
   V. Undervaluation
     A. Short-term results versus long-run investment programs
     B. Market below replacement cost
  VI. Information and signaling
 VII. Agency problems and managerialism
     A. Protect or build the empire
     B. Free cash flow theory
VIII. Winner's curse—Hubris
  IX. Market power
   X. Tax considerations
  XI. Redistribution

DIFFERENTIAL EFFICIENCY   The most general theory of mergers involves differential efficiency. If the management of firm A is more efficient than the management of firm B and if after firm A acquires firm B, the efficiency of firm B is brought up to the level of efficiency of firm A, efficiency is increased by merger. Note that this outcome would be a social gain as well as a private gain. The level of efficiency in the economy would be raised by such mergers.

    Firms operating in similar kinds of business activity would be most likely to be the potential acquirers. They would have the background for detecting below-average or less-than-full-potential performance and have the managerial know-how for improving the performance of the acquired firm.

INEFFICIENT MANAGEMENT   Inefficient management may simply represent management that is inept in an absolute sense. Almost anyone could do better. The differential efficiency theory is more likely to involve management that is superior because it has experience in a particular line of business activity. The differential-efficiency theory is more likely to be a basis for horizontal mergers. The inefficient management theory could be a basis for unrelated mergers.

    The inefficient management theory may be difficult to distinguish from the differential efficiency theory previously discussed or the agency problem which is treated later. In one sense, inefficient management is simply not performing up to its potential. Another control group might be able to manage the assets of this area of activity more effectively.

Operating Synergy

Operating synergy or operating economies may be involved in horizontal and vertical mergers. For horizontal mergers the source of operating economies must represent a form of economies of scale. These economies, in turn, may reflect indivisibilities and better utilization of capacity after the merger. Or important complementarities in organizational capabilities may be present that result in gains not attainable from internal investments in the short run.

Another area in which operating economies may be achieved is vertical integration. Combining firms at different stages of an industry may achieve more efficient coordination of the different levels. The argument here is that costs of communication, and various forms of bargaining, and opportunistic behavior can be avoided by vertical integration (Williamson, 1971; Arrow, 1975; Klein, Crawford, and Alchian, 1978).

Financial Synergy

The possible financial synergies involve some unsettled issues of finance theory. Nevertheless, empirical analysis of mergers may shed light directly or indirectly on the fundamental issues. Financial synergy argues that the cost of capital function may be lowered for a number of reasons. If the cash flow streams of the two companies are not perfectly correlated, bankruptcy probabilities may be lowered; and this consequence may decrease the existing present value of bankruptcy costs.

This debt-coinsurance effect benefits debt holders at the expense of shareholders (Higgins and Schall, 1975). However, this effect can be offset by increasing leverage after the merger, and the result will be increased tax savings on interest payments (Galai and Masulis, 1976). The increase in debt capacity (defined as the maximum amount of debt that can be raised at any given interest rate) due to merger has been explicitly analyzed by Stapleton (1982) in the context of the option pricing theory. In his theory, the increase in debt capacity does not require the existence of bankruptcy costs.

Another dimension, emphasized by Levy and Sarnat (1970), is economies of scale in flotation and transaction costs that may be realized in conglomerate firms. Arguments may be raised about the potential magnitude of these financial factors. Further questions could be raised as to why joint activities might not be taken by unmerged firms to achieve the same economies of scale in flotation and transaction costs. However, the heterogeneity of firms and the costs of contracting would seem to make such activities prohibitive since such joint activities are not observed in the real world.

A fundamental type of financial synergy may be of greater importance than the previous types discussed. This theory holds that bidders have excess cash flows, but lack good investment opportunities. In contrast, targets are said to need additional funds to finance an abundance of good available growth investment opportunities. An example would be the acquisition by Philip Morris of General Foods in 1987 and of Kraft Foods in 1988. Philip Morris had large cash flows from their tobacco operations which appeared to be shrinking because of the mounting efforts to achieve a "smoke-free society." The food industry offered opportunities for growth, particularly since new product developments are an important source of expansion for such industries.

Strategic Realignment

The literature on long-range strategic planning has exploded in recent years. This literature is related to diversification through mergers. The emphasis of strategic planning is on areas related to firms' environments and constituencies, not just their operating decisions (Summer, 1980).

The strategic planning approach to mergers appears to imply either the possibilities of economies of scale or utilization of unused capacity in the firm's present managerial capabilities.[1] Another rationale is that by external diversification, the firm acquires management skills for needed augmentation of its present capabilities. This approach still leaves some questions unanswered. New capabilities and new markets could be developed internally. The less risky strategy may be to buy established organizations, but a competitive market for acquisitions implies that the net present value to acquirers from such investments is likely to be small. Nevertheless, if the changes in the environment call for a rapid adjustment, combinations of existing firms may have significant positive benefits. Furthermore, if these investments can be used as a base for still additional investments with positive net present values, the strategy may succeed.

Undervaluation

Undervaluation has a number of aspects. The nature and implications of each are somewhat different.

SHORT-TERM MYOPIA   The problem here is said to be that market participants, especially institutional investors, emphasize short-term earnings performance. As a consequence, it is argued that corporations with long-term investment programs are undervalued. When firms are undervalued, they become attractive targets to other firms or individual investors with large resources at their command (raiders).

MARKET BELOW REPLACEMENT COST   One reason that firms have stepped up diversification programs is that in recent years entry into new product market areas could be accomplished on a bargain basis. Inflation had a double-barreled impact. For various reasons, stock prices were depressed during the 1970s and did not recover until the latter part of 1982 as the level of inflation dropped and business prospects improved. The second impact of inflation was to cause current replacement costs of assets to be substantially higher than their recorded historical book values. These twin effects resulted in a decline of the q-ratio, defined as the ratio of the market value of the firm shares to the replacement costs of the assets represented by those shares.

In recent years the q-ratio had been running between 0.5 and 0.6. If a company wished to add to capacity in producing a particular product, it could acquire the additional capacity more cheaply by buying a company that produces

---

[1] For an elaboration of these themes, see also Chung and Weston (1982), and Chung (1982).

the product rather than building brick-and-mortar from scratch. If firm A seeks to add capacity, this activity implies that its marginal q-ratio is greater than 1. But if other firms in its industry have average q-ratios of less than 1, it is efficient for firm A to add capacity by the purchase of other firms. For example, if the q-ratio is 0.6 and if in a merger the premium paid over market value is 50 percent (which is the average figure for recent years), the resulting purchase price is 0.6 times 1.5 which equals 0.9 This outcome would mean that the average purchase price would still be 10 percent below the current replacement costs of the assets acquired. This potential advantage would provide a broad basis for the operation of the undervaluation theory in recent years as the q-ratio has declined.

For companies in natural resource industries, q-ratios have been as low as .2 because of high estimated values of reserves in the ground used in the denominator. The low q-ratio provided a basis for even more substantial premiums where natural resource firms were involved in mergers. For example, although U.S. Steel paid a substantial premium over market value in the Marathon merger, Marathon shareholders threatened suit because they stated that independent appraisals had estimated the current value of Marathon assets at more than double the price paid by U.S. Steel. Of course, these appraisals were subject to considerable uncertainty. Witness the sharp decline in oil prices that began in early 1983.

Information and Signaling

The announcement of merger negotiations or of a tender offer may convey information and/or signals to market participants. The announcement of a merger or tender offer may convey information that the target is "sitting on a gold mine" or signal that the old management will receive a "kick in the pants" from the new owners. A variation of this theme is that the announcement of a merger or tender offer conveys signals that future cash flows are likely to increase and that future values will increase accordingly. Thus, the announcement may signal that bidders see a potential for future value increases.

Agency Problems and Managerialism

Jensen and Meckling (1976) formulated the implications of agency problems. An agency problem arises when managers own only a fraction of the ownership shares of the firm. Partial ownership may cause managers to work less vigorously than otherwise and/or to consume more perquisites (such as luxurious offices, company cars, memberships in clubs) because the majority owners bear most of the cost. The argument can be made that in large corporations with widely dispersed ownership, individual owners do not have sufficient incentive to expend the substantial resources required to monitor the behavior of managers. A number of compensation arrangements and the market for managers may mitigate the agency problem (Fama, 1980).

Another market mechanism is the threat of takeovers. The threat of a takeover may substitute for individual shareholders' efforts to monitor the managers. The agency explanation of mergers extends the previous work by Manne (1965). Manne emphasized the market for corporate control and viewed mergers as a threat of takeover if a firm's management lagged in performance either because of inefficiency or because of agency problems.

A variant of the agency problem is the managerialism theory of conglomerate mergers as set forth by Mueller (1969). Mueller hypothesized that managers are motivated to further increase the size of their firms. He assumed that management compensation is a function of the size of the firm, and argued that managers adopt too low an investment hurdle rate. But in a study critical of earlier evidence, Lewellen and Huntsman (1970) presented findings that managers' compensation is significantly correlated with the firm's profit rate, not its level of sales. The basic premise of the managerialism theory, therefore, is doubtful.

The free cash flow theory of Jensen (1986, 1988) is based on the inherent conflict of interest between managers and shareholders. It adopts Mueller's theory that managers seek to protect or build their empires to increase perks and salaries. Funds beyond what a firm requires to invest in all available positive net present value investments are termed *free cash flow* by Jensen; such excess cash should be paid out. Jensen recommends substituting debt for equity or increasing debt ratios by other methods for such firms. He argues that this provides bonding that the managements of such firms will pay out excess cash flows in the future. Growth firms that have investment opportunities may properly retain cash flows to finance profitable investments.

Agency theory suggests that when the market for managers does not solve the agency problem, the market for firms or merger activity will come into play. This theory suggests, therefore, that merger activity is a method of dealing with the agency problem. The managerialism theory argues that the agency problem is not solved, and that merger activity is a manifestation of the agency problems of inefficient, external investments by managers.

Winner's Curse—Hubris

When bidding takes place for a valuable object with an uncertain value, the winning bid is likely to represent a positive valuation error. This result is likely to hold even though the valuable object is worth the same amount to all bidders (a common value auction) and the estimates of value are unbiased, so the mean of the estimates is equal to the common value of the valuable object. The positive valuation error represents the winner's curse. Capen, Clapp, and Campbell (1971), based on their analysis of sealed-bid competitive lease sales, present a diagram which depicts the relation between the high estimate to true value as a function of the degree of uncertainty and the number of bidders. Roll (1986) analyzes the effect in takeover activity. Postulating strong-market efficiency in all markets, the prevailing market price of the target already reflects the full value of the firm. The higher valuation of the bidder (over the target's true economic value), he states, results from hubris—the bidder's excessive self-confidence (pride, arrogance). Hubris is one of the factors which causes the winner's curse phenomenon to occur.

Market Power

The argument can be made that increasing the size of the firm will result in market power. What market power means or how it is achieved through greater size usually is not spelled out. In the case of horizontal mergers, the argument is sometimes made that the decrease in the number of firms will increase recognized interdependence or the possibility of collusion among the remaining firms in the industry.

Tax Considerations

Tax considerations also are involved in mergers. One example is the substitution of capital gains taxes for ordinary income taxes by acquiring a growth firm with a small or no dividend payout and then selling it after its growth to realize capital gains. Although the Tax Reform Act of 1986 eliminated preferential tax rate treatment for capital gains, there is still the advantage of deferral or choosing the time at which the capital gains will be realized and subject to tax.

Another tax factor is the sale of firms with accumulated tax losses. Although a business purpose also must be demonstrated, a firm with tax losses can shelter the positive earnings of another firm with which it is joined. The Economic Recovery Tax Act of 1981 provided for the sale of tax credits from the use of accelerated depreciation. These transactions often involved sale and lease-back arrangements. This tactic suggests that whether tax considerations induce mergers depends on the availability of alternative methods of achieving equivalent tax benefits.

Another strong tax incentive is to acquire firms in order to achieve a stepped-up basis for depreciable assets. This is one way of avoiding the disadvantage of low depreciation based on older historical costs during a period of inflation.

Still other tax effects are associated with inheritance taxes. A closely-held firm may be sold as the owners age because of the uncertainty of the value placed on the firm in connection with estate taxes. Also a sale may be made to provide greater liquidity for the payment of estate taxes.

A study of mergers in the newspaper industry illustrates the effects of the two previous tax influences (Dertouzos and Thorpe, 1982). The stepped-up basis for depreciable assets leads to competition among bidding firms resulting in premiums paid for newspaper companies acquired. These high, demonstrated market values are then used by the income tax service in setting values on newspaper companies for estate tax purposes. But the realization of the tax benefits of the higher depreciable values requires an actual transaction. This realization stimulates the purchase of individual newspaper companies by newspaper chains.

Redistribution

Tax saving is a form of redistribution from the tax collector to the firm that achieves tax benefits. Other forms of redistribution may be involved. Some argue that the gains achieved by mergers and tender offers go to the shareholders. It is argued that the source of the gains represent redistribution to the shareholders from a number of other stakeholders. These include bondholders in the form of reduced values, labor in the form of reduced wages and/or reduced employment, and consumers in the form of restricted supply and/or higher prices.

ISSUES IN EMPIRICAL STUDIES

There are a number of issues and questions that empirical studies may potentially elucidate. First and foremost, the goal is to provide tests of alternative theories. Another important objective from a public policy standpoint is to determine whether or not social value is enhanced by mergers. If, for example, the basic driving force for mergers is improved efficiency, the improvement represents a social gain regardless of the theory that explains how it is achieved.

If value is increased by mergers or tender offers, is it maintained? Is value maintained in the short term only for a period of six months or less? Or should the tests cover a subsequent period of five to ten years? Do value increases represent social gains or merely redistribution?

Additional questions relate to how the gains are divided between bidders and targets. Questions have been raised as to whether bidders gain. A related issue is determination of the effects on other firms in the same industry.

TESTS OF MERGER THEORIES
BY RESIDUAL ANALYSIS

Residual analysis basically tests whether the return to the common stock of individual firms or groups of firms is greater or less than that predicted by general market relationships between return and risk. Most merger studies in recent years have made use of residual analysis. These studies have sought to test whether merger events provide positive or negative abnormal returns to the participants.[2] The studies of abnormal returns provide a basis for examining the issue of whether or not value is enhanced by mergers.

The studies cover different time periods and different sample sizes. The

---

[2] The definition of *merger event* varies in the studies. In our judgment the announcement date is preferred to the actual consummation of the merger. Indeed, the evidence strongly suggests information leakage even before the announcement date.

studies are sometimes limited to conglomerate mergers. Other studies include horizontal and vertical mergers as well. Many studies deal with tender offers only. Some studies use monthly data; some use daily data; and some focus on individual mergers. At least one study analyzes firms engaged in programs of merger and tender offer activity over a period of years (Schipper and Thompson, 1980).

While there is widespread agreement on the use of residual analysis, its application is subject to variation. One problem is the choice of a reference period for obtaining parameters to be used in calculating excess returns caused by the events such as mergers and tender offers that are studied. If the reference period chosen is too long or far removed from the event, then the risk characteristics of the sample firms may have changed in the interval. If the reference period is too short, it may not represent a valid benchmark.

Another problem is the question of whether the market index used in the analysis is a valid measure of the market in relation to the underlying theory. However, the market model is widely used. Nevertheless, an alternative technique is sometimes employed. This method avoids use of the market model. It simply takes a reference period before and after (or before only, or after only) a window of 10, 20, or 30 days around the event date. This approach also has problems. One is the choice of the length of the reference period. Another is the width of the window to be employed.

Even if all of the uncertainties with regard to the use of residual analysis were resolved, there remain difficult problems in interpreting empirical results. Table 10.2 lists variables that could potentially influence the nature of empirical results. Twenty factors are listed. No attempt is made to discuss each one of these in detail. The table provides a checklist which is drawn upon in our interpretation of empirical data. We now turn to the empirical studies themselves.

EMPIRICAL RESULTS ON SUCCESSFUL BIDS

The *Journal of Financial Economics* published a compendium of studies of mergers and tender offers in 1983. In their comprehensive summary article, Jensen and Ruback (1983) reviewed 13 studies with sample data ending mostly in the late 1970s. Six of the studies were on mergers and seven on tender offers.

Returns to Targets

The summary table of Jensen and Ruback shows a 30 percent positive return to target shareholders in successful tender offers and a somewhat lower return of 20 percent to targets in successful mergers. (In mergers usually the larger firm is designated as the acquiring firm and the smaller firm as the acquired or target.)

Jarrell, Brickley, and Netter (1988) summarize results for 663 successful

TABLE 10.2
Variables Influencing Empirical Results for M&A Studies

1. Merger
   Tender offer
	12. Bidder—«/high-growth versus low-growth
	   industry
	   Target—«/high-growth versus low-growth
	   industry

2. Friendly Hostile (Resistance)	

3. Uncontested
   Contested
	13. Bidder—«/high-growth versus low-growth
	   firm in investment opportunities
	   Target—«/high-growth versus low-growth
	   firm in investment opportunities

4. Single bidder Multiple bidders	

5. Successful now
   Successful later
   Unsuccessful
   Unsuccessful acquired later
	14. Bidder—high versus low cash flows
	   Target—high versus low cash flows

	15. Bidder—high versus low leverage Target—high versus low leverage

6. Single acquisition
   Program of acquisition
	16. Stock market conditions favorable
	   Stock market conditions unfavorable

7. Tax effects involved
   a. Use of NOL
   b. Step up
   c. Defer gains
   d. Estate tax administration
	17. Spread between short and long rates wide
	   Spread between short and long rates nar-
	   row

	18. Spread between governments and
	   medium-grade corporates wide
	   Spread between governments and
	   medium-grade corporates narrow

8. Cash payment Securities payment	

9. Insider holdings high
   Insider holdings low
	19. Foothold percentage of bidder high
	   Foothold percentage of bidder low

10. Institutional holdings high
   Institutional holdings low
	20. Government regulations
	   Williams Act of 1968
	   13 (d) «/10%—1970—5%
	   14 (d) «/public tender offer—disclose its in-
	   tentions and business plans

11. Anticipated Unanticipated	

tender offers covering the period from 1962 through December 1985. They observe that premiums to targets in successful tender offers averaged 19 percent in the 1960s, 35 percent in the 1970s, and 30 percent for the period 1980–1985 (p. 51). Similar results were obtained by Bradley, Desai, and Kim (1988). For the period July 1963 to June 1968, the returns to targets were 19 percent. For the subperiod July 1968 to December 1980, they were 35 percent and for the period January 1981 to December 1984, the returns were 35 percent. Their study covered 236 successful tender offer contests completed between 1963 and 1984.

It is clear that targets in successful tender offers or mergers earn substantial premiums. It is clear also that the time trend of returns to targets has been upward. The reasons for the upward time trend may be summarized. In July 1968 the Williams Amendment gave the Securities and Exchange Commission (SEC) the power to regulate tender offers. In the same year the first state antitakeover law was passed by Virginia. The effect of government regulation was to require publication that a foothold position had been taken by the acquiring firm. In addition, government regulations provided for a delay before a tender offer could be completed. This enabled the targets to develop defenses and counterbids.

The period after the Reagan administration took office in early 1981 has its own distinctive characteristics. The regulatory agencies announced new standards toward mergers and takeovers which permitted horizontal and vertical mergers that would have been contested in earlier years. These developments were also accompanied by a rapid pace of innovations by financial intermediaries to finance mergers and tender offers. A counterdevelopment was the emergence of a wide array of defenses against takeovers. These included supermajority and fair-price amendments to corporate charters as well as the use of poison pills and various restructuring defenses. (These are all discussed in later chapters.)

Opposing forces are operating. However, it is clear that after the enactment of government regulations in the late 1960s, the returns to targets in successful tender offers increased from below 20 percent to somewhat over 30 percent on average.

While there is no question of large positive gains to target shareholders, Jarrell, Brickley, and Netter (1988, p. 52) observe that the evidence "probably understates the total gains to these shareholders." They observe that an active market for information develops about impending takeover bids. They point to a number of identifiable influences on prebid trading. These include articles in the financial press, information that develops on the bidder's foothold acquisition in the target, and in friendly bids there may be preliminary communications. They argue that factors such as these influence the earlier price runup and that these influences are distinct from illegal insider trading. Overall the shareholders of targets benefited by a substantial degree in successful tender offers and mergers. The evidence for bidders or acquiring firms, for unsuccessful events and for total value increase requires a more careful assessment to which we now turn.

Returns to Bidder Firms

There is no doubt that the returns to target shareholders are positive. The only issue is their magnitude. It is less clear whether or not the excess returns to the shareholders of bidder firms are positive. If the market for corporate control is perfectly competitive, we expect the excess returns to the shareholders of bidding firms to be zero. Bidders would earn only normal returns under competition. If this were the case, then overall M&A activity would be value increasing. The gains to the targets are positive and substantial. If the excess returns to bidder firms are zero, then overall the gains to the M&A activity would necessarily be positive. Only if the excess returns to bidder firms were negative would there be a possibility that the overall gains could be negative.

In their summary of the evidence, Jensen and Ruback (1983) concluded that the excess returns to bidder firms in successful tender offers was a positive 4 percent. They estimate zero returns to bidder firms in mergers. Jarrell, Brickley, and Netter (1988) examine the data on returns to shareholders of acquiring companies for a sequence of decades. For the 1960s, they obtain about the same result as

Jensen and Ruback for tender offers. For a window of ten days before the announcement date to five days after, the excess returns to successful bidders in tender offers are 4.4 percent. When the window is extended to 20 days after the event date, the cumulative excess returns rise to 4.95 percent and are highly significant from a statistical standpoint. The increase in excess returns during the subsequent 15-day period indicates that the postevent performance of the bidders improved somewhat with the longer postevent time period for analysis.

For the 1970s the excess returns to successful bidders drop to about 2 percent, statistically significant. For the 1980s, the excess returns become negative at about 1 percent but are not statistically significant.

Bradley, Desai, and Kim (1988) find similar results for tender offers. For subperiods approximating the 1960s, the excess returns to acquiring firms are slightly over 4 percent. For a period roughly corresponding to the 1970s, the excess returns are 1.3 percent. For the 1980s, the excess returns become negative at slightly under 3 percent. The data for the 1960s and the 1980s are significant at the 1 percent level. The excess returns to acquiring firms for the total period 1960–1985 for Jarrell, Brickley, and Netter and 1963 through 1984 for Bradley, Desai, and Kim are positive and significant. Bradley, Desai, and Kim also calculate the dollar amount of wealth change. They find that the combined results for target and acquiring firms are positive for each of the subperiods, including the 1980s when the excess wealth return to acquirers is negative.

The preceding evidence suggests that the returns to target firms increased over the decades as government regulation increased and as sophisticated defensive tactics by targets were developed. The excess returns to bidding firms decreased over the decades for the same influences operating in the reverse direction. But even for the most recent period of the 1980s, it appears that the total wealth increase from M&A activity is positive.

These conclusions are also supported by the frequency distribution analysis of You, Caves, Smith, and Henry (1986). The mean return to target companies for 133 mergers during the period 1975 through June 1984 is about 20 percent. The excess returns to shareholders of bidder companies are a negative 1 percent. In addition to mean returns, You, Caves, Smith, and Henry present frequency distributions. For target companies, 82 percent had positive excess returns. In fact, 20 percent of the companies had positive excess returns exceeding 40 percent. But 18 percent of the target companies had negative returns. For bidder companies, about 47 percent had positive returns while about 53 percent of the bidder companies had negative returns. However, most positive returns for bidder firms were modest in size. Twenty-five percent of the bidder companies had positive returns of from 0 to 5 percent. This is also true for the bidders that experienced negative returns—28 percent had excess returns of from 0 to −5 percent.

Thus, the mean returns cover up the wide diversity in experience both for target and bidder companies. Although bidder companies for some time period experienced negative returns, there is always a substantial fraction of the bidder companies who experience positive returns. This may provide motivation for bidder firms to continue to engage in M&A activity, although average results may be unfavorable. Each firm, based on the evidence, may formulate the judgment that its own results can be positive.

THE EFFECT OF METHOD OF PAYMENT AND MANAGERIAL RESISTANCE

While we analyze method of payment in more detail in Chapter 13, we want to note the effect of method of payment to place the previous data in perspective. Huang and Walkling (1987) analyzed acquisitions by tender offer versus merger, by payment method, and by target management's attitude. Like the previous studies, they found that tender offers yielded significantly higher returns than mergers. They found, however, that tender offers are generally for cash and more likely to be resisted than mergers. Mergers on average tend to be friendly transactions.

In their regression analysis, Huang and Walkling (1987) controlled for form of payment and degree of resistance; no significant difference remained between tender offers and mergers. They found that resisted offers earned somewhat higher returns to targets than unresisted offers, but the difference was not significant from a statistical standpoint. They argue that the overall impact of resistance is difficult to judge. There is always the possibility that target resistance may cause the bidder to abandon attempts which otherwise might have been profitable. The abandoned tender offers might not even reach the announcement stage in many instances.

The Effect of NASDAQ Trading

Most of the studies of M&A activity are for New York Stock Exchange and American Stock Exchange targets. A study was made for NASDAQ targets for 1984 (Asquith, 1988). In Table 10.3, the results are shown for all offers. For the period -10 days to the announcement date, the excess return to targets is 19.0 percent. However, for day -1 to the announcement date the return is 10.7 percent. This is the order of magnitude of the data for NYSE and ASE companies. The results are not greatly different when broken down between successful and unsuccessful offers and between uncontested and contested offers.

UNSUCCESSFUL TAKEOVERS

Jensen and Ruback (1983) found that for unsuccessful tender offers both target and bidder companies experienced negative excess returns of modest size, but not statistically significant. In mergers, target firms also experienced negative,

TABLE 10.3

Cumulative Abnormal Returns to Tender Offers, NASDAQ Targets, 1984

				ALL OFFERS			
				CAR	T-STAT	%POS.	N
Day −60	to	20	:	0.32344	11.53	86.	44.
Day −60	to	−21	:	0.07105	5.40	74.	50.
Day −20	to	20	:	0.26231	13.22	86.	44.
Day −20	to	−11	:	0.04596	4.33	58.	50.
Day −10	to	0	:	0.18969	19.40	93.	45.
Day 1	to	10	:	0.01910	2.74	65.	49.
Day 11	to	20	:	0.00261	0.25	47.	49.
Day −4	to	−2	:	0.03294	4.12	62.	47.
Day −1	to	0	:	0.10675	28.48	76.	49.

Source: Daniel Asquith, "Evidence on Theories of Volume, Bid-Ask Spreads, and Return Premia Among NASDAQ Targets of Tender Offer Bids," Doctoral Research Paper, November 1, 1988.

but statistically insignificant returns. For bidder firms in mergers, the excess negative return was 5 percent and it was statistically significant.

Returns to Targets

In discussing a sample of 112 unsuccessful takeovers, Bradley, Desai, and Kim (1983) divide the targets into three groups. The first group (58 percent of the sample) is subsequently taken over within 60 trading days after the announcement date (day zero). The cumulative abnormal return (CAR) is almost 50 percent during the two-day period (−1 to 0) and rises to over 66 percent by the end of the 60 trading days. A second group (19 percent of the sample) is taken over after 60 days, but before five years. Their CAR for the two-day period (−1 to 0) is about 23 percent. By day +60, their CAR rises to over 55 percent. So they do almost as well as the first group, but the market does not react until later when the probability of a subsequent bid increases. For the third group (23 percent of the sample) which is not taken over within the five-year period, the CAR which is initially about the same as for the second group, becomes negative after two years and drifts between a range of a negative 5 to 10 percent during the subsequent three years.

Bradley, Desai, and Kim (1983) argue that these data on targets of initially unsuccessful takeovers are consistent with a synergy theory, but not an information theory. Roll (1987, p. 80) suggests an alternative explanation. He states:

> . . . what if the tender offer revealed the *probable* existence of private positive information about the target, not the certainty of such information? One would expect that those firms for which such information did exist might be more likely candidates for further bids. Since each bid has some chance of success, such firms would also be more likely to enter a subsequent combination. Firms for whom there was

no private information in the first place would be less likely to elicit further bids since there would be little incentive for a potential acquiring firm to make a bid. Thus, firms which never enter a combination should experience a fall in price back to the original level. Information whose *possible* existence was revealed by the initial unsuccessful tender offer turns out not to exist in these cases.

Returns to Unsuccessful Bidders

In discussing unsuccessful bidders, Bradley, Desai, and Kim (1983) divide their sample into two groups. Group 1 bidders lose out to a rival bidder by the end of 180 trading days after the announcement date. Their CAR is a negative 8 percent by the end of the 180 days. For group 2 bidders, no rival bidder has succeeded within the 180 days subsequent to the initial announcement. At the end of 180 days, these bidders experience a small positive, but not significant CAR.

Bradley, Desai, and Kim (1983, p. 204) rule out an information explanation of these patterns. They state:

> Thus, the information hypothesis predicts no difference in the returns to the stock-holders of the unsuccessful bidding firms in the two subsamples. Unlike the information hypothesis, the synergy hypothesis provides at least a plausible explanation for the relation between the returns to unsuccessful bidding firms and the ultimate disposition of control of the target resources. The data are consistent with the joint hypothesis that the ultimately successful bidding firm possesses a specialized resource that allows for a higher-valued offer and that the synergy created by combining with the target places the unsuccessful bidding firm at a competitive disadvantage in the marketplace.

Again, Roll (1987, pp. 80–81) suggests that the data are equally consistent with an information explanation.

> But doesn't the information hypothesis really imply the same thing? The appearance of a rival bid increases the probability that there exists positive non-public information about the target firm but it *decreases* both the probability that the initial bidder has exclusive possession of the information and the probability that the initial bid will succeed.

We next turn to further evidence on returns to unsuccessful bidders.

Further Analysis
of Unsuccessful Bidders

The results for the unsuccessful acquiring firms are of interest because of the impact on total value. As observed previously, if the returns to acquiring firms are sufficiently negative, this could cause the total activity to be a negative net present value activity rather than one that created positive values.

Bradley, Desai, and Kim (1983) found that for the period 1963–1980, the unsuccessful bidders in the multiple-bidder contests on average lost 8 percent of their preoffer value. They observe that the gains to successful bidders in multiple-bidder contests during the same period were not significantly different from zero. They conclude that it is better to win than to lose in a multiple-bidding contest. But this conclusion does not hold for the 1981–1984 period during which successful bidders in multiple-bidder contests lost 5.1 percent (highly significant) (Bradley, Desai, and Kim, 1988).

For a larger sample of tender offers, Opler (1988) finds that for the period 1981–1986, unsuccessful bidders earn a positive .68 percent, marginally significant. The results for unsuccessful acquiring firms depend on a number of other variables, however. These influences are examined in greater detail. In Figure 10.1, a breakdown is made between unsuccessful acquiring firms which made a later takeover and those which did not. The cumulative average abnormal return was a positive 10 percent 18 months after termination during which a later takeover had occurred. When no later takeover occurred, the cumulative average abnormal return, however, was negative by about 5 percent.

The results differ also depending on whether the unsuccessful acquiring firms experience positive CARs for the announcement period (the day before through the day after the announcement date). Figure 10.2 shows that for the subsample of bidders which had positive announcement CARs and which made a later takeover during the subsequent 18 months, the cumulative abnormal returns by the end of the 18 months were 20 percent. For unsuccessful bidders with initial positive returns, but which made no later takeover, the cumulative average abnormal return was only slightly above zero.

In Figure 10.3, the patterns are shown for those unsuccessful acquiring firms which experienced negative announcement period CARs (−1, +1 days).

FIGURE 10.1   CARs to Unsuccessful Bidders, Later Takeover, No Later Takeover, All, 1980–1986

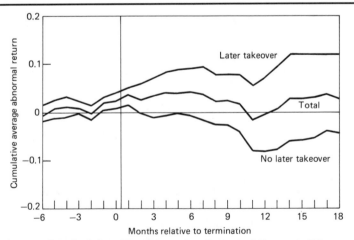

SOURCE: Tim C. Opler, "The Information Content of Corporate Takeover Announcements: Issues and Evidence," Anderson Graduate School of Management, University of California, Los Angeles, October 1988.

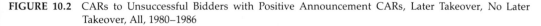

FIGURE 10.2   CARs to Unsuccessful Bidders with Positive Announcement CARs, Later Takeover, No Later Takeover, All, 1980–1986

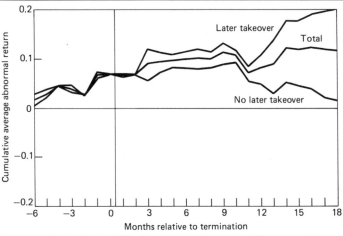

SOURCE: Tim C. Opler, "The Information Content of Corporate Takeover Announcements: Issues and Evidence," Anderson Graduate School of Management, University of California, Los Angeles, October 1988.

For such unsuccessful acquiring firms which made a later takeover within the 18 months after the announcement date, the cumulative return was positive for most of the 18-month period, but returned to approximately zero by the end of the 18 months. For those unsuccessful acquiring firms which made no subse-

FIGURE 10.3   CARs to Unsuccessful Bidders with Negative Announcement CARs, Later Takeover, No Later Takeover, All, 1980–1986

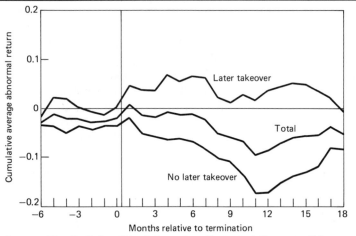

SOURCE: Tim C. Opler, "The Information Content of Corporate Takeover Announcements: Issues and Evidence," Anderson Graduate School of Management, University of California, Los Angeles, October 1988.

quent takeover, the CARs declined sharply to about -18 percent by the twelfth month following the announcement date and then recovered to about a -10 percent CAR by the end of the 18 months.

These data and related patterns show that the experiences of unsuccessful acquiring firms are quite different depending on the initial response in the announcement period and also whether or not the acquiring firm made a later takeover. However, no inference on causality appears possible because the better performance of unsuccessful bidders making later takeovers may not be the result of such a takeover, but simply be due to a selection bias (that is, better performance led to takeovers).

THE CORRELATION
OF ABNORMAL RETURNS

Residual analysis studies can be extended to pinpoint more closely the behavior of abnormal returns. Three alternative hypotheses can be tested more directly. The managerialism hypothesis argues that firms pursue size maximization rather than value maximization. This hypothesis implies high agency costs and excessive premiums paid to acquired firms. These excessive premiums will have adverse effects on acquiring firms. This hypothesis predicts a negative correlation between buyer-and-seller returns.

The inefficient management hypothesis states that mergers and acquisitions occur because the target-firm managements are not performing up to the full potential for the firm. This hypothesis implies that agency costs are high and the current owners are unable to replace management. No presumption is made of greater than average management efficiency in the acquiring firm. Since a number of buyers could improve the performance of the target firm, competition in the takeover market would cause most of the gains to go to the sellers. This theory predicts zero correlation between buyer and seller returns.

The synergy theory states that by combining two entities, efficiencies and economies not otherwise achievable will be obtained. Managerial synergy implies that complementarity exists between the capabilities of the combining firms. The buyer has underutilized managerial resources that can be effectively applied in the combined firm. Financial synergy suggests economies in financing as a result of the merger. Illustrative types are: (1) better utilization of internal cash flows, (2) increased debt capacity, and (3) economies of scale in flotation costs. The synergy theory also predicts a positive correlation between buyer and seller returns.

Tests of the alternative theories were performed using the Federal Trade Commission (FTC) large-merger series for 1958–1977.[3] The sample consisted of 49

---

[3] Data on merger activity through 1987 are now available from W. T. Grimm, but this series does not go back beyond 1967. The data for the FTC series used here are not available beyond 1979.

pure conglomerate mergers (PCMs) and 68 product-extension mergers (PEMs). The market model was used with parameters estimated over months $(-84$ to $-25)$ relative to the merger-announcement month. The variables investigated were:

RET1   Sum of acquired firm residuals over months $[-3$ to $0]$

VAL   Market value of common equity of the acquired firm in month -4

RET2   Same as RET1 except that returns are adjusted for industry effects (residuals estimated with the industry return added as the second factor in the market model)

A "B" is placed in front of the variables to indicate buyer firm. SIZE is then defined as the ratio of the market value of target equity to the market value of buyer equity (VAL/BVAL) at the end of month -4. Three tests were performed:

1 Regress BRET1 on RET1 for correlation between buyer and seller returns.

2 BRET1 = f(RET1, SIZE)—effect of acquiring different relative size targets.

3 BRET1 × BVAL = f(RET1 × VAL)—correlation of dollar returns. Dollar returns = RET1 × VAL and BRET1 × BVAL.

These three tests also were performed using RET2 and BRET2, the returns adjusted for industry effects using three-digit SIC codes. The summary statistics are presented in Table 10.4. Based on the average market values, the acquiring firms are five times as large as the acquired firms for the pure conglomerate mergers. For the product-extension mergers, the relative size relationship is 5.7 times.

TABLE 10.4
Summary Statistics of Variables

VARIABLE	PCM (PURE CON-GLOMERATE)			PEM (PRODUCT EX-TENSION)		
	N	MEAN	STD. DEV.	N	MEAN	STD. DEV.
ACQUIRED FIRMS						
RET1 (%)	49	22.9	29.2	68	23.9	24.5
VAL ($ million)	49	132.0	218.6	68	92.4	98.6
RET1×VAL ($ million)	49	19.8	55.2	68	13.1	14.3
RET2	25	20.5	26.8	29	18.0	16.6
VAL	25	124.8	140.2	29	91.6	71.7
RET2×VAL	25	14.9	30.0	29	13.5	14.1
ACQUIRING FIRMS						
BRET1	49	−0.6	16.2	68	3.1	16.0
BVAL	49	710.5	1461.1	68	530.4	689.7
BRET1×BVAL	49	−9.9	68.8	68	6.1	52.9
BRET2	25	−1.1	9.8	29	2.8	14.6
BVAL	25	502.4	533.6	29	485.3	556.4
BRET2×BVAL	25	−3.9	23.6	29	4.4	47.8

TABLE 10.5
Estimates of Regression Coefficients[a]

DEPENDENT VARIABLE	CONST.	RET1[b] OR (RET2)	SIZE	RET1×VAL[b] OR (RET2×VAL)	R²	N
1. PURE CONGLOMERATE MERGERS						
BRET1	−4.14	0.16 (1.99)			0.08	
BRETI	−9.34	0.23 (2.62)	8.46 (2.58)		0.22	49
BRET1 XBVAL	−24.61			0.74 (2.77)	0.14	49
BRET2	−4.70	0.17 (2.60)			0.23	25
BRET2	−5.76	0.19 (2.53)	1.59 (0.50)		0.24	25
BRET2 ×BVAL	−6.30			0.16 (0.87)	0.03	25
2. PRODUCT-EXTENSION MERGERS						
BRET1	−0.49	0.15 (1.80)			0.08	68
BRET1	−9.06	0.21 (2.39)	18.78 (2.80)		0.21	68
BRET1 ×VAL	−9.72			1.21 (2.15)	0.09	68
BRET2	−3.15	0.33 (1.75)			0.12	29
BRET2	−7.98	0.37 (1.95)	10.15 (1.29)		0.19	29
BRET2 ×VAL	−6.81			0.83 (1.26)	0.07	29

[a]t-values are in parentheses.
[b]If the dependent variable is BRET1 then RET1 is used and if it is BRET2 then RET2 is used.

The regression results are presented in Table 10.5. For the market model without industry adjustments, the buyer abnormal returns are significantly positively correlated with seller returns for all three tests. The results are similar for both the PCMs and PEMs. The dollar-gain coefficient is not significantly different from 1, which suggests evenly divided gains after the buyer incurs the costs of the merger. The costs of the merger are represented by the intercept terms, which are $24.6 million for PCMs and $9.7 million for PEMs. The industry-adjusted results (RET2, BRET2) are less strong. There is still significant positive correlation between buyer and seller returns. The relative size and dollar-gain results are not significant. The tests are consistent with the efficiency or synergy theory. The results are clearly inconsistent with the managerialism theory since the signs are never negative.

EFFICIENCY VERSUS MARKET POWER

The empirical studies suggest that value is increased by merger activity, which does not support the managerialism theory. The evidence is strong that the shareholders of acquired firms gain. Whether the gains to the shareholders of acquiring firms are statistically significant is not clear. The possibility remains that the value gains result from increases in market power, however, rather than from increases in efficiency. A number of studies are relevant to these issues.

Ellert (1975, 1976) studied these issues at great length. He analyzed the data for 205 defendants in antimerger complaints for the period 1950–1972. He found that for four years before the filing of the complaint, the residual performance was positive and statistically significant for the defendants. As expected, the residuals become negative upon the filing of a complaint. However, the negative residuals were relatively small. Ellert observed that the record of effective asset management in the years preceding merger activity by acquiring firms may result in complaints by their rivals to antitrust authorities. Ellert termed such legal actions a "harassment" hypothesis. He indicated that incentives exist for complaining rivals to follow this course. The government agencies bear the costs of prosecution; and if successful, the complaining firms' actions will handicap their rivals. The complaining parties may then file private treble damage suits. The harassment hypothesis is clearly the opposite of a monopoly explanation of merger activity. In addition, if a doubt exists about whether the acquiring firms obtain gains from the merger, this doubt itself is inconsistent with the monopoly theory. If the monopoly theory is valid, both parties should gain from the merger.

The monopoly theory has been pursued even further in studies by Stillman (1983) and Eckbo (1981) who looked at the residuals of the rivals of firms participating in mergers. The problem is complex because at the theoretical level a number of alternative hypotheses can be formulated as illustrated in Table 10.6.

Three studies appear to support the efficiency basis for mergers. Ellert emphasized that acquiring firms had positive residuals in prior years, and acquired firms had negative residuals in prior years. Stillman's evidence showed that rival firms did not benefit from the announcement of proposed mergers which is inconsistent with the concentration-collusion hypothesis. Eckbo found positive residuals on the merger announcement but no negative effects on rivals when it appeared that the merger would be blocked by the antitrust authorities. He interpreted this pattern of relationships as indicating that the main effect of the merger is to signal the possibility of achieving economies for the merging firms and to provide information to rivals that such economies may also be available to them.

TABLE 10.6
Alternative Hypotheses of Merger Effects

	PARTICIPATING FIRMS	RIVAL FIRMS
	I. ANNOUNCEMENT OF MERGER	
Collusion	+ Higher profits from colluding	+Are part of the collusion
Efficiency	+External investment with large positive NPV	+Demonstrate how to achieve greater efficiency
		−Tougher competition
		0Competition in marketplace un-affected by purchase of under-valued firm
	II. ANNOUNCEMENT OF CHALLENGE	
Collusion	−Collusion prevented	−Collusion prevented
Efficiency	−Prevents a positive NPV investment, also litiga-tions costs	+Threat of more efficient rivals reduced
		−Also prevented from mergers for efficiency
	0Could do same thing internally	0Can do internally
	III. ANNOUNCEMENT OF DECISION	
Collusion	−Collusion definitely prevented	−Collusion prevented
		+Defendants prevented from be-ing more efficient
	0(1)Negative impact already, at challenge date	0(1)Negative impact already, at challenge date
	(2)Leakage of likely judicial decision during trial	(2)Leakage of likely judicial deci-sion during trial
	(3)Underlying economics of the industry not af-fected	(3)Underlying economics of the industry not affected
Efficiency	+Increased efficiency	+Can now legally merge for effi-ciency
		−Tougher competition
		0Could have accomplished the same thing internally

Note: The +, −, 0 signs denote the predicted positive, negative, and zero impacts, respectively, on the firms' values.

CONCLUSIONS

The first six theories listed in Table 10.1 are inefficient management, operating synergy, financial synergy, strategic realignment, undervaluation, and information and signaling. From the empirical evidence, it is difficult to distinguish among these six explanatory theories. But they are all consistent with the empirical evidence that value is created by mergers and takeovers.

The remaining five theories are agency problems, winner's curse (hubris), market power, tax considerations, and redistribution. These theories cast doubt on whether value is created by mergers and takeovers. The agency problem theory argues that the motive is empire building and that the M&As should not have been made in the first place. The winner's curse is more ambiguous in its prediction. Bidders could pay too much for targets and still have value created by the combination. This is suggested by the data. Market power would also create gains to shareholders, but at the expense of consumers or owners of input factors. Tax factors could create gains to shareholders at the expense of the tax collector. Redistribution would benefit shareholders at the expense of other stakeholders.

The preponderance of empirical evidence supports the judgment that merger activity is usually rational, value-maximizing behavior. On average, residuals measured as rates of return or in absolute amounts associated with the merger events are positive; and the residuals do not decline significantly after merger events. The evidence does not support the managerialism theory of mergers which holds that managements merge to increase the size of firms to increase their own compensation, or for the prestige of running giant organizations. However, individual examples of mistakes, excesses, hubris, and financial self-dealing can be cited.

The major studies of the monopoly versus efficiency issue obtain complex empirical patterns. However, all interpret their results as supporting the efficiency theory.

If bankruptcy costs are significant, the existence of a corporate income tax may confer benefits because the merger may reduce expected bankruptcy costs and result in increased debt capacity. Also, mergers of failing or floundering companies take place to preserve organization values. Mergers as a substitute for bankruptcy are consistent with the existence of large, indirect bankruptcy costs. More than pure diversification effects are involved if organizational values are destroyed by bankruptcy, but can be preserved or enhanced by mergers. Other empirical evidence is consistent with the proposition that firms with under-utilized managerial capabilities acquire firms in industries with relatively more favorable investment prospects.

The q-ratio, the measure of market values to replacement costs, leads us to additional insights on merger activity. In different types of economic environments, different types of merger activity take place. Merger activity was positively correlated with the q-ratio during the 1960s. With the increased emphasis on strategic planning and aligning the firm to its changing environments, the relatively low q-ratios in the 1970s facilitated investment and diversification into attractive areas at "bargain prices."

Mergers and takeovers appear to represent a response to the characteristics of the economic environment. Specifying the economic environment permits a prediction of the level of merger activity as well as the forms that mergers take.

M&A activity is also seen as a part of a broader resource allocation process. Even conglomerate acquisitions were concentrated in certain industries which changed in different economic environments. The high rate of divestitures—40 percent to 45 percent of all merger activity in recent years—is also consistent with a resource reallocation function.

Whether on balance the current wave of restructuring is socially beneficial must await our further analysis in subsequent chapters. We cover additional important aspects of managerial and broader social issues in the chapters which follow.

QUESTIONS

1. If residual analysis indicates positive abnormal returns to merging firms, what theory (or theories) of mergers is supported? If residual analysis indicates negative abnormal returns, what theory (or theories) is supported?
2. How do abnormal returns vary for acquiring and acquired firms during the period well before any merger announcement? What do these returns imply?
3. How do state and federal regulation affect returns to merging firms?
4. a. What do the following merger theories predict about the correlation between abnormal returns of buyer and seller returns in mergers:
   Managerialism
   Inefficient management
   Synergy/efficiency
   b. Discuss the empirical results of tests of the correlation between buyer and seller returns.
5. How should the returns to rivals of the merging firms be affected under the market power (monopoly) and efficiency theories?
6. What can residual analysis tell us about aggregate merger activity in the economy as a whole?

REFERENCES

ALEXANDER, GORDON J., P. GEORGE BENSON, and JOAN M. KAMPMEYER, "Investigating the Valuation Effects of Announcements of Voluntary Corporate Divestitures," *Journal of Finance,* June 1984, pp. 503–517.

ARROW, K. J., "Vertical Integration and Communication," *Bell Journal of Economics,* Spring 1975, pp. 173–183.

ASQUITH, DANIEL, "Evidence on Theories of Volume, Bid-Ask Spreads, and Return Premia Among NASDAQ Targets of Tender Offer Bids," Doctoral Research Paper, Anderson Graduate School of Management, University of California, Los Angeles, November 1, 1988.

ASQUITH, P., "Merger Bids, Uncertainty, and Stockholder Returns," *Journal of Financial Economics,* April 1983, pp. 51–84.

———, and E. HAN KIM, "The Impact of Merger Bids on the Participating Firms' Security Returns," *Journal of Finance,* December 1982, pp. 1209–1228.

BRADLEY, M., "Interfirm Tender Offers and the Market for Corporate Control," *Journal of Business,* October 1980, pp. 345–376.

———, ANAND DESAI, and E. HAN KIM, "Specialized Resources and Competition in the Market for Corporate Control," University of Michigan, September 1982.

———, "The Rationale Behind Interfirm Tender Offers: Information or Synergy?" *Journal of Financial Economics,* 1983, pp. 183–206.

———, "Synergistic Gains from Corporate Acquisitions and their Division Between the Stockholders of Target and Acquiring Firms," *Journal of Financial Economics,* 21, 1988, pp. 3–40.

CAPEN, E. C., R. V. CLAPP, and W. M. CAMPBELL, "Competitive Bidding in High-Risk Situations," *Journal of Petroleum Technology,* June 1971, pp. 641–653.

CHOI, DOSOUNG, and GEORGE C. PHILIPPATOS, "On the Economic Rationale for Corporate Divestitures and Spin-Offs," presentation at the 1982 Annual Meeting of the Financial Management Association, San Francisco, CA, August 1982.

CHUNG, K. S., "Investment Opportunities, Synergies, and Conglomerate Mergers," Ph.D. dissertation, Anderson Graduate School of Management, University of California, Los Angeles, 1982.

———, and J. FRED WESTON, "Diversification and Mergers in a Strategic Long-Range-Planning Framework," Chapter 13 in M. Keenan and L. J. White, eds., *Mergers and Acquisitions,* Lexington, MA: D. C. Heath, 1982.

CHUNG, K. S., "The Correlation of Abnormal Returns for Acquired and Acquiring Firms in Conglomerate Mergers," Rutgers University, January 1983.

COPELAND, THOMAS, E, and J. FRED WESTON, *Financial Theory and Corporate Policy,* 3rd ed., Reading, MA: Addison-Wesley Publishing Company, 1988.

DANN, L. Y., and H. DEANGELO, "Standstill Agreements, Privately Negotiated Stock Repurchases, and the Market for Corporate Control," *Journal of Financial Economics,* April 1983, pp. 275–300.

DEANGELO, H., and E. M. RICE, "Antitakeover Charter Amendments and Stockholder Wealth," *Journal of Financial Economics,* April 1983, pp. 329–360.

DERTOUZOS, JAMES N., and KENNETH E. THORPE, "Newspaper Groups: Economies of Scale, Tax Laws, and Merger Incentives," Santa Monica, CA, Rand Corporation, R-2878-SBA, June 1982.

DODD, P., "Merger Proposals, Management Discretion, and Stockholder Wealth," *Journal of Financial Economics,* June 1980, pp. 105–137.

———, and R. RUBACK, "Tender Offers and Stockholder Returns: An Empirical Analysis," *Journal of Financial Economics,* December 1977, pp. 351–374.

DODD, P., and J. B. WARNER, "On Corporate Governance: A Study of Proxy Contests," unpublished manuscript, University of Chicago, September 1981.

ECKBO, B. E., "Examining the Anti-Competitive Significance of Large Horizontal Mergers," unpublished Ph.D. dissertation, University of Rochester, 1981.

ELGERS, P. T., and J. J. CLARK, "Merger Types and Shareholder Returns: Additional Evidence," *Financial Management,* Summer 1980, pp. 66–72.

ELLERT, J. C., "Antitrust Enforcement and the Behavior of Stock Prices," doctoral dissertation, University of Chicago, June 1975.

———, "Mergers, Antitrust Law Enforcement, and Stockholder Returns," *Journal of Finance,* May 1976, pp. 715–732.

FAMA, E., "Agency Problems and the Theory of the Firm," *Journal of Political Economy,* April 1980, pp. 288–307.

GALAI, D., and R. W. MASULIS, "The Option Pricing Model and the Risk Factor of Stock," *Journal of Financial Economics,* January/March 1976, pp. 53–82.

GROSSMAN, S., "The Allocational Role of Takeover Bids in Situations of Asymmetric Information," *Journal of Finance,* May 1981, pp. 253–270.

HALPERN, P. J., "Empirical Estimates of the Amount and Distribution of Gains to Companies in Mergers," *Journal of Business,* October 1973, pp. 554–575.

HIGGINS, R. C., "Discussion," *Journal of Finance,* May 1971, pp. 543–545.

———, and LAWRENCE D. SCHALL, "Corporate Bankruptcy and Conglomerate Merger," *Journal of Finance,* March 1975, pp. 93–113.

HUANG, YEN-SHENG, and RALPH A. WALKLING, "Target Abnormal Returns Associated with Acquisition Announcements," *Journal of Financial Economics,* 19, 1987, pp. 329–349.

JARRELL, G., and M. BRADLEY, "The Economic Effects of Federal and State Regulations of Cash Tender Offers," *Journal of Law and Economics,* October 1980, pp. 371–407.

JARRELL, G. A., J. A. BRICKLEY, and J. M. NETTER, "The Market for Corporate Control: The Empirical Evidence Since 1980," *Journal of Economic Perspectives,* 2, Winter 1988, pp. 49–68.

JENSEN, M. C., "Agency Costs of Free Cash Flow, Corporate Finance and Takeovers," *American Economic Review,* May 1986, pp. 323–329.

———, "The Takeover Controversy: Analysis and Evidence," Chapter 20 in *Knights, Raiders, and Targets,* J. C. Coffee, Jr., L. Lowenstein, and S. Rose-Ackerman, eds., New York: Oxford University Press, 1988.

———, and W. MECKLING, "Theory of the Firm: Managerial Behavior, Agency Costs and Ownership Structure," *Journal of Financial Economics,* October 1976, pp. 305–360.

JENSEN, M. C., and R. S. RUBACK, "The Market for Corporate Control: The Scientific Evidence," *Journal of Financial Economics,* 1983, pp. 5–50.

KLEIN, B., R. G. CRAWFORD, and A. A. ALCHIAN, "Vertical Integration, Appropriable Rents and the Competitive Contracting Process," *The Journal of Law and Economics,* 21, October 1978, pp. 297–326.

KUMMER, D. R., and J. R. HOFFMEISTER, "Valuation Consequences of Cash Tender Offers," *Journal of Finance,* May 1978, pp. 505–516.

LANGETIEG, T. C., "An Application of a Three-Factor Performance Index to Measure Stockholder Gains from Merger," *Journal of Financial Economics,* December 1978, pp. 365–383.

LEVY, H., and M. SARNAT, "Diversification, Portfolio Analysis and the Uneasy Case for Conglomerate Mergers," *Journal of Finance,* September 1970, pp. 795–802.

LEWELLEN, W. G., and B. HUNTSMAN, "Managerial Pay and Corporate Performance," *American Economic Review,* September 1970, pp. 710–720.

MALATESTA, P. H., "The Wealth Effect of Merger Activity and the Objective Functions of Merging Firms," unpublished manuscript, University of Rochester, March 1982.

MANDELKER, G., "Risk and Return: The Case of Merging Firms," *Journal of Financial Economics,* December 1974, pp. 303–335.

MANNE, H. G., "Mergers and the Market for Corporate Control," *Journal of Political Economy,* April 1965, pp. 110–120.

MUELLER, D. C., "A Theory of Conglomerate Mergers," *Quarterly Journal of Economics,* November 1969, pp. 643–659.

NELSON, RALPH L., *Merger Movements in American Industry 1895–1956,* Princeton, NJ: Princeton University Press, 1959.

OPLER, TIM C., "The Information Content of Corporate Takeover Announcements: Issues and Evidence," ms., Anderson Graduate School of Management, University of California, Los Angeles, October 1988.

ROLL, RICHARD, "The Hubris Hypothesis of Corporate Takeovers," *Journal of Business,* April 1986, pp. 197–216.

——, "Empirical Evidence on Takeover Activity and Shareholder Wealth," Chapter 5 in *Modern Finance & Industrial Economics,* Thomas E. Copeland, ed., New York: Basil Blackwell, 1987, pp. 74–91.

SCHIPPER, K., and R. THOMPSON, "Evidence on the Capitalized Value of Merger Activity for Acquiring Firms," Carnegie-Mellon University Working Paper, 1980.

STAPLETON, R. C., "Mergers, Debt Capacity, and the Valuation of Corporate Loans," Chapter 2 in M. Keenan and L. J. White, eds., *Mergers and Acquisitions,* Lexington, MA: D. C. Heath, 1982.

STILLMAN, R. S., "Examining Antitrust Policy Towards Horizontal Mergers," *Journal of Financial Economics,* April 1983, pp. 225–240.

SUMMER, C., *Strategic Behavior in Business and Government,* Boston, MA: Little, Brown and Company, 1980.

WANSLEY, JAMES W., WILLIAM R. LANE, and HO C. YANG, "Abnormal Returns to Acquired Firms by Type of Acquisition and Method of Payment," *Financial Management,* Autumn 1983, pp. 16–22.

WILLIAMSON, O. E., "The Vertical Integration of Production: Market Failure Considerations," *The American Economic Review,* May 1971, pp. 112–123.

YOU, VICTOR, RICHARD CAVES, MICHAEL SMITH, and JAMES HENRY, "Mergers and Bidders' Wealth: Managerial and Strategic Factors," *The Economics of Strategic Planning,* Lacy Glenn Thomas, III, ed., Lexington, MA: Lexington Books, 1986.

CHAPTER 11

Timing of Merger Activity

As noted in Chapter 1, merger activity has fluctuated throughout the periods of recorded merger activity. This fluctuation poses a challenge to the theory of mergers to explain the timing or determinants of aggregate merger activity. It also provides an opportunity to test the validity of theories of mergers. A complete theory of mergers should have implications on the timing of aggregate merger activity. As the matter stands, there does not exist an accepted theory which simultaneously explains motivations behind mergers, characteristics of acquiring and acquired firms, and the determinants of the levels of aggregate merger activity.

Many authors, including Nelson (1959, 1966) and Melicher, Ledolter, and D'Antonio (1983), who studied the timing question were not guided by any general merger hypothesis and only established links between merger activity and stock prices, industrial activity, and interest rates. In the absence of a theory, the mere knowledge of association between variables cannot establish causal relationships between them. Other omitted variables may have caused the fluctuations in the variables that are found correlated over time. The correlation becomes meaningful only when there is a theory which predicts a causal relationship.

In the following we first describe the time series merger data which have been used in most studies of aggregate merger activity. Second, previous work on the timing and determinants of merger activity is reviewed. This review introduces various explanations offered regarding the association between merger activity and stock prices, the business cycle, interest rates, and so on. Third, the statistical properties of merger activity are considered in connection with the work by Shughart and Tollison (1984) who dispute the notion that mergers occur in "waves" rather than randomly. Fourth, implications of the merger hypothesis presented in Chapter 3 are derived with respect to aggregate merger activity and an empirical model is presented. Finally, significant timing-related aspects of merger activity are described and analyzed.

MERGER STATISTICS

There are two currently published sources of merger statistics, W. T. Grimm & Co. and *Mergers and Acquisitions* magazine. For past periods, there are five time-series statistics of mergers in manufacturing and mining industries. Each of these series covers a different and largely nonoverlapping period. These are:

1 Nelson (1959) for 1895–1920
2 Thorp (1941) for 1919–1939
3 Federal Trade Commission (FTC, 1972) for 1940–1971
4 FTC (1981) "overall merger series" for 1972–1979
5 FTC (1981) "large merger series" for 1948–1979

These series are not completely comparable as they are constructed based on different information sources, different standards of inclusion (or size-based cutoff points), and different size measures of firms acquired or consolidated. Therefore, the different series cannot be spliced or combined to form a consistent time series for longer periods without necessary adjustments which may not entirely be possible. For certain kinds of work, the data can be transformed into different series such as quarterly percentage changes to cover longer periods. It appears that the data sources covering recent years give very different time-series behavior for certain periods, especially when quarterly data are used. One reason for this difference is that mergers are either recorded as they are announced as in the Grimm series, or as they are consummated as in the *Mergers and Acquisition* magazine series.

The Nelson Series for 1895–1920

The series compiled by Nelson (1959) includes consolidations whose size was greater than $1 million for the period 1895–1914 or $2 million for the 1915–1920 period in which price rose rather "rapidly." The list also includes acquisitions that were greater than $35,000 for the 1895–1914 period or $65,000 for the later period. The measure of merger activity is available both by the number of net firm disappearances through consolidations or acquisitions, and by the size of consolidations or acquisitions.

In the Nelson series, size of a consolidation or a merger by acquisition is measured as the authorized capitalization of the firm resulting from a multifirm consolidation or a merger by acquisition. Because of this, the Nelson series by size is subject to an upward bias relative to the currently conventional measurement of size by the value paid to the acquired firm's shareholders or the total asset value of the acquired firm. For the 1895–1920 period of merger activity, approximately 70 percent of the firms that disappeared were absorbed into multifirm consolidations, while the remaining 30 percent disappeared through merger by acquisition. The Nelson series was compiled on a quarterly basis. The rule used in assigning dates was to record the date of transfer of control of the acquired firm or the date of incorporation in consolidations.

The Thorp Series for 1919–1939

The Thorp (1941) quarterly series overlaps the Nelson series in 1919 and 1920 and includes about three times as many firm disappearances as the Nelson series. The principal reason for the difference, as suggested by Nelson, is that the information source for the Thorp series was the *Standard Daily Trade Service* which probably reported small mergers more completely than the publication which Nelson relied on. The Thorp series gives only the number of disappearances, and not by size, in mining and manufacturing industries.

The FTC Series for 1940–1971

After 1939, the Federal Trade Commission (1972) continued to compile merger series which maintained comparability to the Thorp series. Data were limited to mergers and acquisitions reported by Moody's Investors Service, Inc. and Standard and Poor's Corporation. This series was discontinued in 1972 when the FTC introduced the Overall Merger Series. Combined with the Thorp series, this FTC series is the longest time series of merger activity in the United States.

The FTC Overall Merger Series
for 1972–1979

In 1972, the FTC introduced a new series which was not comparable to the 1940–1971 series for several reasons. First, the Overall Merger Series was compiled from a greater number of source materials than previously used. Second, it included acquisitions of firms outside manufacturing and mining industries, while still excluding industries over which the FTC did not have jurisdiction (commercial banks, transportation entities, and communication concerns). Third, in the previous series, a count was made of partial acquisitions where less than 50.1 percent of a company had been acquired. This was no longer done in the Overall Merger Series. Fourth, a distinction was made between completed and pending acquisitions, and the new series included the completed ones only. The full series is available as FTC (1981) which has been the last merger-related publication by the FTC.

The FTC Large Merger Series
for 1948–1979

To be included in this series, the acquired firm must be a manufacturing or mining concern having assets of at least $10 million at the time of acquisition. The sources used in compiling the series were Moody's manuals, Standard and Poor's stock exchange reports, newspapers, company annual reports, and FTC premerger notification information. The list shows acquired and acquiring company names, asset and profit data, industry classification, date of consummation, and type of acquisition (horizontal, vertical, or conglomerate). In addition, the list shows the extent of acquisition (partial or whole), the medium of exchange (cash or securities), and the consideration (amount) paid by the acquiring company.

Because all manufacturing corporations (and, since 1974, all mining corporations) with assets of $10 million or more are covered by the FTC's *Quarterly Financial Report* series, the Large Merger Series is believed to be comprehensive and historically consistent. One problem in the series, however, is the artificial trend built into the series due to the $10 million floor which falls over time in constant-dollar terms. The number of mergers as well as the size of mergers is increased because of inflation. In analyzing merger activity via the Large Merger Series, one would have to eliminate the artificial trend. Further, the proportion of firms belonging to the size class of above $10 million in constant-dollar terms increases over time as firms grow in size, and this should also cause the series to be biased upward over time.

The W. T. Grimm Series Since 1963

The Grimm series represents all publicly announced formal transfers of ownership of at least 10 percent of a company's assets or equity. The purchase price must be at least $500,000 and one of the parties a U.S. company. The number and size of transactions are recorded as they are announced, not as they are completed. This makes the series unique and more useful than the series described earlier. It is well known that mergers are generally completed five to ten months after their announcements. In studying the correlation between merger activity and industrial production, for example, merger dates based on announcements should yield a more accurate relationship. Cancelled transactions are deducted from total announcements in the period in which the cancellation occurred. The series is available both on an annual basis (since 1963) and on a quarterly basis (since 1974).

The Grimm statistics also record divestitures, medium of payment, industry classification, foreign acquisitions of U.S. companies, and U.S. acquisitions of foreign companies. The series includes tender offers since 1974. Grimm also provides its own analyses of various aspects of merger activity.

The *Mergers and Acquisitions* Magazine Series Since 1972

The *Mergers and Acquisitions* magazine reports transactions valued at $1 million or more in cash, market value of capital stock exchanged, or debt securities. Partial acquisitions of 5 percent or more of a company's capital stock are included if the size requirement is met. Transactions in the real property area are not included. The series is based on the completion date.

The magazine also presents profiles of each transaction, the acquired and the acquiring firms. Included in the "Roster" are the merger/acquisition activity of U.S. firms, takeovers of U.S. companies by foreign companies, and acquisitions of foreign companies by American corporations.

MERGERS AND THE MACROECONOMY

Statistical Relationships: Nelson (1959, 1966) Studies

Merger activity appears closely associated with the business cycle. Nelson (1959) investigated the lead and lag relationships between merger activity and the general business cycle, industrial production, stock prices, stock trading, and business incorporations. For the 1897–1954 period, there were 14 cycles in general business activity and 12 merger cycles. A definite timing relationship to the reference cycle turning points was found in 11 of the 12 merger cycles. The two reference expansions (1911–1913, 1921–1923) for which there was no corresponding merger expansion were either of short duration or of moderate amplitude. The reference cycle contraction of 1953–1954 had no corresponding merger contraction and was one of the mildest contractions in the six-decade period.

One characteristic of the procyclical movement of merger activity was that its peaks usually preceded the peaks of the reference cycle. However, the time sequence for troughs was less consistent than for peaks. Nelson (1959, p. 112) suggests that this irregular time sequence of merger activity indicates "that economic forces in a depression are likely to be diffuse and weak, compelling no great uniformity in the response of merger activity."

Comparison of the merger series with the other specific economic series revealed that merger activity was closely related to stock trading, stock prices, and business incorporations. The average lead and average lag between these series and merger activity were less than three months, both at peaks and troughs. In particular, the peak in merger activity was reached one month earlier than stock prices, but its trough lagged the trough in stock prices by three months.

Further analyses based on detrended series showed that mergers were more positively correlated to stock price changes than to changes in industrial production in periods of high merger activity. Conversely, mergers were more positively (or less negatively) correlated to industrial production in periods of low merger activity. Nelson (1959, p. 119) states:

> This suggests that capital market conditions or their underlying causes were of leading importance in periods of high merger activity, and that their role in times of low merger activity was not important. While industrial production was the more important factor in times of low merger activity, the correlations were so low that no strong cause-and-effect connection is suggested.

These results are consistent with what Weston (1953) and Markham (1955) found earlier. Using regression analyses, Weston showed that merger activity was statistically significantly related to stock prices but not to industrial production. Markham calculated correlation coefficients which were statistically significant, but were larger between mergers and stock prices than between mergers and industrial production. The lower correlation between mergers and industrial production may be attributed in part to the larger differences in the timing of turning points of the two series as found by Nelson. (Mergers led industrial production by more than five months.)

In a follow-up study, Nelson (1966) found that merger activity for the 1919–1961 period peaked on average five months before the peak in stock prices, whereas peaks in plant construction contracts and equipment orders were almost coincident with those in stock prices. His interpretation for this result was that external growth through mergers was selected by firms early in a stock price rise and before they undertook internal investments. One reason that was offered by Nelson is that in stock-for-stock transactions, one is faced with the problem of predicting stock prices of both firms and therefore the involved firms have the mutual willingness to avoid the uncertainty contained in such a "double-contingency" decision by consummating mergers early in the expansion phase. Another reason suggested by Nelson is that the phenomenon reflects the immediacy with which mergers start to produce revenues and profits. Internal investments may involve a protracted waiting period.

In the same study, it was found that a peak in merger activity, on average, came 19 months following the trough in the reference cycle or at about the two-thirds point in a reference-cycle expansion lasting about 29 months. This dismisses any impression that mergers occur so early in business upturns that they set the stage for subsequent economic expansion. The fact that mergers peak before overall economic activity may reflect that there is at any one time a pool of firms suitable for acquisitions and, as they are acquired in a period of high merger activity, the pool is diminished and merger activity returns to a low level.

Statistical Relationships: Recent Studies

The relationship between merger activity and such macroeconomic variables as industrial activity, business failures, stock prices, and interest rates was analyzed by Melicher, Ledolter, and D'Antonio (1983) in a time-series analysis context.

They used the FTC quarterly merger data for 1947 through 1977 (*not* the Large Merger Series). Each time series was transformed into white noise (that is, uncorrelated random variables or residuals from univariate time-series models) and correlated with other prewhitened series to find lead and lag structures. Among their findings are:

1 An increase (decrease) in stock prices is followed in a quarter by an increase (decrease) in merger activity. Since merger negotiations begin on average about two quarters before consummation, merger negotiations may precede stock price movements by about one quarter.

2 Mergers respond inversely to prior changes in bond yields, although this relationship is weaker than the case of mergers and stock prices. Further, an increase in bond yields decreases stock prices in the same period, but an increase in stock prices leads to an increase in bond yields in the following period (due to an increase in business activity).

3 Changes in merger activity and changes in stock prices both lead changes in industrial production.

4 Merger activity precedes business failures by one quarter and the relationship is negative.

Melicher, Ledolter, and D'Antonio went on to build a model which would explain future merger movements as a function of stock prices and bond yields. The results were consistent with the argument that capital market conditions (stock prices, interest rates) or their underlying causes could explain aggregate changes in merger activity. Since merger negotiations begin about two quarters before consummation, increased merger activity may reflect the expectation of rising stock prices and declining interest rates.

Linkages between mergers and the macroeconomy have also been studied by Becketti (1986). He used the FTC Large Merger Series for 1948–1979 and the *Mergers and Acquisitions* magazine data for 1979–1985. In modeling the merger activity, the two quarterly merger series were made comparable by first eliminating the part of each series that can be predicted by its own recent past levels and then by normalizing the remaining portion of each series. He related the combined merger series to a stock price index, the yield on three-month Treasury bills, the stock of money, the stock of domestic nonfinancial debt, the capacity utilization rate, and GNP. The results show that past values of the stock price index, capacity utilization rates, and the stock of debt are positively correlated with current merger activity, while past values of the T-bill rate and GNP are negatively correlated. These relationships are not always statistically significant; statistical significance varies depending on the measure of the merger series (number versus value of mergers) and the short-run versus long-run effects.[1]

The stock price index coefficients are generally insignificant and GNP has significantly negative coefficients. These unexpected results may be due to the inappropriate use of trended variables to explain a dependent variable, either without a trend or from which the trend has been eliminated. Another reason for

---

[1] The joint statistical significance of the lag coefficients of an explanatory variable is regarded as a significant short-run effect. The statistical significance of the sum of the lag coefficients is regarded as a significant long-run effect.

the negative association between past values of GNP and current values of mergers may be the fact that peaks in mergers come before peaks in general economic activity. Becketti interprets the other results as follows:

1 Changes in the interest rate affect the cost of mergers by changing the cost of borrowed funds which are often used in acquisitions or by changing the return to lending cash.

2 In the short run, an increase in capacity utilization rate leads to an increase in mergers. This implies that firms regard mergers as a way of speeding up the increase in capacity normally achieved through internal investments. However, fluctuations in the capacity utilization rate appear to have no long-run effects on merger activity (since the sum of the lagged coefficients are not statistically significant).

3 Both the stock of debt and the stock of money have no consistent effect on merger activity.[2]

Golbe and White (1987) study the determinants of merger activity. They test (1) a bargains hypothesis holding that mergers rise when a firm's asset price is low relative to the replacement value of assets, (2) a market change hypothesis holding that relative price shifts signal changes in the efficient industry scale and lead to mergers, (3) a cost of capital hypothesis maintaining that the real cost of capital influences the timing, financing costs, and expected profitability of mergers, (4) a tax regime dummy for tax law changes in 1954, 1963, and 1981, and (5) a divergence of opinion hypothesis suggesting that merger activity rises with divergence of opinion as to future price movements.

Golbe and White spliced the FTC large firm series with the domestic series from *Mergers and Acquisitions,* as was done by Becketti (1986). To test their hypotheses with multiple regression, they proxied for the cost of capital with the real interest rate and for the divergence of price opinions with the coefficient of variation of the Livingston panel one-year advance forecast of the CPI. Their regressions find a strong relation between both nominal GNP and Tobin's q (proxying for bargains hypothesis) and merger activity. *T*-statistics were not significant for any other variables. The positive coefficient on the Tobin's q variable is inconsistent with the bargain theory which predicts a negative relation between Tobin's q and mergers.

Their results also show that mergers follow strong autoregressive patterns. Autoregressivity is not necessarily inconsistent with wave patterns in the merger series. Since Shughart and Tollison (1984) cannot reject the hypothesis that the merger series is a white-noise process, Golbe and White provide a nonparametric "runs" test to check if low and high merger periods were clumped together in runs (a pattern that would be inconsistent with a white-noise process). They found the number of runs to be fewer than expected from a random drawing—a result supporting the characterization of waves in the merger data.

While Dennis Mueller (1969) was one of the first authors to discuss mergers

---

[2] These results may be because of the presence of interest rates in the econometric model which account for the credit availability in the economy. Also, the stock of money alone cannot measure credit availability. It should be measured relative to economic activity.

as a form of investment, only recently has the issue been considered in depth. George Bittlingmayer's (1987) paper, "Merger as a Form of Investment," begins by characterizing the decision to merge as an outgrowth of the decision to invest. This rather simple observation is backed empirically at an industry level by a positive correlation between merger capitalizations per unit of book value and new capital investment per employee. The results are $\rho = .273$ for the United States, 1948–1979 and $\rho = .576$ for Germany, 1973–1982. These correlations do indicate a relation between merger activity and investment but are not in themselves conclusive. The strength of Bittlingmayer's merger-as-investment framework is its ability to explain other findings about mergers. First, the framework suggests that the frequently observed absence of supernormal returns to acquiring merger partners is a natural result of the tendency for rates of return to equalize on all forms of investment. Second, the strong relation between mergers and asset prices, argues Bittlingmayer, reflects the real phenomenon of high expectations of returns on future investment. An increase in expected returns should concurrently raise asset prices and increase investment (namely, merger) activity. One conceptual weakness of Bittlingmayer's framework is its omission of an explanation of the circumstances in which merger serves as a superior form of investment to assembly of a firm from separated inputs.

Bittlingmayer also finds that increases in Department of Justice and Federal Trade Commission antitrust cases were negatively related to the *number* of mergers from 1948–1979. This result is consistent with Bittlingmayer (1985) which finds a close temporal relationship between key antitrust cases and merger innovations from 1890–1902.

Interpretation of Statistical Relationships

The consistent pattern that emerges from the statistical investigations is that merger activity is procyclical. Merger activity is roughly coincident with stock price movement. (It leads the stock price movement by about one quarter according to Nelson. It lags stock price changes according to Melicher, Ledolter, and D'Antonio and Becketti.) The peak in merger activity comes earlier than the peak in the general business cycle. Recent studies also report that an increase in interest rates is followed by a decline in merger activity.

Many different reasons have been advanced to explain these phenomena. Some of them may in fact be valid, but generally they are not presented in a coherent fashion and thus are not convincing. This state of the matter still reflects the lack of a general hypothesis which Markham (1955, p. 143) pointed out three decades ago. For example, the mere fact that stock prices are positively correlated with merger activity does not tell us much about why mergers occur or why merger activity fluctuates. The stock price itself is affected by such underlying factors as profit expectations, business risk, and interest rates. Without a theory, it is difficult to determine which of these factors are responsible for fluctuations in merger activity. Or does the stock price change itself cause the fluctuations?

The following are among the reasons often suggested for the observed association between mergers and macroeconomic variables.

1   Firms regard mergers as an opportunity for immediately increasing capacity and for gaining greater control over the market in a period of expanding and favorable economic conditions (Nelson, 1955; Becketti, 1985).

2   Mergers are an alternative to purchases of new plants and equipment. Since transactions involving stocks of firms are subject to less uncertainty than internal investments in plant and equipment, mergers are selected earlier than internal investments to avoid the greater uncertainty (Nelson, 1966).

3   Expectational differences between stockholders and outsiders become larger in periods of rising stock prices. These valuation differences or "economic disturbances" lead to acquisitions of firms that are low-valued from the viewpoint of outsiders (Gort, 1969).

4   The "expansiveness" of the businessperson during periods of economic prosperity often expresses itself in the merger movement and increased size of business organizations (Thorp, 1931; Reid, 1968; Roll, 1986). The constraint on managerial pursuit of own goals is likely to weaken as rising returns to stockholders in an upswing increase their optimism and confidence in their managers. The stock market becomes more receptive to managerial pursuit of growth objectives when stock prices rise (Mueller, 1977).

5   Acquiring firms rely heavily on borrowed funds (Melicher, Ledolter, and D'Antonio, 1983) and bond purchases are an alternative use for the cash that is used for corporate acquisitions (Becketti, 1986). Thus, lower interest rates lead to more acquisitions.

The validity of these explanations requires testing by the microeconomic aspects of the theory on which the explanation relies. Unfortunately, however, in most cases the theory itself is not well stated or is missing entirely. Derivation of implications that are testable with firm or industry data is difficult because the explanations are not based on a complete theory and are often offered on an ad hoc basis. Later we present our own account of the fluctuations in merger activity which is based on the theory presented in Chapters 2 and 3.

TESTS OF THE MERGER WAVE HYPOTHESIS

It is a widely held perception that mergers occur in waves. The previous figures appear to confirm that the perception is in fact valid. Crudely, the wave notion implies that merger activity increases for some periods and then declines. If mergers occur in waves, then this is a systematic pattern that can be exploited, for example, in developing predictive models of merger activity.

Shughart and Tollison (1984) have been the first to put the merger wave hypothesis to rigorous statistical tests. Specifically, they test the opposite hypothesis that historical merger activity can be represented as a white-noise process, that is, that the first differences in the merger series appear to be random with possible drift. This random-walk model can be written as

$$X_t - X_{t-1} = m + e_t$$

where X_t is the number (or real value) of the mergers occurring in period t, m is a constant term representing the drift, and e_t is the noise term having zero mean and uncorrelated with any of its previous values. The nature of the random-walk process is such that "the series will proceed by a sequence of unconnected steps, starting each time from the previous value of the series" (Shughart and Tollison, 1984, p. 503).

They also consider, as alternatives to the random-walk model, the class of stationary models in the levels of merger activity:

$$X_t = \beta_0 + \beta_1 T + \alpha_1 X_{t-1} + \alpha_2 X_{t-2} + \ldots + \alpha_n X_{t-n} + e_t$$

where T is a linear time trend and e_t is the random error term. Using the Nelson, Thorp, and FTC merger series for the 1895–1947 period and also the FTC Large Merger Series for the 1948–1979 period, Shughart and Tollison find that the white-noise model or the (first-order autoregressive) model (with $\alpha_1 < 1$)

$$X_t = \beta_0 + \alpha_1 X_{t-1} + e_t$$

quite adequately fits the historical annual merger series. This means that the series advances in steps, with the observation in any given period starting from the previous value of the series.

As Shughart and Tollison note, the implication of this finding is that merger values for most previous years except for the last year will have no role to play in explaining current merger activity. An economic model generating mergers in a given year does not include as explanatory variables the levels of merger activity occurring more than one year earlier. However, the "results in no way detract from the idea of searching for the empirical determinants of merger activity" (Shughart and Tollison, 1984, p. 509).

The finding is in some ways to be expected. First, as we have noted in the first chapter, mergers occur in response to changes in economic and business conditions such as technological advances, developments in transportation and communication, changes in industry regulation, and so on. As long as these changes occur randomly, merger activity will also be characterized by random-ness. Second, as is argued in the next section, mergers occur to capture invest-ment opportunities and more mergers will occur when favorable investment opportunities are expected. If expectations change randomly and quickly, then merger activity will also change similarly. Third, as Nelson (1959, pp. 116–117, 126) argued based on empirical observations, historical merger activity was char-acterized by large bursts of activity separated by long intervals of low activity. This discontinuous pattern and in particular the long intervals of low activity reflects the absence of continuously strong underlying forces. Also, the influence of external economic changes in periods of low merger activity is diffuse and erratic. If the wave hypothesis is tested with data characterized by lengthy periods of low activity and only few occasional waves, then the result will certainly reject the hypothesis. Finally, the Shughart and Tollison analysis was conducted using annual time series of mergers. If the waves are of short duration extending over several quarters, then the use of quarterly data may yield a different result.[3]

It is not easy to abandon a common notion. And mergers may really occur in waves. If aggregrate expectations change only gradually, merger activity may also change gradually in a certain direction. New events may occur randomly, but the reaction to the event can appear gradually as the market digests the implications of the event over some periods. New tests of the wave hypothesis seem warranted.

A MODEL FOR AGGREGATE CONGLOMERATE MERGER ACTIVITY

One hypothesis that can potentially provide consistent answers to many questions regarding mergers is the investment opportunity synergy (IOS) hypothesis presented in Chapter 3. This hypothesis argues that the acquiring firm seeks to internalize investment opportunities in the acquired firm's industry by realizing managerial and/or financial synergies. Based on the hypothesis, this section explains the fluctuations in aggregate merger activity.[4] An empirical model is derived from the hypothesis and is estimated with the FTC Large Merger Series. The IOS hypothesis predicts and the regression analyses below show that both aggregate investment opportunities and financial market conditions determine aggregate merger activity for the period 1957–1977 when conglomerate mergers predominated.

Implications of the IOS Hypothesis for Aggregate Merger Activity

According to the IOS hypothesis, a conglomerate merger may achieve benefits. If the expected benefits are greater than the costs, a merger occurs. And more mergers occur when economic conditions make benefits to mergers greater because some potential mergers with otherwise unprofitable prospects become profitable, and because detection of merger opportunities is easier with greater benefit/cost ratios.

Here the level of merger activity, the dependent variable, is measured by the number N of mergers completed in a year and also by the sum of total assets of the acquired firms in those mergers. The profitability of mergers which determines this number is dependent on the variables affecting (1) aggregate invest-

---

[3] Shughart and Tollison mistakenly state that there are no quarterly time series. However, the series that they employ in their study are all available in quarterly measurements.

[4] This section draws on Chung (1982).

ment opportunities and (2) financial market conditions (at least for the pure conglomerate merger). Among the variables that may be implied by the hypothesis, only those that vary over time are useful. Two variables are identified which determine aggregate investment opportunities and another two relate to the financial market conditions.

AGGREGATE INVESTMENT OPPORTUNITY   Investment opportunities are a factor giving rise to conglomerate merger processes. Excess demand for factor inputs results when investment opportunities rise. The product-extension merger (PEM) can be an efficient means of reallocating managerial capabilities, from the acquiring to the acquired firms and industries. The pure conglomerate merger (PCM) is directly motivated by greater investment opportunities in the acquired-firm industry and represents an efficient means of reallocating financial resources. Greater intensity in conglomerate merger activity should result when a greater number of industries are associated with better investment opportunities and thus when general business prospects turn favorable.

The strength of investment opportunities from the returns side is determined by expected long-term growth of industries. It is well established that the growth potential of individual industries is generally a function of the prospective real growth rate of the economy as a whole. Since expectations are generally based on factual observations, the actual growth rate of the economy can potentially affect and represent the expected growth rates of industries as a whole. In other words, the growth rate of the economy is larger when many industries are expected to grow faster. Hence, one proxy for the strength of investment opportunities that stimulate conglomerate merger activity is the growth rate G of real GNP.

From the point of view of firms, investment opportunities are determined relative to the cost of capital. A higher long-term cost of capital should mean "smaller" investment opportunities, and hence the number of conglomerate mergers will be smaller. A difficulty with this variable is that it should be a real expected long-term rate of interest. For convenience, the realized real rate on high-grade corporate bonds r is used. This rate was calculated by Ibbotson and Sinquefield (1979). Alternatively, Tobin's q (the ratio of market value to current replacement value of a firm's nonfinancial assets) that has been used in previous studies as an important determinant of aggregate investment may substitute for these two variables, G and r, thereby avoiding the difficulty in measuring the expected real interest rate.

FINANCIAL MARKET CONDITIONS   The potential relevance of the cost of capital in explaining at least PCMs is provided by the cyclical behavior of macrofinancial variables. An obvious difficulty in using these variables for the present purposes is that theories are not so well developed as to explain their determination and intertemporal fluctuations. Nonetheless, employing both theoretical and intuitive reasoning, two financial variables are selected for use in the regression model.

The risk premium included in the returns to risky corporate securities fluctuates because the degree of perceived risk varies with general economic expectations. Since diversification through a PCM can reduce the variability of the output pattern, it may reduce bankruptcy risk. It is likely that when the perceived degree of bankruptcy risk on securities is higher, the absolute reduction in this risk (or the probability) through merger is larger. Hence, mergers bring greater absolute reductions in risk premium in times when the risk is high. This effect will generally be large when one of the merger partners (the acquired firm in the hypothesis) has differentially higher risk premiums on its securities.

The relative number of conglomerate mergers can then be expected to be larger when the market risk premium is larger. A measure of the risk premium is the difference between the yields on bonds of differing risks but with equal maturities. To eliminate the effects of inflation from the measure, it is measured in a slightly different form. This variable (PREM) is obtained as $[(1 + r_1)/(1 + r_2) - 1]$, where r_1 and r_2 denote the yields on BAA and AAA corporate bonds, respectively.[5]

The characterization of the acquired firms also suggests another financial variable, a measure of monetary stringency, to be included in the equation. To the extent that the high costs of capital of these firms are related to their lower cash flow rates, the demand for external financing is greater for them than for others. When the availability of funds is tight or, in general, when the markets are not stable, their flotation costs and their costs of capital may rise differentially relative to large, well-known firms due to greater increases in risk premiums charged by underwriters (and possibly by investors and lending organizations as well). The reason suggested in the underwriting cost literature (Dyl and Joehnk, 1976; Ederington, 1976) is that underwriter risk is increased in tight and unstable markets as a result of greater uncertainty over investor demand, which can be reduced only by incurring information costs. Demand uncertainty and informational requirements increase when tight-money conditions prevail or the market is perceived to be unstable. The result is that underwriter spreads are increased more for smaller and less-known (acquired) firms. A measure of the tightness of external fund availability is the spread between short- and long-term interest rates, proposed by Evans (1969, pp. 139, 188–194) and used in the investment literature. This variable (SPD) is measured here as $[(1 + r_3)/(1 + r_4) - 1]$, where r_3 is the yield on four- to six-month prime commercial paper, and r_4 the yield on AAA corporate bonds. Its value is normally negative. A greater

---

[5] Measuring the default risk premium from BAA and AAA rates, rather than from (or including) the yield spread between corporate AAA bonds and default-risk-free government bonds, serves an important practical purpose. The best that a combined firm can expect, it would seem, is to reduce the extra risk faced by one or both of the merging firms to the level of risk characterizing the "AAA firms." The latter default premium involving the government and AAA bonds can be properly considered a general indicator of the overall business risk in the economy and is unavoidable even by the most stable firms in the economy. Thus, all firms may be subject to the latter premium.

The measure used here is in addition to this inevitable overall business risk premium and, as far as it is reducible via merger, a higher level of it should induce more mergers. The alternative premium measured from the government and AAA bonds is appropriately included in the interest rate governing general business investment opportunities and should have a *negative* effect on mergers.

algebraic value of this variable implies tighter financial conditions, and hence the hypothesis predicts that it will be positively correlated with the rate of merger activity.

Since the maturities of the two underlying securities in *SPD* are different, the effect of changing inflation expectations will not in general be absent from this variable. However, it may initially be assumed that there is no theoretically valid reason for inflation per se to affect the rate of merger activity. In this case, once we find *SPD* is statistically significant in explaining merger activity, the desired inference is possible. On the other hand, inflation itself may influence merger activity. This can result from the relationship between interest payment requirements and cash flows of a firm. Higher expected inflation for a short period, by increasing the short-term rate (more than the long-term rate), may cause some firms with low current cash flow rates to be unable to borrow. When investment opportunities are captured sequentially, the high nominal rate of interest may therefore motivate these firms to merge to secure investment funds. When higher inflation is expected to last for a short period, *SPD* takes a larger value. Thus, inflation may directly affect the level of merger activity and *SPD* would capture this effect in addition to the tight-money effect that we expect.

In summary, four variables (or three if Tobin's q is used) have been identified for use in testing the IOS hypothesis from annual time series data. The model is then

$$N = f(PREM, SPD, G, r)$$

or

$$N = f(PREM, SPD, q)$$

where:

N = the number of conglomerate mergers

$PREM$ = the modified default risk premium measured from the yields on the long-term corporate BAA and AAA bonds

SPD = the modified yield spread between the short-term (four- to six-month) prime commercial papers and the AAA corporate bonds

G = the growth rate of the real GNP

r = the inflation adjusted long-term, high-grade corporate bond return taken from Ibbotson and Sinquefield

q = Tobin's q

The hypothesis predicts that the variables *PREM*, *SPD*, *G*, and *q* should have positive coefficients and *r* a negative one. The sum of the total assets of the acquired firms (ASSET) will alternatively be used as the dependent variable.

The Data and Equation Specification

Variables N and *ASSET* are obtained from the FTC Large Merger Series. Use of these data requires caution. The FTC Large Merger Series includes only those mergers in which the acquired firm's assets are $10 million or over in current dollars. The major problem of this cutoff is obviously that inflation causes the asset valuation and the number of mergers to be inflated over time. The data are adjusted for inflation by converting the asset figures to constant dollars and eliminating mergers that fall below the $10 million bottom line.[6]

The number of mergers as reported by the FTC is also affected by the fact that average firm sizes grow over time. Even if the annual total number of mergers stays constant, the FTC series shows increasing numbers of mergers for this reason. It appears that this artificial trend in mergers built into the FTC Large Merger Series is manifestly stronger in the earlier years of the series starting in 1948. This is at least partly because the $10 million minimum asset size was too large for most of the conglomerate mergers in the earlier years to be included in the series. For example, the number of PCMs in the series is zero for three consecutive years up to 1950 and one in 1951 compared to an annual average of 21 mergers and a minimum of six mergers in that category for the period since 1957. Since the size distribution of firms at any point in time is such that at least for the relevant range there are more firms in a smaller-size class, the steep increase in the FTC series mergers in the earlier years is to be expected. This is because a given size class in terms of absolute dollar amounts becomes a smaller relative size class next year as firm sizes grow over time. This consideration suggests it appropriate that the estimation be performed for a later period for which the data should be more meaningful.

Allowance for lag in response to changes in the explanatory variables is also necessary since the data are compiled based on the completion dates. Cross-sectional merger studies have found that information on upcoming mergers reaches the market many months before the announcement of a merger agreement, which in turn precedes the completion of the merger usually by several months. Allowing for the time spent in searching for merger partners, a minimum lag of at least one year seems necessary. To account for this effect, all independent variables are entered as the sums of their current and two lagged values.[7] Note that this creates no particular econometric problem, since only the independent variables are summed.

[6] The conversion of assets into constant-dollar amounts was done by dividing the assets by the average of the current and last four-year GNP deflators. The average for 1951 was set at unity. The five-year period is chosen arbitrarily. This adjustment, however, did not affect the substantive results.

[7] The results indicated that the three-year sums perform slightly better than the two-year sums. This seems reasonable because the independent variables themselves are annual averages, and thus the three-year sums allow a minimum lag of only 13 months. For example, a merger initiated in December of year $t - 2$ and completed in January of year t took 13 months but requires the year $t - 2$ data. If some mergers took 24 months or more to their completion, the three-year period might not be enough.

If there exists a kind of "adjustment lag" because the merger market has to learn the impacts on merger benefits of a change in economic conditions, presumably from the experience of other contemporary mergers, the lag allowance will have to be longer than without the adjustment lag.

TABLE 11.1
Regression of the Numbers of Large Conglomerate Mergers, 1957–1977[a]

DEPENDENT VARIABLE	CONST.	G	r	q	PREM	SPD$_{-1}$	$\bar{R}^2$	DW	F-TEST
1. Investment Opportunity Variables Only									
Pure	15.54	0.04	−0.45				0.21	0.60	3.63
conglomerate		(0.08)	(−2.69)						
mergers	−0.97			5.33			0.02	0.43	1.32
				(1.15)					
Product-	6.20	1.92	−0.67				0.34	1.16	6.22
extension		(2.52)	(−2.60)						
mergers	−43.43			21.81			0.35	0.88	11.62
				(3.41)					
2. With Financial Variables Added									
Pure	−37.28	2.73	−0.43		15.77	6.13	0.81	1.37	22.97
conglomerate		(6.28)	(−4.78)		(6.39)	(6.79)			
mergers	−62.41			17.78	12.22	3.48	0.50	1.05	7.56
				(3.04)	(2.96)	(3.01)			
Product-	−30.62	4.47	−0.46		11.54	9.08	0.68	1.80	11.13
extension		(4.55)	(−2.23)		(2.07)	(4.44)			
mergers	−55.92			24.84	4.25	4.08	0.42	1.13	5.82
				(2.33)	(0.57)	(1.94)			

[a]All explanatory variables are the sums of the current and two lagged values. The *t*-values are in parentheses.
SOURCE: Kwang Chung, "Investment Opportunities, Synergies, and Conglomerate Mergers," doctoral dissertation, University of California, Los Angeles, 1982.

Results

Estimations have been made for the period 1957–1977[8] and the results are presented in Table 11.1 for the regression of N and in Table 11.2 for the regression of ASSET.[9] In both tables, the first four regressions use the investment opportunity variables only, that is, G and r or q, whereas the rest are based on the fully specified model. The objective of these separate estimations is to see the extent to which investment opportunities alone can explain the different types of conglomerate mergers. The results are essentially the same for the two dependent variables, and thus the following discussion is based on the results for N in Table 11.1.

Although the partial specification results show the existence of autocorrelation, they still provide some information. The results make it clear that PCMs

[8]The starting year is chosen somewhat arbitrarily, although the annual Tobin's q series (taken from the *Economic Report of the President, 1978*) starts in 1955 so that the chosen period is the longest for which the data were available due to the use of two lagged values.
[9]The variable SPD representing monetary conditions improved the estimation when it is lagged one year relative to others. A plausible reason is that this variable is determined with almost no lag by the monetary policy of the government and therefore is more difficult to forecast compared to others. This should imply a longer delay in response. Little improvement is made by doing the same for other variables.

TABLE 11.2

Regression of the Acquired Assets in Large Conglomerate Mergers, 1957–1977[a]

DEPENDENT VARIABLE	CONST.	G	r	q	PREM	SPD$_{-1}$	$\bar{R}^2$	DW	F-TEST
1. *Investment Opportunities Variables Only*									
Pure	907.3	3.4	−43.3				0.20	0.98	3.57
conglomerate		(0.07)	(−2.67)						
mergers	−41.0			306.9			−0.03	0.70	0.44
				(0.67)					
Product-	138.9	79.4	−34.8				0.35	0.85	6.45
extension		(2.24)	(−2.92)						
mergers	−2005.5			930.7			0.28	0.63	8.77
				(2.96)					
2. *With Financial Variables Added*									
Pure	−4154.9	240.2	−47.9		1494.5	440.9	0.63	1.65	9.63
conglomerate		(4.05)	(−3.86)		(4.43)	(3.57)			
mergers	−5454.5			1394.5	1044.8	245.1	0.24	1.12	3.06
				(1.99)	(2.12)	(1.77)			
Product-	−2286.9	222.6	−28.3		740.2	421.6	0.70	1.62	12.44
extension		(5.05)	(−3.07)		(2.96)	(4.60)			
mergers	−3679.5			1283.9	382.0	188.4	0.38	1.03	5.07
				(2.50)	(1.05)	(1.85)			

[a]All explanatory variables are the sums of the current and two lagged values. The *t*-values are in parentheses.
SOURCE: Kwang Chung, "Investment Opportunities, Synergies, and Conglomerate Mergers," doctoral dissertation, University of California, Los Angeles, 1982.

require some factors in addition to investment opportunities. However, a substantial portion of the cyclical variation in PEMs seems to be explained by investment opportunity variables alone. These results are consistent with the predictions of the hypothesis. As they are based on managerial capacity considerations, PEMs are largely determined by the investment activities in the economy. On the other hand, PCMs occur to capture investment opportunities through financial advantages and therefore are determined by financial market conditions as well as investment opportunities. This a priori reasoning is further confirmed by the second set of regressions which use both financial and investment opportunity variables.

With the financial variables added, the DW statistics are significantly improved and are either in the indeterminate ranges (at the 1 or 5 percent level) or show no autocorrelation.[10] Equality of all the (slope) coefficients across the two types of mergers is rejected at the 1 percent level. After adjusting for the differences in variances for the two samples, the *F*-tests result in $F = 7.78$ (with 3 and 34 *d.f.*) or $F = 8.98$ (with 4 and 32 *d.f.*) depending on the explanatory variables used. Relative to the partial specification results, the fit is now better for PCMs

---

[10]Adjustment for the serial correlation in the regressions using the Cochrane-Orcutt iterative procedure does not change the qualitative aspects of the results that we discuss presently.

than for PEMs. Further, whereas all variables are highly significant in the PCM regressions, the financial variables in the PEM regressions are either insignificant or less strongly significant. In particular, the risk premium variable, *PREM* is insignificant in a regression of PEMs, suggesting that financial synergy in the specific sense of reducing risk premiums on securities may be more important for PCMs than for PEMs. This is presumably because PCMs can generally realize greater diversification effects.

The variable *SPD,* derived from the short-term and long-term rates of interest, stays significant for both types of mergers. This is consistent with the hypothesis that instability in the financial market adversely affects acquired firms to a greater extent than others, and mergers with firms having excess internal funds are a way to meet investment needs. Obviously this effect can be present not only in PCMs but also in other types of mergers, as the results indicate. However, this variable might be a proxy for other variables not identified in the model, due to the possible presence of inflationary expectation effects, as discussed earlier. Nonetheless, this at best should be only partially true because the results with *SPD* are simply a reconfirmation of the results by Nielsen and Melicher (1973). Their findings indicate that the rate of premium paid to the acquired firms as an approximation to merger gains is greater when the cash flow rate of the acquiring firm is greater and that of the acquired firm is smaller. This should imply that there is redeployment of capital from the acquiring to the acquired firm's operation.

The results with the variables *G* and *r* which together determine investment opportunities suggest that such opportunities are a determinant of conglomerate mergers. This interpretation may seem to be tentative since the measure of *r* may not fully capture the structure of the real expected rate of interest. However, use of Tobin's q instead of *G* and *r* does not change the results qualitatively. Therefore, the result on investment opportunities seems robust.

Finally, the negative coefficient for the real long-term interest rate is in accord with Melicher, Ledolter, and D'Antonio and Becketti. However, it contrasts with the results of Beckenstein (1979) who used the FTC Large Merger Series including all types of mergers and such independent variables as the nominal GNP, stock price index, and short-term nominal interest rates. Although Beckenstein found a positive coefficient for the nominal interest rate, both empirical and theoretical considerations suggest that this might have represented a spurious correlation. First, both the FTC series and the nominal rate include the effects of inflation whose rate has increased over the 1960s and 1970s almost linearly. The effects of inflation could bias the results. Second, the premise on which Beckenstein based the inclusion of the interest rate in his equation is the managerialism hypothesis (for example, Mueller). However, it is not at all clear how this hypothesis implies the supposed positive association between the cost of capital and merger activity. If the manager's discount rate moves in the same way as the true market determined cost of capital, so that the spread between the two stays constant, the interest rate is irrelevant in explaining the merger activity. Further, even if it were implied by the managerialism hypothesis, it is the long-term rather than the short-term rate that approximates the cost of capital for a firm or a project.[11]

Conclusions from the Econometric Analyses

Four variables have been considered to explain fluctuations in conglomerate merger activity. Product-extension conglomerate mergers are highly correlated with investment opportunity conditions in the economy. According to the IOS hypothesis, this implies that these mergers are motivated by the possibility of transferring managerial resources and the demand for such transfer is larger when greater investment opportunities exist in the economy. Pure conglomerate mergers cannot be explained by investment opportunity variables alone. The results indicate that macrofinancial variables measuring risk premiums and monetary conditions are required to account for cyclicality in PCMs. This is consistent with the hypothesis that these mergers occur to capture investment opportunities through the realization of financial economies arising from diversification effects and internal transfer of funds. The role of financial variables is weaker in effecting PEMs, although it seems that the money market condition also influences the occurrence of these mergers. Overall, these results are consistent with those obtained from the firm- and industry-level tests of implications of the theoretical framework presented in Chapters 4 and 10.[12]

An inspection of the data for the four variables suggests that the merger boom in the late 1960s was caused by the general perception of prevailing investment opportunities coupled with tight money and capital market conditions culminating in the 1966 credit crunch. For the increase in merger activity starting in 1976, it appears that the changing industrial structure in the U.S. economy giving rise to the growth of some industries and the high default risk premium required on low-grade securities since the oil crisis have been responsible.[13] The

---

[11] Apart from all these reasons, a more conclusive evaluation is obtained by applying Beckenstein's best-performing equation (other than those with dummy variables) to the period 1961–1977. Note that this period is relatively freer from the artificial trend built into the FTC series than the period including earlier years. The estimated equation is

$$MGR = -21.6 - 3.55\,GNP + 1.30\,SP + 4.56\,PRATE \qquad \bar{R}^2 = .05\ DW = .71$$
$$\ (-1.28) (1.62) (0.84)$$

where the t values are in parentheses and where MGR = the total number of large mergers, GNP = the nominal GNP, SP = Standard and Poor's 500 stock price index, and PRATE = four- to six-month prime commercial paper rate. Not only the coefficients are insignificant but the F-value (= 1.30) indicates a failure. Further, the coefficient for GNP has a wrong sign.

In comparison, when our model is fitted to this particular period, the results are approximately the same as those in Table 11.1 (F = 7.15):

$$MGR = -135.0 + 54.3\,PREM + 19.9\,SPD_{-1} + 12.0\,G - 1.2\,r \qquad \bar{R}^2 = .60$$
$$\ (3.20) (3.74) (3.73)\ (-2.62) \qquad DW = 1.49$$

[12] See also Chung (1982, Chapters 4 and 5).

[13] A number of mergers in the late 1970s involved the oil and gas, financial services, and other newly growing industries (for example, the cable TV industry).

tightening of credit conditions since 1978 along with continued industrial restructuring prolonged the merger activity until the end of the 1970s.

Latest data show that merger activity declined during the brief recession in 1980, increased briefly afterwards, and then decreased in the 1981–1982 recession. Lower interest rates and improved business prospects in the mid-1980s as evidenced by historical advances in stock prices have brought another historical wave of merger activity in the United States.

OTHER TIMING-RELATED PHENOMENA

Merger statistics reveal a number of interesting phenomena accompanying the fluctuations in merger activity. These include, among others, the time-series behavior of the divestitures, the medium of payment, and the premium or P/E ratio paid over the market. Ultimately, merger theory will have to incorporate these phenomena and provide explanations of all relevant aspects of merger activity.

SUMMARY

Fluctuations in merger activity over the years have stimulated a number of attempts to explain the determinants of merger timing. These studies have been able to demonstrate an association between merger activity and various macroeconomic characteristics. However, since they have not been founded in a general theory of merger activity, they have not been able to demonstrate causation. Time-series data on merger activity have been recorded in one form or another since 1895. A number of separate series of data covering various periods compound the problem of analysis, since the series often do not use the same data sources, size criteria for inclusion, or date of recording (for example, as announced versus as consummated).

Studies based on these data have attempted to relate merger activity to the business cycle measured by industrial production, stock prices and trading, business incorporations, interest rates, and so on. The findings of these studies are that merger activity is cyclical and roughly coincident with stock price movements. The peak of M&A activity tends to precede the peak in the general business cycle, and increases in interest rates precede declines in M&As. Based on these associations, hypotheses of merger timing are formulated:

1 Mergers are used to increase capacity immediately to get into an expanding market.
2 Mergers are a less risky alternative to purchasing new plants and equipment.
3 Expectational differences between shareholders and outsiders increase during periods of rising stock prices resulting in an assessment of undervaluation by outsiders.

4 Management optimism during economic upturns is expressed in increased merger activity.
5 Since acquiring firms rely heavily on borrowed funds, increases in interest rates affect merger activity adversely.

For some periods, the data are consistent with one or more of the preceding hypotheses but none has general explanatory power. The economic rationale for and the relationship between the alternative theories of timing have not been adequately developed. Other studies have focused on whether or not merger waves exist; Golbe and White (1987) concluded that merger activity is not random, while Shughart and Tollison (1984) found that previous years' merger activity (except for the most recent) had no value in predicting merger activity for the current years.

In previous work the present authors developed an econometric model explaining the timing of conglomerate merger activity. We restricted the analysis to conglomerates because most activity between 1950 and 1980 represented conglomerate mergers. We distinguished between product-extension conglomerate mergers and pure conglomerate mergers. Two investment opportunity variables, the growth rate of real GNP representing growth opportunities and expected real long-term interest rates representing the basic discount rate, successfully explained product-extension mergers. The pure conglomerate mergers required two additional explanatory macrofinancial variables. A risk premium was measured by the difference between AAA and BAA bond rates. The ease or tightness of monetary conditions was measured by the spread between short-term versus long-term rates (the difference between the yields on four- to six-month prime commercial paper and the yields on longer-term AAA corporate bonds). We recognize that since 1980 more horizontal and vertical mergers have been permitted by the new federal government policies. Thus, another discontinuity in the nature of mergers has occurred. Different economic circumstances in each of the major merger movements since the 1890s have produced discontinuities which make it difficult to find one general model which successfully explains the timing of merger activity over the past 100 years.

QUESTIONS

1. What information do studies of the timing of mergers provide when the focus is on the link between merger activity and stock prices, business cycles and industrial activity?
2. Discuss the evidence in support of and refuting merger waves.
3. What factors determine the profitability of mergers overall, that is, not the profitability of individual mergers?
4. Discuss the effect of the following variables on merger activity:
   a. The growth rate of real GNP, G.
   b. The real interest rate, r.

    c. Tobin's q-ratio.

    d. The market risk premium, *PREM.*

    e. Monetary stringency, *SPD.*

5. To what extent are pure conglomerate mergers versus product-extension mergers explained by the preceding variables?

REFERENCES

BECKENSTEIN, A. R., "Merger Activity and Merger Theories: An Empirical Investigation," *Antitrust Bulletin,* 24, Spring 1979, pp. 105–128.

BECKETTI, S., "Corporate Mergers and the Business Cycle," *Economic Review,* Federal Reserve Bank of Kansas City, May 1986, pp. 13–26.

BITTLINGMAYER, GEORGE, "Did Antitrust Policy Cause the Great Merger Wave?" *Journal of Law and Economics,* April 1985, pp. 77–118.

———, "Merger as a Form of Investment," *Science Center Berlin,* mimeo., January 1987.

CHUNG, K. S., *Investment Opportunities, Synergies, and Conglomerate Mergers,* unpublished doctoral dissertation, University of California, Los Angeles, 1982.

DYL, E., and JOEHNK, M., "Competitive Versus Negotiated Underwriting of Public Utility Debt," *Bell Journal of Economics,* 7, Autumn 1976, pp. 680–689.

EDERINGTON, L., "Negotiated Versus Competitive Underwriting of Corporate Bonds," *Journal of Finance,* 31, March 1976, pp. 17–28.

EVANS, M. K., *Macroeconomic Activity: Theory, Forecasting, and Control,* New York: Harper & Row, 1969.

Federal Trade Commission, *Current Trends in Merger Activity, 1971,* Washington, DC: Government Printing Office, March 1972.

———, *Statistical Report on Mergers and Acquisitions,* Washington, DC: Government Printing Office, July 1981.

GOLBE, DEVRA L., and LAWRENCE J. WHITE, "A Time Series Analysis of Mergers and Acquisitions in the U.S. Economy," mimeo., Presented at National Bureau of Economic Research Conference on Mergers and Acquisitions, February 1987.

GORT, M., "An Economic Disturbance Theory of Mergers," *Quarterly Journal of Economics,* 83, November 1969, pp. 624–642.

IBBOTSON, R. G., and R. A. SINQUEFIELD, *Stocks, Bonds, Bills, and Inflation: Historical Returns (1926–1978),* Charlottesville, VA: Financial Analysts Research Foundation, 1979.

MARKHAM, J. W., "Survey of the Evidence and Findings on Mergers," in *Business Concentration and Price Policy,* Princeton, NJ: Princeton University Press, 1955, pp. 141–212.

MELICHER, R. W., J. LEDOLTER, and L. D'ANTONIO, "A Time Series Analysis of Aggregate Merger Activity," *The Review of Economics and Statistics,* 65, August 1983, pp. 423–430.

MUELLER, D. C., "A Theory of Conglomerate Mergers," *Quarterly Journal of Economics,* 83, 1969, pp. 643–659.

———, "The Effects of Conglomerate Mergers," *Journal of Banking and Finance,* 1, 1977, pp. 315–347.

NELSON, R. L., *Merger Movements in American Industry, 1895–1956,* Princeton, NJ: Princeton University Press, 1959.

———, "Business Cycle Factors in the Choice Between Internal and External Growth," *The Corporate Mergers,* W. W. Alberts and J. E. Segall, eds., Chicago: University of Chicago Press, 1966.

NIELSEN, J. F., and R. W. MELICHER, "A Financial Analysis of Acquisition and Merger Premiums," *Journal of Financial and Quantitative Analysis,* 8, March 1973, pp. 139–162.

REID, S. R., *Mergers, Managers, and the Economy,* New York: McGraw-Hill, 1968.

SHUGHART, W. F., II, and R. O. TOLLISON, "The Random Character of Merger Activity," *Rand Journal of Economics,* 15, Winter 1984, pp. 500–509.

THORP, W. L., "The Merger Movement," in Temporary National Economic Committee Monograph No. 27, Washington, DC: U.S. Government Printing Office, 1941.

WESTON, J. F., *The Role of Mergers in the Growth of Large Firms,* Berkeley and Los Angeles: University of California Press, 1953, Chapter 5.

CHAPTER 12

Tax Planning Options

Another theory of mergers suggests that tax effects are an important motivating factor in some instances. The tax synergy argument is that mergers facilitate the utilization of tax shields not fully available in the absence of an acquisition transaction (Eckbo, 1983, p. 244). Leveraged buy-outs (discussed in Chapter 16) are a prime example. Tax effects explain much of the value increase. The buy-out transaction itself revalues the assets, resulting in a greater depreciation tax shelter than previously possible. In addition, the high degree of leverage produces a greater interest tax shelter than before (although why the reorganized firm should experience such an increase in debt capacity is subject to debate). Even in combinations undertaken for other motives (for example, to achieve operating synergies), transactions are structured to maximize tax benefits and minimize tax liability while complying with Internal Revenue Code regulations. Tax effects can make a marginal investment more profitable, or cause an otherwise acceptable transaction to be abandoned, if, for example, the IRS hands down an unfavorable private ruling on a proposed merger plan.

SOURCES OF TAX BENEFITS

There are several sources of merger-related tax benefits:

1 Market value of depreciable assets in excess of book value.
2 Substitution of capital gains for ordinary income.

3 Unused and/or unusable NOL and tax credit carry-overs.
4 Uncertainty of valuation for estate tax purposes.

Market Value of Depreciable Assets in Excess of Book Value

Changes in the value of a target's assets can provide a powerful tax incentive for mergers. By accounting convention, a firm's balance sheet reflects the historical cost of its assets. Although replacement cost information may be provided, depreciation charges are based on these historical costs. If the current market value of the assets greatly exceeds the historical cost (as is often the case, especially in a period of inflation), a potential for a greater depreciation tax shelter is achievable if the asset is revalued by a sale transaction. The acquiring firm can achieve a stepped-up asset basis reflecting the purchase price, resulting in a greater depreciation tax shelter than the target firm enjoyed on the same assets. The increased depreciation tax shelter is available only to the new owner, but the price paid in the acquisition allows the original owner to recoup some of the value increase.

Substitution of Capital Gains for Ordinary Income

A growth firm with many investment opportunities generally follows a policy of no dividends, and attracts a shareholder clientele with a preference for such a policy. As growth slows and investment opportunities diminish, the risk increases that the IRS may impose a penalty tax on improperly accumulated earnings if the no-dividend policy is continued. If the firm's stock is publicly traded, its shareholders can simply sell their shares to others with less aversion to dividend income. The market price of the stock should reflect a capitalization of expected future earnings, and selling shareholders will realize capital gains rather than receiving dividends subject to the ordinary personal income tax. If the firm is closely held, the shareholders' only alternative may be to sell out to another firm, the acquisition price likewise reflecting a capitalization of future earnings.

Unused and/or Unusable NOL and Tax Credit Carry-overs

A firm with net operating losses in excess of what it can utilize may be an attractive merger partner for a firm with positive earnings to shelter. Or a firm may have investment tax credits or foreign tax credits it cannot use. The Economic Recovery Tax Act of 1981 provided a means for effectively "selling" tax credits but these provisions were subsequently severely curtailed. Absent this device, a properly structured merger might be the sole means of realizing the value inherent in the carry-overs.

Uncertainty of Valuation
for Estate Tax Purposes

The sale of a closely-held firm before the owners' death provides both a certain valuation for estate taxation purposes as well as the liquidity for the heirs to meet the estate tax liability.

Dertouzos and Thorpe (1982) emphasized the combined influence of estate tax and asset basis step-up considerations in their study of mergers in the newspaper industry. The ability to step up the basis for depreciable assets results in higher prices for the companies acquired. These high prices establish market values which are then used by the tax authorities in valuing other companies for estate tax purposes. But in order to realize the tax benefits of the stepped-up basis, a sales transaction must take place. This encourages mergers to make possible the tax savings from increased depreciation charges for tax purposes.

The mechanics of the merger transaction in large part determine whether potential tax benefits will be realized and how their value will be allocated among the parties involved. These aspects are next discussed.

TAXABLE ACQUISITIONS VERSUS
TAX-FREE REORGANIZATIONS

Although the IRS distinguishes between taxable and tax-free takeover transactions in terms of target shareholder gain recognition, its basic position is that all takeovers are taxable events. The IRS holds that there can be no tax benefit without a corresponding "toll charge" or tax liability. Within this global stance, a transaction qualifies as a so-called tax-free reorganization under IRC 368(a)(1) if certain conditions are met. The distinguishing characteristic of tax-free reorganizations is that the primary consideration paid to obtain the voting stock or assets of the target firm must be voting stock of the acquiring firm.

There are three forms of tax-free reorganizations. Type A reorganizations include statutory mergers (in which the target firm is absorbed by the acquiring firm) and consolidations (in which both firms cease to exist as such and a new entity is created) with the approval of a majority of both target and acquiring firm shareholders. In a merger, target firm shareholders exchange their target stock for shares in the acquiring firm; in consolidations, both target and acquiring firm shareholders turn in their shares and receive stock in the newly created company.

Type B reorganizations are similarly stock-for-stock exchanges; following a Type B reorganization, the target may be liquidated into the acquiring firm or maintained as an independent operating entity.

Type C reorganizations are stock-for-asset transactions with the requirement that at least 80 percent of the fair market value of the target's property be acquired. Typically, the target firm "sells" its assets to the acquiring firm in exchange for acquiring firm voting stock; the target then dissolves, distributing the acquiring firm stock to its shareholders in return for their (now-cancelled) target stock. In general, Types A and B reorganizations use the pooling of interests method of accounting, while Type C reorganizations use the purchase method.

Notwithstanding compliance with the preceding requirements, acquisitions carried out solely with the acquiring firm's voting stock may still be considered taxable transactions if a valid business purpose beyond tax avoidance and substantial continuity of ownership and operation cannot also be demonstrated. Even then, the reorganizations are tax free only to the extent that target shareholders are not required to immediately recognize any gain (or loss) on the excess of the market value of acquiring firm stock received in trade over their basis in the target firm's stock. They must, however, recognize the gain if and when they sell the stock received; that is, their basis in the acquiring firm's stock is the same as their original basis in the target stock. (Unless, of course, they die without selling the acquiring firm stock, in which case its basis as part of their estate is stepped up to its market value at the time of death; and any gain resulting from the takeover transaction is truly tax free.) Thus, in most cases, tax-free reorganizations might better be categorized as only tax deferred, which is, after all, better than nothing.

Acquisitions are taxable when the medium of exchange is cash or non-equity securities of the acquiring firm. The target may be absorbed into the acquiring firm, or maintained as a separate operating entity.

The impact of acquisition method on tax effects varies. An overview is set forth in Table 12.1. The stepped-up asset basis is available to the acquiring firm only in taxable transactions. Thus, target firm shareholders must immediately (that is, in the year of the sale) recognize any resulting capital gains. If, in addition, the target firm has used accelerated depreciation, a portion of any gain that is attributable to excess depreciation deductions will be recaptured to be taxed as ordinary income rather than capital gain, the amount of recapture depending on the nature of the property involved. In tax-free acquisitions, the target's asset basis is transferred intact to the acquiring firm (carry-over basis). Thus, if the target's basis were greater than its market value (and purchase price), an acquirer would most likely prefer a tax-free reorganization. In Type C (stock-for-asset) tax-free reorganizations, depreciation recapture is deferred until the assets are subsequently disposed of in a taxable transaction; obviously, this permits the possibility of indefinite deferral.

Net operating losses are available to the acquiring firm only in tax-free reorganizations; and they can only be used to shield future income, not to recapture past taxes paid. Furthermore, even in tax-free reorganizations, if the target is maintained as a separate operating entity within the acquiring firm

TABLE 12.1
Tax Effects

	ACQUIRING FIRM	TARGET FIRM
Tax-free reorganizations	Carry-over asset basis NOL carry-over Tax-credit carry-over	Deferred gains for shareholders
Taxable acquisitions	Stepped-up asset basis	Depreciation recapture[a] Immediate gain recognition by target shareholders

[a]Any tax effects for the target firm (as opposed to its shareholders) ultimately impact the acquiring firm.

following a Type B transaction (stock-for-stock), the carry-over remains with the "target/subsidiary" rather than transferring to the "acquirer/parent," and can be used only to shelter target earnings; the target must be liquidated following the transaction to make the NOL carry-over available to the acquiring firm. Liquidation, in turn, can trigger depreciation recapture and other negative tax consequences for the target firm (now a part of the acquiring firm). Transactions can be structured to utilize NOL carry-forward regardless of whether the loss firm is the target or the acquirer, so long as the arrangement is not solely for the purpose of tax avoidance; that is, the combination must have a justifiable business purpose. In taxable transactions, the net operating loss carry-over simply vanishes and is not available to anyone. Tax credits such as the investment tax credit or foreign tax credits are treated in the same way as net operating losses.

PRE-TEFRA TAX PLANNING

The Tax Equity and Fiscal Responsibility Act of 1982 (TEFRA) contained a variety of complex provisions affecting both individuals and businesses. Tax planning patterns had to be changed as a consequence of the legislative changes. We look at tax planning pre-TEFRA in this section. The following section covers post-TEFRA tax changes up to the next major tax law changes which occurred in 1986. The Tax Reform Act of 1986 made many additional fundamental changes which are also reviewed.

As noted earlier, the IRS distinction between taxable and tax-free reorganizations focuses on the consideration paid (voting stock of the acquirer versus other) and target shareholder tax liability (deferred versus immediate). Within this framework, and depending on the specific tax attributes involved, it is often the case that transactions which benefit acquiring firms do so by creating tax liabilities for target firms and/or their shareholders (and vice versa). For example, a stepped-up asset basis (beneficial to the acquiring firm) is generally available only in a taxable takeover; but this would mean immediate capital gains recognition and recapture income for the target, which might demand a higher purchase price to compensate for the anticipated tax burden.

It has been noted that tender offers are characterized by higher premiums (greater gains for target shareholders) than mergers. This may, in part, be due to the fact that tender offers are more often than not taxable events, and thus target shareholders demand a higher pretax return, whereas mergers are often treated as tax-free reorganizations. The creativity and expertise of corporate legal advisers is called into play because companies, not unnaturally, want to "have their cake and eat it too." They seek to realize maximum tax benefits immediately while indefinitely deferring tax liabilities. Complex plans are devised and reworked with every change in the tax laws. Laying aside for the moment the IRS dichotomy between taxable and tax-free transactions, we now discuss various means by which firms have been able to achieve desired tax goals regardless of medium of exchange or target shareholder tax consequences.

One popular plan grew out of the General Utilities rule that a corporation does not recognize gain on the distribution of appreciated property with respect to (in redemption of) its shares [Section (311)(d)(2)(B)]. Such stock redemptions enable companies to dispose of appreciated assets without recognizing capital gain or depreciation recapture income, while passing benefits of the transaction on to their shareholders in the form of capital gains rather than dividend income. Ginsburg (1983) provides several case illustrations. The 1980 Mobil-Esmark transaction is one example. Esmark wanted to sell its Vickers Energy Corporation. Mobil Corporation wanted to buy TransOcean Oil, a subsidiary of Vickers. Instead of simply buying TransOcean Oil stock, which would have resulted ultimately in a capital gain for Esmark, Mobil made a cash tender offer for Esmark stock. Mobil then redeemed its Esmark stock in exchange for shares of Vickers Energy Corporation (which by that time held TransOcean Oil stock as its only asset). Esmark was not required to recognize any gain on the distribution of appreciated property (the Vickers stock) to a shareholder in a redemption. Esmark shareholders were free to choose whether they wanted to participate in the transaction; presumably those who tendered their shares to Mobil did so willingly, and took their returns in the form of capital gains. Had Esmark sold the TransOcean Oil stock or assets to Mobil more directly, its gain, net of tax, would conceivably have been passed on to Esmark shareholders eventually in the form of dividends, taxable as ordinary income, whether the shareholders wished to receive them or not.

Ginsburg (1983) also describes a similar arrangement involving Dome Petroleum's tender offer purchase of Conoco stock which it then redeemed in exchange for Conoco's interest in the Hudson's Bay Oil and Gas Co. In this case, Conoco was an unwilling participant in the transaction, whereas Esmark, in the previous instance, was cooperative. The results, however, were the same: A parent firm was able to (or forced to) effectively sell appreciated assets without recognizing gain or recapture income; those of its shareholders who wished to participate benefited in the form of capital gains; and the acquiring firm's asset basis reflected the price it paid to tendering parent firm shareholders. On the other hand, many stock redemption transactions have been struck down, the IRS forcing both the parent firm and its shareholders to recognize gain as if the transaction had been carried out as a sale of the subsidiary's assets followed by a cash distribution in redemption of shares (to those shareholders who tendered to the acquiring firm). In particular, the IRS has ruled against cases where shell subsidiaries were created and endowed with appreciated assets for the sole purpose of transferring such assets to an interested buyer via a stock redemption.

Another device, partial liquidation within a consolidated balance sheet (IRC 346), grew out of the pre-TEFRA requirement that in order to achieve stepped-up asset basis following a stock purchase, the target had to be liquidated into the acquiring firm. Consider cash mergers, for example. If the acquiring firm wants to achieve a stepped-up asset basis, the transaction should be structured as follows: The acquiring firm and the target firm would first agree to merge; then as part of the merger plan, target shareholders would exchange all of their target shares for cash. For tax purposes the transaction is treated as if the target had sold all of its assets to the acquiring firm and simultaneously liquidated, distributing the cash proceeds to its shareholders in redemption of their shares. Target shareholders would receive capital gains treatment, the acquiring firm would achieve a stepped-up asset basis, and there would be no recognition of recapture income by the acquiring firm. (If, on the other hand, the acquiring firm preferred carry-over asset basis treatment, the transaction would be structured with the stock purchase from target shareholders preceding the merger, so that at the time of the merger, the target is a wholly-owned subsidiary of the acquiring firm. The tax results would be identical except that the acquiring firm would obtain carry-over basis.)

The advantage of the partial liquidation device was that it gave acquiring firms great latitude in selecting basis treatment for target firm assets following a stock purchase transaction. For example, stepped-up asset basis treatment for a subset of target assets could be obtained without the assumed asset sale and simultaneous complete liquidation of the target considered earlier. A partial liquidation plan might be structured as follows: The acquiring firm buys the stock of the target (at least 80 percent control), via whatever medium of exchange. Following the stock purchase, the target firm's operations are included in the consolidated financial statements of the acquirer. Then, at some point, the acquiring firm redeems some, but not all, of its target shares in exchange for a subset of target firm assets with a fair market value equivalent to what the acquiring firm had paid for the surrendered shares. The basis for this subset of target assets is thus stepped-up to the basis of the shares redeemed. The transaction involves no investment tax credit recapture for the target, and no immediate depreciation recapture (although depreciation will be recaptured over time as the acquiring firm depreciates the assets each year). Target assets not involved in the partial liquidation maintain their original basis. A complete liquidation of the target in a situation like this would have resulted in immediate investment tax credit and depreciation recapture income recognition within the consolidated financial statements of the acquiring firm.

POST-TEFRA TAX CHANGES

Perhaps the most significant change brought about by the TEFRA legislation was new code Section 338 which diminished the importance of the structure of a transaction in determining the tax consequences, in particular, whether the acquisition was carried out via an asset purchase or a stock purchase.

Although carry-over asset basis has been and continues to be the general rule following a stock purchase transaction, the IRS has always permitted the acquiring firm to elect stepped-up asset basis treatment at a toll charge measured by recapture taxes imposed upon the target, now part of the acquirer (and sometimes avoided/deferred). Pre-TEFRA, however, this "election" for stepped-up basis had to take the form of a costly liquidation of the target into the acquirer (old Section 334). Current law now enables qualified stock purchase acquisitions to be treated as if they were asset sales under previous Section 337 if the acquiring firm wants to obtain stepped-up basis. Old Section 337 applied to those cases where the target firm sold all its assets to the acquiring firm and simultaneously liquidated; the target corporation recognized no gain on the sale, however, recapture provisions applied and were reflected in the acquiring firm's stepped-up asset basis calculations. By making a (new) Section 338 election, the acquiring firm can cause a stock purchase to be treated as a 337 asset sale as of the date 80 percent stock control is acquired. Technically, the transaction is considered to be an asset sale by the "old" target to a clone "new" target; the "old" target liquidates; the acquiring firm is considered to own "new" target stock; any recapture income as a result of the transaction is included in the "old" target's final tax return, and not on the acquiring firm's.

Parent firms may still, of course, liquidate controlled subsidiaries; however, it is the 338 election rather than the liquidation which determines the basis of the assets for the parent. Only if the 338 election is made does the process result in stepped-up basis; without the 338 election, the parent obtains carry-over basis.

Section 338 also addresses the perceived abuse inherent in partial liquidations, that is, selectivity as to which acquired assets receive stepped-up basis and which carry-over basis treatment, via its *consistency requirement*. The consistency requirement essentially says "all or nothing"; a 338 election for stepped-up basis for one subsidiary of an acquired target is deemed to be a 338 election for the entire target firm. It also applies to the mode of acquisition. If the acquirer purchases the assets of one target subsidiary while purchasing the stock of another subsidiary (of the same target), the asset purchase is deemed to be a Section 338 election for both subsidiaries.

Among the overall goals of the new legislation was to achieve a closer correlation between tax benefits and toll charges as a result of acquisition transactions. Applied to stock redemptions, this effectively denies the General Utilities doctrine that companies recognize no gain on the distribution of appreciated assets with respect to their stock by more closely relating asset basis step-up by

the distributee (the "acquirer") to recognition of gain by the distributing corporation (that is, the parent of the target). As the code now stands, a corporation
distributing appreciated assets in a stock redemption must recognize gain equivalent to what would have been required had the property been sold on the
redemption date. For the shareholder/recipient, tax consequences now hinge
upon this entity's corporate-noncorporate status. For noncorporate shareholder/
recipients, the distribution is treated as payment in exchange for stock; the
recipient must recognize capital gain (or loss), and obtains stepped-up asset
basis. For corporate form shareholder/recipients, the distribution is treated as an
intercorporate dividend, subject to carry-over asset basis, so long as the distribution is pro rata to all shareholders. (In non-pro rata distributions, the corporate
shareholder/recipient can get stepped-up asset basis, and must recognize capital
gain, if the distribution is substantially disproportionate or terminates the corporate shareholder's interest.)

THE TAX REFORM ACT OF 1986

What started out as a "tax simplification" effort ended up being a "tax complica-
tion" law. The Tax Reform Act of 1986 resulted in the enactment of a 1986
Internal Revenue Code that made many fundamental changes from the previous
1954 Code.

The Tax Reform Act of 1986 had a number of impacts on merger and
acquisition transactions. (1) It severely restricted the use of net operating loss
carry-overs. (2) The preferential rate on corporate capital gains was repealed. (3)
A minimum tax was imposed on corporate profits. (4) The General Utilities
doctrine was repealed. (5) Greenmail payments could not be deducted.

Net Operating Loss (NOL)
Carry-overs

The new tax reform act provides that if there is greater than a 50 percent ownership change in a loss corporation within a three-year period, an annual limit on
the use of NOLs will be imposed. The amount of an NOL that may be used to
offset earnings is limited to the value of the loss corporation at the date of
ownership change multiplied by the long-term tax-exempt bond rate.

For example, assume a loss corporation is worth $10 million immediately
before an ownership change, the tax-exempt bond rate is 7 percent, and the
corporation has a $5 million loss carry-forward. Then $700,000 ($10 million ×
7%) of the NOL can be used annually to offset the acquiring firm's taxable
income.

In addition, a loss corporation may not utilize NOL carry-overs unless
it continues substantially the same business for two years after the change

in ownership. If this requirement is not met, all of the losses generally are disallowed.

Corporate Capital Gains Tax

The corporate capital gains tax rate had been 28 percent. For taxable years beginning on or after July 1, 1987 long-term as well as short-term corporate capital gains are taxed as ordinary income subject to the maximum corporation tax rate of 34 percent. Since many individuals will be taxed at less than the top corporate rate of 34 percent, this could stimulate more acquisitions through master limited partnerships (MLPs) or through use of S corporations. The use of MLPs or S corporations enables profits to flow directly to the partners or to the S corporation shareholders. This achieves a lower tax rate and avoids double taxation on both earnings and dividends.

Minimum Tax on Corporate Profits

Before the Tax Reform Act of 1986, a corporation paid a minimum tax on specific tax preferences in addition to its regular tax. The old add-on minimum tax is replaced by an alternative minimum tax with a flat rate of 20 percent. Thus, corporations pay taxes to at least 20 percent of their income above the exemption amount. This has a negative impact on leveraged buy-outs and acquisitions of mature companies where effective tax rates are below 20 percent.

General Utilities Doctrine

Under the General Utilities case decided in the 1930s and incorporated in later code sections, corporations did not recognize gains when they sold assets in connection with a complete liquidation if the requirements of Section 337 were met. This required adoption of a plan of liquidation and sale with distribution of assets within a 12-month period. Distribution of assets in kind in liquidation also were not subject to tax. The provisions were repealed by the TRA of 1986. Most of the exemptions from the new rules are for relatively small and closely-held corporations or provide for limited transitional periods.

Greenmail

The Tax Reform Act of 1986 also limited the extent to which amounts paid as greenmail to corporate raiders could be deducted for tax purposes. This change plus the others listed previously move in the direction of being less favorable to merger and acquisition activity. However, there is a long history of tax planners coming up with creative new ideas for avoiding the adverse impact of tax law changes.

EMPIRICAL TESTS OF TAX EFFECTS

The most thorough empirical study of the effects of taxes on the merger decision was made by Auerbach and Reishus (1986). Their sample was divided into five groups. Group I firms have positive tax payable and no credits carried forward. This is where the majority of firms in the study were located. Group II firms have no current federal tax liability. Tax losses and credits are being carried back against prior year's taxable income. These firms have little capacity to absorb tax transfers through mergers. Group III firms possess unused tax credits carried forward. They have no tax losses. Group IV firms possess both tax losses and tax credits carried forward.

A fifth group have tax loss carry forwards as well as positive taxes currently payable. Although this is somewhat confusing, the type of firm that may exhibit this tax treatment is a life insurance company, or an organization which consolidates its financial statements.

Gains from the transfer of tax benefits were measured as the maximum amount of the constrained firm's tax benefits which could be used over a three-year period by a Group I firm with constant taxable income during that period. Example: Firm A has taxable income, firm B has tax losses and credits carried forward. Multiply the taxable income of firm A by 3, and compare this to B's losses. If these losses exceed A's three-year income, then this amount times t (corporate tax rate) equals the benefit. If B's losses are less than A's income, then the credits are offset against the remaining income.

Of the 442 firms studied, Auerbach and Reishus found that Group I contained 234 acquired and 260 acquiring firms. Group I acquisitions of Group III or IV firms resulted in 40 mergers. Group I firms acquired by Group III or IV firms totaled 21 mergers. Group I and Group I combinations had nine mergers. Therefore, the potential tax benefit is 20 percent of all mergers studied.

Potential tax benefits are present in almost one fifth of the mergers studied. The average gain (calculated as percentage of combined value of the acquired firm's equity plus debt) is just over one tenth of the target firm's value.

Transference of unused tax benefits is economically relevant in few mergers. One third of the mergers studied had benefits in excess of 10 percent of the acquired firm's market value. The mean benefit was 10.5 percent. Weighted for size of the firm, the result is 6.1 percent. This indicates that a tax-oriented merger is more important with smaller targets.

The basis step-up benefits they found were smaller than the tax-loss benefits. Of the 275 firms studied, seven produced gains from a basis step-up greater than 5 percent of the target firm's value. Of the 40 cases where the target also had unused credits and losses, the basis step-up was only 2 percent.

The authors looked at the debt ratio two years before a merger and two years after a merger to determine the company's long-run debt/equity ratio.

Equity was defined as the year-end market value of common stock. Debt was calculated from the book value of long-term debt.

Long-term debt as a percentage of debt plus equity increases from an average of 30 percent to 32 percent, a weighted increase of 25.4 percent to 26.7 percent. These changes in the sample are not considered significant.

The combined debt ratios of merged firms with a target market value between 25 and 50 percent of the parent's experience a decrease in debt ratio from 40.4 percent to 38.3 percent. With an acquired firm's market value greater than 50 percent of the parent's, the debt market value ratio increased from 32.1 percent to 35.3 percent, weighted.

CONCLUSIONS

Tax effects are important in virtually all corporate restructuring events, and in some cases are the primary reason for the event. Among the most important considerations are asset basis treatment and gain recognition, as well as NOL and other carry-overs. Tax planning becomes complicated when, say, the tax goals of target and acquiring firms are inconsistent, or do not seem to conform with Internal Revenue Code conventions. Successive changes in tax laws in response to perceived inequities in the code with respect to corporate combinations spawn a succession of new tax plans to achieve the same or similar ends.

Under the Tax Reform Act of 1986, significant changes were made in the laws. As a consequence of experience under the tax law of 1986, many additional changes in the tax laws might be made as a consequence of the Treasury's study and recommendations.

QUESTIONS

1. How can personal taxation affect mergers?
2. Discuss the advantages and disadvantages of stock-for-stock versus cash-for-stock transactions from the viewpoint of acquired and acquiring firm shareholders.
3. Given: Beta Company transfers assets with a fair market value of $200 to Alpha Company for voting stock valued at $160 and cash of $40. No liabilities are assumed. Beta Company uses the $40 to pay its liabilities, distributes the stock to its shareholders, and then liquidates.
   a. What type of reorganization is this?
   b. If Beta Company's assets have a basis of $100, does it have to recognize a gain? If so, how much?
   c. What is Beta's basis in its Alpha voting stock?
   d. What is the basis of the assets in Alpha's hands?

     e. What is the basis of the assets in Alpha's hands if Beta liquidates and distributes Alpha stock plus the $40 cash to its shareholders?

     f. What happens if, in the original case, Alpha transferred stock of $120, cash of $40 and assumed liabilities of $40 for Beta's $200 fair market value in assets?

     g. What happens if, in the original case, Alpha transferred stock of $120 and assumed liabilities of $80?

4. How do a firm's growth prospects affect its potential for being involved in a tax-motivated merger?

5. How have TEFRA and the Tax Reform Act of 1986 affected merger planning?

REFERENCES

AUERBACH, ALAN J., and DAVID REISHUS, "Taxes and the Merger Decision: An Empirical Analysis," Cambridge, MA: National Bureau of Economic Research, Working Paper No. 1855, March 1986.

BIERMAN, HAROLD, JR., "A Neglected Tax Incentive for Mergers," *Financial Management*, Summer 1985, pp. 29–32.

CURTIS, MICHAEL R., "Tempered Benefits on NOLs and Capital Gains," *Mergers & Acquisitions*, January/February 1987, pp. 48–49.

DERTOUZOS, JAMES N., and KENNETH E. THORPE, "Newspaper Groups: Economies of Scale, Tax Laws and Merger Incentives," Santa Monica, CA, Rand Corporation, R-2878-SBA, June 1982.

ECKBO, B. ESPEN, "Horizontal Mergers, Collusion, and Stockholder Wealth," *Journal of Financial Economics*, 11, 1983, pp. 241–274.

GINSBURG, MARTIN D., "Taxing Corporate Acquisitions," *Tax Law Review*, 38, 1983, pp. 177–319.

HAYN, CARLA, "The Role of Tax Variables in Corporate Acquisitions," Working Draft, December 1985.

SMIRLOCK, MICHAEL, RANDOLPH BEATTY, and SAMAN MAJD, *Taxes and Mergers: A Survey*, Monograph 1985-3, New York: Salomon Brothers Center for the Study of Financial Institutions at the Graduate School of Business Administration of New York University, 1985.

WOOD, ROBERT, W., "General Utilities Repeal: Injecting New Levies Into M&A," *Mergers & Acquisitions*, January/February 1987, pp. 44–47.

CHAPTER 13

Methods of Payment and Leverage

Related corporate finance theory implies that the method of payment used in a merger or tender offer may influence the returns to the stockholders of both the bidder and target firms. Of particular relevance is the theory of Myers and Majluf (1984) which holds that the method of financing an investment conveys information. They argue that when the firm sells common stock to finance a new project, it is because the managers judge the common stock to be overvalued. When the firm uses debt to finance a new investment, this implies that management judges its common stock to be undervalued. In addition, empirical studies suggest that there are negative returns to shareholders when new outside financing is used whether in the form of debt or equity. (See our previous discussion in Chapter 5.)

First we review the empirical studies of the effects of method of payment in a corporate takeover on shareholder returns. Next we attempt to relate the empirical evidence to a number of alternative theories. Third, since debt is one of the methods of payment, we also analyze whether significant leverage changes have taken place as a consequence of mergers and tender offers. Further theoretical discussions appear in Appendix A.

EMPIRICAL STUDIES OF EFFECTS
OF METHODS OF PAYMENT

The earlier studies by Gordon and Yagil (1981) and by Wansley, Lane, and Yang (1983) found higher abnormal returns for cash offers than for stock offers. The

Gordon and Yagil study examined completed pure conglomerate mergers over the period 1948–1976. The Wansley, Lane, and Yang work covered mergers for the period 1970–1978. Wansley, Lane, and Yang found that the target firm cumulative average residual for the 41 days through the announcement date when the method of payment was cash was 33.54 percent as compared with 17.47 percent when securities were used. When the method of payment represented a combination of cash and securities, the CAR was 11.77 percent. They discuss the role of taxes in impacting these differential abnormal returns. They also observe that when stock is used, the bidding firm must go through Securities and Exchange Commission registration which may take several months. Cash offers can be accomplished much more rapidly. The longer time to complete a takeover gives target management more possibilities for developing a defense to the takeover. They can stimulate additional bids and may encourage such bids by selectively disclosing important information to selected potential bidders.

Later studies by Travlos (1985, 1987) analyze the impact of methods of payment on both bidders and targets. For *target firms*, his results are similar to those of Wansley, Lane, and Yang. The two-day announcement period abnormal cumulative portfolio return when common stock is used is 12.04 percent. They find that significant positive abnormal returns start appearing a week before the announcement appears in *The Wall Street Journal*. In cash transactions the two-day abnormal return is 17.06 percent and highly significant. Again some significant abnormal returns are observed in the preannouncement period.

For the *bidding firms*, Travlos finds that when stock is used as the method of payment, the two-day announcement period CAR is minus 1.47 percent, which is significant at the .01 level. Thus, the effect is small but still statistically significant. He observes that Gordon and Yagil found positive abnormal returns of 5.3 percent over the eight-month period prior to the completion date of the merger, but that the long period may confound the influence of other factors. The results of Travlos are more comparable to those of Eger (1983) who found in a sample of 37 pure common stock exchange mergers that bidding stockholders lose about 3 percent during the event period.

However, the results are different when the buying firms use cash to acquire target firms. The two-day announcement period cumulative abnormal return is .24 percent which is insignificant. Travlos concludes that on average shareholders of bidding firms earn only normal rates of return when their firms pay cash in a takeover. Again his results differ from those of Gordon and Yagil who found an abnormal cumulative (monthly) return of 7.9 percent over the eight-month period prior to the merger completion date.

The findings by Travlos on the results for bidder firms have great significance both for theory and practice. Studies which have found negative returns to bidding firms have argued that shareholders of bidding firms are penalized by takeover activities. They argue that an agency problem is involved. But if only normal returns are experienced when cash is used, this reflects the highly competitive nature of the takeover market. The negative returns when common stock exchanges are employed may simply reflect the negative information implications set out by Myers and Majluf (1984). When the studies do not distinguish between cash and common stock exchange takeovers, the average result may simply reflect the method of payment rather than a meaningful measure of the performance of bidding firms.

Franks, Harris, and Mayer (1987) compare the effects of means of payment in takeovers for the United Kingdom as well as for the United States. Their results are summarized in Table 13.1.

From Table 13.1 it can be seen that acquired firm returns are higher for cash offers than for all equity offers both in the United States and in the United Kingdom. For the event month the effects are stronger in the United Kingdom. For the period encompassing four months prior and one month after the event month, the effects are about the same in both countries. For bidders during the event month, all cash offers yield small positive abnormal returns that are statistically significant in the United States, but not significant in the United Kingdom. All equity offers have negative returns that are significant in the United States, but not in the United Kingdom. For the longer period of analysis covering months −4 to +1, cash offers yield small positive abnormal returns both in the United States and the United Kingdom and have some statistical significance. All equity offers carry no statistical significance.

TABLE 13.1
Abnormal Returns in Cash Versus All Equity Offers for the U.K. and the U.S.

ACQUIRED	MONTH 0		MONTHS −4 TO +1	
	U.K.	U.S.	U.K.	U.S.
All cash	.302	.254	.305	.363
	(28.07)	(42.29)	(11.56)	(24.67)
All equity	.151	.111	.182	.156
	(12.88)	(25.90)	(6.34)	(14.86)

BIDDER	U.K.	U.S.	U.K.	U.S.
All cash	.007	.020	.043	.026
	(.75)	(3.56)	(1.98)	(1.89)
All equity	−.011	−.009	.018	.006
	(−.95)	(−2.23)	(.63)	(.61)

SOURCE: Julian R. Franks, Robert S. Harris, and Colin Mayer, "Means of Payment in Takeovers: Results for the U.K. and U.S.," ms., 1987.

Queen (1989) also studied the effects of the form of payment. Queen brings in another variable, the extent to which the tender offer may have been antici- pated prior to the announcement date. Her results can be summarized in the following matrix of returns:

	PREANNOUNCEMENT	AROUND-ANNOUNCEMENT	TOTAL PERIODS
Target	noncash > cash	noncash < cash	noncash = cash
Bidder	noncash = cash	noncash = cash	noncash = cash

It can be seen that her results when measured around the announcement date are similar to the results for the studies previously described. However, she extends the analysis into the preannouncement period. Here the target receives more in a noncash tender than for a cash tender offer. For bidders abnormal returns are the same whether the method of payment is cash or noncash. When she combines the two periods, Queen finds that for the total periods, the abnor- mal returns to both the target and bidder are the same whether cash or noncash is employed. Queen, therefore, concludes that observed differences are simply because the extent to which the tender was anticipated was not adequately analyzed in the previous studies.

A study by Huang and Walkling (1987) combines the analysis of method of payment with acquisition form and managerial resistance. Whereas previous studies found higher abnormal returns (30 to 35 percent) for tender offers than for mergers (15 to 20 percent) for target shareholders, such studies did not consider the effect of payment method and target management resistance. Huang and Walkling find that when method of payment and degree of resis- tance are taken into account statistically, abnormal returns are no higher in tender offers than in mergers. Managerial resistance carries somewhat higher abnormal returns, but the results are not statistically significant. These results are not affected after controlling for form of payment and form of acquisition. The most powerful influence they find is the method of payment. After control- ling for type of acquisition and for managerial resistance, cash offers have much higher abnormal returns than stock offers. The average CAR for cash offers is 29.3 percent compared with 14.4 percent for stock offers. For mixed payments, the average abnormal return is 23.3 percent, which falls between the values reported for stock and cash offers.

Huang and Walkling subject the results to regression analysis. This enables them to take the effects of form of payment, managerial resistance, and form of acquisition into account holding two of the influences constant while the third varies. The difference between the abnormal returns of tender offers and merg- ers disappears when the influence of the form of payment and managerial resis- tance are taken into account. But the difference between cash and stock offers remains strong even after controlling for resistance and the form of acquisition, merger or tender offer.

THEORIES OF THE INFLUENCE
OF METHOD OF PAYMENT
ON ABNORMAL RETURNS

The studies of the empirical results on the influence of method of payment consider a number of alternative theories to explain their results. The leading theories involve tax factors, information effects, and signaling.

The main tax effects considered are tax deferral, a capital gains tax, and asset write-ups. A stock-for-stock exchange enables the target shareholders to avoid taxes at the time of the takeover. However, when they sell the equity received in the exchange transaction, it will then be subject to a capital gains tax. Hence, the tax is deferred and in addition it is in the form of a capital gains tax rather than an ordinary tax. (With the Tax Reform Act of 1986, the capital gains tax advantage is lost as the capital gains treatment is removed.) Tax deferral is of benefit to the target shareholders. When cash is used, the capital gains tax has to be paid immediately by the target shareholders. This reduces the after-tax returns to the target shareholders. Some, therefore, argue that the premiums and abnormal returns in cash payments must be higher to offset this tax disadvantage.

The potential for writing up assets to recover a higher amount of depreciation tax shelter is an advantage that is realized by the bidder. This may lead the bidder to pay a higher premium to the target. The advantage of asset write-up to the bidder may help explain the small positive gain observed when cash is used by bidders as the method of payment in a takeover.

Information Effects

This refers to the Myers and Majluf (1984) hypothesis which holds that when equity is used it gives the information that the bidder judges its equity to be overvalued. This should cause the returns to bidders to be negative. However, since the market will see through this information, it should have no effect on the returns to the target. But we do observe that targets have much higher returns when cash is used than when there is a stock exchange.

Signaling

The third theoretical thread is signaling in the sense of indicating future investment opportunities or cash flows. The use of cash can be a positive signal in many ways. For the bidder, it may signal that cash flows from its existing assets will be large. If this signaling effect exists and if internal financing as opposed to external financing facilitates investments, then it may have a derived effect. That is, it can signal the ability of the bidder to exploit the investment opportunities possessed by the target or created by synergy effects. Cash payment may also signal the bidder's private information on the profitability of the takeover.

The use of equity has opposite effects. It is a negative signal about prospects for the bidder. It may also be a negative signal for the takeover in the sense that the ability of the combined firm to internalize the investment opportunities is not great with respect to internal financing. Hence, bidders using stock as the method of payment will experience negative abnormal returns. Targets should gain but they would not gain as much as when cash is used and gains from the takeover are shared by the bidder and the target.

We have now completed a review of the empirical studies on the effects of methods of payment in a corporate takeover on shareholder returns. We have also related the empirical evidence to three alternative theories. We next turn to the third segment outlined at the beginning of the chapter, the effects of takeover activity on leverage ratios. Closely related to the topic of method of payment is the new development that occurred in recent years, the use of high-yield bonds (generally referred to as junk bonds) in M&A activity.

THE ROLE OF JUNK BONDS

Junk bonds are high-yield bonds either rated below investment grade or unrated. Using Standard & Poor's ratings, junk bonds are defined at below BBB−; using Moody's the level is below Baa3. Allegations have been made that junk bonds have contributed to excessive takeover activity and resulted in unsound levels of business leverage. Taggart (1986) has addressed these issues with empirical data and analysis.

Trends in the Use of Junk Bonds

There have always been high-yield bonds. But prior to 1977, high-yield bonds were "fallen angels," bonds initially rated investment grade but whose ratings had been subsequently lowered. The first issuer of bonds rated below investment grade from the start is said to be Lehman Brothers in 1977. Drexel Burnham Lambert soon became the industry leader. Competition followed, but Drexel still had 45 percent of the market in 1986 and 43.2 percent of the market through mid-November 1987 (Frantz, 1987). However, as a result of its legal problems, Drexel's share of public underwritings of junk debt fell to only 16 percent in the first quarter of 1989 (Laing, 1989). Between 1970 and 1977, high-yield bonds represented on average about 3 to 4 percent of total public straight debt bonds. By 1985, this share had risen to 14.4 percent. These are shares of the stocks of public straight bonds outstanding. As a percentage of yearly flows of new public bond issues by U.S. corporations, the straight junk bond shares had risen from 1.1 percent in 1977 to almost 20 percent by 1985. Clearly junk bonds have come to play a significant role in bond financing. Further dimensions of the market are presented in connection with an evaluation of the issues raised by junk bond financing after the economic factors which stimulated this financial innovation are reviewed.

Financial Market Setting of Junk Bond Issuance

The relatively high rates of inflation from the mid-1960s through the early 1980s increased the need for external financing by business firms. At high price levels, the same physical volume of business activity will require more financing. With rising inflation, the same physical volume of sales will grow in inflated dollars and any growth in the physical volume of sales will be magnified by inflation (Weston and Copeland, 1986, pp. 247–249). Under plausible relationships, with higher inflation, more external financing will be needed. Also business fluctuations will cause swings in the extent of external financing required.

With greater dependence on external financing, business managers have sought to be as efficient as possible in the use of outside funds. Business firms responded by greater use of international financing, the Eurodollar bond financing by U.S. corporations reaching $20 billion in 1984. Business firms have also financed directly from investors. One such form is the commercial paper market whose outstandings increased fourfold to $80 billion between 1978–1985. At the same time, deregulation of financial institutions increased competition and lowered fees and earnings of financial intermediaries. Investment bankers earned less in their traditional business activities as did commercial banks. Financial intermediaries sought new areas of growth and profitability.

Increased competition in most industries was stimulated by new technologies, new products, and the globalization of markets with international competition. The advantage of mass-production industries diminished in the face of consumer demand for more variety and the need for increased flexibility in production technologies. New medium-sized competitors emerged. They needed financing and only 6 percent of 11,000 public corporations could qualify for investment grade ratings (Taggart, 1986, quoting Paulus, 1986).

Investment bankers sought new customers just as commercial banks increased their efforts to finance customers who could not qualify as prime-rate borrowers. The rapidly changing economic environment led to mergers and acquisitions and a wide range of forms of corporate restructuring. Firms moved in and out of new and old industries and product markets. The need to mobilize capital quickly to meet new opportunities and challenges created changed market opportunities for investment bankers and commercial bankers. Thus, the economic conditions were ripe for the expansion of the high-yield bond market and financial innovators responded to this new market opportunity.

We next consider issues related to whether the growth in the high-yield bond market is good or bad for the economy. A number of public policy issues have been raised by the use of junk bonds and the conditions which gave rise to them. This discussion is stimulated by Taggart (1986).

Performance of Junk Bonds

To date junk bond returns have been larger than for higher-grade bonds (Altman and Nammacher, 1986). For the period 1974–1985, the annual default rate on rated junk bonds averaged 1.53 percent versus 0.09 percent for all rated public straight bonds. But the nominal yields of junk bonds are also higher. For 1978–1985 Altman and Nammacher (1986) found a compound annual rate of return of 12.4 percent for junk bonds compared with 9.7 percent for the Shearson Lehman Long-Term Government Bond Index. During the period 1976–1985, the average total reinvested return for mutual funds with an investment emphasis on high-yield bonds was 206.8 percent versus 178.0 percent for U.S. government bond funds. Other studies by Blume and Keim (1984) found similar results.

A study by Asquith, Mullins, and Wolff (1989) questions these earlier find-ings on the basis that the rapid growth of junk bond issuance inflates the denomi-nator in the default ratio. When a given group of junk bonds is followed over the years, they find that the default ratios rise to 19 to 34 percent. The reason is that default rates rise with the age of the junk bonds. For an investor who continued to shift to newer bonds, the lower default ratios might be experienced. But this requires expert management and assumes that the shifts can be made before the market discounts the prospective default.

However, the period covered by all these studies was one of relatively high rates of business activity and favorable conditions in the financial markets. The junk bonds have yet to be tested by a serious recession. The market crash of October 1987 gives some information. A study of common stock performance of 13 companies associated with Drexel's junk bonds was made between August 26, 1987, the day after the market's peak, and November 18. During this period the S&P index of 500 stocks was down 27 percent, while the Drexel index was down 40 percent. An index of 30 companies with high levels of corporate debt was down 31 percent for the same period. While stock prices were down for high debt users, their bond values were up. An index of 110 companies with the largest outstanding junk bonds showed their bond prices had increased 2.6 percent between October 19 and November 18, 1987. This reflected the policy of the Federal Reserve System to provide ample liquidity to the financial markets and caused government bonds to rise by 13 percent over the same period.

Junk Bonds and Merger Activity

Much concern has been expressed about the use of junk bonds in leveraged buy-outs (beginning in 1981) and in takeovers (beginning in 1983). In the process a potential acquirer receives commitments from investors to purchase a specified amount of securities (which may include junk bonds) if a specified fraction of target shares is tendered in response to the offer. The securities sold to the investors may be issued by a shell corporation created specifically to acquire the target's shares; but the securities issued are not collateralized by the shares tendered. If the bidder succeeds in obtaining control, the target company's as-sets can then be used as collateral for additional financing that may be needed to complete the acquisition. The investors may be compensated with a commitment fee ranging from 0.5 to 1.0 percent of the funds committed whether or not the tender offer succeeds.

The advantage of the prior commitment is the ability to pounce on a target with speed before the target can mount its defenses. The role of a financial intermediary like Drexel Burnham in arranging such commitment can be a very vital one. Another practice is for a number of large investors to help finance one another in successive takeovers. The Federal Reserve Board sought to discourage the shell financing structure by a rule adopted in January 1986. The Fed imposed margin requirements on stock purchases by shell corporations, but provided for many exceptions to the rule.

The Fed had estimated that in 1984, $6.5 billion, 41 percent of total publicly-issued junk bonds, were related to M&A activity in some way. It further estimated that $4.3 billion in junk bonds that were privately placed were merger related. This would bring the total to $10.8 billion. These Fed figures on the estimates of the extent to which junk bond usage was merger related are much higher than the estimates of Drexel Burnham and also much above the somewhat higher estimates of Morgan Stanley. But even the Fed's estimates represent about 9 percent of 1984 total merger and acquisition activity. The percentage could be higher for 1985, but not likely to be more than 20 percent using the Fed's estimates. Morgan Stanley's estimates for 1985 place the use of junk bonds at 4.5 percent of the total value of M&A activity for the year. These data suggest that junk bonds represent a relatively small fraction of total M&A activity.

Junk Bond Holdings by Savings and Loans (S&Ls)

Another concern is that some S&Ls have invested heavily in junk bonds relying on federal insurance [The Federal Savings and Loan Insurance Corporation (FSLIC)] to bail them out if necessary. Federally chartered S&Ls can invest up to 11 percent of their assets in junk bonds. But federally insured S&Ls in 1985 held about .05 percent of their total assets in junk bonds. However, in mid-1985, ten S&Ls (of a total of 3,180 FSLIC-insured S&Ls) accounted for 77 percent of total junk bond holdings by S&Ls, representing about 10 percent of their total assets. Also state-chartered S&Ls may invest higher percentages. One California S&L held 16 percent of its assets in junk bonds.

While pricing deposit insurance and limiting S&L risk pose serious unresolved issues, junk bonds represent only a relatively small part of the S&L problem.

Effect on Other Bondholders

When measured at book values, leverage has increased in recent years. In some highly publicized corporate restructurings, leverage has increased substantially for individual firms. Evidence of rising leverage ratios is the downgrading of corporate debt. In 1985 alone Moody's downgraded about 16 percent of the total par value of corporate bonds outstanding. Restructuring was associated with 38 percent of the downgrades.

But while downgrading may be associated with decline in bond values, the preponderance of empirical evidence shows little effect of restructuring on bond-holders while beneficial to shareholders. If bondholders were harmed in the past, they are likely to require compensation in future financing in the form of higher rates and terms. New protective mechanisms will be required to sell future bond issues. Illustrative are issues of bonds containing "poison put" provisions. These give their holders the option to exchange their bonds for cost or stock if a change occurs in the control of the issuing firm.

Conclusions on Effects of Junk Bonds

Newly issued junk bonds represent a financial innovation of the 1980s. They represent a response to the changed economic and financial environment. These new factors include increased external financing by business firms, heightened interest rate volatility, deregulation and increased competition among financial institutions, and an increase in the pace of industrial restructuring.

The use of junk bonds may have increased the extent of M&A activity and corporate restructuring. But the conclusion set forth by Taggart (1986) seems reasonable. His view is that the junk bond market itself is unlikely to have a major impact on the aggregate level of debt or the safety of the financial system. It is likely also that M&A activity and related corporate restructuring is determined by more fundamental economic and financial forces than the emergence of newly issued high-yield debt.

POSTMERGER FINANCIAL LEVERAGE

Most earlier studies of the impact of mergers found that leverage increased as a result of merger activity. All of these studies were completed by 1980 and generally found increased leverage after mergers. Before 1980 most mergers were of the conglomerate type because the courts and regulatory authorities had virtually barred horizontal and vertical mergers. Therefore, the results might be different for mergers taking place after 1980. However, as the preceding discussion on the use of junk bonds suggests, takeovers in the 1980s have increasingly been financed with funds raised by debt issues. Leveraged buy-outs and leveraged cash-outs are new phenomena that developed in the 1980s. Hence, it appears that the findings of the earlier studies are valid also for the takeovers that have occurred in the 1980s.

Shrieves and Pashley (1984) provide the results of an elaborate test of the increased-leverage theory. After controlling for firm size and industry effects, they found that mergers resulted in significant increases in financial leverage.

(They were also able to reject the latent debt-capacity hypothesis as opposed to the increased debt-capacity hypothesis.) Weston and Mansinghka (1971), Melicher and Rush (1974), and Stevens (1973) find that conglomerate mergers yielded significant postmerger increases in debt-to-equity ratios. Similarly, Markham (1973, pp. 88–89) reports that the interest payments of the acquired firm (or the new division) increased after the merger, which also implies an increase in leverage. Kim, McConnell, and Greenwood (1977) provide further evidence on increased leverage. Finally, conglomerate firms are characterized by a significantly higher degree of financial leverage compared to all other manufacturing firms (Chung, 1982).

The systematic increase in leverage following conglomerate mergers is consistent with reduced expected values of bankruptcy costs. It is also consistent with the (Galai and Masulis, 1976; Higgins and Schall, 1975) proposition that risk is lowered for bondholders and then is moved toward its previous level for bondholders by increased leverage. The leverage increases that take place should also yield increased tax savings.

We describe more fully the evidence developed by Chung (1982) as illustrative of the quantitative aspects of increased leverage associated with mergers in the pre-1980 period. Two different types of tests were used. The first examines whether diversified or conglomerate firms use a greater amount of debt than nondiversified firms. The second is a direct test of the increase or decrease in financial leverage after a pure conglomerate merger compared with product-extension mergers.

The first test compares a group of diversified firms with another group of nondiversified firms with respect to three financial ratios, debt to (stockholders') equity, return on total capital employed, and net income to equity. The latter two ratios are included in order to ascertain the extent to which financial leverage benefits the conglomerates.

Two samples of multi-industry firms (or conglomerates) were obtained. One comprises 44 firms from the *Forbes* (January 7, 1980) classification and the other 58 firms from the study by Weston and Mansinghka. The two samples are not entirely distinct, as a total of 27 firms belong to both samples. The nondiversified-firm group consists of all manufacturing firms on the Standard and Poor's 1979 Compustat Annual Industrial tape, excluding of course those classified as the conglomerates in each test. Firms whose data are not completely available were eliminated. In addition, if a firm's equity is negative, if the rate of return on equity is greater than 100 percent in absolute value, or if the debt/equity ratio is greater than 100, that firm was dropped from the sample.

The financial data used for both groups are also from the Compustat tape. The tests were performed for the five-year period from 1974 through 1978. For the period, variables were calculated as denominator-weighted averages.

The results presented in Table 13.2 show that the conglomerates are more heavily levered than the large manufacturing firm sample. The data with respect to the rates of return clearly reflect this leverage difference. In order to test the effects of financial leverage on equity return more directly, the increase in return

TABLE 13.2

Comparison of Financial Leverage Between Conglomerates and Other Manufacturing Firms, 1974–1978

	CONGLOMER- ATES		MANUFACTURING FIRMS		t-VALUE FOR MEAN DIFFERENCE
	n	AVERAGE (%)	n	AVERAGE (%)	
1. Forbes sample	44		1194		
a. Return on capital		8.91		9.77	−1.67[a]
b. Return on equity		11.52		11.05	0.62
c. Debt to equity		104.		58.	3.15[b]
d. (b − a)		2.61		1.28	3.68[b]
2. Weston and Mansinghka sample	58		1180		
a. Return on capital		9.51		9.75	−0.56
b. Return on equity		12.19		11.02	1.71[a]
c. Debt to equity		86.		58.	2.80[b]
d. (b − a)		2.68		1.27	3.95[b]

[a]Statistically significant at the 10% level (two-tailed test).
[b]Statistically significant at the 1% level (two-tailed test).

SOURCE: Kwang Chung, "Investment Opportunities, Synergies, and Conglomerate Mergers," doctoral dissertation, AGSM-UCLA, 1982.

was measured as the difference between the rates of return on equity and on capital employed, and the mean difference test was applied to this measure. Although the means of the measure are positive for both conglomerates and the manufacturing firms as expected, that of the former is significantly larger than that of the latter. Conglomerates improve their rate of return on shareholders' equity by about 1.3 percentage points more than the manufacturing firms by using greater leverage. It is worth noting that while the return on capital is generally lower for conglomerates, the return on equity is higher for them than for manufacturing firms.

The second test directly examines the change in financial leverage following a pure conglomerate merger. Thus the premerger and postmerger leverage ratios for the merged firms are compared to those for a control group. The control group is here taken as the weighted average of the industries of the acquired and acquiring firms. The leverage ratios, defined here as long-term debt (LTD) to total assets (TA), were obtained as follows. First the ratios for each firm and industry are calculated as the two-year averages $(LTD_{-1} + LTD_0)/(TA_{-1} + TA_0)$ for the premerger period, with the subscripts denoting years and year 0 as the merger announcement year. Then the "firm" leverage ratio is obtained as the weighted average of the two ratios for the acquiring and acquired firms, using the firms' total assets as the weights. Likewise, the industry (or control group) leverage ratio is calculated from the two industry ratios, again using the firms' total assets as the weights. The postmerger ratios are similarly constructed with

TABLE 13.3

Postmerger Financial Leverage Changes for 36 Pure Conglomerate Mergers

	PREMERGER LEVERAGE	POSTMERGER LEVERAGE	POSTMERGER VERSUS PREMERGER	
			AVERAGE DIFFERENCE	t-VALUE
Firm	0.230	0.285	0.055	4.37[b]
Industry	0.199	0.214	0.016	2.83[b]
Firm−Industry	0.030	0.071	0.040	2.00[a]

[a]Statistically significant at the 5% level (two-tailed test).
[b]Statistically significant at the 1% level (two-tailed test).

SOURCE: See Table 13.2.

data for years 2 and 3. The data for this test are taken from the Compustat tapes and Moody's Industrial Manual.

The average leverage ratios and the test results are shown in Table 13.3. Both the firm and the industry leverages increased significantly during the period around a merger. However, the increases for the merging firms were significantly greater than for their industries. But we note that the levels were low (about 25 percent) and the increases were only 3 to 5 percentage points.

Following the same procedure as described above for the pure conglomerate mergers, Chung obtains the results on leverage changes for the product-extension mergers as shown in Table 13.4. Both the combined firms and their industries have increased financial leverage around the time of merger. The increases for the firms, however, are not statistically significantly different from the increases for the industries. This indicates that the leverage effects are relatively small or nonexistent for the product-extension mergers.

Another detailed study was performed by Auerbach and Reishus (1986). Their main interest was the impact of taxes on the merger decision. Their analysis included measures of the change in leverage for the firms in their sample.

TABLE 13.4

Postmerger Financial Leverage Changes for 37 Product-Extension Mergers

	PREMERGER LEVERAGE	POSTMERGER LEVERAGE	POSTMERGER VERSUS PREMERGER	
			AVERAGE DIFFERENCE	t-VALUE
Firm	0.162	0.199	0.037	2.74[b]
Industry	0.176	0.187	0.011	2.64[a]
Firm−Industry	−0.014	0.012	0.026	0.51

[a]Statistically significant at the 5% level (two-tailed test).
[b]Statistically significant at the 1% level (two-tailed test).

SOURCE: See Table 13.2.

Their data ended in 1982 but since they studied debt/equity ratios two years after the merger, no mergers beyond 1980 were included in their calculations.

Auerbach and Reishus begin with the discussion of what they term a "serious conceptual problem." Usually the impact of a merger on leverage is measured by calculating the fraction of total capitalization that is debt before and after the merger. But they argue that this procedure fails to take into account dynamic changes. They point out that a firm may build up retained earnings in anticipation of a merger. This would cause the debt/equity ratio to fall. When it actually makes the acquisition, it may use borrowed funds in addition to its own equity accumulations. The debt/equity ratio would increase mainly because of the "lumpiness" of the project. In a longer perspective no fundamental change in underlying financial policy may have taken place.

Despite this bias toward overstating the impact of mergers on leverage ratios, for their sample of 162 pairs of merging firms for which a leverage analysis could be made, Auerbach and Reishus found only a minor impact. Long-term debt as a fraction of long-term debt plus equity changed only from an average of 30 percent to 32.1 percent. The weighted average ratio increases from 25.4 percent to 26.7 percent—an even smaller impact.

When the preceding evidence is added to the findings of Taggart discussed in Chapter 5, it appears that merger activity has not been a determining influence on leverage ratios in the economy as a whole. Nevertheless, there are dramatic and well-publicized individual cases in connection with restructuring where leverage ratios were greatly increased. Without question, the higher leverage ratios make the economy and individual firms more vulnerable to economic downswings. Increased leverage results in increased financial risk. For firms with leverage ratios above 100 percent debt to equity, the increased risk must be substantial.

SUMMARY

Empirical studies have shown that the method of payment used in mergers has a significant effect on bidder and target returns. Abnormal returns to target shareholders are higher in cash offers (17 to 34 percent) than in stock offers (12 to 17 percent). Bidder returns are also higher in cash offers, although abnormal returns are zero reflecting a competitive takeover market. The return differences between mergers and tender offers disappear when management resistance and the method of payment are considered; of these two, method of payment was found to be the more powerful influence on returns.

Several theories attempt to explain the effect of method of payment. Target shareholder taxable gains in stock-for-stock exchanges may be deferred indefinitely, while the taxes on gains in cash transactions are payable immediately. Cash offers must therefore be higher to compensate. The availability of asset write-ups for future depreciation tax shelters may also explain the higher return to bidders in cash offers. Some writers argue for the information effect of stock versus cash. Using stock implies that the bidder thinks its stock is overvalued. The signaling hypothesis says that using cash is a positive signal that future cash flows will be large enough to exploit investment opportunities or the takeover will generate large cash flows; using stock suggests that the bidder may not have sufficient internal financing.

Original high-yield or junk bonds are a recent phenomenon that has received much attention in relation to merger and acquisition activity, although statistically they represent only a small fraction of merger financing. Junk bonds are defined as bonds which are subinvestment grade from the date of issuance. They arose in response to changing conditions in the economy and in financial markets. Deregulation and increased competition among financial institutions were important factors. Default rates on junk bonds have been low when measured against the total outstanding in a given year. But if the bonds issued in a given year are followed through, their subsequent experience default rates rise to the 20 to 30 percent range.

Most early studies found that mergers increase leverage and that the increase is due to increased debt capacity rather than utilization of latent debt capacity. This may be related to the fact that most merger activity during the 1950–1980 period under study was conglomerate. Studies show that diversified (conglomerate) firms use more leverage than nondiversified firms and by doing so increase their return on equity by over one percentage point even though their return on total assets is lower. Other studies suggest a smaller impact on leverage and point out that a bias toward overstating the impact of mergers on leverage may be created if firms build up retained earnings in anticipation of a merger.

Leverage measured by the ratio of interest-bearing debt to shareholders' equity at book value has risen from about 45 percent during 1970–1983 to about 65 percent by the end of 1988 for all manufacturing. In industries in which LBOs have been taking place, the leverage ratio has risen to about 100 percent; in other industries, leverage remained at about 50 percent. Dramatic increases have been observed in the restructuring activities of individual firms.

QUESTIONS

1. What are the results of empirical studies on the effect of method of payment on bidder and target returns?
2. What is the relationship between method of payment used in mergers and each of the following:
   a. Tax factors
   b. Information effects
   c. Signaling
3. How have junk bonds performed relative to investment grade bonds through 1988?

4. Describe the procedure for the use of junk bonds in takeover financing.
5. What is the effect of mergers on leverage according to the empirical studies discussed in the chapter?
6. What information is conveyed to the market when stock is used to finance an investment?

REFERENCES

ALTMAN, E. I., AND S. A. NAMMACHER, "The Default Rate Experience on High Yield Corporate Debt," New York: Morgan Stanley & Co., March 1985a.

———, "The Anatomy of the High Yield Debt Market," New York: Morgan Stanley & Co., September 1985b.

———, "The Anatomy of the High Yield Debt Market: 1985 Update," New York: Morgan Stanley & Co., June 1986.

ASQUITH, PAUL, DAVID W. MULLINS, JR., and ERIC D. WOLFF, "Original Issue High Yield Bonds: Aging Analyses of Defaults, Exchanges, and Calls," Harvard Business School, ms., March 1989.

AUERBACH, ALAN J., and DAVID REISHUS, "Taxes and the Merger Decision: An Empirical Analysis," Cambridge, MA: National Bureau of Economic Research, Working Paper No. 1855, March 1986.

BLUME, M. E., and D. B. KEIM, "Risk and Return Characteristics of Lower-Grade Bonds," Working Paper, Rodney White Center for Financial Research, The Wharton School, December 1984.

CARLETON, W., D. GUILKEY, R. HARRIS, and J. STEWART, "An Empirical Analysis of the Role of the Medium of Exchange in Mergers," *Journal of Finance*, 38, June 1983, pp. 813–826.

CHUNG, KWANG S., "Investment Opportunities, Synergies and Conglomerate Mergers," unpublished doctoral dissertation, AGSM-UCLA, 1982.

EGER, CAROL ELLEN, "An Empirical Test of the Redistribution Effect in Pure Exchange Mergers," *Journal of Financial and Quantitative Analysis*, 18, December 1983, pp. 547–572.

FRANKS, JULIAN R., ROBERT S. HARRIS, and COLIN MAYER, "Means of Payment in Takeovers: Results for the U.K. and U.S.," ms., June 1987.

FRANTZ, DOUGLAS, "Crash Hasn't Shaken Drexel's Faith in the Value of 'Junk Bonds,' " *Los Angeles Times*, November 19, 1987, Part IV, p. 1.

GALAI, D., and R. W. MASULIS, "The Option Pricing Model and the Risk Factor of Stock," *Journal of Financial Economics*, 3, January/March 1976, pp. 53–81.

GORDON, MYRON J., and JOSEPH YAGIL, "Financial Gain from Conglomerate Mergers," in *Research in Finance*, 3, 1981, pp. 103–142.

HANSEN, R. G., "A Theory for the Choice of Exchange Medium in Mergers and Acquisitions," *Journal of Business*, 60, January 1987, pp. 75–95.

HIGGINS, R. C., and L. D. SCHALL, "Corporate Bankruptcy and Conglomerate Merger," *Journal of Finance*, 30, March 1975, pp. 93–113.

HUANG, YEN-SHENG, and RALPH A. WALKLING, "Abnormal Returns Associated with Acquisition Announcements: Payment, Acquisition Form, and Managerial Resistance," *Journal of Financial Economics*, 19, 1987, pp. 329–350.

KIM, E. H., J. J. McCONNELL, and P. GREENWOOD, "Capital Structure Rearrangements and Me-First Rules in an Efficient Capital Market," *Journal of Finance*, 32, June 1977, pp. 789–810.

LAING, J. R., "Up and Down Wall Street," *Barron's*, April 10, 1989, pp. 1, 49–50.

MARKHAM, J. W., *Conglomerate Enterprises and Public Policy*, Boston, MA: Harvard Graduate School of Business Administration, 1973.

MELICHER R. W., and D. F. RUSH, "Evidence on the Acquisition-Related Performance of Conglomerate Firms," *Journal of Finance*, 29, March 1974, pp. 141–149.

MYERS, STEWART C., and NICHOLAS J. MAJLUF, "Corporate Financing and Investment Decisions When Firms Have Information That Investors Do Not Have," *Journal of Financial Economics*, 13, June 1984, pp. 187–221.

PAULUS, J. D., "Corporate Restructuring, 'Junk', and Leverage: Too Much or Too Little?, *Economic Perspectives*, New York: Morgan Stanley & Co., March 12, 1986.

QUEEN, MAGGIE, "Market Anticipation of Corporate Takeover and the Gain for the Bidders," unpublished doctoral dissertation, UCLA, 1989.

SHRIEVES, R. E., and M. M. PASHLEY, "Evidence on the Association Between Mergers and Capital Structure," *Financial Management*, 13, 3, Autumn 1984, pp. 39–48.

STEVENS, D. L., "Financial Characteristics of Merged Firms: A Multivariate Analysis," *Journal of Financial and Quantitative Analysis*, 8, March 1973, pp. 149–165.

TAGGART, R. A., JR., "Have U.S. Corporations Grown Financially Weak?," in *Financing Corporate Capital Formation*, B. M. Friedman, ed., Chicago: University of Chicago Press, 1986, pp. 13–33.

TRAVLOS, NICHOLAOS G., "Corporate Takeover Bids, Methods of Payment and Stockholders' Returns: Some New Insights," ms., July 1985.

———, "Corporate Takeover Bids, Methods of Payment, and Bidding Firms' Stock Returns," *Journal of Finance*, 42, September 1987, pp. 943–963.

WANSLEY, JAMES W., WILLIAM R. LANE, and HO C. YANG, "Abnormal Returns to Acquired Firms by Type of Acquisition and Method of Payment," *Financial Management*, 12, Autumn 1983, pp. 16–22.

WESTON, J. FRED, and THOMAS E. COPELAND, *Managerial Finance*, 8th ed., Hinsdale, IL: The Dryden Press, 1986, pp. 247–249.

WESTON, J. FRED, and S. K. MANSINGHKA, "Tests of the Efficiency Performance of Conglomerate Firms," *Journal of Finance*, 26, September 1971, pp. 919–936.

CHAPTER **14**

Joint Ventures

Mergers and tender offers involve a complete fusion of two independent firms or other entities into a single decision-making unit. Many other forms of relationships between firms take place. They can range from licensing or cross-licensing of particular technologies, joint bidding on an individual contract, franchising or other forms of short-term or long-term contracts. Joint ventures represent another form of relationship between two or more business entities and are widely used by business firms. During the period 1972–1979 it has been tabulated that 7,000 U.S. corporations engaged in intercorporate joint ventures (McConnell and Nantell 1985, quoting *Mergers and Acquisitions* magazine).

Examples of joint ventures abound. In an early study Bachman (1965) describes the entry of oil and gas companies into chemicals using joint ventures to a considerable degree. For the early 1960s some illustrative joint ventures and the products they produced included:

Alamo Polymer (Phillips Petroleum and National Distillers)—polypropylene
American Chemical (Richfield Oil and Stauffer)—vinyl chloride, ethylene
Ancon Chemical (Continental Oil and Ansul)—methyl chloride
Avisun (Sun Oil and American Viscose)—polypropylene resins
Goodrich-Gulf (Gulf Oil and Goodrich Rubber)—S-type rubber
Hawkeye Chemical (Skelly Oil and Swift)—ammonia
Jefferson Chemical (Texas Co. and American Cyanamid)—ethylene, propylene, and others
National Plastics Products (Enjay and J. P. Stevens)—polypropylene fiber

Sun Olin (Sun Oil and Olin)—urea, ethylene, and others

Witfield Chemical (Richfield Oil and Witco Chemical)—detergent alkylate

In an excellent in-depth study, *Business Week* (1986) listed a number of joint ventures and the reasons for the associations. These are listed in Table 14.1. The reasons for the joint ventures are varied. They are illustrative of the wide range of motives for joint ventures.

Joint venture participants continue to exist as separate firms with a joint venture representing a newly created business enterprise. The joint venture may be organized as a partnership, a corporation, or any other form of business organization the participating firms might choose to select.

In contract law, joint ventures are usually described as having the following characteristics:

1 Contribution by partners of money, property, effort, knowledge, skill, or other asset to a common undertaking
2 Joint property interest in the subject matter of the venture
3 Right of mutual control or management of the enterprise
4 Expectation of profit, or presence of "adventure"
5 Right to share in the profit
6 Usual limitation of the objective to a single undertaking or ad hoc enterprise

Thus, joint ventures are of limited scope and duration. Typically they involve only a small fraction of each participant's total activities. Each partner must have something unique and important to offer the venture and simultaneously provide a source of gain to the other participants. However, the sharing of information and/or assets required to achieve the objective need not extend

TABLE 14.1

Examples of Joint Ventures and Their Objectives

PARTNERS	PRODUCT	STRATEGIC OBJECTIVE
AT&T/Olivetti	Computers	Foreign market
Boeing/Mitsubishi/Fuji/Kawasaki	Small aircraft	Cut costs, share technology
Corning/Ciba-Geigy	Lab instruments	New market
Ford/Measurex	Factory automation	Cut costs
GM/Toyota	Autos	Cut costs
GTE/Fujitsu	Communications equipment	Cut costs, better marketing
Kodak/Cetus	Biotech diagnostics	New market, better distribution
3M/Harris	Copiers	Better marketing
U.S. Steel/Pohang Iron & Steel	Steel	Raise capital, expand market
Westinghouse/General Electric	Power semiconductors	Cut costs, better marketing

SOURCE: *Business Week*, "Corporate Odd Couples," July 21, 1986, p. 101.

beyond the joint venture. Hence the participants' competitive relationship need not be affected by the joint venture arrangement.

It has been found that joint ventures and mergers display similar timing characteristics. For the period 1972–1977 the correlation between completed mergers and joint venture start-ups was over .95, highly significant from a statistical standpoint. We have already commented that merger activity is highly correlated with plant and equipment outlays. Both joint ventures and mergers are likely to be stimulated by factors which affect total investment activity generally.

JOINT VENTURES IN BUSINESS STRATEGY

In recent years, joint ventures have come to be called "strategic alliances." A number of motives have stimulated joint ventures:

1 Share investment expenses or combine a large company that has cash to invest with a smaller company with a product or production idea but with insufficient funds to pursue the opportunity. This is a somewhat inaccurate description. If a product idea is clearly a good one, financing will usually be forthcoming. Financing is likely to be a problem when the outcome is highly uncertain (risks are high) and the payoff may not come until years into the future. While outside investors may be reluctant to take high risks even on an equity basis, a business firm may be interested because it has more information on the project or has other projects that may benefit from the learning experience that may be gained from the joint venture.
2 The second strong motive is the learning experience that may be achieved.
3 Even for a large company, a joint venture is a method of reducing the investment outlay required and sharing the risk. In addition, the activity may represent a significant learning experience.
4 Antitrust authorities may be more willing to permit joint ventures than to permit mergers (*Los Angeles Times*, 1984). While mergers result in a reduction in the number of firms, joint ventures increase the number of firms. The parents continue in operation and another firm is created. Particularly, joint ventures in research and development areas are likely to receive endorsement from government agencies.

Joint ventures may be used to acquire complementary technological or management resources at lower cost, or to benefit from economies of scale, critical mass, and the learning curve effect—all elements of strategic alliances. The "go together-split" strategy achieves these ends in the usual 50–50 or 60–40 joint venture of limited scope and duration, while the successive integration strategy uses joint venturing as a way of learning about prospective merger partners to full merger or acquisition.

Firms may also use joint venturing as an element of long-run strategic planning. The spider's web strategy is used to provide countervailing power among rivals in a product market and among rivals for a scarce resource. Thus, a small firm in a highly concentrated industry can negotiate joint ventures with several of the industry's dominant firms to form a self-protective network of counterbalancing forces. Indeed, it is reported that large companies such as General Electric are involved in over 100 joint ventures and that IBM, GM, AT&T, and Xerox participate in more than a dozen joint ventures. Companies of the type listed have both financial resources plus managerial and technical competence to bring to a joint venture (*Business Week*, 1986). This strategy presupposes, of course, that the small firm has something unique to offer the industry leaders.

Joint Ventures and Complex Learning

The expressed purpose of 50 percent of all joint ventures is knowledge acquisition (Berg, Duncan, and Friedman, 1982). The complexity of the knowledge to be transferred is a key factor in determining the contractual relationship between the partners.

Where the knowledge to be transferred is complex or embedded in a complicated set of technological and organizational circumstances, learning-by-doing and teaching-by-doing (L/TBD) may be the most appropriate means of transfer. Successive adaptations to changing internal and environmental events may be necessary to achieve efficiency in the process being taught. It may be very costly or even impossible to give training in complex production tasks in a classroom situation—the atmosphere (operations, machines, work group) may be essential. In addition, job incumbents, no matter how skilled, may be unable to describe job skills to trainees except in an operational context. The demands of the task may make joint venture the most appropriate vehicle for the knowledge transfer; L/TBD may not be possible outside the joint venture setting.

Tax Aspects of Joint Ventures

Tax advantages may be a significant factor in many joint ventures. If a corporation contributes a patent or licensable technology to a joint venture, the tax consequences may be less than on royalties earned through a licensing arrangement. For example, one partner contributes the technology, while another contributes depreciable facilities. The depreciation offsets the revenues accruing to the technology; the joint venture may be taxed at a lower rate than any of its partners; and the partners pay a later capital gains tax on the returns realized by the joint venture if and when it is sold. If the joint venture is organized as a corporation, only its assets are at risk; the partners are liable only to the extent of their investment. This is particularly important in hazardous industries where the risk of worker, product, or environmental liability is high.

A number of other more technical tax advantages may tip the scale towards the use of joint ventures in many circumstances. These include the limitation on operating loss carry-over, the partnership status of unincorporated commercial joint ventures, the use of the equity method of incorporating the joint venture into the partners' financial statements, and the benefits of multiple surtax exemptions.

International Joint Ventures

Finally, joint ventures can be used to reduce the risk of expanding into a foreign environment. In fact, there may even be a legal requirement of a local joint venturer in some foreign countries. The contribution of the local partner is likely to be in the form of specialized knowledge about local conditions, which may be essential to the success of the venture.

RATIONALE FOR JOINT VENTURES

The previous section indicated typical reasons given by firms for engaging in joint ventures. A survey of the literature indicates a number of general reasons which can be summarized as follows:

1 To augment insufficient financial or technical ability to enter a particular line of business
2 To share technology and/or generic management skills in organization, planning, and control
3 To diversify risk
4 To obtain distribution channels or raw materials supply
5 To achieve economies of scale
6 To extend activities with smaller investment than if done independently
7 To take advantage of favorable tax treatment or political incentives (particularly in foreign ventures)

In view of alternative forms of business relationships, a basic issue is why the use of joint ventures versus other forms of contractual arrangements is justified. The literature suggests that the underlying theoretical justification for joint ventures lies in the transaction cost theory of the firm, as discussed in Chapter 2.

Every exchange between productive agents involves transaction costs. The benefits of interaction arise from using resources efficiently, but resources are used up by the organizing activity itself through obtaining information on exchange opportunities, negotiating and enforcing contracts, and so on. The exchange and organizational patterns viewed in the marketplace are responses to varying levels of transaction costs, which affect the allocation of resources in society. According to the theory, resource misallocation cannot exist in the absence of transaction costs.

Complementary production refers to the joint use of assets or inputs to create products which cannot be unambiguously attributed to any single input. Nor can the inputs simply be summed to yield the total output of the process, that is, synergy. A complementary asset is one whose value in a production process depends on its combination with other assets or a specifically chosen technology. The difficulty arises when these inputs are owned by different firms.

In general, an asset's productivity increases with its specialization to other inputs used in the production process. However, specialization also increases the risk of loss to the owner of the complementary asset if the other inputs are withdrawn. Complementary or composite quasi-rent is the economic term for the investment cost of the complementary asset which is nonrecoverable if the other inputs with which it is used are withdrawn. Thus, the owners of the other inputs, by threatening to remove their inputs, can expropriate the owner of the complementary asset by taking a larger share of the return from the process (which, by definition, cannot be unambiguously attributed to any single input).

Input owners will choose the organizational form which minimizes transaction costs. Long-term explicit contracts and common ownership of the complementary assets are possible solutions to the problem. However, a flexible contract may result in litigation for interpretation. A comprehensive contract is costly both to write and to enforce. These costs may outweigh the benefits of the contract. Business complexity increases the number of contingencies that might arise, thus increasing the cost of enumerating contingencies, the risk of omitting to specify contingencies, and costs of monitoring in a contractual relationship.

Finally, the greater the frequency of exchange of inputs, the greater the likelihood of joint ownership. The prospect of recovering the investment cost of specialized assets increases with the frequency of the transaction. In a contractual relationship, repetitive activity would mean repetitive contracting and thus higher contracting costs. The specialized organizations required in common ownership are easier to justify for recurring transactions than for identical transactions occuring only occasionally.

In some cases, common ownership might extend to complete merger, but in general, joint venture is appropriate where:

1 Complementary production activity involves only a limited subset of the firms' assets.
2 Complementary assets have limited service life.
3 Complementary production has limited life.

Reasons for Failure

Joint ventures are a form of a long-term contract. Like all contracts they are subject to difficulties. As circumstances change in the future, the contract may be too inflexible to permit the required adjustments to be made. There is also evidence that in many joint ventures, the participants early become enamored of the idea of the joint activity, but do not spend sufficient time and effort to lay out a program for implementing the joint venture. *Business Week* (1986) refers to independent studies by McKinsey & Co. and Coopers & Lybrand which found that about 70 percent of joint ventures fell short of expectations or were disbanded. Other studies suggest that on average joint ventures do not last as long as one half the term of years stated in the joint venture agreement (Berg, Duncan, and Friedman, 1982). An independent survey by the present authors uncovered many examples of joint ventures that came apart either before they started or early into the venture. Some of the reasons for the abortive lives of joint ventures are:

1 The hoped-for technology never developed.
2 Preplanning for the joint venture was inadequate.
3 Agreements could not be reached on alternative approaches to solving the basic objectives of the joint venture.
4 Managers with expertise in one company refused to share knowledge with their counterparts in the joint venture.
5 Management difficulties may be compounded because of inability of parent companies to share control or compromise on difficult issues.

Some joint ventures raise critical issues of public policy and long-term strategies of individual business firms. The announcement of a joint venture between Boeing Co. and a group of Japanese companies touched off much controversy (Harris and Wysocki, 1986). Boeing is the world's largest airplane builder accounting for the production of 60 percent of the world production of jetliners. In early 1986 it was announced that Boeing had entered into an agreement to form a joint venture with three Japanese companies—Kawasaki Heavy Industries Ltd., Mitsubishi Heavy Industries Ltd., and Fuji Heavy Industries Ltd. The joint venture would build a new 150-passenger airplane that would be ready in the early 1990s. The Japanese would contribute $1 billion of the $4 billion or more expected development cost. In return they would receive a share of the profits and learn about the manufacturing, marketing, and servicing of jetliners through their association with Boeing.

Great concern was expressed by a number of Americans that the Japanese would learn the secrets of aircraft manufacturing from Boeing. Since some of the key Boeing civilian aircraft had developed from military versions, concern was also expressed that this would help Japan build up a military aircraft production capability. But the major concern was that the Japanese would become leaders in commercial aviation as they had in autos, electronics, steel, and construction by copying and improving on American methods.

Boeing officials said that they were aware and concerned about such possibilities. But they pointed out that the Japanese companies had solicited joint venture proposals from other Western companies including Airbus, McDonnell Douglas, and Fokker of the Netherlands. Hence, in part, the Boeing action to agree to form the joint venture was a defensive strategy. As the president of Boeing, Frank Shrontz, stated: "We'd rather work with them (the Japanese) than have somebody else work with them and against us" (Harris and Wysocki, 1986, p. 1).

Early in the negotiations, the usual problems with joint ventures began to crop up. The Japanese complained that Boeing assigned to the project too many young, inexperienced executives who did not understand Japanese business practices. Americans complained that the Japanese negotiators lacked technical knowledge. But more significant is the basic national policy issue that the Boeing-Japanese joint venture raised.

Joint ventures offer many attractive opportunities. But they also pose difficult challenges. Illustrative are the summaries of articles on joint venture problems given in the appendix to this chapter.

JOINT VENTURES AND ANTITRUST POLICY

A problem that may be faced by joint ventures are legal challenges. Although we have distinguished joint ventures from mergers, they are often subject to the same regulatory scrutiny and challenge by self-identified rivals; for example, the Chrysler challenge and Federal Trade Commission analysis of the General Motors-Toyota joint venture. Court actions have been brought under the Clayton Act (for real or potential anticompetitive effects) and under the Sherman Act (for cartel behavior, boycotts, and exclusion of competitors).

Until recently the courts have adhered to the structural approach (first set forth by Kaysen in a shoe industry case in the 1950s) in analyzing the effects of both mergers and joint ventures. The structural approach is based on the theory of collusion which proposes that enhancement of monopoly power is the only motive for corporate combinations. Cost reduction and productive efficiency justifications (including the transaction cost/expropriation rationale discussed earlier) are given only perfunctory attention. Structuralists assume that competition is a function of the number of rival firms in a market; since horizontal joint ventures (where the venture partners and the joint venture are all in the same industry) increase concentration, they increase the likelihood that the partners will coordinate their efforts beyond the joint venture activity as well. Brodley (1982) takes industry concentration as fully determinative of the ease of and gains to general coordination achieved through joint venture. Three landmark cases illustrate the application of the structural approach against joint ventures in the past. The main objections raised are the threat of industry-wide collusion, loss of potential competition, and restraints on distribution.

A number of factors led to the antitrust decision in the 1950 *U.S. v. Minnesota Mining and Manufacturing Co. et al*. These included the implied market dominance of the joint venture partners, the existence of a joint sales agency, and concern of spill-over of joint venture cooperation into collusion. The venture was formed in 1929 to export coated abrasives for its nine partners. The partners could not export except through the joint venture; however, they could, and did, set up foreign manufacturing subsidiaries to supply foreign buyers. The joint venture had competition from both American and foreign firms; the market share of the nine original firms (five had dropped out of the venture by 1950) had declined from 86 percent in 1929 to 60 percent by 1948. The joint venture export firm often suspended or limited sales through the joint venture when it was more profitable to supply foreign buyers through local subsidiaries. The courts ruled that this represented an illegal conspiracy and further suggested that the joint venturers would compete less vigorously in the American market as well.

In 1964, the main issue in *U.S.* v. *Penn-Olin* was the loss of potential competition. An Oregon firm, Pennsalt, wanted to penetrate the southeastern U.S. market for sodium chlorate, a bleaching agent used in paper pulp processing. The southeastern region accounted for 50 percent of all U.S. sales of sodium chlorate; however, two firms already dominated this area with a combined market share of 91.3 percent in 1960. Pennsalt's first step was to form a sales arrangement with Olin-Mathieson, a firm which did not manufacture sodium chlorate, but which had a marketing presence in the Southeast. The success of this arrangement and projections of future capacity shortages in the area led to the formation of a 50–50 joint venture in 1960. A local manufacturing plant was operated by Pennsalt, while Olin continued to market the output.

The court's decision focused on whether the firms would have entered the market independently in the absence of the joint venture. That is, say Pennsalt entered the market independently; would Pennsalt and the other firms in the market view Olin as a threatening potential entrant? Would Olin view itself as a potential entrant, or would it drop out of the race, abandoning the idea of entering the market? If both firms could have seriously considered entering independently, then the joint venture has decreased potential competition (by adding only one new productive entity to the market instead of potentially two). The final decision permitted the joint venture. Independent entry by both firms was judged to be improbable due to the low expected rate of return (as a result of the high cost to a single firm of building an optimum-size plant) and due to possible excess capacity if two optimum-size plants were constructed.

The structuralists' argument with respect to loss of potential competition alleges that the joint venture will affect the market price level and reduce the elasticity of demand for firms already in the market. But the meaning of potential competition is vague, and evidence in support of this argument would require estimates of market entry costs for various potential competitors as well as the demand elasticity of extant firms, neither of which can be made precisely.

Pitofsky (1969) examined antitrust issues in joint venture cases with specific reference to Penn-Olin. His main focus was on the spill-over of information beyond the joint venture, leading to coordination of pricing and production decisions by the venture partners and reduction of competition. The habit of cooperating within the joint venture was assumed to lead to further cooperation whether by written or tacit agreement. Furthermore, when the parents are direct competitors, they must consider the effects of each other's price and production policies when setting their own. Since the parents work together in setting price and production levels for the joint venture's output (which may also be in competition with the parents' outputs) with an eye to both the success of the joint venture and its effects on the parents' sales, a web of interlocking considerations leads to coordination of both prices and production among the joint venture and its parents. Or the spill-over of information may be more indirect. If the joint venture's output is sold through one parent's selling organization (as in Penn-Olin), or is used as an input in a parent's own production, the exchange of information required to set joint venture production levels may reveal a great deal of information about the parents to each other with or without any overt collusive intent. Pitofsky argued that if the joint venture and its parents were actual competitors, the parents would prevent the joint venture from pricing aggressively or pursuing other actions which might be detrimental to parent company sales. And if the joint venture were only a potential competitor, the parents would block any product or geographic expansion that would threaten the parent.

In another analysis of the Penn-Olin case, Meehan (1970) concluded that joint ventures were the optimal entry strategy where potential market entrants seek to minimize losses rather than to maximize profits. If this were true, however, we would likely see many more joint ventures for the purpose of market entry than are found.

The decision against the joint venture in *Yamaha v. FTC* (1981) was based on many factors (loss of potential competition, high industry concentration, spill-over collusion, potential permanence of the joint venture). However, the distin-guishing feature in terms of this discussion involves the collateral agreements between the venture partners. In 1972, Brunswick and Yamaha formed a joint venture to produce and sell outboard motors; the joint venture was to have a ten-year life with automatic three-year extensions. The same motor produced by the venture would be sold through Yamaha dealers as a Yamaha and through Bruns-wick dealers as a Mariner. (Brunswick had been selling motors worldwide since 1961, and Mariner was to be its second line.) Collateral agreements restricted distribution by assigning exclusive rights to sell the joint venture motor in certain parts of the world. Brunswick had North America, Australia, and New Zealand; Yamaha had exclusivity in Japan, and the rest of the world was open to competi-tion. Other collateral agreements restricted competition beyond the joint ven-ture. Yamaha could not make or distribute any motor similar to the joint ven-ture's, and Brunswick was prohibited from making any products then produced by Yamaha (except snowmobiles).

The court determined that the joint venture eliminated Yamaha as a poten-tial entrant (prior to the joint venture Yamaha had twice attempted unsuccess-fully to penetrate the U.S. market) and that such independent entry would have reduced concentration in an industry becoming increasingly highly concentrated due to firm exits. It was felt that Brunswick would not allow the joint venture motor to compete with its other line, and therefore the joint venture could not be treated as a new entrant. The court found no efficiencies inherent in the collat-eral agreements restricting distribution and production. They were judged to be anticompetitive and thus potentially collusive.

The first hurdle for legitimacy in these and other cases is based on structural criteria, and concentration is used as a predictor of firm behavior. Structuralism is, however, incomplete and outdated as a theory of external market relationships. Focusing on buyer or seller concentration neglects the effects on competition of product differences, supply and demand elasticity and cross-elasticity, differences in manufacturing and distribution costs and risk.

Some industry conditions make collusion more likely. Other industry condi-

TABLE 14.2
Industry Characteristics and Possibility of Collusion

COLLUSION POSSIBLE	COLLUSION DIFFICULT
Product homogeneity	Heterogeneous products
Equality of costs across firms	Inequality of costs
Stability of demand, supply, and technology	Rapid and unstable changes in demand, supply, and technology
Difficulty of entry and expansion	Ease of entry and expansion
Similarity in firm strategies and policies	Dissimilarity in firm strategies and policies
Few firms	Many firms
Low costs of enforcing collusive agreement and of being detected relative to benefits	Difficulties in enforcing collusion; high risk and cost of being detected
Low price elasticity of demand	High price elasticity of demand

tions make collusion difficult and probably impossible. These characteristics are summarized in Table 14.2. Any one condition in the second column of conditions which make collusion difficult is enough to deny the validity of the structural approach. Contemplation of the characteristics of most actual industries in the United States would indicate characteristics that make collusion difficult. These would include heterogeneous products, inequality of costs, rapid and unstable changes in demand, supply, and technology, dissimilarity in firm strategies and policies, substitutability among products on the demand side, and the likelihood of additions to the supply of products by other firms if one firm restricted supply.

CASE STUDY OF THE GM–TOYOTA
JOINT VENTURE

A case study will bring together a number of the theoretical arguments and legal issues involved in connection with evaluating joint ventures. The GM–Toyota joint venture provided for production of a subcompact car in a GM plant in Fremont, California that previously had been closed down. The plan was approved by a 3–2 majority of the Federal Trade Commission (FTC) in December 1983. After approval by the FTC, Chrysler brought suit to stop the joint venture. After a series of legal skirmishes, Chrysler withdrew its suit. The following is an analysis of the joint venture made by one of the authors (Weston, 1984).

The business reasons underlying the GM–Toyota joint venture are straightforward. GM hopes to obtain hands-on experience in the advanced management technology of building small cars, and to add this experience to other efforts underway to become more cost efficient in producing a family of small cars.

For its part, Toyota aims to test its production methods in a new setting with different labor and supplier relationships. Each firm is seeking to become more efficient to meet the tough competition in the automobile industry. Because the cars will be produced at an unused plant in Fremont, California, the new investment costs are reduced. Hence, the risk/return prospects of the venture are improved compared with alternative methods of achieving their objectives.

In contrast to previous joint ventures that have been found illegal, this agreement expresses the intention of both parties to compete vigorously in all their markets for every product. This joint venture, as codified by the conditions of the FTC consent order, is quite circumscribed. It limits the annual volume of the one model the joint venture can produce for GM to 250,000. It limits the duration of the venture to a maximum of 12 years. It restricts the exchange of information that can pass between the parties. The order also requires that records be kept of certain contacts between the parties, and that both companies file annual compliance reports with the FTC.

Yet, despite all these safeguards, the critics have voiced skepticism. The many darts thrown at the joint venture do not pierce its fundamental efficiency motive. While some of the criticisms make good rhetoric, they do not stand up to careful analysis.

The first criticism is that the joint venture will increase the already excessive concentration of market positions in the auto industry. Only under the outdated structural theory would concentration measures command center stage. The new wisdom recognizes that the economic facts of life of an industry are more to the point.

For example, take the government's prosecution of IBM for anticompetitive behavior, which was dropped in 1982. Carl Kaysen, who as an economic adviser to U.S. District Judge Charles Wyzanski in the early 1950s set the pattern for the structural theory in a shoe-industry case, has argued that the circumstances in the IBM case were different and that the government's position was without merit (Kaysen, 1983). While IBM's share of the computer market was large, Kaysen has written, it had been declining. Superior new technologies were appearing with "breathtaking speed." IBM's main customers were large and sophisticated, with the ability to seek out and even create alternative sources of supply. These arguments were the thrust of the IBM defense and evidently helped persuade the Justice Department to drop the case (Fisher, McGowan, and Greenwood, 1983).

But even under older structuralist standards, the data on the venture are consistent with dynamic competition. One of the ways of measuring concentration endorsed by the Department of Justice guidelines (1982 and 1984) is called the HHI index, which sums the squares of the market percentage shares of each firm (the squaring has the impact of giving greater weight to the large-firm shares). An HHI above 1800 in an industry is considered excessive concentration; below 1000 is considered unconcentrated. Between the two ranges, the guidelines suggest further study of such market factors as prices, product quality, and service to customers. The HHI for the world auto market in 1981 was 680—clearly in the acceptable range and even lower than the HHI of 896 ten years earlier.

To narrow the market definition to subcompact autos sold in the United States would be to carve up the market in an artificial way because of competition between different models. But this is how the structuralists like to define the game, and we will therefore play it for the moment. For the subcompact segment, the HHI was, predictably, somewhat higher, at a level of 1316 for 1982 car deliveries. There was no dominant firm: Ford had slightly over 20 percent of the market, with GM and Toyota following close behind. In all there were 13 major international competitors with appreciable market shares.

A wide range of assumptions could be made about how the single joint venture car model would impact this narrow subcompact segment. It is likely that there would be an increase in subcompact sales overall, and some substitution of the joint venture car for other subcompacts. But a reasonable assumption is that the market share of the joint venture would be about 6 percent. And if the venture is treated as a separate entity, the HHI for this industry segment would drop to under 1200, near the acceptable area under the government guidelines. All reasonable assumptions point to a negligible impact of the joint venture on concentration measures. Thus, even under the older structural approach, the GM–Toyota joint venture does not raise serious antitrust concerns.

But looking at concentration numbers is the outmoded way of judging the joint venture. The right way is to recognize that there are many substitutes for the products sold by GM and Toyota. Since consumers have good alternatives, and since other firms are ready to augment output if GM or Toyota individually or jointly attempt to control supply, one conclusion is inescapable: The two firms do not have monopoly power, nor do they have the potential to collude effectively. The original provisions for limiting the venture, now codified in the FTC consent order, further guarantee against anticompetitive effects.

A second criticism leveled at the joint venture is that it will help solidify "collusive price leadership" in autos (that is, all of the automakers will march in step with the industry leader's prices). Past studies of the U.S. auto industry found no evidence to support such claims, and the joint venture will not change the situation. The special conditions that must be present for collusive price leadership do not exist in the auto industry. Its products are highly differentiated. Costs vary greatly among rival firms. Fluctuations in demand and supply are large and continuous. Technology is subject to continuous change. Entry by foreign firms has taken place in markets throughout the world. The market shares of the auto firms have been fluctuating, and concentration has been decreasing in all major market segments. The cross-elasticity of demand among auto models is high, so that any attempts to elevate prices in some segments of the market would be met by a loss of sales to competing firms and models.

There is no basis in logic or fact to support allegations of collusive price leadership in the industry. While it is argued that some firms announce prices before others, what is more relevant is that prices continually change throughout a given model year. The forms of price change are numerous, including extra bonuses to dealers for exceeding quotas, different strategies for pricing "extras," and so forth.

Thus, the idea that Toyota and GM can ignore market forces and raise prices at will is pure fantasy. To do so would mean huge losses in sales and profits and corresponding gains to competitors. Such behavior would clearly be irrational.

The FTC majority saw no basis for concern, even if concentration, by some measures, were to increase under the joint venture. A preponderance of theory and evidence support the FTC decision, which, rather than creating new rules, is consistent with both the older structural theory and the newer emphasis on efficiency in antitrust policy.

A third criticism is that the pricing formula, based on the prices of competing models, would lead to an upward spiral in auto prices. Such an argument is pure conjecture and fails to take into account market mechanisms that determine auto prices. What is fundamentally involved is supplier relationships. All kinds of purchasing activity is required in doing business and supplier-buyer prices must be "set." To call the GM–Toyota relationship "price fixing" in any sense is to regard all supplier-price relationships as suspect—which they clearly are not.

More important, after the car is transferred to General Motors, neither the joint venture nor Toyota plays any further part in pricing the vehicle. General Motors, within the boundaries set by the competition of the marketplace, arrives at a set of price relationships with dealers. Dealers, of course, then negotiate final prices with consumers, and at this point even GM is out of the picture.

The joint venture realizes a net amount which is equal to a competitive price less a relatively fixed distributor margin. If the joint venture is highly efficient and keeps its costs low, it has the potential for making high profits. If the joint venture is inefficient, it will suffer losses.

It is important to note that the pricing of the joint venture car produces an inherent conflict of interest between GM and Toyota that is procompetitive. GM as distributor would like to buy at as low a price as possible; it receives 100 percent of the benefits of a low purchase price, whereas it receives only half the profits from the joint venture. However, Toyota shares only in the profit from the joint venture's sales; it would thus be motivated to have as high a price as possible while keeping costs low. GM also wants the joint venture to achieve low costs, so that it can learn to manufacture small cars more efficiently. The logic of the joint venture is to provide the correct efficiency incentives at each stage of the relationship.

Finally, opponents of the venture argue that it will lead to the exchange of competitive-sensitive information. Obviously, they speculate, GM and Toyota will have to talk about such things as new models, output, and prices, and it will be to their advantage to exchange as much information as possible.

Of course, by jointly investing in this particular project, GM and Toyota will have to produce and share information. GM will seek to learn about Toyota's superior approaches to stamping facilities, plant layout, quality control, inventory control, assembly and related production activities, and management of the work force. For its part, Toyota will learn about operating in the United States, particularly in connection with supplier and labor relations.

But there will be self-limiting controls on the exchange of information. Consider, for example, GM's marketing of the joint venture product. Advance information of GM's consumer-research and marketing strategy would be useful to its rivals, among them Toyota. Since such information could be used to inflict competitive harm on General Motors, GM is not likely to want to share it with anybody. Similarly, it would not be rational for Toyota to share with GM product design and research for other vehicles, since it is competing for the same customers.

This logic is reinforced by the absence of collateral restraints in the joint venture agreement. By means of collateral restraints, parties to a venture impose limits on competition between themselves in certain areas. For example, collateral restraints were the reason that the joint venture agreement in 1972 between Yamaha and Brunswick to produce outboard motors was declared illegal. These included division of markets in which each could sell and limits on each to produce competing products. But no such limits are found in the GM–Toyota agreement. The significance of the absence of these collateral restraints is that each firm intends to be a more vigorous competitor with the other as well as with all other rival companies.

Other critics say that it is not just sharing of information that poses a competitive threat but the fact that the venture will make GM more efficient in general. Indeed, some of GM's competitors have stated publicly that the venture will enable GM to produce cars at a lower cost. The following syllogism is then implicit: As a consequence of the joint venture, GM will become more efficient. If GM is more efficient, this will make life more difficult for its other domestic rivals. Therefore, the knowledge gained by GM and the joint venture will be anticompetitive.

But our antitrust laws were not intended to protect competitors. They were designed to stimulate competition. Greater efficiency forces greater competition. In addition, history tells us that when superior efficiency enters into the management experience of some companies in the United States, it becomes diffused to other companies. If the joint venture is successful, the new management technology learned by GM will be diffused to other firms in the auto industry as well as to other industries.

Another claim is that the GM–Toyota joint venture would stimulate similar arrangements by other companies. But this is evidence of the basic procompetitive nature of the joint venture. Other firms may indeed be forced to strive harder, by whatever means they can, to stay competitive. But this is the essence of the competitive process.

Furthermore, the GM–Toyota joint venture is of limited scope and duration. The histories of other joint ventures tell us that most were dissolved before their half-lives had been completed. This is so, in part, because the purposes of the joint ventures had been achieved, but perhaps also because the inherent difficulties and animosities that arise in operating under a long-term contractual arrangement will cause joint ventures to come asunder. A joint venture is not a marriage intended to bind the parties for eternity. Rather, it is a temporary arrangement that the parties will terminate when short-term needs have been satisfied. Thus, very likely the GM–Toyota venture will be of shorter duration than the 12-year maximum life.

The FTC majority weighed efficiency benefits against anticompetitive costs: "To the extent the Fremont venture can demonstrate successfully that the Japanese system can work in America, the Commission finds that this will lead to the development of a more efficient, more competitive U.S. automobile industry."

The GM–Toyota joint venture will achieve an important management technology transfer to the United States. It reinforces GM's strong commitment to the small-car market and provides incentives for other U.S. firms to do likewise.

In the shorter term, the venture will yield substantial benefits to consumers and workers. Consumers will benefit from lower prices and a greater range of choice in new cars. Workers will benefit from the reopening of the Fremont plant, which will create approximately 3,000 jobs (closer to 12,000 if jobs stemming from new orders to suppliers are taken into account). Without the joint venture's cars, more Japanese imports might be sold in the United States, which means fewer jobs for Americans.

In the longer term, the improved efficiency will spur other U.S. rivals to improve efficiency, enhancing total U.S. competitiveness in the industry. The joint venture thus has the potential to produce thousands of new jobs that might well be lost to other countries unless the U.S. companies become more efficient. Ford's proposed new joint venture plan in Mexico and rumors of similar moves by other U.S. firms are clear warnings of what could happen.

The dynamics of competition in the auto industry, despite various artificial barriers created by governments, guarantee against effective collusion. Attempts at collusion would, indeed, be ineffectual. High product substitutability and numerous rivals will continue to guarantee strong competition in the industry.

EMPIRICAL TESTS OF THE ROLE
OF JOINT VENTURES

Much of the early literature on joint ventures focused on anticompetitive effects. These analytical studies often used inappropriate and relatively unsophisticated methodology (for example, correlation analysis to infer causality) and suffered from other shortcomings as well.

Earlier Studies

Fusfeld (1958) found anticompetitive effects as a result of joint ventures in the iron and steel industry due to the horizontal relationships (and limited number) of joint venture parent firms. While risk reduction was a beneficial effect of the joint venture activity, it had potential anticompetitive side effects.

Boyle (1968) focused on the size of parent firms and found that joint venture participation increased with firm size, in spite of smaller firms' presumably greater need for external resources. Since the joint ventures' industries were related to the parents' industries in 90 percent of the cases and were relatively small, he concluded that the potential for social benefit was small, while the potential for anticompetitive effect was great.

Mead (1967) examined a restricted sample of joint ventures formed specifically for the purpose of bidding on government-owned resources, such as timber and oil and gas leases. He found that joint bidding resulted in fewer and lower bids (but not in every region) and concluded implicit collusion was occurring.

Pfeffer and Nowak (1976) examined interindustry variation in joint venture activity based on two-digit SIC codes to define horizontality and concentration. They found greater joint venture activity in industries characterized by medium concentration, and concluded that highly concentrated industries do not need joint ventures to monitor competitors' reactions (and thus reduce uncertainty), while in unconcentrated industries, joint ventures would have little impact in reducing uncertainty. The main criticism of Pfeffer and Nowak is their use of two-digit SIC codes, which are far too aggregated to enable inferences of horizontality and concentration to be drawn. Pfeffer and Nowak did, however, find a correlation of joint venture activity with research and development intensity, suggesting the potential importance of investigating the purpose of a joint venture when evaluating its potential impact.

While the preceding studies tend to focus on anticompetitive effects, others have stressed the efficiency gains resulting from joint ventures, even in the company of anticompetitive effects.

Bachman (1965) surveyed more than two dozen joint ventures in the petrochemical industry during the 1950s and early 1960s. The chemical industry is characterized by a large degree of risky, long-term investment in research and development. Bachman found that joint ventures could reduce risk through the combination of specialized technological know-how, and that this factor was more important than any economies of scale which might be involved. He found intensified research efforts and vigorous price competition associated with joint ventures. In fact, price increases by industry leaders were often rescinded. The development of man-made fibers accelerated and productive capacity was increased. Bachman (1965, p. 23) found that joint venture partners did "not use a kid glove approach in other markets in which the parents meet," and concluded that joint ventures, in chemicals over the period surveyed, were a strong competitive force.

Hlavecek, Dovey, and Biondo (1977) put forth a basic view of the joint venture as a means of acquiring external knowledge and focused on joint ventures between large and small firms (which may represent a significant portion of joint venture activity), where the smaller firms brought technology and the larger firms brought marketing expertise to the venture. They found synergistic gains for both firms. They went on to develop an approach for small firms seeking joint venture partners, and cautioned that financial complementarities alone are probably not enough of a basis for a successful venture. On the other hand, Edstrom (1976), in a study of Swedish joint ventures found significant relationships between joint ventures and financial variables.

Perhaps the most comprehensive and methodologically robust study of joint venture activity is that of Berg, Duncan, and Friedman, reported in their 1982 book, *Joint Venture Strategies and Corporate Innovation*. They identify three primary incentives for joint venture participation: (1) risk avoidance; (2) knowledge acquisition; and (3) market power. Using cross-firm and cross-industry analysis on a large sample of joint ventures from the period 1964–1973, they use multiple regression to evaluate the relationships between joint ventures and concentration, research and development (R&D), financial variables, and firm size.

They found that industry joint venture participation also rose with average firm size, average capital expenditure, and average profitability. Technologically-oriented joint venture participation also rose with average R&D intensity. Within each industry, they attempted to distinguish the characteristics of those large firms engaging in joint ventures from those that did not, and found firm size to be the *only* pervasive influence across industries.

Cross-firm patterns indicated that joint ventures substitute for research and development in the chemicals and engineering industries, but not in resource-based industries, and found that the long-term R&D substitution effect was stronger than the short-term substitution effect. Joint ventures were also found to have a significant negative impact on large firms' rates of return in chemicals and engineering in the short run, although the long-run effect on rate of return was not significant.

At the industry level, technologically-oriented and nonhorizontal joint ventures showed strong positive effects on R&D intensity, indicating that joint ventures and R&D are complements at the industry level. These same types of joint ventures also have a significant negative impact on industry average rates of return, consistent with the reduced risk or reduced time lag that may result from technological or commercial knowledge-acquisition joint ventures. The result is also consistent with using joint ventures as a vehicle for new market entry.

Nontechnologically-oriented and horizontal joint ventures produced significant positive impact on industry average rates of return. While this evidence was not strong, it did suggest to Berg, Duncan, and Friedman that some potential for collusive behavior did exist in parent-parent horizontal ventures.

McConnell and Nantell

The most thorough study of the performance of joint ventures was conducted by McConnell and Nantell (1985) using residual analysis. Their study covered a selection from all joint ventures reported in *Mergers and Acquisitions* for the period 1972–1979. Their sample consisted of 210 firms engaged in 136 joint ventures. The average size of the joint ventures was about $5 million. The two-day announcement period abnormal return was 0.73 percent which was significant at the 1 percent level. The cumulative average residual (abnormal return) over the 62-day period ending on the event day (announcement day) was 2.15 percent, significant at the 10 percent level. The cumulative average residual remains at 2.15 percent after 60 days subsequent to the joint venture announcement, indicating no further valuation effect following the initial announcement.

McConnell and Nantell compare the size of the abnormal return with the results for companies involved in mergers using a representative study of mergers by Asquith (1983). Asquith found excess returns for the two days ending in the announcement to be 6.5 percent for the target firm and 0.3 percent for the bidding firm. Since joint ventures do not identify an acquiring and acquired firm, their results should fall between the two, which they do. Asquith found that over a 60-day period prior to the merger announcement the CAR increases by 11 percent for acquired firms and is unchanged for the acquiring companies. Again the CAR for joint ventures lies between.

Since real estate and entertainment joint ventures constitute 23 percent of their sample, McConnell and Nantell also test for overrepresentation by calculating results without this group. Their results are similar. They also eliminate firms for which other information was released near the joint venture announcement date. Again the results are not changed.

McConnell and Nantell also study the relative size effect. They note that in mergers, the dollar value of gains appears to be evenly divided between the two companies. But if the acquiring company is 20 times as large as the target which gains 10 percent in market value, the acquiring company will gain only 0.5 percent in stock value. Accordingly, the firms in their joint venture sample are divided into large and small groups based on the total market value of their common stock 61 trading days before the announcement of the joint venture. Information was available to do this for 65 joint ventures, but not for 80 other companies which were placed into a third, "all other," category. The statistical tests were repeated for the three groups. The small firms gained 1.10 percent, the large firms gained 0.63 percent, and all others gained 0.57 percent—all of these statistically significant. The dollar gain to the small-firm sample was $4.538 million and for the large-firm sample, it was $6.651 million. Thus as in mergers, the dollar gain is about evenly divided, but the percentage gains are much higher for the smaller firms.

When the dollar gains are scaled by the amounts invested in the joint venture, the average premium is 23 percent (after removing one outlier). This result lies in the range of premiums observed in mergers and tender offers. McConnell and Nantell observe that the gains in mergers and tender offers could be from either synergy or displacement of less effective management. Since joint ventures do not change the managements of the parents, McConnell and Nantell (1985, p. 535) conclude that "we are inclined to interpret our results as supportive of the synergy hypothesis as the source of gains in other types of corporate combinations."

SUMMARY

Joint ventures are new enterprises owned by two or more participants. They are typically formed for special purposes for a limited duration. This brings the participants into what is essentially a medium- to long-term contract which is both specific and flexible. It is a contract to work together for a period of time. Each participant expects to gain from the activity but also must make a contribution. For example, in the GM–Toyota joint venture, GM hoped to gain new experience in the management techniques of the Japanese in building high-quality, low-cost compact and subcompact cars. Toyota was seeking to learn from the management traditions that had made GM the number one auto producer in the world and in addition to learn how to operate an auto company in the environment under the conditions in the United States, dealing with contractors, suppliers, and workers.

To some degree the joint venture represents a relatively new thrust by each participant, so it is often called a strategic alliance. Probably, the main motive for joint ventures is to share risks. This explains why joint ventures are frequently found in bidding on oil contracts and in drilling oil wells, in large real estate ventures, in movies, plays, and in television productions. The second most frequently cited aim in joint ventures is knowledge acquisition. One or more participants is seeking to learn more about a relatively new product-market activity. This may be in all aspects of the activity, or in a limited segment such as R&D, production, marketing, or servicing products.

Other reasons for joint ventures are numerous. One frequently encountered is the small firm with a new product idea that involves high risk and requires relatively large amounts of investment capital. A larger firm may be able to carry the financial risk and is interested in becoming involved in a new business activity that promises growth and profitability. By investing in a large number of such ventures, the larger firm has limited risk in any one and the possibility of very high financial payoffs. In addition, the larger firm may thereby gain experience in a new area of activity that may represent the opportunity for a major new business thrust in the future.

A basic tension is often found in joint ventures. Each participant hopes to gain as much as possible from the interaction, but would like to limit the gains to the other participants. This is particularly true when the firms are competitors in other areas of their activities.

Antitrust authorities often view joint ventures with suspicion. One concern is that each of the participants might have entered the new area independently. Hence, they reason that absent the joint venture, multiple new competitors might have emerged. But it is also possible that the risk to reward outlook is so uncertain that absent the joint venture, no additional competitors would have emerged. In areas of research and development activities, the antitrust authorities are more favorably disposed. For one reason, R & D activity is recognized to be inherently risky. For another, if the R & D joint venture effort turns out to be successful, it may contribute to the economic and competitive strength of the nation as a whole in the world economy.

On balance, the most thorough study of the value effects of joint ventures finds that positive returns are achieved. By the standard abnormal returns or residual analysis, joint ventures result in positive gains for the participants. When scaled to the size of investments, joint ventures appear to achieve about a 23 percent return higher than predicted by general capital market return-risk relationships. This may be biased somewhat upward, since only joint ventures that have actually been formed and been in operation for some time are included in the sample. The many joint ventures that never even reached the launching pad and those aborted shortly after take-off could not be included in the sample. On the other hand, some joint ventures that might have been spectacular successes may have been discouraged or prevented. Worthwhile joint ventures may have not come into being because of negative attitudes of the antitrust authorities. Or the inherent tensions and difficulties of forming and operating an enterprise involving two companies which formerly had been completely independent in their decision-making activities may have prevented the launching of a successful new activity. But overall joint ventures appear on average to make important contributions to the well-being of business firms and to the economy as a whole.

APPENDIX: EMPIRICAL ANALYSES
OF JOINT VENTURE PROBLEMS

The following summaries of articles on joint venture activity in the past describe the status of many joint ventures, identify problems faced, analyze the reasons for the problems, and draw important lessons for future joint venture activity.

1. "Foreign Investors Say 'Sayonara' to 308 Companies They Managed," *Japan Economic Journal*, September 12, 1978, p. 4.
   Foreign investors have pulled capital out of 10 percent (308/3,003) of enterprises set up in Japan since World War II (1950–1977).

   Reasons: Poor business in 57 percent of cases.
   Expiration of terms of technical tie-ups in 15 percent of cases.
   Japanese domestic recession 1975–1977.
   Circumstances affecting the investors in 7 percent of cases.

Entry of huge multinationals has apparently ended for the moment. Despite withdrawals, the indication is that the role of foreign capital in Japanese economy will continue to increase: Sales share of foreign capital firms to combined sales of all firms in Japan rose from 1.37 percent in March 1965 to 2.1 percent in March 1977.

2. "How Companies Resolve Common Problems in Japanese Joint Ventures," *Business Asia*, September 10, 1976, pp. 289–291.

Problems: Product—must be suitable to Japanese market, Japanese competition not too strong.

Differences in objectives—both partners may have been forced into joint venture structure by circumstances, when their objectives might have made another structure more appropriate.

Poor management—Japanese partner may use joint venture as dumping ground.

Communication—distance and language barrier; don't rush to conclude joint venture agreement before ironing out all the problems.

List of 147 joint ventures with changes in equity position. Of 1,000 significant joint ventures in Japan, only about 200 have had to alter their equity position, and 50 of these maintained some form of joint ownership, so problems are not insurmountable.

3. "Joint Venture Problems in Japan," *Economist*, May 14, 1977, pp. 100–101.
Sixty-five joint ventures ended or passed into Japanese hands in 1976; joint venture activity seems to have peaked although foreign investment is still high.

Reasons: Easier to set up wholly-owned subsidiary in Japan; awareness of problems with joint ventures.

Hazards of joint ventures: 50–50 management difficult at best.

Declining Japanese need for technology.

Lower profits, higher debt ratios than foreign partners preferred. Japanese recession.

Lessons: Joint day-to-day decision making not workable; analyze motives carefully; keep an eye on the bottom line.

Successful foreign companies in Japan: (1) Stalwarts—founded pre-1967; mainly wholly owned. (2) Go-go companies—more likely to buy out Japanese partner than to sell out.

4. Alan Otten, "Japanese Firms Press European Ventures to Help Profits, Deter Protectionism," *The Wall Street Journal*, April 16, 1982, p. 54.
European pressure on Japan to limit exports, allow more imports from Europe to Japan and for Japanese to invest in job-creating European plants. Attractiveness of European investment: Large market, increasing shipping costs, safe place to invest and earn good profits. Japanese motive: To get foothold against possible future restrictions and to soften anti-Japanese mood by creating jobs. Domestic content issue important in Common Market; point of argument in joint venture negotiations.

5. Mike Tharp, "Uneasy Partners: More U.S. Businesses Pull Out of Ventures Set up with Japanese," *The Wall Street Journal*, November 8, 1976, pp. 1, 28.
U.S. firms pulling out of joint ventures with Japanese in Japan. U.S. partner had provided technological know-how in exchange for Japanese sales and distribution access. Never amounted to a very large share of all industries in Japan.

Reasons: Japan's lessening need for foreign technology; Japanese recession; misunderstandings over joint venture goals.

Examples: General Mills–Morinaga—too much red tape in management, need to translate all documents; high costs of Telex, phone calls to United States;
charges of technology theft.

AMAX—10 Japanese firms—disparity in sizes, goals of Japanese partners;
opposition from environmentalists; changing market for product (molyb-
denum); changing economic conditions; years of planning with no
result.

Sterling Drug–Nigata—profitable at first; problems arose over who really
controlled. Not really "joint," Japanese looked at joint venture as a subsidiary. Switch to a licensing arrangement.

6. "When Joint Ventures Come Unglued," *Business Week*, April 26, 1982, p. 100.
Difficult and costly to untangle alliance; difficult to value partners' contributions
(e.g., expertise). Still, industrial joint ventures on the rise (to share know-how, to
break into unfamiliar markets, to build large manufacturing plants): 212 in 1981
versus 183 in 1980.

Problem: Joint venture is separate entity with debt financing that doesn't appear on
either partners' balance sheet. Lender has recourse only to joint venture
assets in event of failure. Partners have moral obligation only. Lending
institutions getting tougher requiring letters binding partners, restrictive
covenants requiring certain capital structure, recourse to joint venture
partners' assets. Joint venture partners also learier of being left holding
the bag.

7. L. G. Franko, *Joint Venture Survival in Multinational Corporations*, New York:
Praeger, 1971.

Harvard Business School Project based on 1,100 joint ventures with 314 instances
of instability.

High degree of tolerance for joint ventures: Foreign product diversity, introduction of new products overseas, ability to live with policy diversity.

Low chance of joint venture success: Constrained to particular product or customer group.

Causes of joint venture instability:

Cost cutting: Commitment to end rather than means, to market rather than set of tools
useful in many markets.

Eventually company will find it necessary to increase demand and grow
by cutting prices and costs, typically by elimination of competing
production facilities.

Production rationalization—product differentiation, or by taking advantage of scale economies in centralized marketing decision making.

Other factors in joint venture instability:

Cultural differences

Whether products are sold to consumers or producers

Tradability characteristics of joint venture products

Importance of financial and other conflicts

Profitability of foreign operations

Tolerance for joint ventures also varies with the organizational stages of multinational growth and development:

Stage 1: (Little joint venture instability)—Strong subsidiary general managers to build
foreign businesses report to president or international division chief with general
management responsibility for all international operations.

Stage 2: (Little joint venture instability)—Worldwide product division form of operations; primary corporate responsibility for foreign operations shifts from international division chief to domestic product division chiefs; recentralization of strategic decision making from worldwide perspective.

Stage 3: (Much joint venture instability)—Area structure: Regional general managers direct either subsidiary managers or functional managers with supranational line responsibility for marketing and production. Area or world functional structure—associated with low product and end-use market diversity.

Purposes of joint ventures: To put together complementary resources of already existing firms.

1   To reduce financial risk of operating in a particular country.
2   To obtain local personal contacts on a committed basis.
3   To obtain marketing channels or skills.
4   To obtain an assured outlet for, or assured source of, raw materials available only from an oligopolistic industry.
5   To obtain access to local cost, market, or technological information.

A company will find joint venture advantageous only when its internal supply of capital, foreign market knowledge, local government contacts, and so on is limited.

Partner contribution is ostensibly specific skills or inputs to a well-defined plannable task. But joint venturers do not behave as if this were the case. Joint ventures do not behave like one-time occurrences without dynamic consequences. Both resources and partners' desires concerning resource allocation may change.

Redefine joint venture as a multifunctional marketing and manufacturing subunit headed by a general manager.

The dimensions of choice a partner can affect go well beyond supplying resources or inputs to a specific task; local choice and local strategy formulation and implementation occur in most joint ventures.

No evidence of relationship between joint venture instability and either volume or complexity of transfers of components among members of multinational systems.

Intermediate goods transfers and transfer pricing problems do not even reach an important level until conflicts also arise over competing production facilities within the corporate system.

Strong intercorrelation between importance of transfer pricing problems and production (rationalization problems with partners) do not become critical until multinational firm wishes to centralize marketing decision making or to eliminate intersubsidiary competition.

8. Yoshi Tsurumi, "The Best of Times and the Worst of Times: Japanese Management in America," *Columbia Journal of World Business*, 13, 2, 1978, pp. 55–61. Three sources of problems for Japanese subsidiaries in America:

1   Supply liaison with headquarters in Japan.
2   Decision making and implementation within the subsidiary.
3   Social interaction of Japanese expatriates with Americans.

Sources of misunderstandings, hostility between Japanese and American managers:

1 Mismatch of leadership styles—consensus on firm goals in Japanese firms allows chief executive to be more aloof from daily problems, interdivisional disputes. Viewed as indecisive, incompetent by American subordinates.

2 Formal versus informal organization—informal more important in Japan. Less reliance on organizational charts for authority boundaries. Aggravated by development of Japanese mafia/grapevine excluding American participation in decisions. Groupthink mentality.

3 Verbal versus written communication—Japanese rely more on verbal; follow up with written memo only after consensus is reached. Due to language barrier, may fall back on written memos as substitute for communication, consultation.

4 Lifetime versus mercenary employment—Japanese managers see American counterparts as money hungry because of frequent job changes.

5 Avoidance of confrontation—Japanese abhor unpleasant personal confrontations; potentially explosive conflicts go unresolved.

6 Management and rank-and-file dichotomy—labor likes Japanese managers' commitment to job security, eradication of social differences between management and labor. American managers feel deprived of perks. Also formal performance reviews and feedback emphasized less by Japanese managers.

7 Size, accommodation, and conflict—subsidiaries small enough to allow intensive interaction between Japanese and American staff have good internal relations. As size grows to 80–120 employees, conflict appears and grows as Japanese executives become more dependent on American managers and supervisors without acknowledging the power shift.

Solutions:

1 Japanese managers must develop intellectual and emotional sympathy with American management culture; be alert to signs of conflict and able to deal with it.

2 Don't choose head of subsidiary from top echelon of parent. Subsidiaries, generally smaller operations, require entrepreneurial executive capable of dealing with daily decisions.

3 Turning over management to younger generation of Japanese managers wouldn't work either because they have not developed the personal contacts within the parent company. Make sure the subsidiary's chief officer has the complete support of the parent's chief executive. Appoint an influential corporate officer, who remains at headquarters in Japan, as official head of the subsidiary; his or her job is to handle the politics of providing support.

9. R. B. Peterson and H. F. Schwind, "Comparative Study of Personnel Problems in International Companies and Joint Ventures in Japan," *Journal of International Business Studies*, 8, 1, Spring/Summer 1977, pp. 45–55.
Problems identified by Western executives in Japan:

1 Communication

2 Lack of initiative by Japanese

3 Inadequacy of furnishing exact information

4 Reluctance to admit mistakes

Causes: Lack of initiative problem due to low value accorded to individual in Japanese society, and emphasis on group decision making. Group decision making is designed for ambiguity with respect to authority and responsibility to protect Japanese managers from loss of face; impolite to inquire who or what caused a failure.

Problems identified by Japanese executives working with Westerners:

1 Communication
2 Way of doing things, decision-making process
3 Handling of promotions—Western promotions based on performance; Japanese promotions based on seniority.

Problems identified by joint venture Western executives (as opposed to Western executives in international companies):

1 Communication problems
2 Difficulty in receiving exact information

Problems identified by international company Western executives (as opposed to Western executives in joint ventures):

1 Lack of taking charge, initiative
2 Lack of imagination in problem solving
3 High personnel turnover
4 Labor unions
5 Reluctance of Japanese to accept responsibility
6 Lack of industry

Analysis: Had expected more problems for joint ventures than for international corporations. For international companies, the managerial system reflects the home office, but strong pressures to accommodate primarily Japanese staff. For joint ventures, there are a number of potential problems: (1) executive may be given ambiguous role by home office; (2) vague functional responsibility of the two parties, due to different philosophies of negotiating the contract; (3) Japanese suspicion of intent of foreign management; (4) primary allegiance of Japanese managers to parent company rather than to the joint venture, feeling by foreigners that the Japanese partner is not supplying its best talent to the joint venture.

However, the sample consisted of 50-50 ventures with very large Japanese companies, staffed mainly by the Japanese partner, resulting in less interaction and fewer problems. In the international companies, the foreign managers had more contact with Japanese subordinates, and more opportunities for confrontation.

Problems identified by American executives in American-based companies:

1 Lack of initiative
2 No open discussion
3 Labor unions
4 Lack of willingness of Japanese to understand point of view
5 Not open minded
6 Reluctance to accept responsibility

Problems identified by European executives in European-based companies:

1 Recruitment of quality personnel
2 Need to push Japanese employees
3 Japanese too talkative

Analysis: Europeans less ethnocentric than Americans, more used to dealing with people of other nations and languages. More contrast between American and
Japanese values than between European and Japanese values (historical
role of feudalism, social ranking).

The following is a sampling of examples of joint ventures that encountered
difficulties and either were never launched or were discontinued after a limited
life.

PARTNERS	DATE OF REPORT	JOINT VENTURE PURPOSE AND LIFE SPAN	REASON FOR CONFLICT
American Micro Devices (U.S.) and Siemens (Germany)	2/79	To manufacture computers in U.S. and Germany; 1 yr.	Conflict over competing products; Siemens made another agreement with Intel to produce a competing product.
Dow Chemical (U.S.) and Korean Pacific Chemicals	6/82	To manufacture plastics chemicals in Korea; started in 1969.	Strife between American managers and Korean government-appointed directors of questionable ability. Perceived lack of contribution by Korean partner.
Fairchild (U.S.) and General Electric (U.K.)	7/80	To manufacture computer components in U.K.; 1 yr.	One partner, Fairchild, was acquired by another company uninterested in the joint venture.
Fujitsu (Japan) and ATC (U.S.)	7/80	To manufacture PBX equipment in U.S.; started in 1976.	Potential conflicts over competing products. One partner, ATC, was taken over by General Dynamics which already had a subsidiary producing a competitive product. Fujitsu concerned over protecting its present stake in U.S. market and future penetration.
Fujitsu (Japan) and TRW (U.S.)	3/83	To market Fujitsu small computers in the U.S.; started in 1980.	Need for one-sided decision process in fast-moving market; need for intimate relationship between development and marketing. Excessive product adaptation required for U.S. market. (Cultural differences not important.) Note: Alternative view: "Failure" of joint venture is part of Fujitsu long-range strategy to enter U.S. market.

PARTNERS	DATE OF REPORT	JOINT VENTURE AND LIFE SPAN	REASON FOR CONFLICT
Intel (U.S.) and Matra-Harris (France)	3/81	To manufacture and market semiconductors in France; never really got started.	French government demands were excessive to Intel, even in view of potentially large French market for semiconductors.
Komatsu (Japan) and Bucyrus (U.S.)	2/80	To manufacture power shovels in Japan; started in 1960s.	Komatsu wants out of Bucyrus' restrictions on competing products in Japan and exports to U.S. now that they have acquired the technological know-how.
Paramount (U.S.) and Sony (Japan)	5/78	To develop VTR software in U.S.; never really got started.	Higher than anticipated costs; staff composed mainly of marketing consultants; risky for Paramount, potential conflict with its motion picture business.
Peugeot (France) and Chrysler (U.S.)	4/83	To build Peugeot subcompact in U.S.; never begun.	Peugeot concluded softening market for subcompacts in view of declining gas prices.
Rank (U.K.) and Toshiba (Japan)	10/80	To manufacture color TVs in U.K.; started in 1978.	Underestimated inflation and interest rates. Wrong product (large sets when market had turned to smaller). Marketing problems involved in selling through both Rank and Toshiba outlets.
Toyota (Japan) and Ford (U.S.)	5/81	To manufacture 200,000–250,000 small vans in U.S.; never got started.	Difficulties seen in 50-50 arrangement; lack of speed in resolving basic issues. Suggestion that Toyota favored licensing over joint venture.
Volvo (Norway and Sweden)	12/78	Holding company started in 1978 for Volvo manufacturing assets and Norwegian petroleum assets.	Hazards—expectations of the two countries perhaps unrealizable. Question of Volvo's viability in European car crunch; possibility that Norwegian oil might turn out to be less of a bonanza than anticipated.

QUESTIONS

1. How do joint ventures differ from merger activity? In what ways are they similar?
2. What are the advantages and disadvantages of joint ventures?
3. How does the concept of complex learning relate to joint ventures?
4. What is the primary difference between a joint venture and a strategic alliance?
5. How can joint ventures be affected by public policy on antitrust?
6. How do joint venture returns compare with returns in mergers and tender offers?

REFERENCES

ASQUITH, PAUL, "Merger Bids, Uncertainty, and Stockholder Returns," *Journal of Financial Economics,* 11, 1983, pp. 51–83.

BACHMAN, JULES, "Joint Ventures in the Light of Recent Antitrust Developments," 10 *Antitrust Bulletin,* 1965, pp. 7–23.

BERG, SANFORD V., JEROME DUNCAN, and PHILIP FRIEDMAN, *Joint Venture Strategies and Corporate Innovation,* Cambridge, MA: Oelgeschlager, Gunn & Hain, 1982.

BOYLE, S. E., "Estimate of the Number and Size Distribution of Domestic Joint Subsidiaries," *Antitrust Law and Economics Review,* 1, 1968, pp. 81–92.

BRODLEY, JOSEPH F., "The Legal Status of Joint Ventures under the Antitrust Laws," *Antitrust Bulletin,* 21, 1976, pp. 453–483.

Business Week, "Corporate Odd Couples," July 21, 1986, pp. 100–105. Department of Justice, *Merger Guidelines,* 1982, 1984.

EDSTROM, ANDERS, "Acquisition and Joint Venture Behavior of Swedish Manufacturing Firms," *Scandinavian Journal of Economics,* 1976.

FISHER, F. M., J. J. McGOWAN, and J. E. GREENWOOD, *Folded, Spindled, and Mutilated,* Cambridge, MA: MIT Press, 1983.

FUSFELD, DANIEL R., "Joint Subsidiaries in the Iron and Steel Industry," *American Economic Review,* 48, 1958, pp. 578–587.

HARRIS, ROY J., JR., and BERNARD WYSOCKI, JR., "Ready for Takeoff?: Venture With Boeing Is Likely to Give Japan Big Boost in Aerospace," *The Wall Street Journal,* January 14, 1986, pp. 1, 22.

HLAVACEK, J. D., B. H. DOVEY, and J. J. BIONDO, "Tie Small Business Technology to Marketing Power," *Harvard Business Review,* 55, 1977, pp. 106–116.

KAYSEN, CARL, "Foreword," in F. M. Fisher, J. J. McGowan, and J. E. Greenwood, *Folded, Spindled, and Mutilated,* Cambridge, MA: MIT Press, 1983.

Los Angeles Times, "Antitrust Chief Urges Ventures Over Mergers" November 3, 1984, Part IV, p. 1.

MCCONNELL, JOHN J., and TIMOTHY J. NANTELL, "Corporate Combinations and Common Stock Returns: The Case of Joint Ventures," *Journal of Finance*, June 1985, pp. 519–536.

MEAD, W. J., "Competitive Significance of Joint Ventures," *Antitrust Bulletin*, 12, 1967, pp. 819–849.

MEEHAN, JAMES W., "Joint Venture Entry in Perspective," *Antitrust Bulletin*, 15, 1970, pp. 693–711.

PFEFFER, JEFFREY, and PHILLIP NOWAK, "Joint Ventures and Interorganizational Interdependence," 21, *Administrative Science Quarterly*, 1976, pp. 398–418.

PITOFSKY, ROBERT, "Joint Ventures under the Antitrust Laws: Some Reflections on the Significance of Interfirm Cooperation," 82, *Harvard Law Review*, 1969, p. 1007.

WESTON, J. FRED, "The GM–Toyota Vows: A Reply to the Critics," *Across the Board, The Conference Board Magazine*, 21, 3, March 1984, pp. 3–6.

Yamaha v. FTC, 657 F 2d. 971 (1981).

CHAPTER **15**

ESOPs and MLPs

An Employee Stock Ownership Plan (ESOP) is a type of stock bonus plan which invests primarily in the securities of the sponsoring employer firm. In a Master Limited Partnership (MLP), the limited partnership interests are divided into units which trade as shares of common stock. Both ESOPs and MLPs have tax advantages, and both have been involved in takeover and takeover defense activities.

A dramatic increase in the use of ESOPs as a takeover defense occurred in 1989. For example, in response to a tender offer by Shamrock Holdings (the investment vehicle for the family of Roy E. Disney, nephew of the late Walt Disney), Polaroid established an ESOP holding 14 percent of Polaroid common stock. Like most large corporations, Polaroid is chartered in Delaware. The Delaware antitakeover statute forbids hostile acquirers from merging with a target for at least three years unless 85 percent of the company's voting shares are tendered. Thus, it is unlikely that Shamrock would be able to obtain 85 percent of Polaroid shares if the ESOP does not tender (Rice and Spring, 1989).

NATURE AND HISTORY OF ESOPs

To analyze the role that ESOPs perform it is necessary to understand their fundamental nature as an employee benefit plan and their relationship to other employee benefit plans. The employee benefit plans involved are pension plans. A pension plan is established by an organization to provide for payments to plan participants after retirement. Such plans are subject to federal government regulation established by the Employee Retirement Income Security Act (ERISA) of 1974.

Types of Pension Plans

ERISA divides employee pension plans into two major types: (1) defined benefit plans, and (2) defined contribution plans. The *defined benefit plans* are what people usually have in mind when they think about a pension plan. It is the type used by most large corporations. According to a formula set in advance, these plans specify the amounts that participants will receive in retirement. A flat benefit formula is a fixed amount per year of service, such as $10 for each year of service. An employee with 30 years of service would receive a pension of $300 per month, subject to a maximum percentage (for example, 60 percent) of (average) final salary. Under a unit benefit formula, the participant receives a fixed percentage of earnings per year of service, such as 2 percent of the average of the last five years. An employee with 30 years of service would receive a monthly pension based on 60 percent of the average final salary. Plans must meet federal fiduciary standards to qualify for favorable tax treatment. They are subject to minimum funding standards and are guaranteed by the Pension Benefit Guarantee Corporation (PBGC).

Defined contribution plans make no fixed commitment to a pension level. Only the contributions into the plan are specified and participants receive over the period of their retirement what is in their accounts when they retire. Defined contribution plans can be of three kinds: stock bonus plans, profit-sharing plans, and money purchase plans. In a *stock bonus plan*, the firm contributes a specified number of shares of its common stock into the plan annually. The value of the contribution is based on the price of the stock at a recent date if it is traded; otherwise, an appraisal is required. The other two forms of defined contribution plans provide for the payment of cash into the plan. Contributions to qualified *profit-sharing plans* are related to profitability rates, so can vary in dollar amounts from year to year. Defined contribution plans are required by law to make "prudent" investments. They are not subject to minimum funding standards, and are not covered by the PBGC.

ESOPs are defined contribution employee benefit pension plans. Under ERISA, ESOPs are stock bonus plans or combined stock bonus plans and money purchase plans designed to invest primarily in qualifying employer securities. The plans may receive stock or cash, used by the plan managers to buy stock. A stock bonus plan can determine each year the amount to invest. A money purchase plan has a specific contribution schedule, such as 4 percent of ESOP salaries per year. ESOPs may also provide for employee contributions.

Since 1977, Treasury Department regulations have permitted ESOP contributions to represent a portion of a profit-sharing plan. But an ESOP is different from an employee stock purchase plan. Stock purchase plans are programs under which a firm enables employees to buy company stock at a discount. The Internal Revenue Code specifies that all or most employees participate and that the shares be sold at 85 percent or more of the prevailing market price of the shares.

ESOPs should also be differentiated from executive incentive programs. These are provided mainly to top management and other key employees. The programs are part of executive compensation packages aimed to align the interests of managers with those of the stockholders. While many forms can be used, the tax laws since 1981 govern two types of plans: incentive stock options (ISOs) and stock appreciation rights (SARs). The exercise price of ISOs must be equal to or greater than the stock price at time of issue. The SARs can have an exercise price as low as 50 percent of the stock price. Both can have a maximum life of ten years from date of issue.

Types of ESOPs

In its reports on ESOPs, the General Accounting Office (GAO) identified four main kinds: leveraged, leveragable, nonleveraged, and tax credit. Each of these is briefly described (GAO, 1986). Leveraged ESOPs were recognized under ERISA in 1974. In a *leveraged ESOP,* the plan borrows funds to purchase securities of the employer firm. The employer firm makes contributions to the ESOP trust in an amount to meet the annual interest payments on the loan as well as repayments of the principal. It is well known that corporations can deduct interest as a tax expense, but not principal. However, contributions by the corporations to ESOPs to cover both interest and principal (subject to some limitations) are fully deductible. Leveragable and nonleveraged ESOPs, also recognized under ERISA, are plans which have not used leveraging. In a *leveragable ESOP,* the plan is authorized, but is not required to borrow funds. The plan documents for nonleveraged ESOPs do not provide for borrowing. *Nonleveraged ESOPs* are essentially stock bonus plans which are required to invest primarily in the securities of the employer firm.

The Tax Reduction Act of 1975 provided for tax credit ESOPs. In addition to the regular investment credit in existence at that time, an additional investment credit of 1 percent of a qualified investment in plant and equipment could be earned by a contribution of that amount to an ESOP. The plans were called Tax Reduction Act ESOPs or TRASOPs. An additional 0.5 percent credit was added in 1976 for companies which matched contributions of their employees of the same amount to the TRASOP. In 1983 the basis for the credit was changed from plant and equipment investments to 0.5 percent of covered payroll. These types of plans were called payroll-based ESOPs or PAYSOPs. TRASOPs and PAYSOPshave been called tax credit ESOPs. The other three types of ESOPs are referred to as ERISA-type ESOPs.

History of ESOPs

The nature of ESOPs has been described. Before analyzing them in detail, it is useful to present a brief history of ESOPs to understand how they came into being and what they were intended to accomplish. The origin of the ESOP was explained in the following terms (Kelso and Kelso, 1984).

> The ESOP was invented in 1956 to enable the employees of a small California newspaper chain, Peninsula Newspapers, Inc., to buy the property from its retiring owner, on non-recourse credit, without diminishing their wages or salaries and without invading their savings. This first ESOP and subsequent ones do utilize in a special way beneficial tax provisions put into the Internal Revenue Code as far back as 1921 to facilitate stock bonus plans.

The stock bonus plans referred to in the preceding quote by the Kelsos grew in popularity during the 1920s with the rising stock market. They contributed to increasing ownership of company stock by employees and were widely acclaimed as a way to develop "people's capitalism." They were associated with the slogan, "a chicken in every pot and a car in every garage." With the stock market crash of 1929, the popularity of stock bonus plans and employee stock ownership decreased. It was not until stock markets rose after World War II that their popularity began to revive.

It is widely acknowledged that the intellectual leadership for increasing employee ownership in the form of ESOPs was provided by Louis Kelso, an attorney in San Francisco, California. In a series of books and pamphlets, some written by himself and others in joint authorship with Mortimer Adler, a distinguished philosopher, and with Patricia Hetter who later became his wife, Kelso set forth his theories (Kelso, 1961; Kelso and Adler, 1958; Kelso and Hetter, 1967). Kelso argued that many of the economic problems of a capitalist society came about because only a relatively small percentage of the population owned most of the securities representing ownership of business. Kelso presented the view that because employees did not own stock, they pushed continuously for wage increases which had inflationary effects. In addition, they viewed profits as simply making the rich richer. They did not appreciate the role that profits played in capital formation and its contribution to economic growth and increased employment. Kelso's idea was that these views could be changed if American workers became owners of common stock and began to have a "second income" from cash dividends to augment their wages.

Kelso believed that new capital investment was financed out of the savings of the rich and added to the skewed distribution of stock ownership. Kelso proposed that corporations should receive incentives to finance new investment in a manner that would enable employees to become owners of the new capital invested in their firms. To bring about employee stock ownership, Kelso proposed that an employee trust would obtain debt financing from an institution to purchase newly issued shares in the firm. The employee trust would pay off the borrowing from the income earned by the new capital. Thus was born the idea of employee stock ownership plans that would enable workers to see profits as a stimulus to economic expansion, increased employment, and their increased ownership of business operations.

Kelso's ideas were communicated to Senator Russell B. Long from Louisiana, Chairman of the Senate Committee on Finance, in the early 1970s. Kelso had direct contact with Senator Long in 1973 when the Finance Committee was developing the provisions of what became the Employee Retirement Income Security Act (ERISA) of 1974. ERISA gave official recognition to ESOPs and exempted them from the general prohibition against using borrowed funds.

The leveraged ESOP was established by ERISA in 1974. Subsequent federal legislation enacted further provisions. As noted earlier, the Tax Reduction Act of 1975 provided for an additional 1 percent to the 10 percent investment tax credit if the corporation contributed that amount or more to a TRASOP. The Tax Reform Act of 1976 permitted an additional 0.5 percent investment tax credit if such an additional amount was contributed to the TRASOP by matching employee contributions. The Economic Recovery Act of 1981 phased out TRASOPs by the end of 1982 to be replaced by PAYSOPs. From 1983 on, companies with PAYSOPs could obtain a tax credit up to 0.5 percent of payroll for contributions of at least that amount. The Tax Reform Act of 1986 repealed the tax credits for PAYSOPs effective December 13, 1986.

Other legislation strengthened the rights associated with the stock that employees received through an ESOP. A 1978 law required that common stock distributed by ESOPs in closely-held firms carry an attached put option. The put option provided that a retired employee would have the right to put the stock to the employer at a specified price even in the absence of a market for the stock.

The Revenue Act of 1978 required that ESOPs in publicly-traded firms provide employees with full voting rights. In privately-held firms, ESOP stock should have the right to vote on major corporate issues. The earlier Tax Reform Act of 1976 specifically authorized ESOPs to pass through to the employees dividends received on the stock held by the ESOP. While they had the power to do so, most ESOPs did not pass through the dividends. The Deficit Reduction Act of 1984 strengthened the incentive to do so by permitting corporations to deduct as a taxable expense dividends paid on ESOP shares when the dividends are passed through to the employee participants. The Deficit Reduction Act of 1984 also permits the lending institution to exclude from income 50 percent of the interest earned on ESOP loans. It also permitted owners to defer taxes on capital gains resulting from the sale to an ESOP of stock in a closely-held firm. The Deficit Reduction Act of 1984 also provided that employers could assume an estate's tax obligation if an equal amount of stock were transferred to an ESOP.

The Tax Reform Act of 1986 contained a number of provisions in addition to repeal of the tax credit for PAYSOPs. For other types of ESOPs a number of other tax benefits were provided. The 50 percent interest income exclusion earned on ESOP loans was extended to regulated investment companies. Dividends paid on stock held by an ESOP could be taken as a taxable expense for the corporation if the dividends were used by the ESOP to reduce principal on ESOP loans. In addition, 50 percent of the proceeds from the sale of employer stock to an ESOP could be excluded from an estate's value.

Clearly, many tax incentives have been enacted on behalf of ESOPs. With this background we are in a position to understand better how ESOPs function and the nature of their impact.

ESOPs have been used in a wide variety of corporate restructuring activities (Bruner, 1988; GAO, 1986). Fifty-nine percent of leveraged ESOPs were vehicles used to buy private companies from their owners. This enabled the owners to make their gains tax free by investing the funds received into a portfolio of securities. ESOPs have also been used in buy-outs of large private companies as well.

Thirty-seven percent of leveraged ESOPs were employed in divestitures. In a very substantial ESOP transaction the Hospital Corporation of America sold over 100 of its 180 hospitals to HealthTrust, a new corporation created and owned by an employee leveraged ESOP.

Leveraged ESOPs have also been used as rescue operations. An ESOP was formed in 1983 to avoid the liquidation of Weirton Steel which subsequently became a profitable company. ESOPs used in the attempt to prevent the failure of Rath Packing, McLean Trucking, and Hyatt Clark Industries were followed by subsequent bankruptcies.

A number of leveraged ESOPs were formed as a takeover defense to hostile tender offers. ESOPs were established as takeover defenses by Dan River in 1983, by Phillips Petroleum in 1985, and by Harcourt Brace Jovanovich in 1987.

The Tax Reform Act of 1986 also permits excess pension assets to be shifted tax free if they are placed into an ESOP. Ashland Oil reverted $200 million and Transco Energy Co. $120 million into new ESOPs.

ESOPs represent one among a number of restructuring activities. ESOPs may be used as a substitute for or in connection with buying private companies, divestiture activities, efforts to save failing companies, as a method of raising new capital, and as a takeover defense.

THE USE OF ESOPs

It is helpful in understanding how ESOPs are used to continue to view them in the setting of a form of employee benefits, particularly as a pension plan. The basic relationships involved in a pension plan are shown in Figure 15.1.

We see in Figure 15.1 that an individual corporation is responsible for setting up the pension fund. It makes dollar contributions either in the form of a defined benefit plan or defined contribution plan, as discussed earlier. The pension fund uses the dollar contributions to make investments in a wide range of securities, real estate, and so on. The implication of ERISA is that prudence generally requires diversification of the pension fund investments. We see further that the benefits of the pension fund accrue to and are finally paid to the pension beneficiaries who are the employees of the company. It is presumed that at least to some degree wages are lower than they otherwise would be because of contributions by the company to the pension fund on behalf of its employees.

FIGURE 15.1 How a Pension Plan Operates

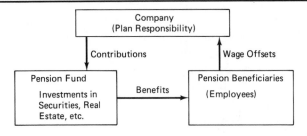

Contributions by a company to a qualified pension fund are tax-deductible expenses at the time of payment by the company. However, these dollar flows are not taxable to the recipient at the time that the pension fund is set up. They are taxable to the recipient only when the benefits are actually received. Since the income of the employees would be expected to be lower after retirement, the employee has the benefit of a lower tax rate on the value of the contributions into the pension fund. In addition, of course, the pension fund earns income which augments the amount of benefits payable to the employees in the future. Both the original payments by the employer into the pension fund and earnings thereon receive the benefit of tax deferral until received by employees.

Concept of a Leveraged ESOP

In an ESOP, the logic of the arrangement is the same as in Figure 15.1. The pension fund would be called an ESOP fund or trust. In a basic ESOP, the contribution by the company could be either cash or securities of the sponsoring company as described earlier. Like ordinary pension funds, ESOPs may also provide for employee contributions. Unlike the general pension fund which is expected to diversify its investments widely for financial prudence, an ESOP is set up to invest in the securities of the sponsoring company. In practice, ESOPs are likely to utilize leverage to increase the tax benefits to the sponsoring company. The nature of a leveraged ESOP is shown in Figure 15.2.

We now have an additional element in the arrangement. This is the financial institution which is the source of the borrowing by the ESOP. As shown in Figure 15.2, the lender transfers cash to the ESOP trust in return for a written obligation. The sponsoring firm generally guarantees the loan. The ESOP trust (ESOT) purchases securities from the sponsoring firm. Since the sponsoring firm has a contingent liability, it does not actually transfer the stock to the name of the ESOP trust until payments are made reducing the principal which the firm has guaranteed. As portions of the principal are repaid, the firm then transfers stock to the name of the ESOP trust. The source of payment of both interest and principal to the financial institution is the cash contributed to the ESOP trust by the company. Both the interest and principal amount transferred by the company are deductible expenses for tax purposes. Subject to the limitations de-

FIGURE 15.2   Illustration of a Leveraged ESOP

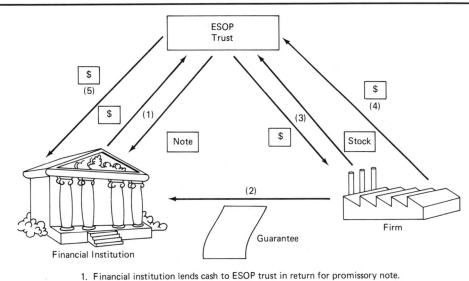

1. Financial institution lends cash to ESOP trust in return for promissory note.
2. Sponsoring firm guarantees note.
3. ESOP trust purchases stock from sponsoring firm.
4. Firm contributes cash to ESOP trust.
5. ESOP trust uses cash to make principal and interest payments on loan.

SOURCE: United States General Accounting Office, *Employee Stock Ownership Plans: Benefits and Costs of ESOP Tax Incentives for Broadening Stock Ownership*, Washington, DC, December 1986, p. 49.

scribed earlier, the total payment by the company to the ESOP is a deductible expense for tax purposes.

Examples of the Use of ESOPs

An example with actual numbers can be used to illustrate the nature of a leveraged ESOP. John Jones was the president and 100 percent owner of Ace Company. His entire estate was represented by the value of Ace. His children were grown and had no interest in running the business. His attorney recommended the sale of Ace since Jones did not have other investments. In the case of his death his estate would be unable to pay the required estate taxes and would be forced to sell the company under unfavorable conditions.

Jones had received an offer from Universal Company. It was to be a share-for-share stock exchange for each of the 300,000 Ace shares outstanding. Universal was trading at around $15 per share. Investment bankers had placed a value on Ace at around $20 per share. Since Jones was only 54 years old, he was reluctant to relinquish ownership and control of his company. Jones recognized the need to increase his liquidity, but did not want to sell the company at this time. We can now illustrate how an ESOP could be helpful. An ESOP is established with all of the employees of Ace Company as beneficiaries. The ESOP borrows $2 million from a bank. These funds are used to purchase 100,000 shares of Ace Company stock from John Jones. The loan from the bank to the ESOP is guaranteed by Ace Company and is secured by the 100,000 shares held in trust. Ace Company agrees to make ESOP contributions to cover both interest and repayment of principal. These are tax-deductible expenses for Ace Company. Note that at this point John Jones has received $2 million in cash; presumably he will place this in a diversified portfolio with a relatively high degree of liquidity and/or marketability. So long as these funds are invested in other U.S. corporations within 12 months, the proceeds are not taxable to Jones at this time (see below for more detail).

As the ESOP repays the loan, the stock held in trust will be allocated to each individual employee's account. When the loan is completely paid off, the ESOP would have received and owned the 100,000 shares of stock representing 33.3 percent of the outstanding stock of Ace Company. These relationships are illustrated in Figure 15.3.

Another example will sharpen the advantages of the use of an ESOP as compared with a merger. It is similar to the previous illustration which was streamlined to bring out the essential nature of a leveraged ESOP. In the present case study, more variables are considered in the analysis. Consider John Doe, the aging owner of 100 percent of the stock of Doeskin Textiles. Most of his personal wealth is tied to the firm's fortunes; he is thinking about retirement and worries about his relatively illiquid position as well as having all his eggs in one basket. In addition, declining health has caused him to consider the effect of substantial estate taxes which might necessitate a hasty sale of the firm by his heirs in the event of his death. All these factors led him to seriously consider a recent overture from Polyestech Corporation to acquire Doeskin in a tax-free exchange of securities for $8,000,000. The offer is acceptable in terms of price, although Doe is somewhat concerned that the value received would deteriorate if Polyestech's

FIGURE 15.3 Leveraged ESOP Example

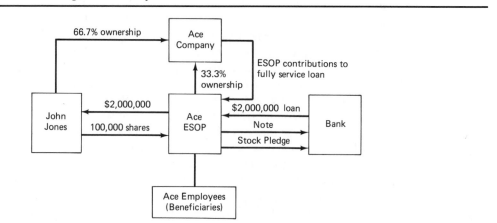

stock price declined. Also, Polyestech has a rather unsavory reputation in terms of labor relations and social responsibility. Doeskin has been the mainstay of the Minnesota community where it is located, and Doe feels quite paternalistic towards his employees and managers. He is uneasy about turning the firm over to outsiders and would like to find another solution. ESOPs offer such a solution.

Suppose Doe would like to withdraw $2,500,000 of Doeskin's $8,000,000 value to invest in a diversified portfolio of publicly-traded corporate securities to provide both diversification and liquidity. He should take the following steps:

1 Doeskin should establish an ESOP.
2 The ESOP should borrow $2,500,000 from a bank, insurance company, or other lender. (Recall that one half the interest income commercial lenders receive on ESOP loans is exempt from taxation—this enhances their borrowing ability.) Doeskin would most likely be required to guarantee the ESOP loan.
3 Doe sells 31.25 percent of his stock to the ESOP for $2,500,000.

As long as Doe invests the $2,500,000 in securities of other U.S. corporations within 12 months, he can defer any federal tax on the transaction. This tax-free rollover is allowable under the 1984 Deficit Reduction Act so long as the ESOP owns at least 30 percent of the firm's stock following the sale and neither the owner nor his family participates in the ESOP once formed. If Doe had sold less than 30 percent, he would have had to pay capital gains tax on the sale, but he would have been able to participate in the ESOP, reducing over time the extent of his ownership dilution.

Doeskin would then make tax-deductible contributions to the ESOP sufficient to repay the loan principal and to pay interest. As the loan was repaid, the Doeskin shares belonging to the ESOP would be allocated to Doeskin employees participating in the plan. Thus, the owner of a privately-held firm can achieve tax-free liquidity without selling his firm to outsiders and even maintaining control, depending on his need for cash and thus the proportion of stock sold to the ESOP.

Among the advantages and disadvantages of the ESOP versus the Polyestech offer are the following:

ESOP:

1 Increased employee loyalty as a result of stock ownership through ESOP.
2 Increased liquidity and diversification for Doe.
3 Dilution of ownership not critical here since Doe maintains control.
4 The tax-free rollover is actually only a tax deferral until the replacement securities are sold.
5 Establishes a market value for Doeskin stock which may help in estate valuation. This may be a positive or negative effect.
6 Provides a market for Doeskin shares if heirs must sell shares to pay estate taxes—avoids "fire sale," and furthermore, 50 percent of the proceeds from the sale of stock to an ESOP may be excluded from the estate's value.

SALE TO POLYESTECH:

1 No liquidity enhancement until Polyestech shares are sold.
2 Potential deterioration of value received.
3 Complete loss of control over firm.
4 Tax advantage in tax-free exchange of securities is one of timing only. Tax must be paid when securities are sold to achieve liquidity.
5 No diversification effect since all eggs would still be in one basket, albeit a different and perhaps more marketable basket.

ESOPs in Lieu of Subsidiary Divestiture

Large corporations often have subsidiaries or plants which they wish to divest for one reason or another. The usual alternatives are to sell the subsidiary to another corporation (although it may be difficult to find a buyer at an acceptable price), or to liquidate the subsidiary's assets which is disruptive for the subsidiary's employees and often for others as well. An ESOP can function well in this type of situation. The subsidiary's employees are likely to be willing purchasers (through an ESOP), since they have a great deal at stake and the alternatives are highly uncertain.

First, a shell corporation is established. The shell establishes an ESOP; the debt capacity of the shell and the ESOP (with the guarantees of the parent corporation) is utilized to arrange financing to purchase the subsidiary from the parent. The shell corporation (now no longer a shell) operates the former subsidiary while the ESOP holds the stock. If successful, enough income will be generated to make the most of allowable tax-deductible contributions to the ESOP, which will enable it to service its debt. As the debt is reduced, the ESOP will allocate shares to the employees' accounts, and over time the former subsidiary will come to be owned by its employees.

This entire transaction is, of course, predicated upon the subsidiary's viability as an independent entity, and its ability to generate sufficient income to cover its financing. In many cases, the original motivation for divestiture is that the subsidiary is in a dying industry or requires extensive modernization of inefficient facilities. If so, selling the subsidiary to the employees benefits neither them nor the economy as a whole in the long run even though short-term disruption might be kept to a minimum. In such cases, liquidation might be the preferred solution.

WORKSHEET ANALYSIS OF ESOPs AND ALTERNATIVES

To understand better the nature of financing through an ESOP, we present another example in which three alternative methods of raising funds are analyzed through detailed worksheets. The first example is of conventional equity financ-

TABLE 15.1
Conventional Equity Financing

		YEAR			
	0	1	2	3	4
Income Statement					
Operating income		$10,000	$11,000	$12,000	$13,000
Interest expense		—	—	—	—
Income before tax		10,000	11,000	12,000	13,000
Income tax @ 40%		4,000	4,400	4,800	5,200
Net income		$ 6,000	$ 6,600	$ 7,200	$ 7,800
Cumulative net income			12,600	19,800	27,600
Capitalization					
Shareholders' equity	$25,000				
	15,000				
Total capital	$40,000	$46,000	$52,600	$59,800	$67,600
Cumulative taxes paid		4,000	8,400	13,200	18,400

Raise $15,000 by selling 1,500 shares @ $10 per share. So total capital rises to $40,000. Original number of shares = 2,500. New total = 4,000. Percent ownership 62.50% × $67,600 = $42,250.

ing. A firm seeks to raise an additional $15,000 by selling 1,500 shares at $10 per share. It starts with shareholders' capital of $25,000 to which is added the $15,000 to raise the capital to $40,000, as shown in Table 15.1. In the income statement, the operating income is shown to rise by $1,000 per year. There is no interest expense, because it is assumed the firm has no other debt. We apply a 40 percent tax rate, which assumes the corporate rate of 34 percent plus state income taxes. Cumulative net income for the four years is $27,600. The capitalization of the company would therefore rise to $67,600. This represents the $15,000 additional equity capital plus retained earnings of $27,600. The original number of shares was 2,500. The new total is 4,000. Thus, the percent ownership of the original stockholders is 62.5 percent. In this sense, dilution of 37.5 percent has taken place.

In Table 15.2, the analysis is made for conventional debt financing. Now, the $15,000 is raised by long-term debt. The debt is to be paid off in four years under the schedule shown in Table 15.2. The interest rate is assumed to be 10 percent of the balance at the beginning of the year, or at the end of the previous year. The logic of the table is as follows: For the first year, $15,000 is owed. Interest is paid at 10 percent, so the amount of interest is $1,500. Repayment of principal is assumed to be $3,000, so $12,000 is owed at the end of the first year. In the second year, therefore, the interest would be $1,200. Principal repayment during the second year of $3,500 is shown, so that long-term debt at the end of the second year is $8,500. And so on.

Cumulative net income at the end of the four years is $25,200. Fifteen thousand dollars of this was used to repay the debt, so the addition to the total capital that existed at the beginning of year 1 after the borrowing is $25,200 less

TABLE 15.2
Conventional Debt Financing

	0	1	2	3	4
			YEAR		
Income Statement					
Operating income		$10,000	$11,000	$12,000	$13,000
Interest expense		1,500	1,200	850	450
Income before tax		8,500	9,800	11,150	12,550
Income taxes at 40%		3,400	3,920	4,460	5,020
Net income		5,100	5,880	6,690	7,530
Cumulative net income		5,100	10,980	17,670	25,200
Repay principal on debt		3,000	3,500	4,000	4,500
Capitalization					
Long-term debt	$15,000	$12,000	$ 8,500	$ 4,500	$ —
Shareholders' equity	25,000	30,100	35,980	42,670	50,200
Total capital	$40,000	$42,100	$44,480	$44,170	$50,200
Principal repayment		3,000	3,500	4,000	4,500
Balance owed		12,000	8,500	4,500	—
Cumulative taxes paid		3,400	7,320	11,780	16,800

Percent ownership of original shareholders = 100 percent
Cash flow = cumulative net income minus debt repayment
     = $25,200 − $15,000
     = $10,200

the $15,000 or $10,200. This is added to the initial capital of $40,000 (the initial equity of $25,000 plus the borrowing of $15,000) to obtain $50,200. Or we could say that total capital at the end of the four years would be the $25,000 plus cumulative net income of $25,200 for a total of $50,200.

It is noted that there is no dilution in equity ownership. However, because of the repayment of the debt and the cost of debt interest, the total capital is about $18,000 less than under the conventional equity financing. But taxes are reduced and ownership higher. So there are tradeoffs between equity financing and debt financing. Perhaps more realistically, one would assume a rollover of the debt financing at the end of the four years so that the process would be continued. This would make the two situations more comparable. This is not intended to be a complete analysis of the use of equity financing versus debt financing. For such an analysis, see any standard textbook in finance. (For example, Weston and Copeland, 1986, Chapter 20.) This analysis is mainly for the purpose of showing the relationship to leveraged ESOP financing to which we now turn.

The same facts as before are assumed, except that the ESOP borrows the $15,000 and uses it to buy the 1,500 shares of stock. The resulting financial patterns are shown in Table 15.3. In the material following line 2 in the table, the relevant ESOP material is given. Line 3 gives the total amount of ESOP payroll.

TABLE 15.3
Leveraged ESOP Financing

1		0	1	2	3	4
				YEAR		
2	*ESOP Data*					
3	ESOP payroll		$12,000	$14,000	$16,000	$18,000
4	Maximum principal repayment (25% of payroll)		3,000	3,500	4,000	4,500
5	Amount owed		12,000	8,500	4,500	—
6	*Income Statement*					
7	Operating income		10,000	11,000	12,000	13,000
8	ESOP contribution—Interest		1,500	1,200	850	450
9	ESOP contribution—Principal		3,000	3,500	4,000	4,500
10	Income before taxes (7−8+9)		5,500	6,300	7,150	8,050
11	Income taxes at 40%		2,200	2,520	2,860	3,220
12	Net income—tax books		3,300	3,780	4,290	4,830
12A	Net income—actual (add line 9 to line 12)		6,300	7,280	8,290	9,330
13	Cumulative net income (actual)		6,300	13,580	21,870	31,200
14	*Capitalization*					
15	Long-term debt	15,000	12,000	8,500	4,500	—
16	Shareholders' equity (13+)	25,000	31,300	38,580	46,870	56,200
17	ESOP obligation	(15,000)	(12,000)	(8,500)	(4,500)	—
18	Net equity = book value (16−17)	10,000	19,300	30,080	42,370	56,200
19	Total capital (15+18)	25,000	31,300	38,580	46,870	56,200
20	Shares outstanding	2,500	2,800	3,150	3,550	4,000
21	Share additions		300	350	400	450
22	Percent original ownership	100%	89%	79%	70%	62.5%
23	ESOP capital cumulative shares		300	650	1,050	1,500
24	ESOP % of shareholders' equity owned		11%	21%	30%	37.5%
25	ESOP equity at book value (24×16)		3,443	8,102	14,061	21,075
26	Cumulative taxes paid		2,200	4,720	7,580	10,800

Book value at time 0 = $10

This information is necessary to meet the regulations with regard to tax-deductible ESOP contributions. Line 4 shows the maximum principal repayment. This is 25 percent of the ESOP payroll. Given the ESOP payroll numbers assumed in line 3, we take 25 percent to obtain the figures in line 4. Line 5 shows the amount owed on the $15,000 loan made to the ESOP at the end of each year.

In line 7 we begin with the data under the Income Statement heading. The operating income is the same as in the previous two examples in Tables 15.1 and 15.2. Now, however, in addition to interest being a deductible expense as it was in Table 15.2 under straight borrowing, the ESOP contribution applied to principal is also a tax-deductible expense. Taxable income before taxes is the lowest of the three examples. Income taxes are also the lowest of the three examples. Cumulative net income is the highest because of tax savings.

As compared with conventional debt financing, shareholders' equity is much larger. In line 20, we show the number of shares outstanding at the end of year 0 as 2,500; in each subsequent year, we transfer shares on the basis of the amount that the ESOP has repaid on principal. By the end of the fourth year, an additional 1,500 shares are outstanding, so that the percent original ownership is exactly the same as under the conventional equity financing, 62.5 percent, assuming that the shares are transferred on the same basis every year. In all of this analysis, it is assumed that the shares were sold at a market price equal to book value, initially $10 per share. But one of the potential advantages of leveraged ESOP financing is that if the funds raised are productive so that the value of the shares increases, a smaller number of shares will have to be transferred. As a consequence, the percent that the original shareholders own at the end of the four-year period would be greater than the 62.5 percent.

The foregoing shows that as compared with conventional equity financing, leveraged ESOP financing has the benefit of transferring the shares on the basis of future market prices which are hopefully higher. As compared with conventional debt financing, repayment of principal is a tax deduction, therefore saves taxes; because of additional tax savings, actual earnings are higher and total capital is higher at the end of the four-year period. We wish to emphasize that it is somewhat artificial to view the firm in terms of a single financing episode like this. Financing is usually on an ongoing basis so that debt is typically rolled over; it is never repaid. But to consider subsequent financings would simply be another illustration of the advantage of ESOP financing.

Similar calculations were made by Bruner (1988). His examples were more complex, taking more variables into account. In one example the outlays in a leveraged ESOP represented by interest expense and principal repayment represent a substitute for pension payments that otherwise would have been made. When this occurs the cash flow advantages to the ESOP are even greater. Another plausible assumption is that the interest rate charged by the lender will reflect all or some of the tax advantage which permits the financial institution to exclude 50 percent of the income on loans to ESOPs from taxable income. This would make the debt interest expense under a leveraged ESOP arrangement lower than under straight debt financing.

Another issue is control of the stock that is placed in the ESOP. Some people argue that management continues to control the ESOP, so that the stock remains in friendly hands. On the other hand, technically the stock belongs to the individual employees, and with a strong union speaking on behalf of the employees, there is always the risk that the employees and/or their union might vote the stock in a way that conflicts with the interests of management. The point was made in connection with Polaroid's establishment of an ESOP that the employees who wished to maintain the status quo and who did not want an outside firm to take over the company would be even more strongly opposed to the takeover than management. Typically after a takeover, employment is reduced, and to protect their positions, the employees are likely to be supporters of management when ESOPs are used as a takeover defense.

The view has been set forth that ESOP transactions represent economic dilution. Potentially they transfer shareholders' wealth to employees (Bruner, 1988). As we observed at the beginning of this chapter, ESOPs represent a form of an employee's pension program. If the ESOP contribution is not offset by a reduction to some degree in other benefit plans, or in the direct wages of workers, employees gain at the expense of shareholders. The argument has also been made that any borrowing by the ESOP uses some of the debt capacity of the firm (Bruner, 1988). It could also be argued that such borrowing substitutes for other forms of borrowing which the firm would otherwise use. To the extent that there is a valid belief that ESOP transactions represent economic dilution to the original shareholders, the price charged to the ESOP for the company stock transferred to it may be at a premium price to compensate for economic dilution. Since the Department of Labor reviews such transactions, this may be a source of its disagreements about the fairness of the price charged by management to the ESOP.

The impact of moving equity shares into the ownership of the employees is apparently an important disadvantage of ESOPs despite their considerable tax advantage. Kaplan (1988, note 12) has expressed this view in the following terms: "The infrequent use of ESOP loans in the sample analyzed in this paper (5 of 76 companies) suggests that the non-tax costs of using an ESOP are high. One such cost is the large equity stake that eventually goes to all contributing employees and significantly reduces the equity stake that can be given to managers and the buyout promoter." The preceding worksheet analysis illustrates how the equity position of original owners is diluted by the sale of shares to an ESOP. A potential advantage is that shares can be sold at higher prices over the years as the ESOP contributes to higher earnings through tax advantages and through the increased incentives and improved motivations of employees as a result of their stock ownership through the ESOP. Further analysis of the reasons for the establishment of ESOPs and their effects on corporate performance are discussed next.

EVIDENCE ON ESOPs

By 1989 over 10 thousand ESOPs had been established. The number of participants reached about 12 million employees (National Center for Employee Ownership, 1989). The volume of public-company ESOP borrowing increased from

TABLE 15.4
Participants and Assets of ESOPs[a]

	PARTICIPANTS		ASSETS[b]		
TYPE	NUMBER (THOUSAND)	PERCENT	TOTAL (MILLION)	PERCENT	MEDIAN/ PARTICIPANT
Tax credit	6,391	90	$14,800	79	$2,952
Leveraged	158	2	1,450	8	8,660
Leverageable	293	4	1,445	8	7,149
Nonleveraged	238	3	961	5	5,098
Other	2	0[c]	1	0[c]	0
Total	7,083	99[d]	$18,660	100.0	$5,226

[a] Based on plans active in 1983, the last year for which complete data are available.

[b] In constant 1983 dollars.

[c] Less than 0.05 percent.

[d] Total does not add to 100.0 percent because of rounding.

Source: United States General Accounting Office, *Employee Stock Ownership Plans: Benefits and Costs of ESOP Tax Incentives for Broadening Stock Ownership*, Washington, DC, December 1986, p. 19.

$1.2 billion in 1986 to an $18 billion annual rate by mid-1989 (Farrell and Hoerr, 1989, p. 118). As shown by Table 15.4, by 1983 almost $20 billion of assets were held by ESOPs. The median amount of investment per participant indicated by Table 15.4 is something over $5,000.

Table 15.4 also shows that 90 percent of the participants in ESOPs are in the tax-credit type. But since the tax-credit ESOPs were terminated as of the end of December 1986, this raises the question of what the present and future role of ESOPs will be. Our discussions with ESOP associations indicate that the role of ESOPs will continue to be important. It appears that many of the tax-credit ESOPs are being changed into leveraged ESOPs. Tax-credit ESOPs had substantial advantages, so while available they were the preferred form. Leveraged ESOPs accomplish almost as much from the standpoint of tax advantages.

In Table 15.5, we consider the reasons for ESOP formation. The main reason indicated is "employee benefit." This is somewhat ambiguous, but it does reflect the fundamental nature of ESOPs in that they are inherently one form of employee pension plan. Tax advantages rank very high as a reason, as does the motive to "improve productivity." Examples of productivity increases in individual companies can be cited (Farrell and Hoerr, 1989) but broader studies thus far do not provide evidence that productivity has been significantly improved.

The one element with respect to the reasons for ESOPs that can be documented concretely relates to tax advantages. It has been estimated that the federal revenue losses from ESOPs for the period 1977–1983 were about $13 billion, an average of $1.9 billion per year (GAO, 1986, pp. 28–31).

Since one of the objectives expressed in the writings in support of the ESOP idea was to achieve "people's capitalism," it is of interest to consider the stock

TABLE 15.5
Reasons for ESOP Formation

REASON	PERCENT
Employee benefit	91
Tax advantages	74
Improve productivity	70
Buy stock of major owner	38
Reduce turnover	36
Transfer majority ownership to employees	32
Raise capital for investment	24
Decrease absenteeism	14
Avoid unionization	8
Make less vulnerable to hostile takeovers	5
Save failing company	4
Exchange for wage concessions	3
Take company private	1
Other	[a]
Total weighted cases	3,698[b]

[a] 0.5 percent or less.
[b] Weighted subtotals do not add up to overall total because of rounding.
SOURCE: United States General Accounting Office, *Employee Stock Ownership Plans: Benefits and Costs of ESOP Tax Incentives for Broadening Stock Ownership*, Washington, DC, December 1986, p. 20.

ownership and control of ESOPs. Table 15.6 shows three fourths of the ESOPs own less than 25 percent of the stock of the associated companies, but the median percent of stock owned is 10 percent. However, only 70 percent of ESOPs hold employer stock with voting rights. Of all plans, the median percent of total voting shares held by the ESOP is 2 percent. Even when stock carries voting rights, the voting rights associated with the stock of ESOP accounts may be exercised by the plan trustees (usually the company management) without input by participants. This has given rise to the charge that ESOPs can be used by management to obtain tax benefits without sharing control with employees. This has been justified in the following terms (Hiltzik, 1984, p. 2):

TABLE 15.6
Ownership of Sponsoring Corporations by ESOPs

	PERCENT
Own up to 25 percent	75
Own more than 25 percent	25
Median percent of stock owned	10

SOURCE: United States General Accounting Office, *Employee Stock Ownership Plans: Benefits and Costs of ESOP Tax Incentives for Broadening Stock Ownership*, Washington, DC, December 1986, p. 39.

"Our programs are the antithesis of workplace democracy," says Joseph Schuchert, managing partner of Kelso & Co., the firm founded by Louis Kelso, which has installed about 800 ESOPs for companies since 1956 and has arranged 80 buy-outs with ESOP participation since 1970. "We've been criticized for not giving workers more participation, but we believe workers are natural shareholders, not natural managers."

There are interesting issues raised in connection with the preceding quote. Apparently the aim of ESOPs is to enable workers to participate in ownership for the purpose of augmenting their income from both dividends and capital gains. But ownership carries the ultimate control power in a corporation. If workers are not to participate in the decision-making process or to exercise ultimate control in their role as shareholders, some unresolved issues are posed.

Studies published through 1986 indicate that ESOPs had not achieved significant improvements in corporate performance. In addition, a number of court cases have raised questions of conflict of interest in the creation and management of ESOPs by managers and their financial consultants. With regard to performance, the most exhaustive study was performed by the General Accounting Office (GAO, 1987) which reviewed a number of prior studies on ESOPs and corporate performance. These are summarized in Table 15.7. None of the studies found significant gains in either profitability or productivity. Only one of the studies reported a significant improvement in the growth rate of sales. No study reported a significant improvement in the growth rate of employment.

These results are in sharp contrast to the results we report in the following chapter for similar studies in connection with leveraged buy-outs (LBOs) and management buy-outs (MBOs). As we see in Chapter 16, significant improvements take place in performance and profitability in LBOs and MBOs. In LBOs and MBOs, the percentage of voting stock held by management increases substantially. Clearly a motivation element is involved since the decision-making powers of managers are strengthened. Their stock ownership represents a high percentage of their present and prospective wealth position. These characteristics do not obtain for ESOPs. As a consequence, it appears that they have not achieved the same positive impacts on motivation and performance as have been documented in LBOs and MBOs.

Of even greater concern are the charges that ESOPs have been used by managements not only as instruments for increasing their control, but to conduct financial transactions in their own interests and to the detriment of the ESOPs and the workers they represent. Some of the court cases in which these issues are at least raised include the following. In Hall-Mark Electronics, employees owned one third of the company stock through their retirement plan. The issue in the court case is the allegation that three Hall-Mark executives arranged to have the ESOP sell its shares back to the company at $4 per share shortly before they participated in the sale of the company for $100 per share (Hiltzik, 1986, p. 1).

Another example is the Chicago Pneumatic Tool Company which established an ESOP in 1985. The controlling trustee was the chief executive of the

TABLE 15.7

Prior Studies on ESOPs and Corporate Performance

STUDY	ESOP SAMPLE	COMPARISON	MEASURE	FINDING IMPROVE	SIGNIFI-CANT
Profitability:					
Conte and Tannenbaum (1978)	Some non-ESOPs	Industry Averages	Pretax Profits to Sales	Yes	No
Tannenbaum, Cook and Lohman (1984)	Some non-ESOPs	Matched Firms	Pretax Profits to Sales	No	No
Livingston and Henry (1980); Brooks, Henry, and Livingston (1982)	Stock Purch. Plans	Matched Firms	Nine Profitability Ratios	Neg Ests[a]	Mixed
Hamilton (1983)	In One Industry	Matched Firms	Net Profits to Net Sales	Some Yrs	No
			Net Profits to Net Worth	Some Yrs	No
			Net Profits to Net Capital	Some Yrs	No
			Net Sales to Net Worth	Yes	Some Yrs
Bloom (1985)	Publicly Traded	Matched Firms	Gross Return on Capital	Mixed Est	Mixed
		Matched Firms and Before and After	Gross Return on Capital	Yes	No
Productivity:					
Marsh and McAllister (1981)	Only ESOPs	Industry Averages	Compensation to Sales	Yes	NR[b]
Hamilton (1983)	In One Industry	Matched Firms	Net Sales per Employee	Yes	No
Bloom (1985)	Publicly Traded	Matched Firms	Sales per Employee	Mixed Est	Mixed
		Matched Firms and Before and After	Sales per Employee	Mixed Est	Mixed
Growth Rates:					
Rosen and Klein (1983)	Some non-ESOPs	Industrial Sector	Employment	Yes	NR[b]
Bloom (1985)	Publicly Traded	Matched Firms	Employment	Neg Ests[a]	Yes
		Matched Firms and Before and After	Employment	No	No
Trachman (1985)	Some in High Technology Firms	High Techn. Firms	Employment Sales	Yes No	NR[b] NR[b]
Quarrey (1986)	Only ESOPs	Matched Firms and Before and After	Employment Sales	No Yes	NR[b] Yes

[a] Negative estimates are only noted if statistically significant.

[b] Not reported

Source: United States General Accounting Office, *Employee Stock Ownership Plans: Little Evidence of Effects on Corporate Performance,* Washington, DC, October 1987, p. 47. For complete descriptions of the studies listed in Table 15.7, see GAO, 1987, pp. 63–65.

company. In March 1986, the company became the target of a hostile takeover. To defeat the bid, it is alleged that the chief executive transferred one million shares from the company's treasury to the ESOP under his own voting control. The U.S. Labor Department (which has responsibility for implementing the provisions of ERISA and of employee pension plans generally) stated that the cost of the transaction to the ESOP was $32.4 million for the shares which were trading at about 30 percent over their historical average because of takeover speculation (Hiltzik, 1986, p. 16).

In 1985, the Labor Department blocked an ESOP-financed $500 million leveraged buy-out of Scott & Fetzer, the publisher of *The World Book Encyclopedia*. The Labor Department objected to the arrangement which provided that the Scott & Fetzer ESOP would invest $182 million in borrowed funds to receive 41 percent of the company in the leveraged buy-out. A group consisting of Scott & Fetzer's top management plus Kelso & Co. were to invest $15 million, for which they would receive 29 percent of the company. The General Electric Credit Corporation which financed the $182 million ESOP loan and provided other financing would receive the remaining 30 percent. The Labor Department alleged that the ESOP was putting up more than 92 percent of the equity investment for only 41 percent of the company. The rebuttal view was that the ESOP investment represented a purchase of shares at market value (or takeover value), not an initial equity contribution. Another issue raised by this case is whether it was appropriate for Kelso & Co., a leading investment banking firm specializing in setting up ESOPs and formulating the terms of the deal, to have a substantial equity participation. It would appear that the possibility of conflict of interest would be involved.

Other cases could be cited. We do not presume to express a judgment on the merits of these cases. That is the province of the courts involved. We present these brief descriptions only to convey that significant issues have been raised with regard to the administration of ESOPs.

The broader economic consequences of ESOPs have also been analyzed (Chen and Kensinger, 1988). If managements also control the ESOPs that are created, no increase in employee influence on the company takes place. While employees may receive stock that may be sold, the additions to their wealth may be relatively small. The amounts received may be insufficient to provide motivation for increased efforts by workers or to achieve harmonious relations between workers and management. On the other hand, if workers did receive substantial increases in control over the company through ESOPs, other harmful results might follow. Workers might use their increased ownership powers to redistribute wealth away from the original shareholders and other shareholders in the firm. The view has also been expressed that reliance can be placed upon market forces to bring about employee ownership where it is appropriate, without the necessity of tax subsidies. The tax subsidies may cause a misallocation of resources. Chen and Kensinger (1988, p. 75) see two risks.

> The tax preferences can keep a dying enterprise limping along, creating an imbalance in its industry which holds back the stronger competitors and so creates

economic inefficiency. Perhaps even more damaging in the long run, these preferences may discourage valuable investment in new technologies and other growth
opportunities by fostering an overly cautious attitude brought on by inefficient
diversification of employees' capital.

They also observe that the greatest potential gains from employee ownership are in smaller high-growth companies in which human capital plays an
important role in productivity performance. But in such companies, typically
growth and profitability provide ample incentives. From a public policy standpoint, the tax preferences granted may cause distortions and departures from
what would occur under the unrestricted operation of market forces. Some
writers have concluded that "mature, diversified corporations with strong labor
unions and few growth opportunities, on balance, are likely to be the best
candidates for ESOP financing" (Chen and Kensinger, 1988, p. 75). In these
situations, however, the advantages and disadvantages of ESOPs should be
compared to alternatives such as takeovers, MBOs, and LBOs. It has been argued that, on balance, these alternatives to ESOPs do not involve tax subsidies of
the same kind or to the same degree. Some even argue that no tax losses result
from the alternatives listed. These are issues that require further research.

MASTER LIMITED PARTNERSHIPS

The corporation has been the dominant form of business organization in the
United States when measured by total assets. When measured by numbers,
proprietorships and partnerships are the most numerous, applying mostly to
relatively small businesses. A corporation has four major advantages in raising
large sums of money. (1) It provides for limited liability of stockholders. Stockholders are not personally liable if the firm is unable to pay its debts. (2) The
corporation has an unlimited life. Managers can come and go and owners may
change, but this does not affect the continuity of the corporation. (3) The ownership shares carry the residual risk, but they are divided into many units. Hence,
investors can limit their risk exposure in any one firm, and this facilitates diversification by investors across many firms. (4) The shares of common stock are
freely bought and sold. This facilitates tradability and transferability of ownership interest in the firm (Weston and Copeland, 1986, pp. 55–56).

The Nature of MLPs

In recent years the master limited partnership (MLP) has taken its place as a new
form of business organization. The MLP is a type of limited partnership whose
shares are publicly traded. The limited partnership interests are divided into
units which trade as shares of common stock. In addition to tradability it has the
advantages of limited liability for the limited partners. The tradability also pro-

vides for continuity of life. While the MLP retains many of the advantages of a corporation, it has a superiority over the corporation in that it eliminates the double taxation of corporate earnings. The MLP is not taxed as an entity; it is treated as any other partnership for which income is allocated pro rata to the partners. Unit holders reflect all income deductions and credits attributable to the partnership's operation in determining the unit holder's taxable income. The Tax Reform Act of 1986 enhances the advantage to MLPs by lowering the top personal income tax rate (28 percent) to below the top corporate tax rate (34 percent).

The Internal Revenue Service has focused on four characteristics in distinguishing between a corporation and a master limited partnership (MLP): unlimited life, limited liability, centralized management, and transferability. To avoid being taxed as a corporation, an MLP may have only two, and no more, of the four corporate characteristics, which are usually centralized management and transferability. MLPs typically specify a limited life of 100 years more or less. The general manager of the partnership has unlimited liability, even though the limited partners do not.

Probably in part because the general partner has unlimited liability, it also has virtually autocratic powers. Once a general partner and the formation of an MLP have been approved by the courts and been reviewed at least by the Securities and Exchange Commission, it would be very difficult to change the general partner in the absence of readily provable fraud or the equivalent. The probability of success of an MLP will be increased if it is structured to achieve an alignment of interests between the general partner and the public unit holders. One way to do this is by using management incentive fees such as providing the general partner with a sharing rule of 4 to 6 percent of the distributable cash flows from the MLP. Alignment of incentives is also achieved because the management of the general partnership also owns a significant number of the limited partnership units.

Different types of MLPs have been identified. Mentz (1987, p. 19) has described four categories of MLPs based on their method of formation:

> (i) "roll-up MLPs," formed by the combination of two or more partnerships into one publicly traded partnership; (ii) "liquidation MLPs," formed by a complete liquidation of a corporation into an MLP; (iii) "acquisition MLPs," formed by an offering of MLP interests to the public with the proceeds used to purchase assets; or (iv) "roll-out MLPs," formed by a corporation's contribution of operating assets in exchange for general and limited partnership interests in the MLP, followed by a public offering of limited partnership interests by the corporation of the MLP, or both. A fifth category of MLP, that may well predominate in the future, is the "start-up MLP," formed by a partnership that is initially privately held but later offers its interests to the public in order to finance internal growth.

It will be noted that some of the distinctions are based on whether the MLP is formed out of a partnership or out of a corporation. Some writers would include the liquidation MLP as a special case of roll-out MLPs. Some writers would also combine acquisition MLPs with start-up MLPs. Our discussion considers three main categories of MLPs: (1) roll-up MLPs, (2) roll-out MLPs, and (3) start-up MLPs.

Roll-ups were the first type of MLPs organized. The roll-ups began with combining limited partnerships formed to invest in programs in the oil industry. The Apache Petroleum Company in 1981 formed the first MLP by rolling up a number of partnership syndications. Before that, the typical practice was to form oil and gas corporations by exchanges of common stock in the newly formed corporation for the previously existing private partnership interests.

Interestingly, computer technology contributed to the timing of the emergence of MLPs. By 1981, Apache had developed the complex computer programs required to report the annual gain, loss, and tax basis of individual partners in a publicly-traded partnership with a relatively large number of investor/participants. Also, Apache was granted a ruling by the IRS that a master limited partnership would be treated as a partnership and not a corporation for tax purposes even though its shares were publicly traded.

The nature of a roll-up MLP is shown in Figure 15.4. The figure depicts three stages. Before the roll-up transaction, there are a number of limited partnerships in existence. The figure shows one general partner in common for all of the partnerships; this was the case with Apache Petroleum which combined a number of limited partnerships that it had previously sponsored. One of the authors was involved in a roll-up transaction in which several different general partners were involved (Pan Petroleum MLP, 1989). They simply entered into an agreement similar to that depicted in the second stage (transaction column) of Figure 15.4. Basically, in return for their shares in the old limited partnerships, units in the new MLP are issued to the old limited partners. The resulting pattern is depicted in the third column, indicating the structure after the roll-up. After the MLP has been formed, there is a general partner for a master limited partnership. It has units which are owned by the limited partners. The units may trade

FIGURE 15.4   Roll-up Master Limited Partnership

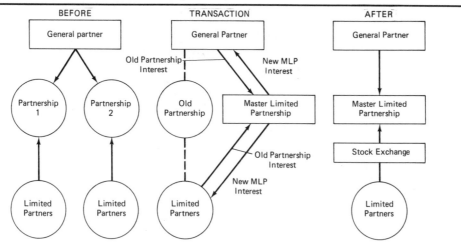

on the stock exchange or they may trade over the counter; we depict the use of a stock exchange in Figure 15.4.

The second major type of master limited partnership is a roll-out, which is sometimes called a spin-off. Roll-outs represent a method by which corporations can transfer assets to avoid the double taxation of corporate dividends or to establish a value on assets that may be undervalued. Roll-out or spin-off MLPs are likely to be used increasingly since corporate tax rates under the Tax Reform Act of 1986 are higher than the top rate for personal taxes. Roll-out or spin-off MLPs are likely to be sold on a yield comparison basis. Transco Corporation, an interstate natural gas pipeline company, in 1983, apparently was the first corporation to spin-off a portion of its assets into an MLP. It transferred its oil and gas reserves into a newly formed partnership and sold about 5 percent of the MLP units to the public. In March 1985, International Paper placed its timberlands into an MLP selling 15 percent of the units to the public. In December 1986, Penn Central Corporation sold its pipeline business, Buckeye Partners, to an MLP raising $240 million.

What takes place in these roll-out or spin-off MLPs is illustrated in Figure 15.5. Before the transaction, the corporation holds a number of business segments. In the transaction, the corporation places the assets of one or more of its business segments into a master limited partnership. The MLP transfers MLP units to the corporation which in turn distributes them to its shareholders. The shareholders continue to own common stock in the corporation, but also own units in the MLP that was formed. In a variation on this pattern, the corporation could have sold a portion or all of the units to the outside public. It is likely that in a roll-out or spin-off, the corporation would designate some of its top officers to constitute the general partner for the MLP. At the completion of the transaction, there will continue to be shareholders in the corporation. It is likely that

FIGURE 15.5   Roll-out or Spin-off Master Limited Partnership

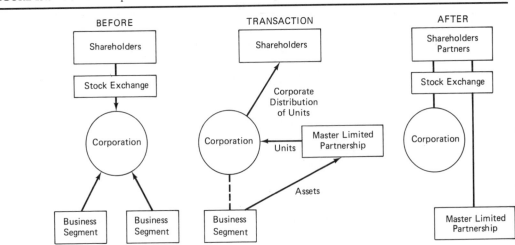

FIGURE 15.6   New Issue, Start-Up, or Acquisition Master Limited Partnership

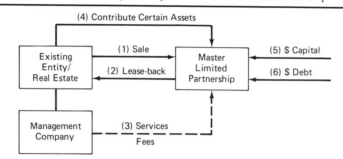

some of the units would be sold to the outside public so there would be a different set of shareholders who owned units in the MLP as well as some of the original shareholders in the corporation conducting the spin-off.

The third major type of MLP is the new issue, start-up, or acquisition MLP. Its nature is illustrated by Figure 15.6. The existing entity transfers assets to the MLP. A management company may be involved which provides services to the MLP and probably will be its general partner. In return, it receives a certain percentage of the cash flow of the MLP. It is probably the key managers of the management company who would serve as the general partners. The general partner does not have to hold units in order to receive income. The partnership agreement provides that a fixed percentage of the income of the MLP is received by the general partners. Notable examples of the start-up MLP include the conversion of the Boston Celtics and Denver Nuggets basketball teams into MLPs. The Boston Celtics transaction in October 1986 raised $48 million. A hoped-for offering price of $20 per unit had to be reduced to $18 for the public offering. One can find a listing of this limited partnership unit in the New York Stock Exchange Composite quotations. As of March 16, 1989, the quotation showed that the 52-week range in price for the units was a high of 15¾ and a low of 12¼.

Various types of MLPs were described in a *Fortune* magazine article (1988). It discussed the business aspects of each of the MLPs. It showed that their prices have fluctuated like common stocks. Although they typically sell on a yield basis (compete with bonds and preferred stock), the value of the MLP units fluctuates with the outlook for the performance of the MLP just as it would for a publicly-traded corporation.

Advantages of MLPs

A strong motivation for the formation of an MLP is the tax advantage, the idea that the MLP is taxed as partnership and therefore avoids the double taxation to which corporate dividends are subject. The nature of the advantage to the use of an MLP is shown by Table 15.8. Under the old tax law, the marginal corporate rate of 46 percent was below the marginal personal rate of 50 percent. It is assumed that for the same $100 of income, the same $20 is required under either

TABLE 15.8
A Comparison of the Tax Benefits of MLPs Before and After the Tax Reform Act of 1986

	PRE-TRA 86		POST-TRA 86	
	CORP.	MLP	CORP.	MLP
Company income	$100	$100	$100	$100
Company tax	46	0	34	0
After-tax income	54	100	66	100
Retained income	20	20	20	20
Payout	34	80	46	80
Personal tax	17	50	13	28
Investor after-tax income	$ 17	$ 30	$ 33	$52

form for reinvestment in the operating activity. The investor would receive $30 under the MLP as compared with $17 under the corporation. This is 76 percent more income.

Under the new tax law, the top marginal corporate rate of 34 percent is now higher than the top marginal personal rate of 28 percent. Under the same assumptions as before, the after-tax income to the investor is $33 under the corporation and $52 under the MLP. The investor receives 58 percent more income under the MLP than under the corporation. The differential under the old tax law was $13; the differential under the new tax law is $19. Thus, the absolute dollar value of benefit is greater under the new tax law. The percentage depends on the patterns of numbers assumed. Also the comparison depends critically on the amount of retained income. This is because the partners pay tax whether the income is retained or not. Also the degree to which there is double taxation depends on the payout; the higher the payout, the more double taxation, so it is difficult to generalize. This also illustrates that the MLP is likely to be most attractive in industries where reinvestment rates are relatively low. This implies high payout rates, and when payout rates are high, the advantage of avoiding double taxation is greater.

Initial Pricing of MLPs

Muscarella (1988) has analyzed the price performance of MLP units. His sample consists of all initial public offerings of MLP units from January 1983 to July 1987. He analyzes the price performance of the MLPs for the 20 days following the initial public offerings. He found no significant underpricing or overpricing for his total sample or any subsample except for a slight overpricing of oil and gas and hotel/motel limited partnerships. This contrasts with substantial underpricing of initial public offerings (IPO) of corporate securities. Ritter (1984), for example, had reported initial average returns of 26.5 percent for 1,028 IPOs from 1977 to 1982. Chalk and Peavy (1987) reported 22 percent initial returns for 649 firms from 1975–1982. Muscarella and Vetsuypens (1988) had found for the period 1983 to June 1987 an initial return of 7.61 percent for 1,184 firms. All of these studies represent substantial underpricing. Theoretical models of IPO underpricing argue that the size of IPO underpricing is related to the degree of uncertainty about the market value of the common stock of the issuing firm. The study of initial price performance of MLP units implies much less uncertainty in the valuation of MLP units. Muscarella is unable to provide an explanation why there should be relatively little uncertainty about the valuation of MLP units.

Case Study: Pan Petroleum MLP

Most of the literature on MLPs has emphasized tax aspects. This case study of the Pan Petroleum MLP, whose formation was reviewed by the courts on April 26, 1989, illustrates the underlying business and economic rationales as well. The 1989 transaction involved a consolidation of a group of 45 oil and gas limited partnerships with Pan Petroleum MLP, a publicly-traded master limited partnership. The consolidated partnership has approximately 4,300 limited partners. It was predicted that as a result of the consolidation, general and administrative expenses would be reduced by as much as $300,000 per year. These savings result from several types of economies of scale resulting from the consolidation. The savings in general and administrative expenses became possible because of the need for only one set of financial records rather than 46, one annual appraisal of mineral properties, one legal entity maintained, and one partnership tax return. Many of the limited partners in the constituent partnerships consolidating with Pan Petroleum MLP were limited partners in more than one partnership. This makes possible further cost savings with respect to record keeping and participant reporting. Many of the constituent partnerships owned interests in the same mineral properties. Duplicate accounting and record keeping could be eliminated as a result of the consolidation. The constituent partnerships participated mainly in wells drilled by two different major exploration companies. The consolidation provided Pan Petroleum MLP with a majority of the working interest in many of the properties. This enables the MLP to conduct negotiations with the two large exploration companies on a more effective basis.

The basis for the consolidation appeared to be efficient and equitable. Engineering surveys established the proved reserves in developed producing properties as well as the nonproducing or undeveloped properties. From the estimates of proved reserves of oil and gas, the amounts of cash flows and their duration were projected. The same was done for the nonproducing or undeveloped properties. The cash flows for this latter group were reduced by 30 percent as an uncertainty factor. The resulting cash flows for both the developed producing properties and for the nonproducing or undeveloped properties were discounted at a 10 percent rate over the expected future economical producing lives of each of the properties. The MLP into which the other constituent partnerships were consolidated had its future cash flows discounted into a value figure on the same basis. For each constituent limited partnership and the Pan Petroleum MLP, the value of other assets and liabilities were also taken into account to arrive at a total "formula value." These were summed to arrive at a total figure of approximately $23 million. Of this amount something over $11 million represented the "formula value" of Pan Petroleum MLP, representing 49.2 percent of the total. Pan Petroleum MLP had 2,571,670 limited partnership units already outstanding. Using these as the reference factor, a total of 5,226,191 MLP units were issued of which Pan Petroleum accounted for 49.21 percent. The other constituent partnerships received MLP units representing the same percentage of the total MLP units issued that their formula value represented in relation to the total formula value. Inherently forecasts and projections were required, but the methodology appears to have represented a rational and equitable basis for making the apportionment of ownership and income rights.

Clearly one of the major advantages to the owners of the constituent limited partnerships is that they would now have ownership rights that could be freely traded, bought, and sold. A number of the constituent limited partnerships would have had to be liquidated and would have ceased to exist except for the consolidation with Pan Petroleum MLP. In addition, by exchanging their limited partnership units for units in the Pan Petroleum MLP, the limited partners now have pro rata ownership rights in an efficient business operation. Even with depressed prices for oil and natural gas, the Pan Petroleum MLP continues to be a viable entity. With improvements in future oil and natural gas markets, the investors in the MLP units have a potential for favorable future returns.

SUMMARY AND CONCLUDING REMARKS

ESOPs were designed ostensibly to promote employee stock ownership and to facilitate the raising of capital by employers. They have a number of shortcomings in the performance of both functions. Nevertheless ESOPs may be quite valuable in a number of circumstances, particularly for privately-held companies engaged in ownership transfer or for firms near the limit of their debt capacity.

The argument for employee stock ownership holds that employees who own stock in their employer are more productive, since as part owners they have a greater stake in the firm's profitability. ESOPs, however, provide a good deal less than direct stock ownership. Participants typically do not receive any distribution of securities from the plan until they separate from service. Dividends and voting rights are passed through only with respect to shares actually allocated to participants' accounts. But most participants are not allowed to sell even those shares which have been allocated to them and thus cannot achieve a level of diversification in their benefit plans. (ERISA excludes ESOPs from the requirement to diversify.) A 1987 report by the General Accounting Office (GAO) concluded that while ESOPs do broaden stock ownership within participating firms, given the limited number of ESOPs within the economy as a whole, the effect is modest overall. Perhaps more important, it found little evidence of improved performance in terms of either profitability or productivity.

As a financing tool, ESOPs provide benefits midway between debt and equity financing. They can bring additional debt capacity to highly leveraged firms or provide a market for equity financing for closely-held firms. They are very useful devices for transferring ownership. The same 1987 GAO report indicated that the use of ESOPs in corporate finance has not lived up to its potential—most leveraged ESOP funds are used to buy back stock from existing shareholders (for instance, retiring major shareholders) and not for capital expansion by the sponsoring firms. Thus ESOPs' contributions to corporate finance have been limited. However, the exploding events in connection with ESOPs during 1989 may substantially alter these earlier patterns. In mid-1989 the IRS ruled that the special tax benefits of ESOP debt would still be allowed even if the debt of the ESOP is traded publicly. Shortly thereafter, however, it was announced that the House Ways and Means Committee was considering a bill to repeal the exclusion (Birnbaum and Winkler, 1989). On June 7, 1989, an IRS private ruling (8921101) held that dividends on ESOP stock were deductible if used to help retire the ESOP loan for leveraged ESOPs. The ruling indicated that companies might transfer stock to leveraged ESOPs from employee profit sharing or stock bonus plans and thereby deduct previously nondeductible dividends. The ruling would also require the ESOP to allocate added stock to employees based on the value of the dividends used for loan payments (Schmedel, 1989). Thus the events of 1989 may have transformed the significance of ESOPs. Their future developments may have great significance for corporate activity and the economy.

The MLP is a new organizational form which offers investors the structure and tax attributes of more traditional partnerships, but differs in one key respect. MLPs offer investors liquidity via an organized secondary market for the trading of partnership interests.

Tax advantages were an important motivating factor in the early development of MLPs. However, some of these advantages have been eroded. The Tax Reform Act of 1986 (TRA 86) eliminated an important tax benefit of corporate-MLP conversions with its repeal of the General Utilities doctrine. Before TRA 86, in a liquidation MLP, the corporate sponsor would contribute assets to the MLP in exchange for units in a roll-out transaction. The units would then be distributed to the corporate sponsor's shareholders in a complete liquidation of the corporation. This transaction would be completely tax free. However, this is no longer the case with the repeal of the General Utilities doctrine. The general rule was that corporate gains from the sale of appreciated assets were taxed at the corporate level at the time of the sale and at the shareholder level when this income was distributed as dividends. Under the General Utilities doctrine, a significant portion of the assets involved in a corporate MLP conversion would escape corporate taxation at the time of conversion. But TRA 86 eliminated this exception and taxed at the corporate level the entire difference between the adjusted basis of the assets and their fair market value. In addition, the shareholders at time of conversion after TRA 86 continue to be taxed on the difference between their basis in the common stock and the market value of the MLP units at conversion.

The main tax advantages of MLPs following TRA 86 are the result of the differential between personal and corporate income tax rates, and the status of MLPs as nontaxable entities. All profits and losses of an MLP flow through to individual investors, to be taxed at lower personal rates, while avoiding the double taxation at both the corporate and personal levels of corporate dividend distributions to shareholders. However, these tax advantages are highly sensitive to an MLP's need to retain earnings, since MLP earnings are taxable to investors whether they are distributed or not.

Thus, the liquidity advantages of MLPs assume even greater importance. Siciliano (1987, p. 1) suggests that this aspect of MLPs has led to "a distinctly different investment and marketing thesis," appealing to investors to view MLP units as simply another component of their equity securities portfolio, rather than "as a long-term method of sheltering income from taxes."

QUESTIONS

1. What are the advantages and limitations of ESOPs?
2. How successful have ESOPs been in achieving their goals of increasing employee stock ownership and facilitating capital raising by employers?
3. How do MLPs differ from ordinary limited partnerships?
4. What are the advantages and limitations of MLPs?
5. Explain the differences between leveraged and nonleveraged ESOPs. Compare the eps and control dilution under equity financing versus financing through an ESOP.
6. How are MLPs similar to corporations? How do they differ?

REFERENCES

BIRNBAUM, JEFFREY H., and MATTHEW WINKLER, "Rostenkowski Acts to Repeal ESOP Provision," *The Wall Street Journal*, June 8, 1989, pp. C1, C17.

BRUNER, ROBERT F., "Leveraged ESOPs and Corporate Restructuring," *Journal of Applied Corporate Finance*, 1, Spring 1988, pp. 54–66.

CHALK, A. J., and J. W. PEAVY, III, "Initial Public Offerings: Daily Returns, Offering Types, and the Price Effect," *Financial Analysts Journal*, 43, September/October 1987, pp. 65–69.

CHEN, A. H., and J. W. KENSINGER, "Beyond the Tax Effects of ESOP Financing," *Journal of Applied Corporate Finance*, 1, Spring 1988, pp. 67–75.

COLLINS, J. MARKHAM, and ROGER P. BEY, "The Master Limited Partnership: An Alternative to the Corporation," *Financial Management*, Winter 1986, pp. 5–14.

ESTRIN, S., P. GEROSKI, and G. STEWART, "Employee Share Ownership, Profit-Sharing and Participation," *International Journal of Industrial Organization*, 6, 1988, pp. 1–6.

"Fabulous ESOPs," *The Economist*, August 6, 1988, p. 13.

FARRELL, CHRISTOPHER, and JOHN HOERR, "ESOPs: Are They Good For You?" *Business Week*, May 15, 1989, pp. 116–123.

HEMPSTEAD, JOHN E., "Have Your Company and Sell It, Too," *Nation's Business*, April 1985, p. 34.

HILTZIK, MICHAEL A., "Do ESOPs Aid Workers or Managers?" *Los Angeles Times*, May 25, 1986, Part IV, pp. 1, 6.

————, "ESOPs Now a Boon for Management," *The Wall Street Journal*, December 30, 1984, pp. 1–2.

KAPLAN, STEVEN, "A Summary of Sources of Value in Management Buyouts," Presentation at the Conference on Management Buyouts, Graduate School of Business Administration, New York University, Salomon Brothers Center for the Study of Financial Institutions, May 20, 1988.

KELSO, L. O., *The New Capitalists: A Proposal to Free Economic Growth from the Slavery of Savings*, New York: Random House, 1961.

————, and M. ADLER, *The Capitalist Manifesto*, New York: Random House, 1958.

KELSO, L.O., AND P. HETTER, *How to Turn Eighty Million Workers into Capitalists on Borrowed Money*, New York: Random House, 1967.

KELSO, L.O., and P. KELSO, "Leveraged Buyouts—Good and Bad," ms., 1984.

LANCASTER, HAL, "Timeout: Despite Success of Celtics Sale, Doubts Remain About Sports Offerings," *The Wall Street Journal*, May 8, 1987, p. 25.

MANEY, KEVIN, "Business of Pro Sports: Money and Great Equalizer," *USA Today*, March 23, 1987, p. 11C.

MENTZ, J. ROGER, Department of the Treasury, Statement on June 30, 1987 in *Master Limited Partnerships*, Hearings before the Subcommittee on Select Revenue Measures of the Committee on Ways and Means, House of Representatives, 100th Congress, First Session, Serial 100-39.

MONROE, ANN, "Master Partnerships Defy Death Notices," *The Wall Street Journal*, March 30, 1987, p. 6.

"More Employees Should Have a Say in ESOPs," *Business Week*, August 15, 1988, p. 134.

MURPHEY, LEE B., "Financing ESOPs: New Opportunities For Lenders," *The Journal of Commercial Bank Lending*, March 1987, pp. 2–9.

MUSCARELLA, C. J., "Price Performance of Initial Public Offerings of Master Limited Partnership Units," *The Financial Review*, 23, November 1988, pp. 513–521.

————, and M. R. VETSUYPENS, "Initial Public Offerings and Information Asymmetry," Working Paper, Southern Methodist University, 1988.

National Center for Employee Ownership, Oakland, California, Telephone Conversation, 3/14/89.

Pan Petroleum MLP, Proposal, March 8, 1989.

RICE, B., and R. SPRING, "ESOP at the Barricades," *Barron's*, February 6, 1989, pp. 38–39.

RITTER, J. R., "The 'Hot' Issue Market of 1980," *Journal of Business*, 57, April 1984, pp. 215–240.

SCHMEDEL, SCOTT, "Tax Report," *The Wall Street Journal*, June 7, 1989, p. A1.

SCHULTZ, E., "All That Payout and Capital Gains Too," *Fortune*, 118, October 10, 1988, p. 28.

Shearson Lehman Brothers Inc., "Meeting Your Goals Under Tax Reform: Partnership and Margin Borrowing," *The Serious Investor*, January 1987.

SICILIANO, JOHN M., "Investment Banking Considerations," in L. M. Allan, *Master Limited Partnerships for Real Property Investments*, Berkeley, CA: California Continuing Education of the Bar, 1987.

Smith Barney, Harris Upham and Co., "Boston Celtics Limited Partnership Preliminary Prospectus," October 26, 1986.

STEIN, BENJAMIN J., "Who Cleans Up From the Roll-Up?" *Barron's*, November 16, 1987, pp. 13, 58–60.

TAUSSIG, JOSEPH K., "ESOPs—A Creative Financial Alternative," Chapter 43 in J. Fred Weston and Maurice B. Goudzwaard, eds., *Treasurer's Handbook*, Homewood, IL: Dow Jones-Irwin, 1976, pp. 942–961.

TELL, LAWRENCE J., "Hottest Thing in Oil: A Look at Master Limited Partnerships," *Barron's*, October 7, 1985, pp. 16, 20.

United States General Accounting Office, *Employee Stock Ownership Plans: Benefits and Costs of ESOP Tax Incentives for Broadening Stock Ownership*, Washington, DC, December 1986.

————, *Employee Stock Ownership Plans: Little Evidence of Effects on Corporate Performance*, Washington, DC, October 1987.

WESTON, J. FRED, and THOMAS E. COPELAND, *Managerial Finance*, 8th ed., Hinsdale, IL: The Dryden Press, 1986.

CHAPTER **16**

Going Private and Leveraged Buy-Outs

"Going private" refers to the transformation of a public corporation into a privately-held firm. There are a number of variations on this theme. In some cases, controlling shareholders seek to eliminate minority interests—called a "squeeze out." A critical element in these going-private transactions is fairness to minority/outside shareholders to avoid accusations of security fraud against controlling shareholders. When structured properly, going private can result in gains to both parties—this is the gains-sharing hypothesis.

Another means of going private, the leveraged buy-out (LBO), has become an increasingly frequent form of corporate restructuring. In general, an LBO is defined as the acquisition, financed largely by borrowing, of all the stock, or assets, of a hitherto public company by a small group of investors. This buying group may be sponsored by buy-out specialists (for example, Kohlberg, Kravis, Roberts & Co.) or investment bankers that arrange such deals and usually includes representation by incumbent management, although hostile LBOs are not unknown. Typically, the buying group forms a shell corporation to act as the legal entity making the acquisition. In the stock purchase format, the target shareholders simply sell their stock and all interest in the target corporation to the buying group and then the two firms may be merged. In the asset-purchase format, the target corporation sells its assets to the buying group. The original shareholders still own the target corporation, now merely a pool of cash with no tangible assets; the target corporation issues a liquidating dividend to its shareholders or becomes an investment company, using the pool of cash to make investments, whose proceeds are distributed to the shareholders. Sometimes the

TABLE 16.1

Going-Private Transactions

YEAR	TOTAL PUBLIC TAKEOVERS	GOING PRIVATE	PERCENT OF PUBLIC TAKEOVERS
1979	248	16	6.4
1980	173	13	7.5
1981	168	17	10.1
1982	180	31	17.2
1983	190	36	19.0
1984	211	57	27.0
1985	336	76	22.6
1986	386	76	19.7
1987	286	47	16.4
1988	464	125	26.9

Note: Included in the table are acquisitions (purchases of a controlling interest) of publicly traded companies.

Source: W. T. Grimm & Co., *Mergerstat Review 1988*, Chicago, IL, Figure 37, p. 91.

management is the prime moving force; these are called management buy-outs (MBOs). Since 1981, going-private transactions in each year represented 10 to 30 percent of all acquisitions of publicly traded companies (Table 16.1). The mean and median purchase prices have generally been increasing in the 1980s and reached $487.4 million and $79.8 million, respectively, in 1988. In the same year, the mean and median premia paid over market price were 33.8 percent and 26.3 percent, respectively (W. T. Grimm, 1988).

In an LBO, debt financing typically represents 50 percent or more of the purchase price. The debt is secured by the assets of the acquired firm and is usually amortized over a period of less than ten years. The debt is scheduled to be paid off as funds are generated by operations or from the sale of assets of the acquired firm. The sale of assets occurs when the investor group has been motivated to take control in part because of what it considers unwise or ill-fitting acquisitions by the firm in the past. There may also be limited equity participation on the part of outside investors such as pension funds and insurance companies, often with the proviso that the equity interest will be repurchased after a predetermined period to provide a specified yield. Following completion of the buy-out, the acquired company is usually run as a privately-held corporation rather than a public corporation, at least for a period of years, after which resale of the firm at a profit is anticipated. LBO activity has been referred to as "inventorying" companies by some analysts.

A variant of the going-private transactions is the unit management buy-out. In a unit MBO, a division or subsidiary of a public corporation is acquired from the parent company by a purchasing group led by (or including) an executive of the parent company or members of the unit's management. Unit MBOs represented more than 10 percent of total divestitures since 1981 (Table 16.2).

TABLE 16.2
Unit Management Buy-Outs

YEAR	DIVESTITURES	MANAGEMENT BUY-OUTS	PERCENT OF TOTAL DIVESTITURES
1978	820	49	6
1979	752	59	8
1980	666	47	7
1981	830	83	10
1982	875	115	13
1983	932	139	15
1984	900	122	14
1985	1,218	132	11
1986	1,259	144	11
1987	807	90	11
1988	894	89	10

Note: The unit MBOs here represent only those instances where it has been publicly announced that an executive of the parent company or members of the division's management were included among the purchasing group. Therefore, any trend depicted here is understated.
SOURCE: W. T. Grimm & Co., *Mergerstat Review 1988*, Chicago, IL, Figure 28, p. 82.

Like most going-private transactions, the majority of unit MBOs are also LBOs in the sense that the buying groups put up only a small part of the purchase price and borrow the rest. The average price paid in unit MBOs was $181.3 million in 1988 (W. T. Grimm, 1988). The average size of unit MBOs is much smaller than that of buy-outs of public companies. But the number of unit MBO transactions is about twice greater than the number of public company buy-outs.

Some corporations or divisions of corporations that had been taken private have recently gone public again. In a recent study, Muscarella and Vetsuypens (1988) estimate that these "reverse LBOs" represented about 5 percent of all LBOs for the period 1981–1986. Since LBOs are a fairly recent phenomenon, it may be expected that reverse LBOs will be more frequently observed in the future.

The LBO and MBO activity burgeoned after 1980 as did the merger and restructuring movement generally. Among the large, well-known companies involved in recent LBOs are Beatrice Foods, City Investing, Conoco Chemical, Denny's, Dr. Pepper, Levi Strauss, Metromedia, Uniroyal, and RJR Nabisco. The Beatrice Foods buy-out is an example of a hostile LBO led by former managers (of Esmark, Inc.) who had been displaced during Beatrice's spate of takeover activity during the early 1980s. The magnitude of buy-out and other restructuring activity reduced the amount of publicly-traded equity available on the stock markets by about $130 billion per year since 1983 (Salomon Brothers, 1987, p. 38). The Beatrice Foods buy-out alone involved over $5 billion in debt.

What developments in the economy caused these corporate control activities? What are the sources of gains, if any, from this type of ownership restructuring? Why would the managers of a public corporation want to take their firm private? What characteristics make for a good buy-out situation? What would induce lenders to permit the high leverage ratios typically involved? These are the questions that we try to answer in the following sections.

GENERAL ECONOMIC AND
FINANCIAL FACTORS

In Chapters 1 and 5 we have presented background on the merger and restructuring movement. We have argued that in substantial measure the increase in the number and dollar volume of merger and restructuring activity particularly since 1980 reflects underlying forces in the economic and financial environments. The same general forces that produced mergers and restructuring appear also to have stimulated increased use of leveraged buy-outs and management buy-outs. Indeed, sometimes an LBO or MBO is a defensive measure against a feared or unwanted takeover. On the other hand, sometimes the announcement of a going-private plan, an LBO, or an MBO will stimulate competing bids by outsiders. Further, unit MBOs have accounted for a consistent 11 percent of divestitures since 1985 (Table 16.2) and divestitures in turn have remained in the narrow range of 35 to 41 percent of the total number of M&A transactions since 1978 (W. T. Grimm, 1988). Thus, there are interactions between takeover and restructuring activity and LBO activity. We briefly summarize here materials we have presented earlier in Chapters 1 and 5 on the financial and economic background that appeared to have stimulated merger and restructuring activity.

One fundamental influence was the period of sustained economic growth since 1982. A new peak in all categories of M&A activity has been reached in this period of sustained business expansion, as all previous major merger waves were also observed in periods of expansionary environments. Total M&A transactions, divestitures, and leveraged buy-outs of public companies and divisions all followed similar patterns in the recent period; total M&A transactions and divestitures peaked in 1986 in terms of the number of transactions while leveraged buy-outs peaked in 1988. (Tables 1.5, 16.1, and 16.2).

Another pervasive influence was (somewhat unanticipated) persistent inflation which began to accelerate in the late 1960s and continued through 1982. The gross national product implicit price deflator during the period 1968–1982 increased by no less than 5 percent. Measured by the Consumer Price Index on all items, double-digit inflation or very close to that level was experienced in six out of the 14 years. The persistence of a relatively high level of inflation had a number of consequences. One was to cause the q-ratio to decline sharply. The q-ratio is the ratio of the market value of a firm to the replacement cost of its assets. When this ratio is less than one it is cheaper to buy capacity in the financial markets than in the real asset markets. The q-ratio moved from a peak of 1.3 in 1965 to a low of .52 in 1981. It began to rise in 1982 with the sharp rise in stock prices after mid-1982. When the q-ratio was as low as .52 in 1981 this meant that a firm could be purchased in the financial markets at almost half of what it would cost to replace the firm's assets in brick-and-mortar and inventories. This undoubtedly motivated some takeovers, although heightened takeover activity also takes place when the q-ratio is high.

In addition, the persistent inflation provided opportunities to realize tax savings through recapitalization. Since coupon payments on existing debt were not adjusted for inflation, real debt obligations declined with rising price levels. Thus the real levels of debt/equity ratios declined over the period of persistent but largely unanticipated inflation. (For the numbers refer again to Chapter 5.) Thus, opportunities existed for greater interest tax shields by releveraging business firms. On the other hand, increased free cash flows reflecting inflation and fixed interest payments (on old debt) may have allowed managers to increase self-aggrandizing but unprofitable expenditures, as suggested by Jensen (1986) when the situation called for increased leverage. For these reasons, firms that lagged in increasing leverage became inviting targets to outsiders who were ready, willing, and able to bring about the restructuring (Shleifer and Vishny, 1988). This in turn stimulated new forms of debt financing such as the use of high-yield bonds in the innovative financial markets. Developments in the financial markets may have been heightened by a succession of laws that deregulated financial institutions.

Other legislative factors also played a role. A succession of new tax laws stimulated restructuring and takeover activity. Particularly, the Economic Recovery Tax Act (ERTA) enacted in 1981 permitted old assets to be stepped up on purchase. These newly established high values could then be depreciated on an accelerated basis. In the period of high inflation, the nominal value of corporate assets was increased above their historical cost, enabling a large step-up in basis. Depreciation recapture was relatively small. Also under the General Utilities doctrine, the sales of assets in the liquidation process (actual or under technical legal terms) were not subject to capital gains taxes at the corporate level. (The General Utilities doctrine was repealed in the 1986 tax reform.)

Another legislative change that encouraged MBOs involved Employee Stock Ownership Plans (ESOPs). While these have been around for some years, the 1981 ERTA increased the ability of ESOPs to borrow from a bank to invest the funds in the firm's shares. The firm is able to treat as a deductible expense for tax purposes contributions to the ESOP sufficient to cover both the interest and the principal payments on the loan. In addition, in 1984 a further tax law change permitted banks to deduct half of their interest income on loans to ESOPs. This enabled the banks to make loans to ESOPs on relatively more favorable terms.

Finally, it is clear that there was a new antitrust climate beginning in 1980 when new appointees to the Federal Trade Commission and to the post of the Assistant Attorney General in charge of antitrust made it clear through public speeches and agency actions that the stringent prohibitions against horizontal and vertical mergers would no longer be supported. Efficiency considerations and a "new economic realism" were substituted for the older structural view which held that the effects on competition could be judged by market concentration ratios. At least three competing explanations for the change in the antitrust regulatory environment have been proffered. One is that the new administration had different political views. Second, the culmination of more than a decade of new empirical research from the academic community provided support for a dynamic competition view of the interactions among large firms. Third, most significant U.S. industries had become subject to intense competition from foreign firms. Thus, competitive pressures provided both the stimulus for restructuring and the recognition of these pressures was the basis for changed public opinion and regulatory policy toward mergers, takeovers, and restructuring.

It was these forces that increased merger activity and restructuring in a wide range of forms. LBOs and MBOs were part of this general pattern. Sometimes LBOs and MBOs were responses to the increased threat of takeover and their announcement often stimulated rival offers by outsiders. There appeared to be interacting influences taking place.

We next illustrate the nature of a typical leveraged buy-out operation. With this as a background, we discuss the conditions and the nature of industries in which LBO activity has taken place. We then review the empirical literature on the effects of LBO activity on shareholder wealth. Finally, we analyze theories on sources of gains in LBO activity.

ILLUSTRATION OF AN LBO

A simplified example will first illustrate the nature of a leveraged buy-out transaction. Wavell Corporation, a successful, publicly-traded manufacturer of glassware, was purchased in the 1970s by Eastern Pacific (EP), a large conglomerate, which during this period seemed bent on buying everything in sight. Eventually, however, Eastern Pacific began to focus its interests predominantly in the transportation, communications, and real estate industries. Wavell did not fit into the EP mold, and languished for a number of years. In 1983, when a small group of disgruntled Wavell executives began to consider the possibility of a leveraged buy-out, EP was more than willing to consider divestiture; Wavell's growth rates did not meet EP's objectives, and EP had never been comfortable with Wavell's product line. Although the glassware industry was not growing rapidly, there was a constant steady demand for Wavell's product. The company had very stable production costs and good contribution margins, which consistently resulted in a strong steady cash flow. The production equipment was old, but in good condition, and its replacement cost far exceeded its book value. Up until the EP acquisition, Wavell had always been managed well, if conservatively, and had little debt.

Wavell's current sales were $7,000,000 with EBIT of $650,000 and net income of $400,000. Negotiations between Wavell management and EP settled on a purchase price of $2,000,000 (representing a P/E ratio of 5). Because of the high replacement cost of Wavell's assets, its strong cash flow, and its relatively unencumbered balance sheet, Wavell was able to take on a large amount of debt. Banks supplied $1,200,000 of senior debt at an interest rate of 13 percent; this debt was secured by the finished goods inventory, and by net property, plant and equipment, and was to be amortized over a five-year period. An insurance company loan of $600,000 was also arranged in the form of subordinated debt, likewise to be amortized over a five-year period. The insurance company also took an equity position worth $100,000; Wavell was expected to repurchase this equity interest after five years for an amount which would provide the insurance company with a 40 percent annual yield. Finally, the Wavell management team put up $100,000 as their own equity position.

The following calculations illustrate the cash flow patterns which might be expected following the LBO. First, amortization tables are provided for the bank and insurance company loans:

Bank Loan[a]

YEAR	INTEREST	PRINCIPAL	BALANCE
1	156,000	185,177	1,014,823
2	131,927	209,250	805,573
3	104,724	236,453	569,120
4	73,986	267,191	301,929
5	39,248	301,929	—

[a] $1,200,000 at 13 percent; annual payment = $341,177.

Insurance Company Loan[a]

YEAR	INTEREST	PRINCIPAL	BALANCE
1	96,000	87,245	512,755
2	82,041	101,204	411,551
3	65,848	117,397	294,154
4	47,065	136,180	157,974
5	25,271	157,974	—

[a] $600,000 at 16 percent; annual payment = $183,245.

The following pro forma cash flow calculations are made on the basis of a number of conservative assumptions. First, no growth is assumed. The tax rate is assumed to be 40 percent. Depreciation is calculated on a straight-line basis over a period of 16.67 years (or 6 percent); accelerated depreciation would clearly enhance cash flows. Furthermore, it is unlikely that debt levels would decline to zero. As the original debt was repaid, it is likely that Wavell would take on additional debt, perhaps long term, to augment the declining interest tax shelter.

Pro Forma Cash Flows

	YEAR 0	YEAR 1	YEAR 2	YEAR 3	YEAR 4	YEAR 5
EBIT	650,000	650,000	650,000	650,000	650,000	650,000
−Interest		252,000	213,968	170,572	121,051	64,519
EBT		398,000	436,032	479,428	528,949	585,481
−Taxes		159,200	174,413	191,771	211,580	234,192
NI		238,800	261,619	287,657	317,369	351,289
+Depreciation		120,000	120,000	120,000	120,000	120,000
CFBDR[a]		358,800	381,619	407,657	437,369	471,289
−Principal Repaid		272,422	310,454	353,850	403,371	459,903
Cash Flow Cushion		86,378	71,165	53,807	33,998	11,386
Equity	200,000	438,800	700,419	988,076	1,305,445	1,656,734
Debt	1,800,000	1,527,578	1,217,124	863,274	459,903	—
Total Assets	2,000,000	1,966,378	1,917,543	1,851,350	1,765,348	1,656,734
% Debt	90%	78%	63%	47%	26%	0%

[a] CFBDR: Cash flow before debt repayment.

If we now assume Wavell is sold at the end of year 5 for book value (again a very conservative assumption given the track record in the pro forma cash flows), we can calculate the annual compounded rate of return on equity as follows:

$$ROE = \left(\frac{1,656,734}{200,000}\right)^{1/5} - 1 = 53\%\ \text{annual compounded rate of return}$$

Since Wavell is required to pay only 40 percent annually on the insurance company's equity interest, a payment of $537,824 would be sufficient to repurchase this equity. This would leave $1,118,910 for the management group, or an annual return of over 62 percent on their investment.

ELEMENTS OF TYPICAL LBO OPERATION

The preceding analysis has been a simplified (and perhaps unrealistic) example of an LBO operation. If we abstract from this example and many more real-world LBOs, the following picture emerges. The first stage of the operation consists of raising the cash required for the buy-out and devising a management incentive system. Typically, about 10 percent of the cash is put up by the investor group headed by the company's top managers and/or buy-out specialists. This becomes the equity base of the new firm. Outside investors provide the remainder of the equity. The managers also receive stock price-based incentive compensation in the form of stock options or warrants. Thus, the equity share of management (not including directors) will grow to a higher percentage, possibly to more than 30 percent. Frequently, managers are also provided with incentive compensation plans based on objective results such as earnings.

About 50 to 60 percent of the required cash is raised by borrowing against the company's assets in secured bank acquisition loans. The bank loan may be syndicated with several commercial banks. This portion of the debt can also be provided by an insurance company or limited partnership specializing in venture capital investments and leveraged buy-outs. The rest of the cash is obtained by issuing senior and junior subordinated debt in a private placement (with pension funds, insurance companies, venture capital firms, and so on) or public offering as "high-yield" notes or bonds (that is, junk bonds). Subordinated debt is often referred to as "mezzanine money" and carries payment-in-kind provisions. If adverse surprises result in the inability to meet interest obligations on portions of mezzanine financing, the debt holders receive more of the same paper in lieu of cash interest payments.

In the second stage of the operation, the organizing sponsor group buys all the outstanding shares of the company and takes it private (in the stock-purchase format) or purchases all the assets of the company (in the asset-purchase format). In the latter case, the buying group forms a new, privately-held corporation. To reduce the debt by paying off a part of the bank loan, the new owners sell off some parts of the corporation and may begin slashing inventory.

In the third stage, the management strives to increase profits and cash flows by cutting operating costs and changing marketing strategies. It will consolidate or reorganize production facilities, improve inventory control and accounts receivables management, change product quality, product mix, customer service, and pricing, trim employment through attrition, and try to extract better terms from suppliers. It may even lay off employees and cut spending on research and new plants and equipment as long as these are necessary to meet payment on the swollen debt. (However, in reviewing business plans, lenders would require that provisions for capital expenditures be adequate.)

In the fourth stage, the investor group may take the company public again if the "leaner and meaner" company emerges stronger and the goals of the group are achieved. This reverse LBO is effected through public equity offering, referred to as secondary initial public offering (SIPO). One purpose of this reconversion to public ownership is to create liquidity for existing stockholders. Aside from this, a study of 72 firms engaging in reverse LBOs over the period 1976–1987 reveals that 86 percent of the firms intended to use the SIPO proceeds to lower the company's leverage (Muscarella and Vetsuypens, 1988). Only eight out of 72 firms raised the funds for capital expenditures. The reverse LBOs are undertaken mostly by ex post successful LBO companies, and indeed the equity participants at the time of the LBO realized a median return of 1965.6 percent on their equity investment, or a median annualized rate of return of 268.4 percent by the time of the SIPO. (The median length of time between the LBO and the SIPO was 29 months.)

CONDITIONS AND CIRCUMSTANCES OF GOING-PRIVATE BUY-OUTS

Typical targets include manufacturing firms in basic, nonregulated industries with at least predictable and/or low financing (capital expenditure) requirements. Stability and predictability of earnings are essential in the face of substantial interest payments and loan amortization. The financing needs of very high-growth firms would be likely to put a strain on debt service capability. High-tech firms are less appropriate since they generally have a shorter history of demonstrated profitability, as well as greater business risk; they generally have fewer leveragable assets. Furthermore they command high P/E multiples well above book value because of growth opportunities (which require financing), whereas the purchase price in LBOs is typically only slightly above book value.

These generalizations are supported by the empirical data developed by Lehn and Poulsen (1988b). They studied a sample of 108 leveraged buy-outs during the period 1980–1984. Almost half of the firms were in five industries, retailing, textiles, food processing, apparel, and bottled and canned soft drinks. Note that these are all consumer nondurable goods industries for which the income elasticity of demand would be relatively low. Hence, these industries would be least subject to fluctuations in sales as the level of gross national product fluctuated. Note also that all of these are mature industries, with limited growth opportunities.

The success of an LBO is enhanced by a track record of capable management. The company should have a strong market position in its industry to enable it to withstand economic fluctuations and competitors' assaults. The balance sheet should be highly liquid; it should show a large, relatively unencumbered asset base for use as collateral, particularly a high proportion of tangible assets whose fair market value exceeds net book value.

The transaction requires sufficient leverage to maximize return on equity, but not so much as to drain funds needed to sustain growth. Lenders are persuaded by interest rates 3 to 5 percentage points above the prime rate and by the characteristics of the company and its collateral. Borrowing capacity is favorably affected by large amounts of cash or cash equivalents, and undervalued assets (hidden equity) whose market value exceeds depreciated book value. Lenders may also look to subsidiaries of the LBO candidate whose liquidation would not impact ongoing operations. In addition, lenders such as venture capital and insurance companies, which also take an equity interest in the LBO, look to the high rate of return they expect on their equity participation. Last, but by no means least, lenders must have confidence in the management group spearheading the LBO, whether incumbent or external. The managers involved typically have a proven record as highly capable executives. They are betting their reputations on the success of the venture, and are highly motivated by the potential for large personal wealth gains which might not be achievable in larger public corporations.

Among the sources of MBO targets are divestitures of unwanted divisions by public companies, privately-owned businesses whose current growth rate is insufficient to provide opportunities for capable management or to attract corporate acquirers, and public companies whose shares are selling at low earnings multiples representing a substantial discount from book value.

EMPIRICAL RESULTS ON GOING PRIVATE AND LBOS

The earliest comprehensive study of going-private transactions was by DeAngelo, DeAngelo, and Rice (1984). Their sample consisted of 72 firms which made 72 initial and nine subsequent (revived) going-private proposals during the period 1973–1980. The median market value of total equity was about $6 million for the sample of 45 pure going-private proposals (that is, without third-party equity participation in the private firm) and somewhat over $15 million for 23 leveraged buy-out proposals. Thus, the firms were relatively small. In addition, management held a relatively large ownership position. In 72 going-private proposals management's mean preoffer ownership fraction was 45 percent with a median measure of 51 percent. For the 23 LBOs with third-party participation, the mean and median were 32 percent and 33 percent, respectively.

DeAngelo, DeAngelo, and Rice found that the average change in stockholder wealth at announcement was a plus 22 percent, which was highly significant from a statistical standpoint. The cumulative increase in stockholder wealth over the 40 days including the announcement date was over 30 percent. They note that public stockholder gains measured as the average premium above market (two months before the proposal) were over 56 percent in 57 sample proposals involving all payment in cash.

DeAngelo, DeAngelo, and Rice also tested for the effects of the announcement of a going-private withdrawal. Their sample was 18 firms for the period 1973–1980. The announcement effect was a negative change in stockholder wealth of almost 9 percent. However, since the cumulative prediction error for the 40 days up to the announcement date was almost 13 percent, the cumulative prediction error for the 40 days through the announcement date was a plus 4 percent. During the subsequent 40 days the cumulative prediction error rises to about 8 percent. They note three potential explanations for the positive returns net of both proposal and withdrawal announcement effects. One is an information effect which causes a permanent upward revaluation of the firm's prospects. Second, a positive probability may remain that managers will revive the going-private proposal at a future date. Third, the positive return may reflect the possibility that another party will offer to acquire the firm.

The Lehn and Poulsen study (1988a) covered 284 going-private transactions for the period 1980–1987. The mean equity value for the Lehn and Poulsen sample was $191 million. The size of going-private transactions increased significantly during the period covered. In a separate study, Lehn and Poulsen (1988b) report that the average pre-LBO debt/equity ratio for a sample of 58 firms was about 46 percent. For the post-LBO period the average debt/equity ratio rose to over 552 percent. Thus, substantial increases in leverage took place.

Lehn and Poulsen (1988b) found that the average net-of-market stock price reaction to the announcement for 92 leveraged buy-outs was slightly over 20 percent, measured over a period of 20 days before the announcement to 20 days after the announcement. The result was highly significant from a statistical standpoint. The average value of the premium paid in the LBO offer compared to the market price of the firm's common stock 20 trading days prior to the announcement was 41 percent, calculated for the 72 leveraged buy-outs in the sample that were all cash offers. These results are somewhat lower than those found by DeAngelo, DeAngelo, and Rice. The Lehn and Poulsen sample represented larger firms for a later period during which there was a more favorable public policy attitude toward LBOs. Also the Lehn and Poulsen study covered LBOs during the 1980–1984 period when the takeover and restructuring market was much more active. In addition, they measured the premium from a reference point 20 days prior to the announcement whereas DeAngelo, DeAngelo, and Rice measured the premium from a reference point two months before the announcement.

Another empirical study was performed by Lowenstein (1985). His sample was 28 management buy-out proposals made from 1979 to 1984; each valued at least $100 million to the shareholders at the winning bid price. The percentage of shares owned by management for the Lowenstein sample was much smaller than for the DeAngelo, DeAngelo, and Rice sample. It was only 3.8 percent when measured by the median and 6.5 percent measured by the mean. In 15 new companies formed as the result of going private, management shares increased to 10.4 percent measured by the median and to 24.3 percent measured by the mean.

Lowenstein also measured the premium of the winning bid over the market price 30 days before the first significant announcement. He found that on all bids the premium was 58 percent measured by the median and 56 percent when measured by the mean. However, the size of the premium was higher the more bids that were involved in the going-private transactions. When three or more bids were received, the premium rose to 76 percent when measured by the median and 69 percent when measured by the mean. The premium of 11 successful third-party bids over the management bid was 8 percent (median) and 14 percent (mean). Lowenstein argues strongly for the creation of an auction which would insure that multiple bids would be received. He acknowledges difficulties in implementing such a proposal. In addition, we would observe that the relatively small percentage of increase in third-party bids over the management bids casts doubt on the need for such a proposal. Furthermore, the Lowenstein findings corroborate those of DeAngelo, DeAngelo, and Rice in observing premiums for public stockholders of 50 percent or more over their market price a month or two before the announcement. This would appear to be a very substantial reward to public shareholders. If they left nothing "on the table" for the entrepreneurs involved in the LBO activity, it would leave little incentive for the transactions to take place. The subsequent losses to the public shareholders would be much greater than the relatively small kicking up of the bid when third-party offers are involved. Besides, market competition assures that if the entrepreneurs are taking too much, this will stimulate other nonmanagement outside offers. But in any event it is difficult to feel that a great injustice is done to the public shareholders or the subsequent minority shareholders since they have received premiums exceeding 50 percent.

Later studies also find large premiums and abnormal announcement returns to prebuy-out shareholders (Amihud, 1988; Kaplan, 1988; Muscarella and Vetsuypens 1988; Travlos and Cornett, 1990).

For divisional management buy-outs, Hite and Vetsuypens (1988) find small but statistically significant wealth gains to parent company shareholders. The mean abnormal return during the two-day period surrounding the buy-out announcement was 0.55 percent for their sample of 151 unit MBOs. Since the mean sale price of the divisions represented only 16.6 percent of the market value of equity of an average seller, the abnormal return would translate into 3.3 percent for a full LBO, which is much lower than the gains found for LBOs above. The authors suggest that divisional buy-outs reallocate ownership of corporate assets to higher-valued uses and that parent company shareholders share in the expected benefits of this change in ownership structure. For a sample of 45 divisional buy-outs which subsequently went public (after an average period of 34 months), Muscarella and Vetsuypens (1988) report a mean abnormal return of 1.98 percent to the seller in the two days around the announcement.

SOURCES OF GAINS AND
EMPIRICAL EVIDENCE

The empirical evidence is consistent among studies in finding that the premiums paid are 40 percent or more of the market price of the stock a month or two before the announcement of the buy-out. The standard residual analysis shows that these gains are substantially sustained in stock price performance after the completion of the change in ownership control. What are the sources of these large gains? A number of explanations have been offered: (1) taxes, (2) management incentives, (3) wealth transfer effects, (4) asymmetric information and underpricing, and (5) efficiency considerations. Each is considered in turn.

Tax Benefits

The tax benefits are clearly there. The question is whether they are the only factor, the major factor, or simply a facilitating factor added to more fundamental business and economic forces. It is difficult to quantify the degree. Some students of the subject ascribe a major role to taxes. Lowenstein (1985), for example, argues that most of the premium paid is financed from tax savings. He states that the new company can expect to operate tax free for as long as five to six years. Of course, an LBO is often sold after about this period of time when its debt/equity ratio has been pulled down from about 10 to 1 or under.

The sources of the tax gain are standard and have been detailed in previous pages. They include the following. The high leverage provides the benefits of interest savings. Asset step-ups can provide higher asset values for depreciation expenses. This tax advantage became much more difficult under the Tax Reform Act of 1986 (Macris, 1988). The accelerated depreciation provisions of the 1981 ERTA had enhanced this benefit. Lowenstein (1985, p. 760) points out that the extent of write-up of assets depended in part on the ability to assign large value to items for which there is little recapture (inventory, film libraries, mineral resources, or real estate) than to items for which recapture may be substantial (equipment).

Tax benefits were further augmented by the Tax Reform Act of 1984 which broadened the benefits of the use of ESOPs. The ESOP purchases the shares using borrowed funds. The borrowings are secured by the employer's schedule of contributions to the fund. Both the interest and principal on the ESOP are deductible and the lender can exclude one half of the interest income from taxable income. These are substantial benefits indeed. These changes increased the use of ESOPs in management buy-outs, representing tangible evidence that this particular tax factor was of importance. However, Kaplan (1988) suggests that ESOP loans are infrequently used due to nontax costs. One such cost pointed out by Kaplan is that all contributing employees share in the equity and this will not leave an adequate equity stake to the managers and the buy-out promoter.

Kaplan also provides empirical evidence on the potential value of tax benefits. While it is not difficult to estimate current tax savings on new buy-out debt, valuation of these savings flows is dependent on, among other factors, whether the debt is permanent and the appropriate marginal tax rate applied to the interest deduction. Further, there is the argument that the interest rate on corporate debt is higher to compensate for higher personal taxation on interest income than equity income, and thus the use of debt to obtain tax savings may have no value. Assuming a marginal tax rate of 46 percent and permanent new debt yielded interest deductions worth a median 1.297 times the premium. A 30 percent tax rate and a maturity of eight years for new debt implied a median value equal to .262 times the premium. In Kaplan's sample of 76 companies, 33 were known to have elected to step up the basis of their assets, and the median value was estimated at .304 times the premium.

These tax benefits appear large but Kaplan argues that they are predictable and thus appropriable by the prebuy-out shareholders. However, Kaplan finds that only a portion of the tax benefits can be attributed to unused debt capacity or the inefficient use of tax benefits prior to buy-out. This implies that a large portion of the tax benefits are the result of buy-out and the buy-out structure may be necessary to realize those benefits. It turns out that the buy-out companies eliminated their federal taxes in the first two years after the buy-out.

In regression analyses, the excess return to prebuy-out shareholders is significantly related to the potential tax benefits generated by the buy-out, but the excess return to postbuy-out shareholders is not. Kaplan interprets this result as indicating that prebuy-out shareholders capture most of the tax benefits. The premium paid to prebuy-out shareholders is also found to be positively related to the pre-LBO tax liability to equity ratio by Lehn and Poulsen (1988b). This is interpreted as evidence that tax benefits play a significant role in LBOs.

The preceding findings on strong tax benefits are at odds with the regression result of Travlos and Cornett (1990) that capital structure change-induced effects fail to explain the abnormal returns experienced at the announcement of buy-outs. One reason for this result might be that both the dependent and the independent variables only partly capture the full effects that they are supposed to measure. Travlos and Cornett (1990, p. 20) defend their results by stating that increased leverage serves no long-term purpose but rather "functions primarily as a part of the mechanism to take the company private" (quoted from Hite and Owers, 1983, p. 15). The temporary nature of at least some portion of the new debt is also shown by Muscarella and Vetsuypens (1988). Their sample of 72 reverse LBO firms has an average debt to total value ratio of over .90 at the time of LBO, an average debt to total asset ratio of .78 prior to the SIPO and the same ratio of .60 after the SIPO.

The preceding results indicate that tax factors can improve a deal, but come into play if some underlying business factors are also operating. This is where other factors come into consideration.

Management Incentives and Agency Cost Effects

It is argued that management's ownership stake is enhanced by the LBO or MBO so that their incentives are stronger for improved performance. Some profitable investment proposals call for disproportionate effort of managers so that they will be undertaken only if managers are given a correspondingly disproportionate share of the proposal's income (Easterbrook and Fischel, 1982). However, such managerial compensation contracts might be viewed as "overly generous" by outside shareholders. In this case, going-private buy-outs facilitate compensation arrangements that induce managers to undertake those proposals (DeAngelo, DeAngelo, and Rice, 1984; Travlos and Cornett, 1990). This reasoning is similar to the argument that the threat of a hostile takeover decreases incentives for managers and employees to invest in firm-specific human capital (DeAngelo and DeAngelo, 1987, p. 107). Going-private buy-outs can guarantee compensation for those investments.

When information on managerial performance is costly, incumbent management can be mistakenly replaced. Managers waste resources to defend their position to potential proxy contestants and to outside shareholders. They may undertake projects that are less profitable but have payoffs more easily observable by outsiders (DeAngelo and DeAngelo, 1985). Going private may eliminate these costs. In many buy-outs, the promoters retain a large equity stake and serve on the board. The equity stake and their desire to protect their reputation as efficient promoters give them the incentive to closely monitor postbuy-out management. This will decrease the information asymmetry between the managers and shareholders. In this view, the concentrated ownership resulting from an LBO represents reunification of ownership and control, which must reduce agency costs.

Finally, free cash flows motivate managers to use them in self-aggrandizing expenditures rather than to pay them out as dividends. Increasing debt through leveraged buy-outs commits the cash flows to debt payment, which is an effective substitute for dividend payment. Managers have less discretion over debt payments than over dividends. Thus, the increased debt reduces managerial discretion in the allocation of free cash flows; the agency costs of free cash flows will be decreased in LBOs (Jensen, 1986). If managers are risk averse, the increased debt will also put pressure on managers and give them an incentive to improve the firm's performance to prevent bankruptcy (since bankruptcy will cause a decline in their compensation and value of human capital). The LBO thus represents a debt-bonding activity; it bonds (precommits) managers to meet newly set targets.

These agency-cost arguments contrast with the notion that the internal controls of the firm already align managers' interests to those of the stockholders. (See Chapter 2.) The internal controls are compensation arrangements and settling up, stock options, bonuses based on performance, and surveillance by the board of directors. If internal controls do not take hold sufficiently, the market for corporate control and the threat of takeovers will insure that managers operate to their full potential. However, a study by Jensen and Murphy (1988) finds that actual executive compensation contracts are insufficient to provide optimal incentives for managers; and that most CEOs hold trivial fractions of their firms' stock, although stock ownership generally swamps incentives generated by compensation. The median fractional ownership of CEOs in their sample of 73 large manufacturing firms is only .16 percent, while the average is 1.2 percent. The CEO salary plus bonus changes only two cents for every $1,000 change in equity value. They ascribe the low relation between pay and performance to pressures from other stakeholders and the public including the media.

Empirical evidence consistent with the management incentive rationale is reported in many studies. First, ownership shares of management are increased substantially after MBOs. For a sample of 76 MBOs in 1980–1986, Kaplan (1988) reports prebuy-out and postbuy-out equity ownership of management. The median prebuy-out ownerships of the CEO, all managers, and all managers and directors are 1.4 percent, 5.88 percent, and 19.3 percent, respectively. (The corresponding mean values are 7.13 percent, 12.20 percent, and 22.89 percent.) The median postbuy-out ownership fractions of the CEO and all managers are 6.40 percent and 22.63 percent, respectively. Thus, in terms of median values, the management ownership increases by about three times the prebuy-out value. For a reverse LBO sample, Muscarella and Vetsuypens (1988) report the before-SIPO (postbuy-out) and after-SIPO management equity ownership fractions. The median before-SIPO fractions for the most highly paid officer, three most highly paid officers, and all officers and directors are 9.2 percent, 26.1 percent, and 61.6 percent, respectively. The management ownership remains high even after the firm goes public through a SIPO. The median after-SIPO fractions are 6.5 percent, 18.8 percent, and 44.2 percent. Evidence on the concentration of ownership is provided by Smith (1989). The median post-MBO ownership share of all officers, outside directors, and other major holders is 95.26 percent. The corresponding pre-MBO ownership share is 75.45 percent.

The second set of evidence on management incentives is provided by Muscarella and Vetsuypens. They document various management incentive plans in LBO firms. Almost all firms in their sample (69 out of 72) had implemented at least one type of incentive plan under private ownership and about 75 percent of the sample firms had at least two separate incentive plans. Among the different types of incentive plans, stock option plans and stock appreciation rights were the most popular. The importance of incentive plans is also vividly described in most anecdotes on individual LBOs. For example, see Anders (1988).

The third and most important evidence on the present hypothesis is the operating performance of LBO firms. However, it should be pointed out in advance that the following results on operating performance may be subject to a selection bias because the reverse LBO firms or firms with postbuy-out data available could be only the more successful ones. Muscarella and Vetsuypens describe the multiple restructuring activities under private ownership. Based on examination of the SIPO prospecti of the firms that went public again after the LBO, they find more than two thirds of all firms (54 out of 72) disclose at least one restructuring activity undertaken since the LBO. Among the activities are asset redeployment (reorganization of production facilities, divestitures, and so on), initiation of cost reduction programs, changes in marketing strategies involving product mix, product quality, pricing, and customer service. Judging from the tone of the offering prospecti, the authors suggest that these activities "represent a significant departure from pre-LBO strategies which would not have been implemented by the predecessor company" (p. 13). As a result of these restructuring activities, the firms under private ownership realized substantial improvement in operating performance. In 35 cases for which data were available, total sales increased by 9.4 percent in real terms for the median firm between the LBO and SIPO (a median period of 29 months) and gross profits and operating profits increased 27.0 and 45.4 percent, respectively.

Kaplan (1988) also provides evidence of improved operating performance following an LBO. The level of operating income in LBO firms increased more than in other firms in the same industry during the first two years after the LBO, but sales growth rates were lower. The results on operating income and sales suggest that the operating margins of LBO firms will improve relative to their industries. Statistical tests by Kaplan confirm this proposition. One potential source of operating improvement was found to be in the area of working-capital management as the inventory/sales ratio declined in the postbuy-out years.

Similar results are obtained by Smith (1989). She finds that both the profit or before-tax operating margin and the ratio of sales to operating assets or employees increase significantly relative to other firms in the same industry. Improvement in working-capital management is evidenced by both a reduction in the inventory holding period and receivables collection period. There is little evidence that cutbacks in research and development, advertising, and maintenance are responsible for the increase in operating cash flows. Although the ratio of capital expenditures to sales is reduced after the MBO, this should not affect the short-run operating gains. Smith also provides regression results that suggest a positive relation between the change in operating returns and the changes in financial leverage and percentage stockholdings by officers, outside directors, and other major stockholders. These results are consistent with the debt-bonding effect, managerial-incentive effect, and the improved monitoring (concentrated ownership) effect. Smith conducts various empirical analyses to provide evidence that the improved post-MBO performance is not attributable to the sample selection procedures in her study. Overall, the results do not tend to indicate selection bias. Smith also considers whether favorable inside information on future cash flows explains the observed increase in operating returns associated with MBOs and provides indirect evidence that the improved performance does not reflect the realization of gains privately anticipated by the buy-out group.

Travlos and Cornett find a statistically significant negative correlation between the abnormal return to prebuy-out shareholders and the P/E ratio of the firm relative to its industry. They interpret this result as being consistent with the joint hypothesis that the more severe the agency problems of the going private firms, the lower their P/E ratios; and that the lower this ratio, the larger the room for improvement, and thus the greater the efficiency gains to be obtained by taking the firm private. But this interpretation may not be correct because a low P/E ratio may simply mean lower growth opportunities. The Jensen hypothesis predicts that the LBO firms are mature firms with limited growth opportunities.

The theory of agency costs involving free cash flow also has empirical support. Lehn and Poulsen (1988a) posit that a direct relationship between measures of cash flows and premiums paid to prebuy-out shareholders is consistent with Jensen's hypothesis. Their data for 149 LBOs in the 1984–1987 period show highly significant direct relationships between the undistributed cash flow to equity value ratio and the premium paid even after controlling for the effects of tax savings (by using the tax to equity variable). The likelihood of going private is also directly related to the cash flow to equity value ratio in their data for LBOs and matched control firms. Further evidence that appears consistent with the free cash flow argument of Jensen includes the results that most LBOs take place in mature industries and that the growth rates and capital expenditures of LBO firms (without controlling for divestitures after the buy-out) are lower than their industry control sample in both the pre- and postbuy-out periods (Kaplan, 1988; Lehn and Poulsen, 1988a).

However, one potential difficulty of the free cash flow argument is that it does not directly predict the strengthened incentive compensation schemes after the buy-out, which are evidenced in the study by Muscarella and Vetsuypens. They also find an elasticity of compensation (defined as salary plus bonus) to sales of 0.46 for the most highly paid officer in their sample, whereas Murphy (1985) reports that the typical elasticity appears to be about 0.3. But it may be the case that going private enables the firm to institute more incentive compensation plans, which may not be possible for public firms due to the political process (Jensen and Murphy, 1988).

Wealth Transfer Effects

Critics of leveraged buy-outs argue that the payment of premiums in these transactions may represent wealth transfers to shareholders from other stake-holders including bondholders, preferred stockholders, employees, and the government. Increased efficiency cannot automatically be inferred from the rise in the equity value. Since debt is increased in LBOs, at least part of the increased value can be offset by a reduction in the value of the firm's outstanding bonds and preferred stock. Many bond covenants do protect existing bondholders in the event of changes of control, debt issues, and so forth, but some do not. The newly issued debt may not be subordinated to the outstanding bonds and/or may have shorter duration than the outstanding bonds. Further, the "absolute priority rule" for a senior security may not be strictly adhered to in bankruptcy court decisions.

Empirical evidence on the change in the value of outstanding debt at the time of LBO announcement is mixed. While Lehn and Poulsen (1988b) find no evidence that (nonconvertible) bondholders and preferred stockholders lose value, Travlos and Cornett report statistically significant losses at the announcement of going-private proposals. However, the losses were small relative to the gains to the prebuy-out shareholders, which implies that wealth transfer cannot be an economically significant factor in explaining the shareholder gain. Such anecdotes as the lawsuit filed against RJR Nabisco by large bondholders do suggest that bondholders can lose substantially in certain cases (Quigley, 1988, pp. 1, 5). In the Nabisco case, it was charged that its $5 billion in highly rated bonds had lost nearly 20 percent ($1 billion) in market value since the announcement of a management-led buy-out proposal involving new borrowing of $16 billion (Greenwald, 1988, p. 69).

Wealth may also be transferred from current employees to the new investors in hostile takeovers (Shleifer and Summers, 1988). The hostile bidder can break implicit contracts between the firm and employees by reducing employment and lowering wages to expropriate quasi-rents accruing to their past firm-specific investments. Whether this argument can be extended to leveraged buy-outs is an empirical question, although the supposed hostility against existing employees does not appear to be present in most LBOs. Management turnover in buy-out firms is lower than in an average firm, although sometimes a new management team is brought in after the LBO (Muscarella and Vetsuypens, 1988). The number of employees grows more slowly in an LBO firm than in others in the same industry and sometimes even decreases, but this appears to be the result of postbuy-out divestitures and more efficient use of labor. (Kaplan, 1988; Muscarella and Vetsuypens, 1988).

There is also the argument that the tax benefits in an LBO constitute a subsidy from the public and cause a loss in tax revenues of the government (Lowenstein, 1985). Indeed, as discussed earlier, there is evidence that the premia paid in LBOs are positively related to potential tax benefits at the corporate level. However, the net effect of an LBO on government tax revenues may be positive (Amihud, 1988; Morrow, 1988). Shareholders pay ordinary income taxes on the capital gains realized on the sale of their stock in the LBO tender offer. Of course, these gains might be realized even without the LBO, but the shareholders could postpone the capital gains taxes to a later date or even eliminate them by bequeathing stocks in an estate. If the firm becomes stronger and goes public at a later date, which is suggested by the empirical evidence reviewed earlier, then the LBO investor group will pay capital gains taxes and the firm will pay more corporate taxes. Amihud also points out that many of the tax benefits could be realized without LBOs and some advantages such as the stepped-up tax basis of assets are almost totally eliminated now.

Asymmetric Information and Underpricing

Large premiums paid by the buy-out investors are also consistent with the argument that managers or the investors have more information on the value of the firm than the public shareholders. In this theory, a buy-out proposal signals to the market that future operating income will be larger than previously expected or that the firm is less risky than perceived by the public.

A variant of this theory is that the investor group believes the new company is worth more than the purchase price and thus the prebuy-out shareholders are receiving less than adequately informed shareholders would receive (Goroff, 1985). This theory amounts to the claim that the MBO proposal cannot reveal much of the information and establish a competitive price for the target firm (despite the fact that a special committee of the board of directors who do not participate in the new company has to approve the proposal).

Kaplan provides evidence that runs counter to these arguments. He finds that informed persons (managers and directors) often do not participate in the buy-out even though these nonparticipants typically hold large equity stakes in the buy-out firm (a median share of 10 percent compared to 4.67 percent held by the management participants). Also, as indicated earlier, Smith (1989) provides indirect evidence that asymmetric information cannot explain the improved performance of bought-out firms. For instance, MBO proposals which fail due to board/stockholder rejection, withdrawal, or a higher outside bid are not followed by any increase in operating returns among the involved firms.

Efficiency Considerations

The other arguments are related to efficiency considerations. The decision process can be more efficient under private ownership. Major new programs do not have to be justified by detailed studies and reports to the board of directors. Action can be taken more speedily, and sometimes getting a new investment program underway early is critical for its success. In addition, a public firm must publish information that may disclose vital and competitively sensitive information to rival firms. These arguments are difficult to evaluate and empirical evidence on these has yet to come. Stockholders' servicing costs and other related expenses do not appear to be a major factor in going private (Travlos and Cornett, 1990).

EVIDENCE ON POSTBUY-OUT
EQUITY VALUE

We now turn to statistical evidence on how the investment in an LBO has fared and what has determined the rate of return. Muscarella and Vetsuypens (1988) first compare the total value of the firm at the time of the LBO (the purchase price paid plus the book value of debt assumed) to the value of the firm at the time of its SIPO (the book value of outstanding debt plus the market value of equity minus any proceeds from the SIPO used to retire existing debt). The median rate of change in firm value for the 41 companies that went public again was 89.0 percent for the entire period between an LBO and the subsequent SIPO. The mean rate was 169.7 percent. The median annualized rate of change was 36.6 percent. The median change in equity value was 1,965.6 percent. The median annualized rate of return on equity was 268.4 percent. Even though the SIPO firms presumably belong to the more successful group among the bought-out firms, these returns are impressive.

The total shareholder wealth change was positively and statistically significantly correlated with the fraction of shares owned by officers and directors. Thus, larger shareholder gains under private ownership are associated with greater managerial stock ownership. Also, the correlation between the size-adjusted measure of salary and shareholder wealth was positive and statistically significant. This finding is consistent with the notion that well-compensated managers work harder to increase shareholder wealth. But the causality might be the reverse. The change in equity values was also associated with the improvements in accounting measures of performance. Thus, it is possible that the improved corporate performance led both to increased managerial compensation and higher equity value. Further, the improved corporate performance does not disprove that exploiting inside information alone can explain postbuy-out shareholder gains.

Other interesting results are also obtained by Kaplan. He first notes that returns on *leveraged* equity in a period of rising stock prices should be very large because interest payments are fixed. Thus, the really interesting comparison should be between the total return to all capital (debt and equity) invested in the buy-out and the return on a stock index like the S&P 500. He finds for his sample of 21 buy-outs that the median excess return to postbuy-out investors (both debt and equity) is 26.1 percent in excess of the return on the S&P 500 (the length of time is not stated). He suggests that this excess return is close to the premium earned by prebuy-out shareholders. This implies that the prebuy-out shareholders actually share handsomely in the gains to the buy-out. Since the 21 companies in the sample had publicly available valuation of their securities, the result may be subject to selection bias; that is, they may represent the more successful of the LBOs.

Finally, Kaplan's regression analysis shows that the excess return to postbuy-out investors is significantly related to the change in operating income, but not to the potential tax benefits. It is shown that the prebuy-out shareholders capture most of the tax benefits which become publicly available information at the time of the LBO.

CONCLUSION:
TOWARDS A THEORY OF MBOs

The empirical evidence available and some of the arguments on the sources of gains provide the possibility of formulating a theory of LBOs. As in the case of M&A activity, a complete theory would have to be able to explain various aspects of LBOs including their motivation, firm and industry characteristics, and their timing. We conclude the present chapter with an attempt to formulate such a theory by employing basic concepts that were introduced in Chapter 2, especially the theory of Alchian and Woodward (1987).

The ownership and organizational structures of the firm depend on its vulnerability to opportunistic behavior among the stakeholders. Two kinds of opportunism are distinguished, holdup and moral hazard. Specialized investments are vulnerable to holdup or expropriation of their quasi-rents. Managers make firm-specific investments (or efforts) and their compensation includes returns, or quasi-rents to such investments. Part or all of these quasi-rents may be expropriated by shareholders, labor and/or other stakeholders. Managers will be led to seek protection of quasi-rents accruing to their firm-specific or activity-specific investments by owning more shares or by holding incentive compensation contracts more tightly related to performance. Such protection is available through MBOs.

Moral hazard arises in debt/creditor relations, among others, and is more likely to arise when the firm's assets are "plastic," allowing a wide range of discretionary decisions by the user. As discussed in Chapter 5, the debt/equity ratio is higher for firms with implastic assets and whose activities are easier to monitor.

These considerations suggest that leveraged buy-outs will occur in firms or industries where managers are vulnerable to expropriation and at the same time assets are implastic to allow greater borrowing to finance buy-outs. These conditions are likely to exist in mature firms with limited growth opportunities and stable cash flows. First, the growth rate of the firm is inadequate to provide managerial incentives in the general form of promotion or managing a larger or more rapidly growing company (usually accompanied with larger compensation). Note that compensation that is not commensurate with the value of contributions represents a form of expropriation. Second, a given improvement in managerial performance in mature firms requires greater strain and more sweat because of less favorable business opportunities relative to growing industries. An application of a typical pay/performance ratio to these firms will be insufficient to compensate managerial efforts in these firms. Third, quasi-rents accruing to team efforts are more vulnerable to expropriation because the sum of the market values of individual resources (managers) is less than the value of their joint product. Mature firms may have better-organized management teams because of their longer history. Thus, the quasi-rents to the management team in a mature firm are likely to represent a greater part of the firm's cash flows than in a new firm. This implies that the managers in mature firms have more to lose relative to their efforts if such events as a hostile takeover occur. Fourth, in multidivisional corporations, the opportunity to redeploy managerial and financial resources among divisions is limited in a mature division. Also in M-form corporations, compensation of divisional managers is often related to overall corporate performance, whether or not it is based on equity (stock prices). This potentially leads to a free-rider problem. Thus, divestiture of a mature division for a unit management buy-out may be efficient.

Finally, financing of a buy-out through increased leverage is facilitated in mature firms. Use of financial resources is easier to monitor as the room for discretionary decisions is small for firms with limited research and other capital expenditure requirements. Moral hazard toward debtors will not be a problem because both the opportunity and incentive to redeploy assets (for example, to increase their riskiness) are limited for mature firms with stable cash flows. The moral hazard problem may also be reduced by the use of strip financing in LBOs. In strip financing, all claimants hold approximately the same proportion of each security (excluding management incentive shares and the most senior debt usually provided by banks). Thus, the holders of risky debt control most of the equity ownership. Jensen (1986) appears to suggest that strip financing in LBOs is limited to nonequity claims and argues that this approach reduces conflicts of interest among classes of nonequity claimants and lowers expected bankruptcy costs. Also, in mature industries, the assets of firms have greater market (liquidating) values as secondary markets for corporate assets operate more efficiently. This will provide increased ability to raise secured debt.

More MBOs occur in periods of economic expansion or of more visible investment opportunities, as in the case of all M&A activities. Management efforts to restructure business operations following the buy-out have greater value when business conditions are favorable. Also, the ability to service debt is enhanced in periods of economic expansion. Further, increased takeover activity stimulates managers to take protective action against expropriation of their firm-specific investments.

The question is often raised why buy-outs are necessary to achieve improved operating performance. From the business community: "Records of dramatic turnarounds after an LBO raise a troubling question. Why were these managers unable to accomplish these feats before the LBO?" (Greenwald, 1988, p. 70). From the academia: "While the evidence suggests that buy-outs generate real economic gains, the question is why they are needed to attain these gains; couldn't the same gains be produced without changing the organizational structure of the firm?" (Amihud, 1988, p. 31). Answers to these questions are found in the theory just proposed. The managers require protection of their firm- and activity-specific investments from expropriation. The flow of quasi-rents apportioned to them has to be a fair amount and guaranteed against both present *and* future opportunistic exploitation. Simply rewriting their compensation contracts to increase incentives may not be a guarantee against future exploitation (for example, in the event of a hostile takeover). The theory of Alchian and Woodward (1987) holds that resource owners more heavily dependent on the performance of the team (the firm) will value more highly the right to control the team and compete to become the residual claimants (the owners). Even rewriting executive compensation contracts to substantially increase incentives may not be feasible in the real world because of the political process involved in the contracting. Jensen and Murphy (1988) argue that the influential third parties in the process (Congress, labor unions, consumer groups, the media, and so on) implicitly regulate executive compensation by constraining the type of contracts and disapproving high rewards. Expensive lawsuits from outside shareholders are also a distinct possibility (Jones, 1980a, 1980b).

Thus, the going-private buy-out may be an efficient vehicle (or "innovation") to implement a substantial adjustment in managerial compensation (Travlos and Cornett, 1990). The theory of the firm predicts that such an innovation occurs through ownership restructuring in firms in which the rents to firm-specific resource owners are subject to a large probability of opportunistic exploitation by holdup. (See Chapter 2.) Going private should not entail large costs in our theory. The firms are already in industries where cash flows are large, investment opportunities are low, and thus outside financing requirements are small. Further, the argument by Amihud (1988) that the management and the buy-out specialist could buy a controlling interest (more than 50 percent of the voting power) in the firm without taking it private and sacrificing the liquidity value of the stock does not appear compelling. Because of wealth and borrowing capacity constraints, the equity base of the firm would have to be small if the management and the buy-out specialist are to acquire a controlling interest. Public trading of the minority shareholdings will not yield much liquidity because these shareholdings represent only a minor percentage of an already small equity base. If the cost of retaining the organizational form of a private corporation becomes large, the firms will reconvert to the form of a public company after the objectives of going private are achieved. Reverse LBOs are frequently observable by now (Muscarella and Vetsuypens, 1988).

The empirical evidence currently available is also consistent with the Jensen hypothesis based on the agency costs of free cash flows. The premium paid to the prebuy-out shareholders is positively related to the cash flow/equity ratio. Buy-out firms are mostly from mature industries and their growth and capital expenditure rates are smaller than other firms in the same industries. This theory, however, does not directly explain why the firm has to go private to commit the cash flows to increased debt payment. Perhaps the shrunk equity base brings more costs than benefits to being a public company. Once it becomes a private concern, the argument can be extended, then it will be able to institute all the managerial incentive plans without worrying about the political process. Still, the question remains, why does the leverage go down again after an LBO? Is it because the free cash flows become smaller? The management incentive theory formulated earlier could respond to this question by saying that the leverage was increased temporarily as a means of taking the firm private to increase managerial incentives.

Clearly, more research is required for us to have a general theory of LBOs or MBOs. Probably the circumstances that influence the financial policies of post-LBO firms and lead some to go public again will provide useful evidence in this regard.

Also we need more analysis of the methods of financing employed. One study states that in 1983–1985 mergers, recaps, and LBOs accounted for 54 percent of all junk bonds. During 1986–1988 they accounted for 83 percent and the creditworthiness of junk bonds dropped (Lowenstein, 1989, p. C2).

QUESTIONS

1. What are the characteristics of industries and firms in which LBOs and MBOs have taken place historically through 1988?
2. a. What is the magnitude of abnormal returns for LBOs and MBOs according to empirical studies?
   b. Would you predict that these returns will go up or down during the next five years?
   c. What are the sources of these gains?
3. What are the advantages and disadvantages of LBOs and MBOs?

4. Discuss the typical types of financing involved in LBOs and MBOs, including two recent variations.

5. What are the reasons for the increase in LBO activity during the 1980s?

6. Why are LBO/MBOs able to use such high leverage ratios compared with other forms of business organizations?

7. Liquidation is usually associated with bankruptcy or financial distress. How can it be used as a successful business strategy?

REFERENCES

ALCHIAN, A., and S. WOODWARD, "Reflections on the Theory of the Firm," *Journal of Institutional and Theoretical Economics*, 1987, pp. 110–136.

AMIHUD, Y., "Management Buyouts and Shareholders' Wealth," ms., New York University, May 20, 1988.

ANDERS, GEORGE, "Leaner and Meaner: Leveraged Buy-Outs Make Some Companies Tougher Competitors," *The Wall Street Journal*, September 15, 1988, pp. 1, 14.

DEANGELO, HARRY, and LINDA DEANGELO, "Managerial Ownership of Voting Rights: A Study of Public Corporations with Dual Classes of Common Stock," *Journal of Financial Economics*, 1985, pp. 33–69.

————, "Management Buyouts of Publicly Traded Corporations," Chapter 6 in Thomas E. Copeland, ed., *Modern Finance & Industrial Economics*, New York: Basil Blackwell Inc., 1987, pp. 92–113.

————, and EDWARD RICE, "Going Private: Minority Freezeouts and Stockholder Wealth," *Journal of Law and Economics*, October 1984, pp. 367–401.

EASTERBROOK, F. H., and D. R. FISCHEL, "Corporate Control Transactions," *Yale Law Journal*, 92, 1982, pp. 698–711.

GOROFF, M., "Leveraged Buyouts of Public Corporations: An Explanation and Defense," mimeo, Harvard Law School, 1985.

GREENWALD, J., "Where's the Limit?" *Time*, December 5, 1988, pp. 66–70.

HITE, G. L., and J. E. OWERS, "Security Price Reactions Around Corporate Spin-Off Announcements," *Journal of Financial Economics*, December 1983, pp. 409–436.

HITE, G. L., and M. R. VETSUYPENS, "Management Buyouts of Divisions and Shareholder Wealth," ms., Columbia University, July 1988.

JENSEN, M. C., "Agency Costs of Free Cash Flow, Corporate Finance, and Takeovers," AEA Papers and Proceedings, May 1986, pp. 323–329.

————, and K. J. MURPHY, "Are Executive Compensation Contracts Structured Properly?" ms., Harvard Business School, February 10, 1988.

JONES, T. M., "An Empirical Examination of the Resolution of Shareholder Derivative and Class Action Lawsuits," *Boston University Law Review*, 1980a, pp. 542–573.

————, "What's Bothering Those Shareholder-Plaintiffs?" *California Management Review*, 1980b, pp. 5–19.

KAPLAN, S., "A Summary of Sources of Value in Management Buyouts, ms., Harvard University, May 20, 1988.

KNOX, ALICE B., "Buyout Blues," *Financial Planning*, May 1986, pp. 5–6.

LEHN, KEN, and ANNETTE POULSEN, "Free Cash Flow and Stockholder Gains in Going Private Transactions," ms., Securities and Exchange Commission, December 21, 1988a.

———, "Leveraged Buyouts: Wealth Created or Wealth Redistributed?" in M. Weidenbaum and K. Chilton, eds., *Public Policy Towards Corporate Takeovers*, New Brunswick, NJ: Transaction Publishers, 1988b.

LOWENSTEIN, LOUIS, "Management Buyouts," *Columbia Law Review*, 85, 1985, pp. 730–784.

LOWENSTEIN, ROGER, "Junk Gets Junkier, and That May Explain Bonds' Current Ills," *The Wall Street Journal*, November 3, 1989, pp. C1, C2.

MACRIS, R. N., "Leveraged Buyouts: Federal Income Tax Considerations," ms., New York University, May 20, 1988.

McCOMAS, MAGGIE, "After the Buyout, Life Isn't Easy," *Fortune*, December 9, 1985, pp. 42–47.

MORROW, D. J., "Why the IRS Might Love Those LBOs," *Fortune*, December 5, 1988, pp. 145–146.

MURPHY, K. J. "Corporate Performance and Managerial Remuneration: An Empirical Analysis," *Journal of Accounting and Economics*, 1985, pp. 11–42.

MUSCARELLA, C. J., and M. R. VETSUYPENS, "Efficiency and Organizational Structure: A Study of Reverse LBO's," ms., Southern Methodist University, November 1988.

QUIGLEY, E. V., "Big Bondholders Launch Revolt Against Nabisco," *Los Angeles Times*, November 18, 1988, Part IV, pp. 1, 5.

Salomon Brothers, Inc., *Prospects for Financial Markets in 1988*, 1987.

SHLEIFER, A., and C. H. SUMMERS, "Breach of Trust in Hostile Takeovers," in A. J. Auerbach, ed., *Corporate Takeovers: Causes and Consequences*, Chicago: University of Chicago Press, 1988, pp. 33–56.

SHLEIFER, A., and R. W. VISHNY, "Management Buyouts as a Response to Market Pressure," in A. J. Auerbach, ed., *Mergers and Acquisitions*, Chicago: University of Chicago Press, 1988.

SMITH, ABBIE, "Corporate Ownership Structure and Performance: The Case of Management Buyouts," ms., University of Chicago, January 1989.

TRAVLOS, N. G., and M. M. CORNETT, "Going Private Buyouts and Determinants of Shareholder Returns," *Journal of Accounting, Auditing and Finance*, forthcoming, 1990.

WELLING, KATHRYN M., "Thank You, Arco, Who's Next?" *Barron's*, May 6, 1985, pp. 8–9, 24, 26, 28, 32.

W. T. Grimm & Co., *Mergerstat Review 1988* Chicago, IL, 1989.

CHAPTER 17

International Mergers
and Restructuring

The growth of international mergers and acquisitions over the past 20 years has been dramatic. Prior to 1973, there was so little activity in this area that the U.S. Department of Commerce did not even bother to systematically collect specific data on foreign transactions. Foreign purchases of American companies in 1968 accounted for a mere 16 transactions (Khoury, 1980, p. 22) out of 4,462 merger-acquisition announcements for that year (*Mergerstat Review*, 1985, p. 3).

Table 17.1 provides data on the number and dollar values of activity by foreign and U.S. buyers for the years 1972–1988. By 1979, foreign acquisitions accounted for over 10 percent of all transactions (236 out of 2,128). In 1988, there were 307 foreign purchases (of a total of 2,258), with a dollar volume of over $55 billion (a large amount in absolute terms, and even more impressive considering that the dollar value was disclosed in only 60 percent of these transactions). American company purchases of foreign companies peaked in 1972 at 531 (out of 4,801 total transactions). In 1986 there were 180 U.S. acquisitions of foreign firms for over $5.2 billion (with only 34 percent disclosure). Table 17.2 shows that 20 of the 100 largest mergers in U.S. history involved foreign companies, all taking place since 1980.

At the end of 1987, U.S. operations abroad totaled $309 billion. At the end of the same year, the direct investments by foreigners in operations in the United States totaled $262 billion. However, the overall net international investment position of the United States has moved from a large positive figure during most of the post-World War II period to a negative position by the mid-1980s. This is explained by the large persistent deficit in the merchandise trade position of the

TABLE 17.1
Number and Values of Foreign and U.S. Acquisitions

YEAR	NUMBER OF TRANSACTIONS			DOLLAR VALUE ($ billions)		
	TOTAL M&As	FOREIGN BUYERS	U.S. BUYERS	TOTAL M&As	FOREIGN BUYERS	U.S. BUYERS
1972	4,801	88	531	16.7	NAᵃ	NA
1973	4,040	143	323	16.7	NA	NA
1974	2,861	173	257	12.5	NA	NA
1975	2,297	184	178	11.8	1.6	0.4
1976	2,276	178	126	20.0	2.4	0.9
1977	2,224	162	112	21.9	3.1	1.0
1978	2,106	199	98	34.2	6.3	0.7
1979	2,128	236	119	43.5	5.8	1.5
1980	1,889	187	102	44.3	7.1	3.8
1981	2,395	234	101	82.6	18.8	1.1
1982	2,346	154	121	53.7	5.1	0.8
1983	2,533	125	146	73.1	5.9	2.5
1984	2,543	151	147	122.2	15.1	2.6
1985	3,001	197	175	179.8	10.9	1.4
1986	3,336	264	180	173.1	24.5	5.2
1987	2,032	220	142	163.7	40.4	11.0
1988	2,258	307	151	246.9	55.5	14.5

ᵃ NA indicates the information is not available.

SOURCE: *Mergerstat Review,* annual issues through 1988.

United States which became very substantial by the mid-1970s and grew to a negative $154 billion by 1987. Thus, in 1985 the overall net international investment position of the United States had reached a negative $111 billion. By the end of 1987, the investment position of the United States had become an even larger negative number of $368 billion (U.S. Department of Commerce, June 1988).

How can we explain these developments? We need to provide a foundation for understanding this substantial expansion of M&A activity in an international setting.

THE THEORY OF THE MNE

To understand international mergers, acquisitions, and tender offers, we must begin with the theory of the multinational enterprise (MNE). This is because a firm which makes an acquisition in another nation thereby becomes a multinational firm. This raises the question of the business or economic reasons for being a multinational firm. More broadly, the issue is why should a firm be a multiplant firm and this particular form of a multiplant firm—the multinational,

TABLE 17.2

Foreign Transactions Included in the 100 Largest Mergers in History Involving U.S. Firms

RANKING	YEAR	BUYER	SELLER	$ BILLIONS
6	1987	British Petroleum United Kingdom	Standard Oil, Ohio	7.8
8	1988	Campeau Canada	Federated Department Stores	6.5
11	1988	Grand Metropolitan United Kingdom	Pillsbury	5.6
13	1984	Royal Dutch Shell Netherlands	Shell Oil	5.5
15	1988	B.A.T. Ind. United Kingdom	Farmers Group	5.2
22	1981	Elf Acquitaine France	Texasgulf	4.3
37	1987	Campeau Canada	Allied Stores	3.2
38	1986	Unilever Netherlands	Chesebrough-Pond's	3.1
40	1988	News Ltd. Australia	Triangle Publications	3.0
41	1984	Nestlé Switzerland	Carnation	2.9
42	1986	Hoechst West Germany	Celanese	2.9
43	1988	Bridgestone Japan	Firestone Tire	2.8
47	1981	Seagram Co. Canada	Conoco	2.6
51	1981	Kuwait Petroleum Corporation	Santa Fe International	2.5
58	1983	Broken Hill Prop. Australia	G. E. (Utah International)	2.4
61	1988	Maxwell Communications United Kingdom	MacMillan	2.3
65	1980	Sun Co. Inc.	Seagram Ltd. Canada	2.3
69	1985	Olympia & York Dev. Canada	Chevron	2.0
70	1987	Sony Japan	CBS (CBS Records)	2.0
89	1988	Private group United Kingdom	Koppers	1.7

SOURCE: *Mergerstat Review*, 1988, pp. 41–46.

multiplant firm? This goes to the even more fundamental issue—the theory of the firm, treated in Chapter 2.

The basic issue in the theory of the firm is what determines whether a firm will use external markets to transact in resources or use managerial coordination within the firm. For international activities, the issues for the firm are why not export and import, or license, or use joint ventures rather than have a plant or plants abroad?

In Chapter 2 on the theory of the firm, we stated that a firm uses internal managerial coordination rather than the external market when the costs are lower or net revenue productivity higher. It is the cost and revenue comparison that is relevant. The basic challenge to the MNE is that when it operates a plant in a foreign country, its costs are likely to be higher and its revenue productivity lower than the indigenous firms with which it competes. The MNE does not know the foreign labor markets, foreign suppliers, local laws, nor culture and customs in the foreign locations. It is costly to learn these things. Why not produce in your familiar home territory and sell abroad, perhaps through a foreign sales agent? Other contractual arrangements such as licensing and or joint ventures may also be considered.

The theory of the MNE is that the use of foreign plants and other operations implies that costs are lower or revenue productivity higher than if alternative contractual arrangements were used. But what is the source of the net revenue advantage to the horizontal MNE—a multiplant firm with plants in different countries? A leading researcher on multinational enterprise asserts that, "The concept that has proved most fruitful for explaining the non-production bases for the MNE is that of intangible assets belonging to the firm" (Caves, 1982, p. 3). Production advantages may also exist, but Caves assembles evidence to show that the most important factors are the intangible assets.

A firm may possess one or more of a number of important intangible assets. The firm may be superior in technology or managerial knowledge. The firm may be a leader in repeated innovations. It may hold patents, trademarks, or branded products. The firm may possess a special competence in styling, continued product quality improvement or in product differentiation. But granting that a firm may have superior technology or managerial knowledge, why not sell it rather than use it in multilocation activities?

The answer provided by the literature of the MNE is illustrated by the special characteristics of the market for knowledge listed by Casson (1987, p. 12):

1 Uncertainty about the quality of the product.
2 The product is indivisible, but the supply capacity of one unit is infinite.
3 The supply of the product is irreversible and cannot be inspected.
4 Property rights to the product are ill defined and costly to enforce.
5 The product may have multiple uses.
6 The marginal cost of supply is low; each customer becomes a potential competitor.

Because of these "public good" characteristics of knowledge, the use of external markets will involve substantial transactions costs required to define property rights and to negotiate, monitor, and enforce contracts. An example based on Caves (1982) illustrates the idea. Assume six producers of widgets each independently owned and located in six different countries. Firm 1 achieves an innovation either in product quality or in the production process which gives it a price or cost advantage. Firm 1 could expand its output and export to the other five countries, but would incur excessive transportation costs if (by assumption) the plants were all efficiently located to begin with. It could license its knowledge but will be unable to achieve revenues to recover its long-run supply price of innovation because of the "public good" nature of knowledge creation. The most profitable solution is for the six plants to combine into one MNE (Caves, 1982, pp. 5–6).

Caves further suggests that an empirical implication of the theory is that MNEs will be found to a higher degree in industries in which intangible assets are important. He also suggests further extensions of the theory. When the MNE utilizes an intangible asset in a foreign subsidiary, this may be viewed as making use of some excess capacity in such assets. An example is the top management capacity in a successful firm. Availability of internal cash flows may also motivate foreign investment, according to Caves (1982, p. 7). He calls a third extension the "going concern" value of a firm. We have referred to this aspect of intangible assets as organization learning. It is interesting to observe that a number of the concepts used in explaining the theory of the conglomerate firm in Chapters 3 and 4 are quite similar to those used by the leading scholars who have developed the theory of the MNE.

We also noted in Chapter 2 that high reputation or high organization capital firms (in the sense of Cornell and Shapiro, 1987) will expand worldwide by direct investment rather than by licensing. The reason is that reputation is not separable from the operation of the firm. Thus, in this case, the intangible asset that is applied to a foreign subsidiary is not a transferrable technology, but rather the general reputation of the firm.

Thus far we have been summarizing the literature on the theory of the horizontal MNE. The theories for vertically integrated MNE or diversified MNEs are somewhat different. The relationships are summarized well by Caves (1982, p. 16): "The vertically integrated firm internalizes a market for an intermediate product, just as the horizontal MNE internalizes markets for intangible assets." As we discussed in Chapters 2 and 4, particular conditions encourage vertical integration and these apply to MNEs as well. The use of impersonal external market transactions may involve higher transactions costs under the following conditions: (1) when it is expensive to shift buyer-seller relationships (high switching costs), (2) when durable, relatively specialized assets are involved, (3) costs of negotiating and monitoring arm's-length contracts are high, and (4) relevant information is difficult to obtain (information impactedness) and some transactors behave deceptively or opportunistically.

The portfolio explanation for the MNE to achieve diversification is less persuasive. The empirical evidence suggests that the higher the ratio of foreign operations to total sales, the lower the variability of a firm's rate of return on equity capital. Other studies of MNEs provide weak support to benefits from international diversification. But the main influences are the systematic forces described earlier and a variety of special factors, such as the inability to repatriate funds from investments made in less developed countries.

Another special influence may be tariffs. When the European Economic Community (EEC) was established after World War II, it provided for reduction or elimination of tariffs within the community, but tariffs against outsiders. This provided increased incentives for U.S. firms (for example) to establish operations within the tariff walls of the EEC. It also gave them the opportunity to utilize their long experience of operating within a large common market as they had been doing for decades in the United States.

Caves (1982, pp. 42–43) notes that exchange-rate relationships may have effects similar to those of tariffs. He observes that many writers have pointed to the positive relation between a strong dollar and increased foreign direct investments by U.S. firms. Similarly, a weak dollar is associated with increased direct investments by foreigners in the United States.

Finally, in this overview of the general theory of the MNE, the factors of experience and risk should also be noted. Researchers have found that the development of foreign operations proceeds on an incremental basis. A firm does well in its domestic operations. As it increases market share at home, the reactions of rivals are likely to intensify. In part, it may represent good strategy to move abroad to utilize its knowledge, experience, and advantages in foreign countries. But conditions are different in foreign countries and different kinds of risk are involved. So the firm may wish to begin by "dipping its toes in the foreign waters" and expanding abroad as it gains experience.

This also provides a stimulus to foreign acquisitions. A foreign firm has a stock of valuable knowledge about its local market conditions. A U.S. firm which acquires a foreign firm may be willing to pay the full going-concern value because it can utilize the knowledge and experience in other or expanded operations—because important synergies may be present. Firms that already have a substantial presence abroad are more likely to establish new foreign subsidiaries by new ventures, rather than by buying existing firms.

REASONS FOR INTERNATIONAL M&As

Many of the motives for international mergers and acquisitions are similar to those for purely domestic transactions, while others are unique to the international arena. These motives include the following:

I. Growth
   A. To achieve long-run strategic goals.
   B. For growth beyond the capacity of saturated domestic market.
   C. Market extension abroad and protection of market share at home.
   D. Size and economies of scale required for effective global competition.
II. Technology
   A. To exploit technological knowledge advantage.
   B. To acquire technology where it is lacking.
III. Extend advantages in differentiated products
   A. Strong correlation between multinationalization and product differentiation (Caves, 1982). This may indicate an application of the parent's (acquirer's) good reputation.
IV. Government policy
   A. To circumvent protective tariffs, quotas, etc.
   B. To reduce dependence on exports.
V. Exchange rates
   A. Impact on relative costs of foreign versus domestic acquisitions.
   B. Impact on value of repatriated profits.

    VI. Political and economic stability
      A. To invest in a safe, predictable environment.
  VII. Differential labor costs, productivity of labor
 VIII. To follow clients (especially for banks)
   IX. Diversification
      A. By product line.
      B. Geographically.
      C. To reduce systematic risk.
    X. Resource-poor domestic economy
      A. To obtain assured sources of supply.

These motives, with examples of each, are now discussed.

Growth

Growth is probably the most important motive for international mergers. Growth is vital to the well-being of any firm. Mergers provide instant growth, and merging internationally adds a whole new dimension to this instant growth. A 1973 study in the *Survey of Current Business* found the size of the target market to be the only significant determinant of foreign direct investment (including mergers and acquisitions) in the United States. The fact that the growth rate of the target market was not found to be meaningful may indicate an emphasis on immediate rather than potential future growth. Factors which may encourage a firm to merge internationally for growth follow.

A profitable firm in a slow-growing economy may be throwing off cash flow beyond its internal investment needs. It makes sense, all else being equal, to invest this surplus cash in a faster-growing economy than in the slow-growth domestic economy.

The company's domestic markets may be saturated, or the domestic economy may simply be too small to accommodate the growth of its corporate giants. Consider, for example, Royal Dutch Shell and Unilever of the Netherlands; the bulk of these firms' sales and growth must come from outside the Dutch economy.

Leading firms in the domestic market may have lower costs because of economies of scale. Overseas expansion may enable medium-sized firms to attain the size necessary to improve their ability to compete. This factor is one explanation for some recent mergers between medium-sized Japanese companies and U.S. firms, notwithstanding the traditional Japanese reluctance to merge with foreign firms. Medium-sized Japanese firms view these transactions as a means of enhancing their own competitive positions in relation to their larger Japanese rivals.

Finally, even with the most efficient management and technology, the globalization of world markets requires an absolute level of size simply to be able to carry out worldwide operations. Size enables firms to achieve the economies of scale necessary for effective global competition.

Technology

Technological considerations impact international mergers in two ways: (1) a technologically superior firm may make acquisitions abroad in order to exploit its technological advantage, or (2) a technologically inferior firm may acquire a foreign target with superior technology to enhance its competitive position both at home and abroad. It is generally accepted that for an investment project (in this case, the acquisition of a foreign firm) to be acceptable, the present value of benefits must exceed the present value of costs. If an asset (the target firm) is correctly priced, the present value of benefits should equal the present value of costs. For positive net present values to occur, an acquiring firm must either be able to buy the target for less than the present value of its benefits (the target must be underpriced), or to increase the present value of future benefits, following the acquisition, over their current level. It is unlikely that target firms are systematically underpriced (even if they were, underpricing would be more difficult to detect in foreign firms in an unfamiliar market than in domestic firms). Hence, the acquiring firm must bring something to the target which will increase the present value of benefits; or the target firm brings something to the acquirer which enables the combined benefits of the merged firm to be greater than the sum of what the individual firms could have achieved separately—synergy.

In domestic mergers, the increased benefits often result when the superior management efficiency of the acquiring firm is applied to the target firm's assets. In international mergers, the acquiring firm may have an advantage in generic management functions such as planning and control or research and development. But capabilities in specific management functions such as marketing or labor relations, for example, tend to be quite environment specific, and are not readily transferable to different surroundings. Such factors may help to explain the predominance of the United Kingdom and Canada as international merger partners of the United States; that is, the common language and heritage, and similar business practices minimize the drawbacks, making such skills more transferable.

Technological superiority, on the other hand, is a far more portable advantage which may be exploited more easily without a lot of cultural baggage. The acquirer may deliberately select a technologically inferior target which, because of this inferiority, is losing market share and thus market value. By injecting technology into the acquired firm, the acquirer can improve its competitive position and profitability both at home and abroad.

Alternatively, one might find acquisitions by cash-rich but technologically backward companies attempting to obtain the technology necessary to remain viable as competitors on the worldwide scene.

In terms of technology transfer, Khoury (1980, p. 241) concluded that, in general, the net flow of technology transfer was into rather than out of the United States. The foreign firms investing in the United States are characterized by a substantial technology base (in addition to financial strength, managerial depth, and powerful marketing organizations).

Examples of international acquisitions to exploit a technological advantage (in this case, specifically in research and development) include Swiss purchases of U.S. drug companies for the production of such drugs as Valium and Librium. (These transactions also illustrate the appropriation of the knowledge advantage via patents.) Another example was the acquisition of the Budd Co., a user of steel in producing rail cars and wheels by Thyssen, a technologically superior diversified German steel firm. The 1986 Boeing Corporation purchase of de Havilland Aircraft of Canada (from the Canadian government as a result of its denationalization policy—see government policy following) for $113.9 million is another example of this type of merger. Federal Express's purchase of Lex-Wilkinson, Ltd. of the United Kingdom would also be expected to result in an injection of the superior technology and efficiencies which have made the U.S. firm so successful, into the British firm.

Acquisitions to acquire technology would include a number of acquisitions by companies from oil-rich but technologically relatively backward nations, although technological backwardness is not an essential ingredient; the American-based Emhart Corporation cited technology acquisition as one motive for its expansion into Asia. Their Tokyo operations have identified potential technological contributions in glass container machinery manufacturing and door hardware (*Mergers and Acquisitions*, March–April 1986, p. 86).

Product Advantages and Product Differentiation

A firm that has developed a reputation for superior products in the domestic market may find acceptance for the products in foreign markets as well. In the early days of the U.S. automobile industry, cars were exported to Europe in large numbers (during the 1920s). This was before the auto industry was developed in those countries. The advantage of the United States in this mass-production industry made the U.S. cars cheaper despite the high foreign tariffs and motivated foreign direct investments. The tables then were turned. First Volkswagens came from Germany to the United States. Later cars from Japan came to have a strong acceptance in the United States. Further, manufacturing operations by foreign makers were established in the United States.

Indeed, the entry of foreign products and makers is likely to intensify competition in the markets in which it takes place. Observers are of the judgment that most major American industries are now subject to international competition.

Government Policy

Government policy, regulation, tariffs, and quotas can affect international mergers and acquisitions in a number of ways. Exports are particularly vulnerable to tariffs and quotas erected to protect domestic industries. Even the threat of such restrictions can encourage international mergers, especially when the market to be protected is large. Japan's huge export surplus, which led to voluntary export restrictions coupled with threats of more binding restrictions, was a major factor in increased direct investment by Japan in the United States.

Environmental and other government regulations (such as zoning, for example) can greatly increase the time and cost required to build facilities abroad for de novo entry. The added cost of compliance with regulation amplifies other effects which may be operating. Thus, the rationale for acquiring a company with existing facilities in place is reinforced by regulation.

Changes in government policy can make acquisitions in various countries more or less attractive. A good example of this was the policy instituted by the Canadian government in 1981 in order to reduce foreign ownership of Canada's energy resources. To implement the policy, the government gave Canadian-owned energy companies advantageous treatment, including subsidizing exploration and development costs, relative to foreign-owned energy companies operating in Canada. The resulting competitive disadvantage suffered by American-owned and other foreign-owned firms reduced their profitability relative to their Canadian-owned counterparts, and accordingly, reduced their market values. This made them attractive acquisition targets for Canadian energy companies. Thus, the government policy was directly responsible for a large number of divestitures of foreign-owned Canadian energy subsidiaries. In terms of U.S. merger and acquisition activity, these transactions show up as foreign acquisitions of (from) U.S. firms. In 1981 and 1982, 62 and 36 such transactions, respectively, represented 25 percent of all transactions for that period, and accounted for 40 percent of reported dollar volume. The 1982 purchase by Aberford Resources Ltd. of Canada of two subsidiaries of Marathon Oil Company for $225 million is typical.

The South African government's policy of apartheid, while not intended as an economic policy as such, has had a similar effect of causing the divestiture of local subsidiaries by U.S. firms in the face of mounting social and economic pressures against investment in that country. For the most part, these subsidiaries are purchased by South African interests, often the management group which had been in charge of the firm.

More recently, the Canadian government has begun to encourage investment in Canada, or at least not to discourage it. Prior to July 1985, virtually all foreign investment in Canada was subject to scrutiny by the Foreign Investment Review Board (FIRA). FIRA has now been replaced with an agency called Investment Canada. (Even the more upbeat name reflects the change in attitude.) The new policy exempts from review altogether most of those transactions which would have required FIRA review, streamlines the review process when it is required, and more clearly defines (and relaxes) the criteria by which transactions are judged. Merger and acquisition opportunities for both Canadian and foreign investors have also been expanded by the Canadian government's decision to privatize many of the companies it currently owns. (The Boeing-de Havilland transaction mentioned earlier in the technology section came about as a result of this decision.)

Exchange Rates

Foreign exchange rates impact international mergers in a number of ways. The relative strength or weakness of the domestic versus foreign currency can impact the effective price paid for an acquisition, its financing, production costs of running the acquired firm, and the value of repatriated profits to the parent. Accounting conventions can give rise to currency translation profits and losses. Managing exchange rate risk is an additional cost of doing business for a multinational firm.

Dramatic examples can be cited. For example, *The Wall Street Journal* of January 21, 1988 carried an article announcing that Japanese acquisitions in the United States during 1987 were almost $6 billion. The article referred to the increased strength of the yen in relation to the dollar (Sesit, 1988).

At about the same time an article in the *Los Angeles Times* refers to the "selling of America." It points out that lower stock prices and the weakness of the dollar in relation to many other major currencies make U.S. properties relatively inexpensive to foreigners (Moskowitz, 1988).

Political/Economic Stability

The relative political and economic stability of the United States have been important factors in attracting foreign buyers. Political and/or economic instability can greatly increase the risk of what is already a riskier situation than purely domestic investments or acquisitions. Political stability considerations run the gamut from outright war (one does not observe many international acquisitions in Lebanon, for example, though presumably there are bargains to be had) to the opposite extreme, with all the variations between. Acquiring firms must consider the frequency with which the government changes, how orderly is the transfer of power, and how much government policies differ from one administration to the next, including the degree of difference between the dominant political parties. They must assess the likelihood of government intervention on both the upside and the downside (for example, subsidies, tax breaks, loan guarantees, and so forth, on the one hand, all the way to outright expropriation on the other hand). Desirable economic factors include low, or at least predictable, inflation. Many South American companies have learned to cope with triple-digit inflation, but it is not very inviting to foreign companies; on the other hand, its near certainty makes it easier to deal with. Labor relations are another important consideration in economic stability. American unions are neither as strong nor as socialistic and militaristic as labor unions in many other parts of the world. Western European labor unions appear to have a far greater voice in the management of companies than do American unions. The stability of exchange rates is yet another factor in economic stability.

The United States excels in virtually every measure of economic and political stability (except exchange rate stability in recent years). It is also a superior target because of the size and homogeneity of the market and the sophistication of its infrastructure. Transportation and communications networks are among the best in the world; the depth and breadth of U.S. financial markets are attractive; there is little risk of expropriation. Indeed, most states offer inducements to investment, and the labor force is relatively skilled and tractable.

Differential Labor Costs, Productivity

We previously raised the issue of labor relations and its effect on the attractiveness of the economic environment. The labor climate clearly impacts the costs of production, but here we are concerned more directly with labor costs and productivity. High labor costs and the declining productivity of the American worker have historically been cited as a barrier to entry in the United States. However, during the 1975–1980 period, declining dollar strength actually caused relative U.S. labor costs to fall, encouraging foreign acquisitions of U.S. firms (*Mergerstat Review,* 1984, foreign buyers section). Labor costs were presumably not equalized by exchange rates for this motive to have an impact. In terms of productivity, although American workers have come in for much criticism, a survey of foreign managers conducted by the U.S. Department of Commerce in 1975 indicated that American workers were considered to be at least the equal of foreign workers in both adaptability and motivation (Khoury, p. 53). Management systems impact labor productivity. When the closed GM Fremont, California plant was reopened under Toyota management, absenteeism dropped and productivity greatly increased.

To Follow Clients
(Especially by Banks)

The importance of long-term banking relationships is a major factor in international mergers in the banking industry. If enough of a bank's clients move abroad, it makes economic sense for the bank to expand abroad as well. Foreign firms abroad may wish to remain loyal to their longstanding, home-country banks. However, if the foreign bank does not have offices available for servicing its clients, it runs the risk of losing business to more convenient local banks. Khoury found a strong relationship between foreign direct investment by manufacturing firms and loan bookings by foreign banks in the host country.

For some time, foreign banks operating in the United States actually had an advantage over U.S. banks, especially in interstate banking, in that they were allowed to have branches in more than one state (with restrictions), while this was denied to U.S. banks. Over the years the playing field has become more equal.

The growth of foreign bank activity in the United States has been dramatic. In the early 1940s, foreign bank assets in the United States were $11 billion. By the end of 1979, they had grown to $168.4 billion. Loan bookings grew from $14.25 billion in 1972 to $94 billion in 1979. Even more relevant, 59 percent of the foreign banks operating in the United States in 1979 had entered the U.S. market by acquisition rather than via de novo entry (Khoury, 1980).

The banking and finance industry was among the top five industries in which foreign firms acquired U.S. companies over the 1981–1985 period, accounting for almost 5 percent of both the total number and total dollar value of transactions. Among the more significant banking industry mergers during the 1980s are the following:

1980—Midland Bank Ltd. of the United Kingdom purchased a 51 percent interest in Crocker National Corporation for $595 million.

1983—Bank of Montreal purchased Harris Bankcorp for $544.2 million; Mitsubishi Bank Ltd. acquired BanCal Tri-State Corporation for $240.3 million; Walter Heller International Corporation divested its commercial subsidiaries to Fuji Bank for $425 million.

1985—Security Pacific Bank acquired Baumeister Kreditbank GmbH for an undisclosed sum.

This is not to say, however, that following clients is the only reason for mergers in the banking industry, or that this motive cannot possibly apply to mergers in any other industry. Khoury found that Japanese banks in California were able to exploit their superior technology to achieve greater processing efficiency, and thus to charge lower interest rates on personal and automobile loans than U.S. banks.

Diversification

International mergers can provide diversification both geographically, and to a lesser extent by product line. International conglomerate mergers are relatively rare; firms appear to be reluctant to add the risk of operating in a new product market to the risks of operating in a new geographic environment. Product diversification in the form of vertical integration, both backward and forward, is more common, and is covered later.

To the extent that various economies are not perfectly correlated, then merging internationally reduces the earnings risk inherent in being dependent on the health of a single domestic economy. Thus, international mergers can reduce systematic as well as nonsystematic risk.

To Assure a Source of Raw Materials

This is an important motivating factor in vertical mergers, especially for acquiring firms from resource-poor domestic economies. Mergers are used as a means to forestall the erection of barriers against the import/export of raw materials. In the case of strategic raw materials, this approach may not be applicable, since many countries, including the United States, have restrictions on foreign owner-ship of such assets.

To this point we have reviewed the theory of the MNE and described a number of reasons for international M&A activity. In light of this background material, let us look at further empirical evidence.

FURTHER EMPIRICAL EVIDENCE

We first consider the industries and countries of acquisitions. In terms of dollar value, Table 17.3 shows that U.S. purchases of foreign companies have been concentrated in financial services and in natural resource areas. By numbers the top industries include the drug industry along with industrial and farm equip-ment and machinery.

Foreign purchases of U.S. companies are shown in Table 17.4. The indus-tries are similar, with chemicals topping the list both in terms of numbers and

TABLE 17.3
U.S. Purchases of Foreign Companies ($ Billion)

	CUMULATIVE TOP 5 INDUSTRIES 1981–1986		
TOTAL =	870	TOTAL =	$13.48
Miscellaneous services	70	Banking and finance	$2.62
Wholesale and distribution	53	Leisure/entertainment	1.40
Drugs, medical supplies		Oil and gas	1.20
and equipment	45	Insurance	.60
Industrial/farm equipment		Household goods	.56
and machinery	43		
Banking and finance	37		
Top 5 as a percent		Top 5 as a percent	
of total =	29%	of total =	47%

	CUMULATIVE TOP 5 COUNTRIES		
TOTAL =	1301	TOTAL =	$13.49
(1977–1986)		(1981–1986)	
United Kingdom	361	United Kingdom	$6.31
Canada	278	Canada	2.64
West Germany	110	Switzerland	1.01
France	107	Italy	.68
Australia	60	Australia	.64
Top 5 as a percent		Top 5 as a percent	
of total =	70%	of total =	84%

Source: *Mergerstat Review*, 1985–1986.

TABLE 17.4
Foreign Purchases of U.S. Companies ($ Billion)

CUMULATIVE TOP 5 INDUSTRIES 1981–1986			
TOTAL =	1125	TOTAL =	$80.3
Chemicals	76	Chemicals	$6.0
Oil and gas	60	Conglomerate	4.6
Printing and publishing	56	Oil and gas	4.5
Miscellaneous services	55	Insurance	2.4
Industrial/farm equipment		Retail	1.9
and machinery	50		
Retail	50		
Wholesale and distribution	50		
Top 5 as a percent		Top 5 as a percent	
of total =	35%	of total =	24%

CUMULATIVE TOP 5 COUNTRIES			
TOTAL =	1909	TOTAL =	$80.3
(1977–1986)		(1981–1986)	
United Kingdom	601	United Kingdom	$18.3
Canada	452	Canada	17.0
West Germany	153	Netherlands	11.3
France	101	France	7.8
Japan	83	West Germany	6.2
Top 5 as a percent		Top 5 as a percent	
of total =	73%	of total =	75%

Source: *Mergerstat Review, 1985–1986.*

dollar amount. These data we believe give support to the material in the section on the theory of the MNEs. There it was argued that horizontal acquisitions involve industries where intangibles are important and vertical acquisitions involve natural resources as a source of stable supply. However, these data are not sufficiently detailed to provide more than an impressionistic survey rather than an in-depth research analysis of the hypotheses. The cumulative top countries represented in U.S. purchases of foreign companies shown in Table 17.3 and foreign purchases of U.S. companies contain a wide degree of overlap. Generally Canada, the United Kingdom, and the developed countries of Western Europe are involved. Notable is the increasing role of Japan as an important foreign purchaser of U.S. companies.

In Table 17.5 the role of divestitures in international M&A activity is treated. In a high percentage of cases, foreign purchases involve foreign-based subsidiaries of U.S. firms. Over the period 1979–1988 this represented almost one fifth of total foreign purchases of U.S. companies. American purchases of American-based subsidiaries of foreign firms averaged 15.4 percent over the period 1980–1988. However, the pattern exhibits a strong upward trend in recent years. The data suggest a pattern of a wide range of restructuring and realign-

TABLE 17.5

Divestitures

	FOREIGN PURCHASES OF FOREIGN-BASED SUBSIDIARIES OF U.S. FIRMS AS % OF TOTAL FOREIGN PURCHASES	AMERICAN PURCHASES OF U.S.-BASED SUBSIDIARIES OF FOREIGN FIRMS AS % OF TOTAL U.S. PURCHASES
1979	14.4	—
1980	15.0	6.9
1981	20.9	10.9
1982	24.0	12.4
1983	19.2	13.0
1984	14.6	15.0
1985	27.4	18.3
1986	13.6	23.9
1987	22.2	17.6
1988	13.7	21.9
Average =	18.5	15.4

SOURCE: *Mergerstat Review*, 1988.

ments typical of M&A activity generally. Data are also available on premiums paid by foreign firms to acquire U.S. companies. As shown by Table 17.6 in most years the premiums paid by foreign firms to acquire U.S. companies have been higher than the average premiums paid by U.S. firms in all of their acquisitions.

The data are not completely reliable. As Table 17.7 shows, the percent disclosing price in foreign acquisitions of U.S. firms is much higher than in U.S. acquisitions of foreign firms. This makes strong conclusions somewhat tentative, but the premiums paid in foreign acquisitions are so much higher that a significant difference probably exists.

There are a number of potential explanations for the higher premiums involved in foreign acquisitions of U.S. firms. First, lack of familiarity may lead to errors in setting an appropriate price. While such errors could just as easily lead to lower premiums, the data are based on successfully completed acquisitions, and the likelihood is greater that the transaction will go through if the acquiring firm has erred on the high side. Foreign firms may also have invested more resources in target selection, and thus have more to lose if the merger is not consummated.

It is more likely that foreign acquisitions will be carried out on a cash basis rather than via an exchange of securities, since most U.S. stockholders are unwilling to accept the securities of any but the most well-known foreign companies. Cash as the medium of exchange has been found to increase the premium to the targets, as we reported in Chapter 13.

Finally, foreign managements often feel strongly that the takeover should not be hostile to avoid ill-will after the takeover. The requirement that the takeover be friendly may lead to higher premiums.

important influence. A strong dollar makes U.S. products more expensive abroad, but reduces the cost of acquiring foreign firms. The reverse holds when the dollar is weak, encouraging U.S. exports and foreign acquisitions of U.S. companies.

Although the risks of operating in a foreign environment are greater, they can be reduced through careful planning, or by an incremental approach to entering the foreign market. Further, to the extent that the foreign economy is imperfectly correlated with the domestic economy, the systematic risk of the company as a whole may be reduced by international diversification.

The increasing globalization of competition in product markets is extending rapidly into internationalization of the takeover market. The best target to achieve a firm's expansion goals may no longer be a domestic firm but a foreign one. International M&A activity has experienced substantial growth over the past 20 years, and this is likely to continue into the future.

QUESTIONS

1. Why acquire a foreign firm rather than license, export, or joint venture the product?
2. a. What is the role of intangible assets in horizontal multinational enterprises?
   b. What factors are more important in vertical MNEs?
3. How will a product-specialized firm choose to enter a large foreign market as compared to a firm offering diverse products in diverse countries?
4. How should a firm react if its domestic market is under attack by a foreign firm that used high profit margins at home to sell at low margins abroad?
5. How should a firm react if a domestic competitor expands into a large and growing overseas market that only provides normal returns?

REFERENCES

Casson, Mark, *The Firm and the Market*, Cambridge, MA: The MIT Press, 1987.

Caves, Richard E., *Multinational Enterprise and Economic Analysis*, Cambridge, MA: Cambridge University Press, 1982.

Cornell, Bradford, and Alan Shapiro, "Corporate Stakeholders and Corporate Finance," *Financial Management*, Spring 1987, pp. 5–14.

Khoury, Sarkis J., *Transnational Mergers and Acquisitions in the United States*, Lexington, MA: Lexington Books, 1980.

Mergers & Acquisitions, March–April 1986.

Mergerstat Review, Chicago, IL: The W. T. Grimm & Co., 1984–1987.

Mergerstat Review, Schaumburg, IL: Merrill Lynch Business Brokerage & Valuation, Inc., 1988.

MOSKOWITZ, MILTON, "Viewpoints," *Los Angeles Times,* January 24, 1988, Part IV, pp. 3, 17.

SCHOLL, RUSSELL B., "The International Investment Position of the United States in 1986," *Survey of Current Business,* June 1987, pp. 38–45.

SESIT, MICHAEL R., "Japanese Acquisitions in U.S. Jumped To $5.9 Billion in '87; Strong Yen Cited," *The Wall Street Journal,* January 21, 1988, p. 18.

United States Department of Commerce, *Survey of Current Business,* Washington, DC: Superintendent of Documents, United States Government Printing Office, 1988.

CHAPTER **18**

Share Repurchase and Exchanges

The topics covered in this chapter represent areas of considerable practical significance to corporate managements. The authors often receive phone calls from high-level executives asking questions related to the topics of this chapter. Their questions are frequently: "We are contemplating repurchase of up to 20 percent of the outstanding shares of our common stock. What will be the effects on share price and will our shareholders be happy or unhappy with this activity?" A related kind of comment is: "We are considering an exchange offer of debt or preferred stock for common stock or vice versa." Similar questions are then raised.

The chapter is divided into two parts. The first deals with share repurchase, the second with exchange offers. The activities are related. Share repurchase generally deals with cash offers for outstanding shares of common stock. This has the effect of changing the capital structure for the firm if nothing else occurs. This is because even if the amount of debt is not changed, the amount of common stock is reduced so the debt/equity ratio or leverage ratio is increased.

Some authors argue that the amount of cash and marketable securities in excess of the transactions needs for a company should be deducted from debt in determining a firm's leverage ratio—a reduction in the leverage ratio. The use of cash to extinguish common stock would magnify the leverage ratio because no longer would debt be reduced by the excess cash and equity would be smaller. Thus, the share repurchase is almost equivalent to a debt for common stock exchange. However, since the two transactions have somewhat different characteristics, we first discuss common stock share repurchases and then in the second part of the chapter deal with exchange offers.

THE NATURE OF CASH SHARE REPURCHASES

A corporation may repurchase its own shares of common stock in the open market, by a tender offer or by a private negotiation. Open-market repurchases of common stock are virtually identical to what occurs when any other investor purchases the company stock through a broker. Open-market share repurchases occur more frequently than tender offers to repurchase. However, open-market repurchases are generally a smaller fraction of total shares outstanding than tender offers. Companies make announcements that their directors have authorized the repurchase of (usually) a specified number of shares of common stock. While such public disclosure is not required by law, repurchase transactions must comply with the antimanipulation and antifraud provisions of the Securities and Exchange Act of 1934 as amended (Dann, 1981). Announcements of open market repurchase programs usually describe them as continuing over a number of months and sometimes over a number of years.

Negotiated repurchases generally involve a smaller number of shareholders who own a significant block of the company's common stock. In recent years negotiated purchases have been associated with unwelcome suitors for the company and are used to ward off a group sometimes called "raiders" who may be making large initial purchases of the company stock as a step toward taking over the company usually by a tender offer. The management of the target firm may arrange for a negotiated repurchase. This is often referred to as greenmail. It sometimes includes a standstill agreement under which the investors in the company agree to sell their stock and not to make any additional purchases for a specified period of time. The greenmail and standstill agreement type of activity may properly be regarded as a merger defense and is discussed in Chapter 20. The main form of common stock repurchasing that is discussed in the present chapter is cash tender offers to repurchase.

Cash Tender Offers to Repurchase

In a cash tender offer the company usually sets forth the number of shares it is offering to purchase and the price at which it will repurchase shares, as well as the period of time during which the offer will be extended. The tender offer price is generally higher than the market price at the time of offer (by approximately 23 percent on average). The tender offer price is usually the net price received by the shareholders who tender their shares. This is because the tendering shareholders pay no brokerage fees and the company generally pays any transfer taxes that are levied.

The number of shares set forth in the tender offer typically represents a maximum number of shares that the company seeks to repurchase. If the number of shares tendered exceeds this limit, the company may purchase all or a fraction of shares tendered in excess of the amount initially set forth. The company also may reserve the right to extend the time period of the offer. If a company purchases less than all shares tendered, the purchases must be made on a pro rata basis from each of the tendering shareholders. The adoption of SEC Rule 13 (e-4) in September 1979 made mandatory the pro rata repurchase of shares when the number tendered exceeds the number the company purchases.

If fewer shares are tendered during the initial offer period than targeted by management, the company may decide to extend the length of the offer period. If the offer period is lengthened, the company is likely to purchase all shares tendered before the first expiration date, and then purchase shares offered during the extension period either pro rata or on the basis of the order in which the shares are offered. The tender offer usually does not permit officers and directors of the repurchasing company to tender their shares. (This has an important implication from the standpoint of the managerial control and signaling that may be involved in a tender offer.)

Empirical Evidence on Cash Tender Offers

Most empirical studies of stock repurchase have focused on cash tender offers. Tender offer repurchases are generally of larger magnitude and over a more accurately measured time period than open market repurchases. For tender offer repurchases one can obtain the announcement date, the actual dates of repurchase activity, and the repurchase price. The market impacts of the repurchase activity will, therefore, be more clearly defined and measurable.

Some interesting materials are provided in the summary by Vermaelen (1981) on undersubscribed versus oversubscribed stock repurchase offers, as shown in Table 18.1.

The CARs are about the same, around 13 percent. The average premium is much higher for oversubscribed issues than for undersubscribed issues, a differential of about 4 percentage points. The average target fraction was only about 13 percent for oversubscribed issues but over 18 percent for undersubscribed issues. The fraction actually purchased was over 16 percent for oversubscribed issues and under 12 percent for undersubscribed issues.

Another interesting set of relationships is provided by Vermaelen (1981) in comparing debt-financed with cash-financed stock repurchase tenders. These are shown in Table 18.2. The debt-financed offers have a much higher wealth effect than the cash-financed offers, 24 percent versus 18 percent. The premium in debt-financed offers is somewhat higher. The target fraction is over 20 percent for debt-financed offers but only about 15 percent for cash-financed offers. The two categories identified as debt financed or cash financed constitute only 62

TABLE 18.1

Summary Statistics on Undersubscribed and Oversubscribed Stock Repurchase Offers Occurring in the Time Interval 1962–1977

	NUMBER BEFORE EXTENSION (1)	NUMBER AFTER EXTENSION (2)	AVERAGE PREMIUM[a] (3)	AVERAGE F^{*b} (4)	AVERAGE F_p^c (5)	CAR'[d] (6)	TOTALR[e] (7)
Oversubscribed	80	86	0.2395	0.1327	0.1619	0.1283	0.1463
Undersubscribed	51	45	0.2047	0.1842	0.1211	0.1377	0.1457
Total	131	131	0.2276	0.1504	0.1479	0.1319	0.1461

[a]Premium is computed as the tender price divided by the price five days before the announcement minus one.
[b]Target fraction.
[c]Fraction purchased.
[d]Cumulative average excess return to remaining shareholders from −5 until day +60.
[e]Average abnormal return to tendering and nontendering shareholders = (3) × (5) + (6) × [1 − (5)].
SOURCE: Theo Vermaelen, "Common Stock Repurchases and Market Signalling: An Empirical Study," *Journal of Financial Economics*, 9, 1981, p. 152.

observations of his total 131 observations. The information effect for his total sample is much lower than for either of the two subcategories. The same is true of the premium.

With this background on the nature of cash repurchases of stock by tender offer, we next turn to some of the basic analytics involved.

TABLE 18.2

Characteristics of the Total Sample, the Sample Financed by Debt and the Sample Financed with Cash (Average Values with Standard Deviations in Parentheses)

	TOTAL SAMPLE	DEBT-FINANCED	CASH-FINANCED
Observations	131	13	49
INFO[a]	0.157	0.236	0.178
	(0.154)	(0.122)	(0.163)
Premium[b]	0.227	0.283	0.268
	(0.179)	(0.139)	(0.214)
F^{*c}	0.151	0.202	0.146
	(0.108)	(0.134)	(0.098)

[a]Total abnormal return to nontendering and tendering shareholders.
[b]Tender price÷the price five days before the announcement−1.
[c]Target fraction.
SOURCE: Theo Vermaelen, "Common Stock Repurchases and Market Signalling: An Empirical Study," *Journal of Financial Economics*, 9, 1981, p. 158.

BASIC STOCK REPURCHASE MODEL

To understand better the implications of stock repurchasing and exchange offers, let us first set out some of the quantitative relationships involved. As is customary, it is necessary to set forth the assumptions of the model employed. The literature on the subject suggests a number of basic conditions involved in the equilibrium pricing of securities (Vermaelen, 1981).

1 The market is efficient in that at any time market prices reflect all publicly available information that influences the prices of securities.
2 This also implies that markets are informationally efficient which specifies that information is costless and is received simultaneously by all individuals. In the economic literature these conditions are generally referred to as the condition of pure competition.
3 There is perfect competition in securities markets. This implies that individual investors are price takers and cannot influence the outcome of a stock repurchase offer.
4 Investors seek to maximize the value of their wealth, after taking into account taxes and transactions costs.
5 After the announcement date investors have homogeneous expectations with respect to the change in value that will be caused by the share repurchase and with respect to the fraction of shares that will be tendered as well as the fraction of shares that will be purchased by the company.
6 Offers are maximum-limit offers. This means that if the offer is undersubscribed, the firm will buy all shares tendered. But if the offer is oversubscribed, the company will buy all shares tendered or will allocate shares pro rata—the company buys back the same fraction of the shares from every tendering shareholder.
7 The price changes analyzed in connection with share repurchase are after adjusting for marketwide price changes.

In the analysis that follows we employ a number of symbols which are now defined:

$$P_O = \text{the preannouncement share price}$$
$$P_T = \text{the tender price}$$
$$P_E = \text{the postexpiration share price}$$
$$N_O = \text{the preannouncement number of shares outstanding}$$
$$N_E = \text{the number of shares outstanding after repurchase}$$
$$W = \text{the shareholder wealth effect caused by the share repurchase}$$
$$F_P = \text{the fraction of shares repurchased} = (N_O - N_E)/N_O$$
$$1 - F_P = \text{the fraction of untendered shares} = N_E/N_O.$$

The basic condition that must be met is set forth in equation (18.1).

$$P_E N_E = P_O N_O - P_T (N_O - N_E) + W \qquad (18.1)$$

Equation (18.1) states that the value of the shares outstanding after expiration of the repurchase offer equals the value of the shares existing before the announcement of the repurchase offer less the value of the shares repurchased plus the change in shareholder wealth associated with the repurchase offer. The source of W, the shareholder wealth effect, will be analyzed subsequently. If we then divide equation (18.1) by N_O and substitute for the definition of fraction of shares repurchased and fraction of shares not repurchased, we obtain equation (18.2).

$$P_E(1 - F_P) = P_O - P_T F_P + W/N_O \tag{18.2}$$

We next divide by P_O and solve for the rate of increase in value or the rate of return created by the repurchase offer. This is shown in equation (18.3).

$$W/N_O P_O = (F_P)\frac{P_T - P_O}{P_O} + (1 - F_P)\frac{P_E - P_O}{P_O} \tag{18.3}$$

Equation (18.3) reveals the two components of rate of return associated with the repurchase offer. The first component is the rate of return received by the tendering shareholders weighted by the percent of shares purchased. The second component is the rate of return received by nontendering shareholders weighted by the percent of nontendered shares.

Dann (1981) found for his sample of open-market share repurchases totaling 143 observations over the period 1962–1976 that the fraction of shares repurchased averaged 20 percent. The shareholder wealth effect was 15 percent. The initial premium represented by the tender offer was 23 percent. From this information we can solve for the relationship between the price of the stock at expiration of the repurchase offer and the initial price, P_O. This is done in equation (18.4).

$$15\% = 20\%(23\%) + 80\% X \tag{18.4}$$

The premium of the expiration price after the share repurchase is therefore 13 percent over the initial share price. Thus, as shown in equation (18.4a), of the 15 percent wealth effect associated with the share repurchase offer, 4.6 percent goes to the tendering shareholders and 10.4 percent goes to the nontendering shareholders.

$$15\% = .2(23\%) + .8(13\%)$$

$$15\% = 4.6\% + 10.4\% \tag{18.4a}$$

The relationship is quite similar for the Vermaelen (1981) study covering 131 open-market share repurchases over the period 1962–1977. The initial premium was the same, 23 percent, but the fraction repurchased was 15 percent. The wealth effect was 16 percent. The relationships are shown in equation (18.5).

$$16\% = 15\%(23\%) + 85\%X$$

$$.16 = .0345 + .85X$$

$$X = .1476 = 14.76\%$$

$$16\% = .15(23\%) + .85(14.76\%) \tag{18.5}$$

The indicated postexpiration price is 14.76 percent over the initial price. Thus, using Vermaelen's data, the 16 percent wealth effect is composed of 3.45 percent to the tendering shareholders and 12.55 percent to the nontendering shareholders. Other studies of open-market share repurchases find similar results; these include Bradley and Wakeman (1983), Brickley (1983), Masulis (1980), and Vermaelen (1984).

Thus, we see that for open-market share repurchases the pattern appears to be consistent. There is about a 23 percent premium reflected in the tender offer price over the preexisting price. The postexpiration price is about 13 percent to 15 percent higher than the preannouncement price. The tendering shareholders receive a higher premium than the nontendering shareholders. But the nontendering shareholders as a group receive the largest portion of the wealth increase. Of course, the basic question is: What is the source of the well-documented and observed wealth increase associated with the share repurchase activity? The alternative explanations are considered in the following section.

THE THEORIES
BEHIND SHARE REPURCHASES

The empirical studies which we summarized show that the size of the premium offered to shareholders to tender their holdings is about 23 percent over the stock price then prevailing. At the expiration of the tender offer period, the price of the stock still remains 13 percent to 15 percent above the pretender offer announcement price. There appears to be a permanent increase in the market price of the firm's common stock as a consequence of the share repurchase program. How is this permanent increase in value to be explained? Six hypotheses have been offered.

1 Dividend or personal taxation hypothesis
2 Leverage hypothesis
3 Information or signaling hypothesis
4 Bondholder expropriation hypothesis
5 Wealth transfers among shareholders
6 Defense against outside takeovers

Each of these is analyzed in turn.

Dividend or Personal Taxation Hypothesis

Cash dividends are taxable at ordinary income tax rates. Prior to the Tax Reform Act of 1986 which provides for a reduction and ultimate elimination of a preferential capital gains tax rate, capital gains were taxed at a preferentially lower rate. The period covered by most of the empirical studies was from the early 1960s to the late 1970s. During this period of time the preferential capital gains tax treatment obtained. Cash received by a shareholder as a result of a stock repurchase was taxable during that period only if the repurchase price exceeded the shareholder's acquisition price and at the preferential lower capital gains tax rate. Section 302 of the U.S. Internal Revenue Code provided that the redemption be "substantially disproportionate to the extent that after the repurchase the percentage ownership of the shareholder must be less than 80 percent of the percentage he held before the repurchase." The empirical studies show that this condition is rarely violated.

The personal taxation argument for explaining the value increase, therefore, suggests that share repurchase enables the stockholder to substitute a lower capital gains tax for a higher ordinary personal income tax rate on the cash received. But both Dann (1981) and Vermaelen (1981) express doubt about the validity of this personal tax savings hypothesis. Both review extensive theoretical literature and empirical studies on the central theoretical proposition involved here. This is the argument from the dividend policy literature that a higher tax rate on dividends versus capital gains implies that a corporation's dividend policy can affect the value of its common stock. The most compelling arguments in this area were made by Miller and Scholes (1978). They describe and illustrate a number of ways that investors can offset personal tax liabilities on dividends. All of these methods, however, involve transactions costs. The argument could then be that share repurchase reduces the transactions costs involved in helping stockholders offset personal tax liabilities on dividends. But share repurchases as a substitute for dividends also involve transactions costs. The question is whether transactions costs are reduced and whether the size of the reduction in transactions costs is sufficient to explain the relatively substantial gain of 13 percent to 15 percent of share price that persists after the expiration date for a tender offer repurchase episode.

There is a very interesting historical and empirical set of observations involved here. Vermaelen (1981) assembles evidence to show that during the period August 1971 to June 1974 a "voluntary" 4 percent limit on dividend increases was imposed as a part of the wage and price controls of the period. During the preceding ten years from 1962 until July 1971, only 32 repurchase offers were observed. During the period August 1971 to June 1974, somewhat less than three years, the number of share repurchases increased to 52 which averages over 17 per year. This increase of over 500 percent Vermaelen (1981, p. 171) refers to as a "dramatic increase in repurchasing activity."

Vermaelen (1981) breaks his data into three subperiods: before, during, and after the controls on dividend increases. We refer to these as periods 1, 2, and 3. During period 1 the abnormal return was 5.6 percent. The premium was 11.6 percent and the target fraction of shares for repurchase was 13.5 percent. The median market value of the firm involved was $59 million. During period 2 the abnormal return jumped to 19.3 percent, and the premium rose to 26.4 percent. The target fraction was 14 percent, while the median market value firm dropped substantially to approximately $22 million. It appears that during period 2, the period of controls on dividend increases, small firms used share repurchase to avoid the controls on dividend increases. In the third period all the variables were similar to those of the second period except that the target fraction rose from 14 percent to 17.2 percent. These data on the nature of the three subperiods are very significant from our standpoint. They shed light on how share repurchases came into being, or at least increased in their frequency. They also indicate the importance of firm size in participating in share repurchase for this period. Our impression is that if these studies were updated through 1986, it would be found that larger firms began to engage in share repurchase to a greater extent after 1980.

The fact that share repurchase was stimulated by controls on dividend increases clearly indicates an association between dividend activity and share repurchase activity. However, the aim appeared to be not so much to obtain the tax advantage of reducing personal taxes on dividends, but rather to achieve dividend increases. But again this suggests that to the owners of small firms dividends do indeed matter. However, the reasons why dividends may matter in these circumstances are not clear.

Leverage Hypothesis

Stock repurchases increase the debt/equity ratio. If the repurchase is financed by excess cash and marketable securities, the extent of the increase depends on the method used to calculate the leverage ratio. If the share repurchase is financed explicitly by an issue of debt, the increase in the leverage ratio is even greater regardless of calculation method. Along with the leverage increase, financing the repurchase with debt also increases the amount of tax-deductible interest payments.

If there is a tax subsidy associated with the deductibility of interest payments on debt, and if this subsidy is passed through to shareholders, the price of the stock would increase. Just as the issue of reduction in personal taxes under the previous point involves the whole issue of dividend policy, the issue of a tax subsidy to debt involves the whole question of debt policy. This entire area is still unsettled. The earlier Modigliani and Miller papers (1958, 1963) developed a model in which there was a tax subsidy to debt. However, Miller (1977) argues that debt is issued to the point where the corporate tax rate equals the personal income tax rate of the marginal bondholder. Under these conditions there exists no optimal debt/equity ratio for the individual firm. Others argue that there is a tax subsidy for debt or for debt substitutes that move the firm toward increased leverage. However, the existence of bankruptcy costs is an offsetting disadvantage so that there is an optimal amount of debt for the individual firm. The issue remains unsettled.

Masulis (1980) gives the greatest weight to the corporate tax shield hypothesis. He divided his sample of 138 share repurchase offers into those with more than 50 percent debt financing and those with less than 50 percent debt financing. The announcement period return for the 45 offers with greater leverage was 21.9 percent, while the 93 offers with a lower percentage of debt financing had announcement period returns of 17.1 percent. Masulis (1980) terms these results as consistent with a corporate tax shield hypothesis.

Vermaelen (1981), however, takes issue with the Masulis (1980) position on the leverage hypothesis as an explanation for the shareholder wealth increase. Vermaelen (1981) develops some regression relationships. He finds that the difference in the size of premiums explains 60 percent of the difference in what he calls information or wealth effect. He observes that the average premium was 27 percent for the more than 50 percent debt-financing group and 23 percent for the less than 50 percent debt-financing group of Masulis (1980). Thus, we have a difference of 4 percentage points in the premium associated with a difference of 4.8 percentage points in the wealth effect between the high-debt and low-debt groups. Employing the 60 percent regression coefficient on the premium explains 2.4 percentage points of the 4.8 percent difference in wealth effect. Vermaelen (1981) also finds positive explanatory power in the fraction of insider holdings, the target fraction of shares in the repurchase offer, and the fraction purchased in relation to the target fraction. Hence, he argues that the significance of the financing effect must be less than the remaining 2.4 percentage points of difference in the wealth effect.

Vermaelen (1981) argues that while the leverage hypothesis may play a role, it is not the predominant explanation for the observed abnormal returns following the share repurchase offer. He argues that the more plausible explanation is the signaling or information effect which we take up next. We may note also that if leverage is regarded as a signal, then it is not possible to separate the leverage signaling effect from the leverage tax effect. We, therefore, turn to the information or signaling hypothesis.

Information or Signaling Hypothesis

The announcement by a company that it is going to engage in a share repurchase program provides an information signal to investors. On first analysis the direction of the signal appears to be ambiguous. On the one hand it may be that the announcement of the use of cash to repurchase its own shares is an acknowledgment by management that it has no profitable investments in which the funds can be employed. But another interpretation is possible. When a company announces that it is willing to buy its shares at a substantial premium above the market price, and as is usually the case insiders cannot or do not participate, this may be taken as inside information that management believes that the common stock of the company is undervalued by the market. One often reads in newspaper accounts of stock repurchase announcements that management states that it feels that investing in its own stock is the best bargain around.

Vermaelen (1981) makes a vigorous case for the information signaling hypothesis. He runs regressions seeking to explain the size of the wealth effect. He successively uses as independent variables the premium in the repurchase announcement, the target fraction the company seeks to repurchase, the fraction of insider holdings in the company, and the fraction of the shares purchased in relation to the target fraction. From this he estimates that the size of the regression coefficient for the premium is .6. The signs on the other variables are always positive and significant in at least one of the nine regressions which he runs with alternative combinations of explanatory variables.

Vermaelen (1981) also reports that tender offers for share repurchase are associated with per share earnings of tendering firms that subsequently are above what would have been predicted by a time series model using preannouncement data. While such prediction methods are subject to limitations, the evidence is still supportive.

Vermaelen (1981) concludes, however, that it is possible that leverage or the financing effect does have some explanatory power. He feels that the information signaling hypothesis carries greater weight in explaining the wealth effect but that the leverage effect may still play a role. Of course, if increased leverage also carries an information, signaling effect, then it is difficult to separate the role of the two alternative hypotheses.

Bondholder Expropriation Hypothesis

Evidence on the effects on bondholders is obtained by analyzing bond price changes around the announcement dates of the equity repurchases via tender offers. Dann (1981) studied 41 issues of straight debt, 34 issues of convertible debt, 9 issues of straight preferred stock, and 38 issues of convertible preferred stock. He analyzed abnormal returns to each of these categories around the announcement date. Significant positive rates of return were observed for the convertible securities, which may be regarded as delayed issues of common stock. The abnormal rates of return were insignificantly different from zero for straight debt and for preferred stock. In addition he found that the correlations between common stock returns and the returns on straight debt as well as preferred stock were positive. This evidence seems inconsistent with the explanation of bondholder expropriation as an important motive for equity repurchases by tender offers.

Wealth Transfers Among Shareholders

Wealth transfers may take place between those stockholders who tender their shares and those who do not. A variety of reasons may exist for these differences in behavior. There may be different constraints and costs among different groups of shareholders. Nevertheless, as the data presented earlier show, the largest portion of the wealth effect goes to the nontendering shareholders. This is because they experience significant gains since the expiration price still remains from 13 percent to 15 percent above the price of the stock before the announcement of the repurchase tender offer. In addition, as a matter of practice, insiders with large shareholdings do not participate in the repurchase tender offer. Hence it would appear that they expect that the stock price at a longer distance into the future will be even more favorable than at the end of the expiration period. This, of course, is consistent with and further supports the information or signaling explanation for the favorable wealth effect.

Defense Against Outside Takeovers

If insiders judge the firm to be undervalued, they may have concerns that the firm is subject to a takeover bid at a relatively small premium. Vermaelen (1984) reports a high correlation for the period 1962–1977 for takeover bid announcements and the number of repurchase tender offers. He suggests that this might protect shareholder interests in that noninsiders may be better off without a takeover bid than with a takeover bid at a low offer premium. The large premium involved in the repurchase tender offer may convey information to the noninsiders that the value of the shares is at least as high as conveyed by the premium and may be perhaps even higher in the future. This could put the market on notice that if a takeover bid is to succeed, it may have to be even higher than the repurchase tender offer premium which, as we have seen, averages 23 percent.

Thus, the personal taxation, leverage, signaling, and takeover defense explanations for the wealth effect in tender offer share repurchases, appear to have explanatory power. Bondholder expropriation and wealth transfers among shareholders appear to be inconsistent with both analysis and empirical evidence. Further understanding of share repurchase tender offers may be gained by an analysis of exchange offers. The evidence on this activity is reviewed in the following section of this chapter.

EXCHANGE OFFERS

An exchange offer provides one or more classes of securities, the right or option to exchange part or all of their holdings for a different class of securities of the firm. Like a tender offer repurchase, an exchange offer is usually open for about one month. However, the offer is frequently extended. To induce the security holders to make the exchange, the terms of exchange offered necessarily involve new securities of greater market value than the preexchange offer announcement market value. Exchange offers usually specify the maximum number of securities which may be exchanged. Also many exchange offers are contingent upon acceptance by a minimum number of securities to be exchanged. On average, Masulis (1980) reports that initial announcement dates precede the beginning of the exchange offer by nine weeks. He states that the average life of the offer is about seven weeks.

Tax Aspects of Exchange Offers

When a company sells bonds at a discount, this generally implies that the coupon interest rate is below the market rate of interest. If the amount of the discount is material, the discount for tax purposes must be amortized over the life of the debt instrument. The amount of the amortized discount is treated as an additional interest payment to make up for the low coupon. It is, therefore, a tax expense to the corporation. When a corporation sells a bond at a premium, this means that the coupon payment is higher than the market rate. The amortization of the premium is a reduction in the interest tax expense to the corporation.

When a firm redeems debt at a price below the issue price, the difference is treated as ordinary income. If debt is redeemed at a price above the issue price, the difference is treated as an ordinary loss. It is generally the case that any change in the corporation's taxable income has an opposite effect on the taxable income of investors acquiring or tendering the debt (Masulis, 1980). When stock is tendered for debt, stockholders incur a capital gains tax liability just as if they had sold their stock for cash. Masulis (1980), therefore, observes that a debt for common stock exchange is likely to occur when stocks are selling at relatively low prices when most shareholders would incur little or no capital gains liability as a consequence.

Empirical Evidence
on Exchange Offers

With some of the characteristics of exchange offers as a background, we next turn to the empirical data. After summarizing the empirical data, we relate the empirical evidence to the explanatory hypotheses. Table 18.3 summarizes the results for exchange offers with positive abnormal returns.

From Table 18.3 it can be seen that an exchange of debt for common stock involves the largest positive returns to shareholders. It is 14 percent, about the order of magnitude of wealth effects observed in stock repurchase tender offers.

TABLE 18.3
Exchange Offers with Positive Returns

P1. Debt for common stock (Masulis, 1983)	+14.0%
P2. Preferred for common stock (Masulis, 1983; Pinegar and Lease, 1986)	+8.2
P3. Debt for preferred stock (Masulis, 1983)	+2.2
P4. Income bonds for preferred stock (McConnell and Schlarbaum, 1981)	+2.2

TABLE 18.4
Exchange Offers with Negative Returns

N1. Common stock for debt (Masulis, 1983)	−9.9%
N2. Private swaps of common for debt (Finnerty, 1985; Peavy and Scott, 1985)	−0.9
N3. Preferred stock for debt (Masulis, 1983)	−7.7
N4. Common for preferred stock (Masulis, 1983; Pinegar and Lease, 1986)	−2.6
N5. Calls forcing debt conversion (Mikkelson, 1981)	−2.1

The exchange of preferred stock for common also carries a large gain of over 8 percent. The exchange of debt or the exchange of income bonds for preferred stock carries small but significant positive returns.

Table 18.4 summarizes the results of exchange offers with negative returns. While the two tables summarize the main empirical findings, how do we explain these results? A number of theories or explanations are possible. The effects appear to depend on whether the exchanges have one or more of the following consequences:

1 Leverage increasing or decreasing
2 Implied increases or decreases in future cash flows
3 Implied undervaluation or overvaluation of common stock
4 Management share ownership is increased or decreased [agency (1)]
5 Control of management use of cash is increased or decreased [agency (2)]

The exchange offers in Table 18.3 have positive returns. They appear to have in common a number of characteristics: they are leverage increasing, they imply an increase in future cash flows, and they imply undervaluation of common stock. In two of the four cases management share ownership is increased, and in three of the four cases the control over management's use of cash is decreased. It is difficult to judge whether the leverage effect is also a signaling effect or whether it is purely a tax effect. It could be argued that the exchange of preferred for common stock does not carry tax implications for the corporation. On the other hand, since 80 percent of the dividends (85 percent before 1986) on preferred stock over the period of these studies could be excluded as income for a corporate investor, the incidence of this tax advantage accrued at least partially to the issuing corporation. This may partly explain why the debt for preferred exchange carries only a small positive return to shareholders. It may be because both convey tax benefits, albeit of a somewhat different nature.

Another curiosity in connection with the leverage-increasing exchange offers is noted by Vermaelen (1981). He points out that 30.1 percent of the leverage-increasing exchange offers in the sample developed by Masulis were announced during the period of dividend controls, roughly from mid-1971 through mid-1974. This suggests that they were by relatively smaller firms which were seeking to avoid the requirement that dividend increases could be no more than 4 percent per year. Of course, another strong external effect came about on the swaps which were stimulated by a tax law change in 1984 documented by Finnerty (1985). Since multiple explanations could account for the positive returns shown by Table 18.3, it is difficult to assign weights to each explanation.

Similarly in Table 18.4, for exchange offers causing negative returns, it appears that the five explanations all run in the opposite direction. It is curious that swaps of common stock or preferred stock for debt carry about the same negative return. However, private swaps of common for debt carry a very small although significant return. Much more detailed studies would be required to attempt to assess the relative weight of each of the potential explanations for the pattern of abnormal returns observed.

Pinegar and Lease (1986) find preferred-for-common exchanges "leverage increasing" with small positive effects on the value of the common and no effects on the value of the preferred. Common-for-preferred exchanges are "leverage increasing" with a small negative effect on the value of the common and a small positive effect on the value of the preferred.

SUMMARY

Share repurchases and exchange offers are significant corporate events. They are covered in the same chapter because they often have similar motives and effects on firms and shareholders. A share repurchase for cash is almost equivalent to a debt-for-common-stock exchange offer in its effect of increasing a firm's leverage ratio. Cash tender offers to repurchase shares have been the subject of empirical studies. They have been found to result in significant positive abnormal returns to shareholders of about 13 percent to 15 percent; returns are even higher when they are financed by debt rather than by cash. Both tendering and nontendering shareholders benefit.

A number of hypotheses have been advanced to explain these gains. Tax effects appear to play a small role; gains to shareholders on repurchase are taxed as capital gains rather than as ordinary income in the case of dividends. This benefit is greatly reduced by the elimination of the lower rate on capital gains by the Tax Reform Act of 1986. Share repurchase represents an alternative means of making payouts to shareholders, which becomes even more important during periods of restrictions on dividends. Increased leverage may also be responsible for some of the shareholder wealth increase, especially in debt-financed repurchases, to the extent that there is a tax subsidy on debt interest payments, or that the firm has been operating at a suboptimal leverage level. Increased leverage is also related to the information or signaling hypothesis, which is another explanation for the source of gains. By increasing leverage, management signals that it believes cash flows will be sufficiently higher in the future to cover higher interest payments. Also, by repurchasing the shares at a premium over the current market price, management is signaling its belief based on inside information that the shares are undervalued by the market. And, since corporate insiders typically do not participate in the repurchase, they are increasing their percentage ownership in the firm, another signal that they are optimistic about the firm's prospects. The share repurchase premium also serves as a takeover defense; it may be higher than the premium offered by a raider. Thus, it alerts shareholders that it is not only the raider who sees the potential for increased value in the firm, but also the firm's own management. The bondholder expropriation theory suggests that the gains to shareholders come at the expense of the bondholders, but there is no evidence to support this hypothesis.

Exchange offers are a way for a company to change its capital structure while holding investment policy unchanged. Debt-for-common-stock offers have the effect of increasing leverage, and vice versa. The theory and wealth effects of exchange offers are similar to those for share repurchase. Among the characteristics which typically result in positive returns to shareholders are: (1) the offer increases leverage; (2) the offer implies an increase in future cash flows; and (3) the offer implies that the common stock is undervalued by the market. Leverage-increasing exchange offers, like share repurchases, are often used as an alternative means of making payouts to shareholders.

QUESTIONS

1. What are three ways to carry out a share repurchase?
2. In a tender offer for share repurchase, how is the wealth increase distributed among tendering and nontendering shareholders?
3. What theory most plausibly explains the positive shareholder wealth effect observed in share repurchases?
4. A company has 8 million shares outstanding. It offers to repurchase 2 million shares at $30 per share; the current market price of the stock is $25. Management controls 500,000 shares and does not participate in the repurchase. What is the signaling cost of the repurchase if the true value of the stock is $20; if the true value of the stock is $29?
5. What types of exchange offers are associated with positive abnormal returns to shareholders and what types are associated with negative returns? What possible sources account for the positive returns?

REFERENCES

BRADLEY, MICHAEL, and LEE M. WAKEMAN, "The Wealth Effects of Targeted Share Repurchases," *Journal of Financial Economics*, 11, 1983, pp. 301–328.

BRICKLEY, JAMES, "Shareholder Wealth, Information Signalling and the Specially Designated Dividend: An Empirical Study," *Journal of Financial Economics,* 12, 1983, pp. 103–114.

Dann, Larry, "Common Stock Repurchases: An Analysis of Returns to Bondholders and Stockholders," *Journal of Financial Economics,* 9, 1981, pp. 113–138.

Feldstein, Martin, and Jerry Green, "Why Do Companies Pay Dividends?" *American Economic Review,* 73, March 1983, pp. 17–30.

Finnerty, John D., "Stock-for-Debt Swaps and Shareholder Returns," *Financial Management,* 14, Autumn 1985, pp. 5–17.

Masulis, Ronald W., "Stock Repurchase by Tender Offer: An Analysis of the Causes of Common Stock Price Changes," *Journal of Finance,* 35, 1980, pp. 305–319.

Masulis, Ronald, "The Impact of Capital Structure Change on Firm Value: Some Estimates," *Journal of Finance,* 38, March 1983, pp. 107–126.

McConnell, John J., and Gary G. Schlarbaum, "Evidence on the Impact of Exchange Offers on Security Prices: The Case of Income Bonds," *Journal of Business,* 54, 1981, pp. 65–85.

Mikkelson, W. H., "Convertible Security Calls and Security Returns," *Journal of Financial Economics,* 9, 1981, pp. 237–264.

Miller, Merton H., "Debt and Taxes," *Journal of Finance,* 32, 1977, pp. 261–276.

———, and Myron S. Scholes, "Dividends and Taxes," *Journal of Financial Economics,* 6, December 1978, pp. 333–364.

Modigliani, Franco, and Merton H. Miller, "The Cost of Capital, Corporation Finance and the Theory of Investment," *American Economic Review,* 48, June 1958, pp. 261–297.

———, Corporate Income Taxes and the Cost of Capital," *American Economic Review,* June 1963, pp. 433–443.

Peavy, J. W., and J. A. Scott, "A Closer Look at Stock-for-Debt Swaps," *Financial Analysts Journal,* May/June 1985, pp. 44–50.

Pinegar, J. Michael, and Ronald C. Lease, "The Impact of Preferred-for-Common Exchange Offers on Firm Value," *Journal of Finance,* 41, September 1986, pp. 795–814.

Vermaelen, Theo, "Common Stock Repurchases and Market Signalling: An Empirical Study," *Journal of Financial Economics,* 9, 1981, pp. 139–183.

———, "Repurchase Tender Offers, Signaling and Managerial Incentives," *Journal of Financial and Quantitative Analysis,* 19, 1984, pp. 163–181.

CHAPTER **19**

Corporate Control Mechanisms

Throughout the book we have emphasized value maximization as a goal. But we also observe that a premium is paid for a control position in a firm. This is not necessarily inconsistent with value maximization. An important motive for control is to ensure that a program for the successful performance of the firm can be carried through without interruption. On the other hand, a management team in a control position may deviate from value maximization in pursuit of self-interests. Managerial ownership and control of voting rights could provide managers with an effective shield against competition from alternative management teams.

In the market for corporate control, managers or teams of managers compete for the rights to manage corporate resources (Jensen and Ruback, 1983). This market operates both within the firm and outside the firm. Transfers of control between management teams are accomplished either through internal control devices typified by the board of directors or through external control mechanisms including proxy contests and hostile takeovers. The control mechanism called upon at a particular instance depends on the ownership structure of the firm, the composition of the firm's board, the availability of outside bidders and dissidents, and so on. The incumbent management may opt to secure its position by increasing its voting power through creation of different classes of common stock or through changes of its financial policies involving debt and assets (Dann and DeAngelo, 1988; Harris and Raviv, 1988; Stulz, 1988). It may also institute antitakeover measures.

In this chapter, we review both theoretical considerations and empirical evidence on (1) the various control mechanisms, (2) the effects of managerial equity ownership, (3) the value of voting rights and control, (4) dual-class recapitalizations, and (5) the role of proxy contests. Other specific takeover defenses including alternative financial policies are discussed in Chapter 20.

INTERNAL AND EXTERNAL CONTROL MECHANISMS

Both internal and external mechanisms for corporate control operate to encourage, monitor and, if necessary, to replace managers. As we have seen in Chapter 2, important internal mechanisms include competition among managers within the firm, the control function of the board of directors, and the monitoring role of large shareholders. When the internal mechanisms fail to solve the problems of the firm, the more expensive external control mechanisms such as tender offers and proxy fights come into play. In this section, we review empirical evidence on the relative efficiency of these control mechanisms in ensuring maximization of shareholder value and on which mechanism is likely to be employed under different circumstances.

Inside versus Outside Directors and CEO Turnover

It is widely believed that outside directors play a larger role in monitoring management than inside directors. Fama (1980), for instance, argues that the inclusion of outside directors as professional referees enhances the viability of the board in effecting low-cost internal transfer of control. This also lowers the probability of top management colluding and expropriating shareholders. Outside directors are usually respected leaders from the business and academic community and have incentives to protect and develop their reputation as experts in decision control (Fama and Jensen, 1983). A study by Weisbach (1988) formally tests the hypothesis that inside and outside directors behave differently in monitoring top management and finds that firms with outsider-dominated boards are significantly more likely than firms with insider-dominated boards to remove the chief executive officer (CEO).

In Weisbach's study, firms are grouped according to the percentage of outsiders (directors who neither work for the corporation nor have extensive dealings with the company) on the board. In his sample of 367 New York Stock Exchange (NYSE) firms, the proportion of outside directors on the board centered around 50 percent, with few firms in the tails of the distribution. In the study, outsider-dominated firms (128 firms) are those in which at least 60 percent of the board are outsiders. Insider-dominated firms (93 firms) have outsiders making up no more than 40 percent of the directors. Firms with between 40 percent and 60 percent outsiders are considered mixed (146 firms). For all the firms in the sample, there were 286 CEO resignations in the period between 1974–1983. In the actual analysis, CEO resignations for reasons that are obviously unrelated to performance are eliminated from the sample.

When stock returns are used as predictors of CEO removal, the results show a statistically significant inverse relation between a firm's market-adjusted share performance in a year and the likelihood of a subsequent change in its CEO. The responsiveness of the removal decision to stock performance is three times larger for the outsider-dominated boards than for the other board types. Resignations are not sensitive to returns from periods preceding the event by more than a year, which suggest that the board's decision to replace the CEO takes place relatively quickly following poor share return performance. Using accounting earnings changes (net of industry effects) as the performance measure gives similar results. Also, there is an indication that the board of directors looks at accounting numbers (earnings before interest and taxes) to evaluate a CEO's performance, possibly more than at stock returns.

Weisbach (1988) also provides evidence that the larger the shareholdings by both the top two officers of the firm and the rest of the board, the smaller the number of outsiders on the board (Table 19.1). As expected, increased shareholdings of the CEO reduce the probability that he or she resigns. However, share ownership by noncontrolling directors (that is, directors excluding two top officers) does not appear to have any explanatory power, in addition to board composition. Thus, Weisbach suggests that the composition of the board rather than its equity ownership is what drives the level of monitoring.

Weisbach (1988) also measures price responses to the announcement of CEO resignations. His results show that the excess returns from a market model are significantly positive and thus imply that more news is revealed by these resignations. This result is different from Warner, Watts, and Wruck (1988), which is reviewed next. Further analyses show that outside and mixed boards increase their firms' values when they replace a CEO, but not for insider-dominated boards.

TABLE 19.1

Management Shareholdings by Board Type for 208 NYSE Corporations in 1980

	BOARD TYPE (%)			ENTIRE SAMPLE (%)
	INSIDE[a]	MIXED[b]	OUTSIDE[c]	
Chairman and President	7.98	2.32	1.57	3.71
Rest of Board	5.26	2.39	1.75	3.01

[a]Inside boards have no more than 40 percent outside directors.
[b]Mixed boards have between 40 percent and 60 percent outsiders.
[c]Outside boards have at least 60 percent outsiders.
SOURCE: M. Weisbach, "Outside Directors and CEO Turnover," *Journal of Financial Economics*, 1988, p. 449.

Stock Prices and Top Management Changes

Warner, Watts, and Wruck (1988) investigate the relation between a firm's stock price performance and subsequent changes in its top management including the CEO, president, and chairman of the board. They also provide new evidence on mechanisms for replacing inefficient managers and encouraging managers to maximize shareholder wealth. The dataset used by Warner, Watts, and Wruck includes top management changes for 269 NYSE and AMEX firms in the period 1963 to 1978.

Consistent with studies of CEO changes (Coughlan and Schmidt, 1985; Weisbach, 1988), Warner, Watts, and Wruck find an inverse relation between the probability of a top management change and share returns. They also document evidence of several internal monitoring mechanisms which include monitoring by large block holders, competition from other managers, as well as discipline by the board. Observing that stock returns adjusted for market factors increase the explanatory power of their analytical procedures, Warner, Watts, and Wruck suggest that management is not held responsible for factors outside its control. The results also indicate that, unless share performance is extremely good or bad, their analytical procedure has no predictive ability. This leads Warner, Watts, and Wruck to raise questions about the strength of the underlying monitoring mechanism.

In contrast with Weisbach (1988), the event study results of Warner, Watts, and Wruck (1988) show little evidence of nonzero abnormal returns at announcement of a top management change. Although many plausible scenarios can be consistent with this finding, "its unimpressive magnitude raises questions about the gains from such an endeavor" (Warner, Watts, and Wruck, 1988, p. 488).

Firm Characteristics and Control Mechanisms

Monitoring by boards of directors can deal with at least some problems facing the firm. This is evidenced by the findings of the studies reviewed earlier that poor performance of the firm increases the likelihood of top management replacement. But there is the alternative view that boards have been ineffective in recognizing the problems of the firm and standing up to top officers, especially when tough decisions are necessary to solve the problems (Jensen, 1986). External control devices such as hostile takeovers have been brought in because of the failure of the board, according to this view.

The work by Morck, Shleifer, and Vishny (1988a) is motivated by these opposing views and provides evidence on when the board can effectively deal with the problems of the firm and when the external control market comes into play. It is the view of Morck, Shleifer, and Vishny that when the company underperforms its relatively healthy industry, it is easier for the board to assess blame and fire the top management; but the board's problem is much harder when the whole industry is suffering. In the latter case, it is difficult to judge whether the management is making mistakes and, even when it is, the board may be reluctant to force the CEO to take painful measures (for example, divest divisions, lay off workers, or cut wages) often required in mature or declining industries. Therefore, under these circumstances, an external challenge to shake up the management and the board may be necessary to enforce shareholder wealth maximization.

The analysis by Morck, Shleifer, and Vishny is based on a sample comprising all publicly-traded 1980 Fortune 500 firms. Of these 454 firms, 34 were acquired in friendly acquisitions, 40 in hostile takeovers, and 93 underwent internally precipitated "complete turnover" of top management in the period 1981–1985. Morck, Shleifer, and Vishny analyze this sample to determine the relationship between the form of control change and a firm's performance problems. The performance measures employed are the Tobin's q for 1980, the cumulative abnormal return on stock over the period 1978–1980 (calculated using the Capital Asset Pricing Model), and employment growth over the 1978–1980 period. The numerator of the q-ratio is the sum of the actual market value of the firm's common stock and estimated market values of preferred stock and debt. The denominator of q is the replacement cost of the firm's plant and inventories.

The results of the analysis can be summarized as follows. Firms experiencing complete management turnover are characterized by their poor performance relative to their own industries and not by poor industry performance. For targets of hostile takeovers, poor industry performance is clearly observed and there is weak evidence that poor company performance is also involved. Targets of friendly acquisitions significantly underperform their industries in terms of stock returns and there is some indication that their industries are characterized by favorable business conditions relative to average industries.

Overall, the results indicate that the board is not completely unresponsive to company problems. When company performance is significantly lower than industry performance, the probability that the board will remove top management rises. But Morck, Shleifer, and Vishny find that the board has not been a major force in removing unresponsive managers in poorly performing industries. Instead, this function has been left with the market for hostile takeovers. When internal control devices such as the boards of directors are ineffective in taking drastic measures to solve industry-wide problems as well as company problems, takeover organizers take advantage of the opportunities.

The evidence on friendly acquisitions allows Morck, Shleifer, and Vishny to suggest that the likely candidates for a friendly acquisition are firms with considerable intangible assets (including growth opportunities) that have recently underperformed their industry. Morck, Shleifer, and Vishny (1988, p. 15) observe, "Targets of friendly mergers are often thought to have considerable intangible assets, such as a growing customer base, to which the acquirer can add management skills or access to capital." Note that the evidence of Morck, Shleifer, and

Vishny with respect to friendly acquisitions is highly consistent with the theory of related and conglomerate mergers presented in Chapter 4.

Finally, Morck, Shleifer, and Vishny report that the characteristics of management also appear to be important in determining the form of control change. The presence of a founding family on the top management reduces the probabilities of both a hostile takeover and complete management turnover. When the top management consists of only one young boss (aged below 60), complete management turnover becomes unlikely and the probabilities of both hostile and friendly takeovers increase. There is also some indication that a larger equity stake of the top executive reduces the likelihood of complete turnover and of a hostile takeover, but increases that of a friendly acquisition.

MANAGERIAL OWNERSHIP AND CORPORATE PERFORMANCE

Equity ownership by managers may have both benefits and costs to corporate performance. It was Berle and Means (1932) who first emphasized that little equity ownership by managers in diffusely-owned corporations will encourage managers to pursue their own interests. When managers' share ownership increases, their interests are better aligned with shareholder interests and thus deviation from value maximization will decline (Jensen and Meckling, 1976). In contrast, managerial ownership and control of voting rights may give a manager enough power to guarantee his or her employment with the firm and pursue self-interest at the expense of shareholder wealth. Firms with insider ownership of over 30 percent are rarely acquired in hostile takeovers (Weston, 1979).

The tradeoff between the alignment of manager/shareholder interests and managerial entrenchment makes it difficult to unambiguously predict the relationship between management ownership and the market value of the firm. Empirical investigation of this relationship will thus be valuable and is performed by Morck, Shleifer, and Vishny (1988a).

A different aspect of corporate equity ownership is that a substantial number of publicly-held corporations are characterized by concentrated ownership, despite the apparent inefficiency in risk bearing (Demsetz and Lehn, 1985). One view on the role of large block holders is expressed in the model developed by Shleifer and Vishny (1986) in which the large shareholder monitors the firm's management and engages itself in jawboning, proxy contests, and takeovers as needed. Stulz (1988) proposes a model in which large block holder managers resist takeover attempts and thereby may cause the takeover premium (and the firm value) to be higher. These different views and predictions on the organizational roles of large block holders motivate Holderness and Sheehan (1988) to empirically investigate the role of large block ownership. We next review their empirical findings and the results of Morck, Shleifer, and Vishny (1988a).

Convergence of Interests Hypothesis versus Entrenchment Hypothesis

Morck, Shleifer, and Vishny (1988a) suggest that the convergence of interests hypothesis predicts a uniformly positive relationship between management ownership and market valuation of the firm's assets, and that the entrenchment hypothesis implies a negative relationship for some range of high ownership stake. Morck, Shleifer, and Vishny argue that the predictions of the entrenchment hypothesis are not clearcut, because entrenchment is not just a consequence of voting power. Entrenchment of a manager is also affected by the manager's tenure with the firm, status as a founder, personality, and by the presence of a large outside shareholder or an active group of outside directors. Morck, Shleifer, and Vishny also point out that diminishing returns might set in before 50 percent ownership is reached so that increases in shareholdings would not allow deeper entrenchment and entail a penalty in market valuation.

In the empirical analysis, Morck, Shleifer, and Vishny look at the relationship between Tobin's q and the shareholdings of the board of directors in a sample of 371 Fortune 500 firms in 1980. In the sample, the mean combined stake of all board members is 10.6 percent whereas the median is only 3.4 percent. In 20 percent of the sample the board owned more than 20 percent of the firm. The results obtained from a variety of (piecewise linear regression) estimations seem to suggest a positive relation between ownership and q in the 0 percent to 5 percent range, a negative relation in the 5 percent to 25 percent range, and perhaps a further positive relation beyond 25 percent. The interpretation suggested by the authors incorporates both the convergence of interests and entrenchment effects. The initial rise in q as ownership rises reflects the incentive effect of rising ownership stakes of managers. Beyond the 5 percent ownership level, managerial ownership increases are associated with other conditions conducive to entrenchment. Whatever its exact source, some form of entrenchment is seen to explain the declining value of assets as managerial ownership rises from 5 percent to 25 percent. In this range, the incentive effect is dominated by the entrenchment effect. Managements with stakes larger than 25 percent are not significantly more entrenched than those with 25 percent ownership. In other words, the board can reject any takeover challenge with an ownership stake greater than 25 percent.

Jensen and Warner (1988, p. 13) express their surpise at the implication that "inside stock ownership as little as 5 percent begins to give managers control powers important enough to cause firm value to fall." They also note that the implication of effective managerial control occurring by 25 percent is inconsistent with the findings of Jarrell and Poulsen (1988). In that study, the largest negative effects of dual-class recapitalizations occur when insider holdings are in the 30 percent to 55 percent range. "If managers of these firms already had effective control at 25 percent, there would be no negative value effects from the additional concentration of voting power in insider hands" following the recapitalization (Jensen and Warner, 1988, p. 13).

Morck, Shleifer, and Vishny (1988a), suggest reasons why their interpretation might not be entirely satisfactory. First, the positive relation between ownership and Tobin's q is not only due to the convergence of interests effect, but also to the fact that managers of high-q firms often receive stock bonuses and exercise their stock options, ending up with more shares. Also, managers may be required to hold more shares when the firm has a lot of intangible assets (causing a larger q) to ensure proper management (Demsetz and Lehn, 1985). Second, the decline of q at 5 percent ownership may reflect the positive correlation between ownership and other attributes facilitating entrenchment. To support this argument, Morck, Shleifer, and Vishny provide the evidence that the presence of a founding family in an older firm decreases q, even after controlling for ownership.

The Role of Majority Shareholders

Holderness and Sheehan (1988) analyze 114 NYSE- or AMEX-listed firms with majority shareholders defined as individuals or entities owning at least 50 percent but less than all of the common stock. The reason for focusing on majority shareholders is that the effects of concentrated ownership should be most accentuated for firms with majority shareholders. For majority holders, most of the wealth effects of their management decisions are internalized and the monitoring by the board or by the external market for corporate control will not restrain their behavior effectually.

Among the 114 firms, 27 became majority-shareholder firms during the period 1978–1984, but only 13 ceased to be such firms during the same period. Thus, there is no apparent net outflow from majority ownership. This result is also confirmed for a much larger base of publicly-traded firms. It appears that majority ownership is surviving as a viable organizational form. In the sample, the majority shareholders are approximately equally divided between individuals and corporations. Firms with individual majority shareholders are typically smaller and firms with corporate majority shareholders are slightly larger than the typical NYSE or AMEX firms. Ninety percent of individual majority shareholders and representatives of 94 percent of corporate majority shareholders are either directors or officers of their firms.

The average majority holding is 64 percent (median 60 percent) for all firms in the sample, which is substantially more than the minimum stock (50 percent) that assures voting control. This evidence appears inconsistent with the proposition that majority blocks are held to expropriate minority shareholders. Expropriation-oriented majority shareholders might want to hold above 66 percent because of supramajority voting provisions in the firm's bylaws or articles of incorporation. However, only 36 percent of the sample firms involve blocks above 66 percent, the typical supramajority requirement, and for these firms the authors find no cases in which the requirement is mentioned in proxy statements.

Holderness and Sheehan (1988) also analyze stock-price reaction to 31 announcements of majority-block trades to study the effect on firm value of changing shareholders. On average, stock prices increase over the day before announcement and the announcement day by an abnormal 7.3 percent, and over the 30-day period around the announcement by an abnormal 12.8 percent. The results also indicate that on average firm value increases more when both the buyer and the seller are individuals, rather than corporations. The abnormal return is higher for announcements involving simultaneous tender offers to minority shareholders (10 out of 31 cases) than announcements with no such tender offers (21 cases). In most of the consummated cases, new directors and officers were appointed after the trades.

When majority-shareholder firms are compared to firms with relatively diffuse-stock ownership, Holderness and Sheehan (1988) find no statistical difference in investment expenditures, frequency of control changes, accounting rates of return, and Tobin's q. However, there is evidence that individual majority-shareholder firms underperform their comparison firms in terms of q-ratios and accounting rates of return, whereas corporate majority-shareholder firms do not.

The preceding results yield several implications. First, the positive stock price reactions are inconsistent with the proposition that majority shareholders' primary objective is to expropriate or consume corporate wealth. If the expropriation hypotheses were valid, majority shareholders would not offer to buy out minority shareholders at substantial premiums. Yet such offers are made in one third of the majority-block trading announcements. Second, majority shareholders or their representatives do not merely monitor management teams but actively participate in management. That the majority shareholder plays a central role in management is consistent with the management and board turnover following majority-block trading. Third, the apparent premise for the antagonism toward large block shareholders (reflected in state regulations limiting their voting rights, antitakeover laws, poison pill charter amendments, and other "shareholder rights" initiatives) is not consistent with the empirical evidence.

As Jensen and Warner (1988) point out, Holderness and Sheehan (1988) do not investigate what characteristics of the firm would make it optimal for a firm to be majority controlled. Additional research is required on the causality between ownership concentration and firm characteristics, on which Demsetz and Lehn (1985) and the studies of leveraged buy-outs (Chapter 16) provide evidence.

VOTING RIGHTS
AND VALUE OF CONTROL

The distribution of voting and cash flow rights among common stockholders on other than a one-to-one basis can be accomplished in a number of ways. With different classes of common stock, one class may be barred from voting in elections for the board of directors, or permitted to elect only a minority of the board. The inferior-vote class of stock may have fewer votes per share, or may have no voting rights at all. Even without different classes of stock, the distribution of shares can alter effective voting rights; especially where cumulative voting is not enforced, the vote of minority stockholders may be rendered virtually meaningless.

Contractual arrangements such as voting trusts and standstill agreements can also impact nominally equal voting rights. In a voting trust, stockholders retain cash flow rights to their shares while giving the right to vote those shares to another entity. Standstill agreements require a shareholder (often a threatening raider) to refrain from acquiring additional stock, and to vote with management over a specified period of time. There may be contingent voting rights for preferred stockholders in the event of missed dividends or, more rarely, for bondholders. Convertible securities as well as warrants and options may also be viewed as conferring contingent voting rights, that is, contingent upon conversion or exercise.

To test the hypothesis that control is valued by the capital market, samples are constructed of firms with dual classes of common stock with identical explicit cash flow rights differing only in voting rights. Any difference in stock price, management ownership, or premium paid in a merger between the two classes of stock then indicates a difference in value attributable to differential voting rights, which can be termed the value of control.

Evidence on Value of Control

Lease, McConnell, and Mikkelson (1983) hypothesize that any voting rights premium, that is, the incremental value of superior-vote stock over inferior-vote stock, must reflect differences in payoffs in future states of nature. The evidence from their sample of dual-class stock firms over the period 1940–1978 supports a price premium for superior voting right, "a consistent relationship between security value and corporate control." For 828 pairs of month-end prices, publicly-traded superior-vote stock commanded a premium 88 pecent of the time; the average premium was 5.44 percent. For a small subsample of firms which also had voting preferred stock outstanding (superior to both classes of common stock), the superior-vote common stock sold at a discount (averaging 1.25 percent) relative to the inferior class of common stock. However, a later study using a sample of British firms found an opposite result—the voting rights premium was even larger in firms having voting preferred stock (Megginson, 1988).

The authors identify and eliminate several possible sources of incremental payoffs which could explain the price premium. In one scenario, controlling shareholders could direct the board to buy back shares of the superior-vote stock at an above-market price; however, this practice is generally prohibited by both charter provisions and the courts. Alternatively, rights to buy new stock at below-market prices could be issued to the superior class of common stock only; while not prohibited, this explanation was not found to drive the results for the sample under study. The authors find a partial explanation for the price premium in the possibility of indirect cash and noncash payments in the form of higher than warranted compensation and/or perquisites for superior-vote stock-holders who are also employees (managers) of the corporation.

Managerial Ownership of Voting Rights

If, as Lease, McConnell, and Mikkelson (1983) argue, the incremental value of control is based to a great extent on the possibility of incremental payoffs to superior-vote stockholders who also happen to be employee/managers of the issuing firm, then we would expect to find ownership of superior-vote stock concentrated in management. DeAngelo and DeAngelo (1985) focus on owner-ship concentration of dual-class stock and confirm that management does, in-deed, seem to place a higher value on voting rights over cash flow rights. For 45 firms with dual-class stock in 1980, 96 percent of all shareholders held inferior-vote stock, with superior-vote stock concentrated in the hands of management. Sixty to 75 percent of the firms were classified as majority controlled by manage-ment (depending on whether the definition of management was extended to include nonofficer directors). Management's median voting rights ownership was 56.9 percent, while median cash flow ownership was only 24 percent.

Other benefits of managerial voting control in addition to incremental sal-ary and perquisites are identified. Vote ownership encourages managers to in-vest in organization-specific human capital. Management performance evalua-tion costs may be high if it is difficult to communicate the information necessary to evaluate performance to outside shareholders; managerial vote ownership protects managers from being removed from office by mistake. For example, a potentially successful long-term strategy may be causing havoc with short-term performance indicators; or an accurate assessment of management performance might require dissemination of proprietary information.

This insulation from competition by other management teams in the mar-ket for corporate control is also the primary cost of managerial vote ownership; however, other substitute discipline mechanisms operate to keep management discretion within bounds. Consistently poor management will result in excessive costs of external capital as well as adverse cash flow consequences for the manag-ers themselves. The significant family involvement in many of these dual-class stock firms provides another potent disciplinary force in the form of social sanc-tions against family member/managers. Many of these firms started as family businesses, but as growth continued, family wealth constraints would have meant foregoing profitable investment opportunities in the absence of external equity. By going public with inferior-vote stock, these companies raise the needed capital without relinquishing control for themselves, and exchanges of stock among family members provide a means to transfer control across genera-tions. (The Ford Company is a notable example.)

Since the sample in this study included many (two thirds) nonpublicly-traded stocks (all of the superior-vote class), the authors did not calculate an explicit market price premium. They did, however, examine selected acquisitions of dual-class stock firms for evidence of a premium paid for the superior-vote stock. Previous studies of acquisition price premiums to superior-vote stock had considered only publicly-traded stock and found a premium in the neighborhood of 5 percent (consistent with the price premium found in the Lease, McConnell, and Mikkelson, 1983 study).

However, open-market trading may not fully reflect the value of the vote, especially in acquisitions, since acquisitions must be designed to keep explicit compensation equal in order to avoid lawsuits blocking or delaying the transaction. Other devices may be used to increase the effective payment to publicly-traded superior-vote stock, such as offering stockholders long-term employment or consulting contracts at above-market rates, or the opportunity to buy a division not wanted by the acquirer at a below-market price. Notwithstanding, the authors were able to identify four transactions (out of 30 acquisitions) in which an explicit premium (ranging from 83 to 200 percent) was paid to holders of nonpublicly-traded superior-vote common stock. The authors estimate that the value of the voting advantage accounted for 47 to 67 percent of the compensation received by these stockholders (DeAngelo and DeAngelo, 1985).

Alternative Hypotheses on Voting Rights Premium

Why should a voting rights premium exist for marginal (noncontrol block) shares of superior voting rights stock? Megginson (1988) addresses this question and provides empirical evidence. He first notes that controlling share blocks sell for more than noncontrolling blocks (Meeker and Joy, 1980). Thus, when superior voting rights shares are a part of a majority block, these shares should sell at a premium over shares of the same voting class that are not part of such a block as well as over shares of another, otherwise identical, class with inferior voting rights. However, the studies by Lease, McConnell, and Mikkelson (1983) and Levy (1983) find a premium for marginal shares of superior voting stock. The premium continues to exist for long periods of time and is involved in trading between investors who do not reap the benefits of control.

Megginson (1988) starts with the critical point that the voting rights premium must reflect rights to future cash flows which ownership of the restricted voting shares does not convey—a point made earlier by Lease, McConnell, and Mikkelson (1983). To identify what the rights entail, Megginson poses three hypotheses. The "extra merger premium hypothesis" involves the possibility that a firm may become the target in a takeover attempt and that a higher price will be paid for the superior voting rights shares. The differential price is a premium for the power to sell control of a company. The rational capital market will capitalize the discounted value of the extra merger premium into the current market price of the superior voting rights stock. Under this hypothesis, the premium will be related to (1) the probability that the firm will become a takeover target and (2) the likelihood that a higher price will be paid for the superior voting shares. One difficulty of the hypothesis is that the observed voting rights premium (such as the 45 percent premium reported by Levy, 1983) appears too large for a discounted expected value of some future takeover premium.

Thus, Megginson (1988) explores a second hypothesis—the "ownership structure hypothesis." It is first noted that managerial shareholdings can have both incentive and entrenchment effects (Grossman and Hart, 1988; Harris and Raviv, 1988a; Morck, Shleifer, and Vishny, 1988a; Stulz, 1988). When managerial shareholdings are large, managers are effectively entrenched in office and it is difficult to discipline them (even through a takeover). As noted earlier, DeAngelo and DeAngelo (1985) document very large shareholdings of insiders in dual-class firms. Further, managers increase their holdings of voting rights after re-capitalizations that introduce a dual-class common stock structure, even as they reduce their fractional ownerships of cash flow rights (Partch, 1987). The entrench-ment effect may lower the market value of dual-class firms. Empirical evidence consistent with this proposition is reported by Jarrell and Poulsen (1988) who document a significant and negative stock price reaction to the announcement by NYSE firms of plans to adopt dual-class equity capitalization after June 1984. Thus, the ownership structure hypothesis states that the entrenchment effect of concentrated insider holders of superior voting stock will cause a discount in the value of inferior voting stock "relative to what their value would be if they had full voting rights." This hypothesis predicts that insider shareholdings of the inferior-vote stock will lower the discount by lessening their incentives to exploit their insider positions at the expense of the inferior-vote stockholders. Conversely, superior-vote stockholdings by insiders increase the opportunistic incentives, and thus the discount (or the voting rights premium) will also be increased. (However, it is not clear whether this ownership structure hypothesis can stand alone with-out the following, third hypothesis, because the marginal shares presumably are not part of the insider shareholdings.)

The third hypothesis is based on the observation that the stability of the controlling coalition of insider shareholders will impact the market value of noncontrol-block shares. Coalition stability affects the probability of a control contest occurring in the future and thus determines the probability that noncontrol-block shares will participate in "any premium payment made to establish voting control." Thus the "voting power hypothesis" is very similar to the extra merger premium hypothesis. It predicts that marginal superior voting shares will sell at a greater premium when control of a corporation is more contestable, that is, when the control coalition is less stable.

To provide empirical evidence on the three alternative, but related, hy-potheses, Megginson (1988) examines a sample of 152 British firms which had two or more common share classes with differential voting rights outstanding at some time during the period 1955–1982. Over 16,000 monthly price pairs were examined. The superior voting rights shares had an average price premium of 13.3 percent over an otherwise equivalent class of restricted voting rights. Liquidity was not causing the premium, because the restricted voting shares traded much more frequently. Liquidity, if anything, attenuated the premium.

Higher prices (an average premium of 27.6 percent) were paid to the superior voting shares in 37 of 43 sample firms that were acquired while they had dual classes outstanding. Since only 28 percent of the firms were acquired during the long period of study and the average takeover premium was 27.6 percent, Megginson (1988) contends that the merger premium (7.8 percent ignoring the time value of money) is too low to explain a stable voting rights premium of 13 percent. When a company was a subsidiary of another firm, the average voting rights premium was lower. The mean premium was 6 percent and significant. This premium is less than half as large as the average for all companies. Megginson (1988, p. 16) interprets this result as being consistent with the extra merger premium hypothesis but "at odds with the voting power hypothesis which predicts no [premium] for subsidiary companies."

Regression analyses showed that the voting rights premium was directly related to insider holdings of superior voting shares and inversely related to insider holdings of restricted voting shares. This result is consistent with the ownership structure hypothesis, but appears inconsistent with the voting power hypothesis (because greater insider holdings of superior voting shares should increase the stability of coalition and thus reduce the voting power of marginal shares and their premium). Thus, the empirical evidence generally supports the extra merger premium and ownership structure hypotheses.

DUAL-CLASS RECAPITALIZATIONS

Dual-class recapitalizations can be used to consolidate control of the corporation by insiders, protecting them from displacement by a hostile takeover. To test this hypothesis, Jarrell and Poulsen (1988) examine shareholder wealth effects of 94 firms recapitalizing with dual classes of common stock with disparate voting rights. The sample firms recapitalized in the period 1976–1986 by either the dividend method (55 percent of the sample), the exchange method (35 percent), and the length of time method (10 percent). The dividend method starts with a stock split or a stock dividend involving distribution of low-vote stock. The previously existing common stock is redesignated as high-vote class B stock usually entitled to ten votes per share and/or to elect a majority of the board of directors. The low-vote stock is usually entitled to one vote per share and/or to elect a minority of the board and sometimes receives a higher dividend. The exchange method issues high-vote stock in exchange for the currently outstanding (low-vote) stock. The low-vote stock generally receives a higher dividend. The length of time method involves a change in voting rights of the existing common stock which becomes entitled to ten votes per share. Newly issued or traded shares become "short term" and are entitled to only one vote. The short-term shares become "long-term" shares and entitled to ten votes per share after being held continuously for a substantial period, such as four years.

Sixty-seven of the 94 firms recapitalized since 1983, and over half of the recent cases represent NYSE-listed firms. For the 62 firms recapitalizing after the NYSE imposed a moratorium in June 1984 on the delisting of dual-class equity firms, the announcement effect of recapitalization was insignificantly negative 0.72 percent for the two-day window of the announcement day and the following day, but was significantly negative 0.55 percent for the day following the announcement. In addition, the fraction of firms with negative abnormal returns was 61 percent (and significantly different from 50 percent) on each of the two days. However, for the premoratorium sample, the abnormal return was insignificant. This latter result is also observed by Partch (1987) who studies 44 dual-class recapitalizations in the premoratorium period and concludes these recapitalizations do not harm shareholders.

Jarrell and Poulsen (1988) provide evidence that the postmoratorium sample (largely NYSE firms) had lower insider and higher institutional holdings. They also find that firms with highest insider holdings do not show negative announcement abnormal returns, but firms in the second and third insider holding quartiles (average holdings of 50.9 percent and 39.9 percent) experience significant negative returns. This evidence leads them to suggest that dual-class recapitalizations are undertaken by firms that are more susceptible to takeover and that they serve to entrench managers. (This interpretation could be more convincing if the lowest insider holding firms showed negative returns at the announcement. But the abnormal returns of these firms are insignificantly different from zero.) The higher institutional ownership may make it easier for insiders to get the recapitalization approved. If this is true, then the stock price should decline more under the insider entrenchment hypothesis when institutional shareholding is higher.

The Jarrell and Poulsen (1988) result or the entrenchment hypothesis raises a question on why the dual-class exchange offers enjoying increased popularity in recent years are voluntarily approved by shareholders. In some cases, the voting power of insiders will be sufficient in achieving shareholder approval, but this cannot explain all approvals. Ruback (1988) develops a model which explains shareholders' behavior in exchange offers in which shareholders are given the opportunity to exchange common stock for shares with limited voting rights but higher dividends. These offers induce shareholders to exchange their shares for limited voting rights shares carrying higher dividends, even though such shareholders are harmed by the exchange as a result of the decline in the share price. In these offers, the wealth of shareholders who retain the superior-vote shares is transferred to shareholders who elect the inferior-vote shares with higher dividends. Thus, all outside shareholders rationally choose the higher dividend. This leads to the approval of the exchange plan and in turn to the decline in their wealth. The shareholders face the prisoner's dilemma. If collective action were possible, outside shareholders would collude to defeat the exchange offer in order to avoid the reduced probability of receiving a takeover bid caused by the recapitalization.

PROXY CONTESTS

Proxy contests represent another aspect of the importance of control and membership on the firm's board of directors. Proxy contests are attempts by dissident groups of shareholders to obtain board representation. Even though technically most contests are unsuccessful to the extent that the dissident group fails to win a majority on the board of directors, proxy contests can and do have significant effects on target firm shareholder wealth regardless of outcome. Some have argued that a better measure of success is whether the dissident group gains at least two members on the board of directors. "We want one person to propose a motion and a second person to second it. Then discussion of the motion will be in the minutes of the board meeting. In this way, we can monitor the majority group and record our views on important policy issues." This quote summarizes views frequently set forth in the financial press in connection with proxy contests.

Studies of proxy contests explain the shareholder wealth effects that take place in terms of the disciplinary value of proxy contests in the managerial labor market, the relationship between proxy contests and other forms of takeover activity, and the value of the vote which takes on greater importance during a proxy contest. The study by Pound (1988) empirically identifies the sources of inefficiency of the present system of proxy contests.

Wealth Effects and Disciplinary Value of Proxy Contests

Dodd and Warner (1983) examined 96 proxy contests for board seats on NYSE- or AMEX-listed firms over the period 1962–1978. They consider several hypotheses to explain why target shareholder returns are positive and significant on average (6.2 percent over the period from 39 days before the contest announcement through the contest outcome) in spite of the fact that dissidents won a majority on the board in only one fifth of the cases studied.

First, even minority board representation allows the dissident group to have a positive impact on corporate policy leading to a permanent share price revaluation.

In cases where no board seats change hands, the fact of the challenge itself may cause incumbent management to implement changes in policy which benefit shareholders (Bradley, Desai, and Kim, 1983, "kick-in-the-pants" hypothesis). Scenarios which hypothesize stock price declines when proxy contests fail were not supported. These hypotheses emphasize the direct costs (in terms of corporate resources) of defending against the dissident group and ignore the possibilities for increased efficiency which may be exposed during the course of the contest. Abnormal returns at the contest outcome announcement were in fact negative for contests in which the dissidents failed to win any seats at all; however, the negative return was only −1.4 percent, not large enough to offset earlier gains and not very significant.

Dodd and Warner (1983) found that almost half the proxy contests were waged by former insiders who had left the target following a policy dispute. This suggests a strong link between proxy contests and competition in the managerial labor market. They also found that few of the dissident groups involved an outside firm, and concluded only a weak relation between proxy contests and merger and acquisition activity. This conclusion is disputed by DeAngelo and DeAngelo (1988) who find a strong link between proxy contests and other types of takeover activity.

The mechanics of waging a proxy contest almost guarantee that there will be leakage of information about dissident activity well before the proxy contest announcement in *The Wall Street Journal.* This is confirmed by significant abnormal returns of 11.9 percent over the period starting 60 days before the announcement through the announcement itself. These returns are not attributable to merger activity, since the results are similar whether the dissident group included another firm or not; the sample did not exhibit unexpectedly higher earnings in the preannouncement period. Thus, the positive returns seem attributable to the proxy contest itself.

Proxy Contests and Value of Control

In terms of the value of control, Dodd and Warner (1983) examine the significant negative abnormal returns (−4.3 percent) found in the interval between the initial contest announcement and the outcome announcement. These negative returns persisted regardless of contest outcome, were more negative for control contests than for participation contests, and did not appear to be caused by selection bias— so what caused them? Dodd and Warner (1983) test the hypothesis suggested by Manne (1962) that part of the increase in share price during a proxy contest is due to the increased value of the share's right to vote. Both dissident activity and incumbent defensive moves increase the demand for voting shares, and thus increase the share price. If this hypothesis is correct, then the stock price should fall when the vote ceases to matter, that is, on the holder of record date for voting in the proxy contest. In particular, if the holder of record date falls in the interval between the contest initiation and outcome announcements, the value of the vote could explain the negative returns during this period. And in fact Dodd and Warner (1983) found significant negative returns (−1.4 percent) at the holder of record date when this date fell in the relevant interval. This affirmation of the value of the vote hypothesis is supported by the fact that there were no significant returns on the holder of record date when the record date was set retroactively to a point before the contest initiation. On the other hand, the negative returns continue following the record date. Ruling out market inefficiency, an additional factor beyond the value of the vote must be operating. The value of the vote hypothesis explains only a portion of the negative returns in the initiation through outcome period.

A later study by DeAngelo and DeAngelo (1988) of 60 proxy contests from 1978–1985 corroborated many of Dodd and Warner's (1983) results. They found significant abnormal returns from 40 days before the contest through the outcome announcement of 6.02 percent, significant returns of 18.76 percent in the 40 days preceding any public indication of dissident activity. As in the earlier study, the gains (particularly those in the precontest period) were not dependent on contest outcome. Like Dodd and Warner (1983) they found negative returns at the contest outcome when the dissidents failed to win any seats on the board. These negative returns were larger than in the Dodd and Warner (1983) study: −5.45 percent over the two-day outcome announcement period. However, most of these negative returns were shown to result from the means by which the dissidents were defeated.   Where the incumbents prevailed in a shareholder vote, the negative return was only −1.73 percent and not significant. However, where the dissidents were defeated by other means, the return was a −7.19 percent (significant). These other means include the expenditure of corporate assets to buy off the dissidents, a white knight acquisition of the target, or court approval of the validity of the incumbent's defense in the face of which the dissidents withdrew. This result appears to imply that when the incumbent management is securely entrenched or the probability of future control contests is reduced, the value of vote and/or the expected takeover premium capitalized in the share price declines.

The Link Between Proxy Contests and Takeover Activity

As in the prior study, the dissidents were successsful in only about one third of the proxy contests. However, DeAngelo and DeAngelo (1988) go on to examine events in the target firm for three years after the contest. It was found that by the end of three years less than 20 percent of the target firms remained as independent publicly-held corporations under the same management as before the contest. For example, in 20 of the 39 firms in which dissidents failed to win a majority, there were 38 resignations of the CEO, president, or chairman of the board over the next three years. These resignations were clearly linked to the proxy contest either explicitly in the financial press, or by the fact that the vacancy was filled by a member of the dissident group. The 60-firm sample included 15 cases where sale or liquidation of the firm in the three-year period following the contest was directly linked to the dissident activity.

In fact, DeAngelo and DeAngelo (1988) conclude that most of the gains to proxy contest activity are closely related to merger and acquisitions activity. The initial gains in the precontest period (approximately 20 percent) are attributed to the increased likelihood that the firm will eventually be sold at a premium at some time following the proxy contest. To support this conclusion, they divide their sample into two groups: those which were eventually sold/liquidated and those which were not. For the "sold" subsample, abnormal returns over the full period of dissident activity were a significant 15.16 percent; while for the "unsold" group, the gain was a less significant 2.90 percent. The fact that the initial run-up was similar for both groups simply indicates that the market revises its opinion of the likelihood of a sale as more information becomes available. To the extent that proxy contests are indeed linked to takeover activity, the goal seems to be to get some representation on the board to persuade the rest of the board to sell or liquidate.

To further test the link between proxy contests and takeover activity, DeAngelo and DeAngelo (1988) focus on the composition of the dissident groups. In 10 of 60 cases, the dissidents included individuals who had been previously employed by the target firm. In 11 of 60 cases, members of the dissident group had reputations as corporate raiders, with previous takeover experience. So why not just take over the firm outright and dispose of the target's assets as owners? In most cases the answer seems to be resource limitations within the dissident group. In 48 of the 60 proxy contests studied, the dissidents consisted entirely of a group of private individuals presumably unwilling to lever themselves to the extent necessary to take over an exchange-listed public corporation. The remaining 12 cases included a public corporation within the dissident group, but the dissident corporation was typically much smaller (one half the size) than the target firm. Furthermore, the equity of the dissident public corporation was dominated by individuals in the dissident group who would have to severely dilute their equity position to raise the necessary funding to take over the target. Other barriers to outright takeover include antitakeover defenses in place and regulatory barriers.

This latter point was emphasized in a *Business Week* article (Power, March 7, 1988, p. 32). The article was headlined, "Why the Proxy Fight is Back: Poison pills and antitakeover laws make it popular again." The article explained that the increased barriers to takeovers had stimulated takeover groups to appeal directly to shareholders to change the composition of the board of directors. This evidence is supportive of some theoretical propositions. One is that the board of directors can indeed be used to monitor management selection and management performance as suggested in Chapter 2. Another is that takeover activity is often stimulated by the belief that changes in management will produce improvement in performance.

Efficiency Problems of Proxy Contests

A traditional view of proxy contests has been that they are an inefficient means of disciplining management and transferring corporate control. During the period 1981–1984, publicly-held corporations in the United States experienced only about 100 proxy contests, of which fewer than 60 were for control, but over 250 tender offers (Pound, 1988). This shows that proxy contests are less frequently used than tender offers for monitoring managers and effecting transfer of control.

Pound (1988) identifies three potential sources of inefficiency in the proxy contest regime and provides empirical evidence on the problems. The first source of inefficiency is the laws governing proxy solicitation. It is argued that the current system imposes high cost and uncertainty because the dissident is required to directly contact shareholders. The proxy card must be delivered to and returned by the shareholder, whereas in tender offers contact is made in one direction only, from the shareholder to the bidder. Share turnover makes it difficult to isolate current voting shareholders and some state laws have provisions making it difficult to determine who possesses the right to vote at any given time. Because of these problems, the management is said to enjoy an advantage in proxy solicitation.

The second problem is related to the composition of the shareholder pool. Small shareholders recognize that their votes are unlikely to affect the outcome and thus tend to remain uninformed about the issues of the contest. Therefore, the most important determinant of efficiency is whether large, informed shareholders have incentives to make the voting process efficient at the margin.

There are alternative hypotheses on the voting behavior of institutional holders and large block holders. One view is that some large block holders maintain strategic alliances with incumbent management. Another is that institutional investors may vote with management because of conflict of interest problems. Many fiduciaries have existing business relationships with incumbent management, as in the case of an insurance company holding a significant portion of a company's stock and concurrently acting as its primary insurer. Despite their fiduciary duties, the institutional investors may choose not to vote against management for fear of undermining their business relationships with the incumbent management.

The third inefficiency is related to the general problem of adverse selection. Proxy contests can be used instead of tender offers when the target undertakes strong defensive initiatives or when the dissident's goal is not to gain full control of the company. Dissident proxy challenges may also be initiated by those who have little confidence in their ex post ability to increase share value. These dissidents will choose proxy fights, rather than tender offers, because they need not be committed with share purchase at a premium. A dissident who seeks personal satisfaction will have to incur only the solicitation costs. Thus, signaling costs have to be incurred by serious dissidents to convey information on the value of their bid to outside shareholders. Available signaling strategies include buying more shares before the proxy vote or a legally binding promise to purchase a fraction of shares contingent on winning control. But these strategies move the proxy contest closer to a tender offer in terms of dissidents' resource commitment.

The data base used by Pound (1988) includes 100 dissident challenges in the period 1981–1985. These challenges cover full control contests, partial control contests to place at least one but less than a majority of directors on the board, shareholder proposals for changes in corporate strategy or structure, and opposition contests against a managerial proposal. The success rates of these contests varied between 40.4 percent (for full control) and 77.3 percent (for partial control), with a full sample average of 51.0 percent.

The data confirm all of the three hypotheses. First, the number of target firm shareholders strongly influences the prospects of contest success; the larger the number of shareholders, the lower the chance of dissident's success. This result is consistent with the hypothesis that dissidents face a significant disadvantage in soliciting votes and that management is better equipped to solicit votes than dissidents. The management's advantage increases when more shareholders must be "tracked down." Also, there was the result that the longer the time available for solicitation, the greater the chance of dissident's victory.

Second, the data show the proxy contest targets have a mean value of institutional ownership of 19.1 percent, which is about 30 percent lower than the market average of 33.5 percent. Further, in successful contests, institutional ownership is lower than the average of target firms. Finally, full-control proxy initiatives involve firms with low institutional holdings relative to other contest targets and the market average. The results are similar with respect to block holdings. These results confirm the conflict of interest theory or the strategic alignment theory on the voting behavior of institutional investors. These theories suggest that higher institutional holdings will deter proxy contests, lower the probability of dissident's success, and discourage full-control challenges.

Finally, Pound (1988) obtains the result that both higher dissident holdings and the existence of a formal offer to buy shares contingent on a victory significantly increases dissident's chances. The average dissident holding in unsuccessful contests is 9.0 percent, while in successful contests it is 14.3 percent. These low dissident holdings even in successful contests may suggest that dissident share purchases is to signal commitment rather than to lock up the vote. These results support the hypothesis that signals in the form of economic commitment by dissidents are demanded by outside shareholders.

Pound (1988) concludes that the three problems identified may prevent some value-increasing proxy contests from occurring. The problems suggest that the current system of proxy voting is not optimally welfare enhancing. Therefore, proposals for regulatory and legal reforms are worth pursuing to the extent that they reduce the solicitation burden and improve fiduciary behavior.

Concluding Remarks
on Proxy Contests

The studies conclude that proxy contests are on average very beneficial to target firm shareholders, whether or not they are successful. Interestingly, DeAngelo and DeAngelo (1988) found the highest abnormal returns (30.12 percent over the full period of dissident activity) for the subset of proxy contests resulting in a compromise outcome. That is, the dissidents obtained some board representation, but not a majority of directorships. On the one hand, the presence of both incumbents and dissidents on the same board could conceivably result in losses to shareholders caused by disagreements over the appropriate corporate policies. However, the results here seem to indicate that the benefits of adversarial mutual monitoring between the two groups outweigh the costs. Given the magnitude of the shareholder gains, it must be that there was great potential for improved performance due either to poor management or to the existence of nontrivial agency problems.

Proxy contests over the right to control increase the likelihood that corporate assets will be transferred to higher-valued uses. They perform an important and effective disciplinary role in the managerial labor market. Finally, they provide yet another approach to takeover activity. Changes in laws and regulations to effect a reduction in the costs of a proxy fight would increase the use of proxy-contest mechanisms in the market for corporate control.

SUMMARY

The empirical evidence reviewed suggests that internal monitoring and control mechanisms are responsive to corporate problems. Poor corporate performance leads to internally initiated turnover of top management. However, external control markets play a role when the problems are industry-wide and thus require tougher managerial decisions to restructure the firm's operation. Managerial shareholdings have both incentive and entrenchment effects. The existence of a majority shareholder does not signal expropriation of minority shareholders but results in active involvement in management by the majority shareholder for value maximization.

There is clear evidence that corporate control is valued in the market. Superior voting rights shares sell at a premium, which may represent the present value of a takeover premium in the future and benefits accruing to insiders with voting control. Dual-class recapitalizations may be initiated by the entrenchment motive of managers as their announcements result in negative abnormal stock returns. Proxy contests provide an alternative means to corporate control, but the present system requires changes to reduce costs of a proxy challenge.

QUESTIONS

1. What conclusions can you draw from the empirical evidence on the value of corporate control?
2. What are the effects of the size of the fraction of equity share ownership by top management on:
   a. q-ratio?

    b. Agency problems?

    c. Probability of a hostile bid?

    d. Level of premium required for a takeover bid to succeed?

3. What was the New York Stock Exchange's main reason for allowing dual classes of stock?

4. What is the stock market's general response to recapitalizations providing for dual classes of stock? Why?

5. Why would any investor purchase an inferior-vote class of stock?

6. What characteristics are typical of firms with dual classes of stock?

7. What effect do proxy contests have on shareholder returns? Why should they have this effect?

REFERENCES

BERLE, A. A., JR., and G. C. MEANS, *The Modern Corporation and Private Property*, New York: MacMillan, 1932.

BRADLEY, MICHAEL, ANAND DESAI, and E. HAN KIM, "The Rationale Behind Interfirm Tender Offers: Information or Synergy," *Journal of Financial Economics*, April 1983, pp. 183–206.

COUGHLAN, A. T., and R. M. SCHMIDT, "Executive Compensation, Managerial Turnover, and Firm Performance: An Empirical Investigation," *Journal of Accounting and Economics*, 1985, pp. 43–66.

DANN, L. Y., and H. DEANGELO, "Corporate Financial Policy and Corporate Control: A Study of Defensive Adjustments in Asset and Ownership Structure," *Journal of Financial Economics*, 1988, pp. 87–127.

DEANGELO, HARRY, and LINDA DEANGELO, "Managerial Ownership of Voting Rights," *Journal of Financial Economics*, 1985, pp. 33–69.

————, "The Role of Proxy Contests in the Governance of Publicly-Held Corporations," ms., January 1988.

DEMSETZ, H., and K. LEHN, "The Structure of Corporate Ownership," *Journal of Political Economy*, 93, 1985, pp. 1155–1177.

DODD, PETER, and JEROLD B. WARNER, "On Corporate Governance: A Study of Proxy Contests," *Journal of Financial Economics*, 1983, pp. 401–438.

FAMA, E. F., "Agency Problems and the Theory of the Firm," *Journal of Political Economy*, 1980, pp. 288–307.

————, and M. JENSEN, "Separation of Ownership and Control," *Journal of Law and Economics*, 1983, pp. 301–325.

GROSSMAN, S. J., and O. D. HART, "One Share-One Vote and the Market for Corporate Control," *Journal of Financial Economics*, 1988, pp. 175–202.

HARRIS, M., and A. RAVIV, "Corporate Control Contests and Capital Structure," *Journal of Financial Economics*, 1988, pp. 55–86.

————, "Corporate Governance: Voting Rights and Majority Rules," *Journal of Financial Economics*, 1988a, pp. 203–235.

HOLDERNESS, C. G., and D. P. SHEEHAN, "The Role of Majority Shareholders in Publicly Held Corporations: An Exploratory Analysis," *Journal of Financial Economics*, 1988, pp. 317–346.

JARRELL, G. A., and A. B. POULSEN, "Dual-Class Recapitalizations as Antitakeover Mechanisms: The Recent Evidence," *Journal of Financial Economics*, 1988, pp. 129–152.

JENSEN, M. C., "Agency Costs of Free Cash Flow, Corporate Finance, and Takeovers," *American Economic Review,* Papers and Proceedings, 76, May 1986, pp. 323–329.

————, and W. H. MECKLING, "Theory of the Firm: Managerial Behavior, Agency Costs and Ownership Structure," *Journal of Financial Economics*, 1976, pp. 305–360.

JENSEN, M. C., and R. S. RUBACK, "The Market for Corporate Control: The Scientific Evidence," *Journal of Financial Economics*, 1983, pp. 5–50.

JENSEN, M. C., and J. B. WARNER, "The Distribution of Power Among Corporate Managers, Shareholders, and Directors," *Journal of Financial Economics*, 1988, pp. 3–24.

LEASE, RONALD C., JOHN J. MCCONNELL, and WAYNE H. MIKKELSON, "The Market Value of Control in Publicly-Traded Corporations," *Journal of Financial Economics*, 11, 1983, pp. 439–471.

LEVY, H., "Economic Evaluation of Voting Power of Common Stock," *Journal of Finance,* 1983, pp. 79–93.

MANNE, H., "The 'Higher Criticism' of the Modern Corporation," *Columbia Law Review,* 1962, pp. 399–432.

MEEKER, L. G., and O. M. JOY, "Price Premiums for Controlling Shares of Closely Held Bank Stock," *Journal of Business,* 1980, pp. 297–314.

MEGGINSON, W. L., "Restricted Voting Stock, Acquisition Premiums, and the Market Value of Corporate Control," ms., University of Georgia, August, 1988.

MORCK, R., A. SHLEIFER, and R. W. VISHNY, "Alternative Mechanisms for Corporate Control," ms., University of Alberta, February 1988.

————, "Management Ownership and Market Valuation: An Empirical Analysis," *Journal of Financial Economics,* 1988a, pp. 293–315.

PARTCH, M. M., "The Creation of Limited Voting Common Stock and Shareholder Wealth," *Journal of Financial Economics,* 1987, pp. 313–339.

POUND, JOHN, "Proxy Contests and the Efficiency of Shareholder Oversight," *Journal of Financial Economics,* 1988, pp. 237–265.

POWER, CHRISTOPHER, "Why the Proxy Fight is Back: Poison pills and antitakeover laws make it popular again," *Business Week,* March 7, 1988, p. 32.

RUBACK, R. S., "Coercive Dual-Class Exchange Offers," *Journal of Financial Economics,* 1988, pp. 153–173.

SHLEIFER, A., and R. W. VISHNY, "Large Shareholders and Corporate Control," *Journal of Political Economy,* 1986, pp. 461–488.

STULZ, R. M., "Managerial Control of Voting Rights: Financing Policies and the Market for Corporate Control," *Journal of Financial Economics,* 1988, pp. 25–54.

WARNER, J. B., R. L. WATTS, and K. H. WRUCK, "Stock Prices and Top Management Changes," *Journal of Financial Economics,* 1988, pp. 461–492.

WEISBACH, M., "Outside Directors and CEO Turnover," *Journal of Financial Economics,* 1988, pp. 431–460.

WESTON, J. F., "The Tender Takeover," *Mergers & Acquisitions,* 1979, pp. 74–82.

CHAPTER **20**

Takeover Defenses

The very terminology used to describe various aspects of takeover activity clearly reveals a distinct lack of harmony on the corporate restructuring scene—raiders, targets, shark watchers and shark repellents, Saturday night specials, scorched earth, poison pills, and so on. The hostile tender offer made directly to a target firm's shareholders, with or without previous overtures to management, has become an increasingly frequent means of initiating a corporate combination. As a result, there has been considerable interest in and energy expended on devising defenses by actual or potential targets (which includes virtually all firms).

Defenses can take the form of general wall building to make the firm less attractive to raiders or more difficult to take over and thus discourage any offers being made. These include asset and ownership restructuring, antitakeover charter amendments, adoption of poison pill rights plans, and so forth. Defensive actions are also taken in response to explicit threats ranging from early intelligence that a "raider" or any acquirer has been accumulating the firm's stock to an open tender offer. Adjustments in asset and ownership structures can also be made even after a hostile takeover bid is announced. A controversial practice in this regard is the targeted block repurchase and standstill agreement. Frequently, the target firm resorts to such strategic maneuvers as filing lawsuits and inviting a white knight bidder.

The issue of whether such actions benefit shareholders is largely unresolved. Defenses may entrench incompetent managers, foil unscrupulous raiders, or maximize the price target shareholders eventually receive. Apologists for defensive actions suggest that such actions will promote an auction for the target firm by allowing time for potential bidders to enter the takeover contest. Opponents of defenses argue that defenses increase the costs of takeover, thereby decreasing the incentive for potential bidders to search for profitable takeover targets or causing an outstanding bid to be withdrawn. For opponents, defensive actions are largely a manifestation of a conflict of interest between management and shareholders. In general, they propose a rule of strict managerial passivity. (See, for example, Easterbrook and Fischel, 1981.) Finally, there is also the view that measures are needed to reduce the conflict of interest in situations involving a change of control. A case in point is golden parachute contracts that provide compensation to managers for the loss of their jobs under a change of control. In this view, shark repellents and other defenses prevent disruption of the contractual relation between managers and shareholders by putting restrictions on hostile tender offers. (See, for example, Knoeber, 1986).

We review the workings of all major types of defenses and also empirical evidence on their effects on shareholder wealth and other aspects. These discussions shed light on the different views of takeover defense. It will be seen that the defenses vary in their impacts on the constituencies involved. Theoretical issues related to takeover defenses will be discussed in depth in Appendix A.

FINANCIAL DEFENSIVE MEASURES

General Considerations

It is possible to identify the characteristics that make a firm a desirable candidate for acquisition from the acquirer's point of view. The factors that make a firm vulnerable to a takeover include:

A low stock price in relation to the replacement cost of assets or their potential earning power.

A highly liquid balance sheet with large amounts of excess cash, a valuable securities portfolio, and significant unused debt capacity.

Good cash flow relative to current stock prices.

Subsidiaries or properties which could be sold off without significantly impairing cash flow.

Relatively small stockholdings under the control of incumbent management.

A combination of these factors can simultaneously make a firm an attractive investment opportunity and facilitate its financing. The firm's assets act as collateral for an acquirer's borrowings, and the target's cash flows from operations and divestitures can be used to repay the loans.

A firm fitting the foregoing description would do well to take at least some of the following steps. Debt should be increased, with borrowed funds used to repurchase equity, thus concentrating management's percentage holdings while using up debt capacity. Dividends on remaining shares should be increased. Loan covenants can be structured to force acceleration of repayment in the event of takeover. Securities portfolios should be liquidated and excess cash drawn down; continuing cash flow from operations should be invested in positive net present value projects or returned to shareholders. Some of the excess liquidity might be used to acquire other firms, possibly in a regulated industry which raiders may want to avoid. Subsidiaries which can be eliminated without impairing cash flow should be divested, perhaps through spin-offs to avoid large sums of cash flowing in. The profitability of all operations should be analyzed in depth to get at the true picture beneath such accounting devices as transfer pricing and overhead allocation; low-profit operations should be divested. The true value of undervalued assets should be realized by selling off or restructuring.

These activities should take place in full public view. Indeed, for a large, publicly-held corporation it would not be possible to take such steps undetected. Management should keep the market informed of its objectives in, for example, increasing the debt ratio so much that the firm's bond rating drops. If applied too vigorously, a scorched-earth effect results. The "lean" restructured company may be less vulnerable to raiders, but it has also given up a great deal of financial flexibility, including the ability to take risks. This may in turn impair its ability to successfully compete as an independent entity with other firms in its industry.

The oil industry in the last decade provides a useful focal point for analysis. The oil companies were, in general, characterized by large cash flows, underutilized debt capacity, and undervalued oil reserves. Restructuring and takeover activity ensued. Arco's major restructuring in the mid-1980s is an example of the type of defenses previously discussed. Arco sold refining capacity, closed 2,000 eastern U.S. gas stations, laid off thousands of workers, cut exploration and production budgets to concentrate in high-profit areas, increased debt, repurchased equity, and increased dividends. The combination of reduced capital spending, lower operating expenses, and increased debt for a lower cost of capital resulted in a higher stock price in spite of a smaller asset base, higher debt ratio, and lower bond ratings. Whether the increased stock price exceeds what Arco shareholders might have received in a takeover is not certain.

Adjustments in Asset and Ownership Structure

Dann and DeAngelo (1988) document attributes and stockholder wealth effects of restructurings announced by 33 target firms in direct response to explicit hostile takeover attempts during 1962–1983. The sample aimed to include all such publicly announced restructurings by exchange-listed targets during the period. It represents 19.3 percent of the hostile takeover bids during the period and contains 35.8 percent (or 19 firms) of such targets during the 1980–1983 subperiod. These statistics suggest that asset and ownership restructurings have become increasingly popular as takeover defenses.

The principal attributes of the sample restructurings are summarized as follows:

I. Acquisitions and divestitures of assets (20 cases)
   A. Purchase of a competitor of the bidder combined with private antitrust litigation.
   B. Counteroffer for control of the bidder.
   C. Sale to a third party of assets in the bidder's line of business.
   D. Cash purchase or sale of assets unrelated to the bidder's line of business.
II. Issuances and repurchases of voting securities (31 cases)
   A. Private block placement.
   B. Repurchases from current public shareholders.
   C. Issuance to dispersed group other than current holders.
   D. Issuance (to current holders) of special voting rights securities that create barriers for extant bidder.

Four economic motivations for the foregoing defensive restructurings are suggested by Dann and DeAngelo. First, 11 cases involve restructurings that create barriers specific to the bidder. These include purchase of assets that cause antitrust problems, purchase of control of the bidder itself, sale to a third party of assets which made the target attractive to the bidder, and issuance of new securities with special provisions conflicting with aspects of the takeover attempt. An example of the last type (of security issues) is found in Lenox's defense against the takeover bid by Brown-Forman Distillers Corporation in June 1983. Lenox declared a dividend of a new class of preferred shares to common stockholders. The preferred stock gave its holders the right to convert their shares into voting shares of a corporation that acquired control of Lenox. This provision was designed to transform the majority ownership of Brown-Forman by the Brown family into a minority interest.

A second common theme was to create a consolidated vote block allied with target management. In 14 cases, new securities were issued through private placements to parties friendly to management, management-allied ESOPs, or to management itself. In five cases, publicly-held shares were repurchased to increase an already sizable management-allied block in place. In some cases, both equity issued through a private placement and repurchase of shares were announced during the control contest.

A third common theme was dilution of the bidder's vote percentage through issuance of new equity claims. The hostile bidder in these cases had apparent resource constraints in increasing its interest proportionately. A fourth theme was divestiture of a major operating unit most coveted by the bidder—the crown-jewel strategy. A variation of this strategy is the more radical scorched-earth approach in which the target sells off not only the crown jewel but also other properties to diminish its worth. Several cases of the crown-jewel strategy were noted by Dann and DeAngelo. In three cases, the divestiture proceeds were planned to be used in stock repurchases.

Dann and DeAngelo find negative effects of defensive restructurings on shareholder wealth. The sample mean abnormal return in the two-day period surrounding announcements of restructurings is a statistically significant -2.33 percent. One possible explanation for the decline in share prices is that managers attempt to entrench themselves by the defensive restructurings. In this view, the restructurings reduce the likelihood of a successful takeover or represent an inferior policy choice causing a decline in corporate profitability. Indirect evidence for the entrenchment interpretation is also provided by the fact that the hostile bidder sometimes reduced its offer in reaction to the planned restructurings and that some restructuring plans were either dropped or modified at the conclusion of the control contest. Further, the fact that managers rarely put the restructuring plans to a shareholder vote may also provide support for the entrenchment view.

An alternative explanation for the share price decline is that the structural change announcement reveals that a multiple bidder auction for the target is not likely. However, Dann and DeAngelo argue that the credibility of this explanation is reduced by the evidence that most target managements did not willingly promote an auction on behalf of shareholders. Incumbents generally preferred not to transfer target control to another management team. A white knight bidder (a third party friendly to incumbent management that is brought in to "rescue" the seller from an undesired takeover) was generally considered only when defensive tactics proved ineffective. In 15 of the 33 contests, there was no evidence that incumbents considered a white knight.

Among the 39 structural change announcements (by the 33 target firms), 25 were actually implemented by target management, ten were dropped or modified in a negotiated settlement with the eventual acquirer (the hostile bidder or a third party), and four were not implemented. The hostile bidder was rarely (three out of 25 cases) successful when the structural changes were actually implemented. In contrast, the hostile bidder was successful in seven of the 14 cases where the change was not implemented. These results suggest that the restructuring defense was often quite effective. The 12 target firms whose incumbent managers retained control (without any offers outstanding) experienced an average share price decline of 9.72 percent at the announcement of the outcome.

Leveraged Recapitalizations

The leveraged recapitalization (or recap) is a relatively new technique of financial restructuring first developed by Goldman Sachs for Multimedia in 1985. It is considered to be a defensive tactic because in most cases the recapitalization, also known as a leveraged cash-out (LCO), has been implemented in response to a takeover bid. All firms that used an LCO have also made charter amendments such as supermajority voting or adopting poison pill voting plans. (See the following related sections.) In a typical recapitalization, outside shareholders receive a large one-time cash dividend and insiders (managers) and employee benefit plans receive new shares instead of the cash dividend. The cash dividend is financed mostly by newly borrowed funds, both senior bank debt and mezzanine debt (subordinated debentures). As a result, the firm's leverage is increased to an "abnormally" high level and this would discourage takeover attempts financed mainly by borrowings against the firm's own assets. The proportional equity ownership of management also significantly rises through the recapitalization. In many cases, new shares, called *stubs*, are issued to replace the old shares. The firm's shares continue to be publicly traded. This appears to be one reason why LCOs are generally implemented by firms larger than those involved in LBOs. The average dollar value of the payouts to shareholders was $1.92 billion for the eight LCO announcements made by early 1987 (Kleiman, 1988).

The terms of exchange in individual recapitalizations often provide more than one alternative for public shareholders (Klein, 1988). Multimedia, the first LCO firm, offered cash, subordinated debentures, and a fraction of a new share in exchange for each old share in one alternative. Another option offered cash and new shares. FMC Corporation's LCO involved three different parties to the transaction and three associated exchange offers. Public shareholders received $70 in cash plus one new share, its thrift plan received $25 in cash plus four new shares, and the management and PAYSOP received 5⅔ new shares in exchange for one old share (Kleiman, 1988, p. 53). FMC's stock price was about $65 two months prior to the announcement of its LCO. All three parties would have received $85 if the new shares sold for $15. The actual stub share price was $16 after the transaction took place. This gave shareholders $86 in total value and management $90. In the Owens-Corning Fiberglass recapitalization, the outside shareholders received $52 in cash, $35 face amount (roughly $19 market value) of junior subordinated debentures, and one new share in exchange for one old share. Thus, this LCO required the public shareholders to do a part of the mezzanine financing. The company's employee benefit plans received seven new shares in exchange for each old share. The two parties to the transaction would have received an equal value at an implied stub stock price of $11.80. One month after the recapitalization, the stub stock price was $12⅜.

LCOs have several important features in common with LBOs (on which the data have been presented in Chapter 16). Leverage is increased substantially both in LCOs and LBOs. Accounting net worth turned negative and interest coverage ratios became less than three times in all six completed LCOs after recapitalization (Table 20.1). Insider equity ownership increases after LCOs and LBOs. Table 20.1 shows that the average insider ownership increased to 29.5 percent after leveraged recapitalizations from a prerecapitalization average of 8.1 percent. The similarity between LCOs and LBOs is also found in firm characteristics. Firms involved in LCOs have low growth rates, mundane product lines not likely to become obsolete, predictable cash flows, and experienced management with a favorable track record (Kleiman, 1988; Klein, 1988). The reduction of debt following either type of restructuring often involves sale of assets after the restructuring.

Some differences are also noted between LCOs and LBOs. In LCOs, the firms remain publicly traded and outside share ownership still represents a majority. Thus, leveraged recapitalizations can partly avoid the criticism that

TABLE 20.1
Financial and Other Aspects of LCOs, May 1985–May 1987[a]

	MUL-TIMEDIA	FMC	COLT	OWENS-CORNING	HOLI-DAY CORP.	HARCOURT BRACE JOVANOVICH
Announcement date	5/1/85	2/22/86	7/20/86	8/28/86	11/11/86	5/26/87
Total assets	$0.4	$2.4	$1.1	$2.5	$2.5	$1.8
Net worth						
Pre-LCO	$0.3	$1.1	$0.4	$1.0	$0.6	$0.5
Post-LCO	($0.6)	($0.7)	($1.1)	($1.0)	($0.9)	($1.6)
Interest coverage						
Pre-LCO	8.7	7.7	16.3	5.9	3.7	1.2
Post-LCO	2.3	2.0	2.9	1.4	2.2	(3.9)
Insider ownership						
Pre-LCO	13%	19%	7%	1%	1.5%	7%
Post-LCO	43%	40%	38%	16%	10%	30%
Stock Price						
2 months before announcement:	$48⅛	$65	$68¼	$46¾	$64	$36
1 month after announcement:	$57¼	$88¾	$93	$97¾	$69⅝	$58
Cash per share to public shareholders	$46[b]	$80	$85	$52	$65	$40

[a]Dollar amounts in billions except for per share data.
[b]There were several other options.

SOURCES: Interest coverage—R. Teters, "The Leveraged Recap: Controversial New Defense Maneuver," *Journal of Business Strategy,* March/April 1988, pp. 26–29; Insider ownership—R. T. Kleiman, "The Shareholder Gains from Leveraged Cashouts," *Journal of Applied Corporate Finance,* 7, Spring 1988, pp. 46–53; Other items—R. Klein, "Leveraged Cashouts: Recapitalization with a New Twist," *Business Forum,* 13, Winter 1988, pp. 10–15.

insiders exploit nonpublic information. On the other hand, Kleiman argues that an LCO does not formally put the company "in play" whereas a buy-out offer does put the company in play, thereby inviting competing bids from potential acquirers. In a buy-out, the company is technically being sold and the value of the firm's shares is actually established. The value is established only after a recapitalization, as the sum of the market price of the stub stock and the cash distributed to public shareholders. This point may add to the appeal of LCOs as an antitakeover strategy. Leveraged cash-outs also have other advantages and disadvantages relative to leveraged buy-outs. The advantages include greater accessibility to capital markets, liquidity of managerial shareholdings, and use of stock prices in devising management compensation packages. The disadvantages include greater monitoring costs resulting from less concentrated outsider share ownership and the costs related to regulatory requirements for public companies. Finally, management of an LCO firm is normally not provided as many stock options or incentive plans as in the case of a buy-out.

The stock market response to LCO announcements has been documented by Kleiman (1988). Over the 60-day period prior to and including the announcement day, the eight firms announcing LCOs (including the six in Table 20.1 and Caesar's World and Allegis) experienced an average market-adjusted return of 33.3 percent. The six "defensive" LCOs in which there were prior public indications of an outstanding or expected takeover bid experienced abnormal returns ranging from −1.3 percent to 20.7 percent in the two-day period including the day before and the day of the announcement. The average two-day return to the six takeover targets was a positive 5.6 percent. In contrast to most other defensive tactics, this implies that LCOs provide returns to shareholders comparable to a takeover.

Golden Parachutes

Golden parachutes refer to separation provisions of an employment contract that compensate managers for the loss of their jobs under a change-of-control clause. The provision usually calls for a lump-sum payment or payment over a specified period at full or partial rates of normal compensation. This type of severance contract has been increasingly used even by the largest Fortune 500 firms as M&A activity has intensified in the 1980s and these firms have become susceptible to hostile takeover. By the mid-1980s, about 25 percent of the Fortune 500 firms had adopted golden parachute features in their employment contracts for top managers (White, 1987).

The majority view on golden parachutes now is that these control-related contracts help reduce the conflict of interest between shareholders and managers in change-of-control situations. However, certain extreme cases of golden parachutes have created a stir among the public and were often viewed as "rewards for failure."[1] An example of an extreme case is the golden parachute payment of $23.5 million to six officers of Beatrice Companies in connection with its leveraged buy-out in 1985. One of the officers received a $2.7 million package even though he had been with the company only 13 months. Another received a $7 million package after being recalled from retirement only seven months before. Also in 1985, the chairman of Revlon received a $35 million package consisting of severance pay and stock options. Even in these extreme cases, the golden parachutes were small when compared to the total acquisition prices of $6.2 billion in the Beatrice LBO and $1.74 billion in the Revlon acquisition. Indeed, the cost of golden parachutes is estimated to be less than 1 percent of the total cost of a takeover in most cases.[2] For this reason, golden parachutes are not considered to be an effective takeover defense.

Excessive use of golden parachutes appears to be infrequent and the new tax law now imposes specific limits. The Deficit Reduction Act of 1984 denies corporate tax deductions for parachute payments in excess of three times the

[1] See, for example, *The New York Times*, "Golden Chutes Under Attack," November 4, 1985, p. D1.
[2] *Fortune*, "Those Executive Bailout Deals," December 13, 1982, p. 86.

base amount on a present-value basis, where the base amount is the executive's average annual compensation over the five years prior to takeover. An executive has to pay an additional 20 percent income tax on "excess parachute payments." To be legally binding, the golden parachutes have to be entered into at least one year prior to the date of control change for the entire corporation or a significant portion of the corporation. In many employment contracts, the severance payment is triggered either when the manager is terminated by the acquiring firm or when the manager resigns voluntarily after a change of control. Coffee (1988, p. 131) reports several cases in which the court invalidated or granted preliminary injunctions against the exercise of golden parachutes especially when the payment could be triggered at the recipient's own election.

The use of golden parachutes has been advocated by economic and legal observers (Coffee, 1988; Jensen, 1988; Knoeber, 1986). One argument is based on the concept of *implicit contracts* for managerial compensation. In general, managers' real contribution to the firm cannot be evaluated exactly in the current period, but can be estimated better as time passes and more information becomes available on the firm's long-term profitability. In this situation, an optimal contract between managers and shareholders will include deferred compensation (Knoeber, 1986). Seniority-based compensation and internal promotion partly reflect this deferred compensation process. Since detailing all the future possibilities and contingent payments in a written contract is costly and very likely futile, a long-term deferred contract will largely be implicit. Another argument presumes existence of firm-specific investments by managers. When the likelihood of an unexpected transfer of control and the loss of their job is high, managers will not be willing to invest in firm-specific skills and knowledge. A related argument is that the increased risk of losing one's job through a takeover may result in managers' focusing unduly on the short-term or even taking unduly high risks (Eisenberg, 1988).

The final, but most obvious, rationale for golden parachutes is that they encourage managers to accept changes of control that would bring shareholder gains, and thus reduce the conflict of interest between managers and shareholders and the transaction costs resulting from managerial resistance. Berkovitch and Khanna (BK, 1988) further analyze the role of golden parachutes in takeover markets in which the bidder has a choice between a merger and a tender offer. In their model, a tender offer is more desirable for target shareholders as more information is released in tender offers and this frequently leads to an auction in which potential acquirers compete for the target. They show that target managers' compensation scheme determines whether a merger or tender offer is selected. If change-of-control payment to the target manager is negative (for example, no compensation for the loss of deferred payment), he or she resists all merger attempts. In this case, only tender offers are possible and potential acquirers with low synergy gains will not bid at all, as they expect to lose in the competition following a tender offer. If the compensation is positive and the same for both mergers and tender offers, then only mergers will occur as the manager accepts all merger bids. The optimal incentive (golden parachute) contract in the BK model calls for granting an amount increasing with synergy gains in the case of mergers. In the case of tender offers, the manager should be paid more than in mergers, although the payment may be independent of synergy gains. Excessive payment will tend to motivate managers to sell the firm at too low a gain. By tying the payment to synergy gains in the case of mergers, the firm can avoid the misuse of golden parachutes. Stock options that are exercisable in the event of a change of control are an appropriate solution and in general increased stock ownership by management will tend to reduce the conflict of interest (Jensen, 1988).

An important question on severance payments relates to the number of managers to be covered. Focusing on the conflict of interest problem in control-related situations, Jensen argues that the contract should cover only those members of the top-level management team who will be involved in negotiating and implementing any transfer of control. The case of Beneficial Corporation which awarded such contracts to over 200 of its managers is seen to be difficult to justify as being in the interest of shareholders. On the other hand, Coffee (1988) emphasizes the implicit contract for deferred payments and the incentive for managers to make investments in firm-specific human capital. This leads Coffee to propose that the control-related severance contracts should be extended to members of middle management.

Empirical evidence obtained by Lambert and Larcker (1985) shows that adoption of golden parachute features in employment contracts results in an average stock price increase of about 3 percent. This result can be due either to the beneficial role of golden parachutes or to the market interpreting the announcement as a signal for increased likelihood of a takeover bid.

Poison Puts

Corporate bond quality often deteriorates following the issuer's leveraged recapitalization, leveraged buy-out, or other forms of control change. Since 1986, some new bond issues have provided their holders with poison put covenants as a protection from the risk of takeover-related credit deterioration of the issuer. This investor protection device, however, has often been viewed as an antitakeover mechanism (Weberman, 1988; *Mergers & Acquisitions*, March/April 1989, p. 17). This view is based on the fact that the right to put is triggered by a change of control, but in most cases does not apply if the change of control is the result of a *friendly* takeover. This kind of put may well protect management but not bondholders. Under a friendly deal, the put is not exercisable even if the change of control hurts bondholders. And in most cases, the put option proved worthless because an agreement was ultimately reached between management and the (initially hostile) bidder or a white knight (Winkler, 1988).

The exercise price of the put option is usually set at 100 or 101 percent of the bond's face amount. Exercise of the put after an unfriendly takeover can be very costly to the bidder even when it can easily finance the required funds. Sometimes the put will prove worthless and impose no cost to the bidder. This will be the case if the bond price prior to the takeover was far above the exercise price and is still higher after the takeover and the resulting deterioration in its quality.

A variety of put covenants have been used with different investor protection and antitakeover implications. A bond issued by UGTC Capital Corporation can be redeemed at the option of management, not the bondholders, in the event of a control change. This is a kind of poison call and is yet to be tested with respect to its efficiency as an antitakeover mechanism. The put option in a subordinated note issued by United Air Lines becomes exercisable if Moody's and Standard & Poor's downgrade the debt as a result of a takeover. Two bond issues from McDermott Inc. do not have the put protection but limit the amount of new debt taken on either by an acquirer or by management itself in an LBO.

A new generation of poison puts was introduced in late 1988 by Harris Corporation and Northwest Pipeline, a subsidiary of Williams Companies. A Eurobond issue by Federal Express Corporation contained a similar provision. These new issues have been called super poison puts as they can "protect" investors under a greater number of circumstances and serve as a more effective takeover barrier at the same time. (See *Mergers & Acquisitions*, March/April 1989, p. 17; Winkler, 1988.) When the issue is downgraded to below investment grade by a rating agency and one of some "designated events" occurs, the holders of the Harris issue can put their bonds at par. As for the Northwest Pipeline issue, if the bonds are trading below par after a designated event occurs, the company will, at its own option, either redeem the bonds at par or increase the coupon rate so that the bonds would trade at par. The designated events include the issuer's merger with another company, an outsider's purchase of 20 percent (or 30 percent) of the common stock of the issuer or its parent, and a major dividend payment or a major stock purchase totaling more than 30 percent of another company. The poison puts of both issues expire in ten years, although both have a 30-year maturity.

The introduction of the super poison puts is believed to have been motivated by the large price declines of bonds of RJR Nabisco, Inc. after the announcement of its leveraged buy-out in December 1988. The LBO triggered several lawsuits by bondholders. It is to be seen whether the stronger safeguards will become a new standard in the future.

"COERCIVE" OFFERS AND DEFENSE: THEORETICAL BACKGROUND

Proponents of antitakeover measures argue that tender offers put individual shareholders under pressure to tender their shares regardless of their collective interest with respect to the offer. In this view, the pressure distorts their decision and its elimination will not only benefit target shareholders but also produce social gains by helping place corporate assets in their most productive uses. Thus, the argument goes, defensive tactics have to be employed by target firms in the absence of regulatory arrangements that presumably are more efficient.

Front-End Loading in Tender Offers

The pressure or "coercion" to tender arises when a takeover bid is front-end loaded, that is, when the offer price is greater than the price of any unpurchased shares. When a bid is front-end loaded, individual shareholders will have the incentive to tender to receive the higher front-end price. It is obvious that front-end loading occurs in two-tier offers. Further, it is commonly believed that partial and any-or-all offers are also front-end loaded.

In a two-tier offer, the bidder offers a first-tier price for a specified maximum number of shares that it would accept and announces at the same time its intention to acquire in a follow-up merger the remaining shares at a second-tier price. In almost all cases, cash is offered for the first-tier transaction, but the second-tier price is typically paid by securities whose market value is often lower than the first-tier value. A partial offer also specifies a maximum number of shares to be accepted, but does not announce the bidder's plans with respect to the remaining shares. Purchase of shares in either two-tier or partial offers is often made conditional on the receipt of a minimum number of shares sufficient to guarantee voting control of the target firm. In two-tier offers, this minimum number is typically equal to the maximum number specified. Partial offers will more frequently be unconditional (Comment and Jarrell, 1987, p. 286). In any-or-all offers, no maximum is specified but none will be purchased if the conditions of the offer are not met. The front-end prices in partial and any-or-all offers are also paid with cash. The back-end value of a partial offer is simply the market value of the remaining shares, whereas in an any-or-all offer, it is given by the terms of a *clean-up* (or *takeout*) merger and typically is equal to the front-end cash offer price.

Front-end loading can occur not only in two-tier offers but also in partial and any-or-all offers. The posttakeover value of remaining (minority) shares is typically lower than the bid price in all three types of offers. This is true even in those any-or-all offers in which cash equal in amount to the front-end bid price is paid in the takeout merger. The reason is that the back-end payment is made only at a later date. More importantly, the lower back-end value observed in most partial offers and in some any-or-all offers is caused by either of the following reasons. In takeout mergers immediately following the takeover, the bidder is allowed to pay minority shareholders a consideration valued lower than the bid price (Bebchuk, 1988, p. 374). According to current takeover law, the acquirer is constrained only by the appraisal rights of the minority shareholders. The appraisal employs data on past earnings and past stock market prices. In takeovers unaccompanied by an immediate takeout that "freezes out" minority shareholders, the acquirer can dilute the equity value of these shareholders. This dilution can be effected by self-dealing (that is, transacting with the target on terms favorable to the acquirer) or by allocating business opportunities to the acquirer. The takeout can be accomplished after the target's earnings are deliberately depressed. Bebchuk (1988) argues that the timing of a takeout merger depends on the ability of the acquirer to dilute the equity value of minority shareholders.

Thus, it is seen that the pressure to tender is not limited to two-tier or partial offers but extends to any-or-all offers. While target shareholders in an any-or-all offer are assured that they will not end up with minority shares if they tender, they still have the fear that their holdings will be diluted if they do not tender. However, the pressure to tender will generally be low in any-or-all offers because the terms of a clean-up merger following such an offer typically provide a back-end value in cash equaling the offer price.

Distortion of Outcome in Coercive Offers

The pressure to tender will lead to a distorted outcome if the acquisition price (or the "blended price") of the offer is lower than the per share value of the target when it remains independent. The acquisition price is a weighted average of the front-end and back-end values, using the fraction of shares receiving each price as the weights. In the notation used by Comment and Jarrell, the acquisition price is expressed as

$$P_B = (F \times P_T) + [(1 - F) \times P_E]$$

where:

P_B = acquisition price (or blended price) of the takeover,
P_T = offer price (i.e., front-end price),
P_E = postoffer market price of remaining shares, and
F = fraction of shares purchased in the front-end offer

Bebchuk and proponents of antitakeover measures argue that the acquisition price can actually be lower than the target shareholders' estimates of the per share value of their shares, even if the acquisition price usually includes a large premium over the prebid market price of the shares. This happens because tender decisions are made many weeks after an initial takeover bid and shareholders' estimates are likely to change following the arrival of new information conveyed by the bid and ensuing events. Typically in hostile bids, the target's management discloses its future plans and proposes a restructuring or recapitalization. The target receives unusual attention and attracts intense investigation by market participants. Therefore, it is not purely hypothetical to suppose that the shareholders' estimates of the value can actually be higher than the acquisition price. It is possible then that in many actual cases individual shareholders are coerced to tender even when their collective value-maximizing action would be to reject the bid.

A Proposal for Remedial Arrangement

The distortion in shareholders' decisions resulting from coercive offers can be prevented by legal rules or charter provisions. An arrangement proposed by Bebchuk (1988, pp. 380–381) would "enable shareholders to express their preference concerning the bid's success separately from their decision to have their shares acquired in the event of a takeover." One version of the arrangement is to let shareholders indicate on the tender form whether or not they "approve" a takeover. Under this scheme all shareholders would rationally tender shares (unless they have other compelling reasons such as tax considerations), but the success of the bid will be determined by the number of approving tenders. To ensure that shareholders express their true preferences, the bidder should be prohibited from penalizing disapproving tenders if the bid is approved. An alternative version of the arrangement is to have a separate voting of the target shareholders prior to the bid's closing. Bebchuk argues that adoption of the arrangement through legal rules would be more efficient than through corporate charter provisions. Provision by law enables the design of a uniform, efficient mechanism and can save transaction and information costs.

One potential drawback of the arrangement is that it would increase takeover premiums and thus would not leave any incentive for prospective bidders to search for potential targets. Indeed, Easterbrook and Fischel (1981, 1982) argue that to provide such incentives, the premium paid to a discovered target should be kept low. However, such an incentive can be provided by the bidder's holdings or secret purchases of target shares prior to its announcement (Shleifer and Vishny, 1986b). Further, the current 5 percent statutory limit on the amount of shares that an acquirer can purchase without a 13D filing could be raised to increase the rewards for search (Bebchuk, 1988, p. 384). Finally, Bebchuk argues that increasing the rewards by sacrificing undistorted decisions might cause a socially excessive level of search. In the extreme, searchers might "raid" a target even in the absence of any efficiency gain.

The Proposed Arrangement versus Related Defensive Measures

It should be noted that the arrangement proposed by Bebchuk still allows all types of tender offers. Thus, front-end loading is possible under the arrangement, but only the pressure to tender is eliminated. The arrangement does not create the free-rider problem pointed out by Grossman and Hart (1980). The free-rider problem arises when a bid is not front-end loaded and when the shareholders are "atomistic" (small). In this case, each shareholder will reason that his or her decision does not affect the outcome of the bid and will refrain from tendering in order to free-ride on the value increases resulting from the takeover. Thus, the bid will fail. Bradley (1980) and Grossman and Hart (1980) suggest that dilution of minority shares or more generally front-end loading should be allowed to overcome the free-rider problem in tender offers.

Certain antitakeover measures adopted by firms eliminate the pressure to tender by creating the free-rider problem. They provide minority shareholders with the option of redeeming their shares at the bid price after the bid expiration. Examples are fair-price charter amendments and some poison pill rights plans. (See the following sections.) In order to allow acceptable bids to go through, the management typically retains the right to make these measures ineffective. This provision encourages bidders to negotiate with target management which is supposed to act in the interest of shareholders, but gives target management the power to prevent a hostile bidder from taking control of the firm and thus to entrench itself in office.

Corporate antitakeover measures are thus seen to have two opposing effects and indeed have led to two competing hypotheses—the shareholder interest hypothesis versus the managerial entrenchment hypothesis. In the following sections we review empirical evidence on the motivation and effects of antitakeover measures adopted by firms. Suffice it here to note that the arrangement proposed by Bebchuk would avoid the managerial entrenchment effect of many antitakeover measures, but be capable of enhancing shareholder interests by eliminating the pressure to tender.

Insignificance of Coercive Effects of Tender Offers: Empirical Evidence

There are both theoretical reasons and empirical evidence that deficiency in bargaining power on the part of small shareholders may not cause significant distortion in their tendering decisions. First, there is competition among management groups including the target managers themselves, which will ensure the acquisition (or blended) price to be adequate (Bradley, 1980; Comment and Jarrell, 1987). The lower limit on back-end value is determined by the appraisal rights of minority shareholders stipulated in state merger statutes. Once this limit on the back-end value is reached, competition among bidders then determines the front-end price. The overall acquisition price can thus be determined at a competitive level. Ruback (1983) provides evidence that the market for corporate control is competitive in the sense that bidders' expected gains from a higher offer than the successful (executed) offer are nonpositive.

Second, the target stock may not be held atomistically because of open-market transactions during the tender-offer period. Large block holdings can be formed by takeover specialists and arbitragers during the period (Demsetz, 1983). The incentive to form a coalition of dispersed shareholders to negotiate with a bidder will only be limited by the marginal cost of cooperation.

Third, Comment and Jarrell (1987) argue that representation by target management is a least-cost vehicle for cooperation of shareholders in most takeover situations. They assume that the agency problems between managers and shareholders can be minimized by side payments from shareholders in the form of control-related severance contracts (such as golden parachutes). Management can influence the terms of an offer by its ability to enter into a merger agreement with a favored bidder and to grant that bidder a lock-up option to buy a block of new shares. This option will significantly disadvantage competing bidders. Because of this power of management, prospective bidders will be induced to negotiate the terms of the offer with management. Bidders thus forego the use of front-end loading to expropriate the wealth of shareholders.

Front-end loading will still be used in negotiated tender offers to penalize shareholders who hold out. Comment and Jarrell (1987) also suggest that the timing advantage of cash transactions necessitates the use of partial or two-tier offers in large acquisitions by cash-constrained bidders. Further, partial acquisitions can serve economic functions and may be desired by bidders. A two-tier transaction can have tax advantages: When less than half of the shares are acquired for cash, the back-end exchange of shares for merger qualifies as a tax-free exchange (Gilson, 1986, p. 459).

Comment and Jarrell (1987) provide empirical evidence that distortion of outcomes in tender offers may not be significant in reality. They study 241 cash tender offers announced between 1981 and 1984. Among these, 210 offers were executed. Only 14 of the 210 target firms had fair-price amendments. Also, the sample period largely precedes the development of a poison pill defense. Among initial offers, about 60 percent of the total were any-or-all offers. Partial and two-tier offers each accounted for 20 percent. Among executed offers, the percentage of two-tier and partial offers was even smaller, 19 and 13 percent, respectively. The average fraction of shares tendered in executed offers was a surprisingly low 67.5 percent and was actually higher in any-or-all offers. These pieces of evidence suggest that, contrary to widely-held perceptions, the pressure to tender is not particularly high in the supposedly more coercive partial and two-tier offers and that two-tier or partial offers are not more frequently used than any-or-all offers.

The degree of front-end loading is smallest in any-or-all offers and largest in partial offers. The mean percentage difference in front- and back-end prices was 2.4 percent in any-or-all offers, 13.8 percent in two-tier offers, and 22.3 percent in partial offers. Comment and Jarrell (1987) suggest that the degree of front-end loading is "surprisingly small" since many two-tier offers are structured as tax-free exchanges of securities for the back-end transaction.

Comment and Jarrell (1987) provide evidence that the target firm management can wield considerable influence over the terms of an offer and over the outcome of the offer. Negotiated offers, in which a written agreement, typically a merger agreement, between the target management and the bidder is present, accounted for half of all initial cash tender offers. Further, four fifths of all executed offers and the terms of almost all two-tier offers were negotiated before expiration. Unnegotiated initial offers were executed only in 31 percent of the cases (38 of 121). Since the sample firms rarely had fair-price amendments or poison pill plans, Comment and Jarrell attribute the apparent bargaining power of management to its authority to enter into merger agreements and to grant lock-up options on the target's unissued shares. The average lock-up option shares (authorized but unissued shares plus managers' personal shares optioned to the bidder) in negotiated offers averaged 15.5 percent of the firm's fully diluted shares outstanding. Thus, the bargaining power of target management tends to offset the bargaining disadvantage of diffuse, atomistic shareholders. Comment and Jarrell (1987) also provide evidence consistent with the view that the problem of diffuse ownership is reduced by a substantial increase in the concentration of ownership during tender offers. On average, more than a third (36.4 percent) of the outstanding shares was traded during an executed tender offer. This quite possibly represents the activities of takeover specialists and arbitragers.

The average premium for the 144 any-or-all offers was 56.6 percent above the preoffer market price. This was not significantly different from the 55.9 percent premium for 39 two-tier offers. On the other hand, the 27 partial offers yielded only 22.8 percent on average. The results also show that shareholders fared equally well on average whether the offer was negotiated or unnegotiated. Overall, Comment and Jarrell (1987) find no evidence that target shareholders are disadvantaged by the two-tier form of tender offer. However, this result may be due to the fact that most executed two-tier offers (36 out of 39) in their sample were negotiated and we cannot entirely eliminate the possibility that hostile, unnegotiated two-tier offers may disadvantage shareholders to a certain extent.

Most corporate charter amendments and proposed regulatory changes on tender offers are designed to provide target management with additional bargaining power against unnegotiated, front-end loaded offers. The evidence presented by Comment and Jarrell (1987) suggest that the benefits to target shareholders from these provisions will be minimal, or may not even exist if managements use these provisions to pursue their own interest by deterring too many offers. Some arrangements like that proposed by Bebchuk (1988) can eliminate the pressure to tender while not yielding pro-management effects. Given that these efficient arrangements can be devised, it is interesting to see what types of antitakeover measures are or will be adopted by firms.

ANTITAKEOVER AMENDMENTS

An increasingly used defense mechanism is antitakeover amendments to a firm's corporate charter, popularly called shark repellents. As with all charter amendments, antitakeover amendments must be voted on and approved by shareholders. To the extent that such amendments may lead to the entrenchment of management, this can sometimes become a delicate matter. Proxy material is required by law to disclose that a proposed change would tend to insulate management from removal; management naturally also puts forth alternative more noble motivations for the proposed amendments. Although 95 percent of antitakeover amendments proposed by management are ratified by shareholders, this may be due to the fact that a planned amendment may not be introduced if management is unsure of its success (Brickley, Lease, and Smith, 1988). Failure to pass might be taken as a vote of no confidence in incumbent management and may provide a platform for a proxy fight or takeover attempt where none had existed before. The evidence provided by Brickley, Lease, and Smith (1988) indicates that institutional shareholders such as banks and insurance companies are more likely to vote with management on antitakeover amendments than others such as mutual funds and college endowments. Note that the former institutions generally have ongoing business relationships with management and thus are more likely to be influenced by management. Brickley, Lease, and Smith (1988) also find that block holders more actively participate in voting than nonblock holders and may oppose proposals that appear to harm shareholders. This result is consistent with Jarrell and Poulsen (1987) who find that those amendments having the most negative effect on stock price (amendments other than fair-price amendments) are adopted by firms with the lowest percentage of institutional holdings and the highest percentage of insider holdings. Jarrell and Poulsen (1987) suggest that these results help explain how harmful amendments receive approval by shareholders. The evidence also suggests that block holders do play a monitoring role. Institutional holders are sophisticated and well informed so that they vote in accordance with their economic interest more consistently than less-informed small investors. However, there still remains some uncertainty because these results on institutional shareholders' voting behavior contrast with the findings of Pound (1988) in the context of proxy contests. (See Chapter 19, Corporate Control Mechanisms.)

Types of Antitakeover Amendments

Antitakeover amendments generally impose new conditions on the transfer of managerial control of the firm through a merger, tender offer, or by replacement of the board of directors. There are four major types of antitakeover amendments.

SUPERMAJORITY AMENDMENTS   These amendments require shareholder approval by at least two thirds vote and sometimes as much as 90 percent of the voting power of outstanding capital stock for all transactions involving change of control. In most existing cases, however, the supermajority provisions have a board-out clause which provides the board with the power to determine when and if the supermajority provisions will be in effect. Pure supermajority provisions would seriously limit the management's flexibility in takeover negotiations.

FAIR-PRICE AMENDMENTS   These are supermajority provisions with a board-out clause and an additional clause waiving the supermajority requirement if a fair price is paid for all purchased shares. The fair price is commonly defined as the highest price paid by the bidder during a specified period and is sometimes required to exceed an amount determined relative to accounting earnings or book value of the target. Thus, fair-price amendments defend against two-tier tender offers that are not approved by the target's board. A uniform offer for all shares to be purchased in a tender offer and in a subsequent clean-up merger or tender offer will avoid the supermajority requirement. Since the two-tier tender offer is not essential in successful hostile takeovers, the fair-price amendment is the least restrictive among the class of supermajority amendments.

CLASSIFIED BOARDS Another major type of antitakeover amendment provides for *staggered,* or *classified,* boards of directors to delay effective transfer of control in a takeover. Management's purported rationale in proposing a staggered board is to assure continuity of policy and experience. For example, a nine-member board might be divided into three classes, with only three members standing for election to a three-year term each year. Thus, a new majority shareholder would have to wait at least two annual meetings to gain control of the board of directors. Effectiveness of cumulative voting is reduced under the classified-board scheme because a greater shareholder vote is required to elect a single director. Variations on antitakeover amendments relating to the board of directors include provisions prohibiting the removal of directors except for cause, and provisions fixing the number of directors allowed to prevent "packing" the board.

AUTHORIZATION OF PREFERRED STOCK The board of directors is authorized to create a new class of securities with special voting rights. This security, typically preferred stock, may be issued to friendly parties in a control contest. Thus, this device is a defense against hostile takeover bids, although historically it was used to provide the board of directors with flexibility in financing under changing economic conditions. Creation of a poison pill security could be included in this category, but is generally considered to be a different and new defensive device. (We examine the poison pill defense in a following separate section.)

Other amendments that management may propose as a takeover defense include:

1 Abolition of cumulative voting where it is not required by state law.
2 Reincorporation in a state with more accommodating antitakeover laws.
3 Provisions with respect to the scheduling of shareholder meetings and introduction of agenda items, including nomination of candidates to the board of directors.
4 Antigreenmail amendments which restrict a company's freedom to buy back a raider's shares at a premium.

The list is not inclusive. A final refinement is the passage of *lock-in* amendments making it difficult to void previously passed antitakeover amendments by requiring, for example, supermajority approval for a change.

Antitakeover Amendments and Stock Prices

Shark repellents may benefit shareholders by allowing diffuse and noncooperating shareholders to respond in unison (through the management) to hostile takeover bids (DeAngelo and Rice, 1983). Most amendments effectively appoint target management as the central negotiating agent of shareholders. Using this leverage, target management may be able to induce competitive bidding from potential acquirers.

This potential benefit from giving management stronger negotiating power will also impose costs on shareholders if management acts in its own interest. The potential conflict between managers and shareholders becomes most acute during control contests. The managers may use the increased veto power over hostile takeover bids to entrench themselves in office. This view of shark repellents may not necessarily be inconsistent with their increased popularity among voting shareholders. Small shareholders may simply vote in accordance with management's recommendations because their economic stake in the firm is small and therefore does not warrant expenditures to become informed.

The effects of antitakeover amendments on stock prices vary; some have a more depressing effect than others, indicating that the management entrenchment hypothesis may dominate. Supermajority amendments appear to be quite damaging, while fair-price amendments seem to have negligible impact. A study by DeAngelo and Rice (1983) of the stockholder wealth effects of all types of antitakeover amendments concluded weak support for the management entrenchment hypothesis. The insignificantly negative stock price effects (about 1 percent) may be due to the fact that the market takes the proposal of antitakeover amendments as a signal that a firm has reason to expect a future attempt. The positive price effects of an anticipated takeover might be offsetting negative effects of substantial significance (DeAngelo and Rice, 1983, p. 355). They suggest one reason shareholders may vote to approve amendments apparently contrary to their own interests may be that the information and transaction costs required to fight antitakeover amendments exceed the benefits if the fight is successful. In contrast with DeAngelo and Rice, Linn and McConnell (1983) find statistically significant positive abnormal returns for antitakeover amendment announcements in the 1960–1980 period for 475 NYSE-listed firms. These conflicting results lead Jarrell and Poulsen (1987) to suggest that shark repellents adopted before 1980 had only a trivial effect on stock prices.

Jarrell and Poulsen (1987) study 649 antitakeover amendments proposed between 1979 and 1985. Of the 649 firms, 554 proposed amendments after 1982. A total of 487 firms adopted fair-price amendments, 104 supermajority amendments, and 58 classified boards, or authorized preferred stock provisions. Their stock returns data show an average abnormal return of −1.25 percent during the 30-day period surrounding the proxy signing date for the entire sample. However, fair-price amendments have very little effect on stock price (−0.65 percent). The other amendments (including supermajority, authorization of preferred stock, and classified board amendments) have a somewhat stronger negative effect (−2.95 percent). These results lend support to the view that the fair-price amendments are less harmful than others and that, since they are the dominant form of antitakeover amendments in later periods, shareholder voting is effective to some degree in monitoring the entrenchment motive of managers.

Jarrell and Poulsen (1987) also find an inverse relationship between stock returns and insider holdings and a positive relationship between stock returns and institutional holdings. They conclude that amendments most harmful to shareholders are more easily approved when insiders have a larger share of votes and institutions have smaller share.

In a later study, McWilliams (1988) finds results that contradict Jarrell and Poulsen. Her sample includes a total of 763 antitakeover amendments by 325 NYSE and AMEX firms in the period 1980–1984. These consist of 231 fair-price amendments, 29 supermajority vote, 158 staggered board, 111 authorizing issuance of common/preferred stock with special voting/dividend rights, 126 requiring director removal only by cause and/or with supermajority vote, and 108 amendments limiting shareholder action only at meetings. She reports a positive stock price effect of amendment proposals and no differences in stock price effects among different types of proposed antitakeover amendments. According to this latter result, no amendment is viewed by the market as being more harmful or more beneficial than another. McWilliams suggests that the discrepancy in conclusions between her study and the Jarrell and Poulsen study may be due to differences in their samples (no OTC firms in McWilliams's sample) and in categorization of sample firms by amendment type. Jarrell and Poulsen place a firm in the fair-price group even if the firm proposes other types of amendments together with the fair-price amendments, whereas McWilliams includes in the fair-price group those firms that propose only fair-price amendments. The results of McWilliams may indicate that the antitakeover amendments represent nonevents in the sense that the market does not view the amendments as effective defenses.

Supermajority and Classified Board Amendments and Takeover Activity

Pound (1987) suggests that the decision to adopt an antitakeover amendment conveys confounding information to the market and that it is this information (and not the structural effects of the amendment) that drives the stock price reaction. One type of such confounding effect is management's assessment of the probability of the firm becoming a takeover target. This information will have a positive effect on stock prices as noted by DeAngelo and Rice (1983). Alternatively, the amendment proposal may send a negative signal about managerial quality because incompetent managers are more likely to attempt to protect themselves from unwanted takeover bids. This signal will have a negative effect on stock price. When these types of confounding information are conveyed by amendment proposals, stock price evidence alone cannot distinguish between the managerial entrenchment and shareholder interest hypotheses.

Thus, Pound (1987) seeks to provide "direct evidence" on the effect of antitakeover amendments on takeover activity. Pound first compares a sample of 100 NYSE-listed firms that adopted supermajority and classified-board amendments in the period 1973–1979 and a complementary control group consisting of

100 firms that adopted neither supermajority nor classified-board amendments. The result of this comparison shows that firms with antitakeover amendments have a 26 percent lower frequency of takeover attempts in the 1974–1984 period than the control sample. Takeover offer frequencies in the period were .28 for the sample with amendments and .38 for the sample with no amendments.

Pound's second empirical analysis is concerned with the effect of anti-takeover amendments on takeover premiums. Takeover bid premiums for 65 targets with supermajority and classified-board amendments average 51.4 percent in the 1974–1984 period, which is not significantly different from an average premium of 48.8 percent for 98 firms with no antitakeover amendments. It thus appears that the two types of amendments do not serve to raise takeover returns to target shareholders while significantly deterring takeover attempts.

A third empirical analysis by Pound shows that costly takeover resistance, including lawsuits and market-based actions, is twice as likely among targets with supermajority and classified-board amendments as it is for target firms without such antitakeover amendments in place. Thus, a part of the deterrent effect of antitakeover amendments comes from an increase in transaction costs that the bidder should expect in its bid to take over a target. Pound also finds that a bidder cannot succeed against continued opposition by management of a target with antitakeover amendments, whereas in the control sample a bidder can succeed with a one third probability even if target management continues to express opposition to transfer of control.

In sum, the results obtained by Pound indicate that supermajority and classified-board amendments increase the bargaining power of management "to the detriment of shareholder wealth." The amendments decrease the frequency of takeover bids while not increasing shareholder gains in actual takeover contests.

Changing the State of Incorporation and Stock Prices

State corporation codes can include takeover-related provisions and may favor incumbent management to the detriment of their shareholders. Changes in the state of incorporation can thus make a hostile takeover of the firm more difficult and may be decided purely in consideration of using takeover defenses. For instance, the Ohio corporation code was changed in November 1986 to "give more leeway to directors in resisting takeovers" (Ryngaert and Netter, 1988). The new Ohio law provides that takeover resistance is consistent with directors' fiduciary duties if it is based on a consideration of long-term as well as short-term interests of the firm's shareholders. In addition, the Ohio law expressly allows the use of poison pills. Romano (1987) argues that the passage of antitakeover legislation may be influenced by incumbent managements of local corporations. Alternatively, Dodd and Leftwich (1980) argue that states competitively adopt corporation codes designed to advance shareholder interests in order to attract firms to their states. According to this view, changes in the state of incorporation would increase stock prices. In their empirical analysis, Dodd and Leftwich (1980) find that changes in the state of incorporation follow a period of superior performance of the involved firms and result in a small positive abnormal return. Romano (1985) reports a statistically insignificant price increase in a subsample of 43 firms which reincorporated as an antitakeover device.

Thus, the empirical evidence is not strong enough to warrant a conclusion on the motives and effects of reincorporation. In particular, there is no evidence that reincorporations deprive shareholders of the benefits from the takeover market. But this is not to deny the possibility that corporation codes in certain states make takeovers more difficult. Ryngaert and Netter (1988) find that the Ohio antitakeover legislation in November 1986 was accompanied by a decline in stock prices of roughly 2 percent for their sample of 37 Ohio firms. Thus, the new law was not seen as beneficial to shareholders. It was seen as benefiting incumbent management or other stakeholders such as workers and the local community.

Effects of Reduction in Cumulative Voting Rights

In some corporations board members are elected through cumulative voting, whereas in most corporations straight voting is used. Straight voting allows each shareholder to cast votes equal to the number of shares held for each director position. In cumulative voting, the shareholder is entitled to cast for each share held as many votes as the number of directors to be elected. Cumulative voting allows minority shareholders to cumulate their votes and cast them for a select number of directors. Thus, it may be possible for a group of minority shareholders to elect some directors even if the majority of shareholders oppose their election. It is easier with cumulative voting for dissident shareholders or corporate raiders to get representation on the board. This can increase the likelihood of a change in control more than with straight voting.

Bhagat and Brickley (1984) report that during the 1962–1982 period at least 52 nationally-listed firms passed management-sponsored charter amendments to eliminate cumulative voting. In the same period 18 other firms passed amendments authorizing cumulative voting. As of December 1982, 383 (approximately 24 percent) of the NYSE-listed firms had cumulative voting. Bhagat and Brickley (1984) also report that the laws of 29 states (including Delaware) permit corporations to adopt cumulative voting and that in 18 states it is mandatory.

The impact of cumulative voting can be reduced not only by eliminating cumulative voting but also by adopting a classified board or by decreasing the size of the board by a firm with cumulative voting. Similarly, the impact of cumulative voting can be enhanced by declassifying a board (that is, by moving to an annual election of all directors) or by increasing the size of the board by a firm with cumulative voting.

Bhagat and Brickley (1984) analyze the effect of these changes in cumulative voting on stock prices. Their sample includes 126 management-sponsored charter amendments affecting cumulative voting rights. For the 84 amendments that reduce the effect of cumulative voting, Bhagat and Brickley find an average return of -0.88 percent during the announcement period (the proxy mailing date and the following day). The two events generating the largest negative stock price reaction are the elimination of cumulative voting and the classification of the board by a firm with cumulative voting. A detailed case analysis shows that the elimination of cumulative voting was used by some firms as an antitakeover tactic in direct response to a takeover bid. Sometimes the change in voting rights was proposed after a state law change permitting such an action. For the 42 proposed amendments that enhance the effect of cumulative voting, Bhagat and Brickley found no significant stock price reaction during the announcement period.

The results of Bhagat and Brickley (1984) suggest that cumulative voting rights can increase firms' values, presumably by increasing the threat of a change in control or by lowering agency costs between shareholders and managers. The results also indicate that management may act to reduce the likelihood of electing minority representatives through cumulative voting even though this reduces share prices. Thus, it is seen that charter amendments reducing the effect of cumulative voting appear to increase management's ability to resist a takeover bid by decreasing the ability of dissident shareholders to elect directors. Finally, the evidence in Bhagat and Brickley (1984) is consistent with Dodd and Warner's (1983) finding that cumulative voting is an important element in proxy contests that benefit shareholders.

Concluding Remarks
on Antitakeover Amendments

Whatever their motivation, antitakeover amendments are increasingly frequent; 195 of the S&P 500 firms had antitakeover amendments in place by the end of October 1984—half of these had been adopted during 1983 and 1984 (Richter, 1985). The trend has been away from supermajority amendments popular in the late 1970s toward less negatively charged fair-price amendments and lock-in provisions to protect previously passed amendments.

Antitakeover amendments certainly do not guarantee a successful fight against a raider. A study of takeover targets during 1974–1979 by the Investor Responsibility Research Center in Washington DC found that 61 percent of a sample of firms with antitakeover amendments succumbed to raiders; however, 39 percent did remain independent, while none of the target firms in the sample without antitakeover amendments were successful in defending against raiders (Richter, 1985). This suggests that delay rather than defeat of raiders may be a significant factor in antitakeover amendments.

POISON PILL DEFENSE

A controversial but popular defense mechanism against hostile takeover bids is the creation of securities called poison pills. These securities provide their holders with special rights exercisable only after some time (for example, ten days) following the occurrence of a triggering event such as a tender offer for control or the accumulation of a specified percentage of target shares. These rights take several forms but all make it difficult or costly to acquire control of the issuer, or the target firm. They economically "poison" the would-be acquirer if swallowed.

Poison pills are generally adopted by the board of directors without shareholder approval. Usually the rights provided by a poison pill plan can be altered quickly by the board or redeemed by the firm (at a prespecified low cost such as three cents per right) anytime before they become exercisable following the occurrence of the triggering event. These provisions force the acquirer to negotiate directly with the target's board and allow some takeover bids to go through. Thus, the proponents argue that poison pills do not prohibit all takeovers but enhance the ability of the board of directors to bargain for a "fair" price. This represents the shareholder interest hypothesis on the effects of poison pill defenses. However, there is the alternative hypothesis that poison pills are one of the most potent devices to entrench management and thus they reduce shareholder wealth.

We will return to these arguments and related empirical evidence after first reviewing the types of poison pill plans.

Types of Poison Pill Plans

Since the first poison pill plan was introduced in late 1982, about 380 firms had adopted variants of (poison pill) rights plans by December 1986 (Ryngaert, 1988). Both Malatesta and Walkling (1988) and Ryngaert (1988) identify and characterize five main types of poison pill plans, summarized in Table 20.2.

PREFERRED STOCK PLANS   Also called *original plans,* these were used exclusively prior to 1984. Five such plans were announced (but only two were implemented) by December 1983 and none thereafter. They no longer appear to be adopted by other firms. In the plan, the firm issues a dividend of convertible preferred stock to its common shareholders. Holders of the preferred stock are entitled to one vote per share and to dividends somewhat higher than the amount of common dividends that would be received after conversion. The issuing firm can redeem the preferred stock only after a lengthy period such as 15 years. In the event that an outside party acquires a large block (for example, 30 percent) of the firm's voting stock, the holder of the preferred stock can exercise special rights. First, preferred stockholders other than the large block holder can require the firm to redeem preferred stock for cash at the highest price the large

TABLE 20.2
Overview of Poison Pill Rights Plans

1. *Original, or preferred stock plans*—dividends of preferred stock convertible into common; if a trigger point reached, can exercise put for cash at highest price paid during past year; if a merger, can convert into common stock of acquirer

2. *Flip-over plans*—rights are a call on the (target) firm's stock far out of the money; (a) in a merger in which acquirer survives, flip over to permit call on *acquirer* stock at price deep in the money (i.e., allow big discount); (b) in a merger in which target survives, become a flip-in

3. *Ownership flip-in plans*—at trigger point, rights flip in to permit call on target stock at price deep in the money, but acquirer's rights are void

4. *Back-end rights plan*—at a trigger point, rights plus stock of target can be put at a value greater than current market; in effect, sets a minimum takeover price

5. *Voting plans*—issue preferred stock with supermajority voting rights to target's shareholders; at trigger point, acquirer's preferred loses voting rights

---

block holder paid for the firm's common or preferred stock during the past year. Second, if the acquiring party merges with the firm, the preferred stock can be converted into voting securities of the acquirer with a total market value no less than the redemption value in the first case. These rights can be modified by the issuing firm's board only if there is no large block holder. Hence, the board can negotiate with a friendly bidder who has not accumulated a large block. When a large block holder exists, modification of the preferred's provisions requires a supermajority vote of the preferred stock.

The original plan is thus seen to be designed to deter coercive two-tier tender offers or to avoid dilution that can be effected by a majority shareholder. A partial tender offer for the preferred stock is likely to fail because holders of the preferred stock have no incentive to tender their shares, as they are guaranteed to receive the highest price paid by the bidder. Modified two-tier offers may still be possible (Ryngaert, 1988, p. 381). For instance, the bidder could buy most of the preferred and half of the common stock at a lower price through a formal merger transaction.

FLIP-OVER RIGHTS PLANS   These plans have been the most popular poison pill defense since first introduced in late 1984. Hundreds of firms, including TRW, Colgate-Palmolive, J. C. Penney, and Time Inc., have adopted this plan. Under this plan, shareholders receive a common stock dividend in the form of rights to acquire the firm's common or preferred stock at an exercise price well above the current market price, and if a merger occurs, the rights "flip over" to permit the holder to purchase the *acquirer's* shares at a substantial discount. For example, a firm whose common stock is selling at $40 issues one right per share to purchase the common shares at $100; in the event of a merger, the rights "flip over" so the rights can now be used to purchase $200 worth of the *acquirer's* stock for only $100.

Usually having a term of ten years, the rights become exercisable ten days (sometimes more) after a person or a group either acquires 20 percent or more, or commences a tender offer for 30 percent or more of the firm's common stock. (The triggering amounts vary across different plans.) When they become exercisable, the rights are separated from the stock and can be traded independently. Before the rights become exercisable, they can be redeemed by the firm's board at a trivial cost (such as three cents per right). This redemption by the board will occur when the board wants to permit a transaction sought by the acquirer to go forward unhindered. The types of transactions that these plans attempt to deter are merger and self-dealing (generally defined as excess compensation, transfer of assets to related entities, and similar transactions). In the event of a merger in which the large block holder is the surviving company, the rights "flip over" and entitle a holder to purchase shares of common stock of the surviving company at a substantial discount, typically 50 percent. Alternatively, in the event of a merger in which the target firm survives, or of a self-dealing defined in the rights agreement, each right *not* owned by the 20 percent or more stockholder is entitled to purchase the target shares at the same discount. The latter case (involving a self-dealing) is called a "self-dealing flip-in."

Note that the flip-over plan does not prevent an acquirer from obtaining a controlling interest in the target. However, mergers or transfers of assets which are the primary goals of most takeovers become prohibitively expensive unless the acquirer obtains most of the rights. Obtaining the rights cheaply will not be possible because of the free-rider problem. Even when the acquirer initiates an offer for any or all shares *and* rights at substantial premiums, holders will not tender their rights because rights still held will presumably be worth much more than the premium offered.

OWNERSHIP FLIP-IN PLANS   An ownership flip-in plan provision may be included in the flip-over plan. This provision allows holders of rights to purchase target shares at a large discount if an acquirer accumulates target shares in excess of a threshold or "kick-in" point (generally 25 to 50 percent). The acquirer's rights are void. This provision imposes losses on the acquirer and dilutes his or her equity. Some plans waive the flip-in provision if the acquisition is pursuant to a cash tender offer for all outstanding shares. Ownership flip-in plans thus deter acquisition of a substantial equity position by any means in most cases or by means other than an all cash tender offer in some cases. Approximately half the flip-over plans contain the ownership flip-in (Malatesta and Walkling, 1988).

BACK-END RIGHTS PLANS   Under these plans, shareholders receive a rights dividend. If an acquirer obtains shares of the target in excess of a limit, holders excluding the acquirer can exchange a right and a share of the stock for senior securities or cash equal in value to a back-end price set by the board of directors of the issuing (target) firm. The back-end price is higher than the stock's market price and thus back-end plans set a minimum takeover price for the firm. Back-end plans deter acquisition of a controlling interest. A conditional tender offer for less than the back-end price will not succeed because rights holders have an incentive to hold out for the higher back-end price. This is again the free-rider problem noted in connection with the foregoing poison pill plans.

VOTING PLANS   A voting plan is implemented by declaring a dividend of preferred stock with voting rights. In some cases, if a party acquires a substantial block of a firm's voting stock, preferred holders other than the large block holder become entitled to supervoting privileges. It is thus difficult for the block holder to obtain voting control. In a different case, long-term (three or more years) holders of preferred stock are entitled to more votes per share than short-term holders. This makes it difficult for a bidder to acquire voting control rapidly. Some voting plans were made illegal by the courts (Malatesta and Walkling, 1988, p. 354).

It is possible to categorize the variants of poison pill plans according to their principal objectives. Four such categories are suggested by Ryngaert (1988):

1 To avoid dilution by a majority shareholder or to prevent a coercive two-tier tender offer (preferred stock plan).
2 To deter formal mergers, substantial asset sales, and self-dealing (flip-over plans).
3 To deter accumulation of a substantial block unless through a cash tender offer for all shares (certain types of ownership flip-in plans).
4 To deter accumulation of a substantial block by any means (some ownership flip-in plans, back-end plans and voting plans).

A common feature of all these poison pill plans is that they promote the free-rider problem, thereby causing a tender offer conditional on shareholders surrendering their pill securities to the bidder to fail. Thus, avoiding the penalties imposed on the bidder by the pills is not generally feasible.

By January 1988, shareholder rights plans were adopted by 559 firms. Of these, 274 plans contain only flip-over provisions and 276 also include an ownership flip-in provision. Back-end rights plans or voting rights plans were adopted by less than ten firms (MacMinn and Cook, 1988).

Hypotheses on Poison Pill Defenses

Poison pill defenses increase the costs of acquiring a firm for merger or merely a controlling interest in the firm. Therefore, management may use a poison pill defense to secure its position. The managerial entrenchment hypothesis emphasizes conflicts of interest between managers and shareholders and argues that a poison pill plan is adopted as a means of enhancing managerial welfare. It is assumed that severance payment arrangements (such as golden parachutes) or threats of director liability suits do not solve the conflict of interest problem in control contest situations. Further, incentive compensation contracts and disciplinary forces such as ex-post settling up in the managerial labor market do not work efficiently to eliminate agency problems in everyday decisions. If this entrenchment hypothesis is valid, the adoption of a poison pill plan will have negative impact on stock prices.

On the other hand, poison pill defenses induce the bidder to negotiate with the target management. This will enable the board to secure a higher price for the firm than would otherwise be paid. Poison pills other than voting plans make coercive two-tiered or partial tender offers ineffective. Also, voting plans can prevent (postacquisition) dilution by inhibiting a bidder from acquiring voting control. These considerations suggest that poison pill plans may be adopted to protect shareholder interests, as argued by all managements initiating these plans. Moreover, as Knoeber (1986) argues, reducing takeover threats may improve managerial incentives to maximize firm value by inducing managers to make more organization-specific investments and by allowing the firm to use performance-based deferred compensation contracts. This shareholder interest hypothesis thus predicts a positive stock price reaction at the time of the rights plan adoption. But the hypothesis requires the further assumption that other mechanisms to protect shareholders from coercive offers do not work adequately, and that such devices as severance payment agreements cannot optimally motivate managers to make investments in firm-specific human capital.

Empirical Evidence

Malatesta and Walkling (1988) study an exhaustive sample of 132 poison pills adopted from 1982 through March 1986; 70 of these are flip-over plans and 46 are ownership flip-in plans. The average abnormal return for a two-day announcement period is significantly negative (−0.915 percent), which is small in absolute value. When the announcement of adoption is reported in *The Wall Street Journal* or *The New York Times*, the average abnormal return is −1.324 percent and significant for the 73 cases included. This result on stock price reaction is consistent with the managerial entrenchment hypothesis.

Malatesta and Walkling (1988) also provide data on managerial ownership which tend to support the entrenchment hypothesis. Firms announcing poison pills have an average managerial share ownership of 9.39 percent, which is significantly smaller than the average managerial ownership of their respective industries (23.12 percent). This is a strong result because firms announcing poison pills are typically smaller than most firms in their respective industries and managerial ownership percentages in smaller firms are typically larger (Demsetz and Lehn, 1985). Lower managerial stock ownership may be consistent with the entrenchment hypothesis because the cost of reduced takeover probability due to the pill defense is smaller to managers. Another piece of evidence consistent with the managerial entrenchment hypothesis is that firms adopting poison pill plans are significantly less profitable than their industry peers. This is consistent with the view that target firms in takeovers are generally less profitable than other firms in their industries (Chung, 1982) and that likely target firms adopt poison pills.

Ryngaert (1988) employs a larger sample of 380 poison pills adopted from 1982 to December 25, 1986. He notes three important points from the data. First, over 80 percent of the adoptions occurred in 1986 which reflects the increased popularity of poison pills. Second, pills that penalize large ownership positions (that is, ownership flip-in plans, back-end plans, and voting plans) became more common in 1986. Third, it became common that firms not confronted with immediate takeover threats adopted pill defenses.

The mean and median management ownership percentages in the sample firms are 6.2 and 3.0 percent, respectively. Management holdings in the poison pill sample are lower than the 13.6 percent average holdings for the antitakeover amendment sample of Jarrell and Poulsen (1987). This result may indicate that management adopts poison pill plans when it lacks voting control of the firm and thus shareholder approval of any antitakeover measures is doubtful. Ryngaert (1988) notes that this is not necessarily consistent with the managerial entrenchment hypothesis because high management shareholdings already give the firm's management effective bargaining power in takeovers, making the poison pill defense unnecessary in promoting shareholder interest. Another interesting aspect of the data developed by Ryngaert (1988) is that over three fourths of the directors of the firms in the sample are outside directors. Thus, if poison pills are adopted primarily for managerial entrenchment, the data indicate that outside directors are not performing their monitoring role efficiently. Finally, the majority of firms in the sample already had antitakeover amendments (staggered boards, supermajority voting, and fair-price amendments).

Stock price reactions to adoption of poison pills are studied for subgroups in Ryngaert's sample. For 283 cases with no actual confounding events (such as initial takeover bid and 13D filings which indicate the acquisition of 5 percent or more of a firm's shares by a single entity), the stock price effect is -0.34 percent for the two-day period around the announcement of the pill adoption. For 57 firms subject to takeover rumors but with no other confounding events, the excess return is -1.51 percent and statistically significant. But 221 adoptions without confounding events and takeover rumors have an average return close to zero (-0.02 percent). This last result may indicate that poison pill defenses are not important to firms which do not have a substantial prospect of becoming a takeover target. Conversely, it may indicate that adoption of a poison pill plan itself signifies that the firm is a likely takeover target. This point is corroborated by the fact that the announcement return is larger for firms which subsequently become subject to new takeover rumors or actual bids unexpected at the time of announcement.

When the sample is divided into subgroups of discriminatory pills and nondiscriminatory pills, the results strongly indicate managerial entrenchment for discriminatory pills. The discriminatory pills are those that penalize acquirers exceeding a given shareholding limit (the kick-in point) and include ownership flip-in plans, back-end plans, and voting plans. The discriminatory pill subgroup of 90 firms not subject to takeover speculation has a statistically significant -0.82 percent return and the same group of 27 firms subject to takeover rumors shows a significant -2.2 percent.

Ryngaert (1988) also examines the effects of court decisions on litigation involving poison pills. It is shown that 15 of 18 pro-management decisions (rejecting requests for temporary restraining orders or preliminary or permanent injunctions against poison pill plans) result in negative excess returns (an average of more than 2 percent in absolute value for all cases) during the day of and the day after the court decision. Six of 11 pro-acquirer decisions result in positive excess returns (an average of more than 3 percent). These results are consistent with the managerial entrenchment hypothesis. The large stock price reactions also suggest that firm excess returns upon poison pill adoption as observed earlier may understate the potential impact of poison pill defenses because of the information on the firm's takeover prospects as conveyed by the poison pill's adoption.

Ryngaert (1988) finds that an unsolicited bid is more likely to be defeated when a poison pill is in place. The firms that defeated an unsolicited tender offer or a merger offer experienced an average excess return of −14.4 percent during the six months following the offer. Most of the defeats resulted from discriminatory poison pills in place rather than nondiscriminatory plans (flip-over plans, preferred stock plans, and ownership flip-in plans permitting cash offers for all shares). However in 52 percent of the cases, firms with poison pill plans in place end up with higher, revised premiums. This suggests that poison pill defenses are not uniformly employed to defeat all unsolicited bids. But the data show that they are no more effective than other defenses in achieving increased bids.

Finally, the evidence shows that poison pill defenses were frequently employed against *existing* bids for *all* the shares of a firm. This result appears to undermine the claim that poison pill defenses are used to protect shareholders from coercive two-tier and partial offers, although the data also show that hostile bids tend to be offers for all shares (33 out of 47 hostile bids) when a poison pill is in place.

Legal Status and Issues of Poison Pill Defense

The legality of poison pills has been questioned because they alter the contractual relationships among the principals (shareholders) without their approval by vote. In most poison pills, the agents (boards of directors) adopt rights plans which treat shareholders of the same class unequally in situations involving corporate control. Thus, poison pills have been vulnerable to court review. Ryngaert (1988) reports that 14 of 21 litigations during the period 1982 through February 1987 resulted in pro-management court decisions refusing to invalidate poison pills, and the rest in pro-acquirer decisions. In his sample, all pro-acquirer decisions except one took place in federal or state courts outside Delaware, while courts in Delaware generally held that poison pills may be a legitimate response to threats to corporate policy and effectiveness. However, Delaware, where almost one half of NYSE-listed companies are chartered, may "not be the haven it used to be" for managers (*Business Week*, December 19, 1988, p. 33). Courts of Delaware have been observed

rights plan provides the firm with flexibility in dealing with potential acquirers, whereas alternative defenses such as scorched-earth tactics irreversibly harm the corporation. The plan can be viewed as preplanned or prospective rather than reactive and reduces the risk of ill-planned reactive devices. While the plan creates the potential for the misuse of authority conferred upon directors, the board armed with a rights plan will possess a bargaining tool to extract concessions from an acquirer. It cannot be assumed that the board will act contrary to shareholder interests. "The adoption of the Rights Plan is an appropriate exercise of managerial judgment under the business judgment rule" (*Moran* v. Household, p. 1083).

In criticizing the court's decision, Jensen (1988) argues that the altruistic model of the board which the court employed is incorrect as a description of human behavior. Although the model has yielded good law for a wide range of cases, it cannot deal with the conflicts of interest between board members and shareholders which are incorporated in the alternative agency models of the corporation. The principal (shareholders) can delegate a set of managerial decision rights to the agent (directors), but it is not sensible to delegate control rights—the rights to hire, fire, and set the compensation of the agent. If the control rights were delegated, the agent would become the effective owner of the decision rights and could be expected to use them in his or her own interests. By applying the business judgment rule to conflicts over control rights between agents and principals, the court effectively allows the agents to change the control rights unilaterally. This interpretation of the contract between the agent and the principal "will destroy (in the long run) the possibility of such cooperative arrangements, because it will leave principals with few effective rights" (Jensen, 1988, p. 43). Finally, Jensen notes that the real problem with poison pills is not in their appropriateness but in their adoption without shareholder approval.

The Future of Poison Pills

Discriminatory self-tender offers are now prohibited by the new SEC rule, but the ability to discriminate against large block holders by a poison pill still survives. However, as indicated earlier, the application of poison pill defenses in actual control contests is not always guaranteed. In addition to the cases previously mentioned in which the court refused to let the targets use the poison pill defense, the Delaware Chancery Court handed down another pro-acquirer decision in *Grand Metropolitan PLC* v. *Pillsbury Co.* On December 16, 1988, the court found that the decision by Pillsbury's board "to keep the pill in place was not reasonable in relation to any threat posed" and thus "the decision was not protected by the business judgment rule" (*The Wall Street Journal*, December 19, 1988, p. A3). The decision was based on facts presumed in the case: The all-cash offer by Grand Metropolitan was considered adequate in relation to the recapitalization plan offered by the target management after being hastily prepared during the ten-week period which the poison pill defense had allowed.

As this case indicates, there is no absolute rule on poison pills as yet. The effectiveness of a poison pill defense depends on individual cases. The court seems to evaluate adequacy of bids and reasonableness of targets' responses. In this, Jensen (1988, pp. 43–44) sees a danger. The current trend, if continued, will lead to the erosion of the limits on judicial interference in corporate management. Ironically, this erosion of the business judgment rule arises out of its continued application to conflicts over corporate control. Jensen (1988) points out that the court is brought into the position of second-guessing managers' business decisions because it understands that the poison pill gives the management great power. Jensen predicts that the trend will be checked and that the court will recognize the problems inherent in the present approach. The solution recommended by Jensen is "for the court to deny protection under the business judgment rule to managerial decisions on control issues" unless ratified by shareholder vote.

Shareholder resistance to adoption of poison pills also seems to be increasing. Antipoison pill proposals requesting management to redeem existing poison pill rights have been taken to annual shareholder meetings in many companies. These resolutions voted on in 1987 received, on average, 29.4 percent of the shares voting (*The Wall Street Journal*, May 25, 1988, p. 3). But the average increased to 39 percent for the 17 antipill measures voted at U.S. companies in early 1988. In 1988, the proposals to eliminate poison pill rights plans received a majority of the votes cast in two companies—USAir Group Inc. and Santa Fe Southern Pacific Corporation. A weakness of the antipoison pill resolutions is that under current law they are only advisory. SEC regulations require shareholder proposals to be nonbinding on the board of directors. Delaware state law also stipulates that directors have discretionary rights on such shareholder decisions.

Meanwhile, the poison pill defense will prove to be effective against coercive and inadequate tender offers. This is because none of the pro-acquirer court decisions in later cases weakens the use of the poison pill defense to "defend" the firm against such bids. Further, the poison pill defense can buy time even in high-premium all-cash offers. Some observers even suggest that Delaware firms can change the state of incorporation (*Business Week*, December 19, 1985, p. 33). Supposedly some state courts are more congenial to management. One example is the state of Pennsylvania whose corporate law appears to allow management to take into account the effects on all stakeholders including employees, the local community, suppliers and customers, as well as shareholders (*Business Week*, December 19, 1985, p. 33).

TARGETED SHARE REPURCHASE AND STANDSTILL AGREEMENTS

In a targeted repurchase, often called greenmail, a target firm repurchases through private negotiation a large block of its stock from an individual shareholder or a subset of shareholders at a premium. The purpose of the premium buy-back presumably is to end a hostile takeover threat by the large block holder or greenmailer. The term *greenmail* connotes blackmail and both payers and receivers of greenmail have received negative publicity. Proponents of antigreenmail charter amendments or legislation which would prohibit targeted repurchases argue that damages to shareholders are caused by greenmailers. In this view, the large block investors are corporate "raiders" who expropriate corporate assets to the detriment of other shareholders. Allegedly, raiding takes the form of using the raiders' corporate voting power to accord themselves excessive compensation and perquisites, receiving on their shares a substantial premium over the market price through greenmail, or "looting" the corporate treasury in some unspecified manner (Holderness and Sheehan, 1985).

An alternative view is that the large block investors involved in greenmail help bring about management changes, either changes in corporate personnel or changes in corporate policy, or have superior skills at evaluating potential takeover targets (Holderness and Sheehan, 1985). In this view, proposals to prohibit targeted repurchases are antitakeover proposals in disguise (Jensen, 1988). Jensen (1988, p. 41) argues that "management can easily prohibit greenmail without legislation; it need only announce a policy that prohibits the board or management from making such payments." He suggests that managers make greenmail payments to protect themselves from competition in the corporate control market.

Often in connection with targeted repurchases, a standstill agreement is written. A standstill agreement is a voluntary contract in which the stockholder who is bought out agrees not to make further investments in the target company during a specified period of time (for example, ten years). When a standstill agreement is made without a repurchase, the large block holder simply agrees not to increase his or her ownership, which presumably would put him or her in an effective control position.

Shareholder Wealth Effects
of Greenmail and Standstill Agreements

Empirical results generally indicate that although a greenmail transaction itself decreases stock prices, the initial stock purchase by a large block investor and related events resulted in a prior positive abnormal return to target shareholders. Dann and DeAngelo (1983) find an average abnormal return on the repurchasing firm's stock of -1.76 percent on the day before and day of announcement for 41 negotiated repurchases involving a premium. The average premium was 16.4 percent. Bradley and Wakeman (1983) report a significantly negative abnormal return of -2.85 percent during the two-day period around announcement for 61 firms that repurchased a single block of common stock, and a return of 1.40 percent for 28 selling firms. Bradley and Wakeman (1983) further find that premium targeted large block repurchases are associated with a takeover bid cancellation. Thus, they suggest that targeted repurchases inflict greater costs to nonparticipating shareholders when they are used to thwart takeover attempts.

These negative effects of targeted repurchases contrast sharply with the typically large positive abnormal returns associated with nontargeted repurchase tender offers. (See Chapter 18, Share Repurchase and Exchanges.)

Dann and DeAngelo (1983) examine the effects of standstill agreements on stock prices. For the 30 firms that repurchased their shares and obtained standstill agreements, they find an average abnormal return of −4.52 percent on the day before and the day of announcement of the agreement. When unaccompanied by repurchase, the agreement resulted in an average abnormal return of −4.04 percent for a sample of 19 firms. Bradley and Wakeman (1983) also find that the announcement of a standstill agreement has the same informational content as the news of merger termination. These results indicate that standstill agreements reduce the wealth of nonparticipating stockholders by thwarting takeover attempts.

Later empirical studies more strongly suggest that prohibition of greenmail payments will not necessarily be in the interests of shareholders. Mikkelson and Ruback (1985, 1986), Holderness and Sheehan (1985), and Klein and Rosenfeld (1988) all find that the initial stock purchase that eventually leads to the repurchase produced significantly positive average abnormal returns both in the initial "foothold period" and in the full purchase-to-repurchase period.

The result of Holderness and Sheehan (1985) in particular is based on the activities of the six controversial raiders including Carl Icahn, Irwin Jacobs, Carl Lindner, David Murdock, Vistor Posner, and the late Charles Bluhdorn. In the six-year period from 1977 to 1982, the six investors or companies affiliated with them made 155 13D filings. No less than 12 cases of greenmail resulted from their initial stock purchases during the period. The general implication of various results from the Holderness and Sheehan (1985) study is inconsistent with the raider image of the six investors; the results show either that the six improve the management of the target firms, or that they consistently identify undervalued stocks.

Mikkelson and Ruback (1986) also find that targeted repurchases do not result in significant decline in stock prices unless they are accompanied by a standstill agreement or preceded by a control contest. Larger stock price declines associated with repurchases with standstills may reflect the possibility that these agreements reduce the probability of a subsequent takeover. However, this expectation is not borne out in their data; the proportions of repurchasing firms with a subsequent control change within three years of the repurchase are the same (28 percent) in the subsample of repurchases with standstill agreements (39 firms) and in the subsample of remaining repurchases (72 firms). Therefore, standstill agreements do not appear to affect the probability of a future takeover following a targeted repurchase. Mikkelson and Ruback (1986) note that the frequency of control changes following targeted repurchases is about three times larger than the unconditional frequency (for a random sample of listed firms during their sample period).

Both Mikkelson and Ruback (1986) and Klein and Rosenfeld (1988) find that the stock price declines at the targeted repurchases are not completely related to the premiums paid in repurchases and thus cannot be attributed solely to a wealth transfer from the nonparticipating to the participating shareholders. Mikkelson and Ruback (1986) also find that the stock price declines are related to the positive stock returns prior to the repurchase. This result suggests that the announcement of a targeted repurchase has the effect of information reversal (that is, a lower takeover probability), but that the information reversal is not complete.

The empirical results further suggest that the initial "foothold" investments that sometimes lead to a targeted repurchase entail many possible outcomes. In addition to repurchase, the possible outcomes include successful takeovers by the initial investor and third-party bids for control. Accordingly, the positive abnormal return during the "foothold period" reflects an expected valuation effect of the possible outcomes, and the negative abnormal return of a repurchase reflects the least favorable outcome for the target's shareholders (Mikkelson and Ruback, 1986). However, as the evidence indicates, the initial investment activity and the subsequent repurchase may induce others to pursue control of the target.

In this connection, Shleifer and Vishny (1986a) present a model in which management resistance including targeted repurchases conveys the unfavorable information that the target does not have access to a white knight, but also raises the prospect of a takeover bid by a third party. In this view, the repurchase and management resistance to takeovers in general may cause stock prices to decline but is value maximizing in the long run. Similarly, Mikkelson and Ruback (1986) argue that a targeted repurchase may reflect management's assessment that ownership of a large block of shares by a particular person is not in the best interest of shareholders. The stock price falls in this case even if the management is acting in shareholders' interests. The reason is that the repurchase signals a lower probability of a lucrative takeover bid than previously expected.

In sum, the whole sequence of events following the initial foothold investment benefits shareholders. It would be costly to restrict or prohibit targeted repurchases. Such regulation would discourage large block stock ownership by outsiders and would reduce investments that lead to closer monitoring of managers and to desirable takeovers.

Antigreenmail Charter Amendments and Shareholder Wealth

Antigreenmail charter amendments prohibit or discourage the targeted repurchase by requiring management to obtain the approval of a majority or supermajority of nonparticipating shareholders prior to a repurchase. Proxy statements proposing antigreenmail amendments typically state that greenmailers pressure the company for a premium buyback with "threats of disruption" including proxy contest and tender offers, that greenmail is inherently unfair to the nonparticipating shareholders, and that the decision-making power for any targeted repurchases should be properly transferred to the hands of those most affected by the repurchase decision. According to Bhagat and Jefferis (1988), proxy statements proposing antigreenmail amendments frequently include one or more of (other) antitakeover amendment proposals. Among a sample of 52 NYSE-listed firms proposing antigreenmail amendments in the 1984–1985 period, 40 firms also offered one or more antitakeover amendments in the proxy material. In 29 cases, shareholders had to approve or reject the antitakeover provisions and antigreenmail amendment jointly.

The average abnormal return for the 52 firms on the announcement period (the proxy mailing day and the following day) is a statistically significant −0.86 percent. When firms contaminated by the release of other information during the announcement period are eliminated, the result is about the same (−0.81 percent for the remaining 39 firms). However, a cross-sectional analysis by Bhagat and Jefferis (1988) reveals that the antigreenmail amendment itself does not significantly decrease shareholder wealth. This is also confirmed by the mean return of −0.04 percent for a clean sample of five firms proposing only the antigreenmail amendment and not contaminated by other information.

Therefore, it appears that the negative abnormal return for their sample is caused by other antitakeover proposals rather than by the antigreenmail proposal. The significant negative effect of antitakeover proposals found by Bhagat and Jefferis (1988) is in contrast with Linn and McConnell (1983) and DeAngelo and Rice (1983). Bhagat and Jefferis suggest several interpretations of this difference in results based on the fact that their sample is drawn from a later time period than the samples analyzed in earlier studies. First, public controversy over antitakeover amendments has increased investor awareness of the potential costs of these amendments. Second, increased takeover activity in the 1980s has increased the opportunity cost of antitakeover amendments. Third, the marginal effect of more recent amendments is greater than those adopted previously because remaining avenues for hostile takeovers are closed.

Bhagat and Jefferis (1988) also provide an interesting theory on the proxy voting process relating to the adoption of antitakeover amendments. They hypothesize and find evidence that the primary role of the antigreenmail amendment is to "hide" other antitakeover agenda items for the annual shareholder meeting. Detailed examination of the notice of annual meeting, in which management summarizes the agenda, reveals that the description of the antitakeover measures is often vague and makes it difficult to determine that an agenda item is related to takeover activity. The antigreenmail amendment, which is assumed to be valuable to shareholders, is routinely used to induce shareholders to accept antitakeover measures that they might otherwise oppose. Managers thus manipulate the voting behavior of uninformed investors. Informed investors such as institutional holders can interpret the implications of any proposed amendments, but they do not undertake a proxy fight or other actions to block the proposed changes if the costs of such actions exceed the benefits. The small decline in shareholder wealth associated with the antitakeover proposal reflects the costliness of informing the uninformed investors. Bhagat and Jefferis (1988) find that an increase in institutional ownership is associated with a statistically significant decline in the occurrence of antitakeover amendments for firms proposing antigreenmail amendments. Thus, the presence of informed investors appears to constrain the behavior of managers, despite the fact that proposals offered by managers are accepted in most cases. This result is at odds with Pound (1987) who finds that full-control proxy initiatives and successes of proxy contests involve firms with lower institutional holdings. (See Chapter 19.) Bhagat and Jefferis (1988) conclude that managerial control of the proxy voting mechanism affords managers an advantage in communicating their views to uninformed shareholders who do not carefully inspect proxy material.

STRATEGIC REACTIONS BY TARGETS

Some of the preliminary defenses described earlier (particularly the poison pill) can also be erected after the fact. However, once an offer is on the table, targets are at a distinct disadvantage with respect to timing. The raider has literally all the time in the world to investigate potential targets, arrange financing, and choose the moment when market conditions are optimal for attack. The unwary target has initially only 20 days in which to respond (the time period required by the SEC that a tender offer remain open).

One way in which targets can gain a bit more time is to make use of a relatively new service offered by proxy solicitation firms referred to colloquially as "shark watching." For a fee, the firms claim to be able to detect and identify early accumulations of stock. SEC regulations do not require that buyers reveal their identity until they have already acquired 5 percent of a firm's stock. Early warning obviously gives the target more time to tailor a defense against the particular purchaser, to look for a more acceptable merger partner (a white knight), and so on. And, if the individual or group buying up the stock is not really a serious acquirer but primarily interested in having his or her stock bought back at a premium, early detection can reduce the amount of greenmail that might ultimately have to be paid to eliminate the threat.

An almost universal first response is for the target to maintain that the acquirer's initial bid is woefully inadequate. The allegation is often supported by an alternative valuation of the target provided by the firm's investment bankers with an explanation why the current market price of the stock is below either of the two figures. The target should be in a position to communicate promptly and accurately both with its own shareholders and the public at large. The shareholder list must be kept current, and ongoing public relations activities are also important in terms of favorable media coverage as well as increasing shareholder loyalty.

Another early response is to file an antitrust or other lawsuit against the bidder or accuse the would-be acquirer of SEC violations. Whether or not there is any merit in the litigation, the judicial process is sure to provide breathing room. Once some time has been gained, the target can pursue other avenues. It may make an acquisition which would create an antitrust incompatibility with the bidder's operations. It may acquire a firm in a regulated industry in order to subject the entire takeover transaction to closer governmental scrutiny. In many cases, however, responses to threats are directed more towards delaying the ultimate takeover with the goal of driving up the price rather than necessarily defeating it altogether.

A recent study of the wealth effects of litigation by targets supports the delay hypothesis (Jarrell, 1985). Although a gamble, litigation was found to be a rational management strategy in keeping with management's duty to maximize shareholder wealth. Litigation is fairly common, found in one third of all public takeover bids for NYSE and AMEX targets over the past 20 years. While there is some risk that litigation may cause shareholders to miss out on takeover premiums altogether by driving off the only suitor in town, the goal in most cases seems to be to drive up the price either from the initial bidder or from other bidders attracted to the target during the interim. Jarrell found that targets are only rarely awarded a permanent injunction against the bidders by the courts. Targets remained independent in only about 20 percent of the litigious takeover group—in some, but not all, of these cases, remaining independent seems to have been management's goal. Since Jarrell found no instances where the target's remaining independent benefited shareholders, these few cases do perhaps reflect a conflict of interest. However, this outcome appears to be an unintended and unfortunate effect of litigation in most cases. Almost two thirds of the takeover events involving litigation resulted in an "auction" for the target, while less than 11 percent of the noncontested takeover sample ended in auctions. Since auctions typically added 17 percentage points to already large initial takeover premiums, what initially might appear to be motivated by management entrenchment is often, in fact, in accord with shareholder wealth maximization.

CASE STUDY OF UNOCAL

An analysis of the Unocal–Mesa/Pickens conflict illustrates most of the defensive maneuvers discussed earlier. On October 19, 1984, Mesa Partners II, an organization headed by T. Boone Pickens, Jr., began buying Unocal shares on the open market; the closing price on October 19, 1984 was $35⅞. On February 14, 1984, there was a report in *The Wall Street Journal* on rumors that Unocal was a takeover target. The next day, the suitor was identified as Mesa. By that time, Mesa had purchased 7.9 percent of Unocal's shares, but denied any intention to take over Unocal. It was not surprising that Unocal immediately began a campaign against the possible takeover attempt. By April 1985, Mesa held approximately 13.5 percent of Unocal stock, and on April 8, 1985, it commenced a cash tender offer for 64 million shares (approximately 37 percent of outstanding shares) at $54 per share, in order to bring its holdings to just over 50 percent. (In mid-April, Unocal was trading at about $48 per share.) This was to be a two-tier offer; once control was gained, the remaining Unocal shares were to be exchanged for junior debt and preferred stock ostensibly worth $54 per share. The debt securities were called "junk bonds" by the Unocal board.

Unocal's corporate charter contained a number of antitakeover provisions, among them a staggered board, a supermajority approval requirement for hostile change of management, and in March 1985 an amendment had been passed blocking shareholder motions submitted within 30 days of the annual meeting. Unocal's annual meeting was scheduled for April 29, 1985. Mesa's tender offer was due to expire on May 3, 1985; that is, Mesa was not allowed to purchase shares under the offer until after that date. Mesa wanted to postpone the annual meeting until June in order to be able to complete the tender offer and nominate its own slate of directors in opposition to the Unocal management slate and they began to solicit proxies to do so.

On April 14, 1985, Unocal's board of directors announced that they had determined Mesa's offer to be inadequate and not in the best interests of Unocal's shareholders. Their response was a conditional offer to buy back 87.2 million Unocal shares in exchange for senior debt securities with an estimated market value of $72 per share. The offer was conditional on the success of Mesa's tender offer, and Mesa's Unocal holdings were exempted from the buyback. This discriminatory self-tender offer could be called a triggered back-end poison pill. The potential outcome of a successful tender offer followed by the exchange offer would be that Mesa's 50 percent ownership of Unocal would effectively become 100 percent ownership of a not very attractive target, the remaining equity having been wiped out and replaced with almost $6.3 billion in debt. The staggered board would prevent Mesa from consolidating control for at least two years during which it would be saddled with the almost $4 billion in debt it took on to finance the takeover as well as Unocal's more than $6 billion in new debt. (Unocal's interest expense alone would be more than seven times greater than the firm's 1984 interest expense, with predictably deleterious effects on net income.)

The conditional exchange offer also included provisions restricting the ability of any acquirer to sell or borrow against Unocal's assets and a measure which would increase the interest rate on the debt in the event of a merger or major sale of assets. Mesa, not surprisingly, labeled Unocal's response a poison pill and filed a number of lawsuits. One maintained that Mesa was unlawfully excluded from the exchange offer; another challenged the time limit for submission of annual meeting agenda items; a third found discrepancies in Unocal's proxy materials. Unocal responded by charging Mesa with securities law violations.

On April 24, in response to rumors that Mesa had lined up sufficient additional financing to sweeten its initial tender offer and expand it to include 75 percent of outstanding shares, Unocal announced a modified exchange offer for 29 percent (or about 50 million) of its shares. The compensation was to be the same as in the previous offer, and Mesa's holdings were still excluded, but the offer was not conditional on the success of the Mesa tender offer. The move appears to have been an attempt to preempt any deal-sweetening Mesa may have been planning. In addition, Unocal proposed spinning off 45 percent of its domestic oil and gas revenues into a master limited partnership, with Unocal's share to be distributed to its shareholders over a period of years.

Meanwhile, legal maneuvering continued. The Delaware courts said that if Mesa succeeded in postponing the meeting, it could bring up new business and nominate new directors. In any event, the meeting was delayed for two weeks while both sides made court-ordered corrections in proxy materials. Unocal challenged Mesa's "junk" financing on the grounds that it did not meet the Federal Reserve Board's 50 percent margin requirements. Unocal sued its own bank for participating in Mesa's takeover financing and subpoenaed the records of other banks involved. Unocal's chairman, Fred Hartley, had purportedly encouraged other corporate managers to pressure their banks not to do business with Mesa, and at least two banks dropped out of the financing consortium. Unocal also accused Mesa of antitrust violations by conspiring to restrain trade in domestic oil and gas exploration; however, a federal court in Louisiana denied an injunction against Mesa on May 8, 1985.

The Delaware Chancery Court ruled on April 19, 1985 that Mesa could not be excluded from Unocal's exchange offer. The market responded favorably to this decision. The price of Unocal shares increased 2.11 percent (net of S&P 500 Index changes) during the day of and the day after the court decision (Ryngaert, 1988). Unocal appealed to the Delaware Supreme Court which held on May 17, 1985 that Unocal was justified in excluding Mesa, given the threat posed by the "grossly inadequate coercive two-tier tender offer coupled with the threat of greenmail" (*Securities Regulation and Law Report*, June 14, 1985, p. 1091). The decision in effect gave Delaware corporations enormous latitude in responding to perceived threats and was possibly reflective of a rising sentiment against hostile takeovers. During the two-day period following the decision, Unocal's stock price declined 2.68 percent net of S&P 500 Index changes.

Ultimately, perhaps to put an end to litigation and eliminate Mesa's threat, Unocal did include 7.7 million of Mesa's 23.7 million shares in the exchange offer. In return, Mesa agreed to dispose of its remaining shares in an orderly fashion on the open market, and not to acquire any more Unocal shares for 25 years. This standstill agreement was announced to the public on May 20, 1985. On the same day, Unocal's self-tender offer expired. Unocal ended up buying back 58 million (one third) of their shares, increasing debt from $1.2 to $5.3 billion.

Financial Effects of the Court Ruling

The court ruling in itself did not impose a halt to Mesa's attempt to obtain control of Unocal. Rather, Mesa's failure was caused by the discriminatory nature of the self-tender offer by Unocal for 29 percent of its outstanding shares or about one third of the shares excluding Mesa's holdings. It was estimated that when Unocal's offer was fully subscribed, the remaining shares would have a value of $35 per share compared to a value of $45–$46 prior to the expiration of the offer

(Kamma, Weintrop, and Wier, 1988). This meant that all of Mesa's 23.7 million shares would experience a substantial decline in value resulting in a capital loss of about $245 million unless the parties settled. Without the standstill agreement Mesa would incur the capital loss regardless of whether it continued to pursue the takeover. Mesa's threat to do this was credible because its ownership should increase to about 19 percent after the restructuring (buy-back of shares) by Unocal. But Mesa preferred to avoid the capital loss and agreed not to pursue the takeover in exchange for the inclusion of Mesa's holdings in the buy-back.

If collective action on the part of Unocal's shareholders had been possible, they would have chosen not to subscribe to the Unocal self-tender offer and to tender their shares to Mesa. This assumes (and it appears to be true) that the per share value of Mesa's offer was larger than the per share value that an average shareholder (excluding Mesa) would have realized by taking advantage of Unocal's discriminatory offer. But the court had a different opinion on the value of Mesa's two-tier offer; it accepted Unocal's contention that the second tier had a value lower than $54, the first-tier value, and therefore the two-tier offer was coercive. The court ruling thus legitimized the imposition of a capital loss on Mesa by holding that the buy-back was valid.

In the end, the expropriation of Mesa's wealth (that is, the imposition of a capital loss) did not occur and Unocal's shareholders ended up with the loss of an opportunity to gain from a change of control.

Investors' Perception of the Court Decision

Kamma, Weintrop, and Wier (1988) conducted a study on investors' perception of the Delaware Supreme Court decision in *Unocal* v. *Mesa*. They estimated the stock price reaction to the court decision for 124 firms that were subjects of 13D filings between March 16 and May 16, 1985. These firms are classified into hostile takeover targets (24 firms) and others under no apparent takeover threats (100 firms) by examining news reports. Each category is further classified according to whether they are chartered in Delaware.

Kamma, Weintrop, and Weir (1988) estimated abnormal performance of the four portfolios of firms on Friday, May 17 and Monday, May 20, 1985. The 14 Delaware firms that were hostile takeover targets earned negative abnormal returns at the conclusion of the Unocal–Mesa case. The two-day abnormal return was −2.36 percent and statistically significant. The other portfolios did not show any significant abnormal performance.

The authors interpret the results as suggesting that the court's decision was perceived as a precedent for future decisions in Delaware cases involving discriminatory repurchase offers. Non-Delaware firms were not seen to be affected by the decision. Further, the negative abnormal returns suggest that discriminatory repurchases are seen as being harmful rather than helpful to shareholders, although the court's decision was aimed at protecting shareholders from "coercion."

SUMMARY AND CONCLUSIONS

Arguments for managerial defensive actions are grounded on the desirability of creating an auction for the target, the coerciveness of tender offers, and the bargaining role of management. Opposing arguments emphasize increased costs of takeovers and the resulting inefficiency in the operation of the market for corporate control. Some argue that coerciveness of tender offers should not be a matter of concern, given that the takeover market is competitive. An interesting proposal that might lay (at least) a part of the debate to rest is that shareholders be given an opportunity to vote on individual bids separately from their tendering decisions. There will probably remain the question of providing optimal incentives for takeover activity. In the meantime, innovations in defensive tactics are likely to continue.

Empirical evidence indicates that the "discriminatory" poison pills, some defensive adjustments in asset and ownership structure, and targeted share repurchases have negative effects on stock prices and reduce the success rate of takeover bids. Negative effects do not appear to be limited to those defensive measures that do not require shareholder approval. Corporate charter amendments instituting supermajority vote and classified boards result in not only a decreased frequency of takeover attempts, but also an increased frequency of resistance by management. There is no clear evidence that these amendments achieve an increase in takeover premia.

Nondiscriminatory poison pills (mostly flip-over plans) and other types of antitakeover amendments including antigreenmail amendments do not show clearly negative effects on stock prices. However, this does not necessarily imply that they are not harmful to shareholders because they may signal an increased likelihood of a takeover bid or because they may not be viewed as an effective defense by the market. Unlike most defensive actions taken in reaction to explicit takeover attempts, leveraged cash-outs show no negative effect on shareholder wealth. Litigation by targets seems to aim at driving up the takeover premium by its delaying effect.

Overall, the suggestion by Jarrell, Brickley, and Netter (1988) that shareholder wealth effects of defensive measures on average depend on whether or not they are voted on by shareholders can be given only limited support. Each type of defensive action appears to have different implications with respect to the direction and degree of its impact as the more recent, detailed studies seem to indicate. For instance, golden parachutes have strong theoretical support for their positive role and show greater (positive) abnormal returns relative to other control-related measures.

Negative stock price effects of some antitakeover measures requiring a shareholder vote raise the question of why they are approved by shareholders. Bhagat and Jefferis (1988) argue that the presence of uninformed investors combined with the high costs of "reaching" those investors by better-informed ones during the proxy voting process is responsible for the result. There is evidence that institutional investors who are presumably better informed vote more actively, and harmful measures are instituted in firms with smaller institutional ownership of voting rights.

Jarrell, Brickley, and Netter (1988, p. 86) express concern that "the business judgment rule is operating too broadly as a shield for defensive actions by target managements." And Jensen (1988) warns that, ironically, the broad application of the business judgment rule will increase judicial interference in corporate management. This fear already appears to have supporting cases. Recent pro-acquirer court decisions in cases involving poison pill defenses have been based on an evaluation by the court of the adequacy of the takeover bid.

QUESTIONS

1. What are the three main types of antitakeover amendments and how do they work to defend a target from an unwelcome takeover?
2. What is the effect of the passage of antitakeover amendments on stock price?
3. What is the role of litigation against a bidder in takeover contests?
4. Under what circumstances are share repurchase and exchange useful as antitakeover measures?
5. How can legislation and regulation serve as merger defenses?

REFERENCES

Alchian, A. A., and S. Woodward, "Reflections on the Theory of the Firm," *Journal of Institutional and Theoretical Economics*, 143, March 1987, pp. 110–136.

Bebchuk, L. A., "The Pressure to Tender: An Analysis and a Proposed Remedy," Chapter 25 in Coffee, Lowenstein, and Rose-Ackerman, eds., *Knights, Raiders, and Targets*, New York: Oxford University Press, 1988, pp. 371–397.

Berkovitch, E., and N. Khanna, "A Theory of Acquisition Markets: Mergers vs. Tender Offers, and Golden Parachutes," ms., University of Michigan, Ann Arbor, April 1988.

Bhagat, S., and J. A. Brickley, "Cumulative Voting: The Value of Minority Shareholder Voting Rights," *Journal of Law and Economics*, 27, October 1984, pp. 339–366.

Bhagat, S., and R. H. Jefferis, "You Can Fool Some of the People All of the Time: The Proxy Voting Process and Antigreenmail Charter Amendments," ms., University of Utah, May 1988.

Bradley, M., "Interfirm Tender Offers and the Market for Corporate Control," *Journal of Business*, 53, 1980, pp. 345–376.

———, and L. Wakeman, "The Wealth Effects of Targeted Share Repurchases," *Journal of Financial Economics*, 11, 1983, pp. 301–328.

BRICKLEY, J. A., R. C. LEASE, and C. W. SMITH, JR., "Ownership Structure and Voting on Antitakeover Amendments," *Journal of Financial Economics*, 20, 1988, pp. 267–292.

CHUNG, K. S., "Investment Opportunities, Synergies, and Conglomerate Mergers," Ph.D. dissertation, University of California, Los Angeles, 1982.

COFFEE, J. C., "Shareholders Versus Managers: The Strain in the Corporate Web," Chapter 6 in Coffee, Lowenstein, and Rose-Ackerman, eds., *Knights, Raiders, and Targets*, New York: Oxford University Press, 1988, pp. 77–134.

COMMENT, R., and G. A. JARRELL, "Two-Tier and Negotiated Tender Offers: The Imprisonment of the Free-Riding Shareholder," *Journal of Financial Economics*, 19, 1987, pp. 283–310.

DANN, L. Y., and H. DEANGELO, "Standstill Agreements, Privately Negotiated Stock Repurchases, and the Market for Corporate Control," *Journal of Financial Economics*, 11, 1983, pp. 275–300.

———, "Corporate Financial Policy and Corporate Control: A Study of Defensive Adjustments in Asset and Ownership Structure," *Journal of Financial Economics*, 20, 1988, pp. 87–127.

DEANGELO, H., and E. M. RICE, "Antitakeover Charter Amendments and Stockholder Wealth," *Journal of Financial Economics*, 11, April 1983, pp. 329–359.

DEMSETZ, H., "The Structure of Ownership and the Theory of the Firm," *Journal of Law and Economics*, 26, 1983, pp. 375–390.

———, and K. LEHN, "The Structure of Corporate Ownership: Causes and Consequences," *Journal of Political Economy*, 93, 1985, pp. 1155–1177.

DODD, P. R., and R. LEFTWICH, "The Market for Corporate Control: 'Unhealthy Competition' Versus Federal Regulation," *Journal of Business*, 53, 1980, pp. 259–283.

DODD, P. R., and J. B. WARNER, "On Corporate Governance: A Study of Proxy Contests," *Journal of Financial Economics*, 11, 1983, pp. 401–438.

EASTERBROOK, F. H., and D. R. FISCHEL, "The Proper Role of a Target's Management in Responding to a Tender Offer," *Harvard Law Review*, 94, 1981, pp. 1161–1204.

———, "Auctions and Sunk Costs in Tender Offers," *Stanford Law Review*, 35, 1982, pp. 1–21.

EISENBERG, M. A., "Comment: Golden Parachutes and the Myth of the Web," Chapter 9 in Coffee, Lowenstein, and Rose-Ackerman, eds., *Knights, Raiders and Targets*, New York: Oxford University Press, 1988, pp. 155–158.

GILSON, R. J., *The Law and Finance of Corporate Acquisitions*, New York: Foundation Press, 1986.

GROSSMAN, S. J., and O. D. HART, "Takeover Bids, the Free-Rider Problem, and the Theory of the Corporation," *Bell Journal of Economics*, 11, 1980, pp. 42–64.

HOLDERNESS, C. G., and D. P. SHEEHAN, "Raiders or Saviors? The Evidence on Six Controversial Investors," *Journal of Financial Economics*, 14, 1985, pp. 555–579.

JARRELL, G. A., "The Wealth Effects of Litigation by Targets: Do Interests Diverge in a Merge?" *Journal of Law and Economics*, April 1985, pp. 151–177.

———, J. A. BRICKLEY, and J. M. NETTER, "The Market for Corporate Control: The Empirical Evidence Since 1980," *Journal of Economic Perspectives*, 2, Winter 1988, pp. 49–68.

JARRELL, G. A., and A. POULSEN, "Shark Repellents and Stock Prices: The Effects of Antitakeover Amendments Since 1980," *Journal of Financial Economics*, 19, 1987, pp. 127–168.

Jensen, M. C., "Takeovers: Their Causes and Consequences," *Journal of Economic Perspectives*, 2, Winter 1988, pp. 21–48.

———, "When Unocal Won Over Mesa, Shareholders and Society Lost," *Financier*, 9, 1985, pp. 50–52.

———, and J. B. Warner, "The Distribution of Power Among Corporate Managers, Shareholders and Directors," *Journal of Financial Economics*, 20, 1988, pp. 3–24.

Kamma, S., J. Weintrop, and P. Wier, "Investors' Perceptions of the Delaware Supreme Court Decision in Unocal v. Mesa," *Journal of Financial Economics*, 20, 1988, pp. 419–430.

Kleiman, R. T., "The Shareholder Gains from Leveraged Cashouts: Some Preliminary Evidence," *Journal of Applied Corporate Finance*, 1, Spring 1988, pp. 46–53.

Klein, A., and J. Rosenfeld, "The Impact of Targeted Share Repurchases on the Wealth of Non-Participating Shareholders," *Journal of Financial Research*, 11, Summer 1988, pp. 89–97.

Klein, R., "Leveraged Cashouts: Recapitalization with a New Twist," *Business Forum*, 13, Winter 1988, pp. 10–15.

Knoeber, C. R., "Golden Parachutes, Shark Repellents, and Hostile Tender Offers," *American Economic Review*, 76, March 1986, pp. 155–167.

Lambert, R., and D. Larcker, "Golden Parachutes, Executive Decision-Making, and Shareholder Wealth," *Journal of Accounting and Economics*, 7, April 1985, pp. 179–204.

Linn, S. C., and J. J. McConnell, "An Empirical Investigation of the Impact of Antitakeover Amendments on Common Stock Prices," *Journal of Financial Economics*, April 1983, pp. 361–399.

MacMinn, R. D., and D. O. Cook, "Antitakeover Activity and the Poison Pill," ms., University of Texas, Austin, September 1988.

Malatesta, P. H., and R. A. Walkling, "Poison Pill Securities: Stockholder Wealth, Profitability, and Ownership Structure," *Journal of Financial Economics*, 20, 1988, pp. 347–376.

McWilliams, V. B., "The Stock Price Effects of Antitakeover Amendment Proposals," ms., Northeastern University, September 1988.

Mikkelson, W. H., and R. S. Ruback, "Targeted Repurchases and Common Stock Returns," ms., University of Oregon, June 1986.

———, "An Empirical Analysis of the Interfirm Equity Investment Process," *Journal of Financial Economics*, 14, 1985, pp. 523–553.

Pound, J., "The Effects of Antitakeover Amendments on Takeover Activity: Some Direct Evidence," *Journal of Law and Economics*, 30, October 1987, pp. 353–367.

———, "Proxy Contests and the Efficiency of Shareholder Oversight," *Journal of Financial Economics*, 20, 1988, pp. 237–266.

Richter, P., "Takeover Targets Show New Vigor Against Raiders," *Los Angeles Times*, April 28, 1985, Part V, pp. 1, 8.

Romano, R., "Law as a Product: Some Pieces of the Incorporation Puzzle," *Journal of Law, Economics and Organization*, 1, 1985, pp. 225–269.

———, "The Political Economy of Takeover Statutes," *Virginia Law Review*, 73, 1987, pp. 111–199.

RUBACK, R. S., "Assessing Competition in the Market for Corporate Acquisitions," *Journal of Financial Economics*, 11, 1983, pp. 141–153.

RYNGAERT, M., "The Effect of Poison Pill Securities on Shareholder Wealth," *Journal of Financial Economics*, 20, 1988, pp. 237–266.

————, and J. M. NETTER, "Shareholder Wealth Effects of the Ohio Antitakeover Law," *Journal of Law, Economics and Organization*, 4, Fall 1988, pp. 373–384.

SHLEIFER, A., and R. W. VISHNY, "Greenmail, White Knights, and Shareholders' Interest," *Rand Journal of Economics*, 17, Autumn 1986a, pp. 293–309.

————, "Large Shareholders and Corporate Control," *Journal of Political Economy*, 94, 1986b, pp. 461–488.

TETERS, R., "The Leveraged Recap: Controversial New Defense Maneuver," *Journal of Business Strategy*, March/April 1988, pp. 26–29.

WEBERMAN, B., "One Man's Poison," *Forbes*, August 22, 1988, p. 117.

WHITE, W. L., "Pulling the Golden Parachute Ripcord," Chapter 30 in M. L. Rock, ed., *The Mergers and Acquisitions Handbook*, New York: McGraw Hill, 1987, pp. 335–342.

WINKLER, M., "Harris, Williams Cos. Unit Are First to Offer Super 'Poison Puts'," *The Wall Street Journal*, November 16, 1988, pp. C1, C15.

Chapter **21**

Regulation of Securities Trading and Takeovers

In this chapter we deal with the laws and rules or regulations promulgated to cover securities trading and takeover activity. We cover securities trading generally as well as takeover activity, the central focus of this book, because the two are so interlinked that they really cannot be separated. Indeed, the laws which were enacted to regulate takeover activity were made a part of the original securities acts enacted in the early 1930s. We also examine the leading cases related to the laws we cover because they give more explicit content to the nature of the law and its intent.

Chapter 22 which follows is titled "Evaluation of Arbitrage and Insider Trading." We begin with the discussion of arbitrage activity since in one respect it is no different from any other form of securities trading. From another standpoint, however, arbitrage activity has become a central ingredient in the takeover activity process. Also, arbitrage activity is an area that is particularly susceptible to the temptations and practices of insider trading. Most large investment banker and brokerage companies have an arbitrage department. They also have a corporate finance department which originates new issues and a mergers and acquisitions (M&A) department which manages merger and takeover activity. Large gains and losses can be realized in the arbitrage department. An important issue is whether investment bankers can really keep the information generated in one activity from being leaked to one of the other activities in violation of the securities laws. Recall that Ivan Boesky was nominally engaged in arbitrage activity, presumably operating independently of investment banking. The academic literature contains articles and books arguing for and against the proposition that insider trading performs necessary and useful economic functions. Chapter 22 summarizes and evaluates this literature. In addition, Chapter 22 presents case studies involving regulation issues set forth in this chapter. Chapter 22 concludes with a summary of the laws and regulations of foreign countries with regard to securities trading, takeover activity, and issues of insider trading.

THE MAIN SECURITIES LAWS

Because wide price fluctuations are likely to be associated with merger and acquisition activity, public policy has been concerned that investors be treated fairly. Legislation and regulations have sought to carry over to the takeover activity of recent decades the philosophy of the securities acts of the 1930s. The aim is prompt and full disclosure of relevant information in the effort to achieve a fair "playing field" for all participants. Some of the earlier legislation is fully applicable, but it has been augmented with additional statutes since the late 1960s.

Since the takeover laws are so closely interlinked with securities laws generally, we begin with a summary of the major securities laws. This provides a framework to which we can relate the laws, rules, and regulations governing takeover activity.

The Special Characteristics of Securities

It is useful to note how securities differ from other goods and services (see Ratner, 1988). This helps us understand why the "rules of the game" applied to securities transactions are somewhat different and rather complicated. First, securities are created as a right to a future stream of income under some specified terms. Unlike goods and services whose values are likely to be related to their size and physical characteristics, a security which trades for millions of dollars may be represented by a small piece of paper or, increasingly, by a computer entry on the books of an organization which performs record-keeping functions. Pieces of paper or computer entries can be produced or issued in vast quantities at an insignificant cost. One of the purposes of securities laws is to insure that there is a valid business and economic basis for their creation.

Second, buyers of securities do not intend to consume them as they would food. The second-hand market in which securities are traded is of much greater volume than the new-issue market. Securities continue to be traded so that a second function of securities laws is to provide for a continuous flow of information that affects the value of securities traded.

Third, since the value of securities depends on future flows upon which securities represent claims, the values of securities are subject to wide differences of opinions with respect to expectations for the future. As a consequence, these expectations may be susceptible to deceptive and manipulative practices.

Fourth, an industry has evolved to perform the buying and selling functions. The individuals and firms which conduct these activities develop specialized knowledge and an expertise. They have responsibilities to conduct the transactions in an efficient, dependable, and trustworthy manner. Trading activity is anonymous in that buyers and sellers do not know each other or the reasons or motivations for the transaction other than their own.

Fifth, because securities transactions are particularly susceptible to fraudulent behavior, laws and regulations have developed to provide penalties for fraud. Violators of the "rules of the game" are subject to penalties. On the one hand, this can be a disadvantage, since laws and rules are subject to interpretation. On the other hand, the effect of having referees to enforce fair rules increases trust in the process. It contributes to active and efficient markets.

Federal Securities Laws

The federal securities laws are mainly seven statutes, six of which were enacted between 1933 and 1940. The seven statutes are:

Securities Act of 1933 (SA)

Securities Exchange Act of 1934 (SEA)

Public Utility Holding Company Act of 1935 (PUHCA)

Trust Indenture Act of 1939 (TIA)

Investment Company Act of 1940 (ICA)

Investment Advisers Act of 1940 (IAA)

Securities Investor Protection Act of 1970 (SIPA)

We first provide a summary of what each of the laws covers to provide an overview of the pattern of legislation. We then develop some of the more important provisions in greater detail. As we have noted, six of the seven major acts were enacted beginning in 1933. There is a reason for the timing. The stock market crash of 1929 was followed by continued depressed markets for several years. Because so many investors lost money, both houses of Congress conducted lengthy hearings to find the causes and the culprits. The hearings were marked by sensationalism and wide publicity. The securities acts of 1933 and 1934 were the direct outgrowth of the congressional hearings.

The Securities Act of 1933 regulates the sale of securities to the public. It provides for the registration of public offerings of securities to establish a record of representations. All participants in preparing the registration statements are subject to legal liability for any misstatement of facts or omissions of vital information.

The Securities Exchange Act of 1934 established the Securities and Exchange Commission (SEC) to administer the securities laws and to regulate practices in the purchase and sale of securities.

The purpose of the Public Utility Holding Company Act of 1935 was to correct abuses in the financing and operation of electric and gas public utility holding company systems and to bring about simplification of the corporate structures and physical integration of the operating properties. The SEC's responsibilities under the act of 1935 were substantially completed by the 1950s.

The Trust Indenture Act of 1939 applies to public issues of debt securities with a value (now, 1988) of $5 million or more. Debt issues represent a form of promissory note associated with a long document setting out the terms of a complex contract and referred to as the *indenture*. The 1939 act sets forth the responsibilities of the indenture trustee (often a commercial bank) and specifies requirements to be included in the indenture (bond contract) for the protection of the bond purchasers. In September 1987, the SEC recommended to Congress a number of amendments to establish new conflict of interest standards for indenture trustees and to recognize new developments in financing techniques.

The Investment Company Act of 1940 regulates publicly-owned companies engaged in the business of investing and trading in securities. Investment companies are subject to rules formulated and enforced by the SEC. The act of 1940 was amended in 1970 to place additional controls on management compensation and sales charges.

The Investment Advisers Act of 1940, as amended in 1960, provides for registration and regulation of investment advisers, as the name suggests.

The Securities Investors Protection Act of 1970 established the Securities Investor Protection Corporation (SIPCO). This corporation is empowered to supervise the liquidation of bankrupt securities firms and to arrange for payments to their customers.

The Securities Act Amendments of 1975 were passed after four years of research and investigation into the changing nature of securities markets. The study recommended the abolition of fixed minimum brokerage commissions. It called for increased automation of trading by utilizing data processing technology to link markets. The SEC was mandated to work with the securities industry to develop an effective national market system to achieve the goal of nationwide competition in securities trading with centralized reporting of price quotations and transactions. It proposed a central order routing system to find the best available price.

In 1978 the SEC began to streamline the securities registration process. Large, well-known corporations were permitted to abbreviate registration statements and to disclose information by reference to other documents that had already been made public. Before these changes the registration process often required at least several weeks. After the 1978 changes, a registration statement could be approved in as short a time as two days.

In March 1982, Rule 415 provided for shelf registration. Large corporations can register the full amount of debt or equity they plan to sell over a two-year period. After the initial registration has been completed, the firm can sell up to the specified amount of debt or equity without further delay. The firm can choose the time when the funds are needed or when market conditions appear favorable. Shelf registration has been actively used in the sale of bonds, with as much as 60 percent of debt sales utilizing shelf registration. Less than 10 percent of the total issuance of equities has employed shelf registration.

THE OPERATION OF THE SECURITIES ACTS

The Securities Act of 1933 has primary responsibility for recording information. Section 5 prevents the public offering and sale of securities without a registration statement. Section 8 provides for registration and permits the statement to automatically become effective 20 days after it is filed with the SEC. However, the SEC has the power to request more information or to issue a stop order which delays the operation of the 20-day waiting period.

It is the Securities Exchange Act of 1934 (SEA) which provides the basis for the amendments which were applicable to takeover activities. Section 12(j) empowers the SEC to revoke or suspend the registration of a security if the issuer has violated any provisions of the 1934 act. The SEC imposes periodic disclosure requirements under Section 13. The basic reports are: (1) The Form 10-K annual report, (2) the quarterly report on Form 10-Q, and (3) a Form 8-K current report for any month in which specified events occur.

Section 14 governs proxy solicitation. Prior to every meeting of its security holders, they must be furnished with a proxy statement containing information specified. The SEC provides procedural requirements for proxy contests. Under SEA Rule 14a-8, any security holder may require management to include his or her proposal for action in the proxy statement. If management opposes the proposal, it must include in the proxy material a statement by the security holder not more than 200 words in length in support of his or her proposal.

TENDER OFFER REGULATION—
THE WILLIAMS ACT

Prior to the late 1960s, most intercorporate combinations were represented by mergers. This typically involved "friendly" negotiations by two or more firms. When they mutually agreed, combination of some form might occur. During the conglomerate merger movement of the 1960s, corporate takeovers began to occur. Some were friendly and not much different from mergers. Others were hostile and shook up the business community.

In October 1965, Senator Harrison Williams introduced legislation seeking to protect the target companies. These initial efforts failed, but his second effort initiated in 1967 succeeded. The Williams Act, in the form of various amendments to the Securities Exchange Act of 1934, became law on July 29, 1968. Its stated purpose was to protect target shareholders from swift and secret takeovers in three ways: (1) by generating more information during the takeover process which target shareholders and management could use to evaluate outstanding offers; (2) by requiring a minimum period during which a tender offer must be held open, thus delaying the execution of the tender offer; and (3) by explicitly authorizing targets to sue bidding firms.

Section 13

Section 13(d) of the Williams Act required that any person who had acquired 10 percent or more of the stock of a public corporation must file a Schedule 13D with the SEC within ten days of crossing the 10 percent threshold. The act was amended in 1970 to increase the SEC powers and to reduce the trigger point for the reporting obligation under Section 13(d) from 10 percent to 5 percent. Basically, Section 13(d) provides management and the shareholders with an early warning system.

The filing requirement does not apply to those persons who had purchased less than 2 percent of the stock within the previous twelve months. Due to this exemption, a substantial amount of stock can be accumulated over years without having to file Schedule 13D. Institutional investors (registered brokers and dealers, banks, insurance companies, and so forth) can choose to file Schedule 13G instead of Schedule 13D if the equity securities were acquired in the ordinary course of business. Schedule 13G is an abbreviated version of Schedule 13D.

More recently, the insider trading scandals of the late 1980s produced calls for a reduction below 5 percent and a shortening of the ten-day minimum period for filing. However, shortening the period would not stop the practice of "parking" violations which were uncovered in the Boesky investigation. Under parking arrangements, traders attempt to hide the extent of their ownership to avoid the 5 percent disclosure trigger by "parking" purchased securities with an accomplice broker until a later date. A related practice is to purchase options on the stock of the target; this is equivalent to ownership since the options can be exercised whenever the holder wishes to take actual ownership.

Schedule 13D identifies the acquirer, his or her occupation and associates, sources of financing, and purpose of the acquisition. If the purpose of the acquisition is to take over the target, the acquirer's business plans for the target must be revealed. That is, does the acquirer plan to liquidate the target, merge it with another firm, or otherwise change its basic corporate structure in a material way? Copies of the 13D must be provided to the target and to all the exchanges on which the stock is traded. Any material changes in the information provided in the 13D must be disclosed promptly in an amended schedule with the same notification requirements. Although these requirements seem fairly specific and straightforward, the language used to respond to them is kept as broad as possible so as to maintain flexibility.

Section 13(g) which requires the filing of Schedule 13G was added to the act in 1972 to apply to all 5 percent owners, regardless of how the 5 percent threshold was reached. Obviously, in the case of takeover contests, the 5 percent interest is amassed fairly quickly; the purpose of adding Section 13(g) was to alert targets to creeping acquisitions over time. The timing requirements for filing 13G are generous. Acquirers have until 45 days from the end of the year during which they reached the 5 percent position, a possible 410-day lag versus only ten days for the 13D. And, if their large block acquisitions push them to a 10 percent ownership interest, they have ten days following the end of the month during which this level was reached to file the 13G with the SEC (a possible 40-day lag).

Section 14

Sections 13(d) and 13(g) of the Williams Act apply to any large stock acquisitions, whether public or private (an offering to less than 25 people). Section 14(d) applies only to public tender offers, but applies whether the acquisition is small or large so its coverage is broader. The 5 percent trigger rule also applies under Section 14(d). Thus, any group making solicitations or recommendations to a target group of shareholders which would result in owning more than 5 percent of a class of securities registered under Section 12 of the Securities Act must first file a Schedule 14D with the SEC. So, an acquiring firm must disclose in a Tender Offer Statement (Schedule 14D-1) its intentions and business plans for the target, as well as any relationships or agreements between the two firms. The schedule must be filed with the SEC "as soon as practicable on the date of the commencement of the tender offer"; copies must be hand-delivered to the target firm and to any competitive bidders; the relevant stock exchanges (or the National Association of Securities Dealers for the over-the-counter stocks) must be notified by telephone (followed by a mailing of the schedule).

Note, however, that the language of Section 14(d) refers to *any* group making recommendations to target shareholders. This includes target management, which is prohibited from advising target shareholders as to how to respond to a tender offer until it too has filed with the SEC. Until target management has filed a Schedule 14D-9, a Tender Offer Solicitation/Recommendation Statement, they may only advise shareholders to defer tendering their shares while management considers the offer. Companies who consider themselves vulnerable often take the precaution of preparing a fill-in-the-blanks schedule left with an agent in Washington, to be filed immediately in the event of a takeover attempt, allowing target management to respond swiftly in making public recommendations to shareholders. Thus, Section 14(d)-1 provides both the early warning system and information that will help target shareholders determine whether or not to tender their shares. SEA Sections 14(d) (4)–(7) regulate the terms of a tender offer, including the length of time the offer must be left open (20 trading days), the right of shareholders to withdraw shares that they may have tendered previously, the manner in which tendered shares must be purchased in oversubscribed offers, and the effect of the bidder changing the terms of the offer. The delay period, of course, also gives shareholders time to evaluate the offer, but more importantly enables management to seek out competing bids.

Also, SEA Section 14(e) prohibits misrepresentation, nondisclosure, or any fraudulent, deceptive or manipulative acts or practices in connection with a tender offer.

INSIDER TRADING

The SEC adopted Rule 14e-3 to apply to insider trading, specifically within the context of tender offers. Table 21.1 summarizes the SEC regulations used to prosecute insider trading cases. To date, the term *insider trading* has not been defined by the SEC. Thus, the SEC now has three broad categories under which insider trading, fraud, or illegal profits can be attacked. Rule 10b-5 has an emphasis on fraud or deceit. Rule 14e-3 applies more directly to tender offers. The Insider Trading Sanctions Act of 1984 applies to insider trading more generally. The very ambiguity of the three sources of power that may be used by the SEC in the regulation of insider trading gives the SEC considerable discretion in its choice of practices and cases to prosecute.

It should be noted also that the traditional regulation of insider trading was provided for under SEA Sections 16(a) and 16(b). Section 16(a) applies to officers, directors, and any persons who own 10 percent or more of any class of securities of a company. Section 16(a) provides that these corporate insiders must report to the SEC all transactions involving their purchase or sale of the corporation's stock on a monthly basis. Section 16(a) is based on the premise that a corporate insider has an unfair advantage by virtue of his or her knowledge of information that is generated within the corporation. This information is available on a privileged basis because he or she is an officer, director, or a major security holder who is presumed to have privileged communications with top officers in the company. Section 16(b) provides that the corporation or any of its security holders may bring suit against the offending corporate insider to return the profits to the corporation because of insider trading completed within a six-month period.

To complete this overview of laws, rules, and regulations applying to ten-

TABLE 21.1
SEC Regulation of Insider Trading

RULE 10b-5

"It shall be unlawful . . . by the use of any means or instrumentality of interstate commerce, or of the mails, or of any facility of any national securities exchange,
- (1) to employ any device, scheme, or artifice to defraud,
- (2) to make any untrue statement of a material fact or to omit to state a material fact necessary . . . or
- (3) to engage in any act . . . which operates . . . as a fraud or deceit . . . in connection with the purchase or sale of any security."

RULE 14e-3

Prohibits "transactions in securities on the basis of material, non-public information in the context of tender offers." Once a tender offer has commenced (substantial steps toward the commencement of a tender offer are sufficient), this rule prohibits trading by any person on the basis of material information which he knows or has reason to know is nonpublic, and which he knows or has reason to know was acquired directly or indirectly from the offering person, the issuer of the securities sought, any officer, director, partner, employee, or any other person acting on behalf of the offeror or the issuer. Trading is prohibited until a reasonable time after the public release of such information.

INSIDER TRADING SANCTIONS ACT OF 1984

Those who trade on information not available to the general public can be made to give back their illegal profits and pay a penalty of three times as much as their illegal activities produced.

---

der offers, insider trading, fraud, and deception, we must make mention of RICO, the Racketeer Influenced and Corrupt Organizations Act of 1970 also covered in Chapter 23. As the name suggests, the act is aimed at companies which engage in acts that defraud consumers, investors, or public bodies such as cities or states, and authorizes triple damages for winning plaintiffs. Furthermore, in a criminal suit brought by any representative of the Department of Justice, RICO permits the court to order that all of the assets of the accused be seized while the case is still being tried. This gives the prosecutor tremendous power. From a practical standpoint, it means that the mere accusation brought under RICO can bring the business of any accused to a halt. If its assets are seized, particularly if it is engaged in securities transactions, it no longer has the means of conducting business. Hence, whether the accused is guilty or not, there is tremendous pressure to settle, because the alternative is to have its business disrupted. And even if after months and months of trial, the accused is found innocent, it is small solace, because the disruption may have resulted in irreparable damage to its business.

We have thus brought together in one place the whole array of laws, rules, and regulations that apply to securities trading including the takeover process. For convenience of reference, we summarize them briefly in Table 21.2.

TABLE 21.2
Summary of Securities Laws and Regulations

Rule 10b-5	Prohibits fraud, misstatements, or omission of material facts in connection with the purchase or sale of any security.
Section 13(d)	Provides early warning to target firms of acquisitions of their stock by potential acquirers: 5 percent threshold, ten-day filing period. Applies to all large stock acquisitions.
Section 14(d) (1)	Requirements of Section 13(d) extended to *all public tender offers*. Provides for full disclosure to SEC by any group making recommendations to target shareholders.
Section 14(d) (4)–(7)	Regulates terms of tender offers. Length of time offer must be held open (twenty days), right of shareholders to withdraw tendered shares, and so on.
Section 14(e)	Prohibits fraud, misrepresentation in context of tender offers. Rule 14e-3 prohibits trading on nonpublic information in tender offers.
Section 16(a)	Provides for reporting by corporate insiders on their transactions in their corporations' stocks.
Section 16(b)	Allows the corporation or its security holders to sue for return of profits on transactions by corporate insiders completed within a six-month period.
Insider Trading Sanctions Act of 1984	
	Provides for triple damages in insider trading cases.
Racketeer Influenced and Corrupt Organizations Act of 1970 (RICO)	
	Provides for seizure of assets upon accusation and triple damages upon conviction for companies which defraud consumers, investors, and so on.

COURT CASES AND SEC RULES

To this point we have described the main statutory provisions which specify the various elements of fraud and insider trading in connection with trading in securities and takeover activities. The full meaning of these statutes is brought out by the subsequent court interpretations and SEC rules implementing the powers granted the SEC by the various statutes.

Liability Under Rule 10b-5
of the 1934 Act

As we have indicated, Rule 10b-5, issued by the Securities and Exchange Commission under the powers granted to it by the 1934 act, is a broad, powerful, and general securities antifraud provision. In general, for Rule 10b-5 to apply, a *security* must be involved. Technical issues have arisen as to what constitutes a security. If securities are involved, all transactions are covered, whether on one of the securities exchanges or over the counter. A number of elements for a cause of action have been set forth in connection with Rule 10b-5, as follows.

1 There must be fraud, misrepresentation, a material omission, or deception in connection with the purchase or sale of securities.

2 The misrepresentation or omission must be of a fact as opposed to an opinion. However, inaccurate predictions of earnings may be held to be misrepresentations and failure to disclose prospective developments may be challenged.

3 The misrepresentation or omission must be material to an investor's decision in the sense that there was a substantial likelihood that a reasonable investor would consider the fact of significance in his or her decision.

4 There must be a showing that the plaintiff actually believed the misrepresentation, relied upon it, and that it was a substantial factor in his or her decision to enter the transaction.

5 The plaintiff must be an actual purchaser or an actual seller to have standing.

6 Defendant's deception or fraud must have a sufficiently close nexus to the transaction so that a court could find that the defendant's fraud was "in connection with" the purchase or sale by plaintiff.

7 Plaintiff must prove that the defendant had "scienter." Scienter literally means knowingly or willfully. It means that the defendant had a degree of knowledge that makes the individual legally responsible for the consequences of his or her act and that he or she had an actual intent to deceive or defraud. Negligence is not sufficient.

These elements represent requirements for a successful suit under Rule 10b-5. Some of the elements were developed in a series of court decisions. The main thrust of Rule 10b-5 is fraud or deceit. The Supreme Court set forth the scienter requirement in two cases: *Ernst and Ernst* v. *Hochfelder,* 425 US 185 (1976); and *Aaron* v. *SEC,* 446 US 680 (1980).

In one legal case it was argued that Rule 10b-5 is applicable only to "investors." This issue was raised in *Hooper* v. *Mountain State Securities,* 282 F.2d 195 (5th Cir. (1960)). This involved a suit by shareholders that alleged that management caused the corporation to be defrauded by issuing shares for inadequate consideration. The defendant argued that the issuance of stock was not a "sale" and that the issuing corporation was not an "investor." The court rejected these arguments, taking the position that the issuance was a sale and pointing out that selling the shares which had economic value placed the corporation in the same position as an investor.

The requirement that the plaintiff be either a purchaser or seller of securities in the alleged fraudulent transaction has also been litigated. The problem arises when a minority shareholder sues on grounds that the sale of a controlling block of stock at a premium over the current market price constitutes fraud or deceit on the minority shareholders. In *Birnbaum* v. *Newport Steel Corp.,* 193 F.2d 461 2d Cir. (1952), the court held that since neither the minority shareholders nor the corporation had purchased or sold any securities, they had no cause of action. In a later decision, the Second Circuit Court held that the transaction in Birnbaum involved a breach of the controlling shareholder's fiduciary duty under state law (*Perlman* v. *Feldmann,* 219 F.2d 173 2d Cir. (1955)).

In addition to its use in fraud or deceit cases, a number of interesting cases have brought out the meaning and applicability of Rule 10b-5 in connection with insider trading. For the present, we refer to insider trading merely as purchases or sales by persons who have access to information which is not available to those with whom they deal or to traders generally. However, there are many court decisions as to what constitutes insider trading and a continued stream of proposals in Congress to clarify the meaning of the term.

An early case was Cady, Roberts & Co., 40 SEC 907 (1961). In this case, a partner in a brokerage firm received a message from a director of the Curtiss-Wright Corporation that the board of directors had voted to cut the dividend. The broker immediately placed orders to sell the Curtiss-Wright stock for some of his customers. The sales were made before news of the dividend cut was generally disseminated. The broker who made the transactions was held to have violated Rule 10b-5.

The Texas Gulf Sulphur Corporation case of 1965 was classic (*SEC v. Texas Gulf Sulphur Company*, 401 F. 2d 833 (2d Cir. (1968)). A vast mineral deposit consisting of millions of tons of copper, zinc, and silver was discovered in November 1963. However, far from publicizing the discovery, the company took great pains to conceal it for over five months, to the extent of issuing a false press release in April 1964 labeling proliferating rumors as "unreliable . . . premature and possibly misleading." Meanwhile, certain directors, officers, and employees of Texas Gulf Sulphur who knew of the find bought up quantities of the firm's stock (and options on many more shares) before any public announcement. The false press release was followed only four days later by another finally revealing publicly the extent of the find. In the company's defense, it was alleged that secrecy was necessary to keep down the price of neighboring tracts of land which they had to acquire in order to fully exploit the discovery. However, the SEC brought and won a civil suit based on Rule 10b-5.

The next case is Investors Management Co. (44 SEC 633 (1971)). An aircraft manufacturer disclosed to a broker-dealer, acting as the lead underwriter for a proposed debenture issue, that its earnings for the current year would be much lower than it had previously publicly announced. This information was conveyed to the members of the sales department of the broker-dealer and passed on in turn to major institutional clients. The institutions sold large amounts of the stock before the earnings revisions were made public. Again the SEC won the suit.

In the next two cases we cover, the SEC lost. The first case involved one of the leading investment banking corporations, Morgan Stanley. The Kennecott Copper Corporation was analyzing whether or not to buy Olinkraft, a paper manufacturer. Morgan Stanley began negotiations with Olinkraft on behalf of Kennecott. Later, Kennecott decided it did not wish to purchase Olinkraft. The knowledge that Morgan Stanley had gained in its negotiations led it to believe that one of its other clients, Johns-Manville, would find Olinkraft attractive. In anticipation of this possibility, Morgan Stanley bought large amounts of the common stock of Olinkraft. When Johns-Manville subsequently made a bid for Olinkraft, Morgan Stanley realized large profits. A suit was brought against

Morgan Stanley. However, the court held that Morgan Stanley had not engaged in any improper behavior under Rule 10b-5.

In the next case, Raymond Dirks was a New York investment analyst who was informed by a former officer of Equity Funding of America that the company had been fraudulently overstating its income and net assets by large amounts. Dirks conducted his own investigation which corroborated the information he received. He told the SEC and a reporter at *The Wall Street Journal* to follow up on the situation and advised his clients to sell their Equity Funding shares. The SEC brought an action against Dirks on grounds that if a tippee has material information knowingly obtained from a corporate insider, he or she must either disclose it or refrain from trading. However, the U.S. Supreme Court found that Dirks had not engaged in improper behavior (*Dirks* v. *SEC*, 463 US 646 (1983)). In Texas Gulf Sulphur, the law made it clear that trading by insiders in shares of their own company using insider knowledge is definitely illegal. But the court held that it was not illegal for Raymond Dirks to cause trades to be made on the basis of what he learned about Equity Funding because the officer who conveyed the information was not breaching any duty, and Dirks did not pay for the information.

So the first principle is that it is illegal for insiders to trade on the basis of inside information. A second principle that has developed is that it is illegal for an outsider to trade on the basis of information which has been "misappropriated." The misappropriation doctrine began to develop in the famous Chiarella case (*Chiarella* v. *United States*, 445 US 222 (1980)). *United States* v. *Chiarella* was a criminal case. Vincent Chiarella was the "markup man" in the New York composing room of Pandick Press, one of the leading U.S. financial printing firms. In working on documents, he observed five announcements of corporate takeover bids in which the targets' identities had presumably been concealed by blank spaces and false names. But Chiarella made some judgments about the names of the targets, bought their stock, and realized some profits. Chiarella was sued under Rule 10b-5 on the theory that like the officers and directors of Texas Gulf Sulphur, he had defrauded the uninformed shareholders whose stock he had bought. Chiarella had been convicted in the lower courts and his case was appealed to the Supreme Court. In arguing its case before the Supreme Court, the government sought to strengthen its case. It argued that even if Chiarella did not defraud the persons with whom he traded, he had defrauded his employer, Pandick Press, and its clients, the acquiring firms in the documents he had read. He had misappropriated information that had belonged to Pandick Press and its clients. As a result he had caused the price of the targets' stock to rise, thereby injuring his employer's clients and his employer's reputation for reliability. The Supreme Court expressed sympathy with the misappropriation theory, but reversed Chiarella's conviction since the theory had not been used in the lower court.

However, in the next case that arose, the SEC used its misappropriation theory from the beginning and won in a criminal case. A stockbroker named

Newman was informed by friends at Morgan Stanley and Kuhn Loeb about prospective acquisitions. He bought the targets' shares and split the profits with his friends who had supplied the information. He was convicted under the misappropriation theory on grounds that he had defrauded the investment banking houses by injuring their reputation as safe repositories of confidential information from their clients. He had also defrauded their clients because the stock purchases based on confidential information had pushed up the prices of the targets.

The misappropriation theory also won in a case very similar to Chiarella. Materia was a proofreader at the Bowne Printing firm. Materia figured out the identity of four takeover targets and invested in them. This time the SEC applied the misappropriation theory from the start and won (*SEC v. Materia*, 745 F. 2d 197 (2d Cir. (1984)).

The SEC also employed the misappropriation theory in its criminal case against *The Wall Street Journal* reporter, R. Foster Winans, the author of the newspaper's influential "Heard on the Street" column. Along with friends, Winans traded on the basis of what they knew would appear in the paper the following day. While his conviction was upheld by the Supreme Court, the four–four vote could not be mistaken for a resounding affirmation of the misappropriation doctrine, and there are those who suspect that without the mail and wire fraud involved in the Winans case, the outcome might have been different.

EMPIRICAL EVIDENCE ON IMPACT OF TENDER OFFER REGULATION

Several empirical studies have attempted to assess the impact of tender offer legislation on returns to takeover participants. Jarrell and Bradley (1981) found significant increases in average cash tender offer premiums following passage of the Williams Act (from 32 percent to 53 percent). Their results (Jarrell and Bradley, 1981, p. 404) for takeovers before and after July 1968 led them to conclude that regulation had the effects of "increasing significantly the purchase price of target firms, decreasing the returns to acquiring firms [although acquiring firm returns were still positive], and reducing the volume and productivity of cash takeovers." The legislation was intended to thwart harmful mergers, but by reducing the incentive of bidding firms to engage in the type of information-producing activity necessary to find appropriate targets, the authors suggest the regulation may also prevent many beneficial mergers.

In another paper, Schipper and Thompson (1981) looked at abnormal returns to shareholders of bidding firms engaged in a program of merger activity over time. Their results indicated that takeover regulation was associated with negative abnormal returns for bidding firm shareholders.

A later study by Asquith, Bruner, and Mullins (1983) used a cutoff date of October 1969 to distinguish between pre- and postlegislation takeovers since it was not until October 1969 that the SEC enacted permanent binding rules implementing the provisions of the Williams Act. Their results confirm Jarrell and Bradley's (1981) conclusion that regulation led to lower positive excess returns for bidding firms—excess returns to bidding firm shareholders were 2.6 percent higher before 1969 than after 1969 (although post-1969 returns were still positive except where the takeover bids were unsuccessful). For target firms, they found little difference caused by legislation; the only significant explanatory variable in a regression of cumulative excess returns over the 1963–1979 period was the eventual success of the merger bid.

Another study demonstrates that the effect of regulation has been to increase the returns to shareholders of target firms and to make it increasingly difficult for shareholders of acquiring firms to earn positive abnormal returns (Bradley, Desai, and Kim, 1988). The Bradley, Desai, and Kim study shows that acquiring firms had slightly over 4 percent cumulative average residuals for the period 1963 through June 1968. This 4 percent was statistically significant. For the next subperiod, July 1968 to the end of 1980, acquiring firms had a modest positive abnormal return of about 1 percent, but it was not statistically significant. For the period between January 1981 and December 1984, acquiring firms had returns of negative 3 percent. This was statistically significant.

OTHER DISCLOSURE REQUIREMENTS

Regulations and legislation have sought to apply to all phases of trading activity generally. We next describe the basic law covering trading by insiders, a topic more fully developed in the following chapter.

Disclosure by Insiders— Section 16 of SEA

Section 16 of the Securities Exchange Act of 1934 was designed to curb insider trading by requiring designated insiders to report all securities transactions and prohibiting insiders from retaining the profits on any purchase and sale (or sale and purchase) of their corporations' stocks within a six-month period. Voluntary changes in stock ownership must be disclosed by the tenth day following the end of the month in which the transaction took place.

An American Bar Association task force has made a number of proposals to modify Section 16 (Grass, 1987). One is to reduce the reporting period to two business days following the transaction, with monetary penalties for late filings. Another is shortening the short-swing trading period from six months to something less, given the almost instantaneous dissemination of corporate information in today's markets. The task force has recommended more specific definitions of such terms as *insider, officer, director,* as well as *beneficial ownership* and *equity security* (in view of the wide range of hybrid securities now available).

Disclosure Requirements
of Stock Exchanges

In addition to the disclosure and notification requirements of federal and state securities regulation, the various national and regional stock exchanges have their own internal disclosure requirements for listed companies. In general, these amount to notifying the exchanges promptly (that is, by telephone) of any material developments that may significantly affect the trading volume and/or price of the listed firm's stock.

The exchanges are naturally reluctant to halt trading in a stock, particularly since institutional investors may continue to trade in the "third market" during a halt. However, it sometimes does so to allow the public time to digest important information which would otherwise result in an order imbalance. A listed company may also request a trading halt. Target companies have sometimes requested halts as a defensive strategy to buy time to find another bidder (a white knight), or to force the initial bid higher. As a result, the NYSE has implemented a policy to limit the length of such voluntary halts. Once a halt is requested, a company has 30 minutes to disclose its news, after which the exchange, not the company, decides when to reopen trading.

Disclosure of Merger Talks

On April 4, 1988, the Supreme Court ruled by a 6–0 vote (three justices not participating) that investors may claim damages from a company which falsely denied it was involved in negotiations that resulted in a subsequent merger. Such denials would represent misleading information about a pending merger which would provide investors who sold stock during the period with a basis for winning damages from the company officers.

The case involved the acquisition by Combustion Engineering of Basic Inc. Executives of Combustion Engineering began talks with Basic officers in 1976. The talks continued through 1977 and into early 1978 when Basic stock was selling for less than $20 per share. The stock began to rise in price, and in response to rumors of a merger, Basic issued three public statements denying that its officers knew of any reason for the rise in the price of its stock. It issued a denial as late as November 6, 1978.

On December 19, 1978, Basic's board voted to approve the sale of the company to Combustion at $46 per share. Some shareholders filed suit against Basic's board claiming that they were misled into selling their stock at the low, premerger price. A district court judge in Cleveland rejected their suit, but a federal appeals court reinstated the suit in 1986 on grounds that the statements made were both significant and misleading. The Supreme Court returned the case to the district court judge for trial. The Supreme Court decision written by Justice Blackmun stated that federal securities laws require that investors be informed about "material developments." What is "material" depends on the facts of the case, but corporate boards may not deny merger talks that reach the point of board resolutions, instructions to investment bankers, and actual negotiations between principals (Savage, 1988).

In a footnote, Justice Blackmun appeared to suggest that refusing to comment might shield a board. Apparently silence is not misleading under Rule 10b-5 of the Securities Exchange Act. This has been interpreted as saying that either the board must put a sufficiently tight lid on any information about mergers so that no rumors get started, or if there are leaks, the board must issue accurate statements of information. The decision appeared to be consistent with the spirit of federal laws and regulations governing securities transactions. Mergers simply represent an area of particular importance because of the large price fluctuations frequently associated with such activity.

REGULATION OF TAKEOVER ACTIVITY BY THE STATES

Before the Williams Act of 1968, there was virtually no state regulation of takeover activity. Even by 1974 only seven states had enacted statutes in this area. This is surprising since states are the primary regulators of corporate activity. The chartering of corporations takes place in individual states. State law has defined a corporation as a legal person subject to state laws. Corporate charters obtained from states define the powers of the firm and the rights and obligations of its shareholders, boards of directors, and managers. But states are not permitted to pass laws that impose restrictions on interstate commerce or that conflict with federal laws regulating interstate commerce.

Early state laws regulating hostile takeovers were declared illegal by the courts. For example, in 1982 the U.S. Supreme Court declared illegal an anti-takeover law passed by the state of Illinois. The courts held that the Illinois law favored management over the interests of shareholders and bidders. The Illinois law was also found to impose impediments on interstate commerce and was therefore unconstitutional.

Recent Developments

To the surprise of most observers, the Supreme Court in April 1987 upheld the Indiana Act. The Indiana Act provides that when an acquiring entity or bidder obtains shares that would cause its voting power to reach specified threshold levels, the bidder does not automatically obtain the voting rights associated with those shares. The transfer of voting rights must receive the approval of a majority of shareholders, not including the shares held by the bidder or insider directors and officers of the target company. A bidder can request a special shareholders meeting which must be held within 50 days of the request with the expenses of the meeting to be borne by the bidder.

Critics of the Indiana Act regard it as a delaying tactic which enables the target to delay the process by at least 50 days. The special requirements in connection with voting make the outcome of the tender offer much more uncertain. The Indiana Act was tested in a case brought by Dynamics Corporation of America chartered in Connecticut. It announced a tender offer to increase its holdings of CTS Corporation (incorporated in Indiana) from 9.6 percent to 27.5 percent. CTS invoked the Indiana Act. Dynamics would not be able to vote either the additional shares or the initial 9.6 percent. Dynamics filed suit arguing that the Indiana Act was preempted by the Williams Act and violated the interstate commerce clause. Dynamics won in the U.S. District Court and in the Appeals Court, but was reversed in the U.S. Supreme Court.

Other states passed acts more moderate than the Indiana Act. The New York-New Jersey pattern provides for a five-year moratorium preventing hostile bidders from doing a second-step transaction such as merging a newly acquired company with another (Veasey, 1988).

A Delaware law was enacted in early 1988. It followed the New York-New Jersey model. The Delaware moratorium on second-step transactions is only for three years; nor does it apply if the hostile bidder buys virtually all of the stock of the target company. A hostile bidder can also obtain the approval of the board of the target company and a two thirds vote of the other stockholders for the transaction to proceed. The board of a Delaware corporation may also vote to "opt out" of the statute within 90 days of its effective date (Veasey, 1988).

The Delaware statute was regarded with great significance because more than half of the Fortune 500 companies are incorporated in Delaware. Also, Delaware's statutes and regulations of corporations are widely regarded as a national model. But in this instance it is argued that Delaware acted because the Delaware state legislators "apparently feared an exodus of companies in search of protection elsewhere" (Bandow, 1988, p. 2).

Issues with Regard
to State Takeover Laws

One reason put forth for state takeover laws is to permit shareholders a more considered response to two-tier and partial tender offers. The other argument is that the Williams Act provides that tender offers remain open for only 20 days. It is argued that a longer time period may be needed where the target is large to permit other bidders to develop information to decide whether or not to compete for the target.

However, in practice it has been found that 70 percent of the tender offers during the years 1981–1984 were for all outstanding shares. The other 30 percent of the offers were split between two-tier and partial offers. The proportion of two-tier offers declined over the period of the study (Office of the Chief Economist, SEC, April 1985).

Furthermore, many companies have adopted fair price amendments which require the bidder to pay a fair price for all shares acquired. Under Delaware, Massachusetts, and certain other state laws, dissenting shareholders may request court appraisal of the value of their shares. To do so, however, they must file a written demand for appraisal before the shareholders meeting to vote on the merger. Tendering shareholders must not vote for the merger if they wish to preserve the right to an appraisal.

Critics also point out that state antitakeover laws have hurt shareholders. Studies by the Office of the Chief Economist of the SEC found that when in 1986 New Jersey placed restrictions on takeovers, the prices for 87 affected companies fell by 11.5 percent (Bandow, 1988). Similarly, an SEC study found that stock prices for 74 companies chartered in Ohio declined an average of 3.2 percent, a $1.5 billion loss after that state passed restrictive legislation. An FTC study estimated that the New York antitakeover rules reduced equity values by 1 percent, costing shareholders $1.2 billion (Bandow, 1988).

For these reasons, critics argue that the state laws protect parochial state interests rather than shareholders. They argue that the states act to protect employment and increase control over companies in local areas. Furthermore, they argue that state laws are not needed. If more shareholder protection were needed, all that would be required would be to amend the Williams Act, by extending the waiting period from 20 to 30 days, for example. It is argued further that securities transactions clearly represent interstate commerce. Thus, it is difficult to argue that the state laws are not unconstitutional. By limiting securities transactions, they impede interstate commerce.

The goal is to achieve a balance. Certainly it is desirable to protect the interests of shareholders. However, it must be recognized that two-tier offers and partial offers are used to prevent free-riding. In the absence of two-tier pricing and post-takeover dilution, shareholders know that their shares will not decline in value if the takeover succeeds. So individual small shareholders will wait until after the takeover in hopes that the changes made by the acquirer will increase the value of the stock. Most individual shareholders may behave this way. Then this "free-rider" behavior will prevent takeovers from being accomplished. (See Chapter 19 and Appendix A for detailed discussions.)

Similarly, if states make takeovers more difficult, the advantage is that time can be extended so that competing bids may be made. The data show that competing bids lead to higher prices for target shareholders. On the other hand, if the impediments to takeover are increased too greatly, bidders will be discouraged from even making the effort. In this case target shareholders will lose all benefits. The argument then concludes that state takeover laws are unnecessary. Applicable federal laws should seek to strike a balance between protecting shareholders and stimulating reasonable competing bidding activity, but not to the point where all bidding activity is discouraged.

It has also been argued that federal laws should prevent "abusive takeovers" where "speculative financing" may be involved. But the critical concepts are ambiguous. What is regarded as abusive or speculative varies with the viewpoints of different decision makers. There may, however, be legitimate concerns that rising debt ratios, whether or not associated with takeovers or restructuring, may amplify financial problems when a future economic downturn takes place.

SUMMARY

Regulation of securities trading is closely related to regulation of merger and acquisition activity, since takeovers are carried out by means of the securities markets. Special characteristics of securities which make them vulnerable to being used fraudulently mandate regulation to increase public confidence in securities markets. The earliest securities legislation in the 1930s grew out of the collapse of confidence following the stock market crash of 1929. The Securities Act of 1933 called for registration of public offerings of securities. The Securities Exchange Act of 1934 established the Securities and Exchange Commission to regulate securities market practices; it also specified disclosure requirements for public companies (Section 13) as well as setting out the procedural requirements for proxy contests. A number of other securities laws in the late 1930s and 1940s applied to public utilities, bond indenture trustees, and investment companies.

The Securities Act of 1933 and Securities Exchange Act of 1934 provided the framework for subsequent regulation. Most of the more recent legislation has been in the form of amendments to these two acts. The Williams Act of 1968 amended the 1934 act to regulate tender offers. Two main requirements were a filing with the SEC upon obtaining 5 percent ownership and a 20-day waiting period after making a tender offer. The disclosure requirements aim to give the target shareholders information that will enable them to receive more of the gains associated with the rise in the share price of the takeover target. The 20-day waiting period gives the target more time to evaluate the offer and/or to tailor a defense or seek multiple bids. Empirical studies on the impact of tender offer regulation on shareholder returns almost universally document significantly higher returns for target shareholders and lower (or negative) returns for bidder shareholders. To the extent that successful tender offers continue to take place, the legislation has achieved its goal of benefiting target shareholders. The risk, however, is that reductions in the returns to bidding firms reduce their incentives to engage in the kind of information-producing activities which lead to beneficial takeovers; thus, the lot of target shareholders in those tender offers which *might* have taken place is not improved.

Historically, insider trading has little to do with M&A activity; it refers to the trading in their own companies' stock by corporate officers, directors, and other insiders. It is largely controlled by Section 16 of the Securities Exchange Act, which requires insiders to report such transactions to the SEC on a regular basis. However, the volatility of stock price changes in connection with M&As creates opportunities for gains by individuals who may not fit the traditional definition of insiders. Rule 10b-5 is a general prohibition of fraud and deceit in the purchase or sale of securities. Rule 14e-3 applies to insider trading particularly in connection with tender offers. The Insider Trading Sanctions Act of 1984 provides for triple damage penalties in insider trading cases, as does the Racketeer Influenced and Corrupt Organizations Act of 1970 (RICO) which also allows immediate seizure of assets and which is invoked in some of the more notorious cases of insider trading. The SEC rules are somewhat ambiguous, but a long series of court cases have clarified key concepts. It is illegal to trade on inside information, whether obtained as a result of one's fiduciary relationship to a firm or through misappropriation.

In addition to federal regulation of M&A activity, a number of states have enacted legislation to protect corporations headquartered within their boundaries. States are the primary regulators of corporate activities. However, there are problems in state regulation of takeovers. Securities markets represent interstate commerce, and state regulations which interfere with interstate commerce are, by definition, unconstitutional. Others argue that state regulations are not necessary, that federal regulations and corporate antitakeover amendments provide sufficient protection. There is even evidence that shareholders are damaged by restrictive state legislation which limits takeovers.

QUESTIONS

1. What has been the effect of state and federal tender offer legislation on returns to target and bidder firms?
2. An ESOP owns 3 percent of ABC Company. The company repurchases one-half of its outstanding shares, but the ESOP does not participate. What, if any, form must the pension fund file with the SEC? How long does the ESOP have to file?
3. What is the rationale for tender offer regulation?
4. Discuss the pros and cons of trading halts as a measure to deal with significant information about a listed firm.
5. Discuss the pros and cons of *state* regulation of mergers and tender offers.

REFERENCES

ASQUITH, P., R. F. BRUNER, and D. W. MULLINS, JR., "The Gains to Bidding Firms from Merger," *Journal of Financial Economics*, 1983, pp. 121–139.

BANDOW, D., "Curbing Raiders Is Bad for Business," *New York Times*, February 7, 1988, p. 2.

BARBER, D. H., *Securities Regulation*, 4th ed., Chicago: Harcourt Brace Jovanovich Legal and Professional Publications, 1987.

BRADLEY, M., A. DESAI, and E. H. KIM, "Synergistic Gains from Corporate Acquisitions and Their Division Between the Stockholders of Target and Acquiring Firms," *Journal of Financial Economics*, May 1988, pp. 3–40.

BROWNE, L. E., and E. S. ROSENGREN, "Should States Restrict Takeovers?" *New England Economic Review,* July/August 1987, pp. 13–21.

GILSON, R., *The Law and Finance of Corporate Acquisitions,* Mineola, NY: Foundation Press, 1986.

GRASS, A., "Insider Trading Report Addresses Reform of Section 16," *Business Lawyer Update,* July/August 1987.

HAYS, L. "Delaware's New Anti-Takeover Law Is Contested by Campeau, Black & Decker," *The Wall Street Journal,* February 3, 1988, p. 8.

HERZEL, L., and L. KATZ, "Insider Trading: Who Loses?" *Lloyds Bank Review,* July 1987, pp. 15–26.

JARRELL, G. A., and M. BRADLEY, "The Economic Effects of Federal and State Regulations of Cash Tender Offers," *Journal of Law and Economics,* October 1981, pp. 371–407.

LANGLEY, M., "Stricter Rules Urged on Informing SEC of Stock Holdings," *The Wall Street Journal,* March 20, 1987, p. 6.

NETTER, J. M., A. B. POULSEN, and P. L. HERSCH, "Insider Trading: The Law, The Theory, The Evidence," *Contemporary Policy Issues,* July 1988, pp. 1–13.

OFFICE OF THE CHIEF ECONOMIST, SECURITIES AND EXCHANGE COMMISSION, "The Economics of Any-or-All, Partial, and Two-Tier Tender Offers," 1985.

RATNER, D. L., *Securities Regulation,* 3rd ed., St. Paul, MN: West Publishing Co., 1988.

ROSENBLUM, K. I., and M. WISE, "Stock Exchange Disclosure Rules," Chapter 38 in M. L. Rock, ed., *The Mergers and Acquisitions Handbook,* New York: McGraw Hill, 1987.

SAVAGE, D. G., "Justices Say Firm Can't Lie About Merger Talks," *Los Angeles Times,* March 8, 1988, pp. 1, 17.

SCHIPPER, K., and R. THOMPSON, "The Impact of Merger-Related Regulations on the Shareholders of Acquiring Firms," Carnegie Mellon University, Working Paper No. 57-80-81, 1981.

——, "Evidence on the Capitalized Value of Merger Activity for Acquiring Firms," *Journal of Financial Economics,* 11, 1983, pp. 85–119.

VEASEY, N., "A Statute Was Needed to Stop Abuses," *The New York Times,* February 7, 1988, p. 2.

CHAPTER 22

Evaluation of Arbitrage
and Insider Trading

Arbitrage is defined as purchasing in one market for immediate sale in another at a higher price. Thus, arbitragers take advantage of temporary price discrepancies between markets. By their actions, the differences are eliminated, driving prices up by their purchases in one market, and driving prices down by their sales in the other. Arbitragers may take offsetting positions in one security in two markets, or in equivalent securities in one or two markets, to make profits without assuming any risk under the theory of pure arbitrage.

RISK ARBITRAGE IN M&A ACTIVITY

In the area of mergers and acquisitions, risk arbitrage refers to the practice of purchasing (that is, speculating in) the stock of takeover targets for short-term (though not immediate) resale at a higher price. Recall that, on average, target shareholders earn excess returns in the range of 20 percent in successful take-overs. By taking a position in the stock of target firms, risk arbitragers are, in effect, betting on the outcome of contests for corporate control. Thus, the term "risk arbitrage" is used differently from the true or original concept of arbitrage.

Illustrative Example

An example will illustrate the arbitrage operation. When a tender is announced, price will rise toward offer price. For example, B selling at $100 may offer $60 for T now selling at $40 (a 50 percent premium). After the offer is announced, the arbitrage firm (A) may short B and go long in T. The position of the hedge depends on price levels after the announcement. Suppose B goes to $90 and T to $55. If the arbitrage firm (A) shorts B and goes long on T, the outcome depends on a number of alternatives. If the tender succeeds at $60, the value of B may not change or fall further, but T will rise to $60, resulting in a profit of at least $5 per T share for A. If the tender fails, T may fall in price but not much if other bids are made for T; the price of B may fall since it has "wasted" its search and bidding costs to acquire T. Thus A may gain whether or not the bid succeeds. If the competition of other bidders causes B to raise its offer further, A will gain even more since T will rise more and B will fall. (Remember that A is short on B and long on T.)

During the stock market crash of October 1987, it was reported that the arbitrage departments of most investment banking firms suffered large losses. The prices of both B and T decreased. It was likely that T fell more than B, since B was likely to reduce or withdraw its offer and acquisition activity dried up in the initial general uncertainty following the market crash. If the arbitrage department (A) was not hedged, but simply long on T, its losses would be even larger.

The increased incidence of hostile takeover activity via cash tender offers in the late 1970s created more opportunities for risk arbitrage and led to dramatic growth of the industry, from about 24 participants in 1976 to about 300 by the end of 1986 (Garcia and Anders, 1986, p. 6). These participants include both free-standing arbitrage funds and partnerships as well as the arbitrage departments now found in most brokerage houses, investment banks and many other financial institutions. Ivan Boesky's famous (now infamous) arbitrage fund was started in 1975 with an initial investment of $700,000, grown to over $1 billion by November 1986, for a compound annual growth rate of 93.6 percent. One of the most recent entrants, Citicorp started up its arbitrage unit in the summer of 1986.

The Nature of the Arbitrage Business

Because risk arbitragers have no intention of maintaining their stock positions on a long-term basis, they have no need to be concerned with the financial and operating risk of the target firm; nor is market risk a consideration. Their only risk is whether the takeover (or other restructuring) will be completed, and at what price.[1] If the event fails to take place, the arbitragers may be left holding a large block of stock purchased at a price above the current market value. Or the attempt may succeed, but at a price barely sufficient, or even insufficient, to cover transaction costs, including the cost of the debt that might have been required to establish the stock position. To reduce their required investment, arbitragers frequently use options to control target stock, rather than buying the stock outright.

Traditionally, arbitragers have responded to announced takeover bids.

---

[1] Opportunities for risk arbitrage arise in a number of corporate restructuring activities, including leveraged buy-outs, reorganizations, liquidations, and so on.

They evaluate the offer and assess its probability of success relative to the value of the target. They must consider the likelihood and consequences of a bidding war between alternative potential acquirers, various takeover defenses, a white knight, greenmail, and so on. However, the arbitragers do not have the luxury of time to perform their analyses; they must act early enough to capture the gains inherent in the transaction. Numerous empirical studies document that target firm stock prices begin to rise even before the first public announcement of a takeover bid.

Information is the principal raw material in the arbitrage business. The vast majority of this information comes from careful analysis of publicly available documents, such as financial statements, and filings with the SEC and/or regulatory agencies. They buy expert advice from lawyers and industry specialists. They may hire investment bankers to assist in their assessment of the offer. In some cases, the investment bankers involved in the transaction may double-check their own assessment of valuation against that of the arbitragers. They attempt to get all available information from the investment bankers representing the target and bidding firms, and from the participants themselves. This phase of information gathering may perhaps cross over the boundary into the gray area of insider trading if the pursuit is too vigorous.

With the increased pace in recent years, arbitragers have, in some cases, attempted to anticipate takeover bids to establish their stock positions in advance of any public announcement, thus increasing their potential return. To do so they try to identify undervalued firms which would make attractive targets, and to track down rumors of impending bids; they may monitor price increases which might signal someone is accumulating stock in a particular company to ferret out potential bidders before the 5 percent disclosure trigger at which the purchaser has to announce his or her intentions. The risk of taking a position based upon this type of activity is clearly greater. Also, if one firm in an industry is acquired, other firms in the industry may be expected to become targets.

Functions of Arbitrage Activity

Aside from providing great wealth to successful practitioners, what useful social purpose, if any, does arbitrage activity provide? One of the main services which arbitragers provide is to allow other target shareholders to cash out before the takeover transaction is completed. Many shareholders lack the expertise, time, and motivation to thoroughly analyze takeover bids for their shares. For example, a shareholder who bought a stock at $10 might be perfectly happy to sell those shares to a risk arbitrager for $15, rather than waiting to get $18 from the bidder at the close of the tender offer period and having to bear the risk that the takeover transaction would not go through and that the stock price would fall back to $10 or even less. So, arbitragers provide risk-bearing services for shareholders who do not want to bear the uncertainty of the takeover (or other corporate restructuring event) eventually taking place, and its final price.

In addition, arbitragers provide indirect service to shareholders who do not cash out early. Because the arbitragers have a larger stake in the outcome of a takeover event than the typical shareholder in a large publicly-held firm, they have the motivation to hold out for the highest possible price, in addition to the necessary skills in valuation and negotiation. Thus, the arbitragers' actions on their own behalf may result in a higher price received by all shareholders who held out through the tender offer period. Bidding firms are not dismayed by this type of activity—far from it; they welcome the arbitragers who can greatly facilitate the entire transaction. The arbitragers will sell their often substantial blocks of stock wherever their value is highest, typically to the highest outside bidder. Target management appeals to their own shareholders tend to be based on less quantifiable factors such as longstanding relationships, loyalty, and so on. Outside bidders welcome holders whose only interest is in a quick sale at the highest possible price. Bidders even enlist the assistance of arbitragers to accumulate enough shares to carry off a deal. In theory, there is nothing illegal about a takeover specialist sharing information he or she has produced with an arbitrager for the purpose of facilitating the takeover. (There are those who argue that this amounts to illegal insider trading, about which there is more in the next section.) There is, of course, always the risk that another bidder will enter the contest, and that the arbitrager with whom the original bidder has shared information will sell out to the new bidder if the price is right.

By taking a position in an announced takeover or other restructuring event, the arbitragers are implicitly valuing the offer, and the likelihood of its success (including assessments of target management defensive maneuverings). Since empirical studies generally reflect a negative stock price reaction to management defenses against takeover bids, the arbitragers would signal their assessment that the management defense would succeed by failing to take a position in the target firm at all.

Brown and Raymond (1986) formulate a model to predict the outcome of corporate takeover contests. They employ the following symbols:

P_{mt} = prevailing market price
P_{Tt} = tender offer price
P_F = price if tender offer fails
x_t = merger probability
$E(\pi_t)$ = expected arbitrage profit

If a takeover is successful, an arbitrager who acquires at the prevailing market price P_{mt} shares in a firm for which there is an outstanding tender offer at the price P_{Tt} will gain a return of $[(P_{Tt} - P_{mt}) \div P_{mt}]$. If the takeover is unsuccessful and the price of the stock falls to P_F, the negative return will be $[(P_F - P_{mt}) \div P_{mt}]$. The expected arbitrage return will be the sum of the probabilities of the positive return and the negative return as in equation (22.1).

$$E(\pi_t) = x_t[(P_{Tt} - P_{mt}) \div P_{mt}] + (1 - x_t) [P_F - P_{mt}) \div P_{mt}] \qquad (22.1)$$

They define the probability x_t that the merger will succeed such that the expected risk arbitrage payoff will be zero. They divide both the numerator and denominator of equation (22.1) by P_{mt} and solve for x_t to obtain equation (22.2).

$$x_t = \frac{1 - (P_F/P_{mt})}{(P_{Tt}/P_{mt}) - (P_F/P_{mt})} \tag{22.2}$$

where:

(P_{Tt}/P_{mt}) = tender premium

and

(P_{Tt}/P_F) = failure premium.

When the numerator and denominator of equation (22.2) are multiplied by P_{mt}, they obtain equation (22.3).

$$x_t = (P_{mt} - P_F) \div (P_{Tt} - P_F). \tag{22.3}$$

Equation (22.3) conveys the intuition that the market as a whole sets the likelihood that the takeover will be successful as the percentage of the incremental tender offer price that already has been assimilated into the market price as of period t. All of the market prices can be observed except the price to which the stock would fall if the takeover fails, P_F. They estimate this value by using the actual market prices of the target firm one, two, three, and four weeks prior to the initial announcement of the attempted takeover. Thus, four separate sets of probabilities are calculated weekly from the resolution date back to the announcement date. In each set, the probability estimates are averaged on a weekly basis from the resolution date.

Some numerical examples will illustrate how their calculations are performed. The stock of a target firm is selling for $20 four weeks prior to the announcement of a tender offer at $30. Assume the market moves to $28, what will be the probability of success of the tender offer according to equation (22.3)? We have $x_t = 8/10 = 80$ percent. If the market moves to $22, we have $2/10 = 20$ percent. We should note that equation (22.3) is restricted to remain within the (0,1) interval. For instance, the market price could go to $32. This is not unusual when the market expects that higher bids will be forthcoming. The computed probability is more than 1, but 1 is used. The market price could fall below the preannouncement market prices. For example, the market expects the takeover to fail because of a defense that impairs the target's value. The estimated failure price is higher than the market price, the numerator is negative, but a probability of zero is assigned. Thus, a successful outcome is predicted with certainty (probability = 100 percent) when the prevailing market price is above the tender offer price; failure is predicted with certainty (probability = 0 percent) when the market price falls below the estimated failure price. Their data consisted of completed and failed takeovers, including competitive as well as noncompetitive bids.

For the completed takeover subsample, the market forecast of successful completion never falls below 70 percent; furthermore, the assessed probability rises steadily up to the time of completion, indicating that the market revises its predictions as the resolution date approaches. For the failed subsample, even the initial assessment of the success probability is not large, never rising above 50 percent, and there is little indication of significant downward revision over time. Interestingly, the market continues to assess a 20 percent probability of success at week 0 (the resolution date) for failed takeovers, reflecting the market's assessment of value of the target based on a probability that another bidder might come along, even though this particular attempt failed.

The authors conclude that market prices during the risk arbitrage stage of a takeover do significantly discriminate between eventual outcomes. These market prices can be used to infer the probability that an acquisition will ultimately take place. They conclude that even though the focus in risk arbitrage is on unsystematic event risk rather than systematic market risk, market prices can still provide useful information.

It has been observed that when investment bankers leak information to favored arbitragers, they are increasing the probability that a takeover will succeed (Herzel and Katz, 1987). When the investment banker leaks information to arbitragers, they accumulate a large number of shares in the target company. The interest of the arbitragers is to turn over their assets as quickly as possible when substantial profits can be realized. If arbitragers accumulate a large percentage of the target shares, the target management may be unable to defend against the takeover. The information leaks facilitate the success of the takeover activity. Although the acquirer benefits and may indeed choose the investment banker because of past success in managing takeovers, when the acquirer learns of the information leaks permitted by the investment banker, he or she may voice objections and register complaints. However, the paradox is that it is the indiscretions of the investment banker that contributed to the success of takeovers generally and which gave him or her the reputation to be hired for this takeover, which also succeeds. Thus, leaks and parking are devices to increase the probability of success of a takeover. They also stimulate continued takeover activity. If takeover activity has a positive social benefit, then information leaks and parking contribute to the continued benefits from takeover activity. We next turn to a consideration of the economic effects of insider trading.

THEORY OF INSIDER TRADING

The theory of insider trading must begin with a consideration of identifying the insiders. One view is that there is simply a continuum. The true insiders are those who have intimate knowledge of firm-specific or transaction-specific information. The other extreme is presumed to be a person who knows only what he or she reads in the newspapers or learns from the radio or TV.

The world probably is not that simple. Table 22.1 suggests a cast of players. It recognizes at least eight categories. The traditional insiders are the top executives or members of the boards of directors of corporations. They are presumed to have the opportunity of learning information about a company before any-

TABLE 22.1
The Cast of Participants in Securities Trading and Takeovers

    I. The Corporations (Bidders and Targets)
        Top executives
        Board of directors
        Secretaries

    II. Investment Bankers
        Top executives
        Arbitrage departments
        Research analysts
        Secretaries

    III. Law Firms
        Lawyers assigned to cases
        Associates with whom they discuss cases
        Secretaries

    IV. Banks and Other Lenders
        Executives who participate in the transactions
        Secretaries

    V. Financial Intermediaries
        Independent arbitrage firms
        Brokers
        Dealers
        Security analysts
        Market letters

    VI. Other Intermediaries
        Journalists
        Proxy solicitors
        Printing firms

    VII. Institutional Investors
        Insurance companies
        Investment companies
        Trust departments of banks
        Pension funds

    VIII. Individual Investors
        Active analysts
        Receives public information only

body else. However, in practice members of the other seven categories could become close students of the corporation's activities, its history, and its future prospects. It has been argued that any individual with a good analytical mind who takes the time can come to know virtually as much as the insiders. A person who follows a company and brings a background from the social and physical sciences to have good judgments of how external developments can affect a company may be in a position to make sound forecasts, perhaps even better than the "corporate insiders." So developing knowledge expertise and making good forecasts about a company does not necessarily involve inside information. The nature of insider information and what constitutes the legal abuse thereof follows.

It is in connection with out-of-the-ordinary or unusual events related to corporate activities that issues with regard to insider trading become particularly important. The particular events would include changes in investment programs, sales, or profitability, management changes, and so forth. Of particular significance are activities in connection with mergers and acquisitions. Here particularly, many entities are involved as outlined in Table 22.1. The table also indicates that members of the business firms who are likely to be involved in M&A activity may range from top or key executives to various types of assistants, including secretaries. So the sources of insider trading may be a wide range of different types of members of many different kinds of organizations. We come back to a consideration of the different types of insiders after a review of theories about insider trading.

Recall what was said about the Texas Gulf Sulphur case in the previous chapter: A vast mineral deposit consisting of millions of tons of copper, zinc, and silver was discovered in November 1963. However, far from publicizing the discovery, the company took great pains to conceal it for over five months, to the extent of issuing a false press release in April 1964, labeling proliferating rumors as "unreliable . . . premature and possibly misleading." Meanwhile, certain directors, officers, and employees of Texas Gulf Sulphur who had learned of the find bought up quantities of the firm's stock (and options on many more shares) before any public announcement. The false press release was followed only four days later by another finally revealing publicly the extent of the find. In the company's defense, it was alleged that secrecy was necessary to keep down the price of neighboring tracts of land which they had to acquire in order to fully exploit the discovery. However, the SEC brought and won a civil suit based on SEC Rule 10b-5, a very general rule prohibiting the use of fraud in connection with the purchase or sale of any security.

Arguments for Insider Trading

Two positive arguments have been made for insider trading. One is that it results in more efficient pricing of securities and in the more efficient operation of securities markets. Two, it is argued that insider trading produces more effective compensation of insiders. (See Manne, 1966, for both these arguments.) The reasoning behind these two arguments goes as follows.

Insiders are said to be the most efficient producers of trading information since they obtain the information in the least costly way. When insiders trade, information is conveyed to the capital markets causing securities to be priced more efficiently and accurately. If insiders were not permitted to trade, the information that they convey would have to be produced in other ways that would involve higher social costs.

Trading by insiders is said to affect the price of securities through direct effects on demand and supply and through signaling information. If insiders have significant information that has not yet been revealed to the market, their purchases will augment demand which causes prices to rise. Their activity may also be taken as a signal that they possess valuable and positive information about prospects for the company.

In addition, it is argued that insider tips can help a firm convey its prospects without providing specific information. Suppose the firm has strategic plans or important developments in technology, production, or marketing that it does not want to reveal to its competitors. The firm desires to convey to investors that its stock is undervalued so that it can obtain additional financing on more favorable terms when its stock price rises. It can tip investment analysts that its outlook has improved without divulging the specifics. It is then argued that investors are more likely to believe the investment analysts' recommendations because the analysts have their reputations to maintain.

Another potential benefit of insider trading is that it may represent an efficient method of compensating management. Permitting insiders to trade on new information is a method of providing additional compensation to managers. Other compensation plans, even if they contain performance incentives, may not be as effective since they might also be withdrawn by the board of directors. By immediate and direct rewards such as insider trading profits, it is also possible that managers will have stronger incentives to accept risky projects supported by shareholders.

Arguments Against Insider Trading

The market efficiency argument is open to question. Insiders have incentives to disguise what they are doing. There are many indirect ways they can benefit without signaling to others what they are doing. Insider trading might also pit one level of employee against another. If it is the lower-level employees who first obtain the information, they may conceal it to benefit themselves in competition with higher-level executives.

It is also argued that compensating executives by insider trading is ineffective. There is no assurance that compensation from insider profits would be related to the performance or value contributed by the executives. Traditional compensation plans with performance incentives at least attempt to align the interests of management and shareholders.

Another defect is that it would represent an unpredictable method of compensation. The size of the insiders' profits could not provide a systematic basis for compensation. It provides incentives to steal valuable corporate property in amounts that cannot be determined in advance. In addition, the information that is appropriated may be used not only to profit the insider, but may signal information to competitors earlier than otherwise.

Finally, insider trading activities could undermine confidence in the securities markets themselves. If the rules of the game are not known in advance or if the rules of the game are perceived as both uncertain and unfair, this could have the effect of reducing the amount of trading activity. The markets would be less efficient. Unless the playing field is perceived as being level and equally fair for all, trading would diminish. Even professionals in the business who take a position in securities—the dealers—would react. If dealers perceive that greater risks are involved because of the advantages of insiders, they would increase the bid-ask spread as compensation for the additional risk that they must bear.

Regulation Policy

Because the public and its legislators have generally been opposed to insider trading, public policy has sought to prevent it. As we have developed in our review of the laws and related rules and regulations, three theories of wrongdoing in connection with insider trading have become firmly established. These are:

Insiders—illegal because they use inside knowledge.
Outsiders using insider information—illegal because of misappropriation of insider knowledge.
Equality for target shareholders—SEC Rule 14e-3.

As we indicated earlier, both Rule 10b-5 and Rule 14e-3 are somewhat ambiguous with respect to their scope and applicability. This gives the SEC the power to take action in a wide range of cases. Indeed, in highly publicized cases such as those involving Ivan Boesky and the Drexel case, these rules were important in establishing the illegality of the practices that were attacked by the SEC and subsequently in criminal cases as well.

In part because these rules are somewhat ambiguous, it has been argued that their application represents an exemplification of a public choice (private interest) theory of regulation (Haddock and Macey, 1987). Haddock and Macey distinguish between true insiders and a particular interest group, the market professionals. They set forth the theory that it is the market professionals who have been influential in setting SEC policy. Haddock and Macey argue that market professionals benefited from SEC rules and suits because they outlawed trading by corporate insiders, but shielded the kind of research and practices that market professionals employ. Since market professionals compete with corporate insiders for access to information, the active SEC prosecution of inside traders protects the interests of the market professionals. They further argue that there was uncertainty as to whether the information developed by the market professionals based on their research and contacts with corporate executives might have represented insider trading. The SEC rules and the litigation generated by the SEC appeared to hold legal the traditional methods of market professionals while it attacked the activities of "true insiders."

Whether the private interest theory of SEC prosecution of insider trading fits the facts has not been fully established. One problem is separating into distinct interest groups the many categories of participants involved. As Table 22.1 demonstrates, the list of participants is indeed a long one. There is an uncertain line which divides "true insiders" from the market professionals. There appears to be a considerable overlapping of both participants and their

On August 4, 1988, five officials of a specialty investment firm by the name of Princeton/Newport Partners along with a former bond trader in Drexel's office in Beverly Hills were indicted by a federal grand jury in New York. They were charged with 35 counts of racketeering, fraud, and conspiracy. This represented the first use of the Racketeer Influenced and Corrupt Organizations Act (RICO) in a securities case. It was the first of a number where it was subsequently used. The six defendants denied wrongdoing. Their lawyers stated that their clients were indicted because they refused to give evidence in connection with the investigations of Drexel and Goldman Sachs. In mid-March 1989, one of the traders at Princeton/Newport testified against Lisa Jones, a Drexel assistant trader. He testified that the chief trader at Princeton/Newport had instructed him to help carry out stock parking deals with Drexel. He testified that Lisa Jones was also involved. Subsequently, Princeton/Newport indicated that the application of RICO made it impossible for them to continue doing business, and the firm's operations were closed. Defense attorneys in the Princeton/Newport case argued that the transactions complained against were tax trades that were common on Wall Street. They were designed to take advantage of capital gains laws which were in effect during the years that the trading took place.

A case paralleling the Winans case in connection with *The Wall Street Journal* "Heard on the Street" column involved S. G. (Rudy) Ruderman, who had been broadcasting the daily stock market radio reports of *Business Week* magazine. According to the complaint, Mr. Ruderman would receive page proofs of the forthcoming issues of *Business Week*. Mr. Ruderman had been *Business Week's* broadcast editor since 1981. He was among the nation's first radio broadcasters to report business news on a regular basis. On the basis of the advance information he received in the page proof about stock recommendations that were to appear in *Business Week's* "Inside Wall Street" column, Mr. Ruderman bought stock. He was charged with illegal insider trading. On December 9, 1988, it was reported that he entered a guilty plea.

Good or Bad Law?

The argument has been made that many of the activities which have been declared illegal in recent cases were for many years common practices in financial trading. One response to this view is that this misses the central objective of SEC Rule 14e-3. The aim is to carry out the intent of the original Williams Act of 1968. This was to be sure that the individual shareholder received as good a price in the takeover as any other seller. The aim of Rule 14e-3 was to insure that the bidder engaged in the takeover will not be able to buy the shares of existing shareholders at depressed prices. If the price of the stock is to rise, this will enable the individual shareholders to receive the benefit of the price rise.

This in turn gives rise to another set of issues. Some would argue that the Williams Act of 1968 was wrong in the first place. They argue that it was passed on an emotional basis because of fears engendered by the active conglomerate merger movement, particularly from 1965 through 1968. It is said that established firms felt threatened by the increased activity in takeovers.

The argument can be made that the raider, the takeover artist, or the firm seeking to acquire another firm have a special competence to bring to the transaction. Why should the source of the improvements that will increase the price of the firm not be permitted to buy on advantageous terms after a 5 percent position is taken? In a study of 236 successful tender offer contests during the period 1963–1984, it was found that the average percent shares held at the time of the tender offer was 9.8 percent. Of the bidder firms, 155 of the 236 acquiring firms held no target shares prior to the offer. Thus, in almost two thirds of the cases, the acquiring firm had no foothold position. On average, the foothold position was relatively small (Bradley, Desai, and Kim, 1988).

The question has been raised, why should the passive shareholders who are holding most of the shares be protected from selling their shares before the price rise associated with the takeover occurs? It is argued that since it is the takeover that produces the increase in value, why should the passive investor be entitled to this large windfall gain? The argument continues that most activities such as parking to conceal that a large foothold position is being taken by the acquiring firm are artificially illegal. By alternative criteria of fairness and equity, it is argued that these are perfectly legitimate business practices. The argument is further made that they increase the probability that such takeover activity will occur, and it is argued that it is this takeover activity that results in value increases and therefore a benefit to the economy as a whole (Jensen, 1984).

Insider Trading—
Some Historical Perspectives

Historically, financial intermediaries have long attempted to trade on the basis of advance information. It is said that the Rothschilds built their fortune by developing advance information. They maintained a network of agents throughout England and much of Europe during the late 1700s and early 1800s when other forms of communication were relatively slow. The agents would convey their information to the Rothschild traders by carrier pigeon, boat, or stagecoach, whichever would convey the news most rapidly. One illustrative case involved the battle of Waterloo (see Herzel and Katz, 1987). The battle came to a climax on Sunday, June 18, 1815. On early Monday, June 19, a newspaper in Brussels published an extra edition proclaiming Wellington's victory at Waterloo. The newspaper was rushed from one Rothschild agent to another until an agent embarked on a Rothschild boat which reached England. The paper was then carried by a Rothschild agent on a speedy horse and delivered to Nathan Rothschild by Tuesday morning. Wellington's official dispatches had not yet reached Downing Street, the domicile of the prime minister. When Rothschild traded on Tuesday morning, June 20, the London financial markets had not received the news of the outcome of the battle of Waterloo. The British government consols were still trading at a steep discount. Nathan Rothschild bought large amounts of the British consols to earn a substantial profit. The gains were as a result of privileged information. Did this represent insider trading? Was it an illegal activity? It played an important role in the making of the Rothschild fortune.

Financial analysts employed by brokerage houses and others working independently have long attempted to develop superior information about the companies that they follow. They build a background of economic information on individual industries and the firms in them. They may study a broad range of economic, social, and political factors that affect the future of the industries and the firms. They develop information from all available printed and verbal sources. They make careful analytical studies. In addition, they visit the chief executives of individual companies to obtain information on a direct, personal contact basis.

Certainly such financial analysts have more information than the individual investor who depends on what he or she reads in newspapers and business journals. The financial analyst has superior information. But is it inside information, and is it illegal? A long tradition holds that such activities by financial analysts are perfectly proper, ethical, and legal. Indeed, it is argued that the ability of financial analysts to receive income from selling such information and/or to profit by trading themselves is a proper economic inducement for such research activities and information gathering to be performed. But some argue that the superior information developed by the financial analysts and the circumstances under which they obtain it are very similar to the kinds of information developed by investment bankers in connection with bringing out a new issue or advising a firm in connection with takeover activity. It has been argued that the main reason the professional security analysts are permitted to engage in such activities is that they represent a more effective pressure group in influencing the policies of the Securities and Exchange Commission.

Thus far in this chapter, we have set forth the theory of insider trading. We have reviewed some arguments that raise questions about whether the laws, rules, and regulations on insider trading represent sound public policy. We next review the laws and regulations on insider trading that have been adopted by other countries.

INSIDER TRADING
AT THE INTERNATIONAL LEVEL

Close links among stock markets in New York, London, and Tokyo were most clearly underscored by the October 1987 stock market crash. Insider trading is also a problem at an international level, although attitudes may vary from country to country. Great Britain's rule against insider trading dates back only to 1980, and differs from American law by its requirement that an individual be "knowingly" involved; thus, a confession is virtually the only certain way to get a conviction. The investigation of the Boesky affair led to exposure of the biggest British financial scandal in years involving the illegal activities of the Guiness Brewing Company in the course of its battle with Argyll Group over the control of Distillers Co. The investigation led to the downfall of the chairman of Guiness, as well as the chief executive, head of corporate finance, and the chairman of Morgan Grenfell, Guiness' merchant banker. The violations included illegal payments of Guiness funds to individuals for various services, including agreements to buy Guiness stock before and after the takeover battle, and the investment of $100 million in a Boesky partnership, which was probably the key which opened the whole Pandora's box of the investigation. The timing of the scandal, 1986–1987, coincided with the deregulation of the London Stock Exchange (the Big Bang), at a time when the British government was particularly anxious to create (and protect) a new breed of private shareholders. Self-regulation was one of the key features of the deregulation plan, with various overlapping agencies (the Takeover Panel, the Serious Fraud Office, the Securities and Investment Board) under the leadership of the British Department of Trade and Industry. Following the Guiness scandal, adjustments were made, particularly giving more enforcement as well as merely investigatory powers to these agencies.

West Germany has only a voluntary code against insider trading, and rules throughout the European communities vary considerably in spite of a drive on the part of the European Commission for a statutory ban on insider trading in all member countries. The French government, embarking on a massive market privatization program of its own, is increasingly concerned about the danger of cross-border financial misbehavior. And even the Swiss appear to have been embarrassed by the use of confidential bank accounts in many of the more notorious illegal transactions, and have shown a willingness to participate in international talks on financial regulation.

Among the foreign countries, Japan particularly has been cited as an example of having a very lax policy towards insider trading. For a long time the criticism was made that there was a lax attitude by Japanese authorities and, in particular, the Ministry of Finance which was supposed to police insider trading. Japanese laws and enforcement procedures traditionally are said to have been aimed at protecting the securities industry, not the individual investor. Individual investors understand that there is insider trading. They buy stocks knowing how the market operates. If they don't like how the market operates, they do not buy stocks. But the volume of stock trading in Japan continues to be very high.

A number of highly publicized cases of insider trading caused Japan's parliament to revise the securities and exchange law in May 1988. The new law was to go into effect in the spring of 1989. It defines insider trading and gives the Ministry of Finance greater investigative powers to enforce the law. Under the new law, an insider trading conviction carries a fine of up to $3,737 and six months in jail. However, the Finance Ministry has limited personnel. Its division consists of 17 persons responsible not only for investigating market manipula-tion and insider trading but also for drawing up new guidelines for futures and options trading.

Nevertheless, government officials in Japan have argued that the Japanese system does provide meaningful deterrence. If cases of stock manipulation and insider trading are publicized by newspapers, radio, and TV, the punishment is substantial. The criminal penalties may be low, but the social punishment is high. The wrongdoers are likely to lose their jobs and their reputations will be destroyed as well. Such punishments, it is argued, represent effective sanctions.

However, highly publicized cases in Japan continue to be reported. On July 29, 1988 at 4 PM, Nippon Steel announced it would buy 18.1 percent of Sankyo Seiki Manufacturing Company for $396 million. On that morning, the share price of Sankyo Seiki began to rise sharply in heavy trading. Trading was sus-pended in the afternoon. The Tokyo Stock Exchange conducted an investigation to determine if senior executives of the two companies bought stock based on inside information in advance of the public announcement in the afternoon. In late August 1988, it was announced that the Tokyo Stock Exchange reprimanded the two companies for insider trading by their employees. Exchange officials announced that 19 employees of Nippon Steel and 15 of Sankyo Seiki bought more than 68,000 shares of Sankyo stock before the announcement of the pur-chase by Nippon Steel. The transaction review section of the Tokyo Stock Ex-change reported that the employees began their purchases as early as four months before the announcement. On the morning of July 29, 1988, the volume of Sankyo shares traded was nearly ten times the level of the previous day. The Tokyo Stock Exchange would not identify any of the 34 employees and said that no charges would be brought.

Another case involving inside information and political bribery has been even more highly publicized and involved the imposition of stronger penalties. The Recruit Co. was originally in the personnel and executive recruiting busi-ness, as its name suggests. It then sought to branch out more widely into other industries. It has been charged that between 1984 and 1986, Recruit's real estate unit, with the name Recruit Cosmos Company, sold shares at discount prices to many Japanese public officials, political officeholders, government bureaucrats, and businessmen. All were able to realize substantial profits when subsequently Recruit Cosmos Co. went public. In November 1988, Hiroshi Matsubara, a former Recruit executive, was indicted for trying to bribe an opposition law-maker into soft-pedaling an investigation of the scandal. On March 6, 1989, it was announced that four Japanese businessmen were indicted on bribery charges, including the founder and former chairman of Recruit Co. The other three businessmen involved were the vice president of a Recruit financial unit and two former executives of Nippon Telegraph and Telephone Corp. The March 18, 1989 issue of the London *Economist* (p. 13) discussed the possibility of an even larger impact of the Recruit scandal. It discussed the possibility that Mr. Yasuhiro Nakasone, the previous prime minister, might also be arrested and held for interrogation in a Tokyo jail. The article commented that if a Nakasone arrest took place, the government of his successor, Mr. Naburo Takeshita, would be likely to fall, and that an early election would probably have to be called. The same issue commented that prosecutions in the Recruit bribery scandal were "inching ever closer to the heart of Japanese politics . . ." (*Economist*, March 18, 1989, p. 30). The foregoing articles cited followed a story carried in *The Wall Street Journal* of March 14, 1989. It announced that three lawmakers from the ruling Liberal Democrat party had admitted receiving checks from Recruit Company during the summer of 1988. All three said that they subsequently returned the money. Also it was reported that 15 lawmakers including one cabinet member had received gifts from Recruit. It was said that opposition party members were bringing increased pressure on Prime Minister Takeshita to either resign or to dissolve Parliament and call an election. Finally, on April 24, 1989, Noboru Takeshita announced that he would resign as prime minister as a consequence of the influence-buying activities of the Recruit Co. in relation to himself and his aides.

EXTENT OF THE PROBLEM

Despite the wide publicity about insider trading, solid evidence on its magnitude is limited. A 1987 study by the Office of the Chief Economist of the SEC focused on insider trading specifically within the context of tender offers. Poulsen and Jarrell (1987) concluded that the prebid target stock price run-up was not necessarily attributable to illegal trading, but to legitimate speculation based on sophisticated analysis of public information. Preannouncement run-up was significant: 22.7 percent, 27.6 percent, and 38.8 percent of the total eventual control premium respectively on days −3, −2, and −1 relative to the announcement date of the tender offer. Poulsen and Jarrell (1987) were able to attribute the run-up to speculation in the media, the size of the foothold acquisition by the bidding firm, and whether the takeover was friendly and negotiated rather than hostile. While the ultimate basis for media speculation might indeed be illegally leaked information, once the rumors are in circulation, the target firm is "in play" for any number of traders. The authors identify a number of completely legitimate sources of information relating to takeovers—the first and foremost, required disclosure under the Williams Act of the bidder's intentions within ten days of acquiring more than a 5 percent equity interest. In addition, there are scores of Wall Street professionals (traders, arbitragers, shark watchers, journalists) dedicated to ferreting out this kind of valuable information. They spot unusual corporate executive activities, meetings, travel, and so on; they use sophisticated computer equipment to monitor accumulations of stock, or unusual trading volume; they focus on industries that have seen recent takeover activity and try to pick out the next target.

Many of the criticisms of insider trading falls into the category of "it's just not right," with little analysis, either legal or economic to back it up. It is this lack of analysis that leads to arbitrary rules such as the short-swing profit rule (six-month holding period). Information is a valuable commodity, and the issue becomes how it will be exploited, and who will benefit from it. At one extreme, Stanley Sporkin, former enforcement chief at the SEC, believed that no one should ever be able to make money by trading on information not available to all regardless of how innocently acquired. His classic example is the investor who sees from the window of a landing airplane that a company's main plant is engulfed in flames; Sporkin's opinion was that trading on this information would be illegal. There are not many who subscribe to such a strict standard. Many feel that anything, including insider trading, which has the effect of moving information to the market faster than it would otherwise arrive is a good thing and should not be curtailed, because it brings stock prices closer to their theoretically correct values. Some argue that insider trading is part of insider compensation, although it is not a particularly efficient or directed means of acquiring this end.

Manne (1966) characterized an excessively paternalistic attitude toward noninsiders as exemplifying a "bumpkin theory of outside shareholders" when, in fact, they may not be quite so naive. The Texas Gulf Sulphur case involved options trading by the insiders, and options traders were included in the protective complaint of the SEC. Manne (1966) refers to options traders as among the "most sophisticated market traders in existence," and suggests that they might even have felt embarrassed by being included. Far from being victimized by the insiders, they were probably able to infer enough from their transactions to theoretically be treated as tippees in the case. Similar criticisms have been offered with respect to the need to protect the naive investing public from junk bonds, when, in fact, they tend to be purchased in large blocks by sophisticated professional traders.

Indeed, part of the problem in insider trading enforcement is the issue of identification of the victims. And, even the perceived need to identify victims, or plaintiffs, is more a reflection of legal versus economic reasoning. To some extent, the problem is eliminated by making the activity a crime, which unlike a civil matter does not require victims. Insider trading regulation has also come up with another means of addressing the problem. Whether or not a corporation has been injured by the short-swing trading of one of its own insiders, the corporation, or any shareholder of the corporation can bring a suit (under Rule 16(b) of the Securities and Exchange Act of 1934) against the insider to recover his or her profits. Such suits are not unusual; one of the more recent cases involved KaiserTech's March 1988 lawsuit to recover damages of at least $4 million from its own chairman, Alan E. Clore.

Short of controlling all the stock in the firm, no one can fully exploit the value of nonpublic information, however acquired. During the insider trading period, many other traders are also dealing in the same stock for a variety of reasons such as portfolio realignment and liquidity needs. (The insider trading period is defined as a period before the public release of the information. In fact, insider trading will stop once the stock price fully reflects the value of the information regardless of whether the information has been officially released or not. The financial literature is full of instances when the official announcement of a given bit of news causes no stock price reaction at all since the information has already been compounded into the stock price.) Given the anonymous nature of the open-market system, it is impossible to distinguish those who traded with insiders from those who traded with noninsiders. As the activities of the insiders affect stock prices, anyone else trading during the period benefits (or loses) accordingly. So, of two simultaneous trades at the same price, one could be considered legal, and the other illegal depending on the information resources of the traders.

Herzel and Katz (1987) also bring up the problem of alternative duties facing the insiders with privileged information that they know will cause their firm's share price to rise. The insider has three options (only two of them legitimate): (1) abstain from trading; (2) publicize the information and then trade on it; (3) trade on the information before publicizing it. If the insider chooses alternative 3, the shareholders selling to the insider may claim to have been injured, since they could have sold their shares at a higher price had the information been revealed earlier. Shareholders accuse the insider of violating securities laws by not publicizing the information (that is, by not choosing alternative 2). However, the insider would also have been in complete compliance with securities laws by doing nothing (alternative 1), and the result for the noninsider would have been identical to the illegal insider trading scenario. (In fact, the outsider may be better off under the illegal scenario, if the insider's activities have the effect of increasing the stock price.) This discussion assumes that the selling shareholders have some reason (other than changes in share price, which in the absence of new information would not change) for choosing this particular time to sell their shares, and would have sold them at this time regardless of the alternative chosen by the insider. However, the outside shareholders benefit under only one of the two equally legitimate alternative actions which the insider could choose. Manne (1966) explores this question of victims and distinguishes between outside investors who trade as a function of time and those who trade as a function of price. Time traders act because of events unrelated to stock price, for example, portfolio adjustment needs; whereas price traders respond to stock price changes regardless of whether or not they know why the stock price is changing. That is, they are more likely to trade based on price changes caused by insiders' actions. The long-term investor is less likely to trade due to price fluctuations, and is thus less likely to be harmed by illegal insider trading. All shareholders who hold on to their stocks throughout the insider trading period will benefit if the new information is good; only the traders will lose. (Of course, the results will be reversed for the "bad news" scenario.) The insider's control over the timing of the release of the information merely benefits or harms a different random group of outside shareholders, and may arguably benefit the corporation, as was suggested in Texas Gulf Sulphur.

PUBLIC POLICY

The term *insider trading* is ambiguously defined by the SEC. Some have suggested that the regulations with respect to insider trading have been kept deliberately ambiguous in order to enable the SEC to encompass a wide range of practices.

Gray areas abound. A corporate raider has inside information about his own intentions as to his next target. Is he prohibited from trading before he has announced those intentions, when he knows the announcement will drive up target stock price? Corporations often repurchase their own shares on the open market without disclosing that they have embarked on an official stock repurchase plan. Should they be required to announce the plan, even if it may drive up the price of the stock, increasing the cost of the repurchase plan, but benefiting those stockholders who sell their shares? If an investment banker's client (a bidding firm) wants information to be leaked so that shares will be bought up by arbitragers with little loyalty to incumbent managers, how can it be misappropriation or a breach of fiduciary duty for the investment banker to leak the information?

Nor is the goal of insider trading regulation to provide a level playing field for all traders. Those who can legitimately amass and more skillfully analyze publicly available information deserve a higher return for their efforts than the proverbial "throw darts at the Big Board" portfolio. Investors will always have differing amounts of information for a variety of reasons, some of them illegal, others a matter of hard, careful analysis, others sheer luck.

So what is the SEC to do? There are those who feel that the current rules are adequate if vigorously enforced (Friend, 1986), while others, notably certain members of Congress, call for more. The SEC wants to maintain public confidence in securities markets, without so much regulation that they cannot function smoothly. Furthermore, even the best of regulations cannot hope to catch all insider trading; in the words of David Ruder, SEC chairman, "greed and lack of ethical standards will always exist." At best, efforts should be directed at catching those they can, and publicizing the arrests for a deterrent effect.

The SEC has relied on the courts to interpret general guidelines such as Rule 10b-5 to create a case law defining insider trading; and the courts have done so, applying Rule 10b-5 over a wide range of activity. However, there are some indications of judicial reluctance to continue to expand the interpretation of Rule 10b-5, creating pressure for a statutory definition. Supreme Court Justice William Rehnquist's criticism (in his opinion in the Blue Chip case) that Rule 10b-5 had grown from a "legislative acorn" to a "judicial oak" is indicative, as is the split decision in the Winans case (discussed earlier) which fell far short of solidly affirming the misappropriation doctrine.

There has been continued pressure from Congress (Representative Edward Markey, D-Mass., has been particularly critical) for a formal definition of insider trading to clarify the theory and strengthen enforcement. The SEC as well as other members of Congress including Representative John Dingell (D-Mich.) has in the past been somewhat reluctant to provide a precise statutory definition of insider trading, believing that to do so would be equivalent to inviting traders to comply with the letter of the law while violating its spirit. However, given judicial reluctance to expand the interpretation of existing rules, the SEC has come up with a number of proposals. One proposed definition (submitted in August 1987) forbids trading "while in possession of material, nonpublic information" obtained by theft, bribery, misrepresentation, or espionage, or used in breach of a duty to keep the information confidential; trading is illegal whether or not that information was the basis for the decision to invest. Another proposal in November 1987 specifically included the misappropriation theory.

SUMMARY

Risk Arbitrage

Risk arbitrage in M&A activity includes simple speculation in the stock of takeover targets. As such, risk arbitragers suffered large losses during the stock market crash of October 1987. To reduce their required investment, arbitragers often use options to control target stock. Traditionally, arbitragers have responded to announced takeover bids. But with the increased pace in recent years, arbitragers have attempted to anticipate takeover bids to establish their stock positions.

One of the main services which arbitragers provide is to allow other target shareholders to cash out before the completion of the takeover transaction. They provide risk-bearing services for shareholders who do not want to bear the uncertainty of the takeover transaction eventually taking place and its final price. They also provide indirect service to shareholders who do not cash out early, through their motivation to hold out for the highest possible price and their skills in valuation and negotiation. Bidders also welcome arbitrage activity since it can greatly facilitate the entire transaction. Bidders even enlist the assistance of arbitragers to accumulate enough shares to carry off a deal.

Empirical analysis shows that market prices during the risk arbitrage stage of a takeover significantly discriminate between eventual outcomes. Thus, these market prices can be used to infer the probability that an acquisition will ultimately take place. If arbitragers accumulate a large percentage of the target shares, the target management may be unable to defend against the takeover. Thus, information leaks by investment bankers to arbitragers and the parking device contribute to an increase in the probability of takeover success.

Insider Trading

Insider trading in the classical sense offers relatively modest opportunities for abnormal profits. Corporate insiders (including anyone owning 10 percent or more of any class of stock) are required by Section 16a of the Securities Exchange Act of 1934 to disclose on a monthly basis any changes in their stock holdings. While several empirical studies (Finnerty, 1976; Givoly and Palmon, 1955; Jaffe, 1974), confirm that insiders are able to beat the market, the disclosure regulation curbs flagrant speculation based on inside information.

Takeovers, on the other hand, offer the prospect of dramatic increases in the stock price and trading volume of the target firm. The insider trading cases that have achieved the most notoriety in the last few years have not involved insiders in the classic sense at all, but outsiders in possession of inside information, specifically risk arbitragers, especially Ivan Boesky, and his co-conspirators in the merger and acquisitions and takeover defense departments of prestigious investment banking firms. Some investment banking firms in fact have both M&A and risk arbitrage departments under the same roof, in theory separated by a so-called "Chinese wall" to prevent information leaks. In practice, these walls have been somewhat less impermeable than the original, and there has been growing criticism of having both functions within the same firm.

Interpreting very general existing legislation, the courts have found it wrong for outsiders to trade on inside information under three kinds of circumstances:

1. *Outsider buys information.* It is wrong to trade if the outsider "buys" information from insiders who breached their fiduciary duty to their company by divulging the information. This includes not only outright purchases of information, but information given in exchange for business or other favors. In Texas Gulf Sulphur, the SEC sought to overturn the trades of those who had received information from insiders on this basis.

Manne (1966) suggested that bartering of information may be a way of coping with Section 16 disclosure requirements. Although insiders may effectively be barred from trading on inside information about their own firms, they may engage in information exchanges with associates who are insiders in another firm, and each would trade on the other's inside information. The Boesky case involved outright purchases, although the purchases were not from insiders in the classical sense, but from "temporary" insiders, employed by investment banking firms assisting their clients in takeover contests, and thus privy to inside information.

2. *The "misappropriation" doctrine.* Court decisions in classic insider trading cases tend to rely heavily on the principle of the fiduciary duty of insiders to the outside shareholders of their own firms. And the principle of fiduciary duty has been extended to include temporary insiders such as accountants, lawyers, and investment bankers whose jobs require that they have access to privileged information, and who are similarly prohibited from using the information at the expense of their client. However, beyond this group the definition of insider begins to become a bit strained, and the SEC has had to stretch to include those

who have no fiduciary duty to the firm in whose stock they are trading. Under the misappropriation doctrine, outsiders are prohibited from trading on the basis of information which they misappropriate, or steal.

3. *Insider trading in tender offers.* Finally, the SEC adopted Rule 14e-3 to apply to insider trading within the context of tender offers specifically.

One argument for insider trading is that it results in more efficient pricing of securities and in the more efficient operation of securities markets. Another is that insider trading produces more effective compensation of insiders. Opponents of insider trading question the validity of these arguments and suggest that insider trading activities could undermine confidence in the securities markets themselves. Unless the playing field (the market) is perceived as being level and equally fair to all, trading would diminish.

Prohibition of insider trading raises many questions in relation to takeover activity. Why should the source of the takeover improvements (namely, the bidder) not be permitted to buy on advantageous terms after a 5 percent position is taken? Why should the passive shareholders who are holding most of the shares be protected from selling their shares before the price rise associated with the takeover occurs? Are corporate raiders prohibited from trading before they have announced their intentions, when they know the announcement will drive up the target stock price? If the bidding firm wants information to be leaked to arbitragers, how can it be misappropriation or a breach of fiduciary duty for the investment banker to leak the information?

It appears that the goal of insider trading regulation is not to provide a level playing field for all traders.

QUESTIONS

1. What is risk arbitrage, and what is good and bad about it?
2. What is the "misappropriation theory" of insider trading? Discuss its application in the Winans case.
3. What is the Public Choice model of SEC prosecution of insider trading set forth in Haddock and Macey (1987)?
4. What social/economic functions do arbitragers provide?
5. What are the major sources of uncertainty in takeover bids?
6. Discuss the arguments for and against insider trading legislation.

REFERENCES

BERG, ERIC N., "Putting the Arbs in the Hot Seat," *The New York Times,* June 8, 1986, Section 3, pp. 1, 25.

BRADLEY, M., A. DESAI, and E. H. KIM, "Synergistic Gains from Corporate Acquisitions and Their Division Between the Stockholders of Target and Acquiring Firms," *Journal of Financial Economics,* May 1988, pp. 3–40.

BROWN, KEITH C., and MICHAEL V. RAYMOND, "Risk Arbitrage and the Prediction of Successful Corporate Takeovers," *Financial Management*, Autumn 1986, pp. 54–63.

Economist, "For the Honour of Japan's Politics," March 18, 1989, pp. 13–14.

Economist, "Unlucky Numbers," March 18, 1989, pp. 30, 32.

FINNERTY, J. E., "Insiders and Market Efficiency," *Journal of Finance*, September 1976, pp. 1141–1148.

FRIEND, IRWIN, "Resisting the Call for More Regulation," *The New York Times*, November 30, 1986, p. 2.

GARCIA, BEATRICE E., and GEORGE ANDERS, "In Arbitrage, Risks are Burgeoning Along with Profits," *The Wall Street Journal*, December 23, 1986, p. 6.

GIVOLY, D., and D. PALMON, "Insider Trading and the Exploitation of Inside Information: Some Empirical Evidence," *Journal of Business*, January 1985, pp. 69–87.

GRAVEN, KATHRYN, "Japan's Efforts to Fight Insider Trading Must Overcome Acceptance of Practice," *The Wall Street Journal*, February 22, 1988.

HADDOCK, DAVID D., and JONATHAN R. MACEY, "Regulation on Demand: A Private Interest Model, with an Application to Insider Trading Regulation," *Journal of Law and Economics*, October 1987, pp. 311–352.

HERZEL, L., and L. KATZ, "Insider Trading: Who Loses?" *Lloyds Bank Review*, July 1987, pp. 15–26.

HOGG, SARAH, "Crime and High Finance," *Britannica Book of the Year*, Chicago: Encyclopaedia Britannica, Inc., 1988, pp. 144–145.

JAFFE, J., "The Effect of Regulation Changes on Insider Trading," *Bell Journal of Economics and Management Science*, Spring 1974, pp. 93–121.

JENSEN, M. C., "Takeovers: Folklore and Science," *Harvard Business Review*, November–December 1984, pp. 109–121.

————, "Don't Freeze the Arbs Out," *The Wall Street Journal*, December 3, 1986, p. 30.

MANNE, H. G., *Insider Trading and the Free Market*, New York: Free Press, 1966.

METZ, TIM, "Highflying Arbitragers are Taking a Beating as Takeover Fever Cools," *The Wall Street Journal*, October 6, 1986, pp. 25, 44.

MILLER, JAMES P., "KaiserTech Sues Its Chairman, Clore, For Alleged Securities-Law Violations," *The Wall Street Journal*, March 2, 1988, p. 10.

NORRIS, FLOYD, "Arb in Orb," *Barron's*, October 7, 1985, p. 13.

POULSEN, A., and G. JARRELL, "Stock Trading before the Announcement of Tender Offers: Insider Trading or Market Anticipation," unpublished manuscript, U.S. Securities and Exchange Administration, 1987.

RICKS, THOMAS E., "SEC Proposes Insider-Trading Measure that Includes Misappropriation Theory," *The Wall Street Journal*, November 20, 1987, p. 4.

SING, BILL, "Beverly Hills Unit of Drexel Fueled Southland Growth," *Los Angeles Times*, March 30, 1989, Part IV, pp. 1, 8.

The Wall Street Journal, "Recruit Gifts to Lawmakers Stir Japanese Opposition," March 14, 1989, p. A16.

WELLS, CHRIS, "Just How Damning is the Case Against Drexel Burnham?" *Business Week*, November 28, 1988, pp. 160–164.

WYSER-PRATTE, GUY P., "Merger Arbitrage," Chapter 21 in Milton L. Rock, ed., *Mergers and Acquisitions Handbook*, New York: McGraw-Hill, 1987, pp. 235–246.

CHAPTER **23**

Antitrust and Public Policies

Some view the merger activity of the 1980s with great alarm. They hold that competition will be decreased, efficiency reduced, and financial instability increased. Others see merger activity as a natural expression of market forces. Mergers and the market for control according to this second view will discipline managers to be efficient and will move resources to their most productive uses. The results will be increased efficiency and an improvement in the ability of business firms to cope with increased international competition.

These opposing views mirror the two approaches to government policy that have been followed.[1] Two major theoretical schools of thought have struggled to shape government policy. This chapter begins with a description of the key statutes which guide the antitrust agencies and the courts in the United States. The two main competing theoretical approaches to interpreting and applying the statutes are explained. Next we sketch some historical background on how the statutes have been applied. Antitrust issues are tested using residual analysis. More recent developments are summarized. Finally, the implications of the preceding materials are considered.

---

[1]Disclosure to readers: At least two schools of thought on industrial organization economics exist—the structural theory versus the dynamic competition theory. The present authors belong to the second school. Those who belong to the first would have written this chapter differently.

THE U.S. ANTITRUST LAWS

Clayton Act of 1914, 1950

Four statutes define the major boundaries of the antitrust laws in the United States. The main statute related to mergers is Section 7 of the Clayton Act originally adopted in 1914. Section 7 of the Clayton Act empowered the Federal Trade Commission (FTC) to prohibit the acquisition by one company of the stock of another if adverse effects on competition resulted. However, the original Section 7 was emasculated by court interpretation. Section 7 could effectively be avoided by purchasing the assets of a company directly or by first purchasing the stock and then the assets of the acquired company. Although control of a company through stock acquisitions might be illegal, the courts held that if the acquired stock were used to absorb the assets of the company before the FTC could file a complaint or complete proceedings under a complaint, the acquisition was not subject to Section 7 of the Clayton Act.[2] This loophole was closed by an amendment to Section 7 of the Clayton Act adopted December 29, 1950.[3] Two important changes were made. First, it enabled the Federal Trade Commission to block asset purchases as well as stock purchases. Second, an incipiency doctrine was added. The Federal Trade Commission could block a merger where it perceived a trend that might ultimately result in a decrease in competition.

Sherman Act of 1890

A second major statute affecting merger activity is the Sherman Act of 1890, Sections 1 and 2. Section 1 of the Sherman Act prohibits contracts, combinations, or conspiracies in restraint of commerce. Section 2 is directed against actual or attempted monopolization. As interpreted by the courts, Section 2 could be used to break up firms that had become "dominant" in their line of business or section of the country. It could also be used to prohibit mergers that would result in a "dominant" firm. The Department of Justice has used both Section 2 of the Sherman Act and Section 7 of the Clayton Act as a basis for evaluating prospective mergers.

Hart-Scott-Rodino Act of 1976

The third major law is the Hart-Scott-Rodino Antitrust Improvements Act of 1976. This was signed into law on September 30, 1976. Some observers consider the Hart-Scott-Rodino Act (HSR) of 1976 of equal importance with the earlier Sherman and Clayton Acts. HSR contains three titles. Title I expands the power

[2] *Thatcher Mfg. Co. v. Federal Trade Commission* and *Swift & Co. v. Federal Trade Commission* (1926), 272 U.S. 554; *Arrow-Hart and Hegeman Electric Co. v. Federal Trade Commission* (1934), 291 U.S. 587.
[3] Public Law No. 899, U.S. 81st Cong., 2nd sess., December 29, 1950.

of the Department of Justice to issue civil investigative demands (CID) in connection with investigations related to the antitrust laws. Title II is the portion of the law which represents the "Pre-Merger Notification Act." It provides for a 30-day waiting period after designated information is submitted both to the Federal Trade Commission and to the Department of Justice before acquisitions or mergers covered by the act may be completed. This waiting period can be extended for an additional 20 days by request of either government agency. The waiting period for tender offers is 15 days which can be extended another ten days upon request by the government.

Generally the notification and waiting period requirements apply to acquisitions of 15 percent or more of the voting securities or assets of an acquired company. There are other requirements related to the size of the purchase and to the size of the acquiring company. Under these provisions, the Department of Justice announced suits against Donald Trump, the Belzbergs, and the Wickes Cos. for arrangements in which it is alleged that they arranged for brokerage firms to obtain control over large blocks of stock under options arrangements (Pasztor, 1988; Redburn, 1988).

Title III is the *Parens Patriae* Act. This expanded significantly the powers of State Attorneys General to institute antitrust triple damage suits on behalf of their natural citizens injured by any violation of the Sherman Act. These suits may be initiated even though the state itself has not been injured by the alleged violation. Damages recovered as a result of a *Parens Patriae* suit may be distributed in any manner authorized by the court.

RICO Act of 1970

Of increased importance is the federal Racketeer Influenced and Corrupt Organizations Act of 1970 (RICO). At first RICO seemed to have narrow applicability and was little used. However, since the late 1970s RICO has been increasingly applied to a wide variety of situations. Illustrative was a RICO suit brought against Laventhol and Horwath, the ninth largest U.S. accounting firm. A class-action suit was brought on behalf of 2,850 investors who lost over $20 million "in a failed tax-shelter program audited by Laventhol" (Berton, 1988). Laventhol lost a jury trial in February 1988 with triple damages yielding a payment of $60 million. In May 1988 Laventhol paid $15 million in an out-of-court settlement of the earlier court decision which Laventhol said it would otherwise have appealed.

Under RICO either governments or private plaintiffs may sue. For example, price fixing could be alleged to represent a form of deceiving customers by charging prices that represent fraud in relation to what competitive prices would have been. Or in connection with a traditional Sherman Act Section 2 case where dominant market power is alleged, RICO could conceivably be invoked because such power would result in noncompetitive (fraudulent) behavior and prices. Similarly, a traditional Section 1 case alleging a conspiracy or a Clayton Act Section 7 case alleging an unlawful combination could invoke RICO on the grounds of deceptive and fraudulent consequences. The demonstrated powerful effect of a RICO suit in securities fraud and insider trading cases may cause its use to spread in the antitrust area. Recall that RICO provides for recovery of treble damages by plaintiff.

The foregoing information represents the bare bones of the main statutes related to mergers, acquisitions, and tender offers in the United States. The critical aspects of the laws have been in their interpretation and application. The key elements involved have been how to determine the effects on competition and how to determine whether a firm is sufficiently dominant to exercise monopoly power. These issues are treated in the next section.

THE STRUCTURAL THEORY VERSUS DYNAMIC COMPETITION

For decades the dominant view in industrial organization was the structural theory. Briefly stated, the structural theory argues that higher concentration in an industry causes (predicts) less competition. If a high enough percentage of industry sales is accounted for by a small enough number of sellers, those companies will develop an awareness of what their rivals are likely to do, leading to a recognized interdependence in pricing and output decisions. The result, it is argued, is tacit coordination or even overt collusion among the largest companies. Under the structural theory, high industry concentration is considered sufficient grounds for antitrust action.

Since the mid-1960s, however, both the theory and the evidence of empirical studies have been challenging the older historical economic reasoning underlying antitrust prosecution. Newer theories of dynamic oligopoly and strategic competition have received increased recognition.

The Structural Theory

The structural theory, which long dominated both academic thinking and public policy, has its roots in the economist's classic model of perfect competition. According to the structural theory, any significant departure from the economy described by this model leads inevitably to collusion by producers on pricing and output decisions, abnormally high profits, and higher prices for consumers.

The building of models in economics, as in any discipline, begins with a set of simplifying assumptions. In examining the structural theory and evaluating its implications for antitrust policy, it is important to keep in mind the special set of assumptions on which the theory rests. The characteristics of a perfectly competitive market, and thus the underlying assumptions of the structural theory, can be summarized as follows:

1 A competitive market comprises a large number of buyers and sellers, large enough that neither individual buyers nor sellers can influence market prices or output.

2 Economies of scale are exhausted at a relatively small company size. Cost efficiencies, therefore, are assumed to be roughly the same across all companies—regardless of size—in a given industry.

3 There are no significant barriers to entry into an industry. Also, there is a ready supply of entrepreneurs available to ensure that all companies are aware of, and capable of exploiting, the latest technology.

4 Constant innovation and the development of new products ensure that no companies maintain more than a temporary "proprietary" position. As a result, there are no significant, lasting differences in quality and product among companies.

5 Complete knowledge of all aspects of the input and output markets is costlessly available. (Advertising and promotion have no economic function in a world of perfect competition.)

The market dictates price; only output (at price equals marginal cost) requires a decision. As a result of the preceding conditions, relative input and output prices adjust such that expected profits are equalized or "normalized" across all industries. No companies or industries, accordingly, can be expected to earn consistently above-normal profits over long periods of time.

The true test of a model, it is important to recognize, is not in the realism of its assumptions, but in its predictive power. The economic model of perfect or atomistic competition has been successfully applied to a number of economic policy problems. Using only the basic notions of downward-sloping demand curves and upward-sloping supply curves, economists can predict with considerable confidence the effects of much government policy on the pricing and output of goods and services. Price or rent controls, for example, give rise to the predicted shortages, while price supports produce excess supplies, without exception.

For policy decisions involving industrial organization, however, the classical model of perfect competition may not be adequate. It may not sufficiently consider the dynamic interactions of business rivalry.

The Dynamic Competition Model

A new model of corporate competition has been challenging the *relevance* of the structural theory of industrial organization. It may be called the dynamic competition model. Its expansion of focus and its new policy implications have been reinforced, moreover, by the separate development of a relatively new field in corporate management: strategic planning. The overlapping literatures of industrial organization and strategic planning have suggested the failure of structural theory to provide the basis for a realistic antitrust policy.

Both the dynamic competition and strategic planning models recognize that the dimensions of corporate decision making extend far beyond the simplified pricing and output decisions of the classic model. Technological leadership, product quality, product variety, promotional efforts, relative cost efficiencies—all of these are strategic business considerations which strongly affect the profitability of corporations. The new research which incorporates these additional factors provides empirical support for the dynamic models, hence, their greater relevance for policy making.

The dynamic competition theory also recognizes that the organizational experience achieved over time is important in the development of an effective business team. Differences in management efficiency among companies, although ignored by the perfect competition model, may not be quickly equalized, allowing for significant and lasting differences in profitability. Because of the persistence of organizational or other efficiency advantages, cost levels and product quality may also vary significantly among firms. Companies that achieve lower costs are likely to increase market share and, at some point, to account for substantial portions of industry output and sales.

High market shares and the resulting high concentration may thus be the result of greater efficiency and *not*, as the structural theory holds, of monopoly power. In the structural theory, high concentration represents market power and is identified as the cause of anticompetitive behavior. But in a business world of dynamic competition, high market shares and high concentration are the *effects* of inequalities in the level of efficiency among competitors.

The structural theory assumes that high concentration or high market shares by a few firms in an industry not only guarantees collusion, but constitutes actual proof of it. This assumption, which governed antitrust policy for many years, depends on the critical assumption that a firm's decisions are limited to output alone.

The dynamic competition theory resists this conclusion. Because there are many other important decisions besides pricing and output in a dynamic business environment, collusion is much more difficult. The instability of—and the resulting uncertainty about—market conditions and costs in the real world make the possibility of widespread collusion even less likely. Also, in such an environment, the potential gains from product innovation, technological leadership, and lower costs are strong motivational forces driving competitive behavior. Corporate executives are likely to judge that the gains from superior performance outweigh the possible profits from collusion—even if collusion were possible in the face of complex, multifaceted, and changing decision processes.

Finally, because organizational learning and other company efficiencies are developed over time, individual companies achieve distinctive advantages over their competitors which are not rapidly equalized. Thus, differences in efficiency among companies can lead to significant differences in profitability which persist for long periods of time. Profits resulting from superior efficiency are the driving force behind the system. Expected profits are the incentive spurring cost control and innovation. For policy purposes, then, efficiency-based profits must be distinguished from monopoly rates of return.

The Evidence

The fundamental differences between the two contending theories can be stated as follows: The structural theory views the degree of concentration as a *cause*, and thus as a predictor, of corporate conduct and performance. Market concentration is viewed as the single most important criterion for public merger policy;

high market share alone is interpreted as evidence of collusive behavior. The dynamic competition theory, on the other hand, sees industrial structure as largely the *result* of the relative efficiency and performance of companies. Thus, high market share may only be reflecting greater efficiency. If so, an antitrust policy narrowly focused on measures of industrial concentration could be penalizing our most efficient firms, thus reducing the efficiency of our economy as a whole.

Economists have attempted to test the claims of these contending theories in a series of empirical studies. The earliest of these provided support for the structural theory. But the more recent and sophisticated research is more consistent with the dynamic competition theory.

We do not present an exhaustive review of the empirical work that has been done to date. (For more complete treatment see Weston, 1978; Weston, 1980.) Here we focus on the central issue in the antitrust controversy, the issue on which the structuralists have based their argument that concentrated industries depart from the competitive norm: the relationship between industry concentration and profits.

The earliest studies found that, on average, profitability ratios were higher in concentrated industries. The best known of these studies, published by Joe Bain (1951), related profits to industrial concentration using a sample drawn from 30 industries. From these findings, the structural theory concluded that in concentrated industries, collusion among companies with high market shares accounted for their greater profitability.

Over time a number of weaknesses in this argument have been pointed out. One objection was that if higher concentration were really responsible for the higher profits, then entry by new companies would eventually eliminate those differential profits. In response to this objection, the structural theory had to be amended to incorporate impediments or barriers to entry. Product differentiation and advertising thus came to be regarded as barriers to entry, allowing "entrenched" companies to shield their "abnormal profits" from new or potential competitors.

The more recent evidence has contradicted the earlier findings on concentration and profits. Even the early study by William Comanor and Thomas Wilson (1967), which is in the spirit of the structural theory, found that the influence of concentration on profitability is no longer significant when other variables such as capital intensity are considered.

In addition, Yale Brozen found that when the data of Bain's sample of 30 industries were extended through later years, the industries showing above-average profitability moved downward toward the average. Those industries with below-average profitability moved up toward the average. The results of Bain's study, Brozen concluded, represent only a "snapshot of resource movement" over a longer period of time. When the longer period of time was examined, the "disequilibrium" situation observed by Bain (that is, the differences in profitability across industries) moved toward equilibrium through the adjustment of profitability performance (Brozen, 1970, 1971a, 1971b).

The static structural model of competition predicts that large companies become progressively larger and more powerful, and that concentrated industries become more concentrated, because of monopoly profits. The evidence suggests a more dynamic picture of industrial evolution. Even the most concentrated industries are subject to the rigors of competition. They, too, exhibit the tendency for higher profits to revert to a more normal or average level of profitability.

The structural theory also implies that if the small number of large firms which dominate an industry collude, they would set higher prices, which in turn would provide an "umbrella" for the smaller firms in the industry. If the smaller companies had similar cost structures, and were indeed pricing under the umbrella of their larger competitors, then we would expect to find the profitability of the smaller companies at least equal to that of their larger counterparts. Harold Demsetz (1973a, 1973b) tested this hypothesis and found that in concentrated industries, the larger companies had higher profits than the smaller ones. He also found that small firms in concentrated industries earned no more than small firms in less concentrated industries. From these results, Demsetz concluded that either (1) a price umbrella was not provided by the larger firms, or (2) the costs of the smaller firms were higher than the costs of the larger firms. Interpreted either way, these data suggest that larger firms are larger because they are more efficient than their smaller competitors.

The structural theory, in short, has been facing an increasingly vigorous challenge, both from new theoretical developments and from the supporting empirical evidence.[4]

APPLICATION OF THE STRUCTURAL THEORY IN MERGER CASES

At the time of the 1950 amendments to the Clayton Act, the structural theory stood virtually unchallenged in the academic world. Subsequent court decisions embraced the structural theory and its policy implications almost without exception. As a consequence, substantial horizontal and vertical mergers were essentially eliminated.

In the Brown Shoe case (1962), the Supreme Court expressed concern that the increased efficiencies achieved through vertical integration might make it more difficult for small nonintegrated firms to compete. While paying lip service

---

[4]See, for example, W. J. Baumol, "Contestable Markets: An Uprising in the Theory of Industry Structure," *American Economic Review*, March 1982, pp. 1–15; J. Fred Weston and Stanley I. Ornstein, *The Impact of the Large Firm on the U.S. Economy*, Lexington, MA: Heath Lexington Books, January 1973; H. J. Goldschmid, H. M. Mann, and J. Fred Weston, eds., *Industrial Concentration: The New Learning*, Boston: Little, Brown and Company, 1974; J. S. McGee, *In Defense of Industrial Concentration*, New York: Praeger Publishers, 1971; Harold Demsetz, *The Market Concentration Doctrine*, Washington, DC: American Enterprise Institute for Public Policy Research, 1973; J. F. Weston, "Concentration and Efficiency: The Other Side of the Monopoly Issue," Special Issues in the Public Interest No. 4, New York: Hudson Institute, May 1978.

to the criterion of "competition," the decision effectively protected "competitors" from "competition" by slowing the drive for greater efficiency.

The first major horizontal merger case following the 1950 amendments was the Philadelphia National Bank (PNB) case decided in 1963. In the PNB case the resulting concentration ratios were deemed to have anticompetitive effects. But both the geographic market and line of commerce were defined artificially. Use of the four-county geographic market defined by Bucks County and three contiguous counties simply reflected state laws on permissible branching. Designating the line of commerce as commercial banking without taking into account competition from finance companies, savings and loan associations, insurance companies, interbusiness financing, investment banking, and the public financing markets unduly exaggerates the role of commercial banking. Banking markets are mainly local or national and international in scope. Market shares in local areas are fundamentally determined by the control of entry by governmental authorities. In the national and international markets the effects of a particular commercial banking merger on concentration measures are small because these markets are large.

Entry into commercial banking is controlled by governmental authorities. It seems illogical to forbid mergers when the government can readily undo their effects by entry policy. Furthermore, in the Marine Bancorporation case, the merger was approved because the court recognized that state law had limits on entry such that merger was the only way that Marine Bancorporation could enter the eastern part of the state of Washington.[5]

In *United States v. Von's Grocery Co.*, decided in 1966, the merger was declared illegal.[6] The resulting firm had accounted for 7.5 percent of grocery sales and 1.4 percent of the number of grocery stores in Los Angeles. Between 1953 and 1962 the number of grocery chains in the Los Angeles market increased from 96 to 150. The 173 entries and 119 exits during this same period along with other market share changes reflected strong and active competition among supermarkets in the area. But the majority opinion of the court emphasized that the number of single-owned stores had declined from over 5,000 in 1950 to under 4,000 by the early 1960s. But this latter trend reflected primarily the increased use of the automobile in grocery shopping which diminished the convenience functions provided by neighborhood Mom and Pop stores. The underlying trends in technology were much more significant in reducing the population of single stores than the merger activity among supermarkets which mainly reflected competitive strategies and counterstrategies.

A series of decisions against mergers of beer companies failed to take into account the significant changes in the nature of competition in the industry [for example, *United States v. Pabst Brewing Co.*, 384 U.S. 546 (1966); *United States v. Jos. Schlitz Brewing Co.*, 385 U.S. 37 (1966); and *United States v. G. Heilman*, 345 F. Supp. 117 (1972)]. Because of improved methods of refrigeration, national adver-

---

[5] *United States v. Marine Bancorporation, Inc.*, 418 U.S. 602 (1974).
[6] *United States v. Von's Grocery Co.*, 384 U.S. 270 (1966).

tising and distribution systems, and greater economies of scale in production, the relevant markets for assessing the level of competition were no longer local or regional as the courts assumed (Ornstein, 1981). Beer markets had become nationwide and even international in scope.

Thus, in a series of cases, the government complaints were upheld. The position of the courts was very clear. An increase in concentration can be equated with a decrease in competition. All horizontal mergers were vulnerable to being declared illegal. Even if market shares were as small as 5 percent, a given merger might be argued to set in train a series of mergers and hence the incipiency doctrine could be invoked. Concentration would be moving in the wrong direction from the standpoint of the courts guided by the structural theory.

Efficiencies and economies were not an adequate defense. Inherently they are difficult to spell out persuasively in a legal, adversary setting. But even if efficiencies could be demonstrated, the courts had spoken. They were willing to pay a price in reduced efficiency and economies to prevent increases in concentration that would come about by mergers.

THE 1968 MERGER GUIDELINES   In setting out its 1968 merger guidelines, the Department of Justice was even more explicit with regard to economies. The Department of Justice held that mergers with market shares high enough to be challenged under the guidelines probably did not involve significant economies of scale. The idea was that the firms were already large enough to have captured most of the potential economies of scale. Furthermore, "where substantial economies are potentially available to a firm, they can normally be realized through internal expansion."[7]

The 1968 merger guidelines set forth specific criteria to assess the degree of concentration in a given industry. The crucial measure of concentration and, hence, of the competitiveness of an industry, was called the four-firm concentration ratio. It was calculated simply by adding the market shares of the largest four companies. In the case of horizontal mergers, it was applied as follows: for industries where the four-firm ratio was under 75 percent, mergers involving acquiring companies with up to 25 percent of the market and acquired companies with about 1 percent of the market share might not be challenged. If the four-firm market share exceeded 75 percent, the permissible numbers fell to 15 percent for the acquiring firm associated with 1 percent for the acquired firm. And if, for instance, the acquiring firm had only a 4 percent market share, the acquired firm could have as high as a 4 percent market share.[8]

---

[7] Department of Justice, "Merger Guidelines," May 30, 1968, p. 12.

[8] The 1982 and 1984 Merger Guidelines substitute the Herfindahl (H) index for the four-firm concentration ratio (CR4). The H index is calculated by summing the squares of the market shares of all the firms in the industry. This effectively provides a broader perspective than the CR4, which considers only the positions of the largest four companies.

Consider, for example, an industry with seven firms, one with 70 percent market share and the remaining six with 5 percent each. In this case, the CR4 would be 85 percent. The H index would be $(70)^2 + 6(5)^2 = 5,050$ which is well above the 1,800 upper limit. A merger between two of the

Further Objections
to the Structural Theory

Besides those shortcomings already mentioned, there are two other important objections to the structural theory underlying these merger guidelines. The first is that domestic concentration measures are not the relevant measures. The large capital-intensive, highly concentrated industries in the United States have been facing growing international competition. The performance of their large international competitors typically has a major impact on the domestic economies of those foreign competitors. Because of intensified international competition, preoccupation with domestic concentration ratios is often completely irrelevant in judging the level of competition in an industry.

The second objection is to the way markets have been delineated. The concentration measures typically defined a market by identifying an historical product or process orientation without considering the broader dimensions of competitive processes. By contrast, modern theories of industrial organization view companies as "bundles of capabilities" rather than producers of individual products. These capabilities include technologies embracing all processes from basic research, product design and development through interrelated manufacturing methods, and postsale consumer service. Electronics technology, for example, has moved from electron tubes to semiconductors to integrated circuitry, silicon chips, and related developments involving a fusion between chemistry and metallurgy.

The method by which markets are defined will, of course, strongly influence concentration ratios. Adopting the broader conception of companies— which considers capabilities rather than specific products—would greatly reduce conventional measures of concentration, giving a more accurate picture of the level of competition facing many large companies in highly concentrated (as conventionally defined) industries.

Conglomerate Mergers

The 1950 amendments to the Clayton Act had considerably less effect in restraining conglomerate mergers. It is more difficult to apply traditional antitrust statutes and precedents to conglomerate mergers because they typically do not affect concentration in individual industries, the touchstone of the structural antitrust philosophy. But the increase in merger activity of the late 1960s, and again in the 1980s, has led to proposals that existing law be modified to restrain conglomerate mergers as well.

---

smaller companies would result in a CR4 of 90 percent, which would be interpreted as a dangerous trend toward monopoly concentration. The H index, however, would become $(70)^2 + (10)^2 + 4(5)^2 = 5,100$. The increase in concentration would be 50 points or less than one tenth of 1 percent. The problem with the CR4 is its failure to distinguish the role of the largest company from that of the other three in producing the "excessive" concentration ratio.

The most serious line of attack against conglomerates argues that the continued merger activities of the past two decades have caused the aggregate concentration ratio (ACR) to rise to an undesirable level. Increases in overall concentration are claimed to strengthen the ability of large firms to exercise political power and control legislation.

The ACR, however, has actually been relatively stable over the past 10 years at about 40 percent when measured by value added in manufacturing. The trend in the ACR is essentially flat, contradicting the unfounded claim that corporate control is becoming steadily more concentrated.

One of the significant findings of this aggregate concentration analysis is that the composition of the largest 50, 100, and 200 companies is constantly changing. Structural theory would predict that the largest companies, through collusion and monopolistic practice, would continually entrench their proprietary positions, growing steadily larger while maintaining profitability. The evidence, however, reveals a pattern of corporate evolution in which older companies (and industries) are continually giving way to new enterprises. This pattern is consistent with the broad conception of the dynamic competition and strategic planning literature.

The conglomerate merger activity of recent decades reflected in part new managerial developments, particularly in strategic planning and in new systems of financial planning and control. Another stimulus was the recognition that higher rates of growth resulted in companies' increased ability to attract top managerial talent—and possibly also to achieve higher valuation in the stock market. Mistakes were made in conglomerate mergers and a high rate of divestiture activity has been the aftermath. But the market has been the source of the corrective activity.

The merger activity of the late 1970s and early 1980s had been influenced by an additional set of factors. Of greatest importance is the fact that the stock prices of many companies have represented substantial discounts from the current replacement costs of their assets. The general investment climate, characterized by higher inflation and the increased risk of government intervention, had resulted in higher required corporate returns on invested capital. Acquiring companies have often found that buying physical assets to add capacity is more expensive than buying other companies even at substantial premiums over their market prices.

ANTITRUST ISSUES TESTED USING RESIDUAL ANALYSIS

Many studies of mergers and other major financial events have been made in recent decades. Many of these studies have been described in other chapters; here we summarize one that focused on antitrust enforcement during the period dominated by the structural theory (Ellert, 1975, 1976). The methodology of the studies of residuals or abnormal returns is first reviewed. The basic idea is that the returns from securities will conform to the risk-return patterns predicted by the security market line. When unusual events occur such as a merger or tender offer, the returns will shift upward or downward, depending on whether the market views the event as favorable or unfavorable. Calculation of the departures from the risk-return relationships predicted by the security market line is a study of the abnormal returns and is known as residual analysis.

In the merger studies using residual analysis, relatively large samples have been used, usually more than 100. The behavior of the returns to the common stocks is studied for as long as 120 months prior to the "merger event" and for the surviving firm for as long as 40 months following the merger. It is important to understand that while the 100 or more mergers may have occurred over as many as 20 or more calendar years, in the analysis, the merger event is the reference date from which analysis of the behavior of returns is made. The procedure begins with an adjustment for the market risk premium. In addition, a wide range of other influences that might occur at a particular time are averaged out over the many different calendar time periods and companies in the merger sample.

On average, securities will yield returns that are related to their underlying risks. However, unusually favorable or unusually unfavorable events will cause security prices to be reassessed. New favorable events will cause security prices to rise so that returns are higher than predicted by the market line relationships between risk and return. Unfavorable events will have the opposite effect. The shifts in returns are called security market line residuals. If no new abnormal events for a firm were occurring, each period's residual would be zero and the cumulative average residuals (CARs) would be flat from that period forward. Comprehensive studies of mergers using this methodology have been made.

Ellert Studies

Ellert (1975, 1976) studied mergers related to antitrust law enforcement. He analyzed the data for 205 defendants in antimerger complaints initiated by the Justice Department and Federal Trade Commission under Section 7 of the Clayton Act for the 1950–1972 period. Of the complaints 121 were issued by the Justice Department and 84 by the FTC. Ellert observes that during the period of the study, the government did not lose a single Supreme Court merger case after the 1950 revision to the Clayton Act. In 60 percent of the cases studied, defendants cancelled merger plans or were ordered to divest part or all of the assets previously acquired. The average duration of litigation measured by the interval between the filing of the complaint and the entry of the last judicial order was 34 months.

Ellert analyzes the behavior of the data for the 205 defendants and also the two groups broken into 123 defendants ordered to divest acquired assets and 82 defendants not required to divest assets. For both groups of defendants during a period preceding the filing of a merger complaint by at least four years, the residual performance was positive and statistically significant for both groups. The cumulative average residual was over 18 percent for defendants ordered to divest and about 13 percent for defendants not required to divest. For the 48 months prior to the filing of the merger complaint, defendants required to divest achieved a further positive residual that was statistically significant. For the same 48 months proximate to the filing of the merger complaint, defendants not required to divest had returns that were not statistically different from the average for the market. In the 12 months preceding the merger complaint, the residual performance was not statistically significant for either class of defendants.

On the filing of the merger complaint, the average portfolio residual declined by 1.86 percent for defendants ordered to divest and 1.79 percent for defendants not required to divest. While these percentages are small, when applied to the large dollar amount of assets involved, they represent substantial absolute amounts. On average in the postwar period these percentages translated into an average dollar loss per respondent of about $7.5 million (in current dollars).

Following the filing of the merger complaint the behavior of the residuals is not statistically significant. This is true for the period between the filing of the merger complaint and the settlement of the litigation. Then in the 48-month period following the settlement of the litigation the behavior of the returns to the companies is not statistically different from the market as a whole. It is of interest to note also that final settlements which resolve future uncertainties are typically followed by nonstatistically significant behavior of the residuals. On the other hand, settlements such as *nolo contendere* which are more likely to be followed by private triple damage suits result in a persistence of negative residuals that are statistically significant. These results are consistent with the underlying logic as well as an indication of the validity of the methodology employed.

It is somewhat surprising that the magnitude of the negative movement in the residuals upon the filing of a complaint is relatively small. The $7 million to $8 million involved is mainly accounted for by litigation costs. A number of possible explanations of this could be offered. One is that there was no basis for bringing the complaint in the first place and that, therefore, nothing really fundamental or basic could be expected to be accomplished in the final action taken by the antitrust authorities. Ellert (1976, p. 727) observes that these results "are also consistent with non-monopolistic hypotheses of merger motivation. If merger is viewed as a means of expanding the operations of an efficient management group, a specific divestiture of assets would not be expected to constitute a large threat to stockholders, particularly if the firm may substitute towards internal expansion or external acquisitions in other markets in the future."

A similar explanation is related to case selection by the FTC and the Department of Justice. Ellert (1975, pp. 66–67) observed the following:

Observance of positive residuals in the pre-complaint stage is also consistent with a "harassment" hypothesis. The argument here is that the administrative procedures of the Commission lead it to select firms which, from a variety of competitive pursuits, have experienced abnormally good stock price performance. Whereas the FTC bears the entire financial burden for prosecuting a case, most of its investigations are prompted by complaints from competing firms. The Commission does not disclose the identity of a complaining party. These arrangements create an incentive to invoke the administrative process as a means to harass competitors. If the objective of harassment is to increase the production costs of a rival, it is likely that the prime targets would be among the innovative and most profitable of firms. By their performance, these firms constitute the greatest threat to the complainants within a dynamic competitive framework.

Similarly on Department of Justice cases Ellert (1975, p. 93) states:

> As with the FTC, "Most of [these] antitrust investigations and cases originate in complaints coming to the Department [of Justice] from the public, about two-thirds of which are from businessmen seeking protection against competitors, groups of competitors, suppliers or other business enterprises."

Ellert concludes that companies acquired were typically those whose pre-merger performance was consistent with ineffective management of assets. This is consistent with the role of mergers as performing a useful economic function in reallocating resources from less efficient to more efficient users. Ellert (1976, p. 729) concludes:

> A public policy concern is that antimerger law enforcement activities may be directed against non-monopolistic accumulations of wealth and toward protection of indigent management rather than being guided by considerations of efficiency in production and exchange.

Mergers for Monopoly Power

Both Stillman (1983) and Eckbo (1981) analyze the residuals of the rivals to firms participating in mergers. They sought to distinguish between the possible efficiency versus monopolization effects of mergers.

Stillman (1983) found that the effect of 30 major challenged horizontal mergers on the residuals of rivals was not statistically significant. The concentration-collusion theory argues that positive residuals should have been observed when the merger was in process and negative residuals when it was challenged. Lack of significance was observed both in relation to the original merger proposal and when it was challenged. That the effect on rivals was not statistically significant casts doubt on the concentration-collusion theory that the mergers were in fact viewed as opportunities for increased possibilities of collusion among the firm's major rivals in the industry.

Eckbo (1981) extended the Stillman study, using a larger sample and a "control" sample of vertical mergers. Eckbo finds that on the announcement of the mergers there are positive residuals both for the participants and their major rivals. This appears to be consistent with the monopoly theory. It is not unambiguous though, because one could also argue that the announcement of the proposed merger conveys information to rivals of opportunities for increased efficiency by expanding scale. Eckbo further finds that at the announcement of the filing of a suit by the antitrust authorities, there is not much effect on the residuals of either the participants or their rivals; in fact, in cases brought by the Federal Trade Commission the effect on rivals is slightly positive. This is consistent with the explanation that the merger partners would have been more efficient and the rivals are protected from this increased efficiency by the Federal Trade Commission suit blocking the merger. Eckbo concludes that the positive performance of rivals of challenged mergers at the time of the original merger announcement reflects information conveyed by the proposed merger that efficiencies can be achieved by expanding scale either internally or externally.

In an extension of Eckbo's earlier work, Eckbo and Wier (1985) paid particular attention to mergers challenged after 1978—that is, following passage of the Hart-Scott-Rodino Antitrust Improvements Act of 1976, which was intended to improve the likelihood that mergers selected for prosecution were truly anticompetitive. Eckbo and Wier (1985, p. 139) found little evidence of improvement; the 17 post-1978 mergers in their study were "economically efficient" and "apparently would not have harmed competition." They lay the blame for this failure on the case selection criteria, that is, inappropriate application of the Department of Justice Merger Guidelines of 1968 and 1982, including the Herfindahl-Hirschman index. While representing an advance in economic thinking, these criteria are still unduly dominated by the older structural theory of antitrust, which holds that the degree of concentration determines industry conduct and behavior.

The preceding studies appear to support the efficiency basis for mergers. Ellert emphasized that acquiring firms had positive residuals in prior years and acquired firms had negative residuals in prior years. Stillman's evidence was that rival firms did not benefit from the announcement of proposed mergers, which is inconsistent with the concentration-collusion hypothesis. Eckbo, and Eckbo and Wier found positive residuals on the merger announcement but no negative effects on rivals when it appeared that the merger would be blocked by the antitrust authorities. They interpret this pattern of relationships as indicating that the main effect of the merger is to signal the possibility of achieving economies for the merging firms, providing information to rivals that such economies may also be available to them.

MORE RECENT DEVELOPMENTS

Some court decisions in the 1970s began to expand the focus of antitrust prosecution beyond traditional concerns with concentration ratios and strict delineation of markets along the lines of historical products. Perhaps the most important of these was the General Dynamics decision (1974), which demonstrated the courts' increased willingness to incorporate economic realism into their decision making. The Supreme Court ruled that an appraisal of the competitive effects of the merger should not rely exclusively on structural tests, but should take into account a much broader range of economic information and business conditions (Bock, 1974). The Department of Justice had analyzed the market in terms of coal sales by a subsidiary of General Dynamics. The Supreme Court instead looked at the market in terms of uncommitted coal reserves. Under this criterion, the effects of the merger on concentration measures were relatively small.

In the more recent Matsushita Electric Industries case, the issue of predatory pricing was raised.[9] Predatory pricing is said to take place when a firm lowers its prices below "cost" until its main competitors are driven out of business when it may then charge monopoly prices. While impressive models of predatory behavior can be constructed, few actual examples in recent decades can be cited. The Supreme Court appears to say in the Matsushita decision that it is skeptical whether predatory pricing conduct has ever existed (Crane, 1987, p. 7; Ginsburg, 1987, p. 11). The reason for the skepticism is that a firm must possess a major share of the market to seek to drive out its competitors (presumably smaller or weaker). Hence, it will suffer substantial losses if it sells below cost. If competitors exit the industry, others will take their place when prices are raised, making it difficult for the predator to recoup its prior losses.

Another important court decision occurred in the Monfort case, initiated as a private antitrust case against a merger.[10] Excell, a wholly-owned subsidiary of Cargill, was the second largest beef packer in the United States. It sought to acquire Spencer Beef, the third largest beef packer. Monfort, the fifth largest beef packer, brought a private antitrust suit against Excell (Cargill) to block the proposed merger. Monfort argued that the combined company would be able to buy cattle at high prices and sell boxed beef at unduly low prices so as to squeeze Monfort's profit margin. The district court accepted Monfort's argument and enjoined the merger.

Excell appealed this decision arguing that any squeeze on profits would reflect increased competition which cannot be an antitrust violation. The court of appeals rejected this argument and affirmed the district court's decision.

The Supreme Court reversed the lower courts by a 6 to 2 decision (one justice did not participate). The court upheld Excell's position that any damage resulting from increased competition did not represent antitrust injury. The antitrust laws should not be used to protect a competitor from price competition even if it was increased by a merger. Moreover, the court held that private litigants, when challenging the merger of two rivals, must have more concrete evidence than mere speculation on potential price squeezes, predatory pricing, and other anticompetitive activities. The decisions of the lower courts reflected the older structural theory. The Supreme Court's reversal reflected the newer theories of dynamic competition.

[9] *Matsushita Electric Industrial Co., Ltd.* v. *Zenith Radio Corp.*, 106 S. Cit. 1348 (1986).
[10] *Cargill, Inc.* v. *Monfort of Colorado, Inc.*, 167 S. Ct. 484 (1986).

Department of Justice 1982 Merger Guidelines

These newer trends in court decisions were paralleled by the changed policies of the main regulatory agencies with jurisdiction over mergers, the Department of Justice (DOJ), and the Federal Trade Commission (FTC). Both issued guidelines statements in the early 1980s, but those of the DOJ had the greatest impact.

The U.S. Department of Justice Merger Guidelines, issued June 14, 1982, codified "the new learning" and represented an official statement of fundamental changes in government antitrust policies. The primary architect of the new policy statement was William F. Baxter, Assistant Attorney General, Antitrust Division, who was on leave from his position as Professor of Law, Stanford University. After summarizing the 1982 guidelines, we comment on their significance.

One major change in the 1982 guidelines was the method of measuring concentration. The previous literature had measured concentration by the share of industry sales, assets, employment or value added of the largest four or largest eight firms. The 1982 guidelines adopted an index developed in the academic literature independently by Professor Herfindahl (1950) and Professor Hirschman (1945). The index is referred to as the Herfindahl-Hirschman Index or HHI. The index is simply the sum of the squares of the market shares of all the firms in the industry. For example, if ten firms each hold a market share of 10 percent, the index would be $10(.1)^2$ which is .1; in the DOJ use of the HHI, market shares are measured as percentages so their HHI would be $10(10)^2$ or 1,000.

The theory behind the use of the HHI is that if one or more firms have relatively high market shares, this is of even greater concern than the share of the largest four firms. An example presented with the announcement of the 1982 Merger Guidelines illustrates this point. In one market, four firms each hold a 15 percent market share, and the remaining 40 percent is held by 40 firms, each with a 1 percent market share. Its HHI would be

$$H = 4(15)^2 + 40(1)^2 = 940$$

In another market, one firm has a 57 percent market share, and the remaining 43 percent is held by 43 firms, each with a 1 percent market share. As in the first market, the four-firm concentration ratio here is 60 percent. However, the HHI would be

$$H = (57)^2 + 43(1)^2 = 3,292$$

Thus, the HHI registers a concern about inequality or the size distribution of firms as well as the degree of concentration.

The HHI can also be related to one of the measures of monopoly power employed, the price-cost margin, defined as price minus marginal cost divided by price. The relationship depends on highly restrictive conditions such as homogeneous goods and the Cournot model which assumes that firm A assumes that other firms hold their output unchanged as firm A restricts output or raises prices. The reaction of rival firms is called "conjectural variation"; the Cournot assumption is that it is zero. From these assumptions a relationship between the price-cost margin and the HHI can be derived (Miller, 1982, pp. 616–618).

The result is shown in equation (23.1):

$$\frac{P - MC}{P} = \frac{HHI}{E_m} \qquad (23.1)$$

where P is price, MC is marginal cost, and E_m represents the market price elasticity of demand. The benchmark of a zero price-cost margin (PCM) reflects the assumptions of models of perfect competition, in which in equilibrium the perfectly atomistic competitive firm chooses its output by equating marginal cost to price. Hence, in the perfect competition model, the price-cost margin is zero. When accounting data are used to measure the PCM, the competitive standard is not zero. One reason is that accountants do not treat the cost of equity capital as a cost. In addition, accounting data do not measure marginal cost nor distinguish between short-run and long-run marginal costs.

Economic theory has moved beyond early structuralist views that the degree of concentration of an industry is inversely proportional to the degree of competition in that industry. Various additional models of single firm or core firm dominance have been developed. They demonstrate that monopoly power, measured by the difference between price and marginal cost, is a function not only of market share or HHI, but also of market demand elasticity, rival firm supply elasticity, market share of competitive firms, firms' reactions to one anothers' changes in price or output (conjectural variation), and differences in cost and risk across firms (Clarke and Davies, 1982; Landes and Posner, 1981; Van Herck, 1982).

One such model for a group of dominant firms surrounded by a group of firms responding as pure price takers is shown in equation (23.2):

$$\frac{P - MC}{P} = \frac{HHI\,(1 + k)}{E_m + E_r S_r} \qquad (23.2)$$

where P is price, MC is marginal cost, HHI is for the dominant firms, k is conjectural variation, E_m is (the absolute value of) market price elasticity, E_r is fringe firms' supply elasticity, and S_r is fringe firms' market supply. Clearly, in this model market power is determined by far more than simply HHI. HHI may be high, but it can be offset by high demand elasticity or high supply elasticity, or by competitive conjectural variation. Conjectural variation ranges from -1.0 to 1.0. If k is positive it reflects coordinated behavior, or collusion. With a negative k any attempt to raise price and restrict output is offset by an opposite reaction from rivals; that is, competitive behavior. Hence, if k is -1.0, or perfect price taking exists, market power, or the markup over price is zero.

A numerical example will help clarify the limited role of *HHI* in determining market power in this dominant firm model. Consider the case of high *HHI* in an industry with competitive behavior, elastic demand, and unitary supply elasticity by a competitive fringe. Assume *HHI* is enormous, 8,100 (0.81), k is -0.5, or competitive, E_m is 2.0, E_r is 1.0, and S_r is .05. In this case the price-cost margin is approximately 20 percent. Given that the average manufacturing industry price-cost margin in the United States (measured by value added less payroll and advertising expenditures in the 1970s) was approximately 26 percent, it is clear that high *HHI* per se is not sufficient for market power.

To this point barriers to entry have not been mentioned. The reason is that the preceding models assume a total absence of entry. They also assume that a unique market exists, perfectly separate from all other markets, goods are perfectly homogeneous, firms face no risk, and technology remains constant. Few if any industries approximate these stringent assumptions. But even under these highly restrictive models which postulate market imperfections in their basic assumptions, market structure alone is seen to be unable to predict price-cost margins. A number of other factors must be taken into account. The guidelines give considerable emphasis to these additional factors that can modify the implications of concentration measurements. These are considered next.

MARKET DEFINITION   The emphasis of the guidelines is to define markets in terms of the underlying concern about market power. The purpose of market definition is to identify all the firms that would have to cooperate in order to raise prices above the competitive level on a sustained basis. The 1982 guidelines suggest that it may be useful to hypothesize a price increase of perhaps 5 percent and then consider whether customers would shift to a different supplier or different product within a year. After the market is defined, standards are used to analyze the effects of the merger. Different standards are used for horizontal mergers versus all other types of mergers.

HORIZONTAL MERGERS   Three levels of concentration are defined:

1 Postmerger *HHI* below 1,000. Market is unconcentrated.
2 Postmerger *HHI* between 1,000 and 1,800. Market is moderately concentrated.
3 Postmerger *HHI* above 1,800. Market is highly concentrated.

When the postmerger *HHI* is below 1,000, it is unlikely to be challenged. When the resulting *HHI* is between 1,000 and 1,800, a challenge is still unlikely if the merger increased the index by less than 100 points. If the resulting *HHI* is over 1,800 and it increased by less than 50 points, a challenge is still unlikely; if the increase in the *HHI* was between 50 and 100, the probability of challenge is increased; with an increase of more than 100 points in the *HHI*, challenge is likely.

But the 1982 guidelines did not stop with measures of concentration. The guidelines state that inferences drawn from the concentration numbers may be adjusted to take account of other factors that influence whether firms may be able to elevate price and restrict output.

OTHER MARKET CHARACTERISTICS   Most important is whether entry is easy or difficult. If output can be increased by expansion of noncooperating firms already in the market or if new firms can construct new facilities or convert existing ones, an effort by some firms to increase price would not be profitable. The expansion of supply would drive prices down. Conditions of entry or other supply expansion potentials determine whether firms can successfully collude regardless of market structure numbers.

Next considered is the ease and profitability of collusion because there is less likelihood that firms will attempt to coordinate price increases if collusion is difficult or impossible. Here the factors to consider are: product differences (heterogeneity), frequent quality changes, frequent new products, technological changes, contracts that involve complicated terms in addition to price, cost differences among suppliers, and so on. Also, DOJ challenges are more likely when firms in an industry have colluded in the past or use practices such as exchange of price or output information or require delivered pricing.

There is consistency between the additional factors the guidelines consider and the economic model reflected in equation (23.2) discussed earlier. Equation (23.2) states that the ability to elevate price above marginal cost does not depend on market structure (the *HHI*) alone. The additional factors are conjectural variation (how competitors react to one another), market demand conditions (the availability of products that are relatively close substitutes to buyers), the portion of the market occupied by the smaller firms, and their ability to increase supply if prices are increased by the dominant firms. The guidelines include these variables suggested by formal economic models and encompass a number of other important real world circumstances as well. The guidelines thus bring increased realism by considering how markets actually operate instead of assuming that all market behavior and performance can be predicted by the degree of concentration in arbitrarily-defined markets.

NONHORIZONTAL MERGERS   The guidelines also include consideration of nonhorizontal mergers. Nonhorizontal mergers would include vertical and conglomerate mergers. Much of the discussion of horizontal mergers is applicable to nonhorizontal mergers. These include market definition, measurement of market concentration, the role of ease of entry, and all the other factors discussed previously. The guidelines express the view that while nonhorizontal mergers are less likely than horizontal mergers to create competitive problems, that "they are not invariably innocuous."

The principal theories under which nonhorizontal mergers are likely to be challenged are then set forth. Concern is expressed over the elimination of potential entrants by nonhorizontal mergers. The degree of concern is greatly influenced by whether conditions of entry generally are easy or difficult. If entry is easy, effects on potential entrants are likely to be small. If entry is difficult, the Department of Justice (DOJ) will examine the merger more closely. The DOJ is more likely to challenge a merger if the number of firms similar in circumstances to a firm that entered a new market by acquisition is less than three. The DOJ will also scrutinize the market share of the acquired firm. No challenge is likely if the market share of the acquired firm is less than 5 percent. The probability of challenge is high if its market share exceeds 20 percent. Toehold entry (market share of acquired firm is less than 5 percent) by either large or small firms will be viewed favorably.

Generally, the effects of a nonhorizontal merger on barriers to entry will be given great weight. The need for two-level entry is considered. If there is sufficient unintegrated capacity in the secondary market to use the products of two plants (firms) of minimum efficient scale in the primary market, the DOJ is less likely to challenge. Hence if entry to the secondary market is relatively easy, the need for simultaneous entry to that market is unlikely to affect entry to the primary market adversely. Generally, the cost of capital is not regarded as a barrier to entry. However, if capital *assets* used in the secondary market are long-lived and specialized, a substantial acquisition in the secondary market may be of increased concern. Nor are economies of scale an entry barrier generally, representing a form of efficiency. But if the capacity of a minimum efficient scale (MES) plant in the secondary market were greater than the needs of a MES plant in the primary market, the DOJ would be concerned about acquisition of a firm in the secondary market.

The guidelines set forth three circumstances under which vertical mergers may facilitate collusion and therefore be objectionable. (1) If upstream firms obtain a high level of vertical integration into an associated retail market, this may facilitate collusion in the upstream market by monitoring retail prices. (2) The elimination by vertical merger of a disruptive buyer in a downstream market may facilitate collusion in the upstream market. (3) Non-horizontal mergers by monopoly public utilities may be used to evade rate regulation.

In the final section of the guidelines, defenses are considered. Mergers for efficiency will generally be approved. But where a merger would otherwise be challenged, efficiencies are not likely to be a valid defense. The "failing firm defense" is recognized as a long-established basis for permitting a merger. The guidelines spell out the conditions under which the failing firm defense will be an acceptable defense.

Basically, the Department of Justice 1982 and 1984 Merger Guidelines applied the new research findings of over a decade which resulted in the "new learning" of dynamic theories of competition. Although a new measure of concentration, the *HHI*, was adopted, the guidelines also encompass many additional dimensions of the behavior and performance of economic markets. The guidelines are rooted in a strong economic framework and sound economic concepts (Ordover and Willig, 1983).

The practical significance of the 1982 guidelines is suggested by a study which analyzed whether leading cases in the past which had been brought to the courts in the past would have been challenged under the 1982 guidelines (Fox, 1982). The study concluded that the following cases which came to the Supreme Court would not have been challenged:

Brown Shoe	Penn-Olin
Alcoa (Rome)	Pabst
Continental Can	Falstaff
Consolidated Foods	Connecticut National Bank
Von's	General Dynamics
Greater Buffalo	Marine Bancorporation
Ford (Electric Autolite)	Citizens & Southern

Of the six cases the study suggests probably would have been challenged, four involve commercial banks. But financial deregulation has increased competition between financial intermediaries so that the four bank merger cases would be unlikely to be challenged after the 1982 guidelines. This would leave only 10 percent of the 20 leading court cases of yesteryear likely to be challenged under the new guidelines.

The 1984 Merger Guidelines

The 1984 guidelines are in the same spirit as the 1982 statement. In market definition, "the 5 percent test" extends the time for competitors to react to two years and applies the test more flexibly. The role of foreign competitors and international competition is given greater emphasis. In markets in which small firms are not likely to have the capacity or capability of expanding output in response to a price increase, acquisitions are more likely to be challenged. Efficiencies and cost savings are considered at an earlier stage. Instead of being treated as a defense, they may influence whether the merger will be considered to have an economic justification or subject to challenge.

The 1984 guidelines indicate a greater willingness to identify economic submarkets. This would have the effect of increasing concentration measures and the likelihood of challenge. On the other hand, the concept of barriers to entry is approached more flexibly. Instead of searching for absolutes such as whether barriers exist, the approach is to consider the nature of barriers, if any, and to analyze their economic significance. The 1984 guidelines also seek to understand the evolution and development of an industry and to place descriptive materials in a historical and dynamic, rather than static, setting.

Thus the 1984 guidelines did not change the 1982 statement in any fundamental sense. Concepts are clarified. Some different aspects are emphasized. The effort to understand the underlying economic dynamics of markets is continued.

IMPLICATIONS
OF THE NEW DEVELOPMENTS

Are the changes in antitrust policy likely to be long-lasting, or do they reflect the impact of one strong-minded president? Do the changes represent sound economic policies or concessions on behalf of "big business?" Strong differences of opinion have been expressed.

Negative Responses
to the New Antitrust Environment

To some the new antitrust environment represents an abdication by the Federal government of its responsibilities toward antitrust. Some argue that actual policy has been more lax than the guidelines themselves (Kolasky, 1988). Others argue that the antitrust policies since the early 1980s represent recognition of research validating new theories of how economic markets function. Regardless of the arguments and disagreements at the theoretical level, concrete actions have taken place as a consequence of the changed government policies toward merger activity.

PRIVATE ANTITRUST SUITS   The attitudes of business competitors have always had a strong influence on antitrust policy. Earlier writers have pointed out that even when government was responsible for most antitrust actions, the investigations usually followed complaints that had been lodged by competitors against the behavior of other firms who were making life difficult for them in the market place.

But it is also argued that the private law suit has always been a temptation to lawyers. The cost of litigation is so high that the threat of a private law suit can sometimes be used as blackmail to pressure the prospective defendant to make a cash settlement (Grundman, 1987). Some basic statistics on private antitrust cases were developed under the auspices of the Georgetown Law School (Pitofsky, 1987; White, 1988). Most private antitrust cases are Sherman Act cases in which plaintiffs challenge cartel behavior. The average private triple damage case takes about 1.5 years to complete compared with nine months for the average civil case including relatively minor court cases. The median award in private antitrust cases is $154,000, about the same as the median award in civil litigation.

The number of private antitrust cases has declined from a high of about 1,600 per year in the late 1970s to about 1,200 in recent years (Pitofsky, 1987, p. 6). Antitrust private triple damage cases are settled before trial 75 percent of the time. This is comparable to all civil litigation, which is settled 72 percent of the time. Of the cases that go to trial, the plaintiff wins about 33 percent, which is somewhat less than plaintiffs win in other kinds of litigation. During the most recent decade about 30 percent of all private triple damage cases were disposed of on summary judgment (Pitofsky, 1987, p. 6). The trend on summary judgment is in an upward direction. Pitofsky (1987, p. 6) presents the view "that judges have caught on to what is going on." He points out that many of the private cases are frivolous with little chance that a trial would bring out evidence of any serious case. Because judges are dismissing such cases early, the number of private antitrust cases has been declining. Nevertheless, the right to bring a private antitrust case remains. The decline in the number of private antitrust cases by about a third during the past decade is inconsistent with the position that government antitrust enforcement has been lax. If it had been truly lax, private parties would have the opportunity to bring suits and the number of suits would have increased rather than decreased.

STATE ANTITRUST ACTIVITY   Another development said to be stimulated by the changed policies of the federal antitrust agencies has been an increase in state activity. The arguments here are also complex and require careful analysis. In the first place the increased power of the states was granted in the Hart-Scott-Rodino Act of 1976 described earlier in this chapter. This was four years before antitrust policies by the federal agencies began to change in 1980. In addition, the federal government gave $10 million to the states to increase their antitrust enforcement efforts under HSR. The Department of Justice reported that during the grant period the number of state actions increased from 206 in 1977 to over 400 in 1979 (Ewing, 1987). Again all of this increase in activity was before the change in policies by the federal antitrust agencies after 1980.

The activity of the states has been increasing. The State Attorneys General have formed a National Association of Attorneys General (NAAG). The National Association of Attorneys General has published both merger and vertical restraint guidelines. In addition, they are developing a legislative program to change by statute the content of the federal antitrust laws.

While the State Attorneys General have been cooperating, there is potential chaos in having 50 different antitrust laws to which business operations may be subject. While cooperation between the State Attorneys General may mitigate this problem, some risk remains. Whenever jobs are threatened in any locality by either the functioning of active free markets or by merger activity, there is a risk that parochial views will dominate what is best for the national economy (Ewing, 1987, p. 109).

The Positive Case
for the New Federal Antitrust Policies

The new antitrust environment as evidenced by emerging court decisions and by the 1982 and 1984 antitrust guidelines promulgated both by the Department of Justice and the Federal Trade Commission after 1980 reflects a dynamic view of competition, just as the earlier 1968 guidelines reflected the older structural theory. A spirited defense of the new policies has been made by administration representatives. One such statement is found in a report of the 35th annual Spring meeting of the American Bar Association summarizing presentations and discussions with the chairman of the Federal Trade Commission and the head of the Department of Justice Antitrust Division. Daniel Oliver, the chairman of the Federal Trade Commission, expressed the philosophy that cartel or monopoly behavior is not likely to be found unless the government itself supports and sustains it. The forces of competition are too strong for such efforts without government support (Oliver, 1987, p. 242). Chairman Oliver nevertheless argued that the Federal Trade Commission has been very active in challenging mergers. In 1986 he pointed out that the FTC attempted to block six transactions which represented more than in any other year since the Hart-Scott-Rodino program began in 1976. He pointed out that another six transactions were abandoned by the parties after the FTC expressed concern (Oliver, 1987, p. 241).

Chairman Oliver also argued that the policy of the administration not to interfere with markets has succeeded. He argued that it had reduced inflation, reduced interest rates, and created millions of new jobs (Oliver, 1987, p. 241). Chairman Oliver also criticized the NAAG horizontal merger guidelines. He argued they defined markets too narrowly and overemphasized concentration data without sufficient consideration of the impact of entry in the form of expansion or new capacity. He also described at length an example of overregulation on the part of the Attorney General of the state of New York in filing suit against an ice cream company on the basis of exaggerated and highly publicized charges unsupported by facts so that the case had to be dropped in 1985 (Oliver, 1987, p. 246).

A similar presentation was made by Charles F. Rule, then Acting Assistant Attorney General, Antitrust Division. He argued that the new policies had made "antitrust viable and credible as a body of law" (Rule, 1987, p. 262). He argued that the 1982 and 1984 guidelines had provided validation and affirmation of the importance of the antitrust laws and had improved respect for merger analysis. He pointed out that during the period of the Reagan administration, the Department of Justice had brought three times the number of criminal cases and obtained two-and-a-half times the fines as did their predecessors in the Carter administration (Rule, 1987, p. 265). These data had also been summarized in an earlier presentation in the conference. The Department of Justice had brought more than 425 criminal cases under the Sherman Act compared with 165 such cases brought during the Carter administration. Its total fines exceeded $110 million compared with $54 million. Its prosecutions had caused 193 individuals to be sentenced to a total of 26,259 days in jail—an average sentence of 136 days per individual. The average jail sentence during the Carter administration had been 91 days (Crane, 1987, p. 12). The head of the Department of Justice Antitrust Division also refuted the claim that since 1981 no merger with a post-acquisition *HHI* of less than 1,800 had been challenged. He stated that almost 20 percent of the cases that had been brought have involved at least one market that was less than 1,800 (Rule, 1987, p. 267).

Mr. Rule also pointed out that some arguments are misdirected. Divestitures, leveraged buy-outs, and pure conglomerate mergers were not prevented by antitrust policy before 1980 and not likely to be subject to antitrust policy in later years. Both Chairman Oliver and Mr. Rule pointed out that many of the big mergers involved natural resource industries which even today, after much merger activity, remain relatively unconcentrated industries. Thus, even under the structural theory the oil industry and other natural resource industries have not violated its tenets and would not have been subject to challenge under the principles of the structural theory itself. Rule expressed concern that the NAAG guidelines could lead to irresponsible use. He observed, "I hope that, despite the fact that the State Attorneys General are elected, they will not succumb to the pressure of using the guidelines to further purely parochial concerns at the risk of great harm to the national commonweal" (Rule, 1987, p. 275).

These views by the head of the Antitrust Division are supported by the Chairman of the Council of Economic Advisors. In its annual report included in the Economic Report of the President transmitted to the Congress, February 1988, Dr. Beryl Sprinkel argues that the economic policies of the administration have brought a new period of prosperity for the nation. The report observes that during 64 months of expansion, the United States has created 15 million new jobs. The unemployment rate has fallen, particularly for minority groups. It is argued that the United States is not deindustrializing. The share of value added by manufacturers in the gross national product has increased since 1960 (Bock, 1987, p. 4). The ratio of manufacturing output to total GNP is back to near its peak for the post-World War II era. The ratio of manufacturing employment to overall employment has declined, but it is argued that this represents a substantial increase in manufacturing productivity, which increases the competitiveness of the U.S. economy.

CONCLUSIONS

The two approaches to antitrust represent matters of differences in philosophy and judgment. Regardless of which point of view is correct, it is clear that antitrust policy in the United States has been subject to change with changes in political administrations. Future presidents may be less tolerant of merger activity than the Reagan administration. Hence, the forces that have led to some aspects of merger and restructuring activity could be subject to legal attack by another administration. Other activities may not be so affected. It is also argued that in bringing cases the Department of Justice and particularly the Federal Trade Commission have found that the courts are still most receptive to the use of the structural theory, using the older court cases of the 1960s as precedent (Calkins, 1988).

It is unlikely, however, that antitrust policy in the United States will go back to the structuralist approach that dominated policy through most of the three decades from 1950 through the late 1970s. Some of the fundamental economic factors have changed. These include:

1 International competition has clearly increased and many of our important industries are now international in scope. Concentration ratios must take into account international markets and will be much lower than when measured on the assumption of purely domestic markets.

2 The pace of technological change has increased and the pace of industrial change has increased substantially. This requires more frequent adjustments by business firms, including many aspects of restructuring which include acquisitions and divestitures.

3 Deregulation in a number of major industries requires industrial realignment and readjustments. These require greater flexibility in government policy.

4 New institutions particularly among financial intermediaries represent new mechanisms for facilitating the restructuring processes that are likely to continue.

Thus, while different political administrations may reinstitute some of the historical challenges to merger and acquisition activity, the extreme standards of the earlier structural theory are not likely to be applied. However, such a position must be expressed with qualification because the various guidelines issued by the NAAG represent the same type of philosophy as was reflected in the structural theory. Thus, the possibility remains of a return to tough antimerger policies in the future. It was these considerations that stimulated many mergers and acquisitions in 1988.

QUESTIONS

1. List and briefly explain the product characteristics and/or management decision variables that make collusion within an industry more difficult.
2. Compare and contrast the structural theory of industrial organization and the dynamic competition model as they relate to antitrust policy.
3. Do empirical studies support or contradict the structural theory?
4. How does the harassment hypothesis explain returns in mergers which result in antitrust complaints?
5. What other factors are considered along with the Herfindahl-Hirschman Index in the government's decision to initiate an antitrust case?
6. What is aggregate concentration? What are its implications? Has recent merger and acquisition activity had any significant effect on trends in aggregate concentration?
7. Do you see any relationship between merger and acquisition activity and the general increase in speculative and gambling activity in the U.S. during the 1980s? Do the increases in legalized gambling (off-track betting, casinos, state lotteries), stock market volatility, insider trading prosecutions, and so on, have anything to do with each other and do they indicate that the U.S. has become a "casino society" with a corresponding decline in moral fiber and the traditional work ethic? If so, what should be done about it?

REFERENCES

ABBOTT, ALDEN F., "Foreign Competition and Relevant Market Definition Under the Department of Justice's Merger Guidelines," *The Antitrust Bulletin*, 30, Summer 1985, pp. 299–336.

Arrow-Hart and Hegeman Electric Co. v. Federal Trade Commission, (1934), 291 U.S. 587.

BAILEY, ELIZABETH E., DAVID R. GRAHAM, and DANIEL P. KAPLAN, *Deregulating the Airlines*, in Richard Schmaler, ed., *Regulation of Economics Series*, Cambridge, MA: MIT Press, 1987.

Bain, J. S., "Relation of Profit Rate to Industrial Concentration: American Manufacturing 1936–1940," *Quarterly Journal of Economics*, 65, August 1951, pp. 293–324.

Baumol, W. J., "Contestable Markets: An Uprising in the Theory of Industry Structure," *American Economic Review*, March 1982, pp. 1–15.

Berton, Lee, "Laventhol Settles Racketeering Suit, Paying $15 Million," *The Wall Street Journal*, May 9, 1988, p. 23.

Bock, Betty, "Rediscovering Economic Realism in Defining Competition," Conference Board, *Record*, June 1974, pp. 6–12.

———, "Introduction," *Restructuring and Antitrust*, The Conference Board Research Bulletin No. 212, 1987, pp. 3–4.

Briggs, John DeQ., "An Overview of Current Law and Policy Relating to Mergers and Acquisitions," *Antitrust Law Journal*, 56, 1988, pp. 657–674.

———, "Appendix—Mergers and Acquisitions: An Outline of General Principles, Current Enforcement Practices, and Recent Contested Cases," *Antitrust Law Journal*, 56, 1988, pp. 675–737.

Browne, Lynn E., and Eric S. Rosengren, "Should States Restrict Takeovers?" *New England Economic Review*, July/August 1987, pp. 13–21.

Brozen, Yale, "The Antitrust Task Force Deconcentration Recommendation," *The Journal of Law and Economics*, 13, October 1970, pp. 279–292.

———, "Bain's Concentration and Rates of Return Revisited," *The Journal of Law and Economics*, 14, October 1971a, pp. 351–369.

———, "The Persistence of High Rates of Return in High Stable Concentration Industries," *The Journal of Law and Economics*, October 1971b, pp. 501–512.

Calkins, Stephen, "Developments in Merger Litigation: The Government Doesn't Always Win," *Antitrust Law Journal*, 56, 1988, pp. 855–900.

Cargill, Inc. v. *Monfort of Colorado, Inc.*, 167 S. Ct. 484 (1986).

Chalk, Andrew J., "Competition in the Brewing Industry: Does Further Concentration Imply Collusion?" *Managerial and Decision Economics*, 9, March 1988, pp. 49–58.

Clark, Barbara A., "Merger Investigations at the Federal Trade Commission: An Insider's View," *Antitrust Law Journal*, 56, 1988, pp. 765–778.

Clarke, Roger, and Stephen W. Davies, "Market Structure and Price-Cost Margins," *Economica*, 49, August 1982, pp. 277–287.

Cohler, Charles B., "The New Economics and Antitrust Policy," *The Antitrust Bulletin*, 32, Summer 1987, pp. 401–414.

Comanor, William S., and T. A. Wilson, "Advertising, Market Structure and Performance," *Review of Economics and Statistics*, 49, November 1967, pp. 423–440.

Constantine, Lloyd, "Current Trends in State Antitrust Enforcement: Current Antitrust Enforcement Initiatives by State Attorneys General," *Antitrust Law Journal*, 56, April 1987, pp. 111–123.

Council of Economic Advisers, "1988 Annual Report," *Economic Report of the President*, Washington, DC: United States Government Printing Office, 1988.

Crane, Mark, "The Future Direction of Antitrust," *Antitrust Law Journal*, 56, April 1987, pp. 3–19.

———, and Michael L. Denger, "Current Trends in State Antitrust Enforcement: Introductory Remarks," *Antitrust Law Journal*, 56, April 1987, pp. 99–101.

Daskin, Alan J., "Horizontal Merger Guidelines and the Line of Commerce in Banking: An Algebraic and Graphical Approach," *The Antitrust Bulletin*, 30, Fall 1985, pp. 651–676.

Demsetz, Harold, "Industry Structure, Market Rivalry, and Public Policy," *The Journal of Law and Economics*, 16, April 1973a, pp. 1–9.

———, *The Market Concentration Doctrine*, Washington, DC: American Enterprise Institute for Public Policy Research, 1973b.

Eckbo, B. E., "Examining the Anti-Competitive Significance of Large Horizontal Mergers," Ph.D. dissertation, University of Rochester, 1981.

———, and P. Wier, "Antimerger Policy under the Hart-Scott-Rodino Act: A Reexamination of the Market Power Hypothesis," *Journal of Law and Economics*, April 1985, pp. 119–149.

Ellert, J. C., "Antitrust Enforcement and the Behavior of Stock Prices," Ph.D. dissertation, Graduate School of Business, University of Chicago, June 1975, pp. 66–67.

———, "Mergers, Antitrust Law Enforcement and Stockholder Returns," 31, *Journal of Finance*, 1976, pp. 715–732.

Ewing, Ky P., Jr., "Current Trends in State Antitrust Enforcement: Overview of State Antitrust Law," *Antitrust Law Journal*, 56, April 1987, pp. 103–110.

Fisher, Alan A., and Robert H. Lande, "Efficiency Considerations in Merger Enforcement," *California Law Review*, 71, December 1983, pp. 1580–1696.

Fox, Eleanor M., "The New Merger Guidelines—A Blueprint for Microeconomic Analysis," *The Antitrust Bulletin*, 27, Fall 1982, pp. 519–591.

Ginsburg, Douglas H., "Antitrust: Public vs. Private Law," *Restructuring and Antitrust*, The Conference Board Research Bulletin No. 212, 1987, pp. 5–13.

Goldschmid, H. J., H. M. Mann, and J. Fred Weston, eds., *Industrial Concentration: The New Learning*, Boston: Little, Brown and Company, 1974.

Grundman, V. Rock, Jr., "Antitrust: Public vs. Private Law," *Restructuring and Antitrust*, The Conference Board Research Bulletin No. 212, 1987, pp. 5–13.

Herfindahl, O. C., "Concentration in the U.S. Steel Industry," Ph.D. dissertation, Columbia University, 1950.

Hirschman, A. O., *National Power and the Structure of Foreign Trade*, Berkeley: University of California Press, 1945.

Kolasky, William J., Jr., "Current Developments: Merger Enforcement by States and Private Parties," *Antitrust Law Journal*, 56, 1988, pp. 839–854.

Landes, William, and Richard Posner, "Market Power in Antitrust Cases," *Harvard Law Review*, 94, March 1981, pp. 937–996.

Matsushita Electric Industrial Co., Ltd. v. Zenith Radio Corp., 106 S. Cit. 1348 (1986).

McGee, J. S., *In Defense of Industrial Concentration*, New York: Praeger Publishers, 1971.

Miller, Richard A., "The Herfindahl-Hirschman Index as a Market Structure Variable: An Exposition for Antitrust Practitioners," *The Antitrust Bulletin*, 27, Fall 1982, pp. 593–618.

Oliver, Daniel, "Interview with Daniel Oliver," *Antitrust Law Journal*, 56, 1987, pp. 239–257.

———, "Current FTC Merger Policy and Enforcement of the Antitrust Laws as They Relate to Mergers," *Antitrust Law Journal*, 56, 1988, pp. 755–764.

ORDOVER, JANUSZ A., and ROBERT D. WILLIG, "The 1982 Department of Justice Merger Guidelines: An Economic Assessment," *California Law Review*, 71, 1983, pp. 535–574.

ORDOVER, JANUSZ A., ALAN O. SYKES, and ROBERT D. WILLIG, "Herfindahl Concentration, Rivalry, and Mergers," *Harvard Law Review*, 95, August 1982, pp. 1857–1874.

ORNSTEIN, STANLEY I., "Antitrust Policy and Market Forces as Determinants of Industry Structure: Case Histories in Beer and Distilled Spirits," *The Antitrust Bulletin*, 26, Summer 1981, pp. 281–313.

PASZTOR, ANDY, "Wickes Settles Options Charges In FTC Case," *The Wall Street Journal*, March 22, 1988, p. 3.

PITOFSKY, ROBERT, "Antitrust: Public vs. Private Law," *Restructuring and Antitrust*, The Conference Board Research Bulletin No. 212, 1987, pp. 5–13.

Public Law No. 899, U.S. 81st Cong., 2nd sess., December 29, 1950.

REDBURN, TOM, "Justice Department to Crack Down on Antitrust Rules," *Los Angeles Times*, March 23, 1988, Part IV, pp. 1, 7.

ROWE, FREDERICK M., STEPHEN G. BREYER, IRA M. MILLSTEIN, and RICHARD A. POSNER, "Restructuring as a Competition Issue," *Restructuring and Antitrust*, The Conference Board Research Bulletin No. 212, 1987, pp. 14–22.

RULE, CHARLES F., "Interview with Charles F. Rule," *Antitrust Law Journal*, 56, 1987, pp. 261–281.

———, "Merger Enforcement Policy: Protecting the Consumer," *Antitrust Law Journal*, 56, 1988, pp. 739–754.

SPRINKEL, BERYL, "A Tour of the Economic Horizon," The National Economists Club, March 28, 1988.

STILLMAN, R. S., "Examining Antitrust Policy towards Horizontal Mergers," *Journal of Financial Economics*, April 1983, pp. 225–240.

Thatcher Mfg. Co. v. Federal Trade Commission and *Swift & Co. v. Federal Trade Commission* (1926), 272 U.S. 554.

U.S. Department of Justice, "1985 Vertical Restraints Guidelines," *The Journal of Reprints for Antitrust Law and Economics*, 16, 1986, pp. 3–57.

———, "1984 Department of Justice Merger Guidelines," *The Journal of Reprints for Antitrust Law and Economics*, 16, 1986, pp. 61–115.

———, "1982 Department of Justice Merger Guidelines," *The Journal of Reprints for Antitrust Law and Economics*, 16, 1986, pp. 119–165.

———, "1982 Federal Trade Commission Horizontal Merger Guidelines," *The Journal of Reprints for Antitrust Law and Economics*, 16, 1986, pp. 169–185.

———, "1980 Antitrust Guide Concerning Research Joint Ventures," *The Journal of Reprints for Antitrust Law and Economics*, 16, 1986, pp. 189–303.

———, "1977 Antitrust Guide for International Operations," *The Journal of Reprints for Antitrust Law and Economics*, 16, 1986, pp. 307–375.

———, "1977 Guidelines for Sentencing Recommendations in Felony Cases Under the Sherman Act," *The Journal of Reprints for Antitrust Law and Economics*, 16, 1986, pp. 379–397.

———, "1968 Department of Justice Merger Guidelines," May 30, 1968, p. 12.

United States v. Brown Shoe Co., 370 U.S. 294 (1962).

United States v. *G. Heilman,* 345 F. Supp. 117 (1972).

United States v. *General Dynamics Corp.,* 415 U.S. 486 (1974).

United States v. *Jos. Schlitz Brewing Co.,* 385 U.S. 37 (1966).

United States v. *Marine Bancorporation, Inc.,* 418 U.S. 602 (1974).

United States v. *Pabst Brewing Co.,* 384 U.S. 546 (1966).

United States v. *Von's Grocery Co.,* 384 U.S. 270 (1966).

Van Herck, G., "Corporate Monopoly Power and Risk," *European Economic Review,* 17, January 1982, pp. 115–124.

Werden, Gregory J., "Challenges to Horizontal Mergers by Competitors Under Section 7 of the Clayton Act," Department of Justice Economic Policy Office Discussion Paper EPO 85-16, December 6, 1985.

Weston, J. Fred, *The Role of Mergers in the Growth of Large Firms,* Berkeley: University of California Press, 1953.

———, *Concentration and Efficiency: The Other Side of the Monopoly Issue,* Special Issues in the Public Interest No. 4, New York: Hudson Institute, 1978.

———, "Section 7 Enforcement: Implementation of Outmoded Theories," *Antitrust Law Journal,* 49, August 1980, pp. 1411–1450.

———, "International Competition, Industrial Structure and Economic Policy," Chapter 10 in I. Leveson and J. W. Wheeler, eds., *Western Economies in Transition,* Hudson Institute, Boulder, CO: Westview Press, 1980.

———, "Trends in Anti-Trust Policy," *Chase Financial Quarterly,* 1, Spring 1982, pp. 66–87.

———, and Stanley I. Ornstein, *The Impact of the Large Firm on the U.S. Economy,* Lexington, MA: Heath Lexington Books, January 1973.

White, Lawrence J., ed., *Private Antitrust Litigation,* in Richard Schmaler, ed., *Regulation of Economics Series,* Cambridge, MA: MIT Press, 1988.

CHAPTER 24

Case Studies of Restructuring and M&A Activity

In the present chapter we focus on case studies of central aspects of M&A activity. The purpose of a chapter on case studies is to develop detailed factors not easily covered in the broader type of statistical studies which represent the bulk of the literature on M&A activity. Our aim is to illustrate the application of concepts, to test the validity of concepts and theories, and hopefully by the review of the experiences of individual companies to spark additional ideas that will be valuable to managers engaged in M&A activity and to provide a guide to formulating sound public policy.

It is useful, therefore, to summarize major themes that were developed in the preceding chapters. We focus on three areas: (1) theories of M&A activity, (2) strategies, and (3) issues related to creating value in M&A activity.

REVIEW OF THEORIES OF M&A ACTIVITY

We have developed the following framework summarized in Table 24.1 on theories of M&A activity. Inherently there is some overlap in the theories of M&A activity. We provide a brief description of what is involved in each. The concept of differential efficiency includes at least two aspects. One is that a particular firm performs better. A second aspect is that a particular firm has a management system that another firm would like to be able to understand better and to copy. For example, the attempt by the American Stores to buy out Lucky Stores in

TABLE 24.1
Theories of M&A Activity

    I. Efficiency
        A. Differential efficiency
        B. Operating synergy
        C. Diversification
        D. Financial synergy
   II. Undervaluation
 III. Information—Signaling
  IV. Agency Problems
        A. Control device
        B. Managerialism
        C. Winner's curse—hubris
    V. Tax Considerations
  VI. Market Power

the spring of 1988 appeared to reflect the recognition that Lucky had developed a very effective management system for competing in the retail grocery market. Accounts in the financial press suggest also that American Stores recognized that the management capabilities of the team running Lucky Stores was of a high level and would be transferable to many of the operations for future expansion of businesses owned by American.

Operating synergy refers to advantages of scale, scope, and organizational learning. Scale refers to reaching a critical size that provides economies of spreading fixed costs over a large number of units. Economies of scope refers to combining activities such that having one activity makes the other activity more efficient. For example, AT&T sought to enter into the computer business because central station telephone exchange systems represent large specialized computers. A broader capability in computers would help make the production of central station telephone apparatus more effective. At the same time, experience with so many aspects of computers in the exchange apparatus and equipment would give AT&T capabilities for competing in the more general computer market. There were broader aspects of this as well since it was recognized that in the information industries of the future there would be a convergence of a wide range of capabilities including computers, transmission equipment, exchange apparatus, printing, copying, and so on.

Diversification refers to spreading risks to preserve organization values by avoiding bankruptcy. The argument for preventing bankruptcy is that organization values would be lost if a firm ceases to exist.

Financial synergy refers to the efficiencies achieved through an internal capital market in firms. Another aspect is economies of scale in flotation and transactions costs of raising funds. A third is combining cash flows that are not perfectly correlated so that debt capacity is increased.

A second major area of merger theories involves undervaluation. This seems to possibly overlap with other factors. For example, undervaluation may occur because the management of a firm is not operating the company up to its potential. This would be an aspect of the inefficient management theory. Another aspect of the undervaluation theory is the difference between the market value of securities and the replacement costs of assets. The inflation of the 1970s caused the current replacement costs of assets to be substantially higher than their recorded historical book values. In addition, until the summer of 1982, market values of equities were depressed. These factors were captured in the q-ratio which was the ratio of market values of equities to the current replacement costs of assets. During the 1970s q-ratios fell to levels well below one.

The next theory is information signaling. One aspect is that a tender offer conveys information that the target shares are undervalued; the offer causes the market to revalue those shares upward. Another possibility is that the offer stimulates the target firm management to implement a more efficient business strategy which increases value.

Agency problems involve several aspects. One is that takeovers represent a control mechanism to unseat inefficient managements. A second aspect is the managerialism view that managers engage in acquisition activity to build larger firms for the sake of size. This reflects either a Napoleonic complex or that managerial compensation is based on sales rather than profit. A third aspect of the agency problem is the hubris theory. This argues that takeovers occur because of overoptimistic expectations of buyers.

A fifth major theory of mergers is that they are propelled by a tax savings. These have been discussed in detail. General studies indicate that the impact of tax is relatively small, but case studies have the potential for further illuminating the subject.

The sixth major merger theory relates to market power. This view holds that firms acquire other firms in their same line of business in order to dominate their markets. As discussed in Chapter 23, for the market power theory to be plausible it would imply that merger activity would make it easier for firms to collude. But as discussed previously, the conditions for effective collusion are such that the theory requires careful evaluation.

These then are the major aspects of merger theory that potentially may be tested by case studies. We keep this framework in mind as we approach case studies.

M&A ACTIVITY TO IMPLEMENT STRATEGIES

We discuss three major approaches: the Boston Consulting Group, the Porter approach, and the eclectic approach.

The Boston Consulting Group emphasized two major ideas. The learning curve argues that a firm with greater cumulative production experience will have lower costs than its rivals. The Boston Consulting Group also emphasizes having a portfolio of business activities which give balance in terms of cash inflow and cash outflow requirements.

The Porter approach emphasizes selecting industries or areas of business activity where entry is difficult or where the main players do not seek to greatly disturb historical patterns of market shares. The major strategic choices are identified as selecting a narrow industry focus or performing over a wide range of products. Another major strategic choice is an emphasis on low cost for wide distribution versus high quality for a strong market position. A third major emphasis of the Porter approach is obtaining a strong position in control over the important value chain activities of the product. A fourth aspect more recently developed (Porter, 1987) emphasizes relatedness to avoid errors in acquisition activity. However, this concept has been in the strategy literature for many years (Steiner, 1979).

A third major approach to strategy is the eclectic approach. This emphasizes developing a sequence of decision steps. It emphasizes process rather than specific goals or objectives. It sees value in the process of iterated "going around the loop" to stimulate new ideas and to review and refine them. Some basic issues are an emphasis on capabilities versus investments and fixed assets. Another important choice is a focus on technology in relation to consumer needs. An important element of this strategy is the recognition of the advantages of product change, product variety, and product differentiation. Related to the effectiveness of this approach is developing efficient information systems, efficient decision systems, and efficient expert systems.

All the preceding approaches to strategy deal with diversification at least to some degree. One element of the theory is to diversify only into related areas, to build a core of capabilities, and to extend them over time. An alternative theory argues that it also makes sense to obtain completely new capabilities through M&A activity and then use these as new core areas for building further growth and related capabilities. Another approach involves investing in areas with favorable growth and profitability opportunities at bargain prices. The question here is, how can this systematically be done in efficient markets?

EMPIRICAL ISSUES

Thus far we have discussed two major areas that may be tested by case studies. One is to test alternative theories of why M&A activity takes place. Another is to test the implementation of strategies related to M&A activity. In this third section we consider some of the major issues that have emerged in empirical studies of M&A activity. There appear to be empirical regularities in gains to targets related to whether a merger (20 percent gain) or tender offer (35 percent gain) is involved. But later studies suggest that other factors may have greater explanatory value. One is whether cash (higher returns to targets) or securities are used as the method of payment. Another set of issues relates to how managers should react to takeover offers. Does resistance by managers increase or decrease values? What is the proper form or pattern of resistance by managers and shareholders? Should multiple bids be stimulated? And from whom and in what forms? Another set of issues relates to whether the successive stages of M&A activity are anticipated by various participants in M&A activity. The degree of anticipation of activities both by bidders and targets may influence empirical results.

THE FOCUS OF CASE STUDIES

A wide range of issues related to theories of mergers, alternative approaches to strategies, factors influencing the empirical data on M&A activity may potentially be tested by individual case studies. Ideally case studies would throw light on these major issues and, in addition, illustrate important concepts or generalizations that might be developed from the vast literature on M&A activity.

Unfortunately, case studies are generally written with a particular interest or point of view. They tend to be descriptive and narrative in nature. They appear to be in the form, "This is how we did it and this is why we succeeded." The existing case studies do not appear to be focused on meeting our needs and objectives of illuminating merger theories, alternative approaches to strategy, or major factors affecting empirical results.

To achieve our underlying goals would require original case studies of our own. This is a project that would involve years and possibly decades. Therefore, for the purposes of the present book we limit ourselves to the existing case materials. We summarize much of the useful case study literature available in published form. In addition, we draw on stories of M&A activity in the financial press to the extent that useful insight material is provided. Finally, in some instances we draw on our personal experiences to attempt to illuminate through case studies some of the broader issues that we have outlined.

RUBACK CASE STUDIES

Richard Ruback (1982, 1983) builds on empirical event studies of takeover activity, but focuses on individual cases rather than averaging across many events. Thus, he can examine in detail the abnormal returns of all takeover participants in response to a series of announcement dates preceding the final outcome. He uses this technique to verify the consistency of stock price reactions with the results of the empirical studies, to provide evidence of their predictive ability, and to test alternative theories. His approach also permits examination of more complex takeover scenarios (including multiple bidders, buybacks, and standstill agreements) which are often eliminated from the samples of event studies to avoid confusion.

Conoco

Ruback (1982) chronicled Du Pont's successful pursuit of Conoco in a multibidder takeover battle in 1981. Throughout the takeover process, Du Pont's returns were consistently negative. However, there were two other competing bidders: Seagram, who initiated the contest, and Mobil who entered about midway through the bidding war.

Seagram's initial bids (June 19, 1981, starting at $70 per share for a 25 percent interest) produced significant positive abnormal returns for both firms, suggesting that the market viewed the combination as value increasing, in spite of Conoco's opposition. Conoco's search for other bidders brought Du Pont into the contest; on July 6, 1981, Conoco and Du Pont announced an agreement in which Du Pont would buy 40 percent of Conoco for cash ($87.50 per share), trading Du Pont shares for the remainder. The agreement included a nine-month option giving Du Pont the right to buy 15.9 million Conoco shares at $87.50, simultaneously increasing the probability that the merger would succeed while providing a hedge against its failure. Even so, the market responded with significant negative abnormal returns for Du Pont (−8.05 percent). Seagram stock also suffered at the announcement, confirming the earlier positive market response; the agreement between Du Pont and Conoco meant that a good investment opportunity for Seagram had probably been lost, or would at the least become more expensive. A bidding war between Seagram and Du Pont followed, and on July 17, 1981, Mobil entered the battle with a $90 per share offer for 50 percent of Conoco (with $90 of Mobil securities for the remainder). However, Mobil's offer was met with no more enthusiasm than Du Pont's. Throughout the rest of July and into August, all three bidders continued to revise their offers. The Department of Justice entered the scene, approving a Du Pont-Conoco merger (pending the elimination of a joint venture between Conoco and Monsanto), but requesting more information from Mobil, thus delaying a Mobil purchase and raising the possibility of antitrust problems.

The contest ended on August 5, 1981 with Du Pont's announcement that it had received tenders for 55 percent of Conoco stock. (The final offer stood at $98 per share for 48 percent with 1.7 Du Pont shares for each remaining share.) A summary of the market's responses to that final announcement, and over the entire period, with Ruback's interpretations follows.

CONOCO   The final announcement caused a small negative reaction, indicating that the market may have been hoping for even higher bids. Overall, Conoco earned significant positive abnormal returns (71 percent from June 17 through August 5, 1981, for an increase in equity value of $3.2 billion); the result is consistent with the broader empirical studies of target returns, although larger than average because of the competing bidders.

DU PONT   The final announcement produced a small positive reaction; in light of earlier negative responses, the end of the battle at least meant that Du Pont would not be making further bids that were even more unprofitable. For the entire period, Du Pont had negative abnormal returns (-9.9 percent, for a loss in equity value of $789 million). The empirical evidence on the returns to bidding firms is less clear, but negative returns are consistent with some studies, notably Dodd's.

MOBIL   Mobil responded positively to the end of the contest. Consistent with negative responses to its earlier bids, the failure was good news. For the entire period, Mobil had significant abnormal losses of -3.05 percent (or $400 million). These losses are too big to be explained by transactions costs alone. This contest may have raised the possibility of antitrust problems in future takeover attempts.

SEAGRAM   Seagram stock responded negatively to the final announcement, consistent with initial positive reactions. The end of the contest indicated Seagram had irrevocably lost a profitable investment opportunity. However, over the entire period, Seagram realized a market adjusted positive, but small, return of 1.13 percent.

Finally, Ruback (1982) attempts to explain the significant revaluation of Conoco, and why Du Pont pursued so vigorously what the market perceived to be a negative net present value investment.

SYNERGY (VERTICAL INTEGRATION, ECONOMIES OF SCALE, MONOPOLIZATION OF PRODUCT MARKETS)   The raw materials produced by Conoco and used by Du Pont are sold in competitive markets offering few, if any, gains from vertical integration. Besides, some of the gains from vertical integration would have gone to Du Pont. The market was aware of the vertical integration aspects of the merger, and still responded negatively. And furthermore, Du Pont could have acquired any oil company if vertical integration were the goal, so why the aggressive pursuit of Conoco, especially when its price continued escalating? Economies of scale were not a major factor, since no explicit combination of assets was contemplated, and the two firms were in different industries. Economies in generic management areas would not have been sufficient to explain the magnitude of the premiums. Monopolization of product markets is also rejected as an explanation, since there were no antitrust objections from the Department of Justice.

MANAGERIALISM (MANAGERIAL DEPARTURE FROM SHAREHOLDER WEALTH MAXIMIZATION)   Conoco did not have a reputation as being badly managed, nor were Conoco's managers replaced after the merger. If it were Du Pont's managers who were departing from wealth maximization, they should have benefited at their shareholders' expense. But on the contrary, Du Pont's managers at best stayed even throughout the transaction, and may even have lost money.

NEW INFORMATION   Some appraisals of Conoco had gone as high as $160 per share, indicating that Du Pont got a real bargain. But other natural resource companies were equally undervalued, so why pursue Conoco so vigorously? Besides, if the natural resources were the goal, *control* would not have been necessary; an investment position could have been obtained without paying such a high premium. Also, the market was aware of the $160 appraisal, and continued to value Conoco at less than Du Pont offered (that is, the investment was a negative net present value investment for Du Pont).

INSIDE INFORMATION   Ruback concludes (somewhat unsatisfactorily) that Du Pont must have had access to inside information not available to the market which led it to value Conoco more highly than the market. Such information must not have been specific to Du Pont (that is, any bidder could have exploited the information), thus it could not be released publicly by either Du Pont or Conoco without increasing still further the cost of the acquisition. To support this hypothesis, Ruback (1982) notes that Conoco allowed Du Pont access to inside information. And further, on the day Du Pont shareholders voted to approve the merger (August 18), Du Pont had significant positive abnormal returns, indicating that Du Pont management may have released enough information to cause the market partially to reevaluate the wisdom of the merger.

Cities Service

In another case study, Ruback (1983) calculated the abnormal returns to participants in the Cities Service takeover of 1982. The contest began on May 28, 1982 with several weeks of offers and counteroffers between Cities Service and Mesa Petroleum bidding for each other. Mesa initially offered a friendly merger at $50 per share for half of Cities Service stock with Mesa securities for the remainder. Cities Service closing stock price was $35.50, so the bid represented a 41 percent premium. Cities Service's counter bid of $17 for 51 percent of Mesa represented only a 1.5 percent premium and was taken to have little chance of success. A second, hostile offer by Mesa at $45 per share for only 15 percent of Cities Service stock indicated Mesa's inability or reluctance to obtain financing for a larger offer. Cities Service countered with a friendly bid of $21 per share for 51 percent of Mesa with Cities Service stock worth $16.31 for each remaining share, and recountered with a hostile bid at $21 for 51 percent.

Gulf's bid for Cities Service on June 17, 1982 ($63 per share for 51 percent plus $63 in fixed income securities for the remainder) effectively put Mesa out of the picture. Gulf's bid was followed by a premium buyback and standstill agreement in which Cities Service repurchased its stock from Mesa and Mesa agreed not to attempt a hostile takeover for five years. Contrary to empirical studies, Cities Service shareholders had no abnormal returns in response to the repurchase (the studies would have predicted negative returns), while Mesa shareholders suffered significant negative abnormal returns of −15.83 percent. This may be due to the fact that while the agreement put an end to Mesa's pursuit of Cities Service, it also ended Cities Service's pursuit of Mesa.

However, a temporary restraining order from the Federal Trade Commission in turn put an end to Gulf's attempt. Cities Service began to actively solicit other takeover bids, and even considered liquidation, when Occidental Petroleum entered the fray with a friendly offer (at $50 per share for 50 percent plus preferred stock and zero-coupon notes for the remainder), followed by revised bids: a hostile offer for 49 percent of Cities Service at $50 per share, and another friendly offer with a $52 per share cash component. Meanwhile, it was becoming evident that no other bidders would materialize. Mobil decided not to bid after being allowed to examine confidential information, and Amerada Hess was supposedly considering an offer, but none was forthcoming. On August 28, 1982, Cities Service accepted a revised Occidental bid ($55 per share for 45 percent with preferred stock and zero-coupon notes for the remainder), and the contest ended.

Cities Service enjoyed significant positive abnormal returns of 12.5 percent, or $352 million over the entire period, consistent with the results of empirical event studies. Occidental Petroleum, the eventual successful bidder had zero abnormal returns, also consistent with several empirical studies. The market appeared to judge the acquisition as a zero net present value investment. Gulf Oil experienced significant negative abnormal returns of 17.6 percent, representing a loss of $1.1 billion. Most of these losses occurred on the day Gulf announced its bid for Cities Service; the offer's cancellation offset some of the initial loss, but not all of it, probably because of a $3 billion lawsuit brought by Cities Service for breach of contract, alleging that Gulf had not tried to resolve the FTC objections. The abnormal returns to Mesa Petroleum are more difficult to interpret, since Mesa was both a target and an unsuccessful bidder in the contest. Overall, Mesa had a 5.9 percent loss, which is puzzling, particularly since they had a gain of $80 million in the premium buyback, but the loss appeared not to be directly related to the Cities Service takeover episode.

CASE STUDIES OF INDIVIDUAL FIRMS

Case studies of individual firms abound in the financial press. If one reads the financial newspapers and magazines, one is served repeated sagas of highly dramatic and often innovative stories. Some of these we have included in this section. Other individual case studies are summarized from other published sources. (See Rock, 1987.)

IC Industries

IC Industries originated as the Illinois Central Railroad, chartered in 1851. Its main line was from Chicago to New Orleans, with about 6,500 route miles in 12 states. A decision to diversify was made in the early 1960s. The goal was to enter businesses that would be less capital intensive, less labor intensive, less cyclical, less government regulated, and with better growth potentials. Because federal law prohibits railroads from owning unrelated businesses, a holding company was organized in 1962 and adopted the name IC Industries, Inc. in 1975.

In 1966 IC Industries developed its first strategic plan. It had four objectives:

1 Modernize the railroad.
2 Merge with another railroad to make IC more efficient and to enable it to expand its service in the growing industrial areas of the South.
3 Develop the company's large real estate holdings.
4 Diversification.

The Illinois Central merged with the Gulf, Mobile and Ohio Railroad reaching agreement in 1966 and obtaining final approval by the Interstate Commerce Commission and the courts in 1972. In 1965 a small builder of heavy electrical equipment was acquired and in 1968 a small manufacturer of precision castings and corrosion-resistant pumps and pumping systems was acquired. In 1968 IC Industries acquired ABEX Corp., a $275 million manufacturer of automotive products, specialty castings, hydraulic equipment, and rail products. The acquisition of ABEX doubled the size of IC Industries.

These three acquisitions were mostly in cyclical markets. To seek stability of earnings, in 1970 IC Industries acquired Pepsi-Cola General Bottlers which had a six-state distribution franchise and sales of $100 million. With this as a base, Dad's Root Beer was acquired in 1971, Bubble-Up Company in 1973, and other Pepsi franchise operations during the 1970s and 1980s.

With further diversification as its goal, in 1972 Midas International, a Chicago-based franchiser of automotive service shops, was acquired (sales of $100 million). In 1982 the cyclical recreational vehicle manufacturing operations of Midas were divested. IC began building a financial services group in the early 1970s which made acquisitions of small financial and life insurance companies. Subsequent developments in the financial services industries indicated that a very large company was required and that competition would be very strong. By 1979 IC divested all its financial service companies.

The second stage of IC's strategic program was to develop further in consumer products and to sell the railroad. In 1978 IC approached Pet, Inc., a nearly $1 billion company which marketed packaged foods and produced food store equipment under the Hussmann name. Pet management initially resisted, but finally agreed to be acquired in a cash tender offer that cost IC $406 million. Between 1978 and 1984 Pet divested 14 businesses that were viewed as "low potential" and made acquisitions of companies in baking and specialty goods and in specialty packaged foods. Eighty percent of Pet's remaining key product lines hold the number one or number two position in their markets.

Stage three of IC's strategic plan was announced in 1981. It was focused on technology and market penetration. In 1982 William A. Underwood, a maker of meat spreads and baked beans was acquired. This was an example of market penetration. Underwood also brought a strong foothold in foreign markets to be used by other food product operations in IC. In October 1984 IC acquired Pneumo Corp. This was a $1.3 billion company producing aircraft landing gear and sophisticated flight control systems.

The main goals of IC Industries were said to have been reached with these acquisitions. IC saw itself as strong in three basic areas: specialty foods (Pet), consumer services (Midas), and commercial products (Pneumo). IC Industries felt that it had achieved growth with stability. Subsequently, in August 1988 Pneumo-ABEX was sold to the Henley Group and Wasserstein, Perella. The railroad was spun off. The remaining parts of IC Industries consisted of consumer products. To emphasize this, the name was changed to Whitman Corporation in December 1988.

A review of the stock price performance of IC Industries indicates that it has indeed achieved success in its diversification program. However, some basic questions need to be raised. IC Industries appears to have violated a number of the key principles of strategy emphasized both by the Boston Consulting Group and the Porter approach. IC emphasized growth and stability. Their acquisitions did not appear to make them leaders in terms of production volume or experience or in achieving a balance of cash inflow and cash outflow activities. Furthermore, they seem to have violated the Porter emphasis on going into industries where entry barriers were high. Certainly the emphasis on diversification from a core into related activities was violated. IC Industries had virtually no experience in the three new major areas into which they moved. They did, however, appear to expand from a base into specialty foods in which they had established their initial position through the acquisition of Pet, a leader in many individual product lines.

In conclusion, IC Industries appears to have violated all of the rules but to have succeeded. This case study suggests that while the general principles would appear to be good guides most of the time, they can be violated and yet achieve a successful diversification and M&A program.

ARA Services

ARA Services started with vending food products in 1936. Their initial product line was relatively narrow (peanuts). From very small beginnings, mergers and acquisitions played an important role in developing ARA Services into a company that by its 1984 fiscal year had revenues of $3.4 billion. In the process they completed more than 300 acquisitions.

ARA Services started with food service from vending machines. This led to a broader range of food and refreshment services for people on the job. These services were extended to students at schools and colleges, hospital patients and staff, senior citizens at community centers, air travelers, and then people engaged in leisure pursuits at parks, stadiums, resorts, and high-level restaurants. It was recognized that food services involved warehousing, inventory control, packing for shipment, distribution (routing trucks), fleet maintenance, and tight accounting and financial controls. With these basic functions, it was a natural

THE FINANCIAL SERVICES INDUSTRY

One of the industrial areas in which the greatest amount of merger and restructuring activity has taken place has been in the area of financial services. Many of the large dollar amounts of merger activity have involved banks and other types of financial institutions. The data show that for the years 1982–1986 the area of banking and finance accounted for 13 percent of merger activity by numbers and 11 percent by dollar amounts and ranked first among industries in M&A activity (W. T. Grimm, *Mergerstat Review*, 1986). We examine the causes and effects of this high level of activity.

Causes of Changes
in the Financial Services Industries

The major forces making for change have been fundamental transformations in the economic environment. Of greatest importance has been increased instability in the economic environment. This has taken the form of fluctuating rates of changes in domestic price levels (inflation). In addition, there has been increased volatility in the relative values of national currencies (foreign exchange rates). Furthermore, the prices (interest rates) and availability of funds have fluctuated to an increased degree.

Financial institutions have been resourceful in creating different kinds of products in a wide range of forms to provide protection against unforeseen developments and benefits under different future states of the world.

The increased pace of technology has caused industries to differ in their relative rates of growth and decline. Great transformations have taken place in industries such as oil, agriculture, real estate, and in commodity prices. Another area where technological change has had a great impact is in transportation and communication. Hence, local and regional markets have become swept up by national and international influences. Major financial markets are worldwide, national, regional, and local.

Another important force has been increased competition in financial services. More products have been created and more firms have entered into financial services. Some of these trends have existed for long periods of time. Their influence has been accelerated by developments described earlier. For example, it is customary for business firms to sell goods to other firms on credit varying from a few days to longer than a year. Trade credit payable is usually the highest percentage of current liabilities on the balance sheet of business firms. In addition, for many years business firms have offered a wide variety of other financial services. This has been particularly true for durable goods. Either the firm itself has extended credit on durable goods or it has established a financial subsidiary to perform these functions.

The Regulatory Environment

It was impossible for the regulatory environment to ignore these fundamental forces of change that affected the financial services industry. Deregulation has taken place in many forms. There is less control over prices that may be charged for financial services or paid for various forms of deposits. In addition, there has been less control over the kinds of products that may be offered by various types of financial institutions. Again, this was in recognition of innovation in formulating products to perform services and functions that nominally were not permitted by the technicalities of the law.

With the wider range of financial services that may be performed by different types of institutions, the distinctions between financial institutions have become increasingly blurred. A succession of legislation has permitted savings and loan institutions to perform almost all the functions performed by commercial banks and to become department stores of finance themselves.

With the advances in both communications and transportation, individual countries in the world have been shrinking in practical consequences. As a result, limits on the size of geographic areas in which financial institutions could operate have become highly artificial. Laws and regulatory policy have been relaxing these restrictions. The Federal Deposit Insurance Corporation (FDIC) helped this development when it permitted Yankee Oil & Gas Co. to acquire Home Savings Bank which was in financial difficulty. Shortly thereafter a major steel company was permitted to purchase several savings and loan associations. The next development was to permit an out-of-state commercial bank to buy savings and loan associations in financial difficulties. Citicorp has been developing the ground work for a nationwide branch system by purchasing problem savings and loan associations in Florida and California. In this connection the Federal Home Loan Bank Board developed the policy of permitting an out-of-state institution with ownership of a savings and loan association in a state as a result of a rescue acquisition to expand by buying other healthy savings and loan associations as though it were an in-state institution.

Another development representing a move toward interstate banking has been the permission of "stake-out" investments. In 1983 an Oregon bank holding company, U.S. Bancorp, purchased 4.9 percent of the voting shares of Old National Bankcorporation in the state of Washington. The Federal Reserve Board approved the investment and its purpose that the two banks would merge in the event that interstate banking became permitted. Cross-state transactions on a regional basis were also supported by a 1985 U.S. Supreme Court decision that supported the concept of regional banking. The court decision approved reciprocal arrangements that allowed a bank in one state to acquire a bank in another state if the laws of the two states permit acquisitions by out-of-state institutions. Statutes granting such reciprocity have been growing in states throughout the country.

What are the consequences of these economic and technological developments and their impact upon the regulatory environment? A wide array of reactions have been taking place among both financial and nonfinancial institutions. Among the developments has been an increased pace of merger and acquisition activity. The purposes of the mergers represent a range of reasons. They include: (1) to expand geographically more quickly than by attempting to begin de novo in new geographic areas, (2) to acquire new organizations with specialist capabilities that are required, (3) to achieve economies of scale, and (4) to shore up weaknesses or to rescue targets with weaknesses. Literally hundreds of examples could be given of these and other developments that have been taking place in the field of financial services. We see some strong trends developing. As a result the future of the financial services industry will look something like the following.

In commercial banking one group will be represented by global banks such as Citicorp that will have activities throughout the world. They will provide a wide range of services. In foreign markets they will often perform services such as merchant banking and make investments in the equities of business firms and engage in other activities that may not be permitted by U.S. laws in the United States.

Another area of activity will be represented by department stores of financial services. Investment banking companies have expanded well beyond their traditional functions. Similarly, bank holding companies have been established which hold commercial banks and a large number of other activities which would be regarded as nonfinancial. Business firms such as Sears Roebuck have expanded into insurance, into financial activities ranging from insurance to real estate finance, and into brokerage services. Sears moved into real estate and financial services with the acquisition of Coldwell Banker, and, with the acquisition of Dean Witter, into brokerage and related activities.

In addition to global department stores of finance there will be other firms that specialize either by regions or by performing a narrow range of specialty functions. They will exist because by concentrating in a particular region or on particular specialty services they will be highly informed and efficient in the areas in which they concentrate. In addition, they can avoid risk areas such as the heavy lending by the international banks to less developed countries, which have been a drain on their financial resources in recent years.

Finally, there will be financial services companies specialized either by locality or specialist services. These will include small institutions in cities or parts of cities. In addition they will include small institutions that become specialists in the particular functions required by the business firms in a particular region. An example would be financing the operations of individual fishermen for individual types of fish such as salmon or tuna in particular coastal cities.

Conclusions on Developments in the Financial Services Industry

The financial services industry illustrates how changes in the economic environment, technological change, and the globalization of markets cause strains in the traditional patterns of providing their services and functions. This in turn led to strains on the existing regulations imposed by governments. As the laws and regulations were changed, further changes took place in the financial markets affected. The resulting shifts in functions and requirements for efficiency in the various financial markets have given rise to merger and acquisition activity, restructuring, and changes both by external acquisitions and by changes internal to the firms. The financial services industry illustrates how M&A and restructuring activity are in considerable measure a response to changes in the economic, technological, and regulatory environment.

SUMMARY

Ideally, in a chapter on case studies one would like to test the main theories. Hence, the chapter begins with a summary of the theory. These were efficiency (synergy), undervaluation, information signaling, agency problems, tax considerations and market power. Since an important aspect of M&A activity is strategy, we review the main theories of strategy. These are the Boston Consulting Group, the Porter approach, the eclectic approach, and alternative theories of diversification strategy. In addition we summarize some of the findings of the broader statistical studies. In these broader statistical studies we have issues such as the effects on premiums of the use of cash versus stock, target resistance, multiple bids, and the extent to which various stages of bidding activity appear to have been anticipated.

In developing case studies, therefore, we focus on trying to find material that would provide an illustration or demonstration of a key conceptual idea. It turns out, however, that existing case studies seem to be written for their own individual purposes. They describe how we succeeded at the A&B Company or see how clever we were at the YZ Company. To develop case studies ourselves to achieve our goals clearly would be a long-term project and, therefore, not feasible for our present purposes. Therefore, we assembled all of the case studies we could from published books, monographs, and the financial press such as *Fortune* magazine, *Forbes*, *The Wall Street Journal*, and *Business Week* accounts of ongoing merger activities. We tried to distill whatever principles were found in the case study write-up or what we could infer from the write-up, even though the study itself might not have contained the ideas. In doing this we have also kept in mind the goals of our final chapter, which is to lay out guidelines for managers contemplating M&A, restructuring, and corporate control activities. So we limit ourselves essentially to a summary of existing case studies. However, we try to approach the studies analytically to illustrate concepts, test theories, and also lay a foundation for guides to management.

We suspect that the success of widely dissimilar strategies and philosophies and the failure of some approaches when the philosophies and strategies are similar, suggests that there is an element of ability involved. Some firms have better players (executives, managers). In other firms a wise philosophy may not be well executed. But nevertheless, we would argue that the probability of success is increased when firms are operating on the basis of sound principles or guidelines of the kinds described in our concluding chapter.

REFERENCES

Galante, Mary Ann, and Martha Groves, "Analysts Debate What Lucky-Alpha Beta Merger Will Cost Customers," *Los Angeles Times,* May 21, 1988, Part I, pp. 1, 4.

Groves, Martha, "American Stores Clears Hurdle in Merger Effort," *Los Angeles Times,* April 1, 1989, Part IV, pp. 1, 4.

Miller, James P., "American Stores Agrees to Buy Lucky For $65 a Share, or $2.51 Billion Total," *The Wall Street Journal,* May 23, 1988a, p. 3.

———, "Supermarket Buy-Out Trend Is Assessed," *The Wall Street Journal,* May 24, 1988b, p. 6.

Porter, Michael E., "From Competitive Advantage to Corporate Strategy," *Harvard Business Review,* May–June 1987, pp. 43–59.

Rock, Milton L., ed., *The Mergers & Acquisitions Handbook,* New York: McGraw-Hill Book Company, 1987.

Ruback, Richard S., "The Conoco Takeover and Stockholder Returns," *Sloan Management Review,* 23, Winter 1982, pp. 13–33.

———, "The Cities Service Takeover: A Case Study," *Journal of Finance,* 38, May 1983, pp. 319–330.

Steiner, George A., *Strategic Planning,* New York: Free Press, 1979.

Wayne, Leslie, "Rewriting the Rules of Retailing," *The New York Times,* October 15, 1989, Sec. 3, pp. 1, 6.

W. T. Grimm, *Mergerstat Review,* 1986.

CHAPTER 25

Management Guides for M&A Activity

Two basic principles should be recognized in the establishment of a sound merger and acquisition program. First, mergers and acquisitions must be related to a firm's diversification program. Second, both programs must be a part of the firm's general planning process. Planning involves both long-range and short-term activities. A brief review of the planning process is therefore necessary.

DIVERSIFICATION AND MERGERS IN A STRATEGIC LONG-RANGE PLANNING FRAMEWORK

This analysis of diversification and mergers in the framework of the strategic long-range planning processes of firms seeks to provide perspective on a number of issues. Initially, it might be argued that taking the viewpoint of the planning activities of firms is simply to analyze the motives for mergers. This argument would then continue that motives are irrelevant—only the effects of diversification and mergers matter.

Certainly any fruitful study of mergers must be related to testable propositions on their effects. But in the merger area a wide variety of models and tests have been employed. Model development is influenced by initial assumptions. Also, the results of tests are influenced by the choice of variables, how they are measured, and how they are combined in the econometric relationships studied.

633

These selections and interpretations are influenced by the conceptions of the underlying processes involved. For example, one of the approaches to mergers is the managerialism school, which is based on a theory of motivation (Mueller, 1969, 1977). It holds that managers control corporations and that they seek mergers for growth's sake because the size, levels of sales, or total assets determine managerial compensation. Such a theory leads to particular empirical tests. Thus, alternative assumptions of managerial motivations may lead to different models or theories and different tests. The purpose of the present approach, therefore, is to provide a basis for evaluating alternative theories of mergers, their tests, and predictions from both social and enterprise perspectives.

The Managerial Capability Perspective

The literature on long-range strategic planning in purposive organizations has exploded in recent years. (See references on long-range and strategic planning at the end of the chapter.) The summary we present is not intended to be a full treatment of the subject. Rather, it represents our interpretation as oriented to the issues raised by diversification through mergers.

The literature views long-range planning and strategic planning as essentially synonymous (Steiner, 1979). The emphasis of strategic planning is on areas related to the firm's environments and constituencies, not just operating decisions (Summer, 1980). In our view, the modern literature on long-range planning indicates that long-range strategic planning involves at least the following elements:

1 Environmental reassessment
2 A consideration of capabilities, missions, and environmental interaction from the standpoint of the firm and its divisions
3 An emphasis on process rather than particular goals or objectives
4 An emphasis on iteration and on an iterative feedback process as a methodology for dealing with ill-structured problems
5 A recognition of the need for coordination and consistency in the resulting long-range planning processes with respect to individual divisions, product-market activities, and optimization from the standpoint of the firms as a whole
6 A recognition of needs to relate effectively to the firm's changing environment and constituencies
7 Integration of the planning process into a reward and penalty or incentive system, taking a long-range time perspective

Earlier, the emphasis of long-range strategic planning was on doing something about the so-called gap. When it is necessary to take action to close a prospective gap between the firm's objectives and its potential based on its present capabilities, difficult choices must be made. For example, shall the firm attempt to change its environment or capabilities? What will be the costs of such changes? What are the risks and unknowns? What are the rewards if successful? What are the penalties of failure? Because the stakes are large, the iterative process is employed. A tentative decision is made. The process is repeated, perhaps from a different management function orientation and at some point, the total enterprise point of view is brought to bear on the problem. At some point, decisions are made and must involve entrepreneurial judgments.

Alternatively, the emphasis may be on broader orientations to the effective alignment of the firm with its environments and constituencies. Different approaches may be emphasized. One approach seeks to choose products related to the needs or missions of the customer that will provide large markets. A second approach focuses on technological bottlenecks or barriers, the solution of which may create new markets. A third strategy chooses to be at the frontiers of technological capabilities on the theory that attractive product fallout will result from such competence. A fourth approach emphasizes economic criteria including attractive growth prospects and appropriate stability.

Other things being equal, a preferred strategy is to move into a diversification program from the base of existing capabilities or organizational strengths. Guidance may be obtained by answers to the following questions: Is there strength in the general management functions? Can the company provide staff expertise in a wide range of areas? Does the firm's financial planning and control effectiveness have a broad carry-over? Are there specific capabilities such as research, marketing, and manufacturing that the firm is seeking to spread over a wider arena?

The firm should be clear on both its strengths and its limitations. To remedy weaknesses, the firm should clearly define the specific new capabilities it is seeking to obtain. If the firm does not possess a sufficient breadth of capability to use as a basis for moving into other areas, an alternative strategy may be employed. This would be to establish a beachhead of capabilities in one or more selected areas. The firm is then in a position to develop concentrically from each of these nuclei.

To understand the potential carry-over even in mergers that may be termed pure conglomerate mergers, one needs to recognize that the nature of firms and the boundaries of industries have become much more dynamic and flexible in recent years. The emphasis of traditional economic theory, as reflected in the Census Bureau's Standard Industrial Classification, is on industry boundary delineation that is mainly product or process oriented. However, organization theory and the behavior of individual firms reflect an emphasis increasingly on missions and capabilities.

In a world of continuous change, managements must relate to *mission*, defined in terms of customer needs, wants, or problems to be solved. In addition to missions, another important dimension of the concept of industries is a range of capabilities. This includes technologies, embracing all processes from basic research, product design and development, and applications engineering through interrelated manufacturing methods and obtaining feedback from consumers.[1]

---

[1] Changing product requirements and changing product-market opportunities require new technologies and new combinations of technologies. To illustrate, the aircraft industry moved through stages in which the critical competence shifted from structures, to engine and other propulsion methods, to

The capabilities concept encompasses important management technologies including planning, information sciences, computerization of information flows, formal decision models, problem-solving methodologies, and behavioral sciences. Thus, managerial capabilities include competence in the general management functions of planning, organizing, directing, and controlling, as well as in the specific management functions of research, production, personnel, marketing, and finance. In addition, they include a range of technological capabilities. Another important dimension is coordinating and achieving an effective organization system.

The development of such a range of capabilities requires substantial investments in the training and experience of people. This includes investments required to hold organizations together during periods of depressed sales. Market demand and supply forces place a high value on executive talent and staff expertise. Their importance in the competitive performance of firms leads to new forms of fixed investment in managerial organizations. The effective utilization of augmented fixed factors leads to firms of larger size and increased diversification. (Fixed factors are investments in plant and equipment or costs of specialist executives.)

The theory of the firm set forth by Coase (1937) predicts these developments. In explaining the role of firms in relation to markets, Coase identified two functions as determinants of the scope and size of firms. One was the relative efficiency of effecting transactions within the firm compared to transactions conducted in the external market place. The other was the effectiveness with which the elements of the firm were coordinated or managed. Coase described possible developments that would affect the size of firms compared to the relative scope of market transactions. Coase's model predicts that the broadening of capabilities encompassed by a firm and developments in managerial technology will result in both an increase in the absolute size of business firms and in the degree of their diversification with respect to capabilities, missions, and markets.

Potential competition has thus been enlarged. Industry boundaries defined by products become less meaningful than industries defined by the ability to perform the critical functions for meeting customers' needs or missions. The ease of entry is increased because the critical factor for success in changing environments may be a range of technologies, experience developed in international markets, or even more general organizational performance capabilities.

---

guidance, and finally to the interaction of structures, propulsion, and guidance as reflected in the concept of aerospace systems. Similarly, in office equipment, products have moved from manual operation to electromechanical, to electric, to electronic, and to the interactions of specialized units in systems. Electronics technology has moved from electron tube to semiconductors to integrated circuitry, involving a fusion with chemistry and metallurgy.

In the consumer nondurable-goods industries, product changes have characteristically been labeled product differentiation, with the unfavorable connotation that fundamental characteristics of products have not altered. Yet even in these industries, fluctuations in consumer income patterns and tastes have created needs and opportunities for basic changes. For example, the need to understand the nature of the impact of foods on people has increased the requirements for competence in the chemical and biological sciences in food industries.

These various approaches are likely to be oriented to business goals and objectives. General goals may be formulated with respect to size, growth, stability, flexibility, and technological breadth. Size objectives are established in order to use effectively the fixed factors the firm owns or buys. Size objectives have also been expressed in terms of critical mass. Critical mass refers to the size a firm must achieve in order to attain cost levels that will enable the firm to operate profitably at market prices.

Growth objectives may be expressed in terms of sales, total assets, earnings per share, or the market price of the firm's stock. These are related to two valuation objectives. One is to attain a favorable price/earnings multiple for the firm's shares. A second is to increase the ratio of the market value of a firm's common stock to its book value.

Two major forms of instability can be distinguished. The first is exemplified by the defense market, which is subject to large, erratic fluctuations in its total size and abrupt shifts in individual programs. Another form of instability is the cyclical instability that characterizes producers of both industrial and consumer durable goods.

The goal of flexibility refers to the firm's ability to operate in a wide variety of product markets. Such flexibility may require a breadth of research, manufacturing, or marketing capabilities. Of increased interest in recent years is technological breadth. With the increased pace of technological change in the U.S. economy, a firm may consider it important to possess capabilities in the rapidly advancing technologies.

Goals may be stated in general or specific terms, but both are subject to quantification. For example, growth objectives may be expressed in relationship to the growth of the economy or the firm's industry. Specific objectives may be expressed in terms of percentage of sales in specified types of markets. The quantification of goals facilitates comparisons of goals with forecasts of the prospects for the firm. If it is necessary for the firm to alter its product-market mix or range of capabilities to reduce or close the planning gap, a diversification strategy may be formulated.

Efforts to achieve multiple goals suggest a broader range of variables in the decision processes of the firm. Decisions involve tradeoffs and judgments of the nature of future environments, the policies of other firms with respect to the dimensions described, and new missions, technologies, and capabilities. In short, to the requirements of operating efficiency and optimal output adjustments has been added the increased importance of the planning processes.

A number of misconceptions are held with respect to the significance of planning in the firm. The misconceptions range between two extremes. One view holds that we have always planned, that planning is nothing new, since the practice antedates biblical times. This view misses the real significance of modern planning, however. Certainly business firms have been planning for decades, with accounting and financial budgeting activities representing one kind of planning. But the important developments that set the new managerial technology of planning apart from its predecessor activities are (1) coordinating research, sales, production, marketing, facilities, personnel, and financial plans, making them consistent with one another, and resolving them into comprehensive planning for the enterprise as a whole; (2) a feedback system; and (3) integration with a reward and penalty (incentive) system. Some U.S. firms developed and practiced such integrated and coordinated planning by the 1920s, but the broad extension of the practice did not occur until after World War II, with substantial gaps still persisting in the understanding and implementation of effective planning among a large number of firms.

The other erroneous view about business planning holds that the heavy investments of capital by large corporations have led them to devise methods for controlling demand and that planning has replaced the market mechanism. Such a view has led one author to sweeping generalizations, unsupported by systematic evidence, such as the following: "It is a feature of all planning that, unlike the market, it incorporates within itself no mechanism by which demand is accommodated to supply and the reverse" (Galbraith, 1967, p. 35).

This represents a basic misconception. Those with experience with purposive organization planning processes recognize that the development of integrated planning is an effort to adapt more responsively to increasingly dynamic environments. Planning and management controls do not remove the uncertainty of market influences; rather, they seek to help the firm adjust more sensitively to change, to new threats and opportunities.

Diversification Planning, Mergers, and the Carry-Over of Managerial Capabilities

From an economic standpoint, does any justification exist for these long-range planning efforts of firms to achieve the regeneration of their organization systems? Particularly, does any justification exist for the use of mergers to seek continuity of firms? We shall not deal with horizontal and vertical expansion by merger activity for practical and theoretical reasons. The practical reasons are that, with the 1950 amendments to Section 7 of the Clayton Act, the ability of government authorities to block horizontal and vertical mergers has become so absolute that mergers are predominantly conglomerate. From a theoretical standpoint, the issues with respect to efficiency and market-position effects of the horizontal and vertical mergers have been well identified. We therefore focus on conglomerate mergers.

Data compiled on conglomerate mergers by the Federal Trade Commission divide them into three groups: (1) product extension, (2) market extension, and (3) others that might be called pure conglomerate mergers. Product-extension and market-extension mergers usually provide opportunities for the carry-over of specific management capabilities such as research, applications engineering, production, marketing, and so on. Pure conglomerate mergers, then, would involve, at least initially, the potential carry-over of only the general manage-ment functions of planning, organizing, directing, controlling, and so on. While finance is a specific management function, its role in the generic functions of planning and control and the broad generality of its applications suggest its treatment as a general management function as well.

One social justification for the continuity of firms whose performance is falling short of their competitors is reducing the expected present value of the costs of bankruptcy. Whether bankruptcy is due to, for example, financial causes, operating or managerial weakness, or inappropriate balance with the environment, one of the potential areas of loss is in organization learning.

In the case of pure conglomerate mergers, it may be presumed that there will be very little carry-over of either firm-specific or industry-specific managerial experience. The carry-over would have to be in the areas of the generic manage-ment functions of planning and control, research, and coordination, as well as in financial planning and control. The initial carry-over is raw managerial experi-ence or capabilities in the more generic management functions. The motivation on the part of the diversifying or acquiring firm is an expectation that it has or will have excess capacity of general managerial capabilities in relation to its existing product-market activities. Furthermore, there is an expectation that in the process of interacting on the generic management activities, particularly overall planning and control and financial planning and control, the diversifying firm will develop industry-specific managerial experience and firm-specific orga-nization capital over time.

But other types of carry-overs were also involved. For example, for Litton Industries the original conception was to apply advanced technologies from its defense business to industries where such applications appeared to have a sound economic and business basis as well as to bring to organization interac-tions a systems approach to management (again developed out of the prior experience of the top managers of Litton). A high percentage of conglomerates came out of the defense industry, not only with organizational capital of the kinds just described and an objective to avoid the destruction of such organiza-tion capital, but also with a need for additional critical managerial capabilities to be successful in the nondefense sector of the economy. Particularly critical for the defense firms was the establishment of a capability for industrial marketing. This suggests that where the desired capability requires an organizational learning and development process that involves time and uncertainties, merger enables the firm to obtain such critical capabilities at their expected values and to avoid the risks of extreme and uncertain outcomes.

Another capability that defense firms had was the ability to manage change, which represented an important contribution to a wide range of nonde-fense industries that had not developed this kind of organization knowledge. Again, even though there appeared to be no relationships between the merging firms, there was a complementarity when firms are viewed as capabilities in the framework of an organization.

THE RULES FOR SUCCESSFUL MERGERS

We feel that a number of important aspects of implementing the general framework discussed in the previous section were provided in the "Drucker Rules." In his editorial page article in *The Wall Street Journal* of October 15, 1981, Peter F. Drucker set forth "The Five Rules of Successful Acquisition." He noted that the current merger movement in the United States paralleled the tremendous wave of acquisitions in Germany in 1920–1922, a period of chronic inflation which preceded the chaotic hyperinflation of 1923. He then went on to observe that during periods of severe inflation, fixed assets can be purchased by buying companies at market prices which are well below book value and even further below replacement costs. The low stock market valuations of companies over the past decade, he argued, were due in large part to sustained underdepreciation of assets because of tax regulations. The basic impetus driving increased merger activity under inflation was said to be the general flight by business persons and investors out of money and into hard assets.

Drucker's Merger Rules

But although Drucker (1981) saw the stimulus for the most recent merger wave as primarily a financial one, he also argues that economically sensible mergers must follow five rules. The Drucker Five Commandments for successful acquisitions are:

1 Acquirer must contribute something to the acquired company.
2 A common core of unity is required.
3 Acquirer must respect the business of the acquired company.
4 Within a year or so, acquiring company must be able to provide top management to the acquired company.
5 Within the first year of merger, managements in both companies should receive promotions across the entities.

Drucker supports his prescriptions by selected examples of successes and failures. The limitation of such a method of proof, of course, is that propositions derived from individual case studies often do not have general validity. There are, however, a large number of systematic empirical studies of mergers that have been performed during the last decade. We discuss the consistency of their findings with Drucker's analysis and prescriptions for acquisitions.

Systematic Studies of M&As

The dollar value of merger and acquisition activity in the United States in recent years has averaged about 20 percent of new plant and equipment expenditures. This relationship, furthermore, is statistically significant. Thus, merger activity appears to be subject to the same influences as investment activity generally, and this suggests that there has been some economic rationale to merger activity in recent years in the United States.

Moreover, there appears to be evidence for Drucker's argument that recent mergers were stimulated by the "low" valuation of assets by the stock market. Statistical tests have revealed a significant relationship between the level of annual merger activity and the q-ratio (also known as Tobin's q). The Tobin ratio is the ratio of the market value of a firm's shares to the replacement cost of the assets represented by those shares. In recent years, the q-ratio has been running between .5 and .6. So, many companies wishing to add productive capacity may have found it cheaper to acquire the additional capacity by buying other companies than building that capacity from scratch. For example, if the average q-ratio was around .6, and if the average acquisition premium paid over market value was 50 percent (which was roughly the average figure in recent years), the resulting purchase price would have been .6 times 1.5, which equals 90 percent of the replacement cost of corporate assets. Thus, the average purchase price may still have been 10 percent below the current replacement costs of the assets acquired.

Yet, we have something of a paradox here in that merger activity during the 1960s appears to have been stimulated by *rising* stock prices and higher q-ratios. Between 1957 and 1968 the q-ratio rose from 1.0 to 1.5. However, this apparently opposite effect of the q-ratio on merger activity may be explained by the fact that the mergers of the 1960s were very different from the most recent merger wave. During the 1960s, conglomerate mergers involving a wide range of industries predominated. But it is instructive to note that almost half of the firms generally regarded as conglomerates had been based in the defense and aerospace industries. Because of the prospects for a drastic reduction in the growth of the defense budget, such firms were seeking participation in a broader spectrum of industrial markets. It was essentially a period of "defensive" diversification into more promising industries by companies facing diminished prospects for growth and profits. This merger movement, culminating in the peak merger activity of 1968 and 1969, was thus driven by companies seeking growth in a relatively strong economy.

In the 1970s, by contrast, natural resource companies were predominant among acquisition targets. The q-ratios of natural resource companies fell as low as .2 based on the estimated values of reserves in the ground. And this alleged undervaluation provided a basis for even more substantial premiums in acquisitions of natural resource firms (although subsequent price developments seem to have undermined this rationale). In fact the W. T. Grimm data indicate that in 1981, over 60 percent of the mergers by value were in the natural resource industries. Another 24 percent were in the financial services industries, where merger was stimulated by deregulation and the changing financial and economic environment.

In short, mergers appear to be influenced by the availability of alternative investment opportunities and, more specifically, by the relative costs of merger as compared with direct internal expansion. But these investment incentives, as the 1960s suggest, operate differently in different economic environments.

Other Significant Determinants of M&As

We would also expect the anticipated profitability of mergers, which presumably determines the rate of merger activity, to depend on the prospects for the general economy (especially for the industry of the acquired firm). Our tests demonstrate that merger activity is positively correlated with rates of growth in real GNP, suggesting that mergers are motivated by the (perceived) availability of investment opportunities, especially in growth industries.

The profitability of investment through merger should also be affected by the relative costs of capital for individual firms. A higher long-term cost of capital should mean fewer investment opportunities and, hence, fewer conglomerate mergers especially. Real long-term rates of interest are a good proxy for the real cost of capital, and lower real corporate bond rates are significantly correlated with the number of mergers in a given period.

In addition, the studies indicate that two other financial variables are particularly important for "pure" conglomerate mergers. Some finance theorists argue that conglomerate mergers may significantly reduce the possibility of bankruptcy, thus reducing borrowing costs or increasing debt capacity. If this were the case, we would expect conglomerate mergers to be on the rise when the general risk of bankruptcy appears greater, and the risk premium on low-grade corporate securities is higher. Using the ratio of the returns on BAA to AAA corporate bonds as a measure of this risk premium, and of bankruptcy costs in general, we find that "pure" conglomerate activity is significantly positively correlated with the size of the risk premium. (It is also interesting to note that this financial variable has virtually no effect on mergers classified as product- and market-extension mergers.)

Another financial variable strongly correlated with conglomerate mergers is the measure of monetary stringency as the spread between short- and long-term interest rates (specifically, one plus the short-term yield on four- to six-month prime commercial paper divided by one plus the AAA bond yield). Acquired firms, in conglomerate mergers, generate less cash flow than their acquiring counterparts. Thus, their need for external financing is generally greater. When the availability of funds is tight in the financial markets, it is plausible that the cost of capital for such firms rises much more for such smaller, less profitable firms due to the higher risk premiums charged by investors, underwriters, and lenders. Therefore, merging with firms with larger internal cash flows and greater access to the capital and money markets may be particularly attractive in periods of tight money. And this is what the statistics seem to bear out.

Overall, then, the results strongly suggest that financial synergy in the sense of reducing the risk premium on securities is far more important for pure conglomerate than for product- or market-extension mergers. And the statistically significant relationship between the level of conglomerate merger activity and the risk premium and monetary stringency seems to attest to the importance of internal funds as a motive in conglomerate mergers.

The Profitability of Mergers to Merging Firms

Most recent studies of the profitability of mergers compare the realized returns to investors at the announcement of mergers and tender offers to returns on the general market. The difference represents abnormal returns, which are interpreted as the market's assessment of the value of the deal to acquiring and acquired firms' stockholders alike. The findings of these studies permit some generalizations.

The value of the merged firms appears to be greater than the sum of the components. This implies that value is created and increased by mergers. This increase in stockholder wealth, in turn, must reflect expected underlying economies and efficiencies from mergers. On the basis of the market's response, therefore, mergers and acquisitions appear, on average, to have followed sound principles or rules. Other findings are:

1 For *acquired* firms during the period just before the announcement date of a merger or tender offer, their shareholders gain by about 15 percent in mergers and about 30 percent in tender offers. However, in earlier periods the abnormal returns of acquired firms were negative, indicating that their managements were not performing up to potential.

2 For *acquiring* firms over the period before the announcement date, their shareholders had modest positive returns but they are not statistically significant. However, in earlier periods their abnormal returns are positive and significant, indicating that acquiring firms had a previous record of managing asset growth successfully.

3 The residuals do not decline after the merger. This further indicates that the mergers on average were based on valid economic or business reasons.

Other studies indicate that acquiring firms generally have higher-than-average leverage ratios while acquired firms have lower-than-average leverage ratios. The studies all show that leverage is increased even further after the completion of the merger or acquisition. One explanation consistent with these findings on leverage is that less risky firms can employ more leverage and become acquirers of more risky firms which have been constrained to employ lower leverage. The risk of bankruptcy and expected bankruptcy costs may be reduced by mergers. Thus, the mergers may cause the cost of capital of the resulting firm to be lower than the simple weighted sum of the cost of capital of the component firms.

Studies also show that new capital outlays for investment in acquired companies' operations increase significantly over premerger outlays. Also, the managerial function of capital expenditure planning is generally relocated to corporate headquarters after acquisitions. These observations suggest that an important motive for mergers is to internalize investment opportunities to take advantage of perceived growth opportunities in the acquired firms' line of business.

Conglomerate Mergers

The studies summarized previously generally include all types of mergers—horizontal, vertical, and conglomerate. Nevertheless, over 75 percent of the mergers and acquisitions between the early 1950s until the late 1970s have been labeled as "conglomerate" by the Federal Trade Commission in compiling its statistics. And "pure"conglomerate mergers would appear to violate the Drucker Rules of relatedness.

However, studies of conglomerate mergers alone yield the same pattern of results as the studies of all mergers. The market's response to conglomerate mergers has not been statistically different from the response to all mergers, nor has their market performance over the years underperformed general market averages or other broad composites such as the returns to mutual funds. In terms of their operating profitability, conglomerates' returns on assets have been slightly lower than the average for all manufacturing firms, but their returns on equity have been higher (reflecting their significantly higher leverage ratios) than the general industry composite.

These findings suggest that conglomerate mergers did not violate the Drucker Rules. Rather there must have been some form of "relatedness." For some companies it was the ability to apply sophisticated financial planning and control systems or other differentially superior general management capabilities (for example, strategic planning, R&D, legal) to firms that could benefit from their application. Some acquiring firms carried over a capability to adjust effectively to changing environments and economic turbulence.

The empirical studies of pure conglomerate mergers are also consistent with the following pattern. The acquiring firms were well endowed with managerial capabilities and cash, reflecting the success of past operations. However, they faced limited investment and growth opportunities in their own industries. On average they acquired firms in industries characterized by favorable demand expectations and greater investment opportunities. Such acquired firms, however, had not generally performed up to the potential realized by other firms in their industries, probably because of limited financial or managerial resources.

Extending the Rules

In general, then, a review of the systematic studies of merger activity supports the Drucker Rules based on individual case studies. Examination of the systematic evidence, however, suggests that the Drucker Rules may be unduly restrictive if interpreted too literally. In essence the Drucker Rules can be boiled down to two statements: (1) merging companies must have activities that are related in some way, and (2) well-structured incentives and rewards must be held out to the management of both firms to help make the merger work, though the acquiring firm should be prepared to cover the departure of the key management of acquired companies.

A less restrictive interpretation of these rules would include the following commentary on the Drucker Pentalogue.

1 Relatedness is a necessary requirement, but complementarities are an even greater virtue. For example, combining a company strong in research but weak in marketing with a company strong in marketing but weak in research may bring blessings to both.

2 Relatedness or complementarities may apply to general management functions such as research, planning and control, and financial management as well as to the more firm-specific operating functions such as production and marketing. This perspective widely increases the basis for relatedness. Thus, companies with cash flows or managerial capabilities in excess of their investment opportunities or available capacity could effectively combine with companies lacking the financial or managerial resources to make the most of the prospects for growth and profits in their industries.

3 Even if the previous rules are followed, an acquiring firm will experience negative returns if it pays too much. It is difficult to fully and accurately evaluate another organization. There may be great surprises on both sides after the marriage, and the problems of implementing complementarities may be substantial. The uncertainty associated with acquisitions is likely to be greater than the uncertainty attending internal investments made in product market areas more directly related to the firm's current activities. The external investments may appear to offer higher rates of return. But financial theory tells us that higher returns on average are associated with higher risks. The prospective high returns from a merger must be based on real economies, whether operating or financial, expected from the combination. Further, the expectation that a firm can improve the average risk-return relationship in an unfamiliar market or industry is likely to be disappointed.

Conclusions

In summary, both the case studies and systematic empirical studies suggest the following guidelines for successful merger and acquisition activity.

1 Be sure there is an element of relatedness, but don't be too restrictive in defining the scope of potential relatedness.

2 Combining two companies is an activity involving substantial trauma and readjustment. Therefore, a strong emphasis on maintaining and enhancing managerial rewards and incentives is required in the postmerger period.

3 The risk of mistakes stemming from wishful thinking are especially great in mergers. The planning may be sound from the standpoint of business or financial complementarities or relatedness. But if the price is not right, someone is going to get hurt.

VALUE-BASED PLANNING

In Chapter 6 we set forth the principles of valuation. In Chapter 7 we applied these concepts to show how a value creation framework could be developed and applied. Our aim was to show how the goal of increasing the value of the firm could be implemented. We set forth a valuation formula which is general and at the same time provides a framework for effective planning in the firm.

The valuation formula we emphasized is valuation with supernormal growth over a limited period of time followed by no growth. The model is shown below in equation (6.5).

$$V_0 = X_0(1-T)(1-b_s) \sum_{t=1}^{n} \frac{(1+g_s)^t}{(1+k)^t} + \frac{X_0(1-T)(1+g_s)^{n+1}}{k(1+k)^n} \qquad (6.5)$$

We also discussed how this simple model could be modified to allow for several stages of supernormal growth. A wide variety of patterns could be envisaged. The most usual pattern might be for supernormal growth to start out low, then increase sharply, then diminish in some pattern followed by no growth. But any pattern observed in actuality could be modeled. The framework is sufficiently flexible to encompass any actual set of empirical patterns.

Any elaboration of the basic formula reproduced as equation (6.5) will still have the same key or critical valuation parameters. These are summarized in Table 25.1.

With the framework provided by Table 25.1, the goal is to relate the qualita-

---

TABLE 25.1
Critical Valuation Planning Parameters

   I. Growth rate (g) in operating income (X) [sales]
      A. Sales growth
      B. Cost control
  II. Achieve a positive margin between profitability on new investments and the cost of capital
      A. Manage profitability rate effectively (r)
      B. Select balanced debt and equity proportions in relation to business risks (k)
 III. Sound management of investment opportunities (b) (N)
  IV. Prudent management of tax obligations (T)

   where:

   X = net operating income (NOI) or earnings before interest and taxes (EBIT) as discussed in Chapter 6

   g = growth rate of X in our models as well as those of Rappaport and other writers. This is also the growth rate in sales, working capital, fixed investment, and so on.

   r = the marginal profitability rate. It is incremental X related to incremental investment requirements including both net working capital and fixed investment requirements.

   k = the firm's weighted marginal cost of capital as discussed in Chapter 7

   b = investment requirements or opportunities in relation to after-tax X

   N = the investment horizon during which supernormal growth takes place, that is, when r is greater than k

   T = the marginal effective corporate tax rate

---

tive aspects of strategy to their quantitative financial results with a view toward value enhancement. As discussed in Chapter 7, this requires using the material on strategy set forth in Chapter 3. It requires use of the business economics framework, plus concepts from the strategy literature integrating them and orienting them to a valuation framework as shown in equation (6.5).

An illustration of how this might be done is provided by Rappaport (1986). A summary of his approach is shown in Table 25.2. Rappaport illustrates how the key valuation parameters which he calls "value drivers" can be related to tactics supporting either a cost leadership strategy or a product differentiation strategy, two major approaches to strategy developed by Porter (1980, 1985, 1987). The key valuation parameters according to Rappaport are:

Sales growth
Operating profit margin
Working capital investment
Fixed capital investment
Cost of capital

While the words are different, the key concepts in Rappaport's model and our model are similar. The basic differences in the two approaches are explained in Chapter 7. Rappaport has a verbal formulation which can be modeled by a somewhat complex computer program. We could do the same with our approach, but we also want to be able to express our formulation in a compact formula. The computer requirements of our formula approach are less onerous. In addition, checks for internal consistency are facilitated. In addition, sensitivity analysis relating key input parameters to valuation results can be performed efficiently.

In Chapter 7 we illustrated how Rappaport's verbal model could readily be translated into our formula approach. The spirit of both models postulates fixed relationships between sales, investments, profitability patterns, in relation to the cost of capital.

Indeed, both models are in the spirit of the early Du Pont approach to investment and financial planning (Weston, 1972). The key relationships of the Du Pont approach are shown in Figure 25.1. The return on investment is obtained by relating turnover to the profit margin on sales. The profit margin on sales reflects effective cost control. Minimizing investment in working capital and fixed assets requires effective investment management. All of this is brought out in the Du Pont chart.

While the Du Pont approach focuses on return on investment, its ultimate goal as revealed in discussions of those who formulated the approach was value-based planning similar to the approach in Rappaport and in our own presentation. For example, Donaldson Brown, who implemented the Du Pont approach at General Motors in the 1920s, wrote articles in the mid 1920s in which he emphasized relating the return on investment to a required cost of capital deter-

TABLE 25.2
Relating Strategy to Key Input Parameters of Valuation Models

VALUE DRIVERS	TACTICS SUPPORTING COST LEADERSHIP STRATEGY
Sales growth rate	• Maintain competitive prices • Pursue market share opportunities to gain scale economies in production, distribution, etc.
Operating profit margin	• Achieve relevant economies of scale for each of the value activities • Introduce mechanisms to improve the rate of learning, e.g., standardization, product design modifications, improved scheduling, etc. • Search for cost-reducing linkages with suppliers based on supplier's product design, quality, packaging, order processing, etc. • Search for cost-reducing linkages with channels • Eliminate overhead that does not add value to the product
Working capital investment	• Minimize cash balance • Manage accounts receivable to reduce average number of days outstanding • Minimize inventory without impairing required level of customer service
Fixed capital investment	• Promote policies to increase utilization of fixed assets • Obtain productivity-increasing assets • Sell unused fixed assets • Obtain assets at least cost, e.g., lease versus purchase
Cost of capital	• Target an optimal capital structure • Select least-cost debt and equity instruments • Reduce business risk factors in manner consistent with strategy

VALUE DRIVERS	TACTICS SUPPORTING DIFFERENTIATION STRATEGY
Sales growth rate	• Command a premium price • Pursue growth in market segments in which buyer is willing to pay premium for differentiation
Operating profit margin	• Choose combination of value activities that create the most cost-effective means of differentiating, e.g., by lowering buyer's cost and risk and by raising performance • Eliminate costs that do not contribute to buyer needs
Working capital investment	• Minimize cash balance • Link accounts receivable policy to differentiation strategy • Maintain inventory level consistent with differentiating level of service • Obtain best terms with suppliers for accounts payable
Fixed capital investment	• Invest in specialized assets that create differentiation • Purchase assets for optimal utilization • Sell unused fixed assets • Obtain assets at least cost, e.g., lease versus purchase
Cost of capital	• Target an optimal capital structure • Select least-cost debt and equity instruments • Increase differentiation and thereby make demand less dependent on general economy

SOURCE: A. Rappaport, *Creating Shareholder Value*, New York: Free Press, 1986, pp. 97–98.

FIGURE 25.1   Du Pont Chart for Divisional Control

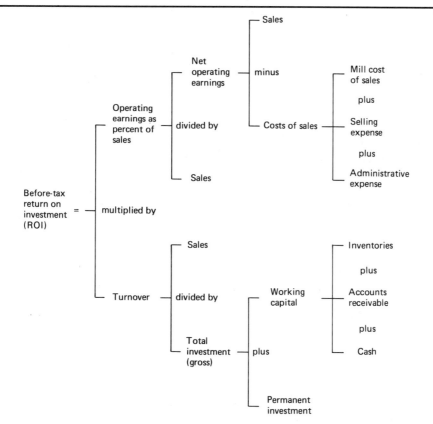

mined by the opportunities and competitive risks of that particular line of business activity (Brown, 1924).

It will be noted that the Rappaport material in Table 25.2 uses two approaches to strategy. Under the cost leadership strategy, sales growth according to Rappaport requires "competitive prices" and an emphasis on increasing market share. Under the product differentiation strategy, Rappaport suggests achieving a "premium price" and finding market segments in which buyers are willing to pay a higher price for a differentiated product. We would comment that premium price is also a competitive price for the buyer-perceived value built into the differentiated product.

Under operating profit margin for the cost leadership strategy, Rappaport suggests achieving economies of scale and mechanisms to improve the rate of learning, as in the Boston Consulting Group approach. Under the product differentiation strategy, Rappaport suggests choosing combinations of activities that help achieve the most cost effective means of differentiating products, as in the Porter approach. Clearly the emphasis is different from that under the cost leadership strategy, but what is actually involved appears to be somewhat vague.

As pointed out, our approach has somewhat different key valuation parameters from Rappaport's. These differences reflect our desire to express our model in a compact formula. In addition, it reflects a different eclectic approach to strategy. We utilize the precepts of the Boston Consulting Group where useful and the precepts of Porter and his associates where useful. But we also see limitations and vulnerabilities in these approaches. Our emphasis is process oriented. It views strategy as efforts that start with identification of the firm's mission. Then it approaches an effective information and feedback system utilizing mechanisms such as iterative "going around the loop." The formulation of the information and decision loops is guided by concepts from specific theories of strategy (like the Boston Consulting Group, Porter, Steiner, etc.), but the emphasis is on process and an adaptive information and communication system (Weston, 1972).

When these processes are performed effectively, they can then be expressed in quantitative terms. The results of applying strategy plus a business economics analysis to the planning framework provided by the critical valuation parameters can then be developed. An illustration of how these results may be applied is shown in the following section.

MERGER ANALYSIS IN A VALUE CREATION FRAMEWORK

In the perspective of alternative merger theories and empirical tests, the foundation has been provided to guide managerial policies with respect to merger and acquisition decisions. From an operational standpoint, mergers and acquisitions should be related to a firm's general planning framework. These requirements have been set forth in detail in other studies (Chung and Weston, 1982). Here, we focus on merger policies in a capital budgeting valuation framework. We make the concepts explicit by using an illustrative case example to convey the ideas.

The Adams Corporation is a manufacturer of materials handling equipment, with heavy emphasis on forklift trucks. Because of a low internal profitability rate and lack of favorable investment opportunities in its existing line of business, Adams is considering a merger to achieve more favorable growth and profitability opportunities. It has made an extensive search of a large number of corporations and has narrowed the candidates to two firms, for a number of considerations. The Black Corporation is a manufacturer of agricultural equipment and is strong in research and marketing. It has had high internal profitability and substantial investment opportunities. The Clark Company is a manufacturer of plastic toys. It has a better profitability record than Black. Relevant data on the three firms are summarized in Table 25.3. Additional information on market parameters includes a risk-free rate, R_F, of 6 percent and an expected return on the market, $E(R_M)$, of 11 percent. Each firm pays a 10 percent interest

TABLE 25.3
Comparative Statistics for the Year Ended 19X0

	BOOK VALUE PER SHARE	PRICE/ EARNINGS RATIO (P/EPS)	NUMBER OF SHARES (millions)	DEBT RATIO, % (D/E)	BETA FOR EXISTING LEVERAGE	INTERNAL PROFIT- ABILITY RATE (r)	INVEST- MENT RATE (b)	GROWTH RATE (g)
Adams	$10	5.40	5	30	1.2	.04	0.1	.004
Black	40	11.70	1	30	1.4	.12	1.5	.18
Clark	40	9.88	1	30	1.6	.14	1.0	.14

rate on its debt. The tax rate, T_c, of each is 50 percent. A period of ten years is estimated for the duration of supernormal growth, n. From the information provided, we can first formulate the accounting balance sheets for the three firms (Table 25.4).

Dividing the internal profitability rate r by $(1 - T_c)$ and multiplying by total assets, we get the net operating income. From the net operating income, we can obtain the market price per share and the total market value that would have to be paid for each of the three companies (Table 25.5). We now have earnings per share, market values per share, and total market values of equity for use in the subsequent analysis.

One popular criterion for evaluating the desirability of making acquisitions from the standpoint of the acquiring company is to determine the effect on its earnings per share. Table 25.6 illustrates these effects based on the data in the present example. It can be seen that either merger would cause the earnings per share of Adams to decline. The percentage dilution in the earnings per share of Adams would be 47 percent if Black were acquired and 39 percent if Clark were acquired. We believe that this widely used criterion is in error. The effects on market values are relevant, and not the effects on earnings per share.

In a valuation framework, it is necessary to make a forecast of the key variables affecting value after the merger has taken place. This requires an in-depth business analysis of each proposed merger in terms of its impact on the key valuation factors. From the background provided, we observe that Adams is

TABLE 25.4
Accounting Balance Sheets ($ Million)

	ADAMS	BLACK	CLARK
Debt	$15	$12	$12
Equity	50	40	40
Total Assets	$65	$52	$52

$$\text{WACC} = k = k_s(S/V) + k_b(1 - T_c)(B/V)$$

$$k(AB) = .1285 \left(\frac{76}{103}\right) + .05 \left(\frac{27}{103}\right)$$

$$= .0948 + .0131 = .1079$$

$$= 10.8\%$$

$$k(AC) = .1375 \left(\frac{76}{103}\right) + .05 \left(\frac{27}{103}\right)$$

$$= .1015 + .0131 = .1146$$

$$= 11.5\%.$$

We now have all the information required to calculate the valuation of the two alternative combinations.

We use the valuation formula for a period of supernormal growth (ten years in this example) followed by zero growth. From Chapter 6 on valuation, this is equation (6.5), reproduced as follows for a leveraged company.

$$V_0 = X_0(1 - T)(1 - b_s) \sum_{t=1}^{n} \frac{(1 + g_s)^t}{(1 + k)^t} + \frac{X_0(1 - T)(1 + g_s)^{n+1}}{k(1 + k)^n} \qquad (6.5)$$

We next insert the numerical values to determine the value of the combined firm if Adams merges with Black (AB) or with Clark (AC). The computations are shown below:

$$V_{AB} = \$18(.5)(.1) \sum_{t=1}^{10} \frac{(1.14)^t}{(1.108)^t} + \frac{\$18(.5)(1.14)^{11}}{.108(1.108)^{10}}$$

$$= .9 \sum_{t=1}^{10} (1.029)^t + \frac{9}{.108}(1.029)^{10}(1.14)$$

$$= .9(1.029)\text{FVIFA}(2.9\%, 10 \text{ yrs.}) + 83.33\text{FVIF}(2.9\%, 10 \text{ yrs.})(1.14)$$

$$= .9261 \left[\frac{1.331 - 1}{.029}\right] + 83.33(1.331)(1.14)$$

$$= .9261(11.414) + 110.91(1.14)$$

$$V_{AB} = 10.57 + 126.44 = \$137.01 \text{ million.}$$

$$V_{AC} = \$16(.5)(.1) \sum_{t=1}^{10} \left(\frac{1.13}{1.115}\right)^t + \frac{\$16(.5)(1.13)^{11}}{.115(1.115)^{10}}$$

$$= .8 \sum_{t=1}^{10} (1.01345)^t + \frac{8}{.115}(1.01345)^{10}(1.13)$$

$$= .8(1.01345) \left[\frac{1.14294 - 1}{.01345} \right] + 69.5652(1.14294)(1.13)$$

$$= .81076(10.63) + 79.51(1.13)$$

$$V_{AC} = 8.62 + 89.85 = \$98.47 \text{ million.}$$

Using the results obtained, we make a summary comparison of the gains or losses from the two alternative mergers shown in Table 25.7.

The data show that, based on estimates of the key parameters, a gain in value of $34 million would result from a merger between Adams and Black. However, the merger between Adams and Clark would result in a loss in valuation amounting to $5 million. The results of this comparison permit some margin of error yet clearly indicate that a merger between Adams and Black is preferable to a merger between Adams and Clark. Indeed, the gain in value of $34 million could be divided between the shareholders of Adams and those of Black. Adams could pay up to a 50 percent premium over the current market price of Black and still achieve a gain in net value that would go to its shareholders.

The foregoing example provides a general methodology for the management analysis of merger activity, which utilizes a number of principles. The acquiring firm is considering several firms as alternative merger candidates. To arrive at a rational basis for analysis, prospective returns and risk from alternative merger combinations must be estimated. While historical data may be used as inputs, a forecast or estimate must be made of the returns and risk that may arise after alternative merger combinations have taken place.

Thus, the forecast of the variables that measure prospective returns and risk for alternative postmerger combinations is critical to a sound evaluation of merger alternatives. The estimates of net operating earnings and their potential growth may or may not reflect synergy between the combining firms depending on the nature and potential of the combined operations. Studies in depth of the relevant product markets and the results of combining the organizations of the

TABLE 25.7
Comparison of Two Mergers ($ Million)

	ADAMS/BLACK	ADAMS/CLARK
Postmerger value, V	$137	$98
Less amount of debt, B	27	27
Value of equity, S	110	71
Less Adams's premerger market value	10	10
Gain in equity value	100	61
Cost if acquired at market price	66	66
Gain in value (loss)	34	(5)

two firms are required. The resulting forecasts are subject to prediction errors, which are sometimes of substantial magnitude.

We may obtain the measures of risk by market-value weighted averages of the betas (the systematic risk) of the combining firms. With the estimates of the new betas, along with a selection of market parameters, we can calculate the new relevant cost of capital for the merged firm, utilizing the security market line relationship. We must also estimate the effect of alternative merger combinations on the cost of debt. With estimates of the cost of equity capital and the cost of debt, we must formulate appropriate capital structure targets for the combined firm and use these to estimate a cost of capital.

Having obtained an estimate of the applicable cost of capital and the estimates of returns discussed earlier, we can apply valuation principles to formulate estimates of the value of alternative merger combinations. From these, we deduct the value of the acquiring firm in the absence of the merger to determine the total value remaining, which we next compare with the cost of acquiring the firm or firms with which a merger is being considered. If the value contributed by the merger exceeds the cost of the acquisition, the acquiring firm has a basis for making an offer that includes a premium to the shareholders of the acquired firm yet still provides an increase in value for the shareholders of the acquiring firm.

SUMMARY

Mergers and acquisitions (M&As) should constitute a part of a firm's diversification program and its overall strategic planning process. The basic elements of strategic planning include an assessment of the firm's environment and an analysis of the firm's resources and capabilities as they relate to the environment. Goals are formulated, and adjustments, which may include mergers and acquisitions, are made to move the firm closer to these goals. The process is never complete, but rather performed iteratively as the firm's capabilities and environments change over time.

Increasingly, firms are defined less in terms of products and markets, and more as a range of capabilities. This creates both opportunities and increasing competitive threats in a dynamic economy. M&As provide a means of preserving the organization capital of those firms which have been less able to adapt to change. They allow more successful firms to acquire needed capabilities faster and with less risk than developing them internally. Even pure conglomerate M&As which start with transferability of only generic management capabilities provide an avenue for the eventual development of increased skills in specific management functions such as production and marketing.

Peter Drucker identifies a financial stimulus for merger activity (that is, merger activity increases during periods of high inflation) and, based on individual case studies and observations, sets forth a set of rules for successful mergers. We agree with his focus on managerial incentives to ease the trauma of adjustment in the postmerger period. We also agree in formulating guidelines for successful mergers on complementarities of capabilities and/or "relatedness."

Systematic studies of M&As enable us to draw a number of conclusions:

1 Value is created by mergers, takeovers, and restructuring; acquired firm shareholders gain 15 to 20 percent on average and acquiring firm shareholders do not lose on average.
2 M&A profitability and activity is positively correlated with GNP growth and favorable investment opportunities.
3 The use of M&As to achieve firm goals is affected by the availability of alternative investment opportunities.
4 Financial variables (including relative costs of capital, monetary stringency, and risk premiums) are more important for pure conglomerate mergers than for product or market extension mergers.
5 Leverage generally increases following M&As.
6 Capital outlays historically have increased following M&As.

The strategic planning framework for M&A analysis is necessarily supplemented by financial analysis of alternative merger candidates. A firm may be an ideal candidate from a strategic planning standpoint, but if the acquiring firm pays too high a price, the transaction will not succeed. There are a number of approaches to this analysis. Our preference is to use compact valuation formulas which can accommodate various assumptions about growth and investment patterns. The variables required by the formulas are supplied by a historical analysis of the candidate along with a business economics-based analysis of what is likely to occur in the future. Our approach and most of the others are related to the traditional Du Pont system of financial control which attempts to maximize return on investment by controlling costs and minimizing investment. The aim is to make positive net present value investments, which may include mergers and acquisitions to achieve business goals.

QUESTIONS

1. What are the basic principles to keep in mind in merger and acquisitions planning?
2. According to Coase, what are the determinants of the scope and size of firms?
3. What are Drucker's rules for successful mergers?
4. How can Drucker's rules be applied successfully?

REFERENCES

BROWN, DONALDSON, "Pricing Policy in Relation to Financial Control," *Management and Administration*, 7, February/March/April 1924, pp. 3–15.

The free-rider problem does arise if the tender offer is made conditional on a minimum number of shares being tendered. Under a conditional tender offer, if $p < v$, it is a *dominant strategy* for each shareholder not to tender his or her shares. So each small shareholder prefers to free ride and the tender fails in the resulting dominant strategy equilibrium.

One solution to the free-rider problem is to allow the bidder to dilute the value of the remaining, nontendered shares of the target firm after takeover. The dilution could be allowed explicitly by limiting the rights of minority shareholders through a corporate charter amendment (Grossman and Hart, 1980). Or the bidder might be able to effect dilution by supplying overpriced inputs to the target or buying underpriced products or other assets from the target. The anticipated dilution induces shareholders to tender their shares at a price below that reflecting the posttakeover improvements. The bidder will be able to profit from the takeover if dilution is possible.

Another method frequently used to avoid the free-rider problem and theoretically equivalent to dilution is to announce a two-tier offer. In such an offer, the bidder will buy target shares up to a certain percentage of the firm at a first-tier price and, after the takeover, the remaining shares at a lower, second-tier price (for a follow-up merger). The second tier will be lower than the value of the target shares under the anticipated improvements so that the takeover will be profitable for the bidder. However, the average price paid may represent a division (equitable) of the improvement in value that conceivably might have been contained in a single price offer were it not for the free-rider problem. (For more discussion, see the section on "coercive offers and defense: theoretical background" in Chapter 20.) Bradley and Kim (1985) show that competition among bidders will lead to maximization of the difference between the first- and second-tier prices in order to maximize the cost to shareholders of declining to tender. The back end price of the offer would be zero if there were no regulation (on redemption prices) and no limits on dilution.

In a study critical of the atomistic-stockholder models which emphasize the free-rider problem, Bagnoli and Lipman (1988) argue that when there are finitely many stockholders, the bidder can overcome the free-rider problem. They show that when there is a finite number of stockholders, some stockholders must be pivotal in the sense that they do recognize that they may affect the outcome of the bid. In their model, making some stockholders pivotal is crucial because it forces them to choose whether or not the bid succeeds. Hence, they cannot free-ride, so exclusionary devices such as dilution and two-tier offers are not necessary for successful takeovers.

A third way of avoiding the free-rider problem, which does not require dilution, is for a large shareholder (or an outsider after "secretly" accumulating a large fraction of the equity) to make a tender offer. This is the subject of the analysis by Shleifer and Vishny (1986a), Hirshleifer and Titman (1988), and Jegadeesh and Chowdhry (1988).

In the framework of Shleifer and Vishny (1986a), a profit after the costs of a takeover can be realized through an increase in value of the shares held by the large shareholder, even though the shareholder does not on average profit from the additional shares purchased through the tender offer. Thus, in the model, it is the large shareholders who perform the functions of monitoring managers and looking for ways to improve the firm's performance. According to the data they present, large shareholdings were prevalent among the *Fortune* 500 firms, with seven out of nine firms having at least one shareholder owning at least 5 percent of the firm. The extent that these large holders are institutional investors is not known. While institutional shareholders are unlikely to initiate a takeover, their presence may (or may not) facilitate takeovers.

In the model of Shleifer and Vishny (1986a), the large shareholder's return on his or her own shares is sufficient to cover the monitoring and takeover costs. However, because the large shareholder internalizes only the gains to his or her shares held prior to the takeover, the monitoring and takeover activity is less than optimal. On the other hand, some privately-held firms do go public despite the value loss associated with the free-rider problem. In order to be able to explain this, one might have to model the factors such as wealth constraint and risk aversion motivating the decision to go public.

The Hirshleifer and Titman (1988) model has a large shareholder who plays the same role as in the Shleifer and Vishny (1986a) model, although the presence of a large shareholder is not necessary as the model can be equally well applied to a bidder who does not have any ownership stake in the target but instead hopes to profit from dilution. More importantly, in the Hirshleifer and Titman model, the takeover bid *may* not succeed because of the randomness of the small shareholder's decision to tender. In the *separating equilibrium* characterized by the Hirshleifer and Titman model, a low-gain bidder offers a low bid and a high-gain bidder bids high; the bid fully reveals information on the gain to be achieved by the takeover. This equilibrium obtains because shareholders are more likely to accept high than low bids. Low-gain bidders bid low to credibly separate themselves from high-gain bidders, but the latter will not offer as low a bid because rejection is more costly to them. In the Hirshleifer and Titman model, the equilibrium bid is not related to the initial shareholding of the bidder, although the bid's probability of success is increased with an increase in the initial shareholding. Hirshleifer and Titman (1988) also derive implications of posttakeover dilution of minority shares and management defenses on the bid price and the probability of success.

The assumption of exogenously determined (that is, fixed) shares of the large shareholders in the Shleifer and Vishny and Hirshleifer and Titman models is relaxed by Jegadeesh and Chowdhry (1988). In the Jegadeesh and Chowdhry model, the bidder's share of the target is an endogenously determined variable and is chosen strategically prior to the announcement of the tender offer. They justify this different assumption by noting that the initial footholdings of the bidders at the time of tender offers show wide cross-sectional variation ranging from zero to nearly 50 percent. This empirical phenomenon reported by Poulsen and Jarrell (1986) contradicts the suggestion that prior to an offer announcement the potential bidder should intensely purchase the target shares in the open market until the stock price is driven up to the postannouncement price.

The Jegadeesh and Chowdhry model assumes, as do the other models discussed, that target shares are held by atomistic shareholders and the potential synergistic gain to be achieved through the takeover is known only to the bidder. In the resulting separating equilibrium, the bidder's pretakeover shareholding is positively related to the value of the potential gain to the takeover. A low-valuation (gain) bidder foregoes the opportunity to acquire as many shares in the open market at the pretender offer price as a high-valuation bidder in order to credibly separate itself from the latter. The separation allows the low-valuation bidder to bid a lower amount in the tender offer than it otherwise would have to. On the other hand, the high-valuation bidder will not mimic the low-valuation bidder because the benefit of a low bid is offset by the cost of mimicking. This cost consists of the lower probability of success which hurts the high-bidder type more and of the smaller share acquisition at the lower preoffer price. The above three models are next explained more fully.

Large Shareholders and Corporate Control: Shleifer and Vishny (1986a)

The pioneering study by Shleifer and Vishny [1986a] explores the implications of an increase in the holdings of the large shareholder. As the proportion of the firm's shares held by L (the large shareholder) rises, a takeover becomes more likely and the price of the firm's shares increases. However, the tender offer premium is actually lower. The reason is that when L owns more, he is willing to take over even if he can only bring about a smaller increase in the firm's value. On the other hand, an increase in the legal and administrative costs of takeovers increases takeover premia but reduces the welfare of small shareholders as bids become less likely.

The Shleifer and Vishny Model

L owns $\alpha(< .5)$ of the firm. For a cost of $c(I)$ for monitoring and research on the firm, L obtains a *probability* I of finding an improvement opportunity of value Z. This random variable has a continuous cumulative probability function $F(Z)$ defined on an interval where the smallest value of Z is greater than zero and its maximum value is Z_{max}. (The mathematical notation for this interval is $(0, Z_{max}]$). That is, after expending $c(I)$, L gets a draw $Z\epsilon(0, Z_{max}]$ with probability I and no draw, or equivalently a draw of 0, with probability $(1 - I)$. The probability I can be thought of as research intensity and $c(I)$ increases with I. Z is interpreted as the increase in discounted profits resulting from replacement of inefficient management or from changing the firm's investment and operating policies.

If L invests $c(I)$ and finds an improvement of value Z, L may bid for $(.5 - \alpha)$ shares that will give him control. Let c_T be the costs of a tender offer that will be incurred by L. The bid price is $q + \pi$; q is the present value of profits under existing management and π is the additional amount paid over q. Note that q must be less than the stock price of the firm since the market price reflects the possibility of a takeover. Therefore, π will be generally larger than the actual premium paid in a takeover. Note also that the final value of the firm after takeover will be $q + Z$. Since $c(I)$ is a sunk cost, L, assumed risk-neutral, will make the offer if (A.1) holds:

$$.5Z - (.5 - \alpha)\pi - c_T \geq 0 \tag{A.1}$$

The small shareholders are assumed to be risk-neutral and have knowledge of α, c_T, and $F(Z)$ only. Z is not known to them. If the level of the bid π is assumed to be uninformative, then their best forecast of Z is given by

$$E[Z|.5Z - (.5 - \alpha)\pi - c_T \geq 0]$$

or

$$E[Z|Z \geq (1 - 2\alpha)\pi + 2c_T]$$

where the conditional expectation is taken with respect to $F(Z)$. They will tender if and only if

$$\pi - E[Z|Z \geq (1 - 2\alpha)\pi + 2c_T] \geq 0 \tag{A.2}$$

It has been assumed that if small shareholders are indifferent between tendering and not tendering their shares, they choose to tender. This is the critical assumption that distinguishes Shleifer and Vishny's (1986a) analysis from Hirshleifer and Titman (1988), where the decision to tender is random.

Let $\pi^*(\alpha)$ be the smallest π that satisfies (A.2). Then L will bid $q + \pi^*(\alpha)$. Given $\pi^*(\alpha)$, the smallest Z that satisfies (A.1) can be determined. This Z is denoted $Z^c(\alpha)$.

The equilibrium values $\pi^*(\alpha)$ and $Z^c(\alpha)$ are functions of α, c_T and $F(Z)$, but are *not* functions of the actual draw Z. The small shareholders will not accept a bid less than $q + \pi^*(\alpha)$, even if it is greater than the current market price. Each small shareholder is atomistic and therefore believes that his individual decision to tender will not affect the outcome. If enough shares are tendered and he holds his shares, his share will be expected to have the value $q + \pi^*(\alpha)$.

A property of $\pi^*(\alpha)$ is that it decreases in α; that is, the more shares L owns, the lower the bid price will be. This is intuitively clear in the context of their model because when L's share is large, his profit from the takeover can be positive even with low-valued improvements and, therefore, the small shareholder's expectation about Z becomes smaller.

This result implies that, given research intensity I, the probability of a takeover increases with α. The cut-off value of Z, called $Z^c(\alpha)$, becomes lower when α is large and, therefore, a takeover is more probable.

Consider now L's optimal choice of monitoring and research intensity. For any draw Z, L is at least as well off and for any draw $Z > Z^c(\alpha)$, he is better off, the larger α is. This is because L receives α of the value of the improvement less the takeover costs, given $Z > Z^c(\alpha)$. Hence, the expected marginal benefit from his holdings dramatically. This is because small shareholders will free-ride on the gains from his increased research and more probable takeover activity. But as long as L already has substantial holdings, in the sense that he is taking over with a positive probability at α_0, he always wants to acquire at least a little more at the new, higher price $V(\alpha,q)$.

However, if L is small and has zero probability of a takeover ($\alpha_0 < c_T/Z_{max}$), he will be made worse off by buying ($\alpha - \alpha_0$) shares at $V(\alpha,q)$ if his takeover probability is positive at α.

These results suggest that once a large block of shares is assembled, the position is unlikely to be dissipated. If L sells his shares to many small shareholders, the possibility of a value-increasing takeover will be diminished. Therefore, large blocks of shareholdings will tend to be sold as a block rather than sold in small quantities, according to the Shleifer and Vishny model.

Share Tendering Strategies and Takeover Bid Success: Hirshleifer and Titman (1988)

In the Shleifer and Vishny (1986a) model, a tender offer will always succeed because the small shareholders choose to tender their shares as long as the offer premium equals their expectation of the posttakeover improvements conditioned on an offer being made. On the other hand, Hirshleifer and Titman (1988) assume that small shareholders' decisions are random when they are indifferent between tendering and not tendering. Therefore, the success of an offer is uncertain.

In this general setting of the Hirshleifer and Titman model, bidders with a low potential gain from the takeover bid low to separate themselves from high-gain bidders. A high-gain bidder, in his effort to ensure success, bids high, and in so doing he unwillingly reveals the fact that his valuation is high. Since shareholders infer higher value of the improvement from a higher bid, the bang-for-buck of raising the bid is reduced; hence, it is hard to ensure success with certainty. Because of low-gain bidders' incentive to bid low and high-gain bidders' incentive to bid high, the information of the bidder is perfectly revealed in the resulting equilibrium, so that the bid exactly equals the expected value of the improvement to be brought about by the takeover.

The Hirshleifer and Titman Model

The Shleifer and Vishny (1986a) notation and assumptions are retained except where noted otherwise. For simplification, the value of the firm under the incumbent management, q, is assumed to be zero. As before, a conditional offer is made for a controlling fraction of the target's shares; the bidder purchases no shares unless the number tendered is at least as large as the number he has bid for. It is assumed that once a bid is rejected, there is no opportunity for later upward revisions.

The cost to the bidder if a bid is rejected will be smaller for a low-Z bidder and larger for a high-Z bidder. Therefore, shareholders infer that low bids are associated with low Zs. This leads to the possibility that shareholders accept low bids. However, to deter high-Z bidders from bidding low, shareholders should reject low bids with sufficient frequency.

In order to have an equilibrium when bids are rejected probabilistically, Hirshleifer and Titman assume that small shareholders who are indifferent between tendering and not tendering their shares make their choices randomly. Let $P(\pi)$ be the probability the bid is accepted, where π is the premium offered (over the nontakeover intrinsic value, but not over the market price) as in the Shleifer and Vishny (1986a) model and let ω be the fraction of the outstanding shares which the bidder offers to buy (ω is equal to $.5 - \alpha$).

Hirshleifer and Titman's objective is to derive a solution for $P(\pi)$ which "supports" the separating equilibrium in which the bid is fully revealing the information with $\pi = Z$. Under the given assumptions, the solution for $P(\pi)$ is the probability of success that obtains in equilibrium. If a bid is made, the level of the bid is chosen to maximize his expected gain, so this problem is

$$\max_{\pi}[\alpha Z + (Z - \pi)\omega]P(\pi) \tag{A.4}$$

The first-order condition with respect to the amount of the bid is

$$0 = P'[\alpha Z + (Z - \pi)\omega] - P\omega \tag{A.5}$$

Investors tender their shares if $\pi > E(Z|\pi)$ and do not tender if $\pi < E(Z|\pi)$. If $\pi = E(Z|\pi)$, they are indifferent and may randomly decide whether or not to tender. For this case, Hirshleifer and Titman assume that the shareholders' tendering strategies are chosen so that the probability of the bid succeeding at different levels of the bid supports the proposed equilibrium behavior of the bidders. Hirshleifer and Titman offer an intuitive justification for such a "mixed strategy" equilibrium: If the bid makes shareholders very nearly indifferent as to whether to tender, then from the bidders' perspective, the actions of the shareholders will appear to be random. That is, although an individual's tendering decision is perfectly determinate, it depends on individual characteristics unknown to the bidder.

The shareholders are indifferent between tendering and not tendering in the case of the proposed equilibrium where the bidder offers a bid of $\pi = Z$. To see that such an equilibrium exists and to solve for the supporting probability schedule, substitute $\pi = Z$ into (A.5) and rewrite the equation in terms of π as

$$\frac{P'}{P} = \frac{\omega}{\alpha\pi} \tag{A.5'}$$

Integrating both sides of (A.5') over π and rearranging terms yields a schedule that expresses the probability of the tender offer success:

$$P(\pi) = k\pi^{\frac{\omega}{\alpha}}$$

where k is a constant of integration. Shareholders accept all bids greater than Z_{max} with certainty because they can do no better by retaining their shares. Therefore, $P(Z_{max})$ must equal 1, so the probability schedule becomes

$$P(\pi) = \left(\frac{\pi}{Z_{max}}\right)^{\frac{\omega}{\alpha}}$$

which increases in π. An increase in the large shareholder's initial holdings, α, also increases the probability of offer success. Large α implies relatively more profits come from initial holdings than from purchased shares. Thus, the incentive to underbid is smaller for large α and the probability of success is larger for large α.

The expected net profit to the bidder should be positive:

$$\alpha\pi P(\pi) - c_T = \alpha\pi^{\frac{5}{\alpha}} Z_{max}^{\frac{-\omega}{\alpha}} - c_T > 0$$

The expected profit is increasing in $\pi (= Z)$. The smallest $\pi = Z$ below which the expected profit is negative has been denoted as Z^c. This critical value is then expressed as

$$Z^c = \left(\frac{c_T}{\alpha}\right)^{2\alpha} (Z_{max})^{2\omega}$$

As in the Shleifer and Vishny (1986a) model, Z^c grows arbitrarily large as α approaches zero. This implies that offers will not be made by atomistic shareholders.

To summarize the preceding discussions, high-Z bidders are induced to submit high bids because this increases the probability of success. Low-Z bidders gain less from a successful offer and thus are less willing to increase their bid to raise the probability of success. High-Z bidders are not motivated to mimic low-Z bidders because their opportunity cost of a failure is high.

Posttakeover Dilution

Hirshleifer and Titman examine the situation in which dilution of the value of the shares of minority shareholders is anticipated after a successful takeover. Let δ be the fraction by which shares may be diluted after the large shareholder takes over the target. Then the posttakeover value of minority shares is $Z(1 - \delta)$. By diluting the minority, the majority shareholder obtains part or all of δZ per minority share, depending on whether there are dead-weight losses to dilution.

In the perfectly revealing equilibrium, small shareholders tender their shares if the bid price is greater than $Z(1 - \delta)$ and are indifferent if the bid equals this value. The bidder's objective function is

$$\max_{\pi}[\alpha Z + (Z - \pi)(.5 - \alpha) + .5 \, \delta Z]P(\pi)$$

The term $.5 \, \delta Z$ reflects the profit to the bidder if dilution has no dead-weight costs. Alternatively, if dilution is costly, after obtaining control of the target, the bidder can make a clean-up offer for the remaining minority shares at the bid price of $Z(1 - \delta)$.

Following the same procedure as previously, Hirshleifer and Titman derive an expression for the probability function. For this case of dilution, the probability of success increases with the amount of dilution. Higher δ increases the cost to underbidding, because a given decrease in the probability of success reduces the expected gain due to the dilution $(.5 \, \delta Z)$ by a greater amount. Therefore, the bidder has less incentive to underbid when δ is high, which leads to higher probability of success.

In the proposed equilibrium, the bid equals $Z(1 - \delta)$; dilution threats are reflected in the "first tier" of the offer. This means that minority shareholders do no worse than those who tender. In an extension of the model, Hirshleifer and Titman show that when managerial defenses operate, "overbidding" is possible, in which case the postoffer share price will be lower than the bid price.

Contingent Cost Defenses
by Management

In extending the basic model, Hirshleifer and Titman examine two categories of defenses: contingent cost defenses, which impose costs on the bidder only in the event of offer success, and litigation. These defensive actions are shown to affect the level of the bid and the tendering decisions of target shareholders. The case of contingent defensive costs is considered here.

Some contingent costs that are imposed on the bidder are redistributed to the target shareholders. In the case of "poison pills," the loss of the bidder is fully redistributed to the remaining target shareholders. In other cases, the costs are not borne by target shareholders. There also are cases in which defensive actions reduce the value of the target (as in "sale of the crown jewels") and thus hurt both the bidder and the target shareholders.

Let $h(Z)$ be the cost per share imposed on the shares held or purchased by the bidder, should the bid succeed. The value per minority share is assumed to be increased by an amount $eh(Z)$, where

$$-1 \le e \le 1, \, h(Z) > 0, \, h'(Z) \ge 0$$

The parameter e represents redistributive efficiency. If $e = 1$, the loss imposed on the bidder is fully redistributed to the target shareholders. But if $e < 0$, the defense that hurts the bidder also reduces the posttakeover value of the remaining target shares.

In the proposed mixed-strategy separating equilibrium, the bid must equal the value of the shares should the takeover succeed, inclusive of redistribution, so that

$$\pi = Z + eh(Z)$$

The bidder's problem is then

$$\max_{\pi}[\alpha Z + (Z - \pi)\omega - .5h(Z)]P(\pi)$$

Following the same procedure as previously, Hirshleifer and Titman obtain a solution for $P(\pi)$, which is similar to the one for the basic model. The probability of success depends critically on the value of the redistributive efficiency ratio e. In the case of poison pills where $e = 1$, the probability of success is unambiguously reduced relative to the basic model for a given level of either the bid or of the improvement. Since defenses such as poison pills redistribute wealth from the bidder to the remaining shareholders, they can be viewed as mechanisms that generate negative dilution. Consequently, their impact on the probability of success for a given level of improvement or on the level of bid is opposite to the impact of dilution. That is, the poison pill unambiguously reduces the probability of success and increases the bid for a given level of the improvement.

When $e = 0$, a cost imposed on the bidder is not shifted to the target shareholders. Charter amendments for staggered terms of directors or supermajority provisions are possible examples of this case. The equilibrium bid is $\pi = Z$ as in the basic model. But the probability of success is lower as a function of either the level of the bid or the size of the improvement. Intuitively, the bidder derives smaller profit from the takeover and this increases the incentive to underbid. To deter underbidding, the probability schedule is reduced relative to the basic model for all bids below Z_{max}.

When $e = -1$, defenses harm the target shareholders as much as the bidder, should the takeover succeed. Examples of these kinds of defenses include "scorched earth" or "sale of crown jewels" defenses, in which the target sells off important business assets having the potential for contributing to the improvement of the firm's performance through corporate combination. This case is equivalent to a reduction in Z at all its value. Therefore, the probability of acceptance *as a function of the bid* [$\pi = Z - h(Z)$] rises from the basic model. However, the bid is reduced, so the probability with a given improvement can be greater, lower, or the same as when there are no defenses. In particular, the probability is increased if the defense decreases the asymmetry of information about the improvement net of defensive costs. Intuitively, asymmetry of information is the cause for bid failure, and to the extent that this can be reduced, the frequency of acceptance is raised. If information is symmetric, that is, if the value of improvement is known to the shareholders, they will certainly accept a bid one cent above the posttakeover value of the share.

Litigation

Incumbent management of a target can directly reduce the probability of success of a bid through litigation. As has been argued previously, defensive actions affect the incentive of bidders to offer high or low premia and therefore influence target shareholders as to their tendering decisions. For litigation by target management intended to reduce the probability of offer success, this adjustment by shareholders could take the form of an increased willingness to tender their shares and partially or even completely offset the direct probability-reducing effect of litigation. For instance, if the probability that the bid is legally allowed rises with the bid, the defense increases the incentive to bid high and so a given bid would become more attractive to shareholders.

On the other hand, if the probability that the bid is legally allowed is not related to the level of the bid, then Hirshleifer and Titman show that the "overall" probability of offer success (the offer being legally allowed *and* accepted by the shareholders) is uniformly reduced. This case is consistent with the evidence of Walkling (1985) that managerial defenses increase tender offer failure. Also, with $P(\pi)$ uniformly lower, the incentive to bid is reduced, so bidders with low improvements are deterred from bidding. This leads to a higher average value of the bids.

However, if the probability of legal acceptance is increased steeply with the bid, overbidding becomes possible and a mixed-strategy equilibrium where bidders offer the true value of improvement becomes infeasible. As an illustration, suppose that all bids lower than Z_{max} are legally disallowed. Then if α is sufficiently high, some low-value bidders will overbid with $\pi = Z_{max}$. In this situation, defenses by management benefit shareholders by increasing the level of the bid and the probability that the tender offer will succeed.

Hirshleifer and Titman observe that defenses can be socially beneficial because by raising bids they can increase the probability of success. This observation is in contrast to the argument that higher bids caused by takeover defenses involve a social cost by deterring potentially profitable synergies. This latter argument is raised by Easterbrook and Fischel (1981), who therefore propose a passivity rule for target management.

The preceding analysis also suggests that the Williams Act, by facilitating defensive actions, may have promoted overbidding in takeover contests. The rise in bid premia since the Williams Act, as reported by Jarrell and Bradley (1980), is consistent with this hypothesis. This prediction is also made by Shleifer and Vishny, but for different reasons. According to Shleifer and Vishny, the average bid premium increases because low-value bidders are deterred from bidding by the rise in the cost of tender offer as a result of the Williams Act. According to Hirshleifer and Titman, it is overbidding that increases the average premium. They emphasize that only overbidding can explain the lower abnormal returns to bidders found by Jarrell and Bradley (1980), after the Williams Act and later state legislations.

Management opposition may also impose a nontrivial cost on bidders prior to the outcome of the bid. If this cost decreases with the bid, then bidders have the incentive to bid high. Therefore, defensive measures can actually increase the probability of takeover success, given a bid is made. An implication of this analysis as observed by Hirshleifer and Titman is that it may be counterproductive for an entrenched manager to use defenses imposing high costs on lower bidders. This is because the probability of low bids succeeding can actually rise. Hirshleifer and Titman further note that social welfare gains might arise from defensive measures (by forcing up the bid or reducing information asymmetry) which lead the bidder to succeed with higher probability.

Empirical Implications

The Hirshleifer and Titman model yields a number of empirical implications. Most of these have been noted in the preceding discussion, but the more significant ones are summarized here.

1 The probability of an offer's success increases with the bid premium and with the initial holdings of the bidder in the target, and is decreasing in the number of shares required to obtain control. The result that the probability of success rises with the bid premium and with the bidder's initial holdings is consistent with the evidence of Walkling (1985).
2 The ratio of the stock price reaction at the announcement of the bid to the bid premium is increasing in the level of the bid and the initial shareholdings of the bidder, and is decreasing in the number of shares required to obtain control.
3 As in the Shleifer and Vishny model, the average bid premium declines with the size of the bidder's initial holdings in the target, and increases with the number of shares needed to obtain control. These implications are consistent with the evidence of Walkling and Edmister (1985).
4 Activities that reduce the degree of asymmetry of information between bidder and shareholders, such as the payment of solicitation fees to persuade shareholders to tender, are predicted to increase the probability of success. Consistent with this prediction, Walkling (1985) found that the payment of solicitation fees does increase the probability of takeover success.

Pretakeover Share Acquisition Strategy: Jegadeesh and Chowdhry (1988)

While bearing close resemblance to the models discussed earlier, the Jegadeesh and Chowdhry model focuses on the bidder's strategy for pretender offer acquisition of target shares. This investigation is motivated by the observation that initial footholdings of bidders vary widely. In the proposed model, low initial shareholding signals that the improvement to be achieved through takeover by the involved bidder will be small and thus enables the bidder to offer a lower premium for target shares.

The Jegadeesh and Chowdhry Model

As in the preceding models, the bidder observes a level of synergy Z which is unknown to the shareholders who are assumed to be atomistically small. The bidder purchases up to α_{max} shares in the open market where $\alpha_{max} < 0.5$. Different target shareholders have different reservation selling prices. These reservation prices, denoted R_i for shareholder i, are unknown to the bidder and can be higher than the prevailing market prices.

After strategically deciding on the open-market purchase α, the bidder launches a conditional tender offer for the balance $(0.5 - \alpha)$ shares required to obtain control of the target at the bid price B. Assuming no dilution of minority shareholders, the risk-neutral shareholders refuse to tender their shares unless the bid is at least as large as the expected synergy conditional on the observed α and B. This "free-rider condition" is expressed as:

$$B \geq E(Z|\alpha,B) \tag{A.6}$$

Shareholder i would tender his shares if $B > R_i$ and condition (A.6) are satisfied. Since the number of shares tendered plus α should be no smaller than 0.5, the probability of success, denoted $P(B)$, is the probability that the bid B is at least as large as the median reservation price. This probability schedule is common knowledge.

Let $V(B,\alpha;Z)$ be the expected value of the tender offer at bid price B to bidder type Z who has acquired α shares in the open market, given that condition (A.6) is satisfied. Assuming that α is obtained at the assumed current market price of zero, the value function is given by

$$V(B,\alpha;Z) = P(B)[.5Z - B(.5 - \alpha)]$$

The risk-neutral bidder's problem is stated as

$$\max_{\alpha,B} V(B,\alpha;Z) \quad \text{subject to } B \geq E(Z|\alpha,B)$$

In order to make the problem on hand interesting and for obtaining insightful results, Jegadeesh and Chowdhry impose two restrictions on the probability distribution function. In particular, these restrictions (assumptions) make the free-rider problem costly to all bidders, which in turn provides incentive for the bidders to separate themselves from higher Z types of bidders.

ASSUMPTION 1   The probability of success is increasing in the amount of the bid at a nonincreasing rate, that is,

$$P'(B) > 0 \quad \text{and} \quad P''(B) \leq 0$$

FIGURE A.1   Expected Value of Takeover Bids

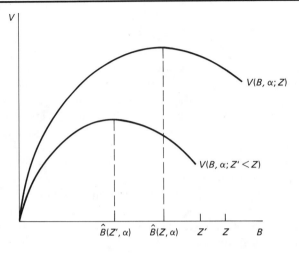

This assumption makes the function V concave in B in the region where V is positive (see Figure A.1). The value of B which maximizes V, denoted $\hat{B}(\alpha, Z)$, is then unique and V is decreasing in B for any value of $B > \hat{B}(\alpha, Z)$. Also, it can be shown that the assumption makes $\hat{B}(\alpha, Z)$ be increasing in α; a large initial foot-holding will cause the expected value of the tender offer to be maximized only at a higher bid.

ASSUMPTION 2   The constraint imposed by the free-rider condition is binding for all bidder types. Formally,

$$Z > \hat{B}(Z, \alpha_{max}) > \hat{B}(Z, \alpha)$$

This assumption implies that the value-maximizing level of bid is smaller than Z; the bidders have the incentive to bid lower in some neighborhood of their respective synergy levels Z.

The preceding assumptions can be shown to imply the relationships depicted in Figure A.1. Note that for any level of bid, the slope of the curve is larger for larger Z and for bids greater than $\hat{B}(Z, \alpha)$, the expected value V declines faster for bidders with $Z' < Z$. In the framework outlined so far, Jegadeesh and Chowdhry establish two interim results which are useful for constructing their final results on the signaling equilibrium.

LEMMA 1. For any given level of initial shareholdings α, the net benefit of bidding low as opposed to high is greater for a bidder with lower valuation Z.

This can be seen easily from Figure A.1 where the difference between $V(B, \alpha; Z)$ and $V(B, \alpha; Z')$ becomes smaller as B is lowered. Intuitively, this result is obtained because a reduced probability of success caused by a lower bid hurts the higher valuation bidder more, while for any given level of initial footholding the benefit of bidding low is the same for all bidder types to the extent that a low bid reduces the cost of purchasing the shares tendered. The higher valuation bidder loses more if the bid fails, since he has more to gain from the success of the offer precisely because his valuation is higher.

LEMMA 2. For any given bid, the cost of choosing a lower level of the initial footholding as opposed to a higher level is identical for all bidders regardless of their types Z.

This is intuitively clear because the additional shares are to be purchased at the given bid price not related to the level of Z if the bid succeeds with probability $P(B)$.

Equilibrium Bids and Shareholdings

The argument is first made by Jegadeesh and Chowdhry that there can be no *pooling equilibrium* in which the size of the initial footholding has no value as a signal and the optimal bids of different bidder types are the same. Then they go on to show the existence of a separating equilibrium in which a low-valuation bidder chooses not to acquire as many target shares as a high-valuation bidder, and thereby credibly separates itself from the latter so that it bids a lower amount.

Suppose there are two types of bidders with Z_L and Z_H, respectively. Assume that $Z_L < Z_M \equiv E(Z) < Z_H$ and that $\hat{B}(Z_H, \alpha_{max}) < Z_L$. In a pooling equilibrium, α has no value as a signal and therefore each bidder will choose α_{max}. Since the bidders must bid at least Z_M by condition (A.6) and prefer to bid low rather than bid high as long as $Z_M > \hat{B}(Z_H, \alpha_{max})$, the pooling equilibrium bid for both bidders will be Z_M.

However, the low-valuation bidder would have an incentive to defect from the equilibrium strategy, since it bids more than its valuation ($Z_M > Z_L$). For the defection to be a credible signal of its type, it must choose a strategy that the high-valuation bidder would not mimic. Suppose that it chooses the strategy in which it bids Z_L with an initial footholding of $\alpha' < \alpha_{max}$, where α' satisfies $V(Z_L, \alpha'; Z_H) = V(Z_M, \alpha_{max}; Z_H)$. That is, the high-valuation bidder is indifferent to mimicking the low bidder's new strategy. For this α', the benefit of bidding low is larger for the low-valuation bidder (see Lemma 1). The cost of choosing a lower initial footholding is the same for both bidders (see Lemma 2). Therefore, since the high-valuation bidder is indifferent, the low-valuation bidder is strictly better off, that is,

$$V(Z_L, \alpha'; Z_L) > V(Z_M, \alpha_{max}; Z_L)$$

The low-valuation bidder will thus deviate from the pooling equilibrium. As a result, that equilibrium cannot survive.

To show the existence of a separating equilibrium, suppose there are only three bidder types Z_L, Z_M, and Z_H. Let $Z_L < Z_M < Z_H$. The bidder with the highest valuation Z_H chooses the maximum possible footholding α_{max}:

$$\alpha_H^* = \alpha_{max}$$

where α^* denotes the optimal α. The medium-valuation bidder now chooses a lower foothold so as to make the high-valuation bidder just indifferent to mimicking its strategy. In other words, α_M^* satisfies the following condition:

$$V(Z_M,\alpha_M^*;Z_H) = V(Z_H,\alpha_H^*;Z_H)$$

Since the high bidder is indifferent, the medium bidder is strictly better off by not choosing the high bidder's strategy (by Lemmas 1 and 2):

$$V(Z_M,\alpha_M^*;Z_M) > V(Z_H,\alpha_H^*;Z_M)$$

If $\alpha_M^* < 0$, the bidder makes negative profits. Its profits are even lower if it mimics the high bidder. In this case the bidder will be driven out of the bidding game. Similarly, the low-valuation bidder chooses α_L^* such that

$$V(Z_L,\alpha_L^*;Z_M) = V(Z_M,\alpha_M^*;Z_M)$$

Again by Lemma 1 and Lemma 2, it can be shown that the low bidder will not mimic the medium bidder:

$$V(Z_L,\alpha_L^*;Z_L) > V(Z_M,\alpha_M^*;Z_L)$$

If $\alpha_L^* < 0$, the bidder is driven out of the bidding. It can be shown that the high bidder will not mimic the lowest valuation bidder and vice versa.

The preceding strategies constitute the equilibrium. Jegadeesh and Chowdhry argue that the separating equilibrium is stable. Consider, for example, a possible defection by the lowest type. Its bid must be at least Z_L (since it is the lowest possible level of synergy) and therefore the initial shareholding must be greater than α_L^* to make it better off. But the medium bidder finds the defection more attractive because it was indifferent to mimicking the low bidder's equilibrium strategy and because the benefits of moving to a higher α are the same for both bidders (Lemma 2) while the cost of having to bid more is less for the medium bidder (Lemma 1). Suppose now that the shareholders believe that if an out-of-equilibrium offer is made, it is made by the highest valuation bidder who could potentially find that offer superior to the equilibrium offer. Under this belief of the shareholders and with the free-rider problem, the out-of-equilibrium offer will be rejected if it is not at least as great as Z_M. Similarly, if there were a bid greater than Z_M that the medium bidder finds attractive, the highest bidder would find that even more attractive. Therefore, all out-of-equilibrium offers would be rejected by the shareholders.

The extension of the preceding analysis to any finite number of bidders is straightforward. Also the intuition obtained from the preceding equilibrium analysis is carried over to the case of equilibrium with a continuum of bidder types. Further, it is noted by Jegadeesh and Chowdhry that, even if we consider issues like dilution, managerial defensive actions, cost of launching a tender offer, and increases in target share prices over the period of foothold acquisition, the nature of the problem is not altered. However, if the costs imposed by tender offer preparation and rising prices of target shares are sufficiently high, some low-valuation bidders would be excluded from the takeover market.

Empirical Implications

The major implication of the results is that the size of the bidder's foothold is positively related to the tender offer premium and to the abnormal returns on the announcement date. This prediction contrasts both with the pooling equilibrium predictions of the Shleifer and Vishny model and the separating equilibrium predictions of the Hirshleifer and Titman model, where α is exogenously specified. In the Shleifer and Vishny model, the tender offer premium is inversely related to the pretender offer shareholdings. In the Hirshleifer and Titman model, the bid premium and α are not directly related, but the average bid premium for bidders with large α will tend to be small.

The prediction of the Jegadeesh and Chowdhry model is claimed by the authors to be supported by empirical results of Mikkelson and Ruback (1985). They use a sample of "acquiring firms" which filed the 13-D schedule with the SEC disclosing their holdings of "target" shares and their intentions. They examine the abnormal returns to various events occurring since the filing. One of the events is "the acquirer increasing the size of its holdings of target shares." Jegadeesh and Chowdhry argue that within the context of their model, this event would occur if the acquirer revises upward its assessment of the value of the synergistic opportunity. Mikkelson and Ruback report that this event is accompanied by a statistically significant positive return of 1.07 percent on the target shares. But this result is also consistent with another implication of the Jegadeesh and Chowdhry model (and also of the Hirshleifer and Titman model) that the size of initial shareholding will be positively related to the probability of success. Walkling (1985) finds a positive relationship. The relationship was particularly strong when the target management resisted the takeover attempt, causing the strategic tendering decisions of the target shareholders to be important in determining the success of the tender offer.

Finally, as in the Shleifer and Vishny model, increasing the cost of tender offers is predicted to increase the average of the actual premium offered in takeover attempts by deterring low-synergy bidders from acquisition attempts.

PREEMPTIVE BIDDING
AND ENTRANCE COSTS

A major difference between tender offers (which the previous models examine) and merger bids is that in the former bids are made directly to shareholders rather than to management. In a conditional tender offer, if target shareholders are small, they believe their decisions cannot affect the outcome of the offer. This leads them to compare only the offer price and the expected value of the share if the bid succeeds. They do not take into account the expected share value conditional on the failure of the offer, because if the offer fails, all shareholders receive that amount regardless of whether they tendered or not.

In a merger bid, however, the target's management decides whether to accept or reject the bid and therefore is concerned with the value of the firm in the case of the offer failure. Management may turn down the present bid if it is likely that a better offer will come from another bidder. Hence, the possibility of competing bids can have an impact on takeover attempts and, in particular, on the strategic decision of the offer price. There is a developing literature on the strategic behavior of bidders and target management in bids made to management. Important studies in this area include Giammarino and Heinkel (1986), Berkovitch and Khanna (1988b), Hirshleifer and Png (1989), and Fishman (1988, 1989).

In modeling the takeover bidding contest, Fishman (1988) describes the process as a special form of auction in which a potential bidder can acquire costly information on the value of the target and then may decide to enter the contest only after a first bidder has made a bid. If the potential (second) bidder should acquire information and bid, then an English auction is triggered. (In an English auction all the potential buyers gather in one place and are free to revise their bids upwards.) A first bidder, in determining his initial offer to the target's management, takes the potential bidder's updating of information and decision to compete into account. In the equilibrium derived by the model, a first bidder may make a high-premium "preemptive" bid that signals its high valuation and deters the second bidder from updating information and competing. This deterrence can be effective because a high valuation by the first bidder lowers the second bidder's expected profit from entering the competition. The model thus explains why bidders frequently offer high premiums on their initial bids rather than making a low bid and being prepared to raise it if there is competition. One important result of Fishman (1988) is that the lower the cost of investigation to the second bidder, the more likely the first bidder will choose to allow investigation. Hence, the expected price of the target will be maximized if the cost of investigation to the second bidder is lowered.

The model employed by Hirshleifer and Png (1989) is similar to Fishman's *except* for the former's assumption that revising a bid is (prohibitively) costly. It is shown by Hirshleifer and Png that facilitating competing bids to the maximum need not maximize the expected takeover price. This is in contrast to a prediction obtained by the Fishman model that lowering the investigation (that is, information) cost of a second bidder will always increase the expected takeover price. In the Hirshleifer and Png model, the expected takeover price is maximized at a cost of investigation that is neither extremely large nor extremely small. The reason is that an extremely low cost of investigation undermines the incentive for the first bidder to make a preemptively high bid. Note that if revising a bid is prohibitively costly, that is, if the bidders can make only one bid, the first bidder's initial bid becomes the final takeover price even if the second bidder makes a bid. (The second bidder's bid will only have to be slightly larger, for example, by a cent.) Hirshleifer and Png also build an example in which each bidder may bid any number of times at a positive cost each time he does so and show that the preceding result still holds. This result has implications for the target management's policy and takeover regulation as they can facilitate or hinder competing bids by affecting the cost of investigation of potential bidders.

Preemptive Takeover Bidding: Fishman (1988)

While the three models reviewed earlier analyze takeover bids made directly to atomistic shareholders, the Fishman study is directed to the takeover process with bids made to management. It models the strategic bidding process among competitors in an environment of asymmetric and costly information. The model developed is capable of providing an explanation for why bidders might make high initial bids and generates testable implications on the interrelationships between bidders' and targets' profits and the effects of takeover legislation.

THE FISHMAN MODEL   It is assumed that there are two management teams called bidders 1 and 2. After observing the initial offer of bidder 1, bidder 2 updates its prior beliefs about bidder 1's valuation of the target. Then, on the basis of these updated beliefs, the second bidder determines its strategy about acquiring information on the valuation of the target. Bidder 1, in determining its initial offer, takes bidder 2's strategy on information acquisition and bidding into account.

Let v_0 denote the target value if there is no takeover. It is assumed to be known to all parties. For $i = 1,2$, let v_i denote bidder i's valuation for the target. At a known cost $c_i > 0$, bidder i can privately observe v_i. The cost includes both direct costs such as investment banker's fees and any opportunity costs involved. The current market value v_0 is assumed to be the minimum acquisition price. There are two states of the world: $s = s^-$ and $s = s^+$. Only in the latter state ($s = s^+$), the target is a potentially profitable acquisition. Bidders never find it profitable to incur the cost of observing their valuations if $s = s^-$ or if the realization of s is unknown. Further, it is assumed that $E(\tilde{v}_i|s = s^-) < E(\tilde{v}_i|s = s^+) < v_0$ for both bidders. This implies that bidders would never find it profitable to bid without observing their valuations. Let $F_i(v_i)$ be the probability distribution function of v_i and $f_i(v_i)$ the density function, both conditional on $s = s^+$. The function $f_i(v_i)$ is strictly positive on the interval $[l,h]$ (where $l < v_i < h$) and zero elsewhere. These distributions are known to all parties.

Bidder 1 privately and costlessly observes s, but bidder 2 does not observe s directly. In state $s = s^+$, bidder 1 pays c_1 to observe $\tilde{v}_1$ and makes a bid if $v_1 > v_0$. Then bidder 2, having observed any offer made by bidder 1, can pay c_2 to observe its valuation $\tilde{v}_2$. If bidder 2 makes a bid, then the bid rises until only one bidder remains. The target accepts the highest remaining bid, given that it is at or above v_0.

Let p $(v_1 \geqslant p \geqslant v_0)$ be bidder 1's initial offer, and let d be bidder 2's decision, where $d = 1$ refers to bidder 2's competing (that is, paying c_2 to observe $\tilde{v}_2$) and $d = 0$ refers to bidder 2's not competing. Bidder i's payoffs as a function of v_1, v_2, p, and d are denoted by $\pi_i(v_1,v_2,p,d)$. Then bidder 1's payoffs are given by

$$\pi_1(v_1,v_2,p,0) = v_1 - p - c_1$$

$$\pi_1(v_1,v_2,p,1) = v_1 - \min\{\max(p,v_2), v_1\} - c_1$$

Bidder 2's payoffs are given by

$$\pi_2(v_1,v_2,p,0) = 0$$

$$\pi_2(v_1,v_2,p,1) = v_2 - \min\{v_1,v_2\} - c_2$$

If bidder 2 does not compete, bidder 1 acquires the target at p. If bidder 2 does compete, he pays to observe $\tilde{v}_2$, and the higher-valuing bidder acquires the target with an offer of $\min\{\max(p,v_2),v_1\}$. That is, if $v_2 > p$, the bid rises to the second-highest valuation.

Finally, it is assumed that the information $v_1 \geqslant v_0$ is not sufficient to deter bidder 2 from competing. Therefore, a preemptive bidder must have a valuation strictly greater than v_0.

ANALYSIS OF EQUILIBRIUM   If bidder 1's valuation (equals or) exceeds a threshold, v', it makes a high-premium, preemptive offer. Otherwise, it offers v_0, the minimum acquisition price. For bidder 2 to be deterred by a first bidder whose valuation exceeds the threshold v', for a preemptive bid p', bidder 2's expected payoff from competing must be nonpositive given that $v_1 \geqslant v'$. This condition is expressed as

$$\int_{v'}^h E\pi_2(v_1,\tilde{v}_2,p',1) \frac{f_1(v_1)}{1 - F_1(v')} dv_1 \leqslant 0 \qquad (A.7)$$

Define r such that (A.7) is satisfied as an equality at $v' = r$. Then it must be true that $v_0 < r < h$ because v_1 must be greater than v_0 for bidder 2 to be deterred. For any $v' \geqslant r$, bidder 2 will be deterred if it is known that $v_1 \geqslant v'$. Now, how much would a first bidder with $v_1 \geqslant r$ be willing to offer to distinguish itself from a bidder with $v_1 < r$, and preempt a second bidder? Since the best alternative to preempting is offering v_0, bidder 1 would offer p' to preempt bidder 2 if the expected benefit of preempting at p' is nonnegative. This can be expressed as:

$$E\pi_1(v_1,\tilde{v}_2,p',0) - E\pi_1(v_1,\tilde{v}_2,v_0,1)$$

$$= E \min\{\max(v_0,\tilde{v}_2),v_1\} - p' \geqslant 0$$

For $v_0 \leqslant v_1 < h$, define $\bar{p}(v_1) = E \min\{\max(v_0,\tilde{v}_2),v_1\}$. This is the maximum initial offer bidder 1 would be willing to make to preempt bidder 2, since $p' \leqslant \bar{p}(v_1)$ from the preceding inequality; $\bar{p}(v_1)$ is increasing in v_1. Intuitively, the higher bidder 1's valuation, the more it expects to lose in the event of an auction, and thus the more he is willing to pay to preempt the competition. Thus, a bidder with $v_1 \geq r$ would be willing to offer $\bar{p}(r)$ to preempt a second bidder, while a first bidder with $v_1 < r$ would not. Note that $\bar{p}(r) \leq r$.

These results imply that it is an equilibrium for bidder 1 to offer $\bar{p}(r) = E$ min$\{$max$(v_0, \tilde{v}_2), r\}$ if $v_1 \geq r$ and to offer v_0 if $v_0 \leq v_1 < r$, and for bidder 2 to be preempted by the former, but not the latter, offer. Under some credibility requirement which restricts the extent of artibrary beliefs formed in response to out-of-equilibrium initial offers, the preceding equilibrium can be shown to be unique. It is a signaling equilibrium. Bidder 1 makes either a preemptive bid, $\bar{p}(r)$, or a zero-premium bid, v_0. The former offer signals that $v_1 \geq r$, in which case bidder 2 is deterred, and the latter signals that $v_0 < v_1 < r$, in which case bidder 2 competes.

The signaling equilibrium is not fully revealing. Therefore, the signaling equilibrium is socially inefficient relative to the equilibrium that would obtain if bidder 2 could directly observe $\tilde{v}_1$. There are cases in which bidder 2 is deterred in the signaling equilibrium but would not be if $\tilde{v}_1$ could be observed directly. Since bidder 2's profit from competing equals the social gain, given its information, its optimal decision coincides with the socially optimal decision when $\tilde{v}_1$ is observable. Therefore, this difference that arises when bidder 2 is deterred plus the investigation cost is the social cost of the incomplete information.

IMPLICATIONS OF THE MODEL   First, consider the changes in c_2. Since r is decreasing in c_2, an increase in c_2 leads to more realizations of $\tilde{v}_1$ for which bidder 2 is preempted. Further, since the preemptive bid is increasing in r, an increase in c_2 leads to a lower preemptive bid. Therefore, bidder 1's equilibrium expected payoff is increasing in c_2. As competing becomes less profitable for bidder 2, preemption becomes cheaper for bidder 1. The target's expected payoff is decreasing in c_2. Both the higher frequency of preemption and the lower preemptive bid decrease the target's expected payoff. Further, it can be shown that the decrease in the targets' expected payoff is equal in magnitude to the increase in bidder 1's expected payoff.

These results with respect to the costs of the competing bidders provide an incentive for targets to take actions that lower the costs. Jarrell (1985) suggests that litigation by targets is undertaken in an attempt to facilitate competing bids by providing more time for a second bidder and thus possibly lowering the second bidder's costs. However, if the target can lower the second bidder's costs to the point where a first bidder's entry would be unprofitable, the first bidder would be discouraged to study the target initially. In this regard, Easterbrook and Fischel (1982) argue that target management should be required to remain passive during takeovers.

The model also has implications with respect to the relationships between initial bids, the number of bidders, and profits. It is easy to see that targets' expected profits conditional on observing high initial bids are greater than their profits conditional on observing low initial bids. Note that the former profits are higher, although there is no competition from other bidders. Further, it can be shown under the model that first bidders' expected profits are also higher conditional on observing a high initial bid and no competing bids. This is in contrast to what one might expect in a model that does not involve preemptive bidding.

In testing these predictions, Fishman cautions that two things have to be taken into account. First, bidders' valuations and the information costs may vary across targets. For instance, targets in single-bidder contests may have lower profits because these contests comprise primarily high-cost cases. Second, it is difficult to distinguish between single- and multiple-bidder contests because second bidders that compete but find lower valuation are not actually observed.

Finally, the impact of federal and state takeover legislation can be analyzed using the model. If legislation lowers the cost to competing bidders, then a target's and second bidder's expected profits would increase and a first bidder's expected profit would decrease. Additionally, there would be a higher frequency of multiple-bidder contests. In empirically estimating the impact of takeover legislation on bidders' profits, it will be crucial to distinguish first bidders from later bidders. This is because the impact will be different between the two groups of bidders and averaging across acquiring bidders will not identify the effects.

Another possible effect of takeover legislation should be noted. As a result of lowering the costs to second bidders, some targets may no longer be profitable for first bidders to study. Thus, fewer firms will be subject to takeover bids and this truncation may increase the measured profits for all bidders and targets.

Facilitation of Competing Bids and Takeover Price: Hirshleifer and Png (1989)

The management of a target firm can affect the cost of information that potential bidders have to incur prior to their decision to make a takeover bid. The study by Hirshleifer and Png examines the effects of the investigation cost of potential bidders on the price of a takeover target. Unlike the Fishman (1988) model, it is shown by Hirshleifer and Png that if revising a bid is costly, the target management would not facilitate competing bids to the maximum. The assumption that the cost of making a revised bid is significant may be justified in actuality as it includes fees to outside advisors, opportunity cost of management's time, the cost of contingent financing for an extended period, and the costs of meeting takeover regulations.

In the first part of the paper, each bidder can make only one bid. The proposition that Hirshleifer and Png derive under this assumption is that the expected takeover price is maximized at a positive value of the second bidder's cost of investigation. The reason: Under the given assumption, the initial bidder's bid becomes the takeover price regardless of the second (potential) bidder's entering the competition, and the first bidder switches to an accommodating bid from a deterring bid when the cost of investigation becomes smaller than some value. Hirshleifer and Png further show that the main results of the paper hold in the more general setting of unlimited number of bids at a fixed cost per bid.

THE BASIC MODEL   Since most of the elements of the Hirshleifer and Png model are the same as those of Fishman, the model is described only briefly and consequently the basic result is also discussed in an intuitive fashion.

There are two potential acquirers, each of which can realize a synergistic gain by taking over a target. Each potential acquirer can learn its valuation of the target at some cost of investigation. The first bidder has the choice between a preemptive bid that deters the second (potential) bidder from investigation and a lower bid that will lead to investigation of the target by the second bidder.

The management of the target seeks to maximize the takeover price, whose minimum is the prevailing market price m. The focus of analysis is what the optimal bid, b, of the first bidder should be after it discovered its valuation, v_1, of the target. In the first part of the paper, Hirshleifer and Png assume that once a bid is made, it cannot be revised nor can it be withdrawn. The bid b by the first bidder must satisfy $m \leq b \leq v_1$.

The second bidder can determine its valuation v_2 with certainty at a cost of c_2. This cost of investigation will include outside fees, opportunity cost of management time, and so on. The target management may increase or decrease this cost by instituting, prior to the first bidder's announcement of its bid, a policy of providing the desired information about itself to the bidder.

The value of c_2 and the distributions of v_1 and v_2 are common knowledge, but the realized values of v_1 and v_2 are private information of the respective bidders.

If the second bidder finds $v_2 > b$, it can acquire the target by matching b and realize $v_2 - b$; otherwise it will realize nothing. The second bidder will investigate only if the expected return from investigation (ERI) is positive:

$$ERI_2(b) = E[\max\{\tilde{v}_2 - b, 0\}] - c_2 > 0$$

Suppose that there exist bids that deter the second bidder from investigating. Then the optimal bid, $b^d(c_2)$, among those that deter competition is the minimum value of b that satisfies $ERI_2(b) \leq 0$, given $m \leq b \leq v_1$. If such a bid exists, b^d does not vary with v_1, but is weakly decreasing in c_2. The expected return to the first bidder from this bid is $[v_1 - b^d(c_2)]$.

Suppose now that there exist bids that allow investigation (that is, that satisfy $ERI_2(b) > 0$ and $b \geq m$). If $v_2 > b$, the second bidder will take the target and the first bidder will realize nothing. If $v_2 \leq b$, the first bidder will realize $(v_1 - b)$ by acquiring the target. Hence, the expected return to the first bidder is $(v_1 - b) \cdot pr(v_2 \leq b)$. Thus, the optimal *accommodating bid*, $b^i(v_1, c_2)$, among those that satisfy $ERI_2(b) > 0$ is that value of b which maximizes $(v_1 - b) \cdot pr(v_2 \leq b)$, given $b \geq m$. Note that the optimal accommodating bid will be independent of c_2, given that it satisfies $ERI_2(b) > 0$.

For those combinations of (v_1,c_2) for which both b^d and b^i exist, b^d will be greater than b^i since $ERI_2(b)$ is decreasing in b. The first bidder will choose the bid that yields the larger expected profit, that is, bid high if

$$v_1 - b^d(c_2) \geq [v_1 - b^i(v_1,c_2)] \cdot pr[v_2 \leq b^i(v_1,c_2)]$$

For some (v_1,c_2), there exist only bids that deter investigation. In these cases, the first bidder will choose from among the deterring bids. In other cases where only bids that lead to investigation exist, one of these bids will be chosen.

OPTIMAL FACILITATION OF COMPETING BIDS   The foregoing discussion of the basic model can be summarized as follows. The first bidder may bid high to be assured of acquiring the target. Alternatively, it may bid low and allow the second bidder to investigate. The cost of a high bid is a smaller profit from the takeover. A low bid is a gamble on the chance that the second bidder will find a low v_2. The first bidder chooses a bid that maximizes its expected profit.

Define $I(c_2)$ as the set of $v_1 \geq m$ such that the first bidder bids $b^i(v_1,c_2)$, and $D(c_2)$ as the set of $v_1 \geq m$ such that the first bidder bids $b^d(c_2)$. It is possible that one of the sets $I(c_2)$ and $D(c_2)$ be empty. The target management sets the cost of investigation before the first bidder announces its bid so as to maximize the expected takeover price which is expressed as

$$p(c_2) \equiv \sum_{v_1 \in I(c_2)} b^i(v_1,c_2) \cdot pr(v_1) + \sum_{v_1 \in D(c_2)} b^d(c_2) \cdot pr(v_1)$$

The investigation cost of the second bidder, c_2, affects this expected price through the values of bids $b^i(v_1,c_2)$ and $b^d(c_2)$ and the choice between bidding to deter investigation and bidding to allow investigation. What Hirshleifer and Png show in the analysis is that this expected price is maximized at a value of c_2 that is neither extremely large nor extremely small. Specifically it is shown that for sufficiently large c_2, a reduction in c_2 increases p or leaves it unchanged; for c_2 close to zero, its reduction leaves p unchanged; and for an intermediate value of c_2, a reduction reduces p. Therefore, p is maximized at a modestly small (or large) value of c_2. A possible example based on this proposition on the optimal bidding strategy as a function of c_2 is depicted in Figure A.2.

An intuitive reasoning for this proposition can be given. Note that in the given model, the first bidder's bid price becomes the takeover price, whether or not a competing bid is offered. At a very low cost of investigation, no deterring bid may be optimal; it is too high to be profitable. But at a higher cost, deterring becomes possible (that is, deterring bids may be optimal) and some will bid high to deter. Thus, the expected takeover price is higher at an investigation cost that is not too low.

In the figure, the highest preemptive bid occurs at c_2^* which is an "intermediate" value of the entrance cost. Note that the accommodating bids can be higher than the market price of the target firm in the absence of a takeover. This is an

FIGURE A.2   Optimal Bidding with Only One Bid Permitted: An Example

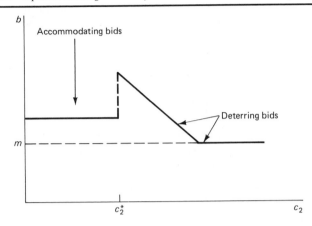

important difference from Fishman's (1988) auction model in which a zero pre-mium bid is made unless the bidder seeks to preempt a potential competitor. In the Hirshleifer and Png model each bidder is allowed at most one bid. Thus, the first bidder makes a premium bid when accommodating investigation in order to increase the likelihood that the second bidder will draw a valuation below the first bid.

In extending the model, Hirshleifer and Png assume that both bidders may bid any number of times at a fixed cost per bid and that bidding ends only when one bidder quits voluntarily. This is an intermediate situation between the pre-ceding case of a prohibitively high cost of revising a bid and Fishman's assump-tion of costless counterbidding. In the new setting, Hirshleifer and Png show that the target's expected price may be *lower* under competitive bidding than if the first bidder makes a preemptive bid. Even if the second bidder competes, the takeover price will not be bid up to the smaller of the two bidders' valuations net of bidding cost. The reason is that once a bidder gets the signal that his value is smaller than that of his competitor, he prefers to quit rather than incur any further cost of bidding. Therefore, as before, lowering the cost of investigation may reduce the expected takeover price.

IMPLICATIONS   The preceding analysis suggests that when the cost of revis-ing a takeover bid is significant, facilitation of competing bids does not always increase the expected takeover price of a target. This result is in contrast to the general belief (or the result from the popular auction model) that lower informa-tion cost would lead to a higher expected takeover price—a belief that is con-firmed by Fishman (1988) if bids can be revised at low costs. Therefore, the effect of assisting competing bidders in their investigation critically depends on the significance or insignificance of the cost of making a revised bid.

One important difference between the results from the auction model and the costly counterbidding model is concerned with the level of an accommodating bid. Only the Hirshleifer and Png model predicts an accommodating bid with a nonzero premium. Spatt (1989) notes that bids at premium to market frequently entail competing bids. This evidence is consistent with the prediction of the Hirshleifer and Png model. Hirshleifer and Png argue that the English auction is a deficient model of takeover bidding.

The cost includes fees for outside advisors, opportunity costs of executive time, and the cost of contingent financing arrangement for the revised bid. This cost is also affected by takeover regulation such as the Williams Act specifying disclosure requirements and a minimum time period a tender offer must remain open. If the time available to competing bidders to investigate is shorter, they will have to rely on more costly methods of collecting information.

The target management can also influence the investigation cost in a significant way. It may adopt a policy allowing free access to information through published reports and frequent press releases. Or it may limit information release to the minimum required by law. With respect to the management's policy, however, there is a problem of commitment. The target management has an incentive to assist potential competitors to the maximum after an initial bid is made, for that could only increase the selling price of the target. This incentive will be stronger if revising a bid is possible to a greater extent.

CHOICE OF THE MEDIUM OF EXCHANGE

As we have seen in Chapter 13, acquiring firms choose equity and debt securities as frequently as cash as the medium of exchange in mergers and acquisitions. When there are no asymmetries in information, no transaction costs, and no taxes, the medium of exchange is not relevant. Thus, the studies which investigate the role of the medium of exchange do so under the assumption that one or more of these conditions, especially the absence of asymmetric information, are violated.

The key difference between a cash offer and a risky securities offer is the contingent-pricing effect of risky securities. When securities whose values are related to the profitability of the target are offered, the price of the target is actually determined ex post. When the profitability of the target turns out to be high (low), the value of the security will also be high (low), implying a higher (lower) payment to the target than otherwise. When the bidders have private information on their valuation of the takeover but the target does not, the value of securities if offered will only be known to the bidders. In this case, securities offers cause an adverse selection problem because the securities offered will be presumed to have a low value, that is, because the bidder will offer cash instead of securities when it knows the securities have a high value. The adverse selection problem will thus lead to the use of cash since no party has private information on the value of cash. The models reviewed earlier assume that only the bidders have private information and therefore consider (justifiably) cash offers only.

The analyses by Hansen (1987) and Fishman (1989) of the role of the exchange medium incorporate the possibility that the target firm has private information on the profitability of the takeover. When the target has private information and cash is offered, the target will accept the offer only when its value is less than the offer made. This then causes the "lemons" problem. To protect itself against this adverse selection, the bidder can make a securities offer whose value is contingent on the future profitability of the takeover. Hansen (1987) considers a bargaining process and shows that a stock offer, having the contingent-pricing effect, increases the probability of a trade occurring. Envisaging an auction process, Fishman (1989) similarly shows that a debt offer (backed by the target's assets) induces the target to make an "efficient" accept/reject decision. According to Fishman (1989), a decision rule is efficient if the target accepts (rejects) the offer when its private information indicates that the acquisition is (is not) profitable, that is, value creating.

According to Hansen (1987) and Fishman (1989), the benefit of a cash offer is not the same. Hansen emphasizes the bidder's private information on its own premerger equity value, and cash is offered if its equity is relatively undervalued. However, in Fishman's auction model, a cash offer signals a high valuation for the target and is made to preempt a potential competing bidder.

Role of Stock Offer: Hansen (1987)

Hansen examines the transacting process of a merger or acquisition to formulate a model for the choice of exchange medium (either cash or stock). The process is treated as a two-agent (the target and a bidder) bargaining game under asymmetric information. Hansen focuses on exchange mechanisms that alleviate the trade-attenuating effects of adverse selection under asymmetric information. Throughout the analysis, the target firm has private information on its value. It first considers the case where the acquirer's premerger value is publicly known and then the case where the acquirer has proprietary information on its value.

The following notations are used:

v = target's asset (equity) value to itself
$F(v)$ = probability distribution of v
$w(v)$ = value of target to acquirer
x = acquiring firm's asset (equity) value

$w(v)$ is increasing in v and $w(v) \geq v$ for all v. The target knows v but the acquirer knows only $F(v)$. Both firms know the function $w(v)$; x is initially publicly known. The case in which only the acquirer knows x is considered later. Throughout, a *first-and-final* offer is assumed to be an optimal bargaining strategy for the acquirer under the given assumptions.

ADVANTAGE OF STOCK TRADES WITH SYMMETRIC INFORMATION ON ACQUIRER'S ASSET VALUE   Hansen first shows that a stock offer can effect trade even when a cash offer cannot. This result can easily be shown by an example. Let v be uniformly distributed over (0, 100), and let $w(v) = 1.5v$. Then no mutually beneficial cash trade exists; if an amount of C dollars is offered, the acquirer expects to receive assets worth only $.75C$. To see this, note that the target accepts the offer if and only if $v \leqslant C$. Then the expected value of the target's assets to the acquirer conditional on the offer being accepted is

$$E[w(v)|v < C] = (1.5)\ E(v|\ v \leqslant C)$$

$$= (1.5)\ \frac{C}{2} = 0.75C$$

Consider now a stock deal in which the acquirer offers an ownership share p of the combined firm. For this case, we can find a stock trade which is mutually beneficial for all v. To be beneficial to the target, the condition

$$p(x + 1.5v) \geqslant v$$

should be satisfied for all v. This will be satisfied for all v when it is satisfied for $v = 100$. (The reason is that the target's minimum acceptable stock offer $p = v/(x + 1.5v)$ is increasing in v.) Thus we must have

$$p(x + 150) \geqslant 100$$

The trade should also be beneficial to the acquirer, conditional on the target always accepting the offer. This occurs when the expected wealth of the acquirer is no smaller than x. Since the expected value of the target's assets to the acquirer conditional on the offer being *always* accepted is 75, the condition for the acquirer should be

$$(1 - p)(x + 75) \geqslant x$$

or

$$p \leqslant \frac{75}{x + 75}$$

The two conditions are graphed in Figure A.3. It is seen that the two conditions can be mutually consistent if $x \leqslant 150$. One mutually beneficial offer that always results in trade would be $p = .55$ if $x = 50$.

The preceding example indicates that stock can effect trade even when cash cannot. The intuition behind this is that by determining the actual acquisition

FIGURE A.3   Mutually Beneficial Stock Trades

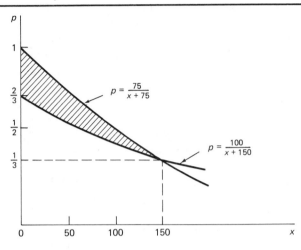

price ex post contingent on the actual value, the acquirer can avoid adverse selection, that is, buying always "lemons" only. Viewing this from the target's side, the stock offer induces the target to sell in more states (of nature) than for a cash offer. This is because when the target knows its assets to be of high value, it can also anticipate its ownership share in the merged firm to increase in value.

In the market for corporate control, we sometimes observe formal contingent pricing (as compared to a stock trade) in the form of conditioning future payments on income of the combined firm. Hansen (1987, note 7) points out that formal contingent pricing as well as using stock will cause incentive problems after the transaction and that the choice between these methods will depend on the relative merits of each method in solving the dual problems of adverse selection and posttransaction moral hazard.

In the preceding example, the size constraint on the acquiring firm ($x \leq 150$) appears because of the contingent-pricing effect; when the acquirer is too large relative to the target, this effect will be negligible. This is a general result that is proved by Hansen. The graph of the example also hints that the probability of trade associated with a stock offer decreases with the relative size of the acquirer. (In the figure, the region of acceptable stock offers decreases as x gets larger.) This result further suggests that for any given firm size, the larger the financial leverage of the acquiring firm and the smaller the financial leverage of the target, the larger the probability of a stock offer. Finally, as Fishman (1989, note 4) argues and the preceding results imply, the optimal securities offer is one backed only by target assets. (However, such an offer will not be feasible, especially in mergers.) The size constraint on the acquirer is always met (that is, becomes irrelevant) when the security offered is backed entirely by target assets. The contingent-pricing effect is the largest in this case.

CHOICE OF CASH VERSUS STOCK WITH ASYMMETRIC INFORMATION ON ACQUIRER'S ASSET VALUE   When the acquiring firm has proprietary information on its own value, another lemons problem arises because the acquiring firm will not offer stock when the target underestimates the value of its offer. The target recognizes this adverse selection problem and must reduce further its estimate of the value of the acquirer's stock. This is one reason why cash offers are often used in actuality; asymmetry of information on the acquirer's asset value offsets the dominance of stock trades. In equilibrium, the chosen medium of exchange and the size of any stock offer are used by the target as signals of acquiring firm value. An optimal choice of the exchange medium and the size of stock offer by the acquirer will take the target's response into account and in equilibrium will sustain the target's beliefs on the signal/value relation.

Let $x(p)$ be the function which the target uses to infer the now unknown value of the acquirer; $x(p)$ must be decreasing in p so that a lower p signals a higher value of x. A firm with a high value of x will choose a low p to signal its high value. In general, false signaling is prevented when the marginal cost of signaling decreases with the true value of the signaler. In Hansen's model, the cost of false signaling arises because a lower p decreases the probability that (or the number of states in which) the target will accept the offer. This cost is larger for a lower-value firm, which is proved by Hansen via a proposition that the acquirer's expected gain from the optimal stock offer decreases with x. [This proposition can also be seen from Figure A.3: The difference between the minimum p-offer acceptable to the target and the maximum p-offer acceptable to the acquirer decreases with x. This implies that the "room" for a (mutually) profitable stock trade decreases with x.] By lowering p, a lower-value firm will incur a greater cost through a reduced probability to make an acquisition that gives greater expected gain than in the case of a higher-value firm.

Hansen argues that the optimal p the acquirer chooses when x is publicly known will no longer be optimal when there is an additional signaling benefit to offering a lower p. Hansen suggests that in equilibrium, the acquirer offers a lower p than it would if x were publicly known. Still, the target correctly infers x from p. A lower p offered when x is not publicly known implies that less trade occurs than would if x were publicly known. The acquirer's expected gain from a stock offer for any x is less with asymmetric information on x than without. This implies that stock will not necessarily dominate cash. Hansen argues that there will generally exist a critical value of x below which (the "overvalued") stock is offered and above which cash is offered. If there exists a net tax benefit from using cash rather than stock, then use of stock will also be decreased. (See Chapter 13.)

Role of the Exchange Medium in Preemptive Bidding: Fishman (1989)

Fishman (1989) focuses on the role of the exchange medium in preempting competition. The model employed is similar to the one in his 1988 study reviewed earlier and in which only cash offers are allowed in an auction process

characterized by asymmetric information between targets and bidders and between bidders. Fishman (1989) considers securities backed by the target's assets
which, as pointed out earlier, should have greater contingent-pricing effect than
those backed by the combined firm's assets. Use of a security backed only by the
target's assets will not be feasible in mergers but could be used in leveraged buy-
outs and leveraged recapitalizations. In Fishman's analysis, securities are used
by lower-valuing bidders and have the advantage of inducing target management to make an "efficient" accept/reject decision, while cash serves to preempt
competition by signaling a high valuation of the target.

THE MODEL   There are two potential bidders for a given target. All are
financed by equity only. The target accepts the offer with the highest value at or
above the target's prebid market value v_0. At a known cost, bidder i can observe a
private signal s_i which conveys information on its own valuation for the target
but is independent of the other. The target costlessly observes a *private* signal, s_0,
which conveys information on both bidders' valuations; $\tilde{s}_0$, $\tilde{s}_1$, and $\tilde{s}_2$ are mutually
independent.

The signal $\tilde{s}_0$ can be either a or b, with respective probabilities $(1 - C)$ and C.
Bidder i's valuation of the target is denoted as $v_i = v^a(s_i)$ when $s_0 = a$, and $v_i = v^b(s_i)$
when $s_0 = b$; v_i increases in s_i, and $v^b(s_i) > v^a(s_i) \geqslant 0$. When $s_0 = a$, acquisition can
never be profitable for both bidders. Also $E[v^b(\tilde{s}_i)] < v_0$ so that it is not profitable
for bidder i to bid without observing s_i.

Initially bidder 1 observes s_1 and decides whether to make a bid. Bidder 2,
after observing this offer, determines whether to observe its own signal at the
known cost and to compete. The media of exchange are cash and debt. The debt
is backed by the target's assets. Suppose that a debt offer with face value p is
accepted. If the target under bidder i's control is worth p or more, the debt
liability is satisfied and, if it is less than p, the bidder defaults on the debt and
turns over the assets. Thus, the target receives either p or v_i and the bidder
receives $v_i - p$ or 0.

The implications, justifications, and other assumptions of the model can be
summarized as follows.

1 The target value if acquired depends on factors specific to the target (s_0) and factors
specific to the bidders (s_1 or s_2). Only the target knows target-specific factors: s_1 (s_2) is
known to bidder 1 (bidder 2) only and is independent of s_2 (s_1).

2 A debt offer with face value p is worth $\min\{v^b(s_i), p\} \geqslant v_0$ if $s_0 = b$ and $\min\{v^a(s_i), p\} < v_0$ if s_0
$= a$. Thus, the target will accept the offer if $s_0 = b$ and reject it if $s_0 = a$. The decision rule is
thus "efficient" because the target accepts the offer only if its private information indicates
that the acquisition can be profitable. In the case of a cash offer, the value of cash is
independent of s_0, so a target may accept an offer even if $s_0 = a$. Thus, a cash offer does not
induce an efficient decision.

3 Suppose that bidder 1 makes a debt offer. If bidder 2 competes, an auction follows. Once
in an auction, there is no incentive to offer cash because of the contingent-pricing property of debt. The bid is made up to the second-highest valuation. (The highest-valuation
bidder needs to offer no more than the other's valuation to win the auction.) This implies
that the expected profit for bidder 2 from competing is decreasing in s_1. Suppose now that

bidder 1 makes a cash offer. If $s_0 = a$, the target accepts this offer without waiting for (the outcome of) an auction. The reason is that only debt offers are made in an auction and the value of debt must be less than v_0 if $s_0 = a$.

OPTIMAL STRATEGIES AND IMPLICATIONS   If bidder 2 believes bidder 1 has a sufficiently high valuation, it chooses not to compete. Bidder 1, in making its initial offer, takes into account the effect of the offer on the beliefs of bidder 2. Bidder 1's optimal strategy is to make either a minimum preemptive offer when it decides to preempt or a debt offer with zero premium when it decides not to preempt.

As in Fishman (1988), it is shown that higher-valuing bidders expect to lose more in an auction than lower-valuing bidders and thus have a greater incentive to deter competition by making higher bids. Further, of the bidders that make preemptive bids, the high-valuing ones use cash and the low-valuing ones use debt. The reason is given as follows. A debt offer is only accepted if $s_0 = b$, while a cash offer is always accepted. A cash offer is a commitment to acquire the target even if $s_0 = a$. The cost of this commitment is the difference between the bid and bidder 1's valuation $[p - v^a(s_1)]$, multiplied by the probability of $s_0 = a$, that is, $(1 - C)$:

$$(1 - C)[p - v^a(s_1)]$$

For $C < 1$, this cost of commitment is decreasing in s_1 and v_1, and thus cheaper for higher-valuing bidders. Therefore, for given preemptive offers, if any bidders use cash it is the higher-valuing ones. Further, this implies that if $C < 1$ (the target possesses private information), the cash offer required to deter bidder 2 is less than the face value of the debt offer required to do the same. Notice that if $C = 1$, the target effectively possesses no private information and cash is equivalent to debt.

Combining these results, Fishman shows that, in equilibrium, low-valuing bidders offer debt and high-valuing bidders offer cash. The optimal strategy for bidder 1 is to make a cash preemptive offer when its valuation is sufficiently high and a debt offer with zero premium otherwise. The cash offer preempts bidder 2, while the debt offer does not. As C (the probability that the acquisition can be profitable) increases, bidder 2 becomes more difficult to deter because the expected profit of bidder 2 from investigating also increases as C increases. Therefore, fewer preemptive bids will be made and securities offers will become less frequent.

The preceding analysis also implies that advance disclosure by the target of its information when $s_0 = b$ makes it more difficult to deter bidder 2, because the disclosure causes C to be unity. Bidder 1's expected profit is lower with the advance disclosure for two reasons. First, preemption by bidder 1 now requires signaling a higher valuation and this is more costly. Second, since bidder 1 can always make a contingent payment offer (debt offer), the advance information yields no benefits. Further, the benefit of using a cash offer to preempt bidder 2 is eliminated. This lowers bidder 1's expected payoff. With advance disclosure, bidder 2's expected payoff is higher because it need not incur the information cost if $s_0 = a$. The target's expected payoff is also higher because there are fewer preemptive bids, and any preemptive bids that do occur are higher. This establishes the rationale for firms to continually release information.

Fishman notes further empirical implications. First, the target is more likely to reject a securities offer as compared to a cash offer. The model suggests that a securities offer can be rejected when the proposed acquisition is not profitable. The decline in the target's share prices when its management rejects a merger offer (Dodd, 1980) may be due to this effect rather than the agency behavior of management. The results must be different for different exchange media. Travlos (1987) reports that, for a merger and tender offer sample, the chance of success is lower if the exchange medium is cash. This contrasts with the prediction of the model. But Fishman suggests that a sample including only mergers is more appropriate for empirical tests of the prediction because, in his model, the accept/reject decision is made by a party with private information on the target and this party is more reasonably interpreted as management rather than shareholders. Further, tender offers are more frequently hostile than friendly and consist of cash.

Second, competing bids are more likely to be observed following an initial securities offer. Third, the share price revaluation for bidder 1 will be higher if it offers cash as compared to securities because cash offers signal high valuation and preempt competing bidders in the model. This prediction is also made for other reasons as noted in Chapter 13.

BIDDER ELIMINATION AND VALUE REDUCTION STRATEGIES

Defensive actions by target management are often taken as evidence of conflicts of interest between managers and shareholders. (See Chapter 20.) However, Spatt's (1989) review of the theoretical literature suggests the potential for benefits to target shareholders arising from management resistance to takeover bids. A frequent theme in this area is that defenses to eliminate a particular bidder or to reduce the target's value to a bidder can increase ex ante the likelihood of contested bids and thus the expected takeover premium. With such defensive actions, potential acquirers may anticipate a bidding war for the target, in which case some will refrain from competing. Some may be reluctant to gather costly information on the target or to incur the bidding costs involved in obtaining advice from investment bankers, arranging for the required funds, and so on. To stimulate bidding, target management may provide uninformed potential acquirers with information on potential synergy gains.

Shleifer and Vishny (1986b) focus on the case of greenmail, but suggest their findings apply to any action taken to eliminate a potential acquirer. They show that managers can increase the expected gains from a takeover by buying the stake of one potential bidder (with low synergies), driving that bidder away with a standstill agreement, and encouraging others to explore taking over the firm. Berkovitch and Khanna (1988b) analyze the beneficial role of defensive strategies such as lock-ups, litigation, and poison pill rights plans. They establish that target shareholders can be made better off through the use of these defensive strategies that discriminately reduce the value of the target to some bidders.

Macey and McChesney (1985) emphasize that the payment of greenmail deals with the free-rider problem in producing costly information on potential synergy opportunities and, therefore, can be in the interest of target shareholders. Hirshleifer and Titman (1988) also find that some defensive measures (for example, litigation) can benefit target shareholders ex ante, by inducing bidders to make higher offers. Other types of management resistance such as rejection of an existing tender offer can also be potentially in the interest of shareholders (Giammarino and Heinkel, 1986). Spatt (1989) provides an example (credited to S. Bhattacharya) in which eliminating some bidders from a fixed number of bidders and reducing the investigation costs increase the common bidding probability obtained in the model. Assuming that only two bidders are needed for the target to capture all takeover gains, the expected gain of the target increases in the example.

Greenmail and the Stock Price: Shleifer and Vishny (1986b)

Shleifer and Vishny show that eliminating a potential acquirer through the payment of greenmail accompanied with a standstill agreement may enable the target to signal that it has not found a "white knight." This elimination of one potential acquirer can encourage others to investigate synergy opportunities with the target and to make competing bids. A white knight is a potential acquirer invited by the target management to top an initial offer opposed by that management. The invitation assures the white knight of the cooperation of the target to profit maximally from the takeover. Shleifer and Vishny suggest that even when the target has a white knight, it may delay the release of that information to promote information acquisition by others to stimulate further bidding.

If the payment of greenmail signals that the target is "weak" (that is, it has not found a white knight), the share price may decline as the market responds to this information. The fall in the share price happens even when managers are attempting to maximize the long-run value of the firm. The analysis by Shleifer and Vishny thus indicates that negative abnormal stock returns found by some event studies of greenmail (see Chapter 20) cannot automatically be taken as evidence of the managerial entrenchment hypothesis.

In reviewing Shleifer and Vishny, we follow the numerical example constructed by Rasmusen (1989, pp. 303–306) which conveys most of the important elements of the original game model in clear and simple fashion. In the model,

FIGURE A.4   Greenmail to Attract New Bidders

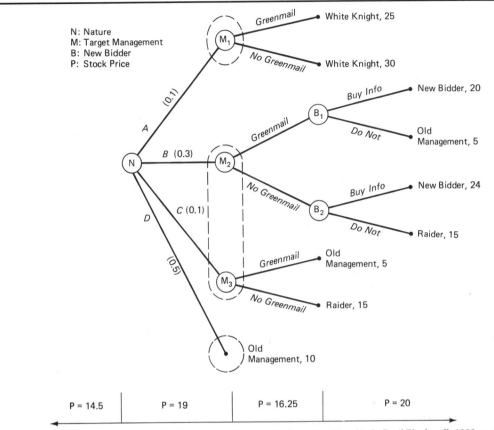

SOURCE: Adapted from Eric Rasmusen *Games and Information*, New York: Basil Blackwell, 1989, p. 304.

the players of the game are the target management, atomistic target shareholders, and potential acquirers. The potential acquirers might have opportunities to create value by taking over the target, but they have to incur investigative costs to collect information required for their valuation. Given that management maximizes the final value of shares, the analysis shows that the payment of greenmail can be an optimal strategy.

For the numerical example, assume that there are four possible states of nature, *A*, *B*, *C*, and *D*, with probabilities 0.1, 0.3, 0.1, and 0.5. These are described as follows and the *game tree* is shown in Figure A.4.

In state *A*, *B*, or *C*, a Raider appears and offers a price of 15. No Raider appears in state *D*. In state *A*, *B*, or *C*, the management considers whether to pay greenmail and extinguish the Raider's offer at a cost of 5 per share.

In state *A*, the management finds a White Knight and supplies all the information required for valuation at no cost. Through bargaining, the White Knight becomes ready to offer 30 if greenmail is not paid to the Raider and 25 if the Raider goes away with the payment of greenmail. Thus, in state A, the management does not pay greenmail and the White Knight takes over the firm at 30 per share.

In state B or C, the target finds no White Knight and does not know which state (B or C) will obtain. If greenmail is paid, a New Bidder will appear in state B but not in state C. The New Bidder can buy information at a cost of 8. If it does, it will find that its valuation of the target is 31 and will make an offer. Assuming that its offer has to be at least 24 if the Raider's offer is not withdrawn and 20 otherwise, it will buy information only if greenmail is paid. Thus, in the present example, the New Bidder has a dominant strategy—buy information and bid 20 if greenmail is paid and not otherwise. Assume that if no New Bidder appears after the payment of greenmail, the incumbent management continues to control the target and in this case the value of the target will be 5. Since state B is three times as likely as state C, the expected value of the firm when greenmail is paid is

$$0.75(20) + 0.25(5) = 16.25$$

which is greater than the Raider's offer of 15. Thus, the management decides to pay greenmail in states B and C.

Finally, in state D in which no Raider appears, the old management continues to control the firm. The final value of the firm in this state is assumed to be 10.

The point that Shleifer and Vishny emphasize is that the share price will fall upon the payment of greenmail, as it signals that the firm is weak. The price of the share before the Raider appears will be

$$0.1(30) + 0.3(20) + 0.1(5) + 0.5(10) = 14.5$$

Upon the announcement of the offer by the Raider, the price will rise to

$$0.2(30) + 0.6(20) + 0.2(5) = 19$$

as state D is eliminated and the market does not know whether the firm has a White Knight or not. When greenmail is paid, the market realizes that the firm does not have a White Knight and consequently the price falls to 16.25.

If the management "deviates" in the information set (B, C) by refusing to pay greenmail, the price may rise to 30 as the market initially believes that the firm has a White Knight. By the time the market realizes that no White Knight offer is forthcoming, the price will fall to 15 since the management will accept the Raider's offer. Note that the New Bidder will not appear since it expects a negative profit in the face of competition from the Raider ($31 - 8 - 24 = -1$). The shareholders will fail to profit from the temporary price of 30. The reason is that when the management indicates overvaluation of the stock to the shareholders, the market will also learn of the overvaluation and refuse to buy.

The negative abnormal return found by some event studies at the announcement of a greenmail payment can thus be explained by the present example. The example also shows that the whole process of "raiding" can be beneficial to the shareholders, as observed by Holderness and Sheehan (1985). Shleifer and Vishny thus show that eliminating a bidder can serve the interests of the target shareholders, although this would not necessarily always be the case in practice.

Value-Reducing Defensive Strategies and Shareholders' Wealth: Berkovitch and Khanna (1988b)

Even if the managerial entrenchment hypothesis is assumed away, the controversy over defensive tactics remains. Opponents argue that management resistance reduces the probability of takeovers and thus is harmful to target shareholders. However, in defense of those tactics, Berkovitch and Khanna (1988b) show that a class of value-reducing defensive strategies (VRDS) enable the target to capture a higher price for the target shares without reducing the probability of takeovers. Ideally, these strategies reduce the value of an acquisition to some bidders but not to others. In many cases, the known intention to use them is sufficient to increase shareholder wealth.

The intuition of the paper is as follows. When managers do not use VRDS, bidders can make preemptive bids to deter competition. When the value to the opening bidder can be reduced by use of VRDS, potential bidders are encouraged to enter and compete, as their offer can now be lower than otherwise. Berkovitch and Khanna show that just the ability to use VRDS can increase the level of the initial (preemptive) bid, as the bidder must bid higher to reduce the target's incentive to actually implement defensive actions. Under several assumptions on the nature of costs imposed by VRDS, it is shown that the use of VRDS does not necessarily reduce the probability of observing tender offers, because VRDS penalize high-value bidders more than low-value bidders and the high-value bidders bid despite the penalty. This is an important argument in view of Easterbrook and Fischel (1981), who suggest that management resistance reduces the probability as the gains from tender offers are reduced.

ANALYSIS UNDER FULL INFORMATION   There are two potential bidders, each of which can generate different synergy gains by taking over a target. Bidder 1 with synergy gains of R_1 makes an opening bid. Bidder 2 with synergy gains of $R_2 < R_1$ must incur a cost, C, of entering the bidding process. If competition occurs, the outcome is determined according to an English (first price open-cry) auction such that the highest-value bidder buys the target for the value of the second-highest bidder. Since $R_2 < R_1$, bidder 2 realizes that he does not have any chance to win and does not bid. Anticipating this reaction by bidder 2, bidder 1 bids $b(R_1)$ equal to the existing market price (plus one cent).

Define a VRDS as follows: A (discriminatory) VRDS of size P against a known bidder is one which reduces its synergy value by P. To be effective (as a threat), the VRDS should be expensive to redeem. Some examples having the required characteristics include litigation, lock-ups, and some types of poison pills.

Assume now that the target management is able to put a VRDS of size P against bidder 1 and reduce its synergy gain to below R_2. Assume that after bidder 1 bids $b(R_1)$, the synergy gain of bidder 2, R_2, becomes public knowledge. At this point, bidder 1 can raise its bid and the target either sells at the new bid or imposes a VRDS against bidder 1. If the target imposes a VRDS, bidder 2 can enter the bidding. In this case, the final bid will be $\min\{R_1 - P, R_2 - C\}$.

Therefore, we can see that: Whenever the target management can threaten to adopt a discriminatory and nonredeemable VRDS, the outcome is that the higher-value bidder bids the value of the lower bidder, less his entry costs, and wins the takeover contest. In the example, bidder 1 bids $R_2 - C$ because he does not wish to be eliminated via a VRDS of sufficiently large size. Consequently, in the complete information case, VRDS are not observed in equilibrium, as the highest-value bidder bids high enough to prevent them. They remain just as credible threats.

ANALYSIS UNDER ASYMMETRIC INFORMATION   Now assume that each bidder's synergy values are known only to itself and can be either L (low) or H (high). The probability of a bidder being a high-value type is q. Let $r = 1 - q$ be the probability of a bidder being a low-value type. These probabilities are common knowledge. Other assumptions in the complete information case are retained.

CASE 1. Assume $C > H - L$. Then bidder 2, irrespective of type, does not find it profitable to compete. Even in the most favorable case where bidder 2 is an H type and bidder 1 an L type, its profit cannot be positive $(H - L - C < 0)$. In the absence of VRDS, bidder 1 will bid the existing market price of the target shares and can still prevent competition. Therefore, VRDS can create competition by decreasing the value of bidder 1. As before, the target is better off with VRDS.

CASE 2. Assume $C < H - L$. Consider two separate possibilities. First, assume that the expected profit of bidder 2 of the H type is negative: $r(H - L) - C < 0$. Under this assumption, when bidder 2 is unable to infer bidder 1's true type from the opening bid (that is, in a pooling equilibrium in which all types of bidders pick the same bid or strategy in all states), bidder 2 will not compete. It is easy to see that VRDS will again improve target payoffs in this scenario.

Second, assume that

$$r(H - L) > C$$

so that bidder 2's expected profit if it is an H type is positive. The following analysis concentrates on this scenario. Berkovitch and Khanna first establish that no pooling equilibrium is possible in this scenario and thus consider only separating equilibria, in which different types of bidders pick different bids.

In a separating equilibrium, *without* VRDS, it must be the case that 1_L (bidder 1 of the L type) bids zero since it does not have to bid higher to signal its type. Bidder 1_H must bid high enough so that the L type does not have an incentive to mimic the high type and stays with a bid of zero. For this, the expected gain of the low type when he bids zero must be no smaller than when he imitates the high type. Let $b(H)$ be the equilibrium bid of the H type. Then this condition can be expressed as

$$L(1 - q) \geq L - b(H)$$

which implies

$$b(H) \geq qL$$

Therefore, in the equilibrium, 1_L bids zero and 1_H bids qL. Bidder 2_L does not enter and 2_H competes if the first bid is below qL, and does not compete if the first bid is qL or higher.

The expected return to the target can be obtained as follows. If 1_L bids zero, 2_H bids L and the probability of this outcome is rq. If 1_H bids qL, no competition occurs and the probability of this outcome is q. Thus, the target's expected gain is $rqL + q^2L = qL$.

Now permit VRDS. If 1_H still bids qL as before, then the target will impose VRDS of size $P = C$ because its expected gain $q(H - C)$ is greater than qL. The expected gain is $q(H - C)$ because the only situation in which it makes positive gains is when the second bidder is an H type. Bidder 2_H must bid $H - C$ to win. Note that we started with $H - L > C$ in case 2, so that $q(H - C) > qL$. Knowing that the target will impose VRDS, 1_H bids at least $q(H - C)$ in a new separating equilibrium.

What happens to the initial bid by 1_L? It still bids 0 unless $rL > C$. If $rL > C$, the expected payoff to the target from using $P = C$, $r(L - C) + q(L - C) = L - C$, is greater than the payoff from using $P = 0$, qL. Therefore, if $rL > C$, 1_L should bid $L - C$ to avoid VRDS. (In this case, it can be shown that 1_H bids $\max\{q(H - C), L - rC\}$ to separate itself from 1_L.)

The preceding results establish that target shareholders are better off when the manager can use VRDS. In extending their analysis, Berkovitch and Khanna show that even when entry costs are incurred by bidder 1 as well as by bidder 2, VRDS can still be attractive to the target. They also show that VRDS are actually imposed whenever the probability of the high type, q, is low enough. The intuition is that whenever q is small, the expected returns from preemption (bidding high) decrease as the risk of competition is smaller. Therefore, the bidder is more willing to take the risk of letting the target trigger VRDS.

Finally, Berkovitch and Khanna argue that many real-life defensive strategies have the appropriate properties of those considered in the analysis. In lock-ups, the target sells a specific asset at a below-market price to a potential bidder conditional on its competing against the other bidder. This reduces the value of the target to the first bidder and gives the second bidder an incentive to compete. A possible limitation of lock-ups is that they require the target to know the identity of the potential bidder. Litigation reduces the value of the bidder taken to court by a greater amount than that of other bidders. However, litigation is less efficient than lock-ups because the target has less control over the cost to the bidder and has to incur litigation costs itself. Purchases of assets to increase the probability of antitrust suits against a specific bidder can work as a VRDS. Some discriminatory poison pills are another possible candidate for VRDS.

OTHER THEMES
IN THEORETICAL MODELS

As the takeover phenomenon continues to attract increased attention of academic researchers, almost all relevant aspects of the takeover process have been subject to theoretical analysis employing formal models. Many of these models have been reviewed in some detail in the foregoing sections, but there still remain many others. In this section, we take up four more topics on the takeover process and describe major elements and insights of the studies on them.

Management Resistance

MANAGERIAL PREFERENCE FOR CONTROL AND THE PASSIVITY RULE: BARON (1983)   In one of the earliest formal models dealing with managerial resistance in takeovers, Baron (1983) assumes private information of target management about the value of the firm and the management's own preference for control. In the model, target management also has a fractional ownership interest and thus may reject an offer for any of three reasons:

1 The offer may be "inadequate" compared to the true value of the target.
2 The offer may be adequate in this sense, but management prefers to await a higher offer in the next period.
3 Target management may reject an offer in order to maintain its control over the target.

The model has two periods. In each period, competition among bidders results in a final offer which causes the expected gain to the bidder to be zero. *After* this final offer is made, target management decides to accept or reject the offer. Thus, the model does not consider the possibility that management resistance causes delay to provide adequate time to allow additional bidding competition or imposes costs on an initial bidder to encourage competing bids, as in Berkovitch and Khanna (1988b).

As offers are made and rejected, some target managements develop a reputation for having a preference for control. This is because the posterior probability that a target has a preference for control becomes larger than the prior probability when it rejects, an offer. Such targets are likely to accept a given offer only when their true value is low (because when both the true value and the preference for control are high, an offer has to be larger for it to be acceptable). This adverse selection reduces the potential gains to prospective bidders. Consequently, the bidding process will generate lower and less frequent offers over time which will further reduce the probability of acceptance. Thus, the market value of the remaining types of targets would decrease over time. This provides an explanation for the findings of Bradley, Desai, and Kim (1983) that targets of unsuccessful tender offers that received no further offer within five years of the unsuccessful offer lost all of their announcement date gains, while those that received another offer and experienced a change in control retained or increased their gains. The model also predicts that the possibility of a preference for control by management reduces the initial prebid market value of the firm below what it would be if there were no such possibility.

Baron further establishes that a passivity rule such as that proposed by Easterbrook and Fischel (1981) is superior to value-maximizing resistance. The reason is that value-maximizing resistance results in an adverse selection problem that makes target shareholders worse off. For a given offer, lower-value types of target firms accept the offer and higher-value types reject it. This will lower the level of any offers that are made. A passivity rule can also eliminate the effect of a preference for control by target management since it is not allowed to resist an offer. Therefore, in Baron's model, a passivity rule increases the initial market value of the target firm. This result is obtained because the model does not incorporate the possibility of increased bidding competition following management resistance. Note that facilitation of increased bidding competition is a basis of the argument against the passivity rule (Bebchuk, 1982).

MANAGEMENT RESISTANCE IN INFORMED VERSUS UNINFORMED BIDDER CONTESTS: GIAMMARINO AND HEINKEL (1986)   Giammarino and Heinkel (1986) set up a model which provides some rationale for value-maximizing management resistance in takeovers, as in Shleifer and Vishny (1986b) and Berkovitch and Khanna (1988b). In their model, the first bidder has information on possible takeover gains while the target and a potential bidder are uninformed. The takeover gains are of common value, that is, independent of the identity of the bidder. Under these assumptions, if both the informed first bidder and the uninformed potential bidder could make as many offers and counteroffers as they wished, it is easy to see that the informed bidder will bid the minimum required amount (for example, a little over the current market price) and the target will accept the bid. The reason is that the uninformed bidder can at best break even and overall will expect to lose from competition with an informed bidder. Since the uninformed bidder has no incentive to enter the bidding and the target will obtain only the minimum possible synergy gain, some form of restricted bidding is favored by the target. The restrictions imposed in the model are: (1) the informed bidder can make only one bid, and (2) if the target rejects the bid, the uninformed bidder can make a bid that is strictly greater than the rejected bid.

The results that Giammarino and Heinkel obtain from their structured model are as follows. The first bidder's incentive to bid an amount lower than the synergy gain is reduced by the possibility of a rejection by management. The motive for the target to reject the initial offer by the informed bidder is to allow a higher counteroffer. However, counterbids by the uninformed bidder do not always materialize. The uninformed bidder sometimes acquires the target at a cost in excess of the realized synergy gains. The structure of the model also gives rise to a white-knight equilibrium, in which the target rejects every bid lower than the maximum possible synergy gain and induces the uninformed bidder to bid more often.

Giammarino and Heinkel note that bitter criticism of the bidding firm by the target management is often observed in actual takeover battles and could be interpreted as the target not only rejecting an initial bid by the informed bidder, but also precommitting not to consider another bid by the same bidder. This precommitment encourages the uninformed bidder to enter the contest, thereby raising the target's expected payoff.

Financing Policies and Corporate Control

MANAGERIAL CONTROL OF VOTING RIGHTS AND VALUE OF THE FIRM: STULZ (1988)   Stulz (1988) analyzes how managerial control of voting rights affects firm value and financing policies. It is shown that the value of the firm is positively related to the fraction a of the voting rights for low values of a and negatively related to a as a becomes large. An important result of Stulz's analysis is that capital structure changes affect the value of the firm through their effect on a.

The model ignores the positive incentive effects of a large a and assumes conflicts of interest between management and outside shareholders, so that in a takeover bid managers do not tender their shares (voting rights) unless the premium offered is sufficiently large. Outsiders randomly decide to tender their shares, and their tendering probability, $S(P)$, is increasing in the premium offered, P. Thus, the fraction tendered for a given P is

$$(1 - a)S(P)$$

This fraction tendered is smaller when management controls a larger fraction of the voting rights. Therefore, when a is large the premium offered has to be large to receive the fraction required for voting control, for example, one half of the total voting rights. On the other hand, when the premium offered has to be large, the probability of a hostile takeover falls.

Stulz shows that for small a the value of the firm increases with a, and for large a the firm value decreases with a so that it reaches a maximum for some positive value of a. Intuitively, when a is increased from a small value, the premium offered is increased but the probability of a hostile takeover bid does not decline much. Therefore, when a is small, increasing a increases the value of the firm which reflects the expected value of the takeover gain. The probability of a successful bid falls as a increases and reaches zero when a equals one half. But the expected premium is bounded by the gain from control for the bidder. Thus, as a becomes large, the product of the probability of a bid being made times the expected premium if a bid takes place becomes small.

The choice of a by management will depend on managers' risk aversion, their wealth, and more importantly on the benefits that managers get from control and on the change in the probability of success of a bid brought about by an increase in a. Since a decrease in the managers' benefits from control decreases a, such a change can be effected by granting management a golden parachute. This suggests that when a is large, a golden parachute can be introduced to increase firm value.

Stulz shows that all financing decisions can affect management's control of voting rights and, therefore, the value of the firm. Managers may wish to change a firm's capital structure for the sole purpose of controlling a larger fraction of the voting rights with a given investment in their firm. In Stulz's model, an increase in leverage which increases a does not necessarily decrease the probability that management will be replaced by a hostile bidder. The reason is that an increase in debt increases a but also decreases the total value of equity, so that it becomes cheaper for a bidder who faces increasing marginal costs of borrowing to acquire control. (The increasing marginal costs may be due to restrictive covenants of existing debt.) However, the covenants attached to new debt, such as a poison put clause, can strengthen management's bargaining position and make a hostile takeover less likely.

A stock repurchase can increase a and hence the stock price of the target, when a is small. The timing in calling convertible securities can be affected by management's desire to maintain its a; forced conversion has a cost created by the redistribution of voting rights. Purchases of shares by the firm's ESOP or pension fund can also affect the value of the firm, since management generally acts as a trustee of these organizations. A standstill agreement typically includes a clause stipulating that the investor will vote with management in a corporate control contest and thus can affect the firm's share price. Stulz suggests that a number of other financial events will have an effect on the value of the firm through their effect on the fraction of voting rights controlled by management.

TAKEOVER METHODS AND CAPITAL STRUCTURE: HARRIS AND RAVIV (1988)   Harris and Raviv (1988) focus on the effect of financial leverage on the takeover methods (proxy fights versus tender offers) and their price effects. The basic idea is that incumbent management of a takeover target can affect the type of takeover attempt and its probability of success by choosing the fraction a of the firm's equity to be held by the management. The change in the fraction a is affected by the amount of debt issued. The management's strategy is based on a tradeoff between the potential gain in firm value due to an improvement in management through takeover and the loss of personal benefits derived

from being in control of the firm. In the model, increases in debt increase a, but reduce the expected benefits of control by increasing the bankruptcy probability, by increasing monitoring activity by creditors, and by reducing the discretion of incumbents in allocating cash flows. It is assumed that if no debt is outstanding, the benefits of control are sufficiently large in relation to the gain in equity value from better management that the incumbent prefers always to vote for itself.

In the model, all parties know that either the incumbent or the rival is best able to manage the firm, but are uncertain about the identity of the better team. The incumbent and the rival do not have better information about their own abilities than the passive investors do. In a control contest, a known fraction of passive shareholders votes with the incumbent but the fraction is dependent on the passive investors' perception of the incumbent's ability. Thus, the *target* management can choose one of three types of control methods and outcomes by choosing an optimal level of a (by changing capital structure). A *successful tender offer* is one in which the rival management (bidder) acquires a sufficient fraction of the equity to guarantee that it captures control even if it is inferior to the incumbent. In an *unsuccessful tender offer*, the incumbent retains sufficient ownership to guarantee that the rival fails to capture control even if it is the superior candidate. One method of guaranteeing control is a leveraged recapitalization. A *proxy fight* is defined as the case in which neither the incumbent nor the rival controls enough votes to win for sure. In a proxy fight the incumbent wins if it is of higher ability; otherwise the rival wins.

Harris and Raviv show that if the incumbent can guarantee itself control without issuing debt, the incumbent prefers an unsuccessful tender offer to determination of control by a proxy fight. Similarly, if a proxy fight is feasible, the incumbent prefers this case to allowing a successful tender offer. The empirical implications derived from the model are:

1 On average, takeover targets increase their debt levels.
2 Targets of proxy fights or unsuccessful tender offers issue more debt on average than targets of successful tender offers.
3 The stock price of target firms increases, on average, in the event of a successful tender offer.
4 The stock price of target firms increases by less, on average, in the event of a successful proxy fight than in the event of a successful tender offer.

To understand the third implication, note that the only reason for the incumbent to choose to relinquish control to the rival, independent of abilities, is to obtain a capital gain on the incumbent's shares. For the fourth implication, Harris and Raviv generally argue that a successful tender offer is chosen when the initial value of the firm is much lower than it is when a proxy fight is chosen, while the final value of the firm under the rival is near the final value in the proxy fight.

In sum, the main insight of the model appears to be that incumbent management can influence the type and outcome of takeover activity by choosing a resistance strategy based on capital structure.

Friendly versus Hostile Bids

There have been relatively few studies on the choice of corporate takeover methods. One such study already reviewed is Harris and Raviv (1988), which focuses on the fraction of share ownership by target management which values control. Also, we introduced in Chapter 20 the study by Berkovitch and Khanna (1988a). In their model, a merger is a bargaining game between the managements of target and acquiring firms, while a tender offer is an auction in which acquirers arrive sequentially and compete for the target. The acquiring firm prefers a merger over a public tender offer because a merger is assumed to be a private negotiation whereas a tender offer releases more information on the target and results in an auction. In equilibrium, there is a unique level of synergy gains below which the acquiring firm makes only a merger attempt, as it expects to lose in a public auction. The target management is given a golden parachute contract and thereby encouraged to force the acquirer into making a tender offer whenever possible. In a later study, Nyborg (1989) develops a model of friendly and hostile bids focusing on posttakeover employment of the human capital owned by the target management. The objective function of the target management is dependent on the premium received and the level of posttakeover employment (identified with control) and is increasing in these two variables. In Nyborg's model, a friendly takeover bid is submitted to the target's management, whereas a hostile bid is submitted to the target's shareholders. This means that for a friendly bid to be successful, it must be approved first by the target's managers and then by shareholders, whereas a hostile bid needs approval from the shareholders only.

The central assumption of the model is that the posttakeover value of the target is a function of how the human capital owned by the target management is employed in the posttakeover organization. The two takeover methods fundamentally differ in that a friendly bid can specify the role the incumbent management will have in the posttakeover management, whereas a hostile bid cannot. In the case of a hostile takeover, the old management's role has to be determined by a posttakeover negotiation between the bidder and the old management of the target. It is assumed that the bidder cannot dictate the role or the level of employment except when the level is going to be zero (that is, all managers of the target are fired).

Since the target management values (posttakeover) control, an optimal use of human capital cannot be agreed upon between the target and the acquirer in a competitive friendly takeover market. The amount of target management's human capital employed will be excessive, as the bidders must give concessions to the incumbents in a friendly bid. Hostile takeovers are used because the bidders sometimes can get closer to the optimal level of employment of the target's human resources by negotiating over these after the actual takeover. One important result obtained by Nyborg is that, under some conditions, hostile takeovers occur more frequently when the size of improvement due to takeover is large, and friendly takeovers occur more frequently when the potential is small. This result suggests that the average abnormal return to targets in hostile takeovers is greater than in friendly takeovers.

Winner's Curse

Common-value auctions are those in which the value of the object being competed for is the same for all bidders but their valuations (estimates of the value) differ. The winner's curse hypothesis states that the winner of a *sealed-bid* common-value auction tends to be the one who most overestimates the true value of the auctioned object. Thus, the winner is likely to be cursed by overbidding. Roll (1986) argues that empirical evidence on bidder returns in corporate takeovers is consistent with his hubris hypothesis that managers infected with hubris try to maximize firm value but make positive valuation errors (that is, stumble into the winner's curse). Giliberto and Varaiya (1989, p. 60) suggest, however, that "the hubris hypothesis itself is premised on an improper recognition of the winner's curse phenomenon by bidding firms" because, "strictly speaking, the usual takeover auction does not conform to the sealed-bid auction framework in which the winner's curse phenomenon can occur." Further, usual takeover contests may be closer to independent private-value (IPV) auctions in which each bidder knows his value with certainty but does not know the values of the object to other bidders.

To avoid the winner's curse in common-value (CV) auctions, bidders should scale down their estimates to form their bids. Optimal bidding strategies in the CV auction call for a decrease in the bid with an increase in the number of competing bidders and the degree of uncertainty about true value.

In IPV auctions, bidders know their valuations precisely and, therefore, there is no need to adjust for winner's curse. An increase in the variance of bidder valuations increases the distance between any two closest valuations. As a result, a bidder can lower his bid without materially affecting the probability of winning the auction. Hence, as in the CV auction, an increase in variance causes a decrease in optimal bids. On the other hand, an increase in the number of bidders increases optimal bids because it is more likely that another bidder's estimate is close to one's own.

Giliberto and Varaiya (1989) employ the data for FDIC sealed-bid auctions of failed banks (1) to test for the presence or absence of winner's curse under the assumption that the FDIC auctions conform to the elements of the CV model, and (2) to determine whether the nature of these auctions can be explained by the IPV model, the CV model without adjustment for the winner's curse, or the CV model with adjustment for the winner's curse. The distinction between the three models is feasible because of their different predictions on the expected winning bid. All three models predict that the expected *winning* bid increases with the number of bidders, but auction theory indicates that the specific pattern of this increase differs across models. Giliberto and Varaiya (1989, p. 64) summarize the differences as follows:

1 In the IPV model, the expected winning bid equals the expected value of the second-highest observation in a random sample of bidder's subjective valuations.
2 In the CV model without adjustment for the winner's curse, the expected winning bid equals the expected value of the highest observation in a random sample of bidder value estimates.
3 In the CV model with adjustment for the winner's curse, the expected winning bid increases in proportion to $1/N$, N being the number of competing bidders.

Tests are conducted for a sample consisting of 219 FDIC auctions in the period 1975–1985. In the first test, bids of all bidders are regressed on the number of competing bidders, the variance of the distribution of value estimates (uncertainty), and other control variables. The result shows that bids are positively related to the number of bidders. Under the assumption that the CV model is appropriate, this indicates that bidders do not adjust for the winner's curse. Note, however, that the result is also consistent with an IPV setting. As predicted by the auction models, bid levels decreased with uncertainty.

In the second test, winning bids are regressed on the number of bidders. The results indicate that expected winning bids appear to increase with the number of bidders. However, it was not possible to reject one model in favor of another. Therefore, the possibility exists that there are significant IPV elements in the auctions. This makes clear interpretation of the first test all the more difficult.

Giliberto and Varaiya caution that the preceding findings may not automatically extend to typical nonfinancial takeovers. First, corporate takeovers are not sealed-bid auctions. Second, the results are consistent with bidder behavior in IPV auctions as well as with bidder behavior in CV auctions without adjustment for winner's curse, and nonfinancial takeovers may have more IPV elements due to "synergistic complementarities" (p. 75).

SUMMARY

As indicated in the introduction, formal models of the takeover process make alternative assumptions and derive different, often conflicting, results. Sometimes, different assumptions are made to focus on specific aspects of the takeover process. Among the many variables and assumptions that are listed in Table A.1, those that are particularly relevant in the models reviewed here are concerned with:

1 Whether bids are made to atomistic shareholders, finite shareholders, or to management.
2 Whether the reservation prices of shareholders are known and identical.

3 Whether initial shareholdings in the target by the bidders are exogenously fixed or endogenously determined.

4 Whether target management has private information on the (takeover) value of the firm.

5 Whether bidders have to incur investigation costs (or information costs or entrance costs) before bidding and whether the costs are different across bidders.

6 Whether revising a bid is costless (as in an English auction), costly, or prohibitive.

7 Whether securities backed by target assets only can be used in takeovers.

8 Whether target management has a preference for control.

Table A.2 classifies the patterns of the models that have been reviewed earlier according to their underlying assumptions and lists their major results and implications. In the following pages, we summarize and compare the findings of these models.

1 *Bids are made to atomistic shareholders; a free-rider problem arises.*

When bids are made to atomistic shareholders, a free-rider problem potentially arises. This problem can be solved either by dilution, two-tier offers, or by a footholding in the target prior to an offer. The models of Shleifer and Vishny (1986a), Hirshleifer and Titman (1988), and Jegadeesh and Chowdhry (1988) address the last case. Shleifer and Vishny assume an exogenously fixed share ownership by the bidder (a large shareholder) and a known, identical reservation price held by all atomistic shareholders. This reservation price is the expected posttakeover value of the firm conditional on the offer being profitable for the large shareholder. The large shareholder bids this expected value and therefore the bid always succeeds. One result of the model is that the larger is the initial shareholding, the smaller will be the takeover premium. The assumption of identical reservation prices is relaxed by Hirshleifer and Titman. They argue that the equilibrium bid must be fully revealing, that is, that each bidder bids the posttakeover value of the firm. They show that the probability of bid success increases with the initial shareholding. Jegadeesh and Chowdhry further relax the assumption of exogenously fixed initial shareholding and show that the equilibrium bid is fully revealing and the equilibrium footholding increases in the bid which is equal to the bidder's valuation of the target.

The three models yield different predictions on the relationship between the initial shareholding and the takeover premium. Shleifer and Vishny predict a negative relationship, Jegadeesh and Chowdhry predict a positive relationship, and Hirshleifer and Titman predict no relationship. In all three models, an increase in the costs of takeovers results in a rise in the average takeover premium by deterring low-synergy bidders from acquisition attempts. But Hirshleifer and Titman additionally show that certain defensive actions induce overbidding, which implies an increase in the average takeover premium but a decline in the returns to bidders.

TABLE A.2
Patterns in Theoretical Models

TOPICS, ASSUMPTIONS, AND AUTHORS	ADDITIONAL ASSUMPTIONS	MAJOR RESULTS
1. *Bids to atomistic sharehold-ers: free-rider problem*		In all models, average takeover premium in-creases with takeover costs.
Fixed initial shareholdings.		
Shleifer and Vishny (1986a)	Known and identical reser-vation prices.	(1) Equilibrium bids equal conditional expectations of posttakeover values. (2) Larger footholding leads to lower bids.
Hirshleifer and Titman (1988)	Unknown and different reservation prices.	(1) Equilibrium bids equal posttakeover values. (2) Larger footholding in-creases success probabil-ity. (3) Defenses may induce over-bidding.
Endogenous initial shareholdings.		
Jegadeesh and Chowdhry (1988)	Unknown and different reservation prices.	(1) Equilibrium bids equal posttakeover values. (2) Higher bids are accompa-nied by larger foot-holdings.
2. *Bids to management: no free-rider problem*		
No private information held by target; significant investigation costs.	Information asymmetry between bidder 1 and bidder 2.	Preemptive bidding is pos-sible.
Fishman (1988)	No costs in revising bids (English auction).	Lowering information costs increases expected payoff to target.
Berkovitch and Khanna (1988b)	No costs in revising bids.	Imposing costs on the first bidder (or threatening to do so) increases expected payoff to targets.
Hirshleifer and Png (1989)	Significant costs in revis-ing bids.	Expected takeover price is maximized at an interme-diate value of informa-tion cost.
Giammarino and Heinkel (1986)	Prohibitive investigation costs to bidder 2; common-value synergy; prohibitive costs in revis-ing bids (only one bid al-lowed).	Rejection by target man-agement can bring a higher counteroffer.

TABLE A.2 (cont.)

TOPICS, ASSUMPTIONS, AND AUTHORS	ADDITIONAL ASSUMPTIONS	MAJOR RESULTS
Private information held by target: adverse selection problem.		Contingent pricing effects of a securities offer increase takeover probabilities.
Hansen (1987)	Use of stock of the combined firm.	(1) Equity of the combined firm introduces another adverse selection problem. (2) Cash offer when stock is undervalued; stock offer when overvalued.
Fishman (1989)	Use of debt backed by target assets.	Cash offer signals high valuation and is used in preemptive bidding; debt offer in accommodating bids.
3. *Managerial resistance, financial policies, and takeover methods*		Managerial resistance and financial policies may affect takeover methods and firm value.
Management preference for control. Baron (1983)	No beneficial role of management resistance; private information held by target management.	(1) Value of unsuccessful targets decreases over time due to reputation and adverse selection effects of management resistance. (2) Passivity rule is superior to value-maximizing resistance due to adverse selection problem (under the given assumptions).
Stulz (1988)	Probability of tendering by outside shareholders increasing in bid; no incentive effect of managerial shareholding.	(1) Takeover premium increases in the share of managerial voting rights. (2) Firm value increases in the share when it is small; decreases in the share when it is large. (3) Financing policies affect firm value through the voting rights share of management.

TABLE A.2 (cont.)

TOPICS, ASSUMPTIONS, AND AUTHORS	ADDITIONAL ASSUMPTIONS	MAJOR RESULTS
Harris and Raviv (1988)	Control benefits decreasing in amount of debt.	Management can influence takeover methods and outcome by choosing its ownership share through capital structure changes.
Nyborg (1989)	Posttakeover value dependent on level of employment of (control allowed to) old management; takeover price and employment level determined prior to takeover in friendly bids.	(1) Hostile takeovers result in more efficient level of employment of target management. (2) Under some conditions hostile (friendly) takeovers are used when improvements can be large (small).
Pure value maximization. Berkovitch and Khanna (1988a)	Mergers consummated in private bargaining; tender offers result in public auctions; possible preference for control by management.	(1) Acquiring firm makes only a merger attempt when synergy level is low (2) Management is encouraged to force the acquirer to make a tender offer through golden parachutes.
Shleifer and Vishny 1986b)	Significant investigation costs for bidders.	Bidder elimination (e.g., by greenmail payment) may be value-maximizing, but result in a decline in the current stock price.

2 *Bids are made to target management; the free-rider problem vanishes.*

When the number of shareholders is finitely large, some stockholders can be made pivotal and thus the free-rider problem is overcome (Bagnoli and Lipman, 1988). The free-rider problem certainly vanishes when bids are made to target management. Most of the other models reviewed in this appendix deal with this case and introduce asymmetric information, investigation (entrance) costs, bidding (revision) costs, managerial preference for control, and defensive actions.

3 *No private information is held by target management and information costs are significant; lowering information costs may or may not increase target payoffs.*

A first set of models assumes that no private information is held by target management on the value of the firm and thus considers only cash bids. Fishman (1988), Berkovitch and Khanna (1988b), Giammarino and Heinkel (1986), and Hirshleifer and Png (1989) all assume investigation (or information) costs faced by potential competing bidders. The significance of information costs is easily seen. If there are no information costs (and no bidding costs), all potential bidders will investigate and compete in an English auction, in which the highest-valuing bidder acquires the target at the second-highest valuation. Preemptive bidding by a first bidder and the role of target management in facilitating competition are impossible or irrelevant in the absence of information costs.

Thus, Fishman (1988) shows that lowering information costs makes preemption by the first bidder more difficult, promotes competition, and increases the expected payoff to the target. Berkovitch and Khanna (1988b) show that potential competition is promoted or the level of a preemptive bid is increased by imposing or threatening to impose costs on the first bidder. Combining these two results, it is seen that promotion of competition or an increase in the level of preemptive bids can be effected both through reduction of investigation costs to potential bidders and through threats of defensive actions against first bidders.

Yet, Hirshleifer and Png (1989) show that if revising a bid is costly, lowering the investigation costs will not necessarily increase the takeover price. The reason is that, when only one bid is allowed (the prohibitive-cost case), the first bidder's bid becomes the takeover price regardless of competition from a second bidder. Lowering the investigation costs sometimes causes the first bidder to give up a preemptive bidding and bid low. Even when many bids are allowed at a fixed cost per bid, competition does not necessarily result in a takeover price larger than a preemptive bid that could have been made had the investigation costs been kept high.

4 *Private information is held by target management; then the medium of exchange becomes relevant.*

When the target management has private information on the firm's true value, a "lemons" problem arises. Hansen (1987) shows that this adverse selection problem can be partly overcome by a securities offer having the contingent-pricing effect. If the security offered is the equity of the combined firm, then another adverse selection problem may be introduced because of asymmetric information on the value of the bidder's assets. Therefore, the dominance of a securities offer is partly offset by this asymmetry of information. In equilibrium, cash will be offered when stock is relatively undervalued and stock will be offered when it is relatively overvalued. Fishman (1989) focuses on the role of the exchange medium in preempting competition. He notes that securities backed only by target's assets, if allowed, dominate other securities as the medium of exchange and induce target management to make efficient accept/reject decisions. In his model, cash is used only to preempt competition by signaling a high valuation of the target. This signaling is effective because a cash offer is a commitment to acquire the target in any states of nature and the cost of this commitment is smaller for firms with high valuation for the target.

5 *Rejection of bids and bidder elimination by target management may be value maximizing.*

Suppose that a first bidder has private information on a *common-value* takeover gain but neither the target nor the potential bidder has such information. Under these assumptions if there were no restrictions (costs) on revising bids (but large information costs as implied by the asymmetry of information), then the informed bidder will bid the current market price (plus one cent) and the target will accept the bid. The reason, of course, is that the uninformed bidder can only expect a nonpositive payoff from competition with the informed bidder and thus has no incentive to enter the bidding. In this case, Giammarino and Heinkel (1986) show that the target management imposes the restriction that the informed bidder can make only one bid and may reject the bid to induce a higher counteroffer by the uninformed potential bidder. Shleifer and Vishny (1986b) argue that greenmail payment and a standstill agreement can potentially increase the payoff to the target. They argue that potential bidders can be encouraged to investigate and compete when an existing bidder is eliminated, for example, by greenmail payment.

6 *Target management has preference for control; the value of the firm, financial policies, and takeover methods are affected.*

Managerial preference for control together with value-maximization motives has been employed in models to explain determination of the market value of the firm, managerial share ownership, capital structure, and takeover methods. In Baron (1983), an increasing reputation for managements' preference for control in unsuccessful targets and the adverse selection problem resulting from managements' private information on firm value together cause a decline in the market value of the remaining (unsuccessful) targets over time. Stulz (1988) shows that the takeover price should increase as the fraction of voting rights held by management which values control, but the probability of a takeover should decline. Thus, in the absence of the incentive effect of share ownership, the market value of the firm increases with the fractional voting rights ownership when the fraction is small but decreases when the fraction is large. In Stulz's model, capital structure changes affect the value of the firm by their effect on the fraction of voting rights held by management.

In Harris and Raviv (1988), the incumbent management can influence the type and outcome of takeover activity (successful and unsuccessful tender offers and proxy fights) by choosing a capital structure which in turn determines its ownership share. In their model, a large amount of debt is assumed to decrease the benefits of control, which reduces management's incentive to increase its ownership share. In Nyborg (1989), there is an optimal level of posttakeover employment of (or control allowed to) the target's old management. A friendly bid which determines the employment level prior to a takeover and an unfriendly bid which determines it following an actual takeover would result in different levels of employment of old managers. In Berkovitch and Khanna

(1988a), the bidder generally prefers a merger which involves private negotiation over a tender offer which results in a public auction. Target management is given a golden parachute contract to get the best bargaining result in a merger and to force the acquirer into making a tender offer whenever possible. A low value of synergy gain to be brought about by the acquirer is likely to lead to a merger rather than a tender offer.

7 *Are the winners cursed in takeovers?*

To avoid the winner's curse in common-value auctions, bidders should scale down their estimates in forming their bids. Optimal strategies in the common-value auction call for a decrease in the bid when more bidders participate in the auction. Empirical evidence provided by Giliberto and Varaiya (1989) indicates either that bidders fail to adjust for the winner's curse or that the alternative, independent-private-value auction model is more appropriate for the takeover process.

REFERENCES

BAGNOLI, MARK, and BARTON LIPMAN, "Successful Takeovers without Exclusion," *Review of Financial Studies*, 1, 1988, pp. 89–110.

BARON, D. P., "Tender Offers and Management Resistance," *Journal of Finance*, 38, 1983, pp. 331–343.

BEBCHUK, L. A., "The Case for Facilitating Competing Tender Offers," *Harvard Law Review*, 95, 1982, pp. 1028–1056.

BERKOVITCH, ELAZAR, and NAVEEN KHANNA, "A Theory of Acquisition Markets—Mergers vs. Tender Offers; Golden Parachutes," ms., University of Michigan, 1988a.

———, "How Target Shareholders Benefit From Value Reducing Defensive Strategies in Takeovers," ms., University of Michigan, 1988b.

BRADLEY, M., A. DESAI, and E. H. KIM, "The Rationale Behind Interfirm Tender Offers: Information or Synergy?" *Journal of Financial Economics*, 11, 1983, pp. 183–206.

BRADLEY, M., and E. H. KIM, "The Tender Offer as a Takeover Device: Its Evolution, the Free Rider Problem, and the Prisoner's Dilemma," ms., 1985.

DANN, LARRY, "Common Stock Repurchases: An Analysis of Returns to Bondholders and Stockholders," *Journal of Financial Economics*, 9, June 1981, pp. 113–138.

DODD, PETER, "Merger Proposals, Management Discretion and Stockholder Wealth," *Journal of Financial Economics*, 8, 1980, pp. 105–138.

EASTERBROOK, F. H., and D. R. FISCHEL, "The Proper Role of a Target's Management in Responding to a Tender Offer," *Harvard Law Review*, 94, 1981, pp. 1161–1204.

———, "Auctions and Sunk Costs in Tender Offers," *Stanford Law Review*, 35, 1982, pp. 1–21.

FISHMAN, MICHAEL J., "A Theory of Preemptive Takeover Bidding," *RAND Journal of Economics*, 19, Spring 1988, pp. 88–101.

——, "Preemptive Bidding and the Role of the Medium of Exchange," *Journal of Finance*, 44, March 1989, pp. 41–57.

GIAMMARINO, RONALD M., and ROBERT L. HEINKEL, "A Model of Dynamic Takeover Behavior," *Journal of Finance*, 41, June 1986, pp. 465–480.

GILIBERTO, S. M., and N. P. VARAIYA, "The Winner's Curse and Bidder Competition in Acquisitions: Evidence From Failed Bank Auctions," *Journal of Finance*, 44, March 1989, pp. 59–75.

GROSSMAN, S. J., and O. D. HART, "Takeover Bids, the Free-Rider Problem and the Theory of the Corporation," *Bell Journal of Economics*, 11, Spring 1980, pp. 42–64.

HANSEN, R., "A Theory for the Choice of Exchange Medium in Mergers and Acquisitions," *Journal of Business*, 60, January 1987, pp. 75–95.

HARRIS, M., and A. RAVIV, "Corporate Control Contests and Capital Structure," *Journal of Financial Economics*, 20, 1988, pp. 55–86.

HIRSHLEIFER, DAVID, and I. P. L. PNG, "Facilitation of Competing Bids and the Price of a Takeover Target," forthcoming, *Review of Financial Studies*, Winter 1989.

HIRSHLEIFER, DAVID, and SHERIDAN TITMAN, "Share Tendering Strategies and the Success of Hostile Takeover Bids," forthcoming, *Journal of Political Economy*, April 1990.

HOLDERNESS, C. G., and D. P. SHEEHAN, "Raiders or Saviors? The Evidence on Six Controversial Investors," *Journal of Financial Economics*, 14, 1985, pp. 555–579.

JARRELL, GREGG A., "The Wealth Effects of Litigation by Targets: Do Interests Diverge in a Merge?" *Journal of Law and Economics*, 28, 1985, pp. 151–177.

——, and MICHAEL BRADLEY, "The Economic Effects of Federal and State Regulations of Cash Tender Offers," *Journal of Law and Economics*, 23, October 1980, pp. 371–407.

JEGADEESH, N., and B. CHOWDHRY, "Optimal Pre-Tender Offer Share Acquisition Strategy in Takeovers," UCLA Anderson Graduate School of Management, Working Paper, September 1988.

MACEY, J., and F. MCCHESNEY, "A Theoretical Analysis of Greenmail," *Yale Law Journal*, 95, 1985, pp. 13–61.

MIKKELSON, W., and R. RUBACK, "An Empirical Analysis of Interfirm Equity Investment Process," *Journal of Financial Economics*, 14, 1985, pp. 523–553.

NYBORG, K. G., "Friendly and Hostile Bids in the Corporate Takeover Process," ms., Stanford University, January 1989.

POULSEN, A., and G. JARRELL, "Stock Trading Before the Announcement of Tender Offers: Insider Trading or Market Anticipation," Working Paper, 1986.

RASMUSEN, ERIC, *Games and Information*, New York: Basil Blackwell, 1989.

ROLL, R., "The Hubris Hypothesis on Corporate Takeovers," *Journal of Business*, 59, April 1986, pp. 176–216.

SHLEIFER, ANDREI, and ROBERT W. VISHNY, "Large Shareholders and Corporate Control," *Journal of Political Economy*, 94, June 1986a, pp. 461–488.

——, "Greenmail, White Knights, and Shareholders' Interest," *RAND Journal of Economics*, 17, 1986b, pp. 293–309.

SPATT, CHESTER S., "Strategic Analyses of Takeover Bids," in S. Bhattacharya and G.

Constantinides, eds., *Financial Markets and Incomplete Information*, Totowa, NJ: Rowman and Littlefield, 1989, pp. 106–121.

STOUGHTON, N., "The Information Content of Corporate Merger and Acquisition Offers," *Journal of Financial and Quantitative Analysis*, 23, June 1988, pp. 175–197.

STULZ, R. M., "Managerial Control of Voting Rights," *Journal of Financial Economics*, 20, 1988, pp. 25–54.

TRAVLOS, NICKOLAOS G., "Corporate Takeover Bids, Methods of Payment, and Bidding Firms' Stock Returns," *Journal of Finance*, 42, September 1987, pp. 943–963.

WALKLING, R. A., "Predicting Tender Offer Success: A Logistic Analysis," *Journal of Financial and Quantitative Analysis*, 20, 1985, pp. 461–478.

———, and R. EDMISTER, "Determinants of Tender Offer Premiums," *Financial Analysts Journal*, 27, 1985, pp. 27–37.

———, and M. S. LONG, "Agency Theory, Managerial Welfare, and Takeover Bid Resistance," *RAND Journal of Economics*, 15, 1984, pp. 54–68.

Numerical Examples of Formal Models

Since the models reviewed in Appendix A are relatively abstract, we seek to convey the intuition and logic of our basic models by numerical examples. The models illustrated are those of Shleifer and Vishny (1986a), Hirshleifer and Titman (1988), Jegadeesh and Chowdhry (1988), and Fishman (1988).[1]

SV MODEL (1986a)

Abbreviations and Symbols

L is a large shareholder; owns $\alpha < .5$ of firm; others are atomistic holders.

c_T is the cost of making a takeover bid; fixed and independent of other factors.

q is the present value of expected profits under existing management; less than V.

V is the current market value; equals q plus expected value of improvements.

Z is the improvement; value of a firm after takeover is $(q + Z)$.

I is the probability of receiving a draw Z from $F(Z)$, that is, finding an improvement.

$F(Z)$ is a continuous probability distribution on $(0, Z_{max}]$.

$c(I)$ is expenditure to receive a draw from $F(Z)$ and increases with probability (or research intensity) I.

π is the premium paid by L over q in the takeover.

[1] For readers who find it helpful to visualize models in more concrete form, this appendix may be studied in conjunction with Appendix A. Since the models were described in detail in Appendix A, the numerical examples are set forth in outline form. We are grateful for the assistance of Dan Asquith, Bruno Gerard, and Kwanho Kim in developing these numerical examples.

FIGURE B.1   Cumulative Probability Function for the Improvement

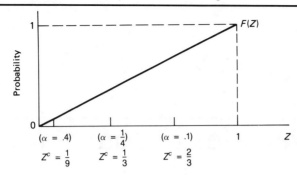

Equation System

L will bid if

$$.5Z - (.5 - \alpha)\pi - c_T \geq 0 \tag{B.1}$$

Small shareholders will tender if

$$\pi - E\,[Z|(B.1) \text{ holds for } L] \geq 0 \tag{B.2}$$

In equilibrium, $\pi^*(\alpha)$ is the smallest π that satisfies (B.2) and $Z^c(\alpha)$ is the smallest Z that satisfies (B.1) given $\pi^*(\alpha)$.

Factors α, c_T, and $F(Z)$ are common knowledge; players are risk neutral and take expectations to solve for the same $Z^c(\alpha)$ and $\pi^*(\alpha)$. Equation (B.1) states that the NPV of L's investment is his share of the improvement (his gross present value, GPV) less the shares he buys times the premium and less the costs of the takeover. Equation (B.2) states the free-rider problem. The small shareholders will infer Z^c from the fact that L makes a bid since α, c_T and $F(Z)$ are known. We can illustrate this for a particular distribution.

Example

Let $c_T = 0$ and let $F(Z)$ be the uniform distribution on $(0,1)$ (for example, zero to $1 million). (See Figure B.1.)

We can solve directly for $Z^c(\alpha)$ in this example if we note that

$$\pi^*(\alpha) = E[Z|Z \geq Z^c] = \frac{1 + Z^c(\alpha)}{2}$$

or the expected value of Z over the relevant segment of the distribution, that is, from Z^c to 1. Then since Z^c is the smallest Z that will allow a bid, it will be the Z such that equation (B.1) just equals 0 given this π^*. Therefore,

$$.5Z^c(\alpha) - (.5 - \alpha)\left(\frac{1 + Z^c\,(\alpha)}{2}\right) = 0$$

$$Z^c(\alpha) = \frac{1 - 2\alpha}{1 + 2\alpha}$$

and

$$\pi^*(\alpha) = \frac{1 + Z^c}{2} = \frac{1}{2} + \frac{1 - 2\alpha}{2(1 + 2\alpha)} = \frac{1}{1 + 2\alpha}$$

So, for example, if $\alpha = 0$, then $Z^c = 1$ and $\pi^* = 1$, which is the Grossman and Hart result. With no shareholding, the bidder has to offer the maximum possible improvement; otherwise the bid fails. If $\alpha = \frac{1}{4}$, then $Z^c = \frac{1}{3}$ and $\pi^* = \frac{2}{3}$. If $\alpha = .4$, $Z^c = \frac{1}{9}$ and $\pi^* = \frac{5}{9}$; the critical improvement is lower and so is the required premium. If $\alpha = .1$, $Z^c = \frac{2}{3}$ and $\pi^* = \frac{5}{6}$; the critical improvement and required premium are higher.

Thus if L bids, the small shareholder knows that L's draw of Z is at least $\frac{1 - 2\alpha}{1 + 2\alpha}$ so the small shareholder will require a premium of at least $\frac{1}{1 + 2\alpha}$. If L's draw is more than Z^c, he will gain more. If L's draw had been less than Z^c, he would not have made the bid.

Summary of Basic Results

LEMMA 1 $\pi^*(\alpha)$ is decreasing in α.

LEMMA 2 $Z^c(\alpha)$ is decreasing in α.

Both have been illustrated numerically by the example. Intuitively, the more L owns of the firm (higher α), the more L stands to make on his own shares and the lower his critical value $Z^c(\alpha)$ will be. When $Z^c(\alpha)$ decreases $\pi^*(\alpha)$ decreases, since this is the expectation over a longer tail of the distribution. (See Figure B.1.)

LEMMA 3 L's optimal choice of research intensity, $I^*(\alpha)$, is increasing in α.

For any draw Z, L is at least as well off (for any $Z > Z^c(\alpha)$ better off) the larger α. So the benefit of $I(\alpha)$ is increasing in α and the cost remains $c(I)$ independent of α. A larger research staff increases probability of finding a target, but does not influence the size of the gold mine which the target is sitting on (improvement).

The market value of the firm, V, is based on the firm value under current management, q, plus the probability of a takeover times the posttakeover increase in value, Z, which are functions of α:

$$V(\alpha, q) = q + I^*(\alpha)\{1 - F[Z^c(\alpha)]\} \cdot E[Z|Z \geqslant Z^c(\alpha)]$$

PROPOSITION 1. An increase in the proportion of shares held by L (α) results in a decrease in the takeover premium (π) but an increase in the market value of the firm (V). Intuition is shown by the example. Consider two values of α.

α	Z^c	π^*	$V = q + I^*(\alpha)[1 - F(Z^c)][E(Z|Z \geq Z^c)]$
.25	⅓	⅔=6⁄9	$= q + (⅔)(⅔)I^*(.25)$
			$= q + .444\ I^*(.25)$
.40	⅑	5⁄9	$= q + (8⁄9)(5⁄9)I^*(.4)$
			$= q + .494\ I^*(.4)$

Note that $I^*(.25) < I^*(.4)$. The intuition is that the smaller Z^c means that a larger range of improvements will be acted on, leads to a lower takeover premium, but the increased probability of implementing an improvement more than compensates for this. (Further, research intensity is larger.) The area under the curve to the right of Z^c (in Figure B.1) is larger, so what is added to q is larger. So for larger α, the premium (π^*) is lower, but V is clearly higher.

HT MODEL (1988)

In the Hirshleifer and Titman model, the notation is about the same except that q is assumed equal to zero. The amount per share bid is denoted here as x instead of $q + \pi$. In their model, $\omega = (.5 - \alpha)$. $P(x)$ is the probability that the bid will succeed. The equation of Shleifer and Vishny, $.5Z - (.5 - \alpha)x - c_T \geq 0$, corresponds to the following equation of Hirshleifer and Titman: $\alpha x\ P(x) - c_T$ is nonnegative. Hirshleifer and Titman argue that $x = Z$ so the preceding equation of Shleifer and Vishny simplifies to $.5x - .5x + \alpha x - c_T \geq 0$ or $\alpha x - c_T \geq 0$. Remember that in equilibrium in Shleifer and Vishny $P(x) = 1$ for optimal bids. Therefore, these equations correspond. This is the condition for a bid to occur.

Shleifer and Vishny have no corresponding equation to the following of Hirshleifer and Titman:

$$\max_x [\alpha Z + (Z - x)\omega]P(x)$$

which is maximized assuming a bid occurs. The term in brackets equals $.5Z - (.5 - \alpha)x$, the first part of equation (B.1) of Shleifer and Vishny because $\omega = .5 - \alpha$. The reason Shleifer and Vishny do not deal with the maximization is that in Shleifer and Vishny $P(x) = 0$ for $x < x^*$ and $P(x) = 1$ for $x \geq x^*$ so that the maximum trivially occurs at x^*.

Hirshleifer and Titman make the information about Z possessed by the target shareholders imperfectly known to the bidder, so that the shareholders' tendering decisions cannot be foreseen by bidders. If shareholders take x to be uninformative, the probability that the offer succeeds is increasing in the bid. This induces the bidders to reveal their level of improvement through their bids. The critical Z^c for Hirshleifer and Titman is:

$$Z^c = \left(\frac{c_T}{\alpha}\right)^{2\alpha} Z_{max}^{2\omega}$$

The tender offer will succeed with probability.

$$P(x) = \left(\frac{x}{Z_{max}} \right)^{\frac{\omega}{\alpha}} \quad \text{for } x \epsilon [Z^c, Z_{max}]$$

Combining these relations, we can illustrate the influence of the key factors, including the share of holdings by L. The bid equals Z and perfectly reveals the bidder's private information for all $Z \geqslant Z^c$ where Z^c is defined as in Shleifer and Vishny.

Explanation of Figure B.2

The probability of an offer's success is depicted in Figure B.2; $Z_{max} = 1$, $c_T = 0.1$, and $\omega = 0.5 - \alpha$ are assumed. The figure illustrates that the probability of success, $P(x)$,

1 increases with the bid premium (x),
2 increases with initial shareholdings (α),
3 is decreasing in the number of shares required to obtain control (assumed $0.5 - \alpha$).

In the figure, the highest possible bid equals $Z_{max} = 1$, and for $x = 1$, $P(x) = 1$. For lower α, the schedule is lower and *steeper* at the right end point. For lower α, underbidding results in larger drop in $P(x)$. The reason is that lower α implies

FIGURE B.2   Probability of Bid Success

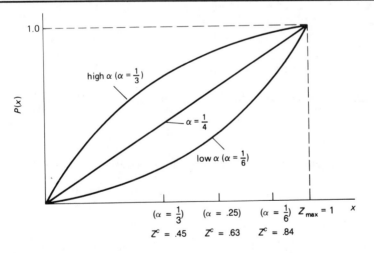

Note: 1. $Z_{max} = 1$, $c_T = 0.1$, and $\omega = 0.5 - \alpha$ are assumed
      2. $Z^c = \left(\frac{c_T}{\alpha} \right)^{2\alpha} Z_{max}^{2\omega}$
      3. $P(x) = \left(\frac{x}{Z_{max}} \right)^{\frac{\omega}{\alpha}}$

relatively lower profits from initial shareholdings compared to purchased shares, which increases the incentive to underbid.

In the figure $Z^c(\alpha)$ decreases with α: increasing α makes it profitable for lower valuation bidders to make an offer, so Z^c (and hence the average bid premium in actual takeovers) declines.

If we used a smaller Z_{max}, $P(x)$ would be higher for any given x satisfying Z^c $\leq x < Z_{max}$. This implies that a reduction in the degree of asymmetry of information, that is, a mean-preserving inward shift in the distribution of Z that lowers Z_{max}, will raise $P(x)$.

JEGADEESH AND CHOWDHRY (1988)

Numerical Assumptions

All numbers used in the following example are illustrative. Assume $\alpha_{max} = .25$.

There are two types of bidders: $Z_L = 80$ and $Z_H = 100$.
There are ½ of each type.
Assume that $P(B) = \frac{\sqrt{B}}{10}$ on $B = (0, Z_{max} = 100)$.
This satisfies Assumption 1 since $P'(B) = \frac{1}{20\sqrt{B}} > 0$ and $P''(B) = \frac{1}{-40} B^{-3/2} < 0$.

Breaking the Pooling Equilibrium

If there exists a pooling equilibrium, α and B must take the following values:

$$\alpha_{pool} = \alpha_{max} = .25 \text{ since there is no advantage to signaling;}$$

$$B_{pool} = E[Z_{pool}|B_{pool}, \alpha_{max}] = Z_M = \tfrac{1}{2} Z_H + \tfrac{1}{2} Z_L = 90$$

The value of each type of being in the pool is shown by the value function:

$$V(B, \alpha; Z) = P(B)[.5Z - (.5 - \alpha)B]$$

$$\text{For } Z_H: V(90, .25; 100) = P(90)[.5(100) - (.5 - \alpha)90]$$

$$= .94868[50 - .25(90)]$$

$$= 26.08879$$

$$\text{For } Z_L: V(90, .25; 80) = P(90)[.5(80) - (.5 - \alpha)90]$$

$$= .94868[40 - .25(90)]$$

$$= 16.60196$$

Z_H is happy in the pool, but Z_L is bidding more than her value of improvement and thus would be better off if she could bid less. To break the pool, Z_L finds the α such that she can bid $Z_L = 80$ and Z_H will not mimic. To do this, Z_L must solve Z_H's value of α such that Z_H is just indifferent. That is:

$$V(80,\alpha_L; Z_H) = V(90,.25;Z_H) = 26.08879$$

$$P(80)[.5(100) - (.5 - \alpha_L)(80)] = 26.08879$$

$$.89443[50 - 40 + 80\alpha_L] = 26.08879$$

$$\alpha_L = .23960$$

To show this breaks the pool, we must demonstrate that Z_L is better off bidding Z_L and acquiring α_L:

$$V(80,\alpha_L;80) = P(80)[.5(80) + (.5 - .23960)(80)]$$

$$= .89443[.23960(80)]$$

$$= 17.14452 > 16.60196$$

Therefore, the pooling equilibrium is broken.

Establishing a Separating Equilibrium

In the separating equilibrium, Z_H will not signal and since her type is identified she must bid Z_H. So she acquires α_{max} and bids $Z_H = 100$ and her value function is

$$V(100,.25;100) = P(100)[.5(100) + (.5 - .25)(100)]$$

$$= 25$$

The α_L such that Z_H will not mimic at $Z_L = 80$ is calculated the same as previously:

$$V(80,\alpha_L;100) = V(100,.25;100) = 25$$
$$P(80)[.5(100) + (.5 - \alpha_L)(80)] = 25$$
$$.89443[50 - 40 + 80\alpha_L] = 25$$
$$\alpha_L = .22439$$

This gives the separating equilibrium:

Z_H bids $Z_H = 100$ and acquires $\alpha_{max} = .25$
Z_L bids $Z_L = 80$ and acquires $\alpha_L = .22439$
If any move with $\alpha > \alpha_L$ is observed, every shareholder believes it is type Z_H that has done this move.

FISHMAN (1988)

Solving the Problem for Uniform Valuation Distributions

Recall the payoff functions:

$$\text{For bidder 1 } \pi_1(v_1,v_2,p,0) = v_1 - p - c_1$$

$$\pi_1(v_1,v_2,p,1) = v_1 - \min\{\max(p,v_2),v_1\} - c_1$$

$$\text{For bidder 2 } \pi_2(v_1,v_2,p,0) = 0$$

$$\pi_2(v_1,v_2,p,1) = v_2 - \min\{v_1,v_2\} - c_2$$

and the distributional assumptions

A.1 $E[v_i|s^-] < E[v_i|s^+] < v_0$

A.2 $E[\max(\tilde{v}_i - v_0,0)|s^-] < E[\max(\tilde{v}_i - v_0,0)] < c_i$

A.3 $E[\pi_2(\tilde{v}_1,\tilde{v}_2,p = v_0,1)] > 0$

Assume that $\tilde{v}_i$ is uniformly distributed. Let

$$\tilde{v}_i \sim U[l^-,h^-] \text{ if } s^- \text{ with probability } 1 - \phi$$

$$\tilde{v}_i \sim U[l^+,h^+] \text{ if } s^+ \text{ with probability } \phi$$

where ϕ, the good state probability, can also be thought of as a mixing probability. For the uniform distribution, we get (ignoring for convenience the superscripts for the end points of the distribution)

$$E[v_i|s] = \tfrac{1}{2}(h + l)$$

$$E[\max(v_i - v_0,0)|s] = \int_l^{v_0} 0 f_i(v_i)dv_i + \int_{v_0}^h (v_i - v_0)f_i(v_i)dv_i$$

$$= \frac{1}{2(h - l)}(h^2 - 2v_0h + v_0^2).$$

Distributional assumption A.2 can be rewritten as

$$E[\max(v_i - v_0,0)] = (1 - \phi)E[\max(v_i - v_0,0)|s^-] + \phi E[\max(v_i - v_0,0)|s^+] \leq c_i$$

Let $\phi_{max}(c_i)$ denote the maximum level of the mixing probability to satisfy A.2.

$$\phi_{max}(c_i) = (c_i - E[max(.)|s^-])/(E[max(.)|s^+] - E[max(.)|s^-])$$

From A.2, we can see also that $c_i^{min} = E[max(.)|s^-]$ for $\phi = 0$.

Determination of r

Since we are in state $s = s^+$, we denote l^+ and h^+ simply as l and h. We can determine r by solving

$$\int_r^h E[\pi_2(\tilde{v}_1, \tilde{v}_2, p, 1)|v_1] \frac{f_1(v_1)}{1 - F_1(r)} dv_1 = 0$$

We have

$$E[\pi_2(\tilde{v}_1, \tilde{v}_2, p, 1)|v_1] = \int_l^h (v_2 - min\{v_1, v_2\} - c_2) f_2(v_2) dv_2$$

$$= \int_{v_1}^h v_2 \frac{1}{h - l} dv_2 - \int_{v_1}^h v_1 \frac{1}{h - l} dv_2 - c_2$$

$$= \frac{1}{2(h - l)} (h^2 - 2v_1 h + v_1^2) - c_2$$

Thus, after substitution and simplifications, r is the solution of

$$\int_r^h \frac{1}{2(h - l)} (h^2 - 2v_1 h + v_1^2) dv_1 - c_2 = 0$$

which yields

$$r = h - \sqrt{6(h - l)c_2}$$

Since the probability of a bid is positive only if $r \geq v_0$, this yields the following condition (which is effectively A.3):

$$c_2 \leq \frac{(h - v_0)^2}{6(h - l)} \text{ and } c_2^{max} = \frac{(h - v_0)^2}{6(h - l)}$$

Note that this last condition and A.2 effectively provide strict bounds to the cost levels that yield an equilibrium. The optimal bid $\bar{p}(r)$ is then

$$\bar{p}(r) = E[min\{max(v_0, \tilde{v}_2), r\}]$$

$$= \int_l^{v_0} v_0 f_2(v_2) dv_2 + \int_{v^0}^r v_2 f_2(v_2) dv_2 + \int_r^h r f_2(v_2) dv_2$$

$$= \frac{h^2 - 2v_0 l + v_0^2}{2(h - l)} - 3c_2$$

Numerical Examples

1. Let:

$v_0 = 10$

$\tilde{v}_i \sim U[1,11]$ if s^-

$\tilde{v}_i \sim U[3,13]$ if s^+

We get, using the preceding formulas

$$E[v_i|s^-] = 6 \quad \text{and} \quad E[v_i|s^+] = 8$$

$$E[max(v_i - v_0, 0)|s^-] = \frac{1}{20} [11^2 - 2(10)(11) + 10^2] = \frac{1}{20} = .05$$

$$E[max(v_i - v_0, 0)|s^+] = \frac{1}{20} [13^2 - 2(10)(13) + 10^2] = \frac{9}{20} = .45$$

$$c_2^{min} = .05 \text{ or } 0.5\% \text{ (of } v_0) \quad \text{and} \quad c_2^{max} = .15 \text{ or } 1.5\%$$

For values of the cost parameter in that range we get

c_2	$\phi_{max}(c_2)$	r	$\bar{p}(r)$
.15	.25	10	10
.125	.1875	10.26	10.075
.10	.125	10.55	10.15
.075	.0625	10.88	10.225
.05	.00	11.27	10.30

2. Let:

$v_0 = 10$

$\tilde{v}_i \sim U[0,10]$ if s^-

$\tilde{v}_i \sim U[3,16]$ if s^+

We get

$$E[v_i|s^-] = 5 \quad \text{and} \quad E[v_i|s^+] = 9.5$$

$$E[\max(v_i - v_0, 0)|s^-] = \frac{1}{20} [10^2 - 2(10)(10) + 10^2] = \frac{0}{20} = .00$$

$$E[\max(v_i - v_0, 0)|s^+] = \frac{1}{26} [16^2 - 2(10)(16) + 10^2] = \frac{36}{26} = 1.385$$

$$c_2^{min} = .00 \text{ or } 0.0\% \qquad \text{and} \qquad c_2^{max} = .462 \text{ or } 4.62\%$$

For values of the cost parameter in that range we get

c_2	$\phi_{max}(c_2)$	r	$\bar{p}(r)$
.462	.333	10	10
.20	.144	12.05	10.785
.10	.072	13.21	11.085
.025	.018	14.60	11.31
.00	.00	16.00	11.385

The range of feasible costs that yield an equilibrium are very restricted and heavily depend on the range of values of v_i^- for c_i^{min} and of v_i^+ for c_i^{max}. Further, each cost level yields a maximum mixing probability for the good state that is positively related to the cost level. This is the consequence of A.2: For any cost levels, the unconditional expected gain from bidding must be lower than the cost of information acquisition. Otherwise bidder 2 types will acquire information in all circumstances, even in the absence of an initial bid. The lower limit on costs is attained for a mixing probability of 0 for the good state of nature.

Note also that even with very low costs and potentially a large acquisition gain, the bid premium is never very large (at least in the preceding computations). For example, with a cost of .25 percent of initial value and the upper valuation at 1.6 times the current value, the deterring bid premium is only 13.1 percent of current value when the valuation differential (takeover improvement) is above 46 percent.

Glossary*

Abnormal return.   In event studies, the part of the return that is not predicted; the change in value caused by the event.

Acquisition.   The purchase of a controlling interest in a firm, generally via a tender offer for the target shares.

Acquisition MLP.   Also called start-up master limited partnership; the assets of an existing entity are transferred to an MLP, and the business is henceforth conducted as an MLP. The Boston Celtics' conversion into an MLP is an example.

ACR.   See *Aggregate concentration ratio.*

Adventure.   A goal in joint ventures (sometimes called joint adventures) in addition to the expectation of profits. Suggests a speculative motive.

Adverse selection.   False signaling. For example, firms with serious problems may signal that they are healthy firms interested in mergers or selling out.

Agency problem.   The conflict of interest between principal (e.g., shareholders) and agent (e.g., managers) in which the agent has an incentive to act in his own self-interest because he bears less than the total costs of his actions.

Aggregate concentration ratio.   Overall concentration nationwide; the percentage of sales controlled by the largest 50, for example, or 100 firms.

Anergy.   Negative synergy. Instead of a "2 + 2 = 5" effect, anergy implies "2 + 2 = 3." Business units actively interfere with each other and may have more value if separated.

Announcement date.   In event studies, typically, the day information becomes public.

Antigreenmail amendment.   Corporate charter amendment which prohibits targeted share repurchases at a premium from an unwanted acquirer without the approval of nonparticipating shareholders.

---

*Technical terms used in explanations are defined in their alphabetical position.

Antitakeover amendment.   A corporate charter amendment which is intended to make it more difficult for an unwanted acquirer to take over the firm.

Any-or-all offer.   A tender offer which does not specify a maximum number of shares to be purchased, but none will be purchased if the conditions of the offer are not met.

Appraisal right.   The right of minority shareholders to obtain an independent valuation of their shares to determine the appropriate back-end value in a two-tier tender offer.

APT.   See *Arbitrage pricing theory.*

Arbitrage.   The purchase of an asset for near-term resale at a higher price. In the context of M&As, risk arbitrage refers to investing in the stock of takeover targets for short-term resale to capture a portion of the gains which typically accrue to target shareholders.

Arbitrage pricing theory.   A general approach to asset pricing which allows for the possibility that many factors may be used to explain asset returns, as opposed to the capital asset pricing model in which the market return is the sole explanatory factor.

Atomistic competition.   Numerous small sellers and buyers, none of which have the power to influence market prices or output.

Atomistic shareholders.   Each shareholder has only a small amount of stock. Small shareholders have less incentive to monitor management than large block shareholders.

Auction.   Two or more bidders competing for a single target. An auction increases the price target shareholders receive.

Back-end rights plan.   A poison pill takeover defense in which target shareholders are issued a rights dividend exercisable if an acquirer obtains over a triggering amount of target stock. Shareholders (excluding the acquirer) may exchange each right-and-share-of-stock held for senior securities or cash equal in value to a back-end price set by the target board. This back-end price is set higher than the market price and becomes a minimum takeover price below which no takeover can succeed.

Back-end value.   The amount paid to remaining shareholders in the second stage of a two-tier or partial tender offer.

Bear hug.   A takeover strategy in which the acquirer, without previous warning, mails the directors of the target a letter announcing the acquisition proposal and demanding a quick decision.

Beta.   In the capital asset pricing model, the systematic risk of the asset; the variability of the asset's return in relation to the return on the market.

Bidder.   The acquiring firm in a tender offer.

Blended price.   The weighted average price in a two-tier tender offer. The front-end price is weighted by the percent of shares purchased in the first step of the transaction, and the lower, back-end price is weighted by the percent of shares purchased to complete the transaction.

Board-out clause.   A provision in most supermajority antitakeover amendments which gives the board of directors the power to decide when and if the supermajority provision will be in effect.

Bottom-up.   An approach to firm strategy formulation based on the aggregation of segment forecasts.

Bounded rationality.   Refers to the limited capacity of the human mind to deal with complexity.

Brand-name capital.   Firm reputation; the result of nonsalvageable investment which provides customers with an implicit guarantee of product quality for which they are willing to pay a premium.

Business judgment rule.   A legal doctrine which holds that the board of directors is acting in the best interests of shareholders unless it can be proven by a preponderance of the evidence that the board is acting in its own interest or is in breach of its fiduciary duty.

Bust-up takeover.   An acquisition followed by the divestiture of some or all of the operating units of the acquired firm which are presumably worth more in pieces than as a going concern.

Buy-back.   See *Share repurchase.*

Capital asset pricing model.   Calculates the required return on an asset as a function of the risk-free rate plus the market risk premium times the asset's beta.

Capital budgeting.   The process of planning expenditures whose returns extend over a period of time.

Capital intensity.   In economics, the ratio of investment required per dollar of sales. In finance, the sales to investment ratio. The steel industry and manufacturing generally are more capital intensive than the wholesale or retail industries.

CAPM.   See *Capital asset pricing model.*

CAR.   See *Cumulative abnormal return.*

Cash cows.   A Boston Consulting Group term for business segments which have a high market share in low-growth product markets and thus throw off more cash flow than needed for reinvestment.

Chinese wall.   The imaginary barrier separating investment banking and arbitrage functions within a financial intermediary.

Classified board.   Also called a staggered board. An antitakeover measure which divides a firm's board of directors into several classes, only one of which is up for election in any given year, thus delaying effective transfer of control to a new owner in a takeover.

Clayton Act.   Federal antitrust law originally passed in 1914 and strengthened in 1950 by the Celler-Kefauver amendment. Section 7 gives the Federal Trade Commission (FTC) power to prohibit the acquisition of one company by another if adverse effects on competition would result, or if the FTC perceived a trend which might ultimately lead to decreased competition.

Clean-up merger.   Also called a take-out merger. The consolidation of the acquired firm into the acquiring firm after the acquirer has obtained control.

Clientele effect.   A dividend theory which states that high-tax bracket shareholders will prefer to hold stock in firms with low dividend payout rates and low-tax bracket shareholders will prefer the stock of firms with high payouts.

Coercive tender offer.   Any tender offer which puts pressure on target shareholders to tender by offering a higher price to those who tender early.

Coinsurance effect.   The combination of two firms whose cash flows are not perfectly correlated will result in cash flows of less variability for the merged firm, thus decreasing the risk to lenders to the firm and thereby increasing its debt capacity.

Collateral restraints.   Agreements between the parties to a joint venture to limit competition between themselves in certain areas.

Collusion.   Illegal coordination or cooperation among competitors with respect to price or output.

Complementarity.   The strengths of one firm offset the weaknesses of another firm with which it combines. For example, one firm strong in marketing combines with one strong in research.

Concentration. Measures of the percentage of total industry sales accounted for by a specified number of firms, such as 4, 8 or 20.

Concentric merger. A merger in which there is carry-over in *specific* management functions (e.g., marketing) or complementarity in relative strengths among *specific* management functions rather than carry-over/complementarities in only generic management functions (e.g., planning).

Conglomerate. A combination of unrelated firms; any combination that is not vertical or horizontal.

Conjectural variation. The reaction of rival firms as one firm, Firm A, restricts output or raises prices. Ranges from -1 to $+1$; a negative conjectural variation indicates competitive behavior, i.e., Firm A's action is offset by the reactions of competing rival firms.

Consistency requirement. Internal Revenue provision (in Section 338) eliminating selectivity as to tax treatment of acquired assets in terms of stepped-up or carry-over asset basis. If stepped-up basis is elected for any subset of acquired firm assets, it is deemed to be an election for stepped-up asset basis for the entire target.

Contingent voting rights. Rights to vote in corporate elections which become exercisable upon the occurrence of a particular event. Examples: Preferred stockholders may win the right to vote if preferred dividends are missed; convertible debt may be viewed as having voting rights contingent upon conversion.

Convergence of interests hypothesis. Predicts a positive relationship between the proportion of management stock ownership and the market's valuation of the firm's assets.

Cost leadership. A business strategy based on achieving lower costs than rivals.

Covenant. See *Indenture.*

Crown jewels. The most valuable segments of a company; the parts most wanted by an acquirer.

Cumulative abnormal return. In event studies, the sum of daily abnormal returns over a period relative to the event.

Cumulative voting. Instead of one vote per candidate selected, shareholders can vote (the number of shares they hold times the number of directors to be elected) for one candidate or divide the total votes among a desired number of candidates. Example: A shareholder has 100 shares; six directors are to be elected. With cumulative voting the shareholder has 600 votes to distribute among six candidates however he or she chooses.

Decision control. Fundamental ownership rights of shareholders to select management, monitor management, and to determine reward/incentive arrangements.

Decision management. Decision functions related to day-to-day operations which may be delegated to managers. Includes initiation and implementation of policies and procedures.

Defensive diversification. Entering new product markets to offset the limitations of the firm's existing product-market areas.

Defined benefit plan. A pension plan which specifies in advance the amount beneficiaries will receive based on compensation, years of service, and so on.

Defined contribution plan. A pension plan in which the annual contributions are specified in advance. Benefits upon retirement depend on the performance of the assets in which the contributions are invested.

Delphi technique. An information-gathering technique in which questionnaires are sent to informed individuals. The responses are summarized into a feedback report and used to generate subsequent questionnaires to probe more deeply into the issue under study.

De novo entry.   Entry into an industry by forming a new company as opposed to combining with an existing firm in the industry.

Differential managerial efficiency hypothesis.   A theory which hypothesizes that more efficient managements take over firms with less efficient managements and achieve gains by improving the efficiency of the target.

Discriminatory poison pill.   Antitakeover plans which penalize acquirers who exceed a given shareholding percentage (the kick-in point).

Dissident.   A shareholder, or group of shareholders, who disagrees with incumbent management and seeks to make changes via a proxy contest to gain representation on the board of directors.

Diversification.   Holding assets whose returns are not perfectly correlated.

Divestiture.   Sale of a segment of a company (assets, a product line, a subsidiary) to a third party for cash and/or securities.

Dividend method dual-class recapitalization.   Most widely used method of converting to dual-class stock ownership. A stock split or dividend is used to distribute new inferior voting stock. The previously existing common stock is redesignated as superior-vote class B stock.

Dogs.   A Boston Consulting Group term for business segments characterized by low market shares in product markets with low growth rates.

Dual-class recapitalization.   Corporate restructuring used to create two classes of common stock with the superior-vote stock concentrated in the hands of management.

Dual-class stock.   Two (or more) classes of common stock with equal rights to cash flows, but with unequal voting rights.

DuPont system.   A financial planning and control system focusing on return on investment by relating asset turnover (effective asset management) to profit margin on sales (effective cost control).

Dynamic competition theory.   A model of industrial organization theory which extends the traditional models of price and output decisions of firms in a static environment to decisions on product quality, innovation, promotion, marketing, and so on in changing environments.

Dynamic oligopoly.   Although an industry may be dominated by a few large firms (oligopoly), recognized interdependence does not occur because decisions must be made on so many factors that actions and reactions of rivals cannot be predicted or coordinated.

Empirical test.   Systematic examination of data to check the consistency of evidence with alternative theories.

Employee stock ownership plan (ESOP).   Defined contribution pension plan (stock bonus and/or money purchase) designed to invest primarily in the stock of the employer firm.

Employment Retirement Income Security Act (ERISA).   1974 federal legislation regulating pension plans including some ESOPs. Sets vesting requirements, fiduciary standards, minimum funding standards. Established Pension Benefit Guarantee Corporation (PBGC) to guarantee pensions.

End of regulation.   A theory hypothesizing that takeovers occur following deregulation of an industry as a result of increased competition which exposes management inefficiency which may have been masked by regulation.

Entrenchment.   See *Managerial entrenchment*.

Equity carveout.   A transaction in which a parent firm offers *some* of a subsidiary's common stock to the general public, to bring in a cash infusion to the parent without loss of control.

ERISA.   See *Employment Retirement Income Security Act*.

ERISA-type ESOP.   Employee stock ownership plans other than tax-credit ESOPs; i.e., includes leveraged, leveragable, and nonleveraged ESOPs recognized under ERISA rather than under the Tax Reduction Act of 1975.

ESOP.   See *Employee stock ownership plan*.

Event study.   An empirical test of the effect of an event (e.g., a merger, divestiture) on stock returns. The event is the reference date from which analysis of returns is made regardless of the calendar timing of the occurrences in the sample of firms.

Excess return.   See *Abnormal return*.

Exchange method dual-class recapitalization.   Means of converting to a dual-class stock corporate structure. High-vote stock is issued to insiders in exchange for their currently outstanding (low-vote) stock. The remaining low-vote stock, in the hands of outside shareholders, generally receives a higher dividend.

Exchange offer.   A transaction which provides one class (or more) of securities with the right or option to exchange part or all of their holdings for a different class of the firm's securities, e.g., an exchange of debt for common stock. Enables a change in capital structure with no change in investment.

Exit-type firm.   In Jensen's free cash flow hypothesis, a firm with positive free cash flows. The theory predicts that for such a firm, stock prices will increase with unexpected increases in payout.

Extra merger premium hypothesis.   The possibility that a higher price will be paid for superior-vote shares if a dual-class stock firm becomes a takeover target causes the price of superior-vote stock to be higher even in the absence of a takeover bid.

Failing firm defense.   A defense against a merger challenge alleging that in the absence of the merger, the firm(s) would fail. The 1982 Merger Guidelines spell out the conditions under which this defense will be acceptable.

Fair-price amendment.   An antitakeover charter amendment which waives the supermajority approval requirement for a change of control if a fair price is paid for all purchased shares. Defends against two-tier offers which do not have board approval.

Fallen angel.   A bond issued at investment grade whose rating is subsequently dropped to below investment grade, below BBB.

Financial conglomerates.   Conglomerate firms in which corporate management provides a flow of funds to operating segments, exercises control and strategic planning functions, and is the ultimate financial risk taker, but does *not* participate in operating decisions.

Financial synergy.   A theory which suggests a financial motive for mergers, especially between firms with high internal cash flows (but poor investment opportunities) and firms with low internal cash flows (and high investment opportunities which, absent merger, would require costly external financing). Also includes increased debt capacity or coinsurance effect, and economies of scale in flotation and transaction costs of securities.

Flip-over poison pill plan.   The most popular type of poison pill antitakeover defense. Shareholders of the target firm are issued rights to purchase common stock at an exercise price high above the current market price. If a merger occurs, the rights flip over and allow shareholders to purchase the acquiring firm's common stock at a substantial discount.

Four-firm concentration ratio.   The sum of the shares of sales, value added, assets, or employees held by the largest four firms in an industry. A measure of competitiveness, according to the structural theory.

Free cash flow hypothesis.   Jensen's theory of how the payout of free cash flows helps resolve the agency problem between managers and shareholders. Holds that bonding payout of current (and future) free cash flows reduces the power of management as well as subjecting them more frequently to capital market scrutiny.

Free-rider problem.   Atomistic shareholder reasons that its decision has no impact on the outcome of the tender offer and refrains from tendering to free-ride on the value increase resulting from the merger, thus causing the bid to fail.

Front-end loading.   A tender offer in which the offer price is greater than the value of any unpurchased shares. Resolves the free-rider problems by providing an incentive to tender early.

Full ex post settling up.   A manager's compensation is frequently adjusted over the course of his or her career to fully reflect his or her performance, thus eliminating an incentive to shirk.

Gambler's ruin.   An adverse string of losses which could lead to bankruptcy, although the long-run cash flows could be positive.

General Utilities doctrine.   An IRS rule which allowed firms to not recognize gains on the distribution of appreciated property in redemption of its shares (e.g., in a "legal" liquidation). Repealed by the Tax Reform Act of 1986.

Generic management functions.   Those functions that are not industry specific and are thus transferrable even in conglomerate mergers. Include planning, organizing, directing, and controlling.

Going-concern value.   The value of the firm as a whole over and above the sum of the values of each of its parts; the value of organization learning and reputation.

Going private.   The transformation of a public corporation into a privately-held firm (often via a leveraged buy-out or a management buy-out).

Golden parachute.   Provision in the employment contracts of top management providing for compensation for loss of jobs following a change of control.

Good will.   The excess of the purchase price paid for a firm over the book value received. Recorded on the acquirer's balance sheet, to be amortized over not more than 40 years (amortization not tax deductible).

Greenmail.   The premium over the current market price of stock paid to buy back the holdings accumulated by an unwanted acquirer to avoid a takeover.

Growth/share matrix.   A guide to strategy formulation which emphasizes attainment of high market share in industries with favorable growth rates.

Harassment hypothesis.   Ellert's theory that Federal Trade Commission antitrust complaints are brought against firms with abnormally good stock price performance, at the instigation of the firms' competitors who are threatened by their superior performance.

Hart-Scott-Rodino Antitrust Improvements Act of 1976.   Expands power of Department of Justice in antitrust investigations; provides for waiting period (15 days for tender offers, 30 days for mergers) following submission of information to Department of Justice and Federal Trade Commission before transaction can be completed; expands power of state Attorneys General to institute triple damage antitrust lawsuits on behalf of their citizens.

Herfindahl-Hirschman Index (HHI).   The measure of concentration under the 1982 Merger Guidelines, defined as the sum of the *squares* of the market shares of *all* the firms in the industry.

HHI.   See *Herfindahl-Hirschman Index*.

Hidden equity.   Undervalued assets whose market value exceeds their depreciated book value, but is not reflected in stock price.

High-yield bond.   See *Junk bond*.

Holding company.   An organization whose primary function is to hold the stock of other corporations, but which has no operating units of its own. Similar to the multidivisional organization which has profit centers and a single central headquarters. However, the segments owned by the holding company are separate legal entities which in practice are controlled by the holding company.

Holdup.   Whenever a resource is dependent on (specialized to) the rest of the firm, there may be a temptation for others to try to expropriate the quasi-rent of the dependent resource by withholding their complementary resources; this is holdup. However, each resource in the team (firm) may be dependent on all the others, and thus all are vulnerable to expropriation.

Horizontal merger.   A combination of firms operating in the same business activity.

Hubris hypothesis.   (Winner's curse) Roll's theory that acquiring firm managers commit errors of overoptimism in evaluating merger opportunities (due to excessive pride, animal spirits), and end up paying too high a price for acquisitions.

IAA.   See *Investment Advisers Act of 1940.*

ICA.   See *Investment Company Act of 1940.*

Implicit claim.   A tacit rather than contractual promise of continuing service and delivery of expected quality to customers and job security to employees.

Incentive stock option (ISO).   An executive compensation plan to align the interests of managers with stockholders. Executives are issued options whose exercise price is equal to or greater than the stock price at the time of issue and thus have value only if the stock price rises, giving managers incentives to take actions to maximize stock price.

Increased debt capacity hypothesis.   A theory that postmerger financial leverage increases are the result of increased debt capacity (as opposed to the firms involved having been underleveraged before the merger) due to reduced expected bankruptcy costs.

Indenture.   The contract between a firm and its bondholders which sets out the terms and conditions of the borrowing, and the rights and obligations of each party (covenants).

Industry life cycle.   A conceptual model of the different stages of an industry's development. (1) Development stage—new product, high investment needs, losses; (2) Growth stage—consumer acceptance, expanding sales, high profitability, ease of entry; (3) Maturity stage—sales growth slows, excess capacity, prices and profits decline—key period for merger strategy; (4) Decline stage—substitute products emerge, sales growth declines, pressure for mergers to survive.

Inferior-vote stock.   In dual-class stock firms, the class of common stock which has less voting power, e.g., may be able to elect only a minority on the board of directors; may be compensated with higher dividends.

Initial public offering (IPO).   The first offering to the public of common stock, e.g., of a former privately-held firm, or a portion of the common stock of a hitherto wholly-owned subsidiary.

In play.   Because of a bid or rumors of a bid, the financial community regards the company as receptive or vulnerable to takeover bids.

Internal rate of return (IRR).   A capital budgeting method which finds the discount rate (the IRR) which equates the present value of cash inflows and investment outlays. The IRR must exceed the relevant risk-adjusted cost of capital for the project to be acceptable.

Investment Advisers Act of 1940 (IAA).   Federal securities legislation providing for registration and regulation of investment advisers.

Investment Company Act of 1940 (ICA).   Federal securities legislation regulating publicly-owned companies in the business of investing and trading in securities; subjects them to SEC rules. Amended in 1970 to place more controls on management compensation and sales charges.

Investment requirements ratio.   A firm's investment expenditures (or opportunities) in relation to after-tax cash flows.

IPO.   See *Initial public offering.*

IRR.   See *Internal rate of return.*

ISO.   See *Incentive stock option.*

Joint production.   Production using complementary inputs in which the output cannot be unambiguously attributed to any single input; and in which the output is greater than the sum of the inputs (i.e., synergy). Problems in assigning returns may arise if the inputs are not owned by the same entity.

Joint venture.   A combination of subsets of assets contributed by two (or more) business entities for a specific business purpose and a limited duration. Each of the venture partners continues to exist as a separate firm, and the joint venture represents a new business enterprise.

Junk bond.   High-yield bonds which are below investment grade when issued, i.e., rated below BBB (Standard and Poor's) or below Baa3 (Moody's).

Kick-in point.   The level of share ownership by an acquiring firm which activates a poison-pill antitakeover defense plan.

Kick-in-the-pants hypothesis.   Attributes the increase in a takeover target's stock price to the impetus given by the bid to target management to implement a higher-valued strategy.

Latent debt capacity hypothesis.   A theory that postmerger increases in financial leverage are due to underleverage in the premerger period.

LBO.   See *Leveraged buy-out.*

LCO.   Leveraged cash-out. See *Leveraged recapitalization.*

Learning by doing.   A means of transferring knowledge which is complex, or embedded in a complex set of technological and/or organizational circumstances, and thus difficult or impossible to transfer in a classroom setting. May motivate knowledge-acquisition joint ventures.

Learning curve.   An approach to strategy formulation which hypothesizes that costs decline with cumulative volume experience, resulting in competitive advantage for the first entrants into an industry.

Leveraged buy-out (LBO).   The purchase of a company by a small group of investors, financed largely by debt. Usually entails going private.

Leveraged cash-out (LCO).   See *Leveraged recapitalization.*

Leveraged ESOP.   An employee stock ownership plan recognized under ERISA in which the ESOP borrows funds to purchase employer securities. (Banks have tax incentives to make loans to ESOPs.) The employer then makes tax-deductible contributions to the ESOP sufficient to cover both principal repayment and interest on the loan.

Leveraged recapitalization.   A defensive reorganization of the firm's capital structure in which outside shareholders receive a large one-time cash dividend, and inside shareholders receive new shares of stock instead. The cash dividend is largely financed with newly borrowed funds, leaving the firm highly leveraged and with a greater proportional ownership share in the hands of management. Also called leveraged cash-out.

Life cycle model of firm ownership.   A theory which suggests firms will attract different shareholder clienteles (high or low tax bracket investors) over different periods of firm development depending on changing investment needs and profitability.

Line and staff.   An organizational form characterized by the separation of support activities (staff) from operations (line).

Liquidation.   Divestiture of all the assets of a firm so that the firm ceases to exist.

Liquidation MLP.   The complete liquidation of a corporation into a master limited partnership.

Lock-in amendment.   A corporate charter amendment which makes it more difficult to void previously passed (antitakeover) amendments, e.g., by requiring supermajority approval for a change.

Lock-up option.   An option to buy a large block of newly issued shares which target management may grant to a favored bidder, thus virtually guaranteeing that the favored bidder will succeed. Target management's ability to grant a lock-up option induces bidders to negotiate.

Logical incrementalism.   A process of effecting major changes in strategy via a series of relatively small (incremental) changes.

M-form.   See *Multidivisional corporation*.

Management buy-out (MBO).   A going-private transaction led by the incumbent managers of the formerly public firm.

Managerial conglomerates.   Conglomerate firms which provide managerial expertise, counsel, and interaction on decisions to operating units. Based on the transferrability of generic management skills even across nonrelated businesses.

Managerial entrenchment hypothesis.   A theory that antitakeover efforts are motivated by managers' self-interests in keeping their jobs rather than in the best interests of shareholders.

Managerialism.   A theory that managers pursue mergers and acquisitions to increase the size of the organizations they control and thus increase their compensation.

Market-adjusted return.   The return for a firm for a period is its actual return less the return on the market index for that period.

Market-extension merger.   A combination of firms whose operations had previously been conducted in nonoverlapping geographic areas.

Market model.   In event studies, the most widely used method of calculating the return predicted if no event took place. In this method, a clean period (with no events) is chosen, and a regression is run of firm returns against the market index return over the clean period. The regression coefficient and intercept are then used with the market index return for the day of interest in the event period to predict what the return for the firm would have been on that day had no event taken place.

Market value rule.   The principle that all decisions of a corporation should be judged solely by their contribution to the market value of the firm's stock.

Master limited partnership (MLP).   An organizational form in which limited partnership interests are publicly traded (like shares of corporate stock), while retaining the tax attributes of a partnership.

Maximum limit offer.   A stock repurchase tender offer in which all tendered shares will be purchased if the offer is undersubscribed; but if the offer is oversubscribed, shares may be purchased only on a pro rata basis.

MBO.   See *Management buy-out*.

Mean adjusted return.   The actual return for a period less the average (mean) return calculated for a time segment before, after, or both in relation to the event.

Merger.   Any transaction that forms one economic unit from two or more previous units.

Mezzanine financing.   Subordinated debt issued in connection with leveraged buy-outs. Sometimes carries payment-in-kind (PIK) provisions, in which debt holders receive more of the same kind of debt securities in lieu of cash payments under specified conditions.

Minority squeeze-out.   The elimination by controlling shareholders of noncontrolling (minority) shareholders.

Misappropriation doctrine.   A rationale for insider trading prosecution of outsiders who trade on the basis of information which they have "misappropriated," e.g., stolen from their employers or obtained by fraud.

MLP.   See *Master limited partnership.*

MNE.   See *Multinational enterprise.*

Money purchase plan.   A defined contribution pension plan in which the firm contributes a specified annual amount of cash as opposed to stock bonus plans in which the firm contributes stock, and profit-sharing plans in which the amount of the annual cash contribution depends on profitability.

Monopoly.   A single seller.

Moral hazard.   One party (principal) relies on the behavior of another (agent) and it is costly to observe information or action. Opportunistic behavior in which success benefits one party and failure injures another, e.g., high leverage benefits equity holders under success and injures creditors under failure.

Muddling through.   An approach to strategy formulation in which policy makers focus only on those alternatives which differ incrementally (i.e., only a little) from existing policies rather than considering a wider range of alternatives.

Multidivisional corporation (M-form).   An organizational form to achieve greater efficiency via profit centers to reduce the need for information flow across divisions and to guide resource allocation to the highest-valued uses. Benefits from large fixed investment in general management expertise (especially strategic planning, monitoring, and control) spread over a number of individual decentralized operations (at which level decision making on specific management functions takes place).

Multinational enterprise (MNE).   A business organization with operations in more than one country, beyond import/export operations.

NAAG.   See *National Association of Attorneys General.*

NASDAQ.   Stock quotation system of the National Association of Securities Dealers for stocks which trade over the counter as opposed to on an organized exchange.

National Association of Attorneys General (NAAG).   An organization of state attorneys general.

Negotiated share repurchase.   Refers to buying back the stock of a large block holder (an unwanted acquirer) at a premium over market price (greenmail).

Net operating loss carry-over.   Tax provision allowing firms to use net operating losses to offset taxable income over a period of years before and after the loss. Available to firms which acquire a loss firm only under strictly specified conditions.

Net present value (NPV).   Capital budgeting criterion which compares the present value of cash inflows of a project discounted at the risk-adjusted cost of capital to the present value of investment outlays (discounted at the risk-adjusted cost of capital).

Niche opportunities.   A business strategy which aims at meeting the needs or interests of specific consumer groups.

NOL carry-over.   See *Net operating loss carry-over.*

Nolo contendere.   A legal plea in which a defendant, without admitting guilt, declines to contest allegations of wrongdoing.

Nondiscriminatory poison pill.   Antitakeover defense plans which do not penalize acquirers exceeding a given shareholding limit. Include flip-over plans, preferred stock plans, and ownership flip-in plans which permit cash offers for all shares.

Nonleveraged ESOP.   An employee stock ownership plan recognized under ERISA which does not provide for borrowing by the ESOP. Essentially the same as stock bonus plans.

Normal return.   In event studies, the predicted return if no event took place, the reference point for the calculation of abnormal, or excess, return attributable to the event.

NPV.   See *Net present value.*

Oligopoly.   A small number (few) of sellers.

Open corporations.   Fama and Jensen's term for large corporations whose residual claims (common stock) are least restricted. They identify the following characteristics: (1) They have property rights in net cash flows for an indefinite horizon; (2) Stockholders are not required to hold any other role in the organization; (3) Common stock is alienable (transferrable, saleable) without restriction.

Open-market share repurchase.   Refers to a corporation's buying its own shares on the open market at the going price just as any other investor might buy the corporation's shares; as opposed to a tender offer for share repurchase or a negotiated repurchase.

Operating synergy.   Combining two or more entities results in gains in revenues or cost reductions because of complementarities or economies of scale or scope.

Opportunism.   Self-interest seeking with guile, including shirking, cheating.

Organization capital.   Firm-specific informational assets which accumulate over time to enhance productivity. Includes information used in assigning employees to appropriate tasks, and forming teams of employees, and the information each employee acquires about other employees and the organization. Alternatively, defined by Cornell and Shapiro as the current market value of all future implicit claims the firm expects to sell.

Organization culture.   An organization's "style" or approach to problem solving, relations with employees, customers and other stakeholders.

Organization learning.   The improvement in skills and abilities of individual or groups (teams) of employees through learning by experience within the firm. Includes managerial learning (generic, as well as industry specific) and nonmanagerial labor learning.

Original plan poison pill.   Also called preferred stock plan. An early poison pill antitakeover defense in which the firm issues a dividend of convertible preferred stock to its common stockholders. If an acquiring firm passes a trigger point of share ownership, preferred stockholders (other than the large block holder) can put the preferred stock to the target firm (force the firm to redeem it) at the highest price paid by the acquiring firm for the target's common or preferred stock during the past year. If the acquirer merges with the target, the preferred can be converted into acquirer voting stock with a market value no less than the redemption value at the trigger point.

Ownership flip-in plan.   A poison pill antitakeover defense often included as part of a flip-over plan. Target stockholders are issued rights to purchase target shares at a discount if an acquirer passes a specified level of share ownership. The acquirer's rights are void, and his or her ownership interest becomes diluted.

Parking.   A securities law violation in which traders attempt to hide the extent of their share ownership (to avoid the 5 percent trigger requiring disclosure of takeover intentions and keep down the price of target stock) by depositing, or parking, shares with an accomplice broker until a later date, e.g., when the takeover attempt is out in the open.

Partial tender offer.   A tender offer for less than all target shares; specifies a maximum number of shares to be accepted, but does not announce bidder's plans with respect to the remaining shares.

Payment-in-kind provision (PIK).   A clause which provides for issuance of more of the same type of securities to bondholders in lieu of cash interest payments.

Payroll-based ESOP (PAYSOP).   A type of employee stock ownership plan in which employers could take a tax credit of 0.5 percent of ESOP-covered payroll. Repealed by the Tax Reform Act of 1986.

Pension plan.   A fund established by an organization to provide for benefits to plan participants (e.g., employees) after their retirement.

Perfect competition.   Set of assumptions for an idealized economic model: (1) Large numbers of buyers and sellers so none can influence market prices or output; (2) Economies of scale exhausted at relatively small size and cost efficiencies are the same for all companies; (3) No significant barriers to entry; (4) Constant innovation, new product development; (5) Complete knowledge of all aspects of input/output markets is costlessly available.

PIK provision.   See *Payment-in-kind provision.*

Plasticity.   (Alchian and Woodward) Resources are considered plastic when a wide range of discretionary uses can be employed by the user. If monitoring costs are high, moral hazard problems are likely to develop.

Poison pill.   Any antitakeover defense which creates securities that provide their holders with special rights (e.g., to buy target or acquiring firm shares) exercisable only after a triggering event (e.g., a tender offer for or the accumulation of a specified percentage of target shares). Exercise of the rights would make it more difficult and/or costly for an acquirer to take over the target against the will of its board of directors.

Poison put.   A provision in some new bond issues designed to protect bondholders against takeover-related credit deterioration of the issuer. Following a triggering event, bondholders may put their bonds to the corporation at an exercise price of 100–101 percent of the bond's face amount.

Portfolio balance strategy.   A balance in business segments based on market-growth/market-share criteria. Combine high-growth/high-market-share (stars), low-growth/high-market-share (cash cows), low-growth/low-market-share (dogs) segments to achieve favorable overall growth, profitability and sufficient internal cash flows to finance positive NPV investment opportunities.

Potential competition.   Firms not in an industry at the present time, but which could enter.

Predatory behavior.   A theory which holds that a dominant firm may price below cost or build excess capacity to inflict economic harm on existing firms and to deter potential entrants.

Premium buy-back.   Refers to repurchasing the stock of a large block holder (an unwanted acquirer) at a premium over market price (greenmail).

Price-cost margin (PCM).   Defined as (Price minus Marginal Cost) divided by Price. That is, operating profit as a percentage of price. A zero PCM reflects perfect competition, i.e., Price = Marginal Cost.

Price pressure.   A theory that the demand curve for the securities of an individual company is downward sloping and that this causes negative stock price effects of large supply increases such as large block offerings.

Price trader.   Outside investors who trade in response to price changes in securities regardless of whether or not they understand the cause of the price change.

Prisoner's dilemma.   A situation in which the inability of individuals to communicate/ cooperate leads them to willingly accept an outcome which leaves them worse off and would not have been chosen had collective action been possible.

Product breadth.   Carry-over of organizational capabilities to new products.

Product differentiation.   The development of a variety of product configurations to appeal to a variety of consumer tastes.

Product-extension merger.   A type of conglomerate merger; a combination between firms in related business activities that broadens the product lines of the firms; also called concentric mergers.

Product life cycle.   A conceptual model of the stages through which products or lines of business pass. Includes development, growth, maturity, and decline. Each stage presents its own threats and opportunities.

Production knowledge.   A form of organization learning; entrepreneurial or managerial ability to organize and maintain complex production processes economically.

Profit-sharing plan.   A defined contribution pension plan in which the firm's annual contributions to the plan are based on the firm's profitability.

Proxy contest.   An attempt by a dissident group of shareholders to gain representation on a firm's board of directors.

Public Utilities Holding Company Act of 1935.   Federal securities legislation to correct abuses in financing and operation of gas and electric utility holding company systems.

Pure conglomerate merger.   A combination of firms in nonrelated business activities that is neither a product-extension nor a geographic-extension merger.

q-ratio.   (Tobin's q-ratio) The ratio of the market value of a firm's securities to the replacement costs of its physical assets.

Quasi-rent.   The excess return to an asset above the return necessary to maintain its current service flow.

Racketeer Influenced and Corrupt Organizations Act of 1970 (RICO).   Federal legislation which provides for seizure of assets upon accusation and triple damages upon conviction for companies which defraud consumers, investors, and so on.

Recap.   See *Leveraged recapitalization.*

Recapture of depreciation.   The amount of prior depreciation which becomes taxable as ordinary income when an asset is sold for more than its tax basis.

Redistribution hypothesis.   A theory that value increases in mergers represent wealth shifts among stakeholders (e.g., a wealth transfer from bondholders to shareholders) rather than real increases in value.

Residual analysis.   The examination of asset returns to determine if a particular event has caused the return to deviate from a normal or predicted return which would have resulted if the event had not taken place. The difference between the actual return and the predicted return is the residual.

Residual claims.   The right of owners of an organization to cash flows not otherwise committed.

Restricted vote stock.   In dual-class stock firms, the stock with inferior voting rights.

Retention ratio.   The percentage of free cash flows retained in the firm.

Reverse LBOs.   Firms, or divisions of firms, which go public again after having been taken private in a leveraged buy-out transaction.

Reverse mergers.   The uncombining of firms via spin-offs, divestitures, and so on.

RICO.   See *Racketeer Influenced and Corrupt Organizations Act*.

Risk-free rate.   The return on an asset with no risk of default. In theory, the return on short-term government securities.

Roll-out MLP.   Also called spin-off MLP. A corporation transfers some of its assets to an MLP to avoid double taxation, for example. MLP units are initially distributed to corporate shareholders, and corporate management serves as the general partner.

Roll-up MLP.   The combination of several ordinary limited partnerships into a master limited partnership.

Royalty trust.   An organizational form used by firms which would otherwise be taxed heavily (due to declining depreciation and increasing pretax cash flows) to transfer ownership to investors in low tax brackets.

Sample selection bias.   Criteria for sample may exclude some relevant categories. Examples: Completed spin-offs will not include spin-offs announced, but not completed. Measures of industry profitability will not include firms that have failed. Studies of leveraged buy-outs that have a subsequent public offering will represent the most successful and exclude the failures or less successful.

Saturday night special.   A hostile tender offer with a short time for response.

Scale economies.   The reduction in per-unit costs achievable by spreading fixed costs over a higher level of production.

Schedule 13D.   The form which must be filed with the SEC within ten days of acquiring 5 percent or more of a firm's stock; discloses the acquirer's identity and business intentions toward the target. Applies to all large stock acquisitions.

Schedule 14D.   The form which must be filed with the SEC by *any* group or individual making solicitations or recommendations which would result in its owning more than 5 percent of the target's stock. Applies to public tender offers only.

Scorched earth defenses.   Actions to make the target less attractive to the acquiring firm and which may also leave the target in weakened condition. Examples are sale of best segments (crown jewels) and incurring high levels of debt to pay a large dividend or to engage in substantial share repurchase.

Secondary initial public offering (SIPO).   The reoffering to the public of common stock in a company which had initially been public, but had then been taken private (e.g., in an LBO).

Second-step transaction.   Typically the merger of an acquired firm into the acquirer after control has been obtained.

Securities Act of 1933 (SA).   First of the federal securities laws of the 1930s. Provides for federal regulation of the sale of securities to the public and registration of public offerings of securities.

Securities Exchange Act of 1934 (SEA).   Federal legislation which established the Securities and Exchange Commission (SEC) to administer securities laws and to regulate practices in the purchase and sale of securities.

Securities Investors Protection Act of 1970 (SIPA).   Federal legislation which established the Securities Investor Protection Corporation empowered to supervise the liquidation of bankrupt securities firms and to arrange for payments to their customers.

Sell-off.   General term for divestiture of part or all of a firm by any one of a number of means, e.g., sale, liquidation, spin-off, and so on.

Shareholder interest hypothesis.   The theory that shareholder benefits of antitakeover defenses outweigh management entrenchment motives and effects.

Share repurchase.   A public corporation buys its own shares, by tender offer, on the open market, or in a negotiated buy-back from a large block holder.

Shark repellent.   Any of a number of takeover defenses designed to make a firm less attractive and less vulnerable to unwanted acquirers.

Shark watcher.   A firm (usually a proxy solicitation firm) which monitors trading activity in its clients' stock to detect early accumulations by an unwanted acquirer before the 5 percent disclosure threshold.

Shelf registration.   The federal securities law provision in Rule 415 which allows firms to register at one time the total amount of debt or equity they plan to sell over a two-year period. Securities can then be sold with no further delays whenever market conditions are most favorable.

Sherman Act of 1890.   Early antitrust legislation. Section 1 prohibits contracts, combinations, conspiracies in restraint of trade. Section 2 is directed against actual or attempted monopolization.

Short-swing trading rule.   Federal regulation under Section 16 of the Securities Exchange Act which prohibits designated corporate insiders from retaining the profits on any purchase and sale of their own firms' securities within a six-month period.

SIC.   See *Standard Industrial Classification.*

SIPO.   See *Secondary initial public offering.*

Sitting-on-a-gold-mine hypothesis.   Attributes the increase in a takeover target's stock price to information disclosed during the takeover process that the target's assets are undervalued by the market.

Small numbers problem.   When the number of bidders is large, rivalry among bidders renders opportunistic behavior ineffectual. When the number of bidders is small, each party seeks terms most favorable to it through opportunistic representations and haggling.

Specialized asset.   An asset whose use is complementary to other assets. For example, a pipeline from producing fields to a cluster of refineries near large consumption markets.

Specificity.   The degree to which an asset or resource is specialized to and thus dependent on the rest of the firm or organization.

Spin-off.   A transaction in which a company distributes on a pro rata basis all of the shares it owns in a subsidiary to its own shareholders. Creates a new public company with (initially) the same proportional equity ownership as the parent company.

Split-off.   A transaction in which some, but not all, parent company shareholders receive shares in a subsidiary in return for relinquishing their parent company shares.

Split-up.   A transaction in which a company spins off all of its subsidiaries to its shareholders and ceases to exist.

Squeeze-out.   The elimination of minority shareholders by a controlling shareholder.

Staggered board.   Also called a classified board. An antitakeover measure which divides a firm's board of directors into several classes only one of which is up for election in any given year, thus delaying effective transfer of control to a new owner in a takeover.

Stakeholder.   Any individual or group who has an interest in a firm; in addition to shareholders and bondholders, includes labor, consumers, suppliers, the local community, and so on.

Stake-out investment.   Preliminary investment for a foothold in anticipation of the future possibility of a larger investment.

Standard Industrial Classification (SIC).   The Census Bureau's system of categorizing industry groups, mainly product or process oriented.

Standstill agreement.   A voluntary contract by a large block shareholder (or former large block holder bought out in a negotiated repurchase) not to make further investments in the target company for a specified period of time.

Start-up MLP.   Also called acquisition MLP; the assets of an existing entity are transferred to a master limited partnership, and the business is henceforth conducted as an MLP. The Boston Celtics' conversion into an MLP is an example.

Stepped-up asset basis.   The provision allowing asset purchasers to use the price paid for an asset as the starting point for future depreciation rather than the asset's depreciated book value in the hands of the seller.

Stock appreciation right (SAR).   Part of executive compensation programs to align managers' interests with those of shareholders. SARs are issued to managers giving them the right to purchase stock on favorable terms; the exercise price can be as low as 50 percent of the stock price at issuance; maximum life is ten years.

Stock bonus plan.   A defined contribution pension plan in which the firm contributes a specified number of shares to the plan annually. The benefits to plan beneficiaries depend on the stock performance.

Strategy.   The long-range planning process for an organization. A succession of plans (with provisions for implementation) for the future of a firm.

Strip financing.   A type of financing, often used in leveraged buy-outs in which all claimants hold approximately the same proportion of each security (except for management incentive shares and the most senior bank debt).

Structural theory.   An approach to industrial organization that argues that higher concentration in an industry causes less competition due to tacit coordination or overt collusion among the largest companies.

Stub.   New shares issued in exchange for old shares in a leveraged recapitalization.

Subchapter S corporation.   A form of business organization which provides the limited liability feature of the corporate form while allowing business income to be taxed at the personal tax rates of the business owners.

Superior-vote stock.   In dual-class stock firms, the class of stock which has more power to elect directors; usually concentrated in the hands of management.

Supermajority.   A requirement in many antitakeover charter amendments that a change of control (for example) must be approved by more than a simple majority of shareholders; at least 67 to 90 percent approval may be required.

Supernormal growth.   Growth due to a profitability rate above the cost of capital.

Swaps.   Exchanges of one class of securities for another.

SWOT.   Acronym for Strengths, Weaknesses, Opportunities, and Threats; an approach to formulating firm strategy via assessments of firm capabilities in relation to the environment.

Synergy.   The "2 + 2 = 5" effect. The output of a combination of two entities is greater than the sum of their individual outputs.

Take-out merger.   The second-step transaction which merges the acquired firm into the acquirer and thus "takes out" the remaining target shares which were not purchased in the initial (partial) tender offer.

Targeted share repurchase.   Refers to repurchasing the stock of a large block holder (an unwanted acquirer) at a premium over market price (greenmail).

Tax credit ESOP (TRASOP, PAYSOP).   An employee stock ownership plan which allowed employers to take a credit against their tax liability for contributions up to a specified amount, based on qualified investment in plant and equipment (TRASOP) and/or covered payroll (PAYSOP). Repealed by the Economic Recovery Tax Act of 1981 and the Tax Reform Act of 1986.

Tax-free reorganization.   A takeover transaction in which the primary consideration paid to obtain the voting stock or assets of the target must be the voting stock of the acquiring firm. (In fact, tax is only deferred until target shareholders sell the stock received.)

Team effects.   A form of organization capital; information which helps assign employees for an efficient match of capabilities to tasks and which helps to match managers and other employees to form efficient teams.

Team production.   Alchian and Demsetz's distinguishing characteristic of a firm. Team output is greater than the sum of outputs of individual team members working independently (synergy); increased output cannot be unambiguously attributed to any individual team member.

Tender offer.   A method of effecting a takeover via a public offer to target firm shareholders to buy their shares.

Third market.   Trading off the organized securities exchanges by institutional investors.

Time trader.   Investors who buy or sell because of events unrelated to stock price fluctuations, e.g., for portfolio adjustment needs.

Top-down planning.   An approach to overall firm strategy based on company-wide forecasts from top management, versus aggregation of segment forecasts.

Total capitalization.   The sum of total debt, preferred stock, and equity.

Total capital requirements.   A firm's financing requirements. Two alternative measures: (1) Total capital = Current Assets minus Noninterest-Bearing Debt plus Net Fixed Assets; (2) Total Capital = Interest-Bearing Debt plus Shareholders' Equity.

Transaction cost.   The cost of transferring a good or service across economic units or agents.

TRASOP.   See *Tax Credit ESOP.*

Trigger point.   The level of share ownership by a bidder at which provisions of a poison pill antitakeover defense plan are activated.

Trust Indenture Act of 1939 (TIA).   Federal securities regulation of public issues of debt securities of $5 million or more. Specifies requirements to be included in the indenture (the agreement between the borrower and lenders) and sets out the responsibilities of the indenture trustee.

Two-tier tender offer.   Tender offers in which the bidder offers a superior first-tier price (e.g., higher or all cash) for a specified maximum number of shares it will accept and simultaneously announces its intentions to acquire remaining shares at a second-tier price (lower and/or securities rather than cash).

Type A, B, C reorganization.   Forms of tax-free reorganizations. Type A—statutory mergers (target merged into acquirer) and consolidations (new entity created). Type B—Stock-for-stock transaction in which target is liquidated into acquirer or maintained as separate operating entity. Type C—Stock-for-asset transaction in which at least 80 percent of fair market value of target's property is acquired; target then dissolves.

Undervaluation.   A firm's securities are selling for less than their intrinsic, or potential, or long-run value for one or more reasons.

Underwritten offerings.   Public securities issues which are sold by a firm to an investment banker at a negotiated price; the investment banker then bears the risk of price fluctuations before the securities are sold to the general public.

Value additivity principle (VAP).   A quality of the NPV method of capital budgeting which enables managers to consider each project independently. The sum of project NPVs represents the value added to the corporation by taking them on.

Value chain.   An approach to strategy which analyzes the steps or chain of activities in the firm to find opportunities for reducing cost outlays while adding product characteristics valued by customers.

Vertical merger.   A combination of firms which operate in different levels or stages of the same industry; e.g., a toy manufacturer merges with a chain of toy stores (forward integration); an auto manufacturer merges with a tire company (backward integration).

Voting plan.   A poison pill antitakeover defense plan which issues voting preferred stock to target firm shareholders. At a trigger point, preferred stockholders (other than the bidder for the target) become entitled to supervoting privileges, making it difficult for the bidder to obtain voting control.

Voting trust.   A device by means of which shareholders retain cash flow rights to their shares while giving the right to vote those shares to another entity.

White knight.   A more acceptable merger partner sought out by the target of a hostile bidder.

White squire.   A third party friendly to management who helps a company avoid an unwanted takeover without taking over the company on its own.

Williams Act of 1968.   Federal legislation designed to protect target shareholders from swift and secret takeovers in three ways: (1) Generating more information during the takeover process; (2) Requiring minimum period for tender offer to remain open; (3) Authorizing targets to sue bidders.

Winner's curse.   The tendency that in a bidding contest or in some types of auctions, the winner is the bidder with the highest (overoptimistic) estimate of value. This explains the high frequency of negative returns to acquiring firms in takeovers with multiple bidders.

WOTS UP.   Acronym for Weaknesses, Opportunities, Threats, and Strengths; a technique to identify these key elements as part of the iterative process used to develop strategy.

Author Index

Subject Index

A

Aaron v. SEC, 540
Abnormal returns
    cash versus all equity offers, 316
    correlation of, 266–69
    measurement of, 217–19
Adaptive processes, 62, 68–69
Advantage of stock trades, 690–91
Agency costs, 201–2, 253–54
    control of, 43–46, 106–12
    investment behavior, 49–50
    LBOs, 407–11
Agency problems (*see* Agency costs)
Aggregate concentration ratio, 590
Aggregate conglomerate merger activity, 287–96
    data and equation specification, 291
    results, 292–95
    conclusions from econometric analyses, 295–96
Aggregate investment opportunity, 288
American Stores–Lucky Stores case study, 625–27
Anticompetitive effects, 83–84
Antigreenmail charter amendments, 518–20
Antitakeover amendments, 497–504, 519–20
Antitrust, 597–610
    implication of new developments, 601–5
    joint ventures, 337–40
    market characteristics, 599
    policies, 597–610
    recent developments, 594–605
    state antitrust activity, 603
    takeover defense, 520–21
    testing antitrust issues using residual analysis, 590–94
    U.S. antitrust laws, 580–82
ARA Services case study, 621–22
Arbitrage
    functions, 554–57
    illustrative example, 552–53
Asset adjustment as a takeover defense, 483–85
Asset structure and investment behavior, 50
Atomisitic shareholders, 661–63, 710
Average investor realized yield, 177

B

Back-end rights plans 507–8
Balance sheet trends, 1970–1986, 123
Baron model, 702–3
Berkovitch and Khanna model, 699–702
Bidder elimination, 695–702, 715
Birnbaum v. Newport Steel Corp., 540
Boesky case, 562–65
Bondholder expropriation, 237, 450
Bond yield plus equity risk premium, 177
Boston Consulting Group, 66–69, 613–14
Brown case, 586–87
Bounded rationality, 29–30, 83–84
Brand-name capital, 51–52, 108–9
Business goals, 71–72
Bust-up takeovers, 241–45